The Naval War in the Mediterranean

Jack Greene, a native of California, has written on a wide range of naval, military and wargaming subjects for over a dozen magazines including *Warship International*, *The Mariner's Mirror*, *Strategy & Tactics* and *Command*. He has self-published two pamphlets, *Handbook on the Italian Army in World War II* (1988) and *Mare Nostrum* (1990). He and Alessandro Massignani have co-authored *Rommel's North Africa Campaign*, *Ironclads at War 1855-1891* and *The Black Prince and the Sea Devils*.

Alessandro Massignani, born in Italy, a former *Bersaglieri* officer, is author of several books and papers on naval and military topics including *Alpini e Tedeschi sul Don* (1991), *Le Truppe D'Assalto Austro-Ungariche nella Grande Guerra* (1995) and co-authored with Andrea Curami *L'Artiglierria Italiana nella Grande Guerra* (1998). There are also Italian editions of Jack and Alessandro's *Rommel in Africa Setterntrionale* (1996) and *Il Principe Nero* (2007).

The Naval War in the
Mediterranean 1940-1943

Jack Greene and Alessandro Massignani

Frontline Books, London

NAVAL INSTITUTE PRESS
Annapolis, Maryland

This book is dedicated to:
Beth, Leilani and Elizabeth
and
Donatella and Valentina

A Greenhill Book

Greenhill Books

First published in Great Britain in 2002 by Chatham Publishing, an
imprint of Greenhill Books, Lionel Leventhal Limited
www.greenhillbooks.com

This edition published in 2011 by Frontline Books,

an imprint of
Pen & Sword Books Ltd.,
47 Church Street, Barnsley, S. Yorkshire, S70 2AS.

Visit us at www.frontline-books.com, email info@frontline-books.com or
write to us at the above address.

Published and distributed in the United States and Canada by
the Naval Institute Press, 291 Wood Road, Annapolis, Maryland 21402-5034
www.nip.org

UK edition: ISBN 978-1-84832-618-7
US edition: ISBN 978-1-59114-561-5

CIP data records for this title are available from the British Library and the
Library of Congress.

Library of Congress Control Number: 2002100310

Printed and bound by CPI Mackays, Chatham ME5 8TD

Contents

List of Plates

Introduction and Acknowledgements

It has been more than a decade since our book was first published. The naval historical landscape has changed with more and more studies appearing over the years. Comparative history, the essence of our study, is a method of historical research where all the possible points of view are taken into account, in order to avoid the reassuring but essentially narrow exposition of facts and interpretations; this requires more research, more effort, an in-depth analysis of the topic.

When we first published *Naval War in the Mediterranean* we strove to present the facts in a scholarly setting and to let the reader decide. This method has advantages over many other academic studies that all too often try to prove this point or that point, like a lawyer in a courtroom, instead of telling the story as best as it can be told based on what occurred.

That was our goal, and we think that by melding together source material from the languages of all the participants we have achieved it.

In that spirit, our new publisher in this edition has encouraged us to correct details wherever possible. Thus, this edition includes a modest number of corrections, mostly of detail, but some of substance. Many of these corrections are due to the fine publications that have appeared since our book was published and correspondence with their authors. We would especially like to thank Enrico Cernuschi, Professor Willard C Frank, Jr., Vincent P O'Hara and Andrew Smith in this regard.

There have been several new arrivals on the scene. We published *The Black Prince and the Sea Devils: The Story of Valerio Borghese and the Elite Units of the Decima Mas* from Da Capo Press in 2004. The Italian edition made the top 20 non-fiction top best-sellers. It expanded on our discussion of the Italian SEALS in *Naval War* and put a spotlight on Borghese's post-war career that most writers deliberately leave in the dark. Vincent P O'Hara's excellent *Struggle for the Middle Sea* (2009) covers the surface naval battles fought in the Mediterranean and Vincent co-authored with Enrico Cernuschi the excellent *Dark Navy: The Italian Regia Marina and the Armistice of 8 September 1943* (2009). Enrico Cernuschi and Vince O'Hara have also contributed essays in the annual *Warship* on important aspects of the Italian navy. Reynolds M Salerno has penned an excellent background study *Vital Crossroads* (2002). Richard L DiNardo has written *Germany and the Axis Powers* (2005) which takes a good look at Italy and the war. John Gooch has produced *Mussolini and his Generals* (2007) that has much on the navy, although largely from an academic perspective. Michael Simpson has published *A Life of Admiral of the Fleet Andrew Cunningham* (2004) based in part on his editing of Naval Records Society *The Cunningham Papers*, Vol I (1999) and Vol II (2006). Taking one up to December 1941 is another addition of a semi-official nature in the Whitehall History Publishing series, *The Royal Navy and the Mediterranean* Vols I and II (2002).

There have been many new books in Italian over the same period and it is unfortunate that they are not being translated into English. Some of the standouts include Francesco Mattesini's *La Battaglia di Capo Teulada* (2000) and *La Marina e l'8 Settembre* (2002), Erminio Bagnasco and Enrico Cernuschi's *Le navi da guerra italiane* (2003), Erminio Bagnasco's *In guerra sul mare* (2005) and *Le navi da battaglia classe Littorio 1937–1948* (2008). Ufficio Storico, the Italian military publishing arm, has continued to churn out many great studies, including official papers/command dairies of *Comando Supremo* and the *Supermarina: Corrispondenza e direttive tecnico-operativo Supermarina* (Rome, 2000) (i.e., the Italian Navy HQ papers). Ufficio Storico also regularly publishes new editions in their Official History series and also produces a long-running series on Italian warships, wonderfully illustrated with numerous diagrams, foldouts and photographs, often in colour, in an oversized format.

Additionally, there have been hundreds of articles by these authors and many others, including Achille Rastelli, Maurizio Brescia and Tullio Marcon in the excellent monthly magazine *Storia Militare* and the Italian naval ministry historical quarterly *Bollettino D'Archivio* (this ceased publication in 2011 although back issues are available). Both are profusely illustrated and the latter over the past two decades usually carried a scholarly essay on a naval battle or activity in the Mediterranean in World War II in every issue. Both are highly recommended.

The thoughtful, and in some ways the father of modern English-language Italian war studies, MacGregor Knox, has added *Hitler's Italian Allies* (2000). This slender study has some information on the Italian navy and takes the view that an invasion of Malta would have likely led to an Axis disaster, which is a view also supported in the latest edition of the Italian official history from Ufficio Storico. Yet, it is our point, that unlike the examples of Sicily or Normandy that Knox cites, Malta's defenders were starving and literally capable of at most twenty-four hours of resistance. We believe that this vital weakness would have countered the poor inter-service and inter-Axis command control problems that would certainly have arisen. Also in regards to the proposed invasion, the air-transportable division, *La Spezia*, might not have been deployed due to the lack of transport aircraft – it was literally on stand-by. There is some historical disagreement over the employment of Colonel von der Heydte's glider battalion in the proposed invasion as an initial raiding force as well. In this vein, we would like to thank John D Burtt and Lieutenant Colonel Davide Pastore, currently working on an alternative history postulating the invasion taking place entitled *Second World War: The Goddess of War: Operation C3: The Invasion of Malta, August 1942*, for their thoughts and comments.

There are several facets of the Mediterranean war that need further study. One major area is the lack of a comprehensive study of intelligence in the war in the Mediterranean that examines all the various services on both sides. The Italian side in particular cries out for a deeper study. Another study needs to be conducted on the range-finding equipment and quality of shells utilized by the British and Italian services. Italian shells appear to have more erratic spreads, but their range-finding equipment may have been superior to the British, though lacking the advantage of radar. Also, the evolution in both services needs to be examined more deeply.

It is interesting to note that Italian studies tend to make greater use of English-language sources then vice-versa. Italian military studies remain a prime source of knowledge that has not been fully mined by English-language scholars.

Another change from when we first published is the Internet sites, some better than others. We would like to suggest: http://www.worldnavalships.com/forums/index.php, http://www.regiamarina.net/, and http://www.italiandestroyers.com.ar/

While our first edition was dedicated to Professors Brian R Sullivan and Lucio Ceva, our families receive the dedication in the second edition of our work. Family trumps their fine academic reputations!

Jack Greene, Paso Robles, California
Alessandro Massignani, Valdagno, Vicenza
May 2011

Glossary and Abbreviations

The PRO is the Public Record Office in Great Britain.

We refer to German submarines as 'U-boats' and all other nationalities as submarines.

AA = anti-aircraft

ACS = Archivio Centrale dello Stato

AOI = *Africa Orientale Italiana* (Italian East African Empire)

AUSSME = *Archivio ufficio storico Stato maggiore Esercito* (Italian Military Archives)

AUSSMM = *Archivio ufficio storico Stato maggiore Marina* (Italian Naval Archives)

BA-MA = *Bundesarchiv-Militärarchiv*

Comando Supremo = Italian Supreme Command

DP = Dual Purpose gun, (capable of A.A. and surface action)

Egeomil = Italian Aegean Command (Dodecanese Islands)

Kriegsmarine = German Navy

NARS = National Archives and Record Services, Washington

Regia Aeronautica = Royal Italian Air Force

Regia Marina = Royal Italian Navy

Sigint = British Signal Intelligence

Superaereo = Air Force Command

Supermarina = Italian Admiralty

CHAPTER 1

The Drift Towards War

On a historical plane, a conflict between Italy and Great Britain is
inevitable.

Benito Mussolini[1]

In the mid to late 1930s the British Empire had several fundamental crises facing her. A resurgent and aggressive Fascist Italy led by the dictator Benito Mussolini declared war on Abyssinia, which adversely affected relations between the two Powers. This was quickly followed by the Spanish Civil War, and all the complications arising from that conflict. This would be a period of mock combat between these countries – the Second World War by proxy allowing preparations for the coming war to become more realistic and intense.

Within the Empire itself there were further conflicts in and around the Mediterranean basin, in part fanned by Italian funds and agents in the 1920s and even more so in the later 1930s. A civil war simmered between Jews and Arabs in strategically-important Palestine, and in Egypt, nominally independent but occupied by British troops, a strong dissident movement opposed to the Imperial presence was gaining momentum. In Morocco (and later in Franco's Spain) Italy had an elaborate spy system in place directed against Gibraltar. Malta would soon witness the expulsion of Italians (and with the coming of war the imprisonment and deportation of Maltese who were thought to be anti-British such as the leaders of the Nationalist Party). In Yugoslavia, both the Croat nationalist movement and the Macedonian separatists were supported and subsidised by Mussolini. Italian propaganda against the British in Egypt and Palestine was strong, she 'flirted' with Saudi Arabia, and money and supplies had been shipped regularly to the Iman of Yemen, with which Italy had a treaty.[2] Neither did the growing ties between Rome, Berlin, and Tokyo bode well for Great Britain. One of the fears dominating British thinking was that in responding to a threat in the Far East, she would be left vulnerable in Europe. Until 1933, Italy had not been considered a likely enemy by British planners. Only Japan, Germany, and the Soviet Union had held that position before then, and the only threat in the Mediterranean was thought to be from Japanese sabotage.

Abyssinia (later Ethiopia), was a large and ancient east African kingdom that had never been conquered by a European nation, bordering on the Italian colonies of Eritrea and Italian Somaliland. Italy had fought, and lost, an earlier war with Ethiopia in the 1890s, and now Mussolini dreamed of revenge for that defeat, and of increasing Italy's empire in the Horn of Africa, which could become an Italian South Africa with the influx of Italian colonists and the development of industry.

As the Abyssinian Crisis grew towards war in the summer of 1935, Great Britain was in a position of naval and military weakness and unpreparedness in the Mediterranean, a theatre she had for too long neglected. Though her position was formidable on paper with bases at each end of the Mediterranean, and Malta in the centre, backed by mutually-supporting air bases and ports from Aden to Iraq to Egypt (and at the beginning of the crisis at Navarino Bay in Greece – 'Base X'), the lean inter-war years had not allowed for any strengthening of those bases. For example, modern anti-aircraft defences were almost non-existent. In strategic terms the Mediterranean route was the quickest way for Great Britain to shift her fleet from Europe to Singapore in response to any threat from Japan to her Far Eastern possessions, the Suez Canal cuttting about 3500 miles off the route to India around the Cape. It was recognised by many in the inter-war period that if war came with Italy, this Mediterranean route would be closed.[3]

France's interests in the Mediterranean lay in communications with her Syrian and North African territories, and also as a route to her eastern European allies. Although she was not formally allied with Britain, the build-up of her fleet was recognised as preparation for possible war with Italy and Germany. France was planning for a fleet to equal 'G + I' (Germany plus Italy). With Hitler in power and German rearmament in full swing, and the Anglo-German Naval Treaty of 1935 seemingly blessing an increase in the German Navy, the French building formula was being put under pressure. The days of a German Navy bound by the Versailles Treaty to 108,000 tons had vanished.[4]

But on the eve of the Abyssinian Crisis, France, with Pierre Laval as Foreign Minister (and after June 1935 also Premier), and Italy formed a *de facto* alliance *against* Germany, to a point where France and Italy withdrew troops from each other's borders, both in Europe and North Africa.[5] Italy had agreed to this arrangement partly because Mussolini thought that Laval had given him a free hand in Ethiopia. Their agreement had several points involving adjustments in colonial borders as well as secret talks involving planning by their respective air, land, and naval staffs for possible war with Germany. The French Navy was the least receptive and talks between them and the Italian Navy never took place. It was 'unlikely that the British knew much if anything about these secret conversations'.[6] France looked to Italy to help her in the web of alliances aimed at Germany which she had established in the inter-war period. With France's alliances with Czechoslovakia, Yugoslavia, Rumania, and Poland, Italy could act as a corridor between her and those nations that were united against a resurgent Germany. For Italy an alliance with France offered the opportunity to further protect a vulnerable Austria from an *Anschluss*.

The most extensive formal discussions were between the French and Italian Air Forces, delineating air sectors and allocations of reinforcements to either one partner or the other, depending upon the German threat. They were in the process of exchanging staff officers and the French had sent sample bombs to Italy to see if the weapons could be made inter-changeable. The French air staff, 'thought fondly of the day when Czech air bases would bring the Italians within striking distance of Berlin, Leipzig, and Hamburg and when French air bases would support Italian raids on the Ruhr'. The army commanders, General Pietro Badoglio for the Italians and General Maurice Gamelin for the French, also met and discussed possible

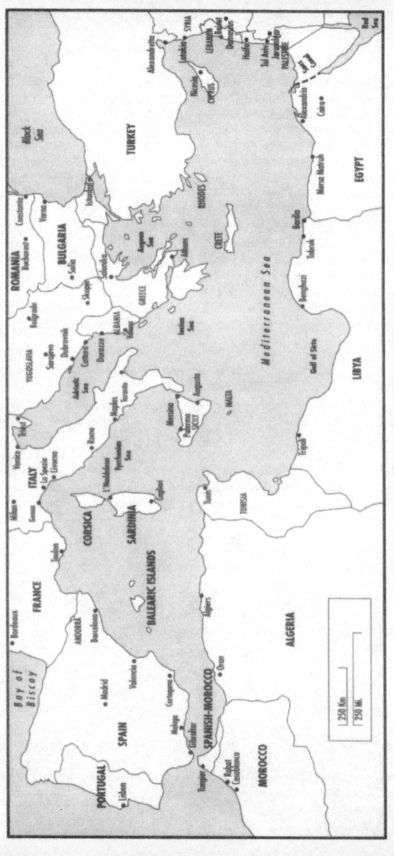

MEDITERRANEAN THEATRE OF OPERATIONS

operations against Germany including an advance on Munich. The French Navy foresaw the Italian Navy helping in convoy duties in the Mediterranean.[7]

However, in the coming Abyssinian Crisis, France had to choose between Italy and Great Britain and she chose Britain. Ironically, the British were even planning for the French Navy to control the Western Mediterranean against Italy and for their Air Force to bomb Italy, at the same time as the French and Italian air staffs were planning on how to attack Germany together! As a result of the French decision, Mussolini would shortly make approaches to Nazi Germany and the Pact of Steel would be the eventual result.

The fact was that Britain needed France. Her naval rearmament in the inter-war years had got off to a slow start and by the mid-1930s had barely started. Of the Fleet Review of 1936 when 160 ships were assembled, Stephen Roskill later wrote that;

> ... it was painfully obvious that the proportion of new ships present was small, and that few of the older ones (many of which were of World War I vintage) had been fully modernised. In truth the shop window was mainly filled with obsolescent goods.[8]

Throughout the 1930s Britain's overall battleship strength would fluctuate as ships were modernised and the *King George V* class battleships were laid down. It would not be until the 1936-37 building programme, with an increase in the budget of £20 million to a total of £81.3 million (this later received a further supplement which brought it to £105 million), that rearmament really got under way, although it is important to note that the Exchequer fought a fierce rearguard action against any substantial increases in the Defence budget. The programme for that fiscal year was to be completed by 1940.

Facing a resurgent Germany and a Japan at war with China for almost the entire decade (and a potential threat to her Far Eastern colonies and Dominions), the recognition of Italy as a potential enemy was an added strain to Britain's already over-extended navy. Salerno has concluded that, 'the inability of the Admiralty to gain approval for a genuine two-power navy contributed to the naval staffs determination not to provoke hostilities in the Mediterranean region'. The British government would therefore spend much of this period attempting to keep Italy out of any war, ultimately unsuccessfully.[9]

Admiral Sir Ernie Chatfield, First Sea Lord 1933-38, would write in 1935 that, '... I am in the unpleasant position of preparing for war and for a war which we have always been told could never happen ... we shall have many losses in ships and men, thereby our world position as a naval power will be weakened'. Great Britain was further alarmed in February 1936 when Germany, now with improving relations with Italy, proposed sending ten small U-boats to Trieste for later assembly at La Spezia.[10] Therefore, as Great Britain faced up to her worldwide commitments, with France refusing to join her in action against Italy, she recognised that any loss of ships, even in what was expected to be a successful war, would leave her weakened. Britain would be left exposed elsewhere, as her rearmament programme was still years from completion.

Contacts between the German and Italian navies in the inter-war years were limited by the political situation. It would not be until the Spanish Civil War, when the Italian Navy gave valuable assistance to the German ships operating in the western Mediterranean, that naval co-operation between the two powers truly began. Before then the Italian Navy had not welcomed the presence of German naval officers as observers aboard their ships, and those present at the 1932 summer naval manoeuvres had to wear civilian clothes and pose as employees of the Zeiss optical instruments company.[11]

However, the German Navy's interest in the Italian fleet could be traced back to the 1925 wargames, in which Italy's role was envisioned as disrupting French seaborne links with her colonies. But later the Germans came not to count on any help from the Italians, as in their words 'we will be those who give and the Italians will be those who will take'. Possibly a strange view coming from a navy reduced to 15,000 men, but the Germans were referring to the technical inferiority of the Italian Navy. The German Fleet Commander, Admiral Boehm, said after the 1932 man-oeuvres the technical know-how and the tactical development of the Italian Navy was inferior to the German. Somewhat arrogantly, Boehm saw the Italians wanting to learn from the German Navy but he also noted that Italy, like Germany, now saw France as her main enemy. Italy could have offered the chance for practical experi-ence and training forbidden in Germany by the Versailles Treaty, especially for the *Luftwaffe*. But technical exchange between all three of the Axis nations was very limited before the war and not extensive during it. This failure was one factor contributing to their defeat.[12]

Military attachés were exchanged beginning in 1927, with the Germans sending officers on 'special missions', since they were not allowed to have military attachés by the Versailles Treaty. According to Admiral Doenitz, relations between the two navies at the time were 'good'. Apparently the Italian Navy did not press for better relations with the Germans, in direct contrast with the Air Force, which supported German rearmament by training pilots. But the Italian naval attaché in Berlin was helpful because of the relative isolation in which the German Navy faced in the first years after Versailles.[13] However, such contacts should not be overrated. At the same time there were excellent relations between the German and the American armies and between the German and Swedish navies. The Spanish Civil War and the help of the Italian Navy in that ideologically attractive conflict helped change the attitudes of the officers of the *Kriegsmarine*, who tended to be opposed to left-wing regimes.[14]

But war between Italy and Great Britain was possible during the Abyssinian Crisis of 1935-36 with Great Britain taking the lead on economic sanctions against Italy brought by the League of Nations. The possible strengthening of those sanctions with the addition of oil to the list, as well closure of the Suez canal, were critical. For this confrontation Britain began increasing her naval strength in the Mediterranean in August 1935.

As the crisis built towards war between Italy and Abyssinia, Italy had one trump card in negotiating with Great Britain: the Italian Military Intelligence Service (*Servizio Informazioni Militari* – SIM) had penetrated the British embassy in Rome and could read many of the British ciphers. This gave Mussolini information concerning the deficiencies of British forces in the Mediterranean, especially the Royal Navy. These shortages included ammunition of all types, anti-aircraft defences, ASDIC-equpped destroyers (furthermore, ASDIC worked poorly near Alexandria due to the discharge of fresh water from the Nile), and resulted in the Royal Navy urging the government to avoid war with Italy. Information like this allowed Mussolini to calculate his moves with a great deal of freedom and strength and allowed him an immense advantage in negotiating with the British and maintaining his own position internally.[15]

But *Il Duce* himself also caused problems for his own armed forces. In 1933 Mussolini took the portfolios for the various armed forces so those who actually ran the various services were the Undersecretaries. This was due to his view of himself as a great war leader, and also to strengthen his hold on power by keeping the armed forces divided into opposing factions so they would not be a threat to him. Thus Admiral Domenico Cavagnari was Navy Undersecretary and Chief of Staff of the Navy, and General Giuseppe Valle was Air Force Undersecretary and Chief of Staff, both reporting (along with the Army) to Mussolini and to the weak General Staff headed by Marshall Pietro Badoglio.

Cavagnari was liked by Mussolini as he was a friend of Admiral Constanzo Ciano, a veteran of the First World War and father of Mussolini's son-in-law Galeazzo. The elder Ciano had helped shape Mussolini's views towards the navy in his early days in power. Furthermore, Cavagnari was not of an aristocratic background and became, as did most who wanted to prosper, a member of the Fascist Party. He wanted to build up the Italian Navy's battleship and submarine strength with the limited funds allocated to the navy. He especially objected to Badoglio having overall control of the armed forces and even issuing directives to the Navy through the Army Staff![16] Mussolini never developed an adequate General Staff or combined Defence Ministry, thus exacerbating inter-service rivalries, as a means to prevent a powerful military leader emerging who might threaten his own power.

To some degree, all the leaders of the Great Powers would lead the war effort of their respective countries in the forthcoming war. Some were more involved in the day-to-day running of their war machines than others, but Mussolini in particular viewed himself as a great war leader, largely thanks to what he regarded as his success in Abyssinia, and he, of all the leaders, was probably the least capable in that role. As MacGregor Knox has written, Mussolini was '. . . incapable of effectively commanding the Italian armed forces, while his insistence on personally conducting the war prevented anyone else from doing so until too late'.[17]

What, therefore, would have happened if war had broken out in 1935-36? The two main naval considerations for Italy in such a war were the need to defend Italy itself, and the need to defend the overseas empire. There were two major aspects to such a naval war. Both of these requirements would be endangered by Britain's naval strength and control over Egypt.

A critical aspect of Italy's position in the Mediterranean was that her long coastlines exposed many of her cities and lines of communication to enemy attack. She did have coast defences, as all the major powers did, but many of the positions were antiquated. Attempts had been made to establish a series of interlocking gun positions up and down the coast, combined with railroad artillery operating on the coastal railroads, and with major bases being defended by her most powerful guns. This was also backed up by the Italian Air Force which had bases throughout the country. But before this current crisis the *Regia Aeronautica* had most of her modern air bases located in the north of Italy, to both defend and attack across her Alpine frontier. She did plan to operate the few new S.81s and the more numerous older Ca.111 and Ca.133s from Sicily, Libya, and Eritrea against the British. But under the circumstances any sustained naval surface attack against almost any point on her coast other than her major naval bases could have succeeded.[18]

Italy's position in the central Mediterranean allowed her to indeed influence, if not control, most east-west movement. But the control of the sea is not like on land where one has an easily defined front-line. The front-line at sea is above, on, and under the water, and remains fluid as ships and planes only control a finite space on an immense sea. Movement across the sea is measured in hours or days at most, and on the eve of this war, it was now being measured in minutes by air. This is not at all like land warfare where a distinct front can change usually no faster than the speed of marching feet, or where a truck can manage to find a road or a unit can be transferred by railway.

Mussolini contemplated an early attack on Alexandria and Malta. The attack on Alexandria would have been a dawn bombardment by a fast cruiser force at the start of the war, while the harbour entrance at Malta would be sealed with blockships. However, previous attempts to use blockships in this manner had met with limited success.

The Italian Navy believed that they would suffer a terrible defeat at sea at the hands of the British. They feared that the 'English battle fleet, escorted by a powerful mass of destroyers . . . [would be] able to ramble about the Mediterranean inflicting whatever damage it wants to our scarcely defended coast'[19] and could not be stopped. This opinion was also shared by the British themselves.[20]

It was at this time that certain forward-thinking young Italian naval officers began developing a weapon that would be one of the few success stories in Italy's coming naval war. The first work on what would eventually become best known as the *X MAS* (*Decima Motoscafi Anti Sommergibili* or Tenth Anti-Submarine Motor-Boat Squadron) began during the Abyssinian Crisis. Two engineer officers, Sub-Lieutenants Teseo Tesei and Elios Toschi, who were serving in the submarine flotilla based at La Spezia, studied the problems facing the Italian Navy. They recognised the overwhelming strength of the British Navy and wanted to see a weapon developed which would be 'new, [an] unforeseen weapon, rapidly produced and instantly employed, to carry destruction into the enemy's camp . . .'. By studying the earlier efforts and successes of Italy's small craft in the First World War, they developed a new weapon system, unique in modern naval warfare. It was a manned torpedo controlled by two frogmen. Its technical name was *Siluro a Lenta Corsa* (SLC) (literally 'Slow Speed Torpedo'). Originally it was planned to deliver the weapon by air so to avoid corrosion, but it was decided instead to employ a submarine to deliver the SLC to a target port. Two frogmen would ride these devices into the port, position them beneath an enemy warship, set the timer, and then leave the area of the impending explosion. Obviously very dangerous work, and yet potentially devastating to an enemy.

The Italian naval hierarchy gave its approval to their work, but set strict conditions. They had to do all work after completing their normal daily assignments, and as they were engineers, not seaman officers, they were not allowed to command the unit once the concept had been proved, although they had developed it. Finally, with the end of the crisis in 1936, the unit was 'casually dissolved' partly because the Italian Admiralty was convinced that any major naval conflict would not be resolved with such weapons, but would be instead fought with the guns of the rival battlefleets.[21] It was this sort of hidebound naval thinking, the 'gun club' dominance of the battleship admirals, which would contribute in part to the failure of the Axis in the Second World War. A trained force with perfected weapons ready for deployment on 10 June 1940 could have made a considerable contribution towards the Italian Navy gaining dominance in the Mediterranean and thus possibly control of the Middle East with its oil.

Another area of weakness was the *Regia Aeronautica* (Royal Air Force). This independent service had adopted the doctrines of General Giulio Douhet, the foremost air power theorist of the inter-war period, and therefore devoted its limited resources to the development of a strategic bomber force for attacks upon an enemy's population centres and industry, and also led the air force's commanders to resist co-operation with both the army and the navy. The result was that, for maritime operations, the *Regia Aeronautica* lacked an adequate torpedo bombing force and her bombs were too small to be effective against enemy ships. One important and often overlooked reason why the Air Force neglected torpedo-planes was that torpedoes cost substantially more than bombs.

The Italian Air Force was the darling of the Fascist regime (Mussolini once said he would black out the sun with his planes!), but it suffered from a fundamental flaw. It 'indulged in the illusion that air forces were the appropriate instrument of war especially for poorer countries'. But what was required for the coming war was either the raw materials and industrial base to build its own aircraft, or the money to purchase foreign designs in quantity, both of which Italy lacked.[22]

Not until 1933 did the Air Force begin a serious programme of development of aerial torpedoes and it did not design a plane specifically for this role. High-altitude bombing, which was the principal tactic of the Italian Air Force, had been proved to be a failure against warships during a exercise in the summer of 1935. The small bombs employed would not significantly damage large armoured warships even if hits were obtained. While some improvements were made between 1935 and 1940, the Air Force simply did not do enough.

The inadequacy of the bombs available for use against naval targets was recognised by Italian leaders during the Abyssinian Crisis. This led Mussolini to an interesting subterfuge. He had Valle 'order' the 15th Bomber Wing, which was equipped with old biplane bombers, to become a suicide unit – the pilots were to crash their planes into British warships in event of war. Mussolini let the British become aware of this, and it was accepted by them as truth. It was all part of Mussolini's political brinkmanship which worked in the short term.[23]

Vice-Admiral W W Fisher commanded the British Mediterranean Fleet. In event of war with Italy, his forces would have first cut off Italian trade at both ends of the Mediterranean, while the Royal Navy in the Red Sea blockaded the Italian ports in Eritrea and Italian Somaliland which were supporting the war against Ethiopia. Vigorous anti-submarine campaigns around Gibraltar and the eastern Mediterranean would also have been launched. Once enough ammunition was available, the Mediterranean Fleet would have conducted an aggressive surface campaign against Italy, sending cruisers and destroyers up and down the Italian and Sicilian coasts 'to spread alarm in Italy and cause dispersion of effort'. As the use of 'Base X' in Navarino Bay had been lost with a change of government in Greece, British plans had changed. Her fleet based at Alexandria would advance into the Central Mediterranean, bombarding Tobruk on the way.

Fisher, an aggressive and skilled commander, proposed air attacks against Catania and Augusta. Later Rear-Admiral Alexander Ramsay, commanding the aircraft carriers, proposed a carrier strike against the main Italian naval base of Taranto, in a night attack with Fairey IIIF bombers and Blackburn Ripon torpedo planes, the aircraft returning in the early morning. Fighters would not be included in the strike force as they lacked the necessary range. It was planned to possibly route the planes through a Greek air base, as the fleet did not want to be within range of the Italian Air Force in the morning. This was the basis for the raid on Taranto in 1940. The British of course recognised that war with Italy would mean the end of shipping through the Mediterranean. Admiral Chatfield thought that slow or fast convoys could be escorted through, but most shipping would have to take the Cape route.

Feelings between the two nations at this time were bad. One example of this is shown by the following account.

> We were guard ship at Port Said for many weeks and used to see the troopships passing. In one of them an Italian sailor peed over the stern to show his feelings for the British. A sailor shouted 'Do it while you can!', which brought the house down, because the Ethiopians were well known for their trick of castrating their prisoners![24]

The French, if they had become involved, which they fought to avoid, would have supplied early warning of Italian air attacks, and would also have entertained the possibility of air attacks from Tunisia against Libya and Sardinia if the British provided aircraft to replace them. They also planned anti-submarine operations near Gibraltar and operating their own submarines off the Libyan coast. Operations with surface forces, at least in the winter of 1935-36 would not have been undertaken, and neither would any land attacks, except possibly an advance against Tripoli if the British attacked from Egypt. This lack of enthusiasm was fuelled by the French desire to maintain their understanding with Italy, an understanding that was already on its last legs.[25]

After the Abyssinian Crisis, a weak Britian still faced threats on three fronts: Germany, the Far East, and the Mediterranean. It would be her policy up to 1939 to seek some sort of understanding with Italy and to treat the Mediterranean as the third priority. An example of Great Britain's dilemma as she hurried to rearm is that as late as October 1937 the dispatch of an anti-aircraft brigade to the Mediterranean (twenty-four guns) was vetoed as this would constitute about 10 per cent of the country's available AA guns![26]

The result of this crisis with Great Britain for Italy was her building bases in the south of the country and switching the emphasis from construction of bases along the traditional Alpine fronts facing France, Yugoslavia, and Austria. Therefore, just as Italy was contemplating war with Great Britain, the British themselves had '. . . no Mediterranean war plans in existence . . .' against Mussolini's Empire! Italy also increased her destroyer, large torpedo-boat, and submarine forces and began supplying larger, but still inadequate, bombs for her aircraft.[27]

For Great Britain there were three main results of this crisis. First, a great amount of money was spent. Secondly, Egypt and Great Britain concluded a favourable treaty that would allow the British to control Alexandria and the Suez Canal for the next 20 years. The Egyptian army would command the anti-aircraft and coastal defences at Alexandria during the Second World War and would fire on attacking Axis aircraft. Thirdly, a substantial naval building programme was undertaken which included two battleships, two carriers of the *Illustrious* class with armoured decks, seven cruisers, and a large number of smaller craft, including the powerful 'Tribal' class destroyers armed with eight 4.7in guns in twin turrets. A supplementary Bill increased the manpower available to the fleet and accelerated work on three new battleships by 6 months. Rearmament was now gaining a real head of steam.

But it was by no means limited to Great Britain. The period after the Abyssinian Crisis, which had also seen other worldwide political developments involving the revisionist powers, saw all major powers increase expenditure on their navies. Japan more then doubled her naval appropriations for new construction, Germany increased her naval budget to the equivalent of £121 million, while Italy increased hers by 41.7 per cent, but that amounted to a total of only £19.1 million – an indication of her economic weakness. Both France and the United States had an increase of almost 17 per cent, bringing the French budget up to £27.4 million. But Britain, no matter how small the actual Italian naval budget was, was not building for war with Italy but against the more immediate threats of Germany in Europe and Japan in the Far East.[28]

CHAPTER 2

The Spanish Civil War

It may therefore be no exaggeration to say that the totally unscrupulous
activities of the Axis navies in the Spanish Civil War ultimately
contributed to their own defeat.

Stephen Roskill[1]

The next confrontation would be during the Spanish Civil War, which grew out the conflict between left and right in Spanish politics. The monarchy had been overthrown in 1931 when King Alfonso XIII was deposed. The military and the right-wing political parties became increasingly concerned by the perceived move to the left by the government. This was brought to a head by the electoral victory in February 1936 of the 'Popular Front', an alliance of left-wing parties which included the Communists. The army led a revolt in July 1936 and fighting broke out immediately.

The French were alarmed by the outbreak of the Civil War, as a weakened Spain might be unable to resist either Germany or Italy, and a Nationalist victory would equally place a potential enemy on her southern border. They were also concerned about control of the Balearic Islands in the western Mediterranean, from which an enemy could threaten communications with their North African colonies. This fear was such that France sent an unofficial delegation from the Ministry of Marine to the British Admiralty in mid-1936 to discuss this potential problem. One of the French officers was Admiral François Darlan, who would command the French fleet at the start of the Second World War. They were also concerned about the Canary Islands in the Atlantic also falling into Italian hands. But this initiative would come to nothing.

However, Darlan had caught the eye of the left-wing French Premier, Leon Blum, and he was appointed Chief of the Naval Staff in January 1937. Darlan, like Blum, opposed Italy and also 'championed the government's social reforms within the navy'. He was a principal figure in French opposition to Italy and he would help persuade Blum to increase new warship construction.[2]

The entire period 1935-38 saw no substantial contacts between the French and British navies. This is remarkable, as the French possessed a modern fleet, by itself superior in strength to the Italian Navy, and had an excellent series of bases, principally in the Western Mediterranean. This lack of co-ordination was a major failure of the Allied nations in the pre-war era and it was Britain that continued to reject France's overtures. As late as 1938 Anglo-French naval discussions concerning the Mediterranean were still precluded by Britain as she sought to seek some form of accommodation with Italy and/or Germany. Not until 1939 was this policy reversed.[3]

With civil war now raging in Spain, both Italy and Germany intervened on the side of the Nationalists and the future Allied nations on the side of the Republicans. The Soviet Union sent the lion's share, including naval officers who would be responsible for much of the poor Republican naval strategy during the war. The British used Gibraltar for their main base of operations for the protection of British trade and interests. Stationed there in command of the destroyer force was Rear-Admiral James Somerville, whom we shall meet later. Gibraltar had not seen much use during the First World War but would become a vital base in the next war.

Italian air and naval forces, as well as ground forces, were heavily involved in the Spanish Civil War. Many of the actions of the Italian Navy were, by International Law, acts of piracy. But, according to Sullivan;

> . . . the navy's limited and often secret and illegal actions were crucial to Franco's victory. The Italian Navy ensured the arrival of the men, arms, and equipment denying similar reinforcements to the Republic. It is difficult to imagine how the Nationalists could have won without such assistance.

This naval help would begin in July 1936 with the convoying of troops and equipment which would last until the autumn. These early operations were vital in holding Tangier and Mallorca as Nationalist ports, especially given that the majority of the Spanish Navy joined the Republican cause. In July 1936 a blockade by Republican ships temporarily isolated key Nationalist units in Spanish Morocco.[4]

The Italian Navy was also instrumental in outfitting auxiliary cruisers for the outnumbered Nationalist Navy, training personnel and improving its equipment. Their presence allowed most of the Nationalist Navy to operate in the Atlantic during the war. The Balearic Islands would be dominated by the Nationalists and the Italians would use them as a base for air and naval units. They had been secured, in part, due to the initiative and energy shown by Captain Carlo Margottini of the Italian Navy who was helped by local Nationalists to gain control of most of the islands.

The Nationalists had failed to secure any of the small Spanish submarines and were desperate to possess at least two. However, by November 1936 they had arranged to have the new German *U-33* and *U-34* operate secretly in the Mediterranean, as well as four Italian submarines, in alternating pairs. The Italian submarines were hampered by restrictive orders, by their poor tactics of simply sitting off Republican ports and by being largely unable to positively identify disguised Republican merchant ships as enemy vessels. One important success was scored by the 'loaned' submarine *Torricelli* (which had an Italian crew but a Spanish Nationalist officer on board as nominal commander), which torpedoed the Republican flagship, the light cruiser *Miguel de Cervantes*, while at anchor off Cartagena on 22 November 1936. Hit by two torpedoes, she would be out of action for most of the war. Fragments of torpedo recovered from the scene, as well as Italian news reports, led the Republicans to conclude that the ship had been attacked by an Italian submarine. Until then they had not feared a submarine attack because they controlled all the available Spanish boats.

The two German U-boats were not successful either during 'Operation Ursula', in late November and early December, failing to score any hits in three attacks. One attack had the *U-34* fire a torpedo at a Republican destroyer, which missed and exploded on the rocky coastline. Fortunately for Germany there was no search for fragments. Berlin became worried that if an unexploded torpedo were recovered, this would positively identify the submarines and therefore they decided to end the operation. However, after previously failing to hit any targets and now operating without orders, *U-34* sighted the Republican submarine *C-3* on the surface off Malaga, and sank her with a single torpedo in 230ft of water. There were only three survivors from her crew of forty-eight. Although they initially suspected an Italian submarine, the Republicans attributed her loss to an internal explosion.[5]

Italy followed this up by deploying fourteen submarines off the Spanish coast where they operated between December 1936 and January 1937. Approximately half had a Spanish 'captain' on board. They sank no ships, but a torpedo fired by the *Jalea* was recovered by the Republican light cruiser *Mendez Nunez* in Barcelona harbour. Clearly of Italian manufacture, it was placed on display for the international community, but the Italian government still denied that its submarines were involved.[6]

In early 1937, Italy secretly transferred two submarines to the Nationalist Navy, along with four motor torpedo boats (*MAS* boats). To try and keep this secret, she had two new submarines building in Italy take the names of the two vessels transferred. The poor sea-keeping characteristics of the *MAS* boats would restrict their operational usefulness; in one planned raid against the port of Almeria they had to be towed, which gave away the element of surprise, and they would remain largely harbour-bound for the duration of the war.

The Nationalist and Republican navies now settled down to trying to build up their strength, and convoy and protect merchant ships bringing supplies and troops. Over 80 per cent of the men and war materials that went to both side 'followed a maritime route'. This would be the main duty of both navies in the coming years of the conflict, though the Nationalist Navy was better led and would slowly grow in strength and presence as the Civil War continued.[7]

In 1937 the Italian Navy conducted two surface raids against Republican Spanish ports with three different light cruisers, all of which were armed with eight 6in guns. On the night of 13 February the light cruiser *Eugenio di Savoia*, commanded by Commander Massimiliano Vietina, arrived off Barcelona and opened fire at 11:00pm. She fired a total of nine salvos of between seven and eight shells each before retiring to the base at La Maddalena, a major Italian anchorage on the north end of Sardinia. Vietini would later become a Rear-Admiral and would command the port of Tobruk where he would become a prisoner of war in January 1941. Barcelona was only slightly damaged in the attack, with casualties of seventeen killed and fifteen wounded.

This was followed up with a raid by the 7th Light Cruiser Division commanded by Rear-Admiral Romeo Bernotti, based in Majorca, on the Republican port of Valencia. Bernotti was a supporter of naval aviation and had been commander of the *Istituto di Guerra Marittima* (Italian Naval War Institute). He was disliked by Cavagnari, who at the start of the Second World War refused him a command saying, 'You would compel me to issue orders I don't want to give'. Thus Italy would lose one of her better admirals. With Bernotti on the *Emanuele Filiberto Duca D'Aosta* was her captain, Commander Alberto Da Zara, who would later command during the only sucessful Italian squadron surface engagement in the Second World War. The other light cruiser was the *Raimondo Montecuccoli*, which covered the operation from the north and did not participate in the bombardment. They left Palma on 14 February, arriving off Valencia just before 10:00pm. The *D'Aosta* fired a total of 125 shells into the city from a range of 6000m. Fire was returned, doing some minor damage to the *D'Aosta*. The cruisers both returned to Italy. Casualties in Valencia amounted to eighteen civilians killed and fifty-seven wounded.[8]

The most notable act of the Italian Navy in this period was to launch the 'Pirate' submarine campaign that lasted from 6 August to 13 September 1937. Initially Cavagnari was in favour of this operation as it gave an opportunity for his submarine force to gain valuable experience. He also saw one of the main roles of the Italian Navy as one of convoying troops and material, and thus supported and developed the convoys carrying troops and supplies to Spain during the war.[9]

Many surface ships were involved as well, operating near Italy, while the submarines operated throughout the Mediterranean, including in the Aegean and off the Spanish coast. The destroyer *Freccia* sank the English tanker *George W McKnight* off Tunisia on 14 August, which was carrying fuel oil for the Republicans. The *Freccia* waited until nightfall and then launched two attacks, firing a total of four torpedoes. She failed to hit in the first attack, but in the second hit with one torpedo. She then chased the limping *McKnight* into Tunisian waters, and shelled her until she burst into flames and eventually sank. Previously the old destroyer *Ostro* had torpedoed and sunk a Republican merchant ship off Bizerta on the evening of 13 August. She then joined up with her sister-ship the *Turbine* and both were successful, torpedoing and sinking a Soviet freighter off Algeria on the 30th.

In fifty-nine patrols, forty-eight Italian submarines fired forty-three torpedoes, but sank only four merchant ships and damaged the Republican destroyer *Churruca*. Despite all the secrecy, the British had been aware of this campaign since the summer of 1937, having broken the Italian naval cipher.[10]

The most exciting submarine action of this period involved an officer who would become one of the most notorious Italian commanders of the Second World War. The submarine *Iride*, commanded by Prince Junio Valerio Borghese, attacked Republican shipping off the port of Valencia on 29 August 1937, without success. Unhappy with the performance of his equipment, he decided to attack again the following night, and attacked what he thought was a Republican destroyer of the *Sanchez Barcaiztegui* class at a range of 700m, but it was in fact the British destroyer HMS *Havock*.

The *Havock* was steaming south from Valencia to Gibraltar and had just altered course to pass Cape San Antionio at 11.30pm when the track of an incoming torpedo was spotted. She turned towards the attack and a lookout reported sighting the *Iride* on the surface. Employing sonar in its first combat situation, *Havock* made contact with what was thought to be a submarine. However, the sighting report and sonar contact conflicted and the *Havock*'s commander chose to depth-charge the sonar contact instead of moving towards the position where the *Iride* was reported seen.

He was criticised for this, and Admiral Somerville made a recommendation for a change in sonar procedures as a result. Throughout the next day (1 September) *Havock* continued her attacks with four other British destroyers and Rear-Admiral Somerville in the light cruiser *Galatea*, but could not maintain sonar contact and was eventually ordered by the Admiralty to break off the hunt. The *Iride* was shaken up, but 'making the appropriate manoeuvres escaped destruction'. This bold attack brought Borghese to the attention of the Italian leadership and he received several decorations including the Bronze Medal for Valor, as well as creating an international uproar over the incident.[11]

The attack on the *Havock*, together with the sinking of the British merchant ship *Woodford* by an Italian submarine shortly afterwards, resulted in Rear-Admiral Somerville, on board the *Galatea*, visiting the commander of the Italian naval forces in Spain, Rear-Admiral Alberto Marenco di Moriondo, at Palma aboard his flagship the old light cruiser *Quarto*, and warning him about the possible consequences of these attacks, which would shortly cease.

The Italian submarines were reasonably successful against merchant ships travelling alone in the Mediterranean, although Cavagnari was not happy with what he saw as a hit rate of only 17 per cent. These successes may have given them a degree of false confidence in their tactics, which they would lose rapidly in the Second World war, but training was intensified. However, it was not just a lack of training that was the problem, but a faulty doctrine. Essentially Italian submarine doctrine called for their boats to operate individually, remaining submerged during the day and waiting for targets to come to them. The German tactic of surface night attacks, where the boats had greater speed, were in fact developed before the outbreak of Second World War, as were 'Wolf Pack' tactics by both the Germans and the Dutch, whose submarines operated in pairs. However, the small number of U-boats available to the *Kriegsmarine* in 1939 meant that these tactics could not be employed immediately. Italian submarines also had certain technical problems as they dove relatively slowly (various figures show they took between two and three times longer to dive than a standard U-boat), and could be seen at shallow depths from the air in the clear Mediterranean waters. It should also be noted that in the Second World War merchant-ship targets were relative scarce in the Mediterranean. The Italian submarines sent to the target-rich Atlantic ocean were quite successful.

By the end of the summer international patrols were instituted to combat these 'unknown' submarines and preparations for convoys were made, but by the time these patrols began in September 1937 the Italians had already called off their campaign. The British employed thirty-six destroyers and two flying-boat squadrons, while the French sent twenty-eight destroyers and some aircraft (the Greeks also instituted patrols in the Aegean). Cavagnari and the Navy had never really been in favour of these 'Pirate' campaigns and they were glad they were over.[12]

These neutrality patrols were useful experience for the navies involved. The Royal Navy especially benefited by learning the advantages and disadvantages of their new sonar equipment. For example they found that it performed poorly at high speeds or in heavy seas, but overall it gave a major new advantage to anti-submarine forces. It was at this time that the Italians transferred four old destroyers to the

Nationalist Navy, which would remain in service long after the end of the Civil War.

Germany also carried out operations in the Mediterranean during the Spanish Civil War and was actually involved in a surface engagement. The *Deutschland* incident would be the most serious of a number of incidents in 1936-37. In December 1936 the United States destroyer *Kane* was bombed by Nationalist aircraft and the gunboat *Erie* was fired on. Both were undamaged and neither returned fire. The French destroyer *Maille Breze* was also attacked by Nationalist forces in early 1937, but again did not respond. Not to be outdone, Republican aircraft attacked the British battleship *Royal Oak* and her accompanying destroyers *Havock*, *Gallant*, and *Gipsy*, which in this case did open fire. As Willard Frank wrote, 'in none of these incidents was there any significant damage'. They were most likely the result of simple errors of identification, a problem that would plague the Italian Air Force in particular throughout the Second World War, with frequent attacks being made on their own ships.[13]

But in May 1937 all this would change. In late May a raid by Russian bombers operating with the Republicans hit Palma twice, damaging an Italian auxiliary cruiser (killing six officers and wounding three) and narrowly missing German vessels and even a British warship. The German ships left the harbour, and the pocket battleship *Deutschland*, accompanied by the large torpedo-boat *Leopard*, steamed to what they thought would be safer waters near the island of Ibiza. At sunset on 29 May two cruisers and eight destroyers were sighted from the *Deutschland*. They were Republican warships out to rendezvous with and escort in an approaching transport loaded with ammunition. As four of the destroyers steamed closer in a detached line about 8 miles from the *Deutschland*, her commander Captain Fanger ordered his ships to be ready in 10 minutes time and recalled men ashore on the island. At that moment, with all attention focused on the approaching ships, two Republican bombers with Russian crews trained in anti-shipping operations appeared from the opposite direction and out of the setting sun. Thinking that they had caught a Nationalist heavy cruiser unawares, they came down to 5000ft and released their bombs, as alarms began to sound aboard the *Deutschland*. One bomb penetrated below decks and started a fire in the paint locker. A second exploded on deck and set fire to the seaplane on the catapult, which spewed burning gasoline down ventilators, starting more fires down below. A third bomb destroyed the captain's gig nearby, while a fourth missed. This attack would cost the German ship thirty-one men killed and seventy-five wounded.

Now, to add to the Germans' discomfort, the Republican advanced destroyer line opened fire, straddling the pocket battleship but scoring no hits. The *Deutschland* tried to fire her 11in main battery in reply but could not man the turrets fast enough before the Republican ships turned away, having finally recognised the *Deutschland* and not wanting to engage that ship and that nation.

After a heated discussion in Berlin which even involved Hitler, Admiral Erich Raeder decided to send the *Deutschland* and her sister-ship the *Admiral Scheer* to bombard Almeria in retaliation. However, only the *Scheer* and three large torpedo-boats were ready. The force was commanded by Captain Otto Ciliax who would later go on to command German surface forces in the Second World War. He had hoped that the old Republican battleship *Jaime I* would be in the harbour at Almeria, but she had departed earlier for Cartagena. In the event, mist covered the town, and the only return fire came from small coastal batteries which were ineffective. The town was hit by ninety-four 11in and one hundred and forty-eight lighter shells that killed nineteen and wounded fifty-five.

A few minor incidents followed this episode, but both Nationalist and Republican forces tried to avoid more international incidents. Germany also laid mines from several S-Boats sent to help the Nationalists. One mine accidently sank the Nationalist battleship *España* while another badly damaged the British destroyer *Hunter* in May 1937. Her engines and boilers were severely damaged and she would not run new trials until November of 1938.[14]

As the war wound down the British were more concerned with the Nationalist and Italian air operations against shipping which continued to take a considerable toll. The Italian anti-shipping operations were carried out from Mallorca in the Balearic Islands, beginning in September 1937. Twelve S.79 bombers, one piloted by Mussolini's son Bruno, attacked Republican ports that were within short range of their base. They were part of the *Aviazione Legionaria Baleri* (Balearic Aviation Legion) that also included a night bombardment group of S.81s, escorting fighters, and a few floatplanes. An additional twelve S.79s were added to the force in January 1938. It must be remembered that these attacks, often against stationary and unarmoured ships, were with small bombs. As Sullivan points out;

> ... in these strikes on port facilities and shipping, the Italians believed that they had inflicted far more damage than they actually did. Nonetheless, along with the Germans, the Italian bombers did sink 115 Republican and fifty-one foreign merchant ships from September 1937 until the end of the war. Adding to their conviction about the efficacy of high level bombing attacks on shipping was the erroneous Italian belief that their S.79 attack on the Republican dreadnought *Jaime I* at Almeria in May 1937 had led to its destruction.

The *Jaime I* was one of three of the smallest class of Dreadnoughts ever built. She also later received attention from the German Condor Legion when on 17 April several He-lllbs carried out an attack on the Loyalist naval base at Cartagena, hitting the battleship again though 'already half-demolished by the S.79s and an internal explosion'.[15]

The fifty-two-year-old General Valle flew a mission over Spain in 1938 which impressed Mussolini. Valle had displayed the Fascist spirit and this would help keep him in power for a little longer, though his errors of judgement would shortly come home to roost when the Second World War showed up the lack of strength and unpreparedness of the *Regia Aeronautica*.

Possibly the worst result for Italy from these air attacks was that it reinforced their belief that high-altitude attacks against shipping would be successful. In addition, the budget for air operations was equal to the entire budget for new Italian aircraft in 1939 ot 650 million lire! This budgetary haemorrhaging combined with the attrition of war material would not help to increase Italy's military strength for the impending war.[16]

On 31 January 1938 a British merchant ship was sunk off Valencia by a Nationalist submarine (one of two transferred by Italy in April 1937), but the submarine campaign was coming to an end by now, due to the wear and tear on the ships and the ending of the 'pirate' patrols.[17] Great Britain also confirmed something she had always thought was true – Italy had lied about the displacement of her ships. The heavy cruiser *Gorizia* was accidentally damaged while at Tangiers and proceeded to Gibraltar for emergency repairs. While there the British carefully measured her and rightly concluded that she exceeded the Washington Treaty tonnage of 10,000 tons, though they took no action as a result. The Italians knowingly violated these treaty limitations, but their ships were also overweight due to their failure to employ weight saving techniques such as welding instead of rivetting.[18]

The Spanish Civil War saw the loss of several large Spanish warships, and these losses were studied by the navies involved to see what lessons could be learnt. A contemporary British assessment concluded that of the eighty warships attacked from the air, seventeen were damaged and none were sunk, while air attacks against eighty-one merchant ships saw six sunk and twenty-nine damaged. British records did not include all the attacks, which makes one wonder if they had been more accurate, would they have spent more time and money on proper AA protection? They recognised the need for AA weapons but it would not be until the Norwegian campaign that the inadequacy of their 4.7in guns with only 40° elevation was proved by both dive-bombing and high-level attacks against warships. This would be further driven home with the terrible losses off Crete in 1941.

More importantly, the British established an Operational Intelligence Centre (OIC) for handling intelligence traffic. This almost immediately led to the establishment of more direction-finding stations, of which only three currently existed. This would help immeasurably in the coming U-boat war. Their first task was to track Italian submarines. Futhermore '... the British benefited from the exercise of putting forces on to a war footing, exposing shortcomings in material and method in good time for remedial action to be taken'.[19] Finally, relations with France had improved. By 1939 Britain would be planning for possible war with Italy. France had arrived at that same conclusion earlier, and they had been planning on the assumption of a hostile Italy since February 1937.[20]

CHAPTER 3

The Final Approach to War

The British were well aware of the limitations on Italy's war-fighting capabilities before 10 June 1940. In February 1938, the Chiefs of Staff had pointed out in their 'Mediterranean Appreciation', that Italy was dependent on seaborne trade and lacked important raw materials, and was therefore incapable of conducting a long war without importing supplies. Furthermore, the supply lines for Italy's *Africa Orientale Italiana* (AOI – the Italian East African Empire) were controlled both by British sea power and her control of the Suez canal.[2]

British naval officers in the pre-war period were not overly impressed with the *Regia Marina*. Its officers, according to Admiral Pound after a visit in 1938, were thought to be 'second rate'. The strength of the Air Force, however, was overestimated, with the British thinking it had 1600 modern aircraft in 1938, but it was believed that shortages of raw materials would make it difficult to replace losses in wartime.[3]

As Lawrence Pratt wrote, on the eve of war 'Britain's strategic planners saw Italy as a second-class military power advantageously placed to secure local and probably temporary successes in a war in the Mediterranean'. But unlike Great Britain, essentially all of Italy's strength was concentrated in one theatre and she did not, with the exception of her African colonies, have the world-wide commitments faced by the British. The Royal Navy knew, after practising running slow and fast convoys from August 1937 to March 1938, that any convoy passing through the Mediterranean with Italy hostile would require a fleet operation in support. It was also recognised that they would be facing Italian air power with long-range bombers, as well as her surface warships and submarines.[4] However, Britain still thought that by appeasing Italy they could maintain a peaceful situation in the Mediterranean. Further, they continued to think that Italy could be still brought into war against Germany and on the side of France for much longer than argued by some historians.[5]

Diplomatically, the major change in 1938-39 was the move to contain German and Italian expansion into eastern Europe and the Balkans, after the Rome-Berlin Axis was suggested in 1938 and signed in 1939. This would culminate with the seizure of Albania in April 1939 and the guarantee by Great Britain and France to Greece (largely to protect Corfu). The British hope of neutralising Italy so that her limited resources could be spared from the Mediterranean would not be totally abandoned until the fall of the Chamberlain government.[6] Both the British and the French also began negotiating with Turkey to strengthen the eastern Mediterranean flank. France concluded a mutual defence treaty on 23 July 1939 with Turkey, which also resulted in the transfer of the disputed Sanjak of Alexandria (a port on the Turkish-Syrian border) to Turkey.

Although by 1938-39 Italy was building up her navy, it was a slow process. All classes of ship, from the new and rebuilding battleships to torpedo-boats, were delayed. The manning of the new ships with skilled crews, especially the new battleships with their large complements, was another problem. Italy's financial and raw material resources were strained to the utmost – the Minister for Exchange and Currency declared 'we are bankrupt'.[7] In 1938 Germany was already aware that Italy's rearmament was proceeding slowly. General Wilhelm Keitel noted that the 'Navy was already very modest in its progress', largely because of shortages of raw materials for new construction. It was recognised that if war came, it had to be short for both Germany and Italy. It is interesting to note that, in the discussions between the two countries, Italy insisted that a 'local' war between just Italy and France was a distinct possibility, but not for two or three years.[8]

The commanders of the German and Italian navies, Admiral Raeder and Admiral Cavagnari, did hold one discussion on the eve of war, at Friedrichshafen on 20-21 June 1939. Raeder opened the meeting by announcing that the German Navy would operate in the Atlantic and not restrict its operations to home waters (but did admit her best units would remain in the North and Baltic Seas). Cavagnari felt that the Italian Navy could control the Central Mediterranean if war came but was concerned about British attacks there and did state that for the Italian Navy '. . . defence was the only possibility'. He also hoped that Germany would vigorously employ her raiders so as to draw off Allied capital ships from the Mediterranean, and therefore offered them the use of ports of the AOI. The agreement also allowed for the exchange of information (one item was the electric torpedo) and delineated world-wide operational zones for the two fleets (Italy was allocated the Indian and Pacific Oceans). It also discussed the build-up of the fleets which saw 144 Italian submarines by 1942, and 188 German U-boats by 1944. Raeder stated the war would not begin before 1942.[9]

By the end of 1938, Admiral Pound viewed an offensive against Libya from French Tunisia and British-occupied Egypt as an excellent tool to hurt Italy and bolster the small Balkan nations. But as late as May of that year he was concerned that British losses could be heavy from Italy's submarine fleet and air force, stating that the Royal Navy 'shall undoubtedly be subject to attrition to a much greater extent than the Italian [navy]'. As First Sea Lord he later advocated a defensive position in the Mediterranean (which Chamberlain and Lord Halifax, the Foreign Secretary, agreed with).[10]

The French Premier Edouard Daladier was so incensed over the Italian seizure of Albania that he directed his military staff to plan for an *offensive* war against Italy. Earlier, in December 1937, the French Navy had called for ' . . . the primary objective of knocking out Italy, an enemy of secondary importance, before attempting a decision against the principal foe, Germany'. This attitude was only further fuelled when Count Galeazzo Ciano, the Italian foreign minister and son-in-law to Mussolini, spoke on 30 November 1938 and called on France to negotiate with Italy on the fate of Tunis, Corsica, Nice and Djibouti.[11]

Admiral Darlan had begun developing an offensive French naval strategy by the time of the *Anschluss*. He ordered the naval staff to develop plans to defeat an Italian landing on the Tunisian coast, and began to plan for attacks on maritime supply lines to Libya 'with certain efficiency'. By 1939-40 there would be plans for a French-led expedition to Salonika and the seizure of several Greek islands, including Crete – with Greece remaining neutral.[12]

This Allied offensive strategy in the Mediterranean was also supported in several mostly unofficial British quarters as well, by Liddell Hart, Admiral Sir Herbert Richmond and Churchill, among others. Hart in particular viewed Italy as the indirect approach, the soft underbelly to be exploited by an offensive that would bring pressure on Nazi Germany. This new strategy may have also been indirectly supported by the United States, by the dispatch of the Pacific Fleet to Pearl Harbor. This relieved Great Britain of some of the burden of shifting her fleet to the Far East to confront Japan, allowing it to be fully deployed against Germany and Italy. But France was in advance of Great Britain in this, and clearly the concept of offensive operations in the Mediterranean was not supported by those in power in Britain.[13]

If France was reasonably strong in the Mediterranean, primarily at sea, and had war plans ready for implementation, Great Britain was still 'unduly weak . . . in comparison with the air forces which Italy can dispose against them', lacked troops, and was still weak at sea. Furthermore, co-operation between the future allies was limited, although Great Britain wanted, and got, the two modern French battle-cruisers, the *Strasbourg* and *Dunkerque*, to operate in the Atlantic so as to chase down modern German surface warships.[14]

However, with talks underway after the fall of Albania, it was decided that an offensive against Libya was possible. This would be primarily from French Tunisia, but the French were concerned that with the end of the Spanish Civil War, a strengthened Spanish Morocco had to be watched and should be attacked first by the Allies if Spain entered the war. In some naval circles, and among certain British politicians, it was thought that Italy was vulnerable and could be taken out of the war with a knock-out punch. But as studies proceeded, and the need to guard against Germany along the French border grew, fewer and fewer troops and planes were available for a war with Italy – and Britain especially wanted to keep Italy out of the war. But if war came, it was to be a war 'against Italy's colonies, its sea communications and its trade'.[15]

When the war did come in September 1939, Italy and Spain both declared that they were 'non-belligerents'. Italy would use the time until her own entry on 10 June 1940 by building up her strength, sending supplies to Germany (with some to France – honouring for the most part pre-war commercial arrangements), and planning.[16] But Mussolini made several key errors at the start of the war as summarised by Angela Raspin:

> Mussolini's policy was based on a series of suppositions: that there would be a long war, that it would be a war of attrition like the First World War, rather than a war of

movement and that the sides would be so evenly balanced that Italian intervention would be effective. All were falsified by the events of 1940. Mussolini was forced to intervene before he was ready and at a time when his intervention was of no importance to his Ally. He intervened on the supposition that it was his last opportunity before a new settlement was reached, and was again proven wrong.[17]

But it may be that Mussolini's decision not to enter the war in September 1939 may have saved Italy from a major naval and possibly also a limited air and land attack from both France and Great Britain. The French Navy, with some British support from submarines and aircraft carriers, would have outnumbered the Italian Navy and with powerful bases in France and North Africa, could have harassed Italy severely though the winter and spring of 1939-40. Nor should it be overlooked, as Salerno has pointed out, that by declaring 'non-belligerence' Italy staved off the Allies' first offensive and kept them completely on the defensive. Certainly the course of the Second World War would have been very different.

* * *

We now turn to the state of the different armed forces in the Mediterranean at the outbreak of war. Numerical strength alone did not determine victory in this theatre, which was also vitally influenced by the success or failure of the élite cutting edge of the combatants' forces, which was itself influenced by levels of training, the size of such forces and the age and capabilities of the equipment available to them. A further factor was the combatants' varying ability to develop new tactics and equipment as a result of war experience. If one side or the other possessed an advantage and used it, it could bring victory. For example, the Axis enjoyed an advantage in the air with the arrival of the Me109 fighter over Malta, but lost it when Germany withdrew those forces to other theatres and the British started moving Spitfires to the island. Furthermore, the advantage that Italy enjoyed in underwater warfare with the *Maiale* (SLC) brought them successes when they were doing badly elsewhere in the Mediterranean.

As the war progressed, equipment changed and developed, and the Italians fell slowly further and further behind, and their ally either would not or could not supply more powerful units or equipment. Italian industry 'failed to provide the unification of types and long production runs that would have allowed mass production by semi-skilled labour . . . Italian war industry remained essentially artisanal: too few highly skilled workers slowly and lovingly hand-crafting obsolete weapons'. This was from an economy that in 1940 had a national income of $5.3 billion compared to France's $12.5 billion and the United Kingdom's $21.9 billion. It is therefore unsurprising that Mussolini received a report in late 1939 that by the middle of 1940 she would have 'war supplies only for three months of war'.[18] Steel production, vital for her war industry, was weak. Italy produced 2.3 million tons of steel in 1938 compared to France's 6.1 million tons and Great Britain's 10.6 million tons. The Axis 'billionaire' of the war, Germany, produced 22.7 million tons in that same year. During the war Italy would be able, despite being blockaded, to just exceed her average yearly output of steel. One interesting issue that might be addressed by a future historian is the contrast with Italy's war effort in the First World War, which was much more impressive.[19]

Italy was backward as a nation, in spite of almost 20 years of the Fascist experiment, with 43 per cent of her population in 1940 being peasants, with high levels of illiteracy. Another weakness was the relative scarcity of motor vehicles in Italian society, which meant there were fewer people with technical know-how to drive and maintain tanks etc. The educated upper and middle classes tended to avoid the military or technical professions.

It should also be remembered that Mussolini did not hold supreme power. The monarchy did impose restrictions on his actions, and eventually deposed him. The Navy was particularly loyal to the King, unlike the *Regia Aeronautica* – the 'pet service' of Fascism.

Nonetheless, this was a nation that between 1935 and 1938 spent about 11.8 per cent of her national income on the military. Germany spent 12.9 per cent, while France and Great Britain spent about half. Much of this went on the war in Abyssinia and then in Spain, and little was in fact spent on upgrading equipment or developing new weapons.[20]

The Italian military budget in the pre-war years broke down as follows:

THE ITALIAN MILITARY BUDGET FROM 1935 TO 1939 (in millions of lire)

	Army	Navy	Air Force	Total
1935/36	2481 (53.5%)	1305 (28.2%)	849 (18.3%)	4635
1936/37	2313 (47%)	1610 (32.7%)	990 (20.3%)	4913
1937/38	2513 (45.5%)	1858 (32%)	1270 (22.5%)	5641
1938/39	2613 (44.3%)	2013 (34%)	1285 (21.7%)	5911
1939/40	3428 (40.8%)	2774 (33.2%)	2190 (26%)	8329
	13,348 (45.3%)	**9560 (32.4%)**	**6584 (22.3%)**	**29,492**

Probably the single most important piece of military equipment in this war was the aeroplane. One had to first win control of the air, even if this control of the air was simply local – such as provided by an aircraft carrier over the fleet. Once command of the air was achieved, naval operations could be more safely conducted and reconnaissance of the enemy was possible.

At the start of the war in the Mediterranean there is no question that the Allies, particularly the British, were heavily outnumbered by the *Regia Aeronautica*. But 'Italian aircraft compared favourably with those of the French in 1939-40, but did not come up to British or German standards'.[21] The exact strength of the Air Force is in doubt and has been debated during and after the war by both officers and historians. Part of this problem is due to the fact that at the time figures were inflated and obsolete aircraft were included in totals to make the Air Force 'look good'. General Valle reported that in the autumn of 1939 that there were 2200 to 2300 combat-ready planes available, and there were 5344 aircraft in total, but this also included the elderly Cr20 fighter, first built in 1926. Because of the poor mobilisation of the *Regia*

Aeronautica and the false numbers put about by Valle, he would be dismissed by Mussolini on 31 October 1939 and replaced by General Francesco Pricolo.[22]

The best figures for reasonably modern Italian aircraft on the eve of war are as follows:

ITALIAN AIR FORCE FRONTLINE UNITS IN 1939

Fighters	Bombers	Ground Support	Aboard Ship
417 Cr32*	413 S79	63 Ba88	101 Ro43
116 Cr42	180 S81	168 Ba65	17 Cant 25
48 G50	19 S85	34 AP1	**Maritime Bombers**
29 MC200	144 BR20	**Naval Recon**	13 S55
1 Re2000	30 Cant 1007	179 Cant 501	80 Cant 506
1 F5	259 Ca133	24 RS14	**Naval Fighters**
2 Ro51**	33 Ca135	**Army Recon**	32 Ro44
	20 P32	172 Ro 37	8 M41bis
	1 P108	173 Ro37bis	
	1 S82	4 Ca311	
		67 Ca309	

*Practically obsolete.

**Two prototypes only.

Italy had the following planes available to her on 30 June 1940. This includes practically everything with wings:

ITALIAN AIR FORCES AS OF 30 JUNE 1940

Area	Fighters	Bombers	Army Recon	Naval Recon	Hydroplane	TOTAL
Italy	994	1142	430	197	109	2872
Libya	212	211	89	7	none	519
Albania	23	37	12	none	none	72
Aegean	32	57	none	none	none	89
AOI	69	241	14	none	none	324
TOTAL	**1330**	**1688**	**545**	**204**	**109**	**3876**

Another view is of aircraft in relation to crews to man them.

	Planes	Day crews	Night crews
Bombers	645	632	355
Fighters	493	642	40
Auxiliary Air Force	92	161	20
Navy	137	157	83
Total	**1367**	**1592**	**498**[23]

To put this in a broader European context, there are some general figures showing the relationship of the *Regia Aeronautica* to the rest of Europe's air forces. This does not take into account aircraft types, quality of pilots, or efficiency of the various services.

EUROPEAN AIR FORCES 1939/40

Nation	Fighters	Bombers	Recon	Transport	Training	Reserve	TOTAL
USSR*	3200	2200	1200	2000	2200	700	11,500
U.K.**	1400	1500	650	180	?	850	4580
Germany	1671	1259	821	589	?	?	4340
Italy***	1213	1510	815	169	?	?	3707
France***	1200	800	800	120	?	?	2920
Poland	260	174	184	25	205	52	900
Yugoslavia	240	180	140	20	120	50	750
Turkey	254	165	53	40	180	30	772
Romania	160	80	90	15	140	35	520
Finland	180	70	60	10	120	45	485
Hungary	120	65	80	10	120	55	450
Belgium	120	70	60	15	140	25	430
Switzerland	210	15	45	15	100	5	390
Bulgaria	68	49	40	12	140	48	357
Netherlands	140	25	35	20	70	20	310
Greece	45	29	36	6	60	14	190
Norway	46	24	24	10	40	10	154
Spain	200	190	93	24	120	40	667

* = 25 per cent located in the Far East ** = includes Fleet Air Arm
*** = includes air units in the colonies, mandates, and/or protectorates

Italy would bring into service 10,389 aircraft between 1939 and 1943, of which three-quarters would be bombers, fighters, transports, and reconnaissance types.[24]

By 10 June 1940, the French air situation had changed radically since the outbreak of war. But unfortunately for the Italians, their intelligence services provided incorrect figures for both the French and the British, giving the French 900 fighters and 1160 bombers, when in fact they had only 87 fighters and 106 bombers (including 38 torpedo bombers) in Corsica and southern France with another 65 fighters and 85 bombers in North Africa when Italy entered the war.[25] Similarly, the British were reported to have a total of 620 aircraft in the Mediterranean, including 140 fighters and 100 bombers in Egypt alone, when the real figures were 75 fighters (which included some Egyptian Air Force Gladiators) and 96 bombers stationed in Palestine and Egypt. Mis-reporting such as this made it difficult for the Italians to plan accurately for war.

One of the most numerous Italian fighters in 1940 was the Fiat Cr42 biplane, which would remain in service throughout the war, although it would be relegated to ground-attack duties in later years.[26] It mostly served in Africa as it lacked the range to fight over the Mediterranean. But this outmoded design was still a serious candidate as late as 1941 to receive the new Daimler-Benz engines from German which were to improve the performance of other more modern fighters.

The Italians built 1553 Cr42s during the war, some as late as June 1943. That such an outmoded aircraft was kept in production so long shows the inefficiency and lack of discipline in the Italian aircraft industry. The numerous manufacturers resented government interference and would not build another firm's aircraft. Pri-colo's dismissal in 1941 was in part due to his pressure for more control over the aircraft industry.[27] Compared to the Morane Saulnier MS 406, France's most numerous modern fighter, the Cr42 was more manoeuvrable, had a higher ceiling and comparable range, but was slower and less heavily armed with only two machine-guns as opposed to the MS 406's two MGs and one 20mm cannon. The British equivalent was the Gloster Gladiator biplane, which was slower than the Cr42 but again more heavily armed with four MGs. A number of these aircraft were deployed in the Mediterranean at the outbreak of war.

The Italians were in the process of introducing monoplane fighters, but only a few were ready in June 1940. The G.50 was the first Italian all-metal monoplane with retractable landing gear, entering squadron service in 1939 (a few examples had fought in the Spanish Civil War). It was faster than the Cr42 but carried the same armament. Also introduced at the same time was the much more successful Macchi MC200 which could make 318mph, but lacked the ceiling of the other two Italian fighters and was still pathetically under-armed with only two machine-guns.

The French counterpart to the MC200 was the powerfully-armed Dewoitine D.520 which mounted a 20mm cannon and two machine-guns, had a top speed of 329mph and a ceiling of over 36,000ft. It was even more manoeuvrable then the Me109E. Few entered service (only thirty-six by May 1940), but they would see duty later in the war with the Vichy forces. The British had the Hawker Hurricane Mk1 which would not be deployed in numbers to the Mediterranean until after the Battle of Britain. It was superior to Italian fighters, though not quite as manoeuvrable at lower altitude, and was heavily armed with eight 0.303in Browning machine-guns. Only later-generation Italian fighters and the German Me109 were superior.

The workhorse of the Italian bomber force would be the S.79 tri-motor, nick-named the *Sparviero* (Sparrowhawk). Originally designed as a bomber, it would perform sterling service as a torpedo bomber. Based on the earlier S.81 design, it had a metal and wood structure with a composite covering. With a crew of six, early versions had a top speed of 267mph and a range of over 1000 miles. The final version was powered by three 1000hp engines that allowed it to reach 297mph. A total of 1217 were built between October 1936 and June 1943. Its replacement, the S.84, of which 309 were built, was slower and was not as popular with its crews. The other main Italian bomber was the larger tri-motor Cant Z1007, known as the *Alcione* (Halcyon). Of all-wooden construction, it had good range and 560 were built, first seeing large-scale use in the Greek campaign.

Italy had many other bombers, some built with very short production runs, and this highlights the basic problem of the Italian aircraft industry, with too many firms (fifteen) building too many different types of aircraft, rather than concentrating on building large numbers of only a few types. In theory, these companies could produce a total of 350 planes a month of which 72 were bombers and 103 were fighters. The Italian aircraft industry was never able to solve its basic problems of needing 'to design new types, go over to all-metal airframes and to introduce assembly line method(s) of construction'.[28]

The Italian aviation industry grew quickly with a workforce of 11,064 in 1934, 51,384 in 1938, 110,366 in 1940 and 149,875 by 1943. In 1939 a further 24,000 men and women were employed building radial engines, but it was these under-powered engines which were the main problem with Italian aircraft, and it was not until they adopted the German-designed Daimler-Benz engines that they built their best planes. The largest aircraft manufacturer was Caproni, employing 28 per cent of the workforce, and Alfa Romeo was the largest engine manufacturer with 33 per cent of the workforce. Italy's automobile industry, the most modern mass-production industry in 1940, switched to the production of aircraft engines during the war and actually exported licensed Daimler-Benz engines back to Germany.[29]

French bombers had little impact on the war. The most common one used by Vichy after the armistice was the LeO 451, a twin-engined aircraft with a crew of four. Faster than the S.79, it carried a bomb load of 4400lbs compared to the S.79's 2756lbs and had a similar range. In the early part of the war, British bombers would have their greatest impact as torpedo bombers.

One area where the Italians were more advanced than their German ally was air-launched torpedoes. From 1922 on the Italian Navy had been developing torpedo warfare, but slowly and in conflict with the *Regia Aeronautica*, as will be detailed in the next chapter. Their early experiments had been with seaplanes, and a purpose-designed torpedo bomber was never developed, although considerable success was achieved with modified S.79s. British torpedo aircraft were the venerable carrier-borne Fairey Swordfish and later in the war the land-based Vickers Wellington and Bristol Beaufort, which were slower than the S.79 but were capable of night operations.[30]

The Italian Naval High Command had considered the development of aircraft carriers but had rejected it (see Chapter 8). The German Official History points out that;

> All in all, the Italian [naval] units were certainly up to international standards. What they lacked most of all was effective air support. More particularly, an aircraft-carrier would have been needed for a balanced fleet structure in modern terms. The inadequate range of land-based aircraft, moreover, had an adverse effect on the operational employment of Italian vessels, as sailing without air cover was regarded as too dangerous. It is true that, even where it should have been possible, naval-air co-operation frequently did not function because the organisational basis was faulty.[31]

The British had fully embraced the aircraft carrier after the First World War and maintained a sizeable force of older ships. The new *Illustrious* class, the main wartime-built fleet carriers, were unique in having armoured hangers and flight decks, which gave them a level of protection against bombing and later Kamikaze attacks which no American carrier could match, but it also reduced the number of aircraft they could carry.

Other factors adversely affected the efficiency of British carrier warfare. When the RAF was created in 1918, it took many of the best men from the old Royal Naval Air Service into it, and the Admiralty did not regain sole control of the Fleet Air Arm until 1937.[32] In contrast, the American and Japanese navies retained control of their own naval air arms and had officers who vigorously developed carrier warfare.

James Goldrick wrote: 'American and Japanese carriers could launch and recover aircraft more rapidly than the British and could marshal their machines in the air more quickly'. The enclosed hangars of British carriers did not allow aircraft engines to be warmed-up below deck, as was possible on American ships with their open hangars. Furthermore, the British practice of stowing the planes before allowing another to move to the flight deck also slowed operations.[33]

These factors, as well as others such as older and less efficient aircraft, would result in slower reaction times, and slower assembling of a force for an attack. The practical result was that the effective range of an air strike from a British carrier was one-third less than from an American or Japanese carrier. But the ability to put up fighter cover over their fleet and launch air strikes against the Italian fleet would be a vital advantage for the British in the Mediterranean, particularly in 1940-41, an advantage the Axis could only partly counter with submarines and land-based aircraft.[34] The French were aware of the need for carriers but did not give their development priority. Their one carrier in service in 1939, the converted battleship *Bearn*, was too slow for fleet operations, and the two other carriers they had under construction were never completed.

The official and semi-official history of the *Regia Aeronautica* and the memoirs of those responsible for it during the Second World War deserve some consideration. General Giuseppe Valle, Chief of Staff and Undersecretary of the Air Force until 9 November 1939, was blamed for the poor state of the air force at the beginning of the war and put on trial. He put his own point of view in his memoirs published in 1958.[35] Although he was later officially cleared, public opinion still held him responsible for the *Regia Aeronautica*'s lack of preparedness for war. His successor, General Francesco Pricolo, remained in his post until 14 November 1941 when he was himself replaced by General Rino Corso Fougier. Pricolo wrote in his memoirs that he was 'surprised' by the state of the air force when he took over, a curious statement from one who had previously been commander of the II Air Zone, responsible for all air units in north-eastern Italy. Fougier likewise expressed 'surprise', and his deputy chief of staff, General Giuseppe Santoro, attempted to blame their predecessors for all the failings of the Air Force. Santoro had considerable influence on post-war Italian air force studies since as chief of the Air Force's historical office, he wrote the semi-official history of the *Regia Aeronautica*, which has appeared in three editions.[36]

There were many problems with the *Regia Aeronautica*, the fundamental one being the difference between the strategic and tactical concepts of the Air Force and the aeroplanes ordered from industry. Another was the shortage of engines powerful enough for modern warplanes. Although Valle's acquisition of German engine designs went some way towards solving this, Italy's weak industrial base was slow to switch over to production of these engines. Alfa Romeo was only able to produce seventy-four of the Daimler-Benz engines in 1941, while those bought directly from Germany were slow to arrive. Furthermore, there was also a shortage of high-octane fuel for aircraft engines. Therefore, when *Officine Meccaniche Reggiane*

(Reggiane) produced a fighter with its own engine design which needed scarce high-octane fuel, but was faster than the MC200 or G.50 fighters, the latter two were preferred by Pricolo, who criticised the Reggiane fighter as too specialised. Another major problem was the relationship between the Air Ministry and the aeronautical industry, particularly FIAT, which received the lion's share of orders. Orders were made more to 'exploit the productive capabilities' of the plants than to obtain good aircraft, which partly explains why the Cr42 biplane was produced until after the Armistice.[37] Development of monoplane fighters was also held back by the Air Force's preference for the aerobatic capabilities of biplanes, which had little to do with modern aerial combat. The lack of powerful engines and other design weaknesses also contributed to the weak armament of Italian fighters.

The Italians were thinking in terms of an 'oceanic navy' by the late 1930s. One proposal submitted to Mussolini in 1936 called for a fleet of nine battleships, three aircraft carriers, thirty-six cruisers (twelve being the small *Capitani Romani* type – see below), and eighty-four ocean-going submarines to be built by 1942. 'Such a force would enable the navy to drive enemy shipping from the Mediterranean and Red Sea, to defend its new *mare nostrum* from outside by sweeps into the Atlantic and Indian oceans, to savage the enemy shipping lanes, and to conduct joint operations with the new German *Kriegsmarine* against the common foe.' Italy could not afford this vast building plan, so only parts of it were adopted later in 1937.[38]

At the outbreak of war, the battleship was still regarded as the principal naval weapon. As 'Jacky' Fisher said, 'The battleship is the embodiment of concentration of force.' Marine Colonel Theodore L Gatchel notes that a 1943 study group established by the Japanese Imperial General Headquarters 'had estimated that a single (modern) US battleship was the equivalent in firepower of five Japanese divisions'. Their role would diminish as the war progressed but they still made an important contribution.[39]

The most modern battleships in the Mediterranean in 1940 were probably the French *Richelieu* and *Jean Bart* (except for their electronics). The Italian *Littorio* class were probably the next best, followed by the British *King George V* class, which suffered in comparison due to their restricted displacement and their use of the troubled 14in gun. However, their modern gunnery radar would have more than made up for any disadvantages they may have had in a ship-to-ship contest.

This introduces an often-overlooked factor in comparing the capabilities of different warships which goes beyond merely 'counting guns'. British radar-assisted range-finding equipment, like that of the Americans and Germans, was excellent, while the Italians and French, despite having good ships, lagged somewhat in this field. The battleships were large enough to mount the largest rangefinders, *ie* those with the longest visual base, and they were also roomy enough to accommodate the new advanced equipment to perform the necessary calculations for naval gunnery.

In the inter-war period the Royal Navy could not afford to modernise all her battleships, unlike the Americans and Japanese, so several ships did not receive all the improved equipment allowing firing at longer ranges. Therefore, when it was learned in the early 1930s that the Japanese were practising firing at 30,000 yards, it spurred the now technologically-inferior British Navy (whose new *Nelson* class battleships' 16in guns were giving 'excessive spreads' in their salvos) with too many unreconstructed battleships to adopt medium-range and night fighting as a response, the means by which the Royal Navy was to gain some of its greatest victories in the coming war. As Jon Sumida has written;

> Preparations for night fighting began to increase dramatically in 1931 and, by 1934, the Royal Navy was investigating situations in which the battle fleet deliberately sought night action against the enemy's capital units. Under successive commanders of the Mediterranean Fleet, the Royal Navy's premier and tactically most influential force, night fighting became standard.

Herein lay the origins of Matapan.[40] In contrast, although the Italians had conducted some 140 night practices including their battleships in the 1920s, in the 1930s a decision was made for the battle fleet to decline night engagements, with light forces warning the main fleet to turn away from the enemy at night, in theory at least. This meant that 8in and larger guns were not supplied with flashless powder, vital for night combat, until *after* the battle of Matapan. Vice-Admiral Angelo Iachino would later write;

> . . . this was surely a serious gap in our preparation for the war, with little explanation because night combat is an action to which the minor navies had to be devoted to, for they can not expose their forces during the daylight to the superior enemy . . . [after the defeat at Matapan] the tactical doctrine for night actions was thus immediately modified. Our ships received in a short time devices for improved night fire control, and the guns were supplied with flash-less charges. Radar, instead, arrived much later and for this reason our ships were never able in the war to meet the enemy in combat in night actions. Our naval actions were thus limited to the daylight hours, while the enemy took profit from this preferring night attacks, when he was in a more favourable conditions of visibility, thanks to radar.

He might have also added British training for night combat to the above.[41] It should also be noted that the Admiralty carefully chose the ships that were to fight in the Mediterranean. It was no accident that the fully-reconstructed, well-trained and excellently-equipped HMS *Warspite* was sent to the Mediterranean when Italy joined the war, and this practice was to continue throughout the war.

The Italians suffered other problems with their gunnery. Too high tolerances for propellant charges caused excessive salvo spread, which was compounded in 8in and lighter twin gun mounts where the guns were placed too close together in an attempt to save weight, so that the shells' flight interfered with each other. In attempts to achieve long-range fire, the Italians designed their guns with very high muzzle-velocities which increased wear on the gun linings, again adversely affecting salvo spread. This increased wear also restricted the number of practice shoots the fleet could carry out. Finally, both their high-explosive and armour-piercing shells had problems with their fuses and duds were common.[42] The problem was only worsened for the Axis with the introduction of range-finding radar, which the Allies developed most throughly and had the greatest success with.[43]

Italy did not begin construction of new battleships until France had announced the construction of the second *Dunkerque* class battlecruiser. They had studied different 'small' battleship designs in the inter-war period, usually in the 18,000-23,000 ton range, but opted for the full-sized 35,000-ton *Littorio* class. The class would exceed this tonnage, displacing 40,516 tons, but the treaty limitations had expired at the end of 1936 and were not renewed. They were armed with 15in guns as this was thought to be ' . . . within Italian industrial capabilities'. In terms of muzzle energy, these were the most powerful guns of their calibre, designed for long-range fire.[44] They also carried a heavy secondary armament of twelve 6in guns because their probable enemy, the French, had numerous large destroyers.[45] Anti-aircraft defence was also strong, although not quite up to Allied standards. The *Littorios* carried twelve 90mm AA guns (comparable to the German 88mm gun) and thirty-two lighter weapons, which would increase in number during the war. In general, Italian AA was slightly better gun for gun at the start of the war, but neither side at that time had as efficient a close-in gun system as the Oerlikon or Bofors would later provide. The Italians would buy some of the Swiss-designed 20mm Oerlikon gun during the war, but shortage of funds restricted the numbers that could be bought. The British had at first rejected both the Bofors and Oerlikon before the war, but quickly adopted them when the need arose – they had a high rate of fire and were very accurate. Ironically, when first seen as a twin-mount on board a Dutch destroyer, and adopted, the 40mm Bofors mount was made by a subsidiary of a German armaments company![46]

The Italians adopted a special underwater protection system developed by General Inspector of the Engineer Corps Umberto Pugliese, in the *Littorios* and their older reconstructed battleships, though the latters' beam was not wide enough for it to work effectively. It was a development of the conventional 'bulge' system. The Pugliese system,

> used a concentric void-liquid-void compartment in various configurations, much like a tin can within a tin can within a tin can, with the middle can being liquid-filled (either water or fuel oil) at all times and the outer and innermost cans being empty. The side of the middle 'can' facing inboard was made up of a 28-40mm layer of silicon-manganese high-tensile steel called *Elevata Resistenza* (ER) steel, which was probably somewhat similar to the British Ducol Steel used for light armour and torpedo bulkhead in WWII.[47]

The system would theoretically contain the explosion of a 350kg warhead by having the first layer forced in against the incompressable liquid in the second layer which would transfer the energy into the empty space behind that and thus contain the damage. It worked well on the *Vittorio Veneto* when she was torpedoed by the submarine *Urge* on 14 December 1941, when the 340kg torpedo warhead caused heavy loss of life, but did not cripple her. However, the efficiency of the system did suffer from being riveted instead of welded, and it became less effective as the beam narrowed towards the bow and stern. Bulge systems would be rendered obsolete both by the increasing power of torpedoes and the development of the magnetic fuse that detonated the torpedo underneath the ship rather than against its side. Combined with the increasing numbers of aircraft and the carriers that launched them, the battleship was doomed.

Instead of building a proposed 26,500-ton battlecruiser armed with six 15in guns in response to the *Dunkerque* class, the Italians decided to extensively rebuild their four old battleships of the *Andrea Doria* and *Conte di Cavour* classes. It has been argued that this was an error as these ships were shown to be 'extremely vulnerable to modern ordnance, and they proved of little value during World War II'. While their combat record was limited, they did perform some excellent missions during the 'Battleship Convoys' in the winter/spring of 1941/42 which delivered critical supplies to the Axis troops in North Africa.[48] They were also powerful AA platforms, though the *Andrea Doria* and *Caio Duilio* were better equipped than their older near-sisters. None of the Italian cruisers were as well armed in this regard, especially the older ones. The latter two battleships were also later fitted with primitive radar sets in 1943.[49] These ships were by any comparison inferior to a modern battleship or battlecruiser, their only advantage being that they were faster than many of the older Allied battleships, and they were certainly much superior to any enemy cruiser. They could also have been successfully used for shore bombardment in the planned invasion of Malta.[50] The money spent on their reconstruction (as well as the fuel and manpower they took up) might well have better been used to build aircraft carriers, leaving the *Littorio* class as the only battleships, but such judgements are easy to make now, and they would perhaps have better repaid the investment in them had they been more aggressively used. As it was, they were capable of taking on the French battlecruisers, even with the powerful French light forces supporting them.

The French began the pre-war battleship race with their excellent battlecruisers, the 26,600-ton *Dunkerque* and *Strasbourg*, capable of 30 knots and armed with eight 13in guns in two quadruple turrets forward. Their main weakness was a thin armour belt (maximum thickness 9in) and a poor AA battery of sixteen 5.1 in dual-purpose guns and lighter machine-guns. The lighter AA guns were to be upgraded but the outbreak of war prevented this. They were followed by two of the finest battleships built in the pre-war era, the *Richelieu* and *Jean Bart*, although neither was completed before the fall of France. Of her older battleships, only the three ships of the *Bretagne* class received extensive modernisation in the inter-war period, being fitted with new 13.4in guns, augmented AA batteries and new oil-fired boilers. However, they were still handicapped by a speed of only 21 knots, significantly slower than their Italian counterparts. France's main base was at Toulon, with others at Mers-el-Kebir near Oran, Algiers, and Bizerta. This gave her a powerful position in the Mediterranean. The lack of exchange of information before the war between the future Allies meant that France, like Italy, entered the war without radar.[51]

When the French laid down their first 'Treaty Cruisers', the heavy cruisers *Duquesne* and *Tourville* of 10,000 tons, Italy replied with the *Trento* and *Trieste*. When France laid down four *Suffren* class heavy cruisers, Italy replied with the very successful *Zara* class. Finally, the last heavy cruisers built by either power saw the French *Algerie* met by the *Bolzano*. The Treaty Cruisers were always thought of as eggshells armed with hammers (the Italian term was 'glass ships with big guns'), and the French probably designed the worst heavy cruisers in the inter-war period. Their first six were almost devoid of protection (the *Tourville* class had only 430 tons of armour), although the French actually added more and more armour to each individual ship as they were begun. The *Algerie* marked a definite change in design philosophy and received a reasonable amount of protection, as well as an improved 8in gun and shell with slightly greater range.

The first two Italian heavy cruisers (and their last one) were slightly less well protected than the *Algerie* while the *Zaras* were some of the best-protected heavy cruisers of the war, with a 6in belt and 6in on the turret facings. They were not as fast as the other Italian or French heavy cruisers, and they were considerably over the treaty weight limits. The *Bolzano* was an improved *Trento* and did not carry as much armour as the *Zaras*.[52] Italian warships did tend to exceed the treaty weight limits, which was certainly an unfair advantage in their design, but in the case of the battleships and the heavy cruisers, especially the *Zara* class, this was not due to superior technology being employed. They were riveted and not electrically welded like German warships, and nor did they reflect any great advantages in armouring beyond their thicker plating – in fact ton-for-ton Italian armour plate was slightly inferior to British and American armour plate.

Italian light cruisers were also built largely in response to the French Navy. Their first four light cruisers, the 'Condottieri' type, were built to counter the large French destroyers of the 1920s. These *Contre Torpilleurs* of the *Jaguar*, *Aigle* and *Lion* classes, sometimes known as 'super destroyers', were over 2000 tons and at least capable of 35 knots. They were themselves developed as a response to such vessels as the Italian *Leone* class flotilla leaders of the First World War and the larger German destroyers, one of which, the 2500-ton *S113*, had been handed to the French as war reparation.[53] The 'Condottieri' class displaced just over 5000 tons, had excellent speed, touching almost 40 knots while partially loaded, and were armed with eight 6in guns. But as time wore on they lost more and more speed due to wear and tear on their engines. They were also very lightly armoured.[54] Against the *Contre Torpilleurs* their speed and armament would have allowed them to choose and maintain the range, but as they aged, their speed dropped, and when they faced British cruisers, which had similar armament and better protection, they would be at a considerable disadvantage.[55]

The Italians would continue to respond to the French light cruiser building programme over the next ten years. The French built twelve light cruisers of varying designs (two were primarily for mine-laying) but it was the final *La Galissonnière* class of light cruisers, laid down in 1931, which would set the highest standards. There were six ships in the class, displacing 7600 tons (allowed by a new treaty limit of 8000 tons for light cruisers), armed with nine 6in guns and having a sustained speed of 34 knots. Their armour actually exceeded that of some French heavy cruisers, with a 4in belt and 4in on the turret faces. The Italians responded with four additional consecutive classes of two ships each which progressively grew larger, better armoured (and therefore slower), and culminated with the two *Abruzzi* class light cruisers laid down in 1933. They were armed with ten 6in guns in four turrets, could steam at 34 knots, and were armoured with a little over 5in on their belt and turret faces. They had now grown in size to almost 10,000 tons. There followed a brief halt to cruiser building as both sides' naval budgets were taken up with paying for the new capital ships.

Construction resumed in 1937 with the French *De Grasse* class of three ships, essentially slightly larger and faster versions of the *La Galissonnière* class. A proposed class of heavy cruisers was authorised in 1940 as a response to the German *Admiral Hipper* class, displacing 14,470 tons and armed with nine 8in guns, but none were built. On the eve of war, Italy ordered two improved version of the *Abruzzi* class (which were never laid down), but then returned to the concepts that had given rise to the 'Condottieri' class. Again as a response to new classes of French *Contre Torpilleurs*, which were now mounting 5.5in guns, the Italians laid down the twelve ships of the 'Capitani Romani' class (all named after Roman generals). Virtually unarmoured, they were armed with eight 5.3in guns, and had a top speed of 41 knots (34 knots sustained), allowing them to out-gun enemy destroyers and escape cruisers with their superior speed. Only three of this class would be completed before the Armistice.

Italian destroyer construction concentrated on large numbers of relatively small vessels, apart from the twelve-strong *Navigatori* class of 1927 with six 4.7in guns and the earlier *Leone* class. The typical Italian destroyer was fast and armed with two turrets with twin 4.7in guns, two torpedo mounts each with two or three 21in torpedoes, a few light AA guns and was also fitted for mine-laying. With limited anti-submarine capability, they were comparable to similar small French and British designs. The Italians planned to have a large number of small economical warships that could be used for many duties in the Mediterranean. Apart from their high speed, they were not really an outstanding design and two would be lost during the war in heavy storms. Each succeeding class tended to become larger and larger, but only those designed during the Second World War exceeded 2000 tons. The Italians had purchased an effective Norwegian-designed torpedo in 1932, and although they recovered a British air-dropped torpedo in 1935, it did not affect their designs.[56]

The French 'super destroyers' were designed to operate in divisions of three ships, and were to converge attacks on the enemy. *The Jaguar* class had five 5.1in guns (which had a range of 20,300 yards, although their inferior rangefinding equipment limited their effective range to about half that), while the latter two classes had 5.5in guns. The early French 5.5in gun fired a heavy shell but had a relatively slow rate of fire, and later weapons adopted the breech design from German ships obtained as reparations after the First World War, which doubled their rate of fire. Before the war, there was a plan to re-arm the *Jaguar* class as AA ships with twin 3.9in dual-purpose guns, and later during the war the British 4in gun was considered for them.[57]

The French also built numerous smaller (1300-ton) *Torpilleurs d'Escadre* armed with four 5.1in guns each and capable of 33 knots speed. The later *Le Hardi* class of twelve ships mounted six 5.1in guns and were approximately 2 knots faster, in order to operate with the new fast capital ships. Their anti-submarine capability was limited, and they were armed with a unique towed anti-submarine torpedo called the 'Ginocchio'. As a result of the lessons of the Spanish Civil War, the French were planning to upgrade the AA armament of their destroyers when war broke out.

Both Italy and France built 600-ton destroyers that the French called 'light destroyers' and the Italians 'torpedo-boats'. These ships were built because the naval treaties placed no limit on the number of ships of this size that could be constructed. The French *La Melphomene* class was armed with two 3.9in guns, two torpedoes, a light AA armament, and one rack of depth charges. They had a speed of 34 knots but were not very seaworthy. On the eve of the war the French began the much larger *La Fier* class of approximately 1010 tons which were interesting in that they were designed for AA and anti-submarine work and would also have carried sonar. The 1933 model 3.9in guns were dual-purpose with mounts capable of 90° elevation and they also carried eight 13.2mm machine guns. None would be completed.[58] The Italians would build the *Spica* class of thirty ships all laid down between 1934 and 1937. By cheating on the 600-ton limit, they weighed in at almost 800 tons and had a speed of 34 knots. Each was crewed by about 118 men, and were armed with three 3.9in guns capable of only 45° elevation, a light AA armament, limited depth charge capability, four 17.7in torpedoes in twin mounts, and were fitted for mine-laying. These little ships would see extensive service during the war and two-thirds of them would be lost, mostly while acting as convoy escorts. The Italians also kept many old destroyers from the First World War in service, likewise classified as torpedo-boats. They would see limited convoy duty during the war in safer areas.

They also built a small class of escorts, the 840-ton *Orsas*, of which more would be built during the war. Designed for only 28 knots, they were like the British 'Hunt' class convoy escorts. The tiny 334-ton *Albatross*, built in 1934, carried the first Italian experimental sonar set at the time of the Spanish Civil War. Sonar was not widely introduced into the Italian fleet until after the war broke out. The *Albatross*' set was called 'peritero' and had a range of about 2000m. In fact, in 1929-31 a French-designed sonar, the Langevin-Florisson set, had been mounted on a torpedo-boat and a destroyer, but it had proved unsatisfactory. But by 1937 the Navy Staff had learnt that foreign countries had better experiences. This led to the mounting of a domestic-produced sonar, the Safar P600, on the anti-submarine corvette *Albatros* in 1939. At the same time the company was selected to produce two types of submarine sonar, SAFAR MC 3000 and GC 3000, which begun to appear at the end of 1942. Since the SAFAR P600 was very slow in production – no sets becoming available until early 1942 – the navy turned to the Germans for help and at the end of 1941 received forty German-built sonar sets. The introduction of sonar to the Italian Navy took place only after 20 months of war and there seemed to be very litle training in its use, as every A/S unit had statistically an average of only 1.5 opportunities to launch practice depth charges.[59]

The modern torpedo-boats *Lince*, *Castore* and *Sagittario* and the escort *Orsa* began to operate with sonar in December 1941, patrolling the Gulf of Taranto with the *Gino Nais* and *Pasman*, two small merchant ships equipped with sonar and depth charges. They did not sink any British submarines but helped to keep the patrolled areas free of them. The installation of sonar began to increase in May 1942 with sixteen further units, and fifty-two more by the end of the year. By the Armistice 101 sets had been installed. The *Orsa* class were among the first to receive it.[60] Otherwise, the older ships had to rely on various types of hydrophones, which were of good quality but of limited capability. The operator had to have particularly sensitive hearing, for one thing. It would not be until August 1941 that the *Antisom* (anti-submarine) school would be established under Rear-Admiral Da Zara. The threat from British submarines lead to the building of a new class of escort destroyers, the sixteen *Animosos*, and the numerous *Gabbiano* class corvettes. Both classes had sonar, and the *Animosos* had a speed of 25 knots and were armed with three 3.9in guns and four 17.7in torpedo tubes. The *Gabbianos* displaced less than 800 tons and could only make 16-17 knots instead of their designed 18, but were nonetheless effective and accounted for several enemy submarines.

Italy specialised in the construction of small *MAS* boats (motor torpedo boats), a legacy of the First World War when she had had some notable successes with similar craft against the Austro-Hungarian fleet. Italy had about fifty high-speed *MAS* boats when the war started, but they were not very seaworthy. At 25 tons, they could make 40+ knots in favourable conditions and were armed with two 17.7in torpedoes and one machine-gun. Improved classes were developed as the war progressed, based largely on German designs. The Italians also built a large number of 60-ton anti-submarine launches (*Vedette Antisommergibili*, or *VAS* boats) during the war for coastal operations with a typical speed of 19 knots and armed with two 17.7in torpedo-tubes, machine-guns and depth charges.[61]

The British, or more properly the Commonwealth, naval effort would fluctuate throughout the war, as a variety of demands were made on the Royal Navy's resources. Most of the older battleships would serve in the Mediterranean at one time or another, but both the eastern and western Mediterranean squadrons usually had at least one modern or reconstructed capital ship capable of long-range fire and an aircraft carrier to provide air cover over the fleet. The older British battleships, like those of the French, were in varying states of reconstruction, the worst being the *Royal Sovereign* class, with a top speed of no more than 20 knots, much slower than their Italian counterparts.

Thanks to her world-wide trade commitments, Great Britain maintained a large cruiser fleet. Of these, the 10,000-ton 'Treaty Cruisers' would mostly not serve in the Mediterranean, being somewhat handicapped by their inadequate armour protection. At the outbreak of war the First World War 'C' class cruisers, armed with five 6in guns in single mounts, were operating in the Mediterranean, but would later be replaced by ships of the same class which had been reconstructed as AA cruisers after the Abyssinian crisis. Their armament varied, but between six and ten 4in guns plus lighter AA was typical.

In contrast, almost all the inter-war light cruisers would serve in the Mediterranean at some point. These included the five *Leander* class ships and the three *Perth* class cruisers built for the Royal Australian Navy, armed with eight 6in guns in four turrets, and the smaller *Arethusa* class of four ships which had one less turret. They were well-armoured (except for the turret faces which had no more than 1in splinter protection), and could make 30 knots, but their small size (under 8000 tons) made them vulnerable to torpedoes. These were followed by the larger 'Town' class laid down between 1934 and 1936. Weighing in at close to 10,000 tons, they were armed with twelve 6in guns in four triple turrets, giving them enhanced firepower. They were a well-balanced design and had good seagoing qualities. Ten were built, although the last two, the *Edinburgh* and *Belfast*, differed from the earlier versions, being slightly enlarged and originally planned for four power-loaded quadruple turrets.[62] The First Sea Lord, Admiral Sir Ernie Chatfield, favoured the building of larger cruisers like the 'Town' class as war approached, as opposed to the smaller *Leanders*. In the inter-war period, Britain had attempted to restrict other naval powers by treaty to building smaller cruisers, so that they could build more cheaper ships, but this had failed and the 'Towns' had to be built as a response to the Japanese *Mogami* class and the American *Brooklyn* class cruisers, both of which were originally armed with fifteen 6in guns in five triple turrets. Therefore, in order to maintain the fleet of seventy cruisers needed to meet the Royal Navy's global commitments, older ships such as the 'C class had to be kept in service.[63]

The British did build another class of light cruiser, the *Didos*, beginning in 1936. They were designed to meet a requirement in 1934 from Vice-Admiral W W Fisher, who wanted small cruisers for scouting purposes in the Mediterranean but which were also capable of contributing to the AA defence of the fleet. Churchill for one disliked them for their small size, but their numerous 5.25in DP guns gave good firepower both in surface actions and air defence, and their small size (5770 tons) reduced their manpower demands. They would prove quite capable of defending themselves against enemy aircraft, only one being lost to air attack, but their small size again made them vulnerable to torpedoes.[64]

The early classes of destroyers built in the inter-war period were fairly small, armed with four 4.7in guns, with the flotilla leaders having five, but when it was realised that three twin turrets cost almost the same as four single mounts, larger ships began to be built, culminating in the sixteen ships of the 'Tribal' class built in 1936-38. Armed with eight 4.7in guns in four twin turrets and four torpedo tubes, they were a response to the larger classes of destroyer built by the French, Italians and Japanese. It was planned that there should be two special squadrons of these powerful ships, one of which would be permanently stationed in the Mediterranean. Later classes mounted six guns in three turrets and increased the torpedo armament to ten tubes.[65] The ships of the 'L' and 'M' classes had 4.7in guns capable of higher elevation firing, but none of the British 4.7in weapons were true dual-purpose guns capable of high-angle fire at aircraft. This was also true for the Italian 4.7in and newly introduced 5.3in guns and for most of the French 5.1in and 5.5in guns. Only the American 5in and later models of the French 5.1in were designed for DP firing.[66]

It is important to be aware that in many cases the ships and equipment of both sides were not necessarily as capable as they appeared on paper. For example, on paper there seems to be little diffrence between the old British battleships *Warspite* and *Resolution*, apart from the latter's lower speed. However, *Warspite* had been fully reconstructed before the war whilst *Resolution* had not, and this would be the deciding factor as to which ship would see service in the Mediterranean.

After her reconstruction between 1934-37, the *Warspite* was a much more capable ship by the outbreak of war. The range of her main armament was increased to 32,000 yards by increasing the elevation of the gun mounts from 20° to 30° and she was also fitted with improved range-finding equipment. Weight-saving reductions were made and her propulsion system was upgraded, giving her a best speed of approximately 23 knots. Limited improvements were also made to her horizontal protection and anti-aircraft armament, which would be further augmented during the war, and radar would be added later.

The *Resolution*, however, did not receive a reconstruction, and so was not as well protected from aircraft, continued with older engines, and the range of her main armament was only 23,734 yards with standard ammunition, although she did have her AA armament improved and received some equipment upgrades before the war. Her sister-ship the *Royal Sovereign* was more thoroughly overhauled but still made only 20 knots best speed, although she had received improved high-altitude range finding equipment for her augmented AA guns on the eve of war. The threat of air attack and the increased danger from plunging fire at the greater gunnery ranges now common led to all navies increasing the horizontal armour protection on their older battleships, especially over the magazines.

Another example were the Italian 'Condottieri' class light cruisers which were credited with a speed of 39-41 knots. They had achieved this on trials in 1931 in a lightly-loaded condition, but at the outbreak of war, with 10 years' wear on their engines, they were really only capable of 33 knots. Wartime modifications would add weight and further reduce their speed. Similarly, in 1940 the Italians still classified the ex-German ships *Bari* and *Taranto* as light cruisers. They had been built in 1912 and had been ceded to Italy as war reparations after the First World War. With a top speed of only 24 knots and armed with worn 5.9in guns with a maximum range of only 17,600 metres, they were in no sense first-line ships, but nonetheless were classified as such.[67]

Italy would also make modifications to her warships both before and during the war, but to a lesser extent than the Allies, in part because in wartime her limited shipbuilding capacity was taken up with repairing damaged ships rather than reconstructing others. Major rebuilding was limited to the four old battleships, but other classes were improved during the war, for example, the *Orsa* class destroyer escorts. The importance of convoy protection in the Mediterranean war led to these four ships receiving extensive modifications, including the replacement of their original AA machine-guns with up to six 20mm Oerlikon cannon, the fitting of additional depth-charge racks and an improved camouflage scheme.[68] The British had a considerable advantage in this area in that they could send ships to American yards, which had vast capacity and could effect repairs very quickly. At the same time, ships under repair commonly received upgraded electronics and improved AA armament.

Italy was well supplied with naval and air bases throughout her territories, but there were still problems. There was a shortage of AA guns and barrage balloons to defend these bases, and many of her airfields had only dirt strips, which were not all-weather capable.[69] British port options were more limited. A large floating dock had to be brought out to Alexandria so large warships could be docked there. Malta was too close to Italian air bases to allow its otherwise excellent facilities to be fully used, while Haifa was too small. At the other end of the Mediterranean there was Gibraltar, a powerful base, but it also lacked repair facilities.

As regards personnel, both the Italian Navy and the Air Force could draw upon higher-quality recruits than the army, due largely to their prestige. However, the overall availability of skilled labour and officer material in Italy was limited in comparison to other Great Powers, which may have contributed to the problems the forces suffered with maintenance of equipment, particularly aircraft. The Navy also suffered from a relative shortage of officers, who made up only 5.4 per cent of total personnel, as opposed to 7.5 per cent in the French Navy and the Royal Navy's 9.2 per cent.[70] At command level, the British had two admirals, Somerville and Cunningham, who had both seen service in the Mediterranean in destroyers and were long-serving sea officers, whereas the Italian fleet commander in 1940, Vice-Admiral Inigo Campioni, had been deputy chief of the Naval Staff, back at headquarters on land, which was to exert so much control of the Italian fleet at sea. One of the main complaints after the war was that Italy had not had the money or the inclination to train her men. Time and again, due to budgetary pressures, training for all three services was insufficient.

In the field of military intelligence, the Allies had what would prove to be a decisive advantage over the Axis. British counter-intelligence cost Italy the services of many of her agents in the Middle East, particularly in Egypt in the run-up to war. Both sides employed aircraft for high-altitude reconnaissance of various important ports, cities, and other installations. Just before the war, the British had sent two agents 'on holiday' to photograph Italian installations in Sicily, Sardinia, Libya and the Dodecanese islands.[71] But it would be ULTRA, the ability of the Allies to decode many Axis radio messages, that would be a decisive factor against the Axis naval effort in the Mediterranean. The Italians had already used eight German Hagelin and Enigma code machines in the Spanish Civil War, prefering the former. Convinced, like the Germans, of the perfect security of this equipment, the Italians purchased several Hagelin machines for use during the war and this would leave them vulnerable to British decoding.[72]

CHAPTER 4

Opening Rounds

Italy is bordered by an inland sea . . . [and] has no free access to the
oceans; Italy is really a 'prisoner' in the Mediterranean . . . The bars of
the prison are Corsica, Tunisia, Malta, and Cyprus; its guards are
Gibraltar and Suez . . . The task of Italy's policy . . . is to break the
prison bars . . . [against] the opposition of Britain and France. To brave
the solution of such problems without first having secured our rear on
the Continent would have been absurd. The Rome-Berlin Axis thus
answers a fundamental historical necessity. The same applies to our
conduct in the Spanish Civil War.

Mussolini 4 February 1939[1]

With Italy's declaration of war on 10 June 1940, the long-awaited conflict in
the Mediterranean had begun, but what did this war offer to the
belligerents?

For the Allies it gave them the opportunity to attack and defeat the weakest of the
Axis powers. Italy's long and vulnerable coastline, her colonies and island possessions, and her fundamentally weaker war machine, left her open to Allied attacks
and meant she would be the first to collapse. Furthermore, control of the Mediterranean allowed the Allies to use the far shorter Suez route to the Far East, and would
also deny resources to both Axis powers.

For the Axis, an early victory in the eastern Mediterranean with the capture of
Suez and the Nile Delta would, if nothing else, have relieved military pressure on
Italy, which could then have concentrated on building up her war industries. As it
was, even though German wartime production outstripped that of Italy, her facto-
ries produced thousands of tanks, trucks and aircraft in this period. In late 1940 and
early 1941, such a success could have been followed up by linking up with the AOI,
or by a foray into the Middle East with its oil supplies, or even a flanking attack
against the Soviet Union in the Caucasus. By 1942 this possible window of opportunity was clearly narrowing, but a threat to India from the west, combined with an
attack from the east by Japan could have brought about the fall of India in 1942, and
maybe even the removal of Churchill from power.

Klaus Schmider argues that this route to the Middle East was a dead end. Even if
the Iranian oil fields had been captured, the time that would be needed to repair the
damaged fields and then to transport the oil to where the Axis could use it made it of
little value. He also argues that the opening of the Suez Canal as a route of attack for
the Axis powers would have been of limited use given the weakness of the Italian
fleet. But he fails to realise that by late 1941 the Royal Navy was itself weak, and if it
had been confronted by an enemy-held shore in the Indian Ocean, and even just a
portion of the Japanese Fleet (with some support from the European Axis powers),
it might have spelt the end for what was the weakest of the Allies.[2]

In what was probably her worst mistake at the outbreak of war, Italy failed to give her merchant fleet sufficient warning of the commencement of hostilities. The Navy insisted that such a warning be given, even though it might alert the enemy to the approaching declaration of war, and a message was broadcast on 5 June 1940. But this was too late, and 254 out of Italy's 786 merchant ships of over 500 tons displacement were either outside the Mediterranean or captured on 10 June, a total of 1,370,822 GRT. To this Germany initially added fifty-four ships already in the Mediterranean giving a total Axis tonnage of 2,135,651.[3] Only seventeen ships sucessfully ran the Allied blockade, so any future additions to her merchant marine would have to be captured ships or new construction, which would place further demands on her already limited shipbuilding capacity. Those shipyards would add 305,733 tons of vessels in the period 1940-42. Furthermore, it had not been until 1936 that all Italian merchant ships had been required to have 'cargo holds suitable for military loads' and be capable of being fitted with guns. Therefore, in 1940, many of the older ships in service were not ideal for convoy work, and many of the smaller ships were unsuitable for the run to Africa.[4]

In fact, Germany opposed Italy's entry into the war at this time. Although they had wanted Italian support in 1939, now with the war going so well for them, it was not required. On 11 June, the day after Mussolini's declaration of war, when Hitler heard that Malta had been bombed for the first time, he commented: 'I would have done everything the other way around'.[5]

* * *

Allied naval strategy made the western Mediterranean France's principal responsibility, whilst Britain was to take care of the eastern Mediterranean. To put the situation in perspective, it is 1850 miles from Gibraltar to Alexandria, equivalent to the distance between Great Britain and Canada. They had thought that the large Italian submarine fleet would be the greatest threat, but it was soon realised that submarine operations in the Mediterranean were not easy, and the Italians were further handicapped by problems with equipment and poor tactics. Furthermore, the Mediterranean was not as target-rich an environment for submarines as the Atlantic.

The commander of the British Mediterranean fleet was Vice-Admiral Andrew B Cunningham, who had spent much of his service life in the Mediterranean. A brilliant and inspiring leader, he was not one to tie his subordinates down with detailed orders, having eliminated many of the 'Standing Orders' for the fleet, giving his subordinate commanders greater freedom of action. Like his French counterpart Admiral Darlan, he believed in taking the offensive against Italy. One of the best Allied admirals of the war, it is our opinion that he will rank in history alongside Howe and Rodney. His first objectives with the entry of Italy into the war were to protect the ports of the Eastern Mediterranean, defend the Suez Canal from possible sabotage, and threaten the Italian Dodecanese Islands. Cunningham would shortly be joined by another great admiral of the Second World War, Philip Vian.

Force H at Gibraltar was commanded by Vice-Admiral James Somerville, another old Mediterranean hand who always went to sea with his Siamese cat Figaro.[6]

A colourful man, Arthur Marder wrote of him that 'he possessed unusual charm, a quick brain, and exceptional energy, and he was a fine seaman in all senses'. Blessed with a good sense of humour (and known as 'Naughty James'), he had once turned to a companion just before a BBC broadcast in 1940 and said 'Good God, they've given me a bottle of water to drink!'. There was certainly no lack of talent in the British Mediterranean Fleet.

Before the war Admiral Darlan had wanted France to have a 'French war strategy (envisioning) first conquering the Mediterranean and terrorising Italy – destroying the Italian fleet and occupying Libya, Spanish Morocco, and the Balearics – while remaining on the defensive in the east and north-east'. This included bombardments of La Spezia, Naples, and the island of Pantelleria. Later Palermo, Genoa, and the small border port of Savona were added to the list. The French also hoped to join with British naval units in neutralising Italian bases in the Dodecanese islands. The French Army and Air Force had opposed this aggressive naval strategy and the German invasion would put paid to much of it, but the navy would still carry out some offensive actions against the enemy they had planned to fight for so long.[7]

* * *

In the centre of the theatre of operations was British-held Malta, a group of two small islands, Malta itself and Gozo, with a total population of 260,000 people. Valletta, the main city, was an important naval base, and in 1939 was the first outside the British Isles to receive a radar set for defence against air attacks.[8] Before the war, Malta had been considered indefensible, particularly by the RAF, but in fact the islands would hold out throughout the war, and furthermore forces based on the island would do serious damage to the Axis war effort. The Governor of Malta for most of the siege was General William Dobbie. He inspired the people of Malta, but seems to have lacked that vital bit of extra energy in getting things done. For example, the slow unloading of ships in the port led to major losses of supplies from ships which had reached Malta, but were sunk there before they could land their cargoes.[9]

The proximity of Valletta to Italian air bases lead the British to develop Alexandria as their main fleet base. Although convenient for defence of the Suez Canal, the permanent docking facilities there could only handle ships no larger than a light crusier, but in 1939 a floating dry-dock capable of accommodating battleships was towed out there from Great Britain. Coast defences were limited except at Gibraltar, Malta and Alexandria, though the latter two had their guns almost exclusively facing the sea. A small port like Haifa was defended, but only with 6in and smaller guns.[10]

As a result of the Pact of Steel between Italy and Germany, the British created the Mobile Naval Base Defence Organisation (MNBDO) to provide the fleet with a base in the eastern Mediterranean. Originally planned for use as 'Base X' in Navarino Bay, it would later be employed in Crete, a small-scale forerunner of the mobile bases that would prove so useful to the Allies in the Pacific War.

* * *

Both sides had some advantages in naval intelligence. The naval intelligence branch (*Servizio Informazioni Segrete* – *SIS*) was the best of the Italian military intelligence services, and had agents successfully monitoring the comings and goings at Gibraltar. Italy's intelligence services had a total of 850 personnel in 1940. They did break several Allied codes during the war, but their tendency to over-estimate the strength of enemy forces would have an adverse effect on planning.[11]

British Intelligence had been reading Italian diplomatic codes for several years and had broken the *Regia Aeronautica* code in 1938, giving them a month's notice of the Italian declaration of war in 1940, and providing information of numbers and deployment of aircraft. But the codes were changed on the outbreak of war and this, coupled with the lack of long-range aerial reconnaisance, made it difficult for the British to gain intelligence of Italian operations. Aerial reconnaisance was largely carried out by flying-boats based at Gibraltar and Alexandria, and from September 1940 by converted Maryland bombers from Malta, but both planes and trained crews were in short supply and it was not until the summer of 1941 that aerial reconnaissance would become really effective.[12]

* * *

The first Italian naval operation was the laying of defensive mine barrages along their coasts. Between 6 June and 10 July 1940, over 10,000 mines were laid from Genoa to the northern Adriatic, as well as off Libya and the Dodecanese. The majority of these were laid deep to defend against submarines. Between 8 and 12 June, offensive mine barrages were also laid in the Sicilian Channel by a mixed force of light cruisers, destroyers, torpedo-boats and converted merchantmen. These operations were covered by a force of three heavy and four light cruisers, with destroyer escorts, commanded by Rear-Admirals Riccardo Paladini and Luigi Sansonetti. In total, the Italians would lay 54,457 mines in the course of the war, 16,134 in the first six months.[13] The Italians had also prepared a special force to cut the submarine telegraph cables linking Malta to the outside world. However, not all were located and cut, leaving the island with some communications, while the Italians were wholly dependant upon radio or couriers for communications with North Africa after November 1941.[14]

Due to the superiority of the Allied navies, the Italian Navy had been told before the war that running convoys to North Africa would not be part of its duties, but this would change with the fall of France. However, in 1938 Admiral Cavagnari had written a memorandum instructing the navy to maintain communications with Libya, in order to supply the proposed invasion of Egypt to seize the Suez Canal, vital for maintaining links with the AOI and allowing the Italian fleet to break out of the Mediterranean. The same document also called for the capture of Malta.[15]

By June *Comando Supremo* was prepared to supply Libya by a combination of air transport, small convoys and freighters operating on the shortest routes from Sicily, fast warships acting as transports, and submarines. Many of the 1,000,000 Axis troops who fought in North Africa arrived by air, while their equipment went by sea. Submarines would be used to run vital supplies across the Mediterranean, beginning on 19 June 1940. In total Italian submarines would carry 10,000 tons of supplies to North Africa in 158 operations, losing six boats to enemy action. The British would also supply Malta in this way, frequently sending submarines loaded with vital aviation fuel. Fortunately, in the first few months of the war the British were too weak to intercept the convoys to Libya and losses in 1940 were minimal.[16]

Offensive operations began with the opening of the submarine campaign. Three of the six British submarines based at Malta were almost immediately lost to enemy action. HMS *Odin* was sunk by the Italian destroyers *Strale* and *Baleno* about 40 miles south of Cape San Vito near Taranto on 13 June, the *Grampus* was lost on 16 June near Syracuse in an action with three Italian torpedo-boats, whilst the veteran destroyer *Turbine* sank HMS *Orpheus* off Tobruk on 16 June. A fourth, the *Olympus*, would be heavily damaged by air attack while in port at Valletta. The heavy losses suffered by the larger British submarines, designed for operations in the Pacific, led the Royal Navy to replace them with smaller boats more suited to conditions in the Mediterranean. It would be the French who would draw first blood against the Italians with the twenty-nine submarines they had deployed, when two Italian merchant ships were sunk by mines laid by the *Saphir* off Cagliari, but on 16 June the French submarine *Morse* was itself sunk by mines off Sfax in Tunisia.[17] But it was the Italians who would receive the rudest shock, losing ten submarines in the first 15 days of the war. Italian submarines were poorly ventilated, especially considering some of the weather conditions they had to operate in, and they were slow to dive (two to three times slower on average than German U-boats). One of their worst faults, and one which they shared with Japanese submarines, was that their large conning towers could be easily picked up on radar at night. Poor operational procedures were also shown up when the submarines *Console Generale Liuzzi* and *Uebi Scebeli* were both spotted by British destroyers while on the surface during daylight at the end of June. Although they managed to dive, they were both rapidly forced to the surface by depth charges. The British recovered the new Italian naval codebooks from the *Uebi Scebeli*.[18]

However, the first Italian submarine success would come when Cunningham's fleet sortied from Alexandria for the first time on 11 June, to test the reaction of the Italian fleet. His fleet was not at full strength as two of the old 'R' class battleships had to be left behind because of their slow speed and the shortage of destroyer escorts. At 3.30am on 12 June, the old light cruiser HMS *Calypso* was torpedoed and sunk south of Crete by the submarine *Alpino Bagnolini*, commanded by Commander Franco Tosoni Pittoni. Thirty-nine men were lost with the first British casualty of the war. Later that year, the *Bagnolini* would be one of the first submarines the Italians would transfer to Bordeaux for operations in the Atlantic.

While the French under Vice-Admiral Godfroy headed north from Alexandria with four cruisers and three destroyers toward the Italian-controlled Dodecanese Islands in the Aegean, Cunningham's main force cruised near Crete. In a subsidiary operation, the light cruisers *Gloucester* and *Liverpool*, accompanied by four destroyers, bombarded Tobruk in a joint attack with the RAF, engaging the old armoured cruiser *San Giorgio*, which was employed as a floating battery, and four gunboats, one of which, the *Giovanni Berta* (620 tons, 9 knots, one 3in gun), was sunk at 5.00am on 12 June, the first Italian surface ship to be lost in action. Her captain, Angelo Palucci, was posthumously awarded the *Medaglia d'Oro*, Italy's highest award for bravery. The *San Giorgio* had been launched in 1908 and had been used many times as a station flagship. Re-equipped on the eve of war as an AA ship, she had sailed to Tobruk to add to the port's anti-aircraft capability. Slow, and employed only as a stationary battery, she still carried four old 10in and eight 7.5in guns, as well as her AA armament. Quickly festooned with protective sandbags, she saw considerable action, being attacked ten times by aircraft including one very heavy raid on 19 November 1940, and she would named 'Lioness of Tobruk' by the garrison. When in January 1941 the British were closing in on Tobruk, she was readied for a sortie from the harbour but it was decided by the Italian High Command that it would not be good for local morale for her to leave. She would later be scuttled in harbour when Tobruk was first captured by the British.[19]

In retaliation for this attack, three older destroyers, led by the ubiquitous *Turbine*, sortied from Tobruk on 14 June. Protected by thick mist, they bombarded Solium on the Egyptian border from 3.49am to 4.05am firing 220 3.9in shells, but poor visibility meant little damage was caused. A second attack in better conditions on 26 June was more successful.

Vice-Admiral Tovey carried out a bombardment of Bardia on the night of 20-21 June with the French battleship *Lorraine* and three British light cruisers in what would be the last French sortie before the Armistice. The operation involved five destroyers conducting an anti-submarine sweep along the coast towards Tobruk, while two French cruisers and three destroyers lay in wait near Tobruk in case any sortie was made from the port by the *San Giorgio* or destroyers. With his flag in the *Orion*, Tovey lead the *Lorraine*, the light cruisers *Sydney* and *Neptune* and four destroyers into the attack at dawn, so the gunners in the coastal batteries would be dazzled by the early-morning sun. Fire was opened at 5.48am and continued for 22 minutes, each ship concentrating on different targets, such as suspected coast defence positions, barracks and areas of the small town. Even the destroyers joined in, firing with their 4.7in guns at a range of 12,000 yards. The larger ships employed spotting aircraft, and there was no reply either from the Italians' non-existant coast defence batteries or by aircraft. The *Lorraine* expended fifty-three 13.4in and thirty-seven 5.5in shells, while the three light cruisers and four destroyers fired off 400 6in and 154 4.7in shells. The only casualty was the *Sydney*'s spotter plane, shot down by RAF fighters! The Italians launched their first air raid on Alexandria on the return of Tovey's squadron, but inflicted no damage. Although these shore bombardments caused little real damage, the morale effect of being under fire from battleship guns should not be underestimated. Such attacks, usually carried out by the Allies, were frequent in the early part of the war, but became less common as enemy air power increased, especially with the arrival of the *Luftwaffe* in the Mediterranean.

In the short time that France remained in the war, she did conduct offensive operations against the Italians at the other end of the Mediterranean. On 14 June 1940, a squadron under Vice-Admiral Emile Duplat, consisting of four heavy cruisers and eleven 'super destroyers', sailed from Toulon to attack targets on the Italian coast. The ports of Vado and Savona were bombarded by the *Algerie* and

Foch of the 1st Cruiser Division supported by six destroyers, while the 2nd Cruiser Division consisting of the *Colbert* and *Dupleix* and the 'super destroyers' *Albatros* and *Vautour* bombarded harbour installations at Genoa, escorted by three destroyers. Visibility was limited due to fog and the bombardments were brief. At Genoa the Italian shore batteries returned fire and some local warships responded to the attack. The French destroyer *Albatros* was hit by a 6in shell and ten men were killed, but the attack by the torpedo boat *Calatafimi* and the 13th Motor Torpedo Boat Squadron failed to stop the French. The four *MAS* boats attacked in two groups of two, one managing to close to within 1800 metres before being driven off. The French fired a total of 1500 8in, 5.5in and 3in shells, killing nine and wounding thirty-six. Ominously for the Italians, there was no response from the *Regia Aeronautica*.

Some minor air attacks by both sides also took place before France's surrender. A single French bomber attacked and damaged some oil tanks at Venice, and a few minor night raids were made on Italian cities. On 14 June one aircraft even dropped leaflets over Rome. The Italians bombed Bizerta, causing some minor damage to an airfield, but little else was accomplished. On 13 June they attacked the airfield at Hyères near Toulon. Twenty-seven Cr42 fighters strafed the field and then some FIAT BR20 bombers also attacked. In this action one French fighter was shot down and several more damaged on the ground. The Italians lost one BR20 shot down in flames and another had to ditch near Cape Noli, between Finale Ligure and Savona.[20]

Between 22 and 24 June, while France was requesting an armistice, Sansonetti's 7th Cruiser Division, made up of four light cruisers and four destroyers, sortied from Caligari in search of French shipping plying between Toulon and Algeria, coming to within 40 miles of Port Mahon on the evening of the 23rd. Next day two floatplanes were launched, but found nothing and the ships retired to Sardinia. This minor operation was nonetheless Italy's first offensive surface operation, and significantly it received no support from the Air Force. If Italy in 1940 was waging a 'parallel war' alongside Germany, it could also be said that the *Regia Aeronautica* was engaged in a 'parallel rivalry' with the Navy. The Air Force had been active in this period, attacking Malta and even targets in Palestine, but just as there was little actual co-operation between the two Axis partners, there was little between the Italian Air Force and Navy. The shortcomings of Italy's naval air arm would soon be shown up by comparison with the successes of Britain's Fleet Air Arm, but these successes would be against her former ally, France.

CHAPTER 5

The Fall of France and the Establishment of Vichy

*Afraid I shall get a colossal raspberry from the Admiralty for letting the
Battlecruiser escape and not finishing off more French ships–we
disposed of three or four big ships in the harbour I believe. In fact I
shouldn't be surprised if I was relieved forthwith. I don't mind because
it was an absolutely bloody business to shoot up these Frenchmen who
showed the greatest gallantry. The truth is my heart wasn't in it and
you've not allowed a heart in war.*

Admiral Somerville[1]

The armistice with France on 22 June 1940 gave the German Navy access to the Atlantic ports for her U-boats and surface warships, but since Italy had made only minor advances into French territory, she could not demand access to vital points in the Mediterranean. If she had annexed Tunisia, or just obtained the right to move troops and supplies to Libya through French territory, the route her convoys would have to take in the next 29 months of war would have been much shorter and safer, being further away from the British bases at Malta and Alexandria. The only drawback to the Tunisian route was that the journey overland to Tripoli and then on to the Egyptian front, already long and costly in fuel, would have been increased, but it would also have been safer. Therefore until November 1942 the Italians would receive only small clandestine shipments of supplies through French North Africa, as the Vichy authorities turned a blind eye to activities that violated the terms of the Armistice.

But it was the fate of the French fleet that was of greatest concern to Churchill. If it was to fall into Axis hands it might prove very dangerous to the Allied cause, especially in the dark days of 1940 when Britain stood alone. According to the Armistice provisions the fleet was to return to Toulon and demobilise, but Churchill hoped that some ships, particularly the almost completed new battleships *Richelieu* and *Jean Bart*, would sail to British ports and fight on. Admiral Darlan, now the French Minister of Marine, had assured the British that the French fleet would scuttle itself before allowing the Germans to take control of it (which indeed it did do very successfully in November 1942). Even if the fleet had been seized intact by the Axis, it would have had to have been manned, co-ordinated with their existing fleets and maintained. There would also have been the logistical problem of supplying ships which had no weapons or equipment in common with the German or Italian ships. It would therefore have taken many months for the Axis to bring the French fleet into service.[2]

But despite Darlan's assurances, Churchill still mistrusted the French after their abandonment of the war by making a separate peace with Germany. Therefore,

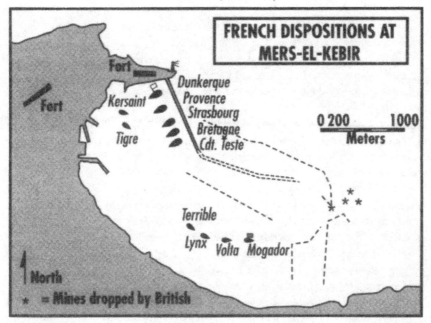

FRENCH DISPOSITIONS AT MERS-EL-KEBIR

0 200   1000
Meters

Fort
Kersaint
Dunkerque
Provence
Strasbourg
Bretagne
Cdt. Teste
Fort
Tigre
Terrible
Lynx Volta Mogador
North
* = Mines dropped by British

largely as a result of the Prime Minister's insistence, the British planned the 'simultaneous seizure, control or effective disablement or destruction of all the accessible French Fleet', in order to deny it to the Axis. Such action would also demonstrate Britain's determination to fight on. The attack on the main French fleet at Oran was christened Operation 'Catapult'.[3]

On the eve of 'Catapult' French ships in British ports, including two old battleships and numerous small craft, were seized by the Royal Navy. Casualties were minimal and 3000 of the 12,000 officers and men aboard the ships later joined the Free French. Churchill later wryly said of this; 'A great act of treachery. Nothing has been more sucessful since the massacre of St Bartholomew's Eve'.[4] But Operation 'Catapult' itself was to be far more dramatic, and costly.

The main French fleet, under Admiral Marcel-Bruno Gensoul, was based at the naval harbour of Mers-el-Kebir, 3 miles west of the Algerian city of Oran. In port were the modern battlecruisers *Dunkerque* and *Strasbourg*, the old battleships *Provence* and *Bretagne*, six 'super destroyers' and the seaplane tender *Commandant Teste*, with twelve aircraft. The harbour was defended by some coastal batteries and there was a nearby air base with forty-two operational fighters (the bombers based there had been disarmed under the terms of the Armistice). There were a further ten light destroyers ('600-tonners') and six submarines (only three of which were operational) at Oran itself, as well as thirteen miscellaneous smaller warships. Gensoul was a rather uninspiring commander who 'went by the book', lacking the flexibility needed in such a situation, but he was in a very difficult position and neither he nor any of his men really believed the British would open fire on them until they actually did.

Force H at Gibraltar, under Vice-Admiral Somerville, was ordered to Oran to deliver an ultimatum to Gensoul and if this was refused, to disable the French Fleet. Somerville had the battlecruiser *Hood*, the battleships *Resolution* and *Valiant* (all three with a main armament of eight 15in guns each), the aircraft carrier *Ark Royal*, two light cruisers and eleven destroyers. *Ark Royal* carried twenty-four fighters and thirty torpedo bombers.

Just past midnight on 3 July 1940, Churchill and Admiral Pound drew up the ultimatum that Somerville was to deliver. This was a common time for them to work – hence the naval staff's nickname of 'midnight follies'. Gensoul could either scuttle his fleet, sail to the French West Indies and be disarmed there, or join the British and continue the war.

Gensoul tried to spin out negotiations as he signalled for help from nearby French naval forces (six *La Galissonnière* class light cruisers were based at Algiers). At about 1.30pm he saw aircraft from *Ark Royal* drop five magnetic mines in the harbour entrance. Gensoul's signal was intercepted by the British, decoded, and as a result London insisted that Somerville act quickly. As Somerville's representative was returning from the last abortive meeting with the French, the British attacked. At 5:55pm the *Hood* led the *Resolution* and *Valiant* in line of battle and opened fire at a range of about 17,500yds (maximum visibility), with aircraft spotting the fall of shot. The range would decrease somewhat during the action, coming down to about 15,300 yards. The French ships were now covered in smoke as they began to raise steam and get under way. Gensoul ordered his ships to leave the harbour with the *Strasbourg* leading the way, followed by the *Dunkerque*, then the *Provence* and *Bretagne*.[5]

The first French ship to open fire was the *Provence*, about 90 seconds after the first British salvo. The French had no intention of fighting from anchor, but to clear harbour each ship had to wait for the vessel ahead of them to get under way. The destroyers were to act independently and had actually begun getting under way just before the fighting began. The French capital ships had moored with their sterns to the quayside, which meant that the two battlecruisers, with their main armament in two quadruple turrets forward, had to get under way and turn to face the enemy before they could open fire.

As both sides had been observing each other for hours and taking the range, and with the French ships stationary, the fire was quite accurate. But the confined waters, the process of getting underway, and the fort of Mers-el-Kebir located on a hill overlooking the harbour, all conspired to make it difficult for the French to return fire accurately. For example, the *Provence*'s first salvo was aimed between the *Dunkerque*'s masts!

The French battlecruisers had each launched two seaplanes to spot the fall of shot just after the action began but their contribution was not significant. They did manage to straddle the *Hood* once or twice, and two of her crew were wounded by splinters, but no other damage was inflicted on the British. The French, however, were not so lucky. The British fired thirty-six salvoes of 15in shells, each one with a time of flight of about 20 seconds. The first shells hit the quayside, sending fragments flying around, and then the *Dunkerque* was hit once, and then by three shells of a single salvo. One shell penetrated 'B' turret, wiping out the crews of one pair of guns, but the armoured bulkhead separating the guns saved the other crews. Another hit the forward engine room and also knocked out her main fire control. The other hits damaged her secondary armament. With this damage, Gensoul ordered the ship not to proceed to sea but to beach herself. She had managed to fire forty 13in rounds, which with the increasing accuracy of the shore batteries' 9.4in and 7.6in guns succeeded in forcing the British battle-line further to the west away from the harbour entrance. She would also fire 152 5.1in shells at the *Ark Royal*'s aircraft, exactly the same number as the *Strasbourg*.

The *Bretagne* was to suffer the worst. She was hit by the second salvo aimed at her as she was getting under way, which caused an immense internal explosion, throwing up a towering pillar of smoke which further obscured the harbour. She capsized and sank in 7 minutes, with the loss of 976 lives. The *Provence* had to wait for the *Dunkerque* to pass her before she could proceed to sea and therefore, as a stationary target, was also hit several times. One 15in shell passed through her 45mm armoured deck and exploded on the opposite side of the ship below sea level. She fired a few shells at the *Hood*, but also had to beach herself.

The destroyers were proceeding independently to sea at about 20 knots, and all would make it except the *Mogador*. She was hit on the stern by a 15in shell, while slowing to let a small ship pass, which set off sixteen depth charges, sending up a plume of smoke almost as high as the one from the mortally-wounded *Bretagne*, and she was forced to anchor. The rest joined the *Strasbourg* which by 5:10pm was in the harbour channel and moving at 15 knots.

Gensoul, after the dropping of the magnetic mines, had ordered the harbour entrance booms opened so as to allow his fleet to escape. Somerville, not having noticed this, thought no ship could escape and so was surprised when one of the *Ark Royal*'s Swordfish reported the *Strasbourg* leaving the harbour. It took a second report 10 minutes later to convince Somerville that one of the big ships was getting away. While escaping, the *Strasbourg* opened fire on the British destroyer *Wrestler* which had been detailed to watch Oran, firing twelve 13in shells at her. The British destroyer promptly hid in a smokescreen. At about 5:12pm the British ceased fire, in part because of the increasing accuracy of the shore batteries, and repeated French requests to cease fire.

Now Somerville was aware of what was happening, the fleet set off in pursuit of the *Strasbourg*, with the fast *Hood* out in front with the destroyers, but by 7.25pm the French ship had escaped. Two of the French 'super destroyers' had attacked the British submarine *Proteus*, operating off Oran, to no effect, while two others fired torpedoes at long range at the *Hood*, which altered course and avoided them. If Somerville had initially deployed further east, the *Strasbourg* might not have escaped and he later accepted this criticism of his deployment.

At one point the *Ark Royal* realised that she was rather too close to the powerful *Strasbourg*, and she turned away at high speed. This change in speed, combined with earlier ones due to flying-off aircraft brought an exasperated Chief Engineer up to the bridge; ' "Could you please give us a little more warning . . . " to which the Navigating Officer replied in a casual tone of voice, "That's all right, old boy, we've only got the *Strasbourg* after us." ' The engineer went quickly back down below!

The *Ark Royal* launched two air attacks against the fleeing *Strasbourg*, one with Swordfish armed with bombs and the second with torpedoes 20 minutes after sunset. It was during the first strike that her escorting Skua fighters engaged several French fighters and one Skua was shot down. The first bombing attack saw the Swordfish dropping from 11,000 to 4000ft, using smoke from a splinter hole in the *Strasbourg*'s funnel as cover. None of the 250lb bombs hit, though one came close – exploding just 25m from stern of the *Strasbourg* as she turned. Two of the attacking aircraft were shot down, but their crews were rescued by the *Wrestler*.

The second torpedo attack by six Swordfish was quite impressive. They attacked after sunset and flew so as to have the coast behind them as they made their final approach at an altitude of 20 feet. They came under AA fire but none were badly damaged. With the *Strasbourg* silhouetted in sunset's afterglow, the six planes attacked in three columns of two each. The attacks were bravely pressed home but no hits were scored.

After passing near Sardinia, the *Strasbourg* and three destroyers made Toulon the next day at 8:10pm, with the rest straggling in shortly after, to the cheers of the sailors in the port. She had suffered an accident in her engine room during the night and five men had been killed.

Two of the light destroyers from Oran also reached Toulon and the *Commandant Teste*, which had not been damaged, joined the *Strasbourg* on 5 July along with the six light cruisers from Algiers. The light destroyers and small craft at Mers-el-Kebir had withdrawn to Algiers, with one sloop, the *Rigault de Genouilly*, being torpedoed and sunk by the British submarine *Pandora*, which fired four torpedoes at 3800 yards. This 1969-ton colonial service sloop with almost 200 seamen aboard was on its way to Bizerta from Oran when she went down. The *Pandora*'s captain had mistakenly identified her as a cruiser.[6]

Somerville did not think that the *Dunkerque* had been completely disabled in the attack on 3 July, a view which may have been reinforced by a radio broadcast by the French naval commander in North Africa, Admiral Jean-Pierre Esteva, in which he had claimed that the ship was not badly damaged.[7] Consequently, an air strike was launched from the *Ark Royal* to finish her off. The Swordfishes' torpedoes were set for a speed of 27 knots and a depth of 13ft, given the shallow waters of the harbour.

The attack went in in three waves, the first consisting of six Swordfish with Skuas as escorts, which met no opposition. The beached *Dunkerque* was surrounded by repair tenders, and the pilots of the first wave thought four hits had been scored. In fact, the single torpedo that did hit the battlecruiser failed to explode while another two hit the jetty and a fourth hit the 780-ton patrol vessel *Terre Neuve*, which was cut in two and sank 30 yards to starboard of the *Dunkerque*. The second wave of three aircraft, now coming under heavy AA fire, failed to hit, but the third group, attacking on the battlecruiser's port side, had more success, despite the intensifying fire and the presence of French fighters. One torpedo hit a tug, destroying it completely, whilst another passed under the keel of the *Dunkerque* and hit the wreck of the *Terre Neuve*, setting off her forty-two depth charges. The massive explosion threw a pillar of water and debris 600 feet into the air and severely damaged the *Dunkerque*. Forty metres of her side were opened up and 154 men were killed or wounded, some by being struck by fragments of her armour belt. Ironically, the ship's very popular captain had remarked earlier of the *Terre Neuve*'s depth charges; 'They'd make a good firework display if ever they did go up'. The ship was effectively out of the war. Temporary repairs were made which allowed her to reach Toulon in February 1942, but she was still out of action when Vichy France was taken over by the Germans 10 months later.

The French lost 1297 men killed and 351 wounded in the attacks of 3 and 6 July. The only British losses were three Swordfish and two Skuas shot down on 3 July, with all but two men rescued. The Vichy government would call the attack a 'massacre' and it turned many Frenchmen against the 'perfidious' British. Somerville himself would never be happy about what he had had to do at Mers-el-Kebir.

There was another French squadron at Alexandria, commanded by Vice-Admiral R E Godfroy, consisting of the battleship *Lorraine*, the heavy cruisers *Duquesne*, *Tourville* and *Suffren*, the light cruiser *Duguay Trouin*, three destroyers and the submarine *Protée*, but here Vice-Admiral Cunningham was able to negotiate their disarming and immobilisation, including the return to France of some of the crews, without bloodshed, despite unhelpful suggestions from Churchill and the Admiralty. The fleet would remain at anchor until August 1943 when it joined the Free French. Despite Cunningham's outstanding success in these negotiations, Churchill would later say (to Vice-Admiral Tovey upon his move from Cunningham's fleet to the Home Fleet) that Cunningham had been 'too pussy-foot' in his dealings with Godfroy.[8]

One result of Operation 'Catapult' was that the German government suspended the armistice article requiring the French fleet to return to ports in Metropolitan France. This removed some of the fear of the French fleet falling into Axis hands, although many warships either already were at Toulon or would arrive there. The French fleet would remain active and did make minor interventions against Allied operations both in the Mediterranean and elsewhere. When the Germans entered Toulon on 11 November 1942 to take control of the fleet, seventy-seven of the eighty ships in port were scuttled, the majority of the French fleet. The Germans were only able to capture some old submarines and small craft at Bizerta in Tunisia. With hindsight, Operation 'Catapult' was probably a mistake. It ensured the hostility of Vichy to the Allies, which would result in further bloodshed, rallied the French empire to them and damaged recruitment to the Free French. If the French really had wanted to attack the Allies, they could have made Gibraltar untenable from their bases in Morocco and Algeria. But it did send an unmistakeable message to the Axis Powers, Franco's Spain and particularly the United States that Great Britain was prepared to fight on.[9]

But even after Operation 'Catapult', the Allies still had to recognise Vichy France, with its fleet and overseas empire, as an important factor in the Mediterranean. It also had to be recognised that, following the collapse of the Third Republic, the French government was now ideologically closer to the Axis than the Allies. With this in mind, on 30 September 1940 the Admiralty ordered that operations against Vichy were to be 'kept down to a minimum'.[10]

Until the invasion of French North Africa, when the British government thought of France they did not think of the Free French led by General Charles de Gaulle, but of Vichy France, understandable as it had the greatest war-fighting capability after the armistice with the Axis.[11]

But de Gaulle himself was not viewed as a strong player and he and Churchill would repeatedly clash over the years. De Gaulle's inability to rally Dakar to the Free French cause later in 1940 was the nadir of his fortunes, and placed Great Britain until November 1942 in an unusual diplomatic situation of negotiating with Vichy and the Free French, whilst at the same time trying to form a third force, in an initiative favoured by Churchill, to be led by General Maxime Weygand to rally French forces to the Allied cause, but this would come to nothing.[12]

After the fall of France, there had been some discussion of withdrawing the Mediterranean Fleet from Alexandria, concentrating some of it at Gibraltar whilst sending the rest around the Cape of Good Hope. Pound at the Admiralty had sent a dispatch about this 'tentative proposal' on 17 June. But it was strongly opposed by Cunningham, who foresaw the devastating effect of abandoning the eastern Mediterranean to the Axis and the probable fall of both Malta and Egypt. He wrote '. . . the effects of this withdrawal would mean such a landslide in territory and prestige . . . Malta, Cyprus, and Palestine could no longer be held, while the Moslem world would regard it as surrender'.[13] Discussions continued in London but on 3 July 1940 Operation 'Catapult' announced to the world that the fleet would stay and fight.

CHAPTER 6

The Battle of Punta Stilo, 9 July 1940

... a disappointing affair but you can't catch ships that go 7 knots faster than you do.

Admiral Cunningham[1]

The first serious clash between the British and Italian fleets would come in the second month of the war. Cunningham maintained an offensive stance from the start, and one of his first successes was against an attempt by the Italians to resupply Tobruk with a high-speed convoy consisting of the old destroyers *Espero*, *Ostro* and *Zeffiro*, under the overall command of Captain Enrico Baroni, carrying two Blackshirt artillery units (from the military arm of the Fascist Party) of about 160 men. On 28 June 1940 the convoy was spotted by two Sunderland flying-boats from Malta, and Vice-Admiral Tovey's 7th Cruiser Squadron, which was in the area to cover the sailing of two convoys from Malta evacuating superfluous personnel and equipment and another sailing to Alexandria from ports in the Aegean, moved to intercept it.

The Italians were first sighted at 6.30pm 100 miles north of Tobruk by HMS *Liverpool*, which opened fire 3 minutes later at a range of 18,000 yards. As the Italians steamed south-west at high speed, Tovey deployed the 1st Division made up of the cruisers *Orion*, *Neptune* and HMAS *Sydney* on the enemy's starboard quarter, and the 2nd Division, the *Liverpool* and *Gloucester*, to port. The 1st Division were older light cruisers with eight 6in guns, while the *Liverpool* and *Gloucester* were larger *Southampton* class ships with twelve 6in guns. Although the Italian destroyers were nominally faster than the British cruisers, their age, laden condition and the sea state meant they were gradually being overhauled.

With their decks cluttered with cargo, the Italian destroyers could not fire torpedoes, but Baroni made good use of smokescreens, and they were hard to hit as the 'action was a chase in rapidly failing light with the enemy against the afterglow of the sunset'. The *Liverpool* and *Gloucester* concentrated their increasingly effective fire at Baroni's flagship the *Espero*, and by 7.20pm the range had closed to 14,000 yards.[2] The *Espero* had been damaged in the chase, but not until the fifteenth salvo, and Baroni turned back to allow his other two ships to escape. With night falling and ammunition running low, Tovey broke off the pursuit, and the *Sydney* closed to finish off the *Espero*. Damage to the British ships was limited to a single hit on the *Liverpool*, on the armour belt 3ft above the waterline, and minor blast damage from their own guns. The *Sydney* picked up forty-seven survivors from the *Espero*. Baroni was killed and would be posthumously awarded the *Medaglia d'Oro*. The two other Italian destroyers reached Benghazi safely on the 29th. The principal lesson of this action for the British was that an excessive amount of ammunition had

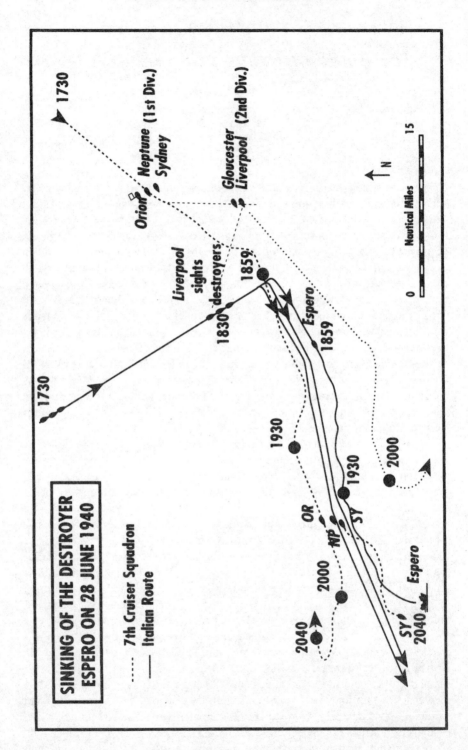

SINKING OF THE DESTROYER ESPERO ON 28 JUNE 1940

----- 7th Cruiser Squadron
——— Italian Route

been used, nearly 5000 rounds, and this sort of action would have to be conducted more economically in future. The resulting shortage of ammunition, as well as the threat of Italian submarines, forced a delay in the sailing of the Malta convoys, and when they did finally put to sea, the battle of Punta Stilo would be the result. The Aegean convoy reached Alexandria without loss, despite coming under air attack.[3]

This action dispelled the myth, prevalent in all navies before the war, that daylight actions at long range could bring about decisive results, when in fact they mostly resulted in massive expenditure of ammunition with little result. For example, in the Pacific War, the battle of the Komandorski Islands on 26 March 1943 was a 3½-hour battle between Japanese and American cruisers in daylight, at the end of which the Japanese withdrew having almost exhausted their ammunition, with only two cruisers and one destroyer damaged. Similarly, it was not until the night action in the Battle of the Java Sea in 1942 that decisive results were achieved. In the final analysis, it was difficult to hit a moving target at long range until the widespread introduction of efficient gunnery radar, and far more shells missed than hit. Daylight actions did not fulfill the expectations that had been held of them before the war.

After the return of the British Fleet to Alexandria, it was the turn of the Fleet Air Arm. Swordfish of 813 Squadron had been deployed forward to Sidi Barrani in Egypt, close to the Libyan border, and on 5 July, nine aircraft attacked shipping in harbour at Tobruk, while the RAF provided fighter cover and attacked nearby airfields. Seven torpedoes were dropped, sinking the old destroyer *Zeffiro* and a merchant ship, and damaging the destroyer *Euro*, a second merchantman and the 15,000-ton liner *Liguria*. At dawn the next day, the light cruisers HMS *Caledon* and *Capetown*, escorted by four destroyers, shelled the port of Bardia at a range of 9000 yards. They were attacked by Italian aircraft but suffered no damage. Later, the guns recovered from the sunken *Zeffiro* were sent to Bardia to augment the coastal defences.[4]

*   *   *

The first confrontation between the two main fleets would again be the result of operations covering convoys. This was the first opportunity for the British to push capital ships into the central Mediterranean and gauge the Italian reaction. After establishing in the first month of the war that the Italian submarines and Air Force were less dangerous than expected, Cunningham planned to test the mettle of the Italian fleet with this operation.

The Italians were running a convoy carrying M.11/39 medium tanks and other supplies to Marshal Graziani's forces in North Africa, while the British were evacuating Italian prisoners, non-essential personnel and equipment from Malta, an operation that had been delayed by Tovey's battle on 28 June. For the Italians, these tanks represented the difference between remaining on the defensive in Libya, or taking the offensive against the British in Egypt. Six small convoys had reached Libya since the outbreak of war, but *Comando Supremo* wanted to ensure the tanks got through and urged the Navy and Air Force to organise a well-protected convoy.

It was to be organised as if Italy were still at war with both France and Britain, as the locations of the mine barrages laid by the French were still unknown. The convoy was authorised in Operational Order No 11, issued on 3 July 1940.[5]

As the main Italian fleet prepared to go to sea, General Francesco Pricolo, the Air Force undersecretary and Chief of Staff ordered bomber units south to assist the passage of this vital convoy. 'X-Day' was to be 6 July, and *Supermarina* requested fighter cover for X-1 and X+3, and for bombers to be available for operations off Sicily and the Gulf of Taranto on X+1 and X+2. But the Italians' greatest problem lay in co-ordinating operations between the Navy and Air Force, which was handicapped by the restrictive chain of command. A fleet commander had to request air support from the local Maritime Command, which in turn had to contact Air Sector command and sometimes even *Superaereo* itself, so by the time the planes actually took off hours could have passed in a fast-moving tactical environment. This centralisation of command and control was a feature of the Fascist regime, and was in stark contrast to Cunningham's more *laissez faire* style. On 5 July Vice-Admiral Inigo Campioni issued General Order of Operations No 6 to the fleet for the convoy, which was to be known as 'TCM'. The new battleships *Littorio* and *Vittorio Veneto* were not to take part, as they were still working-up, despite the request of their captains and the commander of the battleship division.

Cunningham organised two convoys for the Malta operation, MF1 of three fast ships to carry personnel, and five slower ships in Convoy MS1 for the equipment. The destroyers *Jervis* and *Diamond* were sent to Malta to join HMAS *Vendetta* to escort the convoys to Alexandria (see table).

Convoys from Malta

Date	Codename	Ships
9 July 1940	MF 1 (ME 1)	*El Nil, Knight of Malta, Rodi*
10 July 1940	MS 1 (ME 1)	*Kirkland, Masirah, Novasli, Tweed, Zeeland*

Limited air cover would be available, and fleet destroyer detachments would provide distant escort for these ships, which would all reach Alexandria safely. While the convoys were being organised Italian air attacks on Malta were 'now becoming more frequent', and a raid on the docks on 7 July killed sixteen civilians and naval personnel.[6]

Cunningham ordered the main fleet to leave Alexandria on the evening of 7 July, with all ships to have cleared the harbour by 1 minute past midnight. Speed was governed by the *Royal Sovereign* which could manage between only 18 and 20 knots. The fleet was divided into three forces; Force A was the cruisers under Vice-Admiral Tovey; Force B had the *Warspite*, flying Cunningham's flag, and five destroyers, acting as a flying squadron with the additional firepower of *Warspite's* 15in guns and modernised range-finding equipment; and Force C, under Vice-Admiral H A Pridham-Wippell on board the *Royal Sovereign*, consisted of the bulk of the fleet of two old battleships (the other being the *Malaya*), eleven destroyers and the aircraft carrier *Eagle*, with seventeen Swordfish and three Gladiator fighters on board to provide air cover for the fleet and a torpedo strike force. Thanks to the captured Italian codebooks, the British were aware their fleet was at sea on the morning of 8 July. Intelligence profiles had convinced Cunningham that the Italian admiral would attempt to 'lure his opponent into a submarine and aircraft trap by waiting back off the Italian coast'.[7]

On their way out of harbour the British fleet was spotted by a group of eleven S.81 bombers of the 39th *Stormo* attacking Alexandria, but this was not the first warning the Italians had that something was up. Not only had heavy radio traffic aroused their suspicions, but they had also intercepted a message containing a list of ships assigned to 'Operation MA5'. Shortly afterward the fleet was also sighted by the submarine *Beilul*, one of twenty-five boats the Italians had deployed in the Mediterranean for this operation. She reported her sighting, and was attacked by the destroyer HMS *Hasty*, which damaged her with depth charges. At the same time Somerville's Force H (battlecruiser *Hood*, battleships *Valiant* and *Resolution*, aircraft carrier *Ark Royal*, three light cruisers and ten destroyers), made a diversionary sortie from Gibraltar. The Italians were aware of this, and at 1.50am on 6 July Cavagnari had alerted *Comando Supremo* and *Superaereo* that Somerville's ships were about to sail. The *Valiant* had been comprehensively reconstructed before the war, while the *Hood* was the only British capital ship in this operation that could approach the speed of the Italian battleships.

The Italian convoy sailed from Naples on 6 July, made up of a passenger ship and three freighters, escorted by the four *Orsa* class destroyer escorts. That evening it passed through the Straits of Messina and rendezvoused with an additional transport and two torpedo-boats from Catania in Sicily. The convoy now carried 2190 troops, 72 M11 medium tanks, 232 other vehicles, 10,445 tons of supplies and 5720 tons of fuel. On the afternoon of 7 July, the close escort was reinforced by two light cruisers and four destroyers in case of any attack from Malta, while distant escort was provided by the four powerful *Pola* class heavy cruisers and four more destroyers, stationed 35 miles to the west of the convoy to protect it from the cruisers reported to be at Malta. In fact this report was false, the destroyers *Jervis* and *Diamond* having been mistakenly identified as cruisers on their arrival at Malta, which had triggered *Commando Supremo*'s concerns. Campioni's two battleships, four light cruisers and sixteen destroyers now sortied from their various ports

So by 8 July the Mediterranean was filled with naval units. The first sighting of Campioni's two battleships and their destroyer escort was by the submarine *Phoenix*, which reported them 180 miles east of Malta, putting them 500 miles away from the British fleet. The *Phoenix* did make a torpedo attack at extreme range, but failed to hit.[8] Cunningham now knew that the Italian main fleet was at sea, probably covering a convoy to North Africa, and he ordered air reconnaissance from Malta. At 3.10pm a flying boat from Malta reported that the Italian force consisted of two battleships, seven cruisers and seven destroyers, heading south towards Benghazi.

Campioni had launched a Ro43 seaplane from the cruiser *Abruzzi* in his own attempt at aerial reconnaissance, but the British fleet had already been located by two land-based Cant Z506 of the 189th and 148th Squadrons and from 10.00am to 6.40pm Cunningham's force came under heavy air attack. Thirteen attacks were carried out by a total of seventy-two planes, which dropped 102 250kg and 331 100kg bombs, all but one of which missed, although Cunningham reported that 'accuracy was very good'. At one point HMAS *Sydney* was completely engulfed in 'pillars of spray as high as church steeples' and Cunningham signalled the ship: 'Are you all right?' to which her captain replied, 'I hope so'.[9] The attacking aircraft came partly from the *Aeronautica dell'Egeo* in the Dodecanese, which deployed twenty-three S.79 bombers of the 34th and 41st Groups and eleven S.81s of the 39th *Stormo*. A further thirty-eight S.79s of the 10th, 14th and 15th *Stormo* flew from bases in Libya. Only one hit was scored, on the cruiser HMS *Gloucester*, which killed eighteen men including her captain. The ineffectiveness of high-level bombing against warships under way was becoming obvious to all.[10]

At 1.20pm on 8 July two Cant Z506 reconnaissance aircraft took off from Menelao airfield near Tobruk and at 2.40pm spotted the British fleet, shadowing it until 6.40pm. The planes reported to Campioni that the first group was composed of three battleships and eight destroyers, the second of one cruiser and five destroyers, and the third of four cruisers and one destroyer, and at 6.00pm they also accurately reported the British position. The observers were probably confusing ships because the main British group had two battleships and the carrier, while the other battleship (the *Warspite*) was in the central group. When Campioni received the first report at about 3.00pm, he had just ordered the 1st *Squadra*, the two battleships and six light cruisers, to turn, an hour after the same order had been given to the 2nd *Squadra*, six heavy cruisers and six light cruisers. The report from Tobruk of the British Fleet south-east of Crete, heading west, led Campioni to believe that his convoy might be attacked the next day off Benghazi, so he altered course towards Cunningham, informing *Supermarina* of his decision. However, when Mussolini heard of this he ordered that 'our naval forces should not be engaged', and the corresponding order reached Campioni at 6.45pm. *Supermarina* was also receiving intelligence reports from the German radio interception service, *B-Dienst*, in Berlin. At 3.50pm the Germans had reported that the British force consisted of four battlegroups, the leading pair of which would have reached a position 75 miles west of Sicily, near Tunisia.[11]

Meanwhile at 3.10pm a Sunderland of 288 Squadron based at Malta, reported spotting two Italian battleships, six cruisers and seven destroyers and at an hour later also reported their course change towards the British. Accordingly, Cunningham decided to cut across the Italians' return route by steaming towards Taranto.[12] He had the benefit of a branch of the Office of Intelligence-Admiralty which had been established at Malta in April 1939 in response to the threat of war with Italy, which had been transferred to Alexandria the following May. At the outbreak of war, a small group of cryptanalysts from all three services was sent out by the Government Code and Cipher School and General Staff Intelligence to work against Italian radio traffic. In this they were greatly helped by the capture of the new naval code book from the submarine *Uebi Scebeli* on 29 June. As Cunningham later wrote in his report, 'I had the advantage of receiving signification of many Italian C-in-C signals'.[13] But Campioni also enjoyed some intelligence advantages: at 6.15pm *Supermarina* received another message from the *B-Dienst* in Berlin which corrected the reported British position to 75 miles east of Sicily, and passed this to the fleet.

At 6.20pm one of Campioni's destroyers, the *Carabiniere*, reported a possible submarine sighting to starboard of the 3rd Cruiser Division and evasive manoeuvres were made. Then, 8 minutes later, the *Pola* and *Cesare* divisions were attacked by Italian aircraft. No ships were damaged or aircraft shot down in what was to be an all too frequent occurrence during the war.

At this point, the order for the fleet not to engage the enemy was received from *Supermarina*. The high command had taken this decison because it feared a night action, for which the Italians were neither properly trained or equipped, taking place beyond the range of land-based air support. Furthermore, influenced by the air reconnaissance reports, they believed that there were four British battleships at sea, despite intercepted British signals mentioning only three. Four battleships, each with eight 15in guns, would have a total broadside weight of 62,016lbs, compared to the 23,140lb total of the two Italian battleships, each with ten 12.6in guns. The re-tubed 12in guns had a range of 31,280 yards, outranging all the British battleships except *Warspite*, which had a range of 33,550 yards, and their rates of fire were comparable.[14]

Supermarina believed that the British were planning a bombardment of the Sicilian coast, possibly coupled with carrier strikes against the naval bases at Augusta and Messina. Consequently, the Air Force was requested to attack any British ships approaching Sicily, and to commit fighters from bases in Sicily and the Italian mainland for the defence of Augusta, and also to provide air cover for the Italian Fleet the next day. Furthermore, a line of five submarines was also deployed off Augusta to intercept enemy ships entering the Gulf of Squillace.

The supposed greater British battleship strength caused Marshal Badoglio, chief of *Comando Supremo* and Mussolini's 'principal military advisor', to ask *Supermarina* if the *Littorio* and *Vittorio Veneto* could be sent to reinforce Campioni, as the ships' captains had requested. But there had been an electrical fire in one of *Littorio*'s main turrets the previous day, killing one civilian worker and causing damage which would need a month's work to repair. Also, neither ship was fully worked-up and it was more than likely that they would not have been able to reach the fleet in time anyway, so the request was denied.[15] At 10.00pm that night, Campioni received instructions and intelligence reports for the following day. He was informed of the estimated course and speed of the British Fleet, the presence of four battleships and an aircraft carrier, and the deployment of the submarine screen off Augusta.

During the night, Cunningham changed course from 310° to 260°, and slowed the fleet from 20 to 15 knots. At dawn three aircraft were launched from *Eagle* for reconnaissance. At 6.00am on 9 July the British Fleet was deployed in three groups, as follows: the 7th Division (the cruisers *Orion*, *Neptune*, *Sydney*, *Gloucester*, *Liverpool*, and the destroyer HMAS *Stuart*) formed a screen 8 miles ahead of Cunningham's flagship *Warspite*, escorted by the destroyers *Nubian*, *Mohawk*, *Hero*, *Hereward* and *Decoy*, and a further 8 miles astern of this group was the 1st Battle Division consisting of the *Royal Sovereign*, the *Malaya*, the *Eagle* and the destroyers *Hyperion*, *Hostile*, *Hasty*, *Ilex*, *Dainty*, *Defender*, *Juno*, *Janus*, HMAS *Vampire* and HMAS *Voyager*.

At 8.00am a Sunderland was spotted by Campioni's ships. Two were in the area and one had informed Cunningham at 7.32am of the presence of the Italian fleet, composed of two battleships, four cruisers and ten destroyers, 50 miles east of Cape Spartivento. A further report put the enemy in two groups, the second formed of six cruisers and eight destroyers, 20 miles west of the main force. Aircraft from the *Eagle* also took part in the tracking of the Italian ships. Intending to position his forces between the Italian fleet and the Calabrian coast, Cunningham ordered a course of 305°, which took the fleet outside the area covered by Italian aerial reconnaissance.[16]

There was consternation at both *Supermarina* and *Superaereo* when neither aircraft, surface scouts nor submarines could find the British Fleet. Furthermore, Force H was reported to have left Gibraltar numbering three battleships, one carrier, two cruisers and ten destroyers, and three Italian destroyers had to return to port with mechanical problems caused by prolonged steaming at high speed.

At 12.30pm *Comando Supremo* reported that British intentions were unknown. Campioni's plans called for a concentration by 2.00pm 60 miles east of Cape Spartivento to patrol on a southerly course behind a 50-mile wide submarine screen, but Cunningham's course change had placed the submarines to the south-west of his fleet, unable to intercept them, and he was now closing undetected on the Italian Fleet's open flank.

At 11.15am the British located the enemy fleet 90 miles to the north bearing 295° and half an hour later a squadron of Swordfish torpedo bombers was launched from the *Eagle* to attack the Italian ships. Between 1.15 and 1.26pm they attacked what they believed to be the Italian battleships, but were in fact the heavy cruisers. No hits were scored and there was only minor damage to the attacking aircraft. The Italians reported that two were shot down after having launched five torpedoes from about 1000-1500m out, two were against the *Trento*, two against the *Bolzano* and one at the *Zara*. Vice-Admiral Paladini later described the attack.

> Two of the aircraft made a determined effort to attack the head of our line, coming up from astern, and one of these, having penetrated our destroyer screen and avoiding the fire of all our escorts, unleashed a torpedo in a beautiful manoeuvre against the *Pola* from the port at an angle of about 70°, and at a distance of between 1000 to 1500 meters. The *Pola* turned to the port at maximum speed and engaged this aircraft with every weapon that would bear.

Doctrine called for the Swordfish to concentrate against one large enemy ship, but because of the heavy fire and the large number of targets, this was not done.[17]

By early afternoon the fleets were about to meet. Campioni had finally received a report from the Air Force of the British position as of 1.30pm, shortly after the Swordfish attack on the heavy cruisers, and at 2.15pm the commander of the 1st Squadra asked for air support according to plan. Three Ro.43 reconnaissance floatplanes were launched by the cruisers *Da Barbiano*, *Di Giussano* and *Duca degli Abruzzi* and later the *Eugenio di Savoia*, *Garibaldi*, and *Cadorna* launched three more. After half an hour they reported the British position, 30 miles closer than supposed by the earlier reports. None of these aircraft were lost, although the one from the *Eugenio* landed at Messina after coming under fire from Italian cruisers.[18]

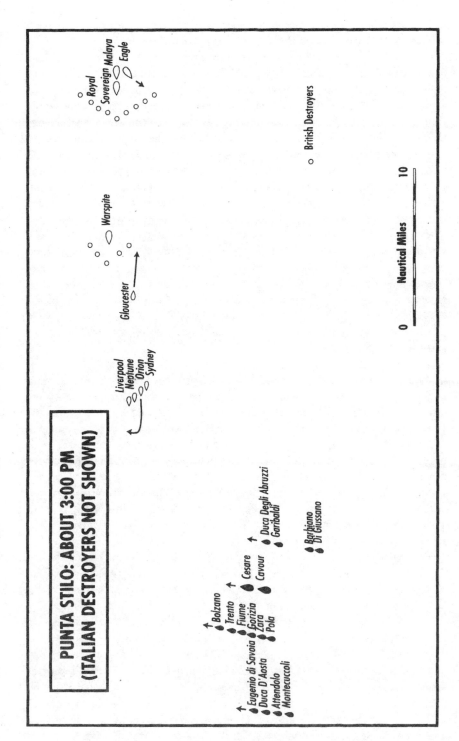

PUNTA STILO: ABOUT 3:00 PM
(ITALIAN DESTROYERS NOT SHOWN)

Royal
Sovereign Malaya
Eagle

Warspite

Gloucester

British Destroyers

Liverpool
Neptune
Orion
Sydney

Nautical Miles

0   10

Bolzano
Trento
Fiume
Gorizia
Zara
Pola

Cesare
Cavour

Duca Degli Abruzzi
Garibaldi

Barbiano
Di Giussano

Eugenio di Savoia
Duca D'Aosta
Attendolo
Montecuccoli

Cunningham's plan had succeeded and by 2.00pm the Italian Fleet was cut off from Taranto. He now ordered the fleet to turn towards the enemy, the destroyers moving to the far side of the capital ships to clear the field of fire. The fleet was held to a maximum speed of 20 knots, the best the *Royal Sovereign* could do. At 2.15pm a Sunderland reported to Cunningham that the Italian warships were turning to the north at a speed of 18 knots, confirming his belief that they wanted to fight him in their own waters. At 2.39pm he was informed by the *Eagle*'s air reconnaissance that the enemy were 30 miles from the *Warspite*, which had moved up in support of the cruisers (the damaged *Gloucester* had been sent back to join the *Eagle*).

At 2.47pm the *Orion* sighted smoke and 5 minutes later the *Neptune* reported two Italian ships ahead, while the *Orion* spotted three destroyers at a range of about 27,300 yards. At 2.58pm three more destroyers and four cruisers were sighted, making smoke. The smokescreen was the result of a false alarm from the destroyers of the Italian 2nd *Squadra* reporting enemy ships to the south-west, and at 3.00pm it was stopped. The first Italian sighting of the enemy came at 3.05pm when the light cruisers of the 4th Division, followed shortly after by those of the 8th Division, spotted units of the British 7th Cruiser Division, but the ships were not positively identified. At 3.10pm the *Eagle* and the old destroyers *Voyager* and *Vampire* left the line of battle and took station 10 miles to starboard of the *Warspite* where they were joined by the damaged *Gloucester*. The remaining British ships were now in two groups, one 8 miles behind the other.

The British had three battleships, one carrier, five light cruisers and sixteen destroyers, mounting in total twenty-four 15in, sixty-eight 6in and sixty-four 4.7in guns, against the Italians' two battleships, six heavy and eight light cruisers and twenty destroyers with twenty 12.6in, forty-eight 8in, fifty-six 6in, and 108 4.7in guns. The Italians could also add 160 bombers from in Sicily and Apulia against the *Eagle*'s aircraft.

The first serious English-language analysis of the forces in this battle was made by Peter Smith, who pointed out that several Italian destroyers had had to leave the fleet due to mechanical problems whilst others had had to be detached to refuel and were on their way back when the action began. Also, the cruisers *Bande Nere* and *Colleoni* and four destroyers had gone on to Tripoli. We give slightly higher totals for the Italian Fleet than Smith, to take into account the four destroyers which rejoined the fleet before the end of the battle.[19]

At 1.10pm *Supermarina* had sent a message to Campioni with instructions for the coming encounter: he was to avoid risking his ships, but he did have permission to engage one or other of the British forces. He was also to develop the action in such a way that the Air Force could join in.[20]

The first shots were fired by the Italian 8th and 4th Cruiser Divisions (*Abruzzi, Garibaldi, Da Barbiano, Di Giussano*), and at 3.18pm the *Orion, Neptune, Liverpool* and *Sydney* returned fire at a range of 22,300 yards, concentrating on the cruisers although *Orion* fired for 3 minutes at a closing destroyer squadron (four destroyers of the 9th Squadron), forcing it to retire. The flagship, the *Alfieri*, suffered splinter damage from a minor hit.

The British thought they were firing on heavy cruisers and supporting destroyers. Both groups had thirty-six 6in guns, as the destroyers were still out of

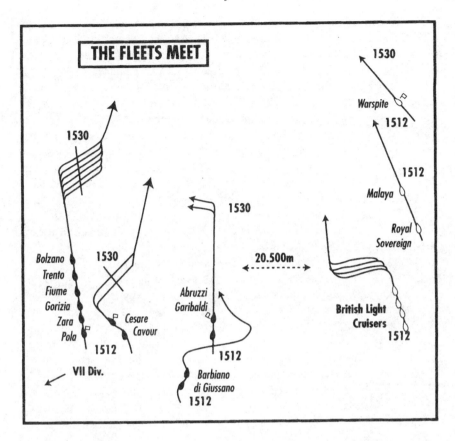

THE FLEETS MEET

1530

1530

Warspite

1512

1512

Malaya

Royal
Sovereign

20.500m

Bolzano
Trento
Fiume
Gorizia
Zara
Pola

1530

1530

Cesare
Cavour

1512

VII Div.

1530

Abruzzi
Garibaldi

1512

Barbiano
di Giussano

1512

British Light
Cruisers

1512

range, but no hits were scored except for one damaged seaplane on the *Neptune*.
Neptune's Rate Officer at the range finder later wrote;

> Once battle was joined everything became very confusing and visibility was obscured
> by cordite smoke, smokescreens, and cascades of water from bursting shells. The
> approaching shells sounded like express trains and the confusion was added to by the
> need to keep shifting targets as cruisers and destroyers appeared through the smoke.

At 3.42pm the Italian heavy cruisers and battleships turned 60° east to come to the
support of the light cruisers, moving to their van. The four Italian light cruisers
opened the range and would eventually move to the rear of the battleships and
heavy cruisers, as four more light cruisers came up. It would be these ships, under
Rear-Admiral Luigi Sansonetti, which would signal the approach of the *Warspite*.

The *Warspite* received the *Neptune's* signal 'Enemy battle fleet in sight' and
shortly afterwards at 3.26pm opened fire on Sansonetti's cruisers, which retreated
under a smokescreen after the battleship had fired ten salvoes. Meanwhile the Italian
heavy cruisers had begun firing on Tovey's light cruisers, which took evasive
action. No hits were scored but they felt uncomfortable under this heavy shelling.
Apparently the Italian battleships did not fire on Tovey's cruisers, while the heavy
cruisers would in part shift fire to the *Warspite*.

The *Warspite* sighted the battleships *Cavour* and *Cesare* at 3.50pm at a range of 26,000 yards and prepared to open fire on the Italian battleships. The *Cesare* opened fire on *Warspite* 3 minutes later at the extreme range of 24,140 yards. The *Cavour* opened fire at 27,400 yards against what her gunners thought was a 'third British battleship', but was in fact the *Warspite*, which had earlier made a complete circle to allow the slower British battleships to catch up. The *Cavour* then fired forty-one shells, her gunnery being affected by the smoke from the *Cesare*, which in turn fired seventy-four rounds. The firing officer on board the *Cesare* had his vision temporarily impaired by the dirty optical equipment when the first salvo was fired.[21] The *Warspite*'s fire was well aimed and her salvoes were tight, while the Italian salvoes were too dispersed. Both sides were straddling their targets, with the *Warspite* doing so on her first salvo. The Italian heavy cruisers joined in, opening fire at 3.50pm at about 24,000 yards.

The *Royal Sovereign* was too slow to reach her assigned position in line and did not take part in the battle. According to Campioni's report, the 15in salvos from the *Warspite* were 'very concentrated'. The *Malaya* did open fire but her salvoes fell far short. In the meantime nine Swordfish attacked the Italian heavy cruisers *Bolzano* and *Trento* at 3.55pm, believing they were the enemy battleships. Despite victorious reports from both sides, no ships were hit and no aircraft shot down.

At 3.59pm the *Cesare* was hit. One 15in shell from the *Warspite* hit the after funnel on the starboard side, opening a 5-6 metre wide hole, then pierced the foredeck, passed through an AA ammunition store and the petty officers' quarters, and stopped on the inner side of the bulwark armour plate. Fire broke out immediately in the damaged areas and smoke was sucked into four of the eight engine rooms by the forced-air turbo system, causing the ship to slow to 18 knots. Giuseppe Grotto was in the aft conning tower aboard the *Giulio Cesare* when the ship was hit, and he recalled that when the shell stuck, all the men in the tower were thrown a half metre in the air. The volume of smoke produced made it seem as if the ship was on fire from stem to stern, and the order to abandon ship was expected, but it did not come and it was then realised that the damage was not as severe as first thought. Campioni likewise thought the *Cesare* had been severely damaged, and ordered the fleet to turn away under cover of smoke, breaking off the action. Cunningham wrote of this, 'I had been watching the great splashes of our 15-inch salvoes straddling the target when, at 4pm, I saw the great orange-coloured flash of a heavy explosion at the base of the enemy flagship's funnels. It was followed by an upheaval of smoke, and I knew that she had been heavily hit at the prodigious range of thirteen miles'.[22]

At 4.12pm the heavy cruisers *Trento* and *Boliano* were unsuccessfully attacked again by Swordfish torpedo planes. The 8in heavy cruiser fire against the *Warspite* did not score any hits. The heavy cruiser *Bolzano*, leading the formation, was hit by three 6in shells from the *Neptune*, one of which hit on the starboard side below the waterline, causing the ship to take on 300 tons of water and damaging the helm, and she changed course by 180°. But the damage was repaired in 6 minutes and she was soon back up to 30 knots, rejoining the line. The second shell hit the torpedo room, killing two, and causing six of the eight torpedoes carried to launch involuntarily, while the

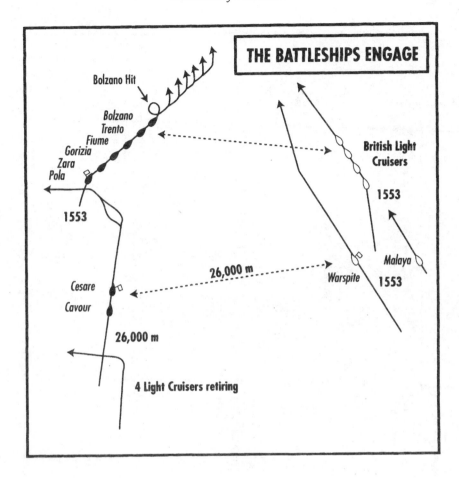

third cut 3ft off the starboard gun of B turret and damaged the other, although both continued to fire.[23]

Campioni said that his decision to break of the action was taken because the *Cesare* was down to 18 knots and the fleet should keep concentrated against a superior enemy (he probably still thought he was facing four British battleships). He could no longer make Taranto with Cunningham blocking his way, and instead headed towards the Straits of Messina. The Italian battleships headed west, steaming towards Messina, while the cruisers put up what the British described as a 'very effective' smokescreen and the destroyers launched torpedoes, but at too great a range to have any chance of hitting.[24] Campioni thought that sustained daylight torpedo attacks against battleships would bring about few results for heavy losses.

Once the fire aboard the *Cesare* had been brought under control, the four boilers shut down due to the smoke were quickly brought back on line and by 4.45pm six of the eight boilers were on line. It was between 4.05pm and 4.45pm that thirty-two torpedoes were launched against the British ships from ranges varying from 5 to 7.7 miles, which was judged by the British as a half-hearted attack. The British

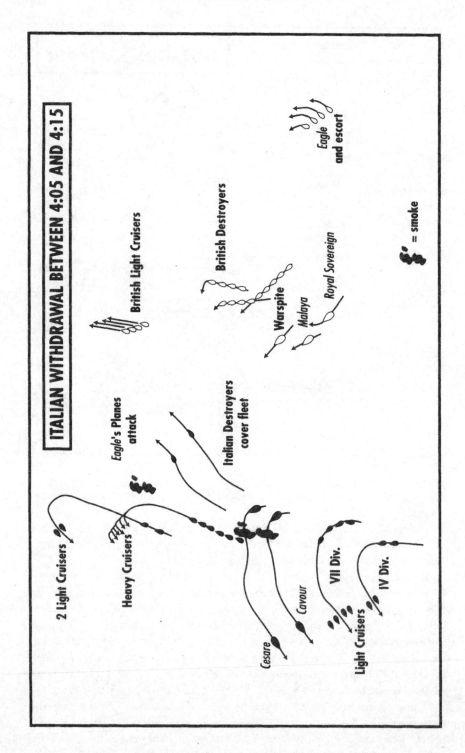

ITALIAN WITHDRAWAL BETWEEN 4:05 AND 4:15

destroyers were ordered to counterattack but they met heavy fire from the Italian cruisers covering the retreat of the battleships, which dodged in and out of the smokescreen, firing as they went, until 4.50pm, when the action ceased.

Cunningham tried to swing around the smokescreen from the north, because from the interception of Italian signals it was clear that the enemy ships were retreating toward a submarine screen and the smoke the Italian ships were dodging in and out of could be a trap. But having reached the northern end of the smoke-screen at 5.35pm only the Calabrian coast was in sight, 25 miles away, and Cunningham also received a Sigint (Signal Intelligence) alert indicating an air-sub ambush. With the smoke and the superior speed of the Italian fleet, the Mediterranean Fleet broke off the pursuit, turning south-south-west, and then changing course again at 7.30pm towards Alexandria.[25]

At that point the *Regia Aeronautica* begun to bomb British and Italian ships alike. Radio communication between Campioni's fleet and the attacking aircraft was not possible, so the aircraft were carrying out the orders they had been issued when the battle was about to begin. Between 4.40pm and 7.00pm, 126 aircraft bombed both fleets, dropping 8 500kg, 236 250kg, and 270 100kg bombs from 12,000 feet. Although the Italian ships had white-painted bows and lacked a distinctive-looking aircraft carrier in their midst, the mistaken attacks continued until some minutes after 7.00pm as they 'bombed both Campioni's and Cunningham's forces impartially until dusk'. A total of 435 bombers took part and four were shot down, two of them by fighters from the *Eagle*, and one by Italian AA. They dropped over 2000 bombs in total during the operation, but caused only minor damage.[26]

The Italian fleet reached port at both Augusta and Messina, Campioni arriving at the latter with the *Cesare* at about 9pm. Several of the undamaged cruisers sailed from Augusta on the 10th to escort a convoy to Benghazi. Admiral Paladini sailed with the undamaged *Cavour* and the bulk of the fleet to Naples, as *Supermarina* had intercepted a signal from Malta that indicated a night attack with Swordfish torpedo planes was planned against Augusta. The following day naval reconnaissance did not sight the Mediterranean Fleet, but message intercepts showed that Cunningham's ships would be between Sicily and Malta on the evening of 10 July, in a good position to launch a air attack. Consequently the base at Augusta was evacuated, while the *Cesare* remained at Messina with her AA crews at action stations. Therefore, when nine Swordfish from the *Eagle* did attack Augusta at 10.00pm that night, in a forerunner of the raid on Taranto, they found few targets. An oiler was damaged and the destroyer *Leone Pancaldo* was sunk (she would later be raised and returned to service), and the Swordfish returned to the carrier via Malta.

On their return to Alexandria, the British fleet was again subjected to heavy bombing by aircraft from Libya, with the *Liverpool* suffering some casualties from near misses and the destroyer *Vampire* taking some splinter damage whilst escorting one of the Malta convoys, but otherwise there were no losses and both convoys made Alexandria safely.

Somerville's Force H had ably supported the Mediterranean Fleet's operations. In order to tie down Italian forces, Cunningham had suggested air attacks against either Naples, or the Sicilian ports of Palermo, Messina or Trapani. However,

Somerville's destroyers lacked the range for such attacks and he chose instead to raid Cagliari in Sardinia. He sortied from Gibraltar on the morning of 8 July with the carrier *Ark Royal*, the battleships *Valiant* and *Resolution*, the battlecruiser *Hood*, three light cruisers, and ten destroyers. The Italians were aware of this and sent air units from Sardinia against the force in a series of high-level attacks. Many near misses occurred from the forty-six Italian S.79s of the 8th and 32nd *Stormo* on 9 July, causing splinter damage to the *Ark Royal*, *Resolution* and *Hood*. The *Ark Royal*'s air group saw action, with three Skuas shooting down a Cant A.506B that had been shadowing the force for 3 hours. The fighters also attacked the 'pretty efficient and determined' Italian bombers, which were operating beyond the range of their own fighter cover. One was shot down and others damaged, with no loss to the Skuas. Somerville decided to retire before attacking Cagliari, to protect his vulnerable carrier. Force H was not located by the Italians on the 10th, so no further air attacks were launched,[27] but as it neared Gibraltar in the early hours of 11 July, the destroyer *Escort* was torpedoed by the submarine *Marconi* at 2.15am. She slowly began to sink, finally going over on her beam ends at 11.00am revealing a 20-foot hole 'from about 4 feet below the upper deck to beyond the keel'. The rest of the force gained port safely.[28]

Considerable concern was caused at *Supermarina* by the mechanical failures suffered by a number of their ships as a result of sustained high speeds. Four ships required repairs lasting from 4 days to a month, whilst several other ships, including two light cruisers, had suffered minor problems and requested to return to base. It was proposed that in future the fleet's cruising speed should be limited to 20 knots. This showed up the shortage of pre-war high-speed exercises.[29]

Italian propaganda attempted to claim that the British had suffered heavy damage at Punta Stilo. A 1940 edition of the weekly *Cronache de Guerra* printed a photograph of the *Malaya* with what looked like a shell hit near the belt and with one 4in and two 6in guns knocked out, which far from being taken after the battle in fact showed the damage she had suffered in a collision with a merchant ship in 1936.[30]

Some of the British ships were badly shaken-up by all the near-misses during the air attacks, and Cunningham did recognise the need to strengthen his fleet. He specifically requested more battleships capable of long-range fire, since the Italian battleships and heavy cruisers 'were straddling us comfortably' at ranges only the *Warspite* could match. In particular he wanted the radar-equipped *Valiant*. He also asked for his own heavy cruisers to support his scouting forces against the Italian heavy cruisers. Cunningham wrote: 'We needed also an armoured aircraft-carrier like the *Illustrious*, with fighters, an anti-aircraft cruiser like the *Carlisle* and a couple of convoy sloops'. With such a force he felt he could dominate the eastern Mediterranean 'indefinitely'. The First Sea Lord, Admiral Pound, would soon take steps to meet these requests, and would additionally send Cunningham some 'G' and 'H' class destroyers.

The Admiralty asked Admiral Cunningham to give his opinions regarding the future composition of naval forces in the Mediterranean, and it was decided to continue maintaining a strong force in the east, and a smaller one at Gibraltar to keep the Italian Navy from passing into the Atlantic, which was thought unlikely as long as Spain remained neutral, which could also be used to raid the Italian coast. Also that summer the British organised the war on economic resources with the establishment of a Special Operation Executive, the task of which was to 'set Europe ablaze'.

The British crews as a whole had their morale boosted by the engagement. They had suffered tremendous bombing with very little damage to show for it, engaged a more numerous fleet (though one inferior in the decisive element in a daylight surface action – battleships), and they had sucessfully got the convoys through. However, Churchill considered the indecisive engagement unsatisfactory and thought Somerville should have been more aggressive.[31]

The Italians had also successfully seen their convoy through to Libya, had likewise suffered little damage, and had fought the mighty Royal Navy and survived. Their principal complaint was, unsurprisingly, with the *Regia Aeronautica*. The fact that it took all of 10 days to unload the convoy at Tripoli also caused concern.[32]

Admiral Campioni did not complain that his ships' guns had worked poorly during the battle, nor did he say much about the accuracy of their fire, only observing that the British salvoes were concentrated and there were two enemy battleships firing (when in fact only the *Warspite* had been in range). Although the guns of the *Cesare* could only be loaded at a fixed elevation of 15°, their rate of fire was the same as that of the *Warspite*. Both Admirals Campioni and Sansonetti considered the fleet's performance in battle as satisfactory, Sansonetti writing in 1946 that it confirmed the fleet's good manoeuvring and training. On the British side the Italian fire was considered good at first, but lost accuracy when they themselves came under fire. That summer the Italian Navy undertook many gunnery exercises.[33]

The accuracy of Italian guns needs some attention, as the action had been decided by the quality of British gunnery. Although *Warspite*'s hit was a lucky one, as Cunningham himself admitted,[34] there was also the effective salvo that hit the *Bolzano*. The Italian heavy gun salvoes were too widely dispersed, which has been commented upon by various authors, among them the Italian historian Alberto Santoni who noted that in 39 months of war Italian naval guns sank only two British motorboats outright. Even if the salvo was well-aimed, the wide dispersion of the fall of shot meant that hits were rare, as was argued by Admiral Angelo Iachino, Campioni's successor as fleet commander.[35] This problem was caused by a number of factors. Firstly, the Italian Navy's pursuit of long-range fire before the war resulted in their guns having excessive muzzle velocities, which led to rapid wear of the barrel linings and consequent loss of accuracy. For example, the 15in Model 1934 guns of the *Littorio* class had a muzzle velocity of 2854f/s, with an approximate life of 110 to 130 firings against 2458f/s of the *Warspite*'s 15in, which had a life of 335 shells. It should be noted that the British 16in was disliked for its wide salvo spreads and its muzzle velocity was consequently reduced, because at 2670f/s 'wear was rapid, accuracy insufficient and the rifling was damaged by hammering of the short-bodied, long headed shell'. The 12.6in guns of the *Cavour* and *Cesare* shared this problem, with a muzzle velocity of 2723f/s giving a barrel-life of 150 rounds, and this was after the original muzzle velocity had been reduced when the guns were re-bored.[36]

Accuracy was further reduced by the poor quality-control in shell production, resulting in a wide variation in the weights of shells. Vice-Admiral Silvio Salza spoke also of 'poor quality' explosive fillings of shells, although he also stressed the lack of training under realistic battle conditions. Admiral Iachino recalled in his memoirs that this situation was well known in the navy before the war. Reports addressed to Cavagnari in July 1939 and signed by Vice-Admiral Salza prove it, saying that scattering of salvoes was too high for 12.6in and 6in guns, while ammunition quality was declining. It is therefore difficult to understand why this state of affairs continued to be accepted by Cavagnari and the Admirals' Committee.[37]

Having seen the influence of the *Eagle* on the battle, Admiral Campioni proposed the introduction of an aircraft carrier in his battle report. The Italian land-based fighters were unable to support the fleet during the battle, allowing the British carrier aircraft to keep the fleet under surveillance. But this did not convince *Supermarina* which even after the attack on Taranto was still sceptical about the utility of aircraft carriers.[38]

By 21 July *Comando Supremo* was aware that, despite the reports of the aircraft crews, the air attacks against the British Fleet had been largely ineffective, as had the submarine screen. One memorandum concluded that it was impossible to deny the passage between Libya, Crete, Tunisia and Sardinia to British naval forces, even if more submarines were deployed and the training of aircrews improved. It was clear that high-altitude bombing was a failure. *Comando Supremo* concluded that the addition of just eighty dive-bombers would enable the Italians to impose a heavy toll on the British forces and proposed to buy these aircraft from the Germans immediately, and one hundred Ju87 Stukas would shortly be supplied to Italy by Germany. No mention was made of torpedo aircraft, an area affected yet again by inter-service rivalry.[39] Shortly afterwards the German liaison officer attached to the *Regia Aeronautica* proposed the deployment of Luftwaffe units in the Mediterranean.

In fact, as Ciano wrote in his diary on 13 July:

> The real controversy in the matter of naval armament is not between us and the British, but between our Air Force and our Navy. Admiral Cavagnari maintains that our air action was completely lacking during the first phase of the encounter, but that when it finally came it was directed against our own ships, which for six hours withstood the bombardment of our aeroplanes. Other information also gives the lie to the glowing reports of our Air Force.[40]

The Italian Navy contradicted the Air Force's reports of heavy damage to British ships, and later German reports confirmed this. It was clear that ship recognition and training should be improved, and that high-altitude attacks had poor results. One *Comando Supremo* memorandum stated that; 'We don't think that the offensive actions carried out by our air force on the days of 8, 9, 11, and 12 July against British naval forces had obtained such results as to give the enemy the impression that high level bombing could be of serious hindrance to the free movements of his fleet'.[41]

During the battle the Italian Navy had shown some unreadiness for war. The German air attaché wrote in his report that on the evening of the 8th; 'Night torpedo attacks against the British fleet were surprisingly not ordered'. Actually, at 7pm Campioni had been instructed by *Supermarina* to launch torpedo attacks with available ships after sunset against British forces heading for Malta, but he had considered that it would be difficult for his destroyers to regain contact with the enemy. The German attaché's initial report was influenced by the Air Force's exaggerated claims of success, but when the true situation became clear, he blamed the poor quality of Italian bombs and the poor deployment of the aircraft. The German *B-Dienst* intelligence service was also criticised for supplying incomplete information to the Italians, for unknown reasons.[42] He also repeated the Italian Navy's claims of scoring some hits, and that a cruiser had been torpedoed at the end of the action. British gunnery was also reported as 'very well aimed' and their salvoes 'concentrated (in one space of not over 70m)'.[43]

The German Naval Staff saw the encounter as a missed opportunity for the Italian Navy, since they had good intelligence on the enemy, superior speed, and the availability of nearby air bases, conditions which '. . . allowed for the collaboration of a friendly air force, submarines and torpedo boats'. The failure to employ destroyers on the almost moonless night that followed that battle was also regarded as a mistake, as was *Supermarina*'s order to Campioni not to engage. The radio intercepts were on the other hand judged to be very good, thanks to the *B-Dienst*, made easier by the 'carelessness of the British conduct in dealing with their messages'. The final assessment was that 'the Italian Navy on 9th and 10th July had lost her decisive opportunity', as such favourable conditions could not be expected to recur in war.[44]

The reports of Vice-Admiral Weichold, appointed as German liaison officer to *Supermarina* in June 1940, were principally responsible for the view formed by Naval Headquarters in Berlin. On 19 July he reported, following the sinking of the cruiser *Colleoni* off Greece, that the Italians 'don't know systematic aerial reconnaissance'.[45] After Punta Stilo, Weichold reported that *Supermarina* proposed a 'common examination of the new strategic situation' following the fall of France and the increased burden upon the British, which could allow the deployment of Italian submarines in the Atlantic. This was a major change, as on 5 July Weichold had reported that the Italians felt such a deployment was impossible due to British surveillance at Gibraltar, and the Germans were pleased at the prospect of more submarines to use against British convoys, possibly under their command. This suggestion came from a re-assessment of the strategic situation by *Supermarina*, in which the future role of the Italian Navy would be to tie up as many British forces as possible.[46]

CHAPTER 7

The Battle of Cape Spada, 19 July 1940

The Battle of Cape Spada . . . painfully revealed that the Italian Navy
was a blind navy.

Franco Maugeri[1]

A lmost before the sound of the guns at Punta Stilo had died away, the next
phase of operations was getting under way. Just before the first of these, on 17
July 1940, the Italians introduced a new cipher, which cost the British much of the
intelligence advantages they had previously enjoyed, until it could be broken by
their cryptanalysts at Alexandria.

Supermarina had decided to send the 2nd Cruiser Division, consisting of the light
cruisers *Bande Nere* and *Bartolomeo Colleoni* under Rear-Admiral Ferdinando
Casardi, into the Aegean to attack British merchant ships plying between Greece
and Turkey, from the Italian base at Portolago on the island of Leros. Casardi's
ships were lightly armoured, armed with eight 6in guns in four twin turrets and after
many years of service able to make just over 30 knots.[2] They had just escorted a
convoy to Benghazi, and had been transferred to Tripoli, out of range of the RAF.
There had been a plan for them to participate in bombardment raids on Sollum and
Mersa Matruh, but *Supermarina* decided against it. Casardi, maintaining radio
silence, was to proceed north of Crete, zig-zagging at 25 knots, refuel at Portolago
and then search for British merchant ships in the Aegean. The Italian naval attaché
in Istanbul was to provide intelligence of possible targets for the cruisers. Yet again,
the main problem for this operation was the absence of effective air reconnaissance.
The Italian Aegean Air Command had attempted to launch four floatplanes early on
19 July, but the very calm sea state meant that the aircraft had to taxi for long
periods with their engines at full power, which meant they overheated and were
unable to take off.

Just after 6.00am on 19 July, the Italian ships were north of Cape Spada (on the
western coast of Crete) when they came upon four British destroyers. The *Hyperion*
(flagship of Captain H Nicholson), *Ilex*, *Hero*, and *Hasty* of the 2nd Destroyer Flotilla
were zig-zagging west at 16 knots in an anti-submarine operation along the north
coast of Crete. HMAS *Sydney*, under Captain (later Vice-Admiral) J A Collins, and
the destroyer *Havock* had been dispatched from Alexandria with orders to support
Nicholson's destroyers and operate to the north of them against any Italian shipping in
the Gulf of Athens. Collins had decided his priority was the support of the destroyers,
so he remained only 40 miles north of Nicholson's ships. In spite of some British
accounts, the destroyers were probably faster than the older Italian cruisers. *Sydney*
was one of the three *Perth* class cruisers of the Royal Australian Navy, armed with
eight 6in guns in four twin turrets, two forward and two aft.

The destroyers were in line abreast when sighted, with appproximately 1½ miles between each ship. Neither side had launched aircraft. The *Sydney*'s floatplane had been lost at the bombardment of Bardia in June and not yet replaced, while Casardi considered the sea state too rough to launch (reporting it as Sea State 5, '*molto agitato*'). It would also have been dangerous for the ships to slow down with enemy submarines possibly in the area, and Casardi had been promised air support from bases in the Aegean.[3]

The British commander later reported that the sea had been calm, directly contradicting Casardi. This may have been because the British ships were operating in the relatively sheltered waters off Crete and the Greek islands, whilst the Italians were approaching from the open Mediterranean. The tendency for Italian ships to roll more than their British counterparts, which adversely affected their gunnery, may have lead to an overestimation of the sea conditions. There was also a rapidly rising undersea ridge which affects the seas where the Italians were. In our opinion, both sides were probably reporting conditions accurately for where they were at the time.[4]

As the two forces closed, G Hermon Gill later wrote;

> In *Hyperion* the ship's company had just been fallen out from dawn action stations, and the smell of breakfast bacon was floating up the bridge voice pipes, when the starboard bridge lookout said: 'Two cruisers on the starboard bow, sir,' adding 'and they're Italian, too'.

The destroyers immediately increased speed to 30 knots and made a 180° degree turn away from the enemy. *Ilex* and *Hyperion*, closest to the enemy, opened fire but their shells fell well short. Likewise, the Italian cruisers increased speed and opened fire at 7.27am at a range of about 19,000 yards. Casardi claimed that he opened fire first and that the British did not reply until the *Bande Nere*'s fifth salvo at 7:32am, although British accounts say they were the first to fire. Firing into the sun, the Italian fire was slow and not very accurate, being correct for range but 'unaccountably out of line'. At 8.00am, thinking the destroyers had fired torpedoes (although they had not), Casardi's ships opened the range to almost 26,000 yards.[5] He did not close with the enemy because, thanks to lack of air reconnaissance, he had no idea whether the destroyers were in fact the screen for a larger force, and he therefore maintained the range and his line-ahead formation, without scoring any hits, as Nicholson continued to head north towards the *Sydney* and the *Havock*. At about 8.05am, the Italians deployed into line abreast and attempted to close with the destroyers, but the extreme range and poor visibility, added to by the British making smoke, meant that there was little firing at only intermittently visible targets, but Nicholson was forced to turn away from his northerly course. At this point an old Greek freighter passed between the two forces, and made off as fast as her tired engines could drive her!

Nicholson had been radioing constant reports of the action which were received by Cunningham at Alexandria as well as Collins, stating clearly that he was engaged with two cruisers, but he was not sure if they were light or heavy cruisers. Casardi had also radioed for help, requesting aircraft from Rhodes. He only transmitted once, even though his position was clearly known by the enemy. Collins had maintained radio silence, so Nicholson thought he was still a full hour away from him, but so far he had suffered no damage.

At 8:20am the *Sydney's* lookouts spied 'volumes of smoke on the southern horizon' and at 8:26am spotted the two Italian cruisers, with the *Bande Nere* leading. At 8:29am the *Sydney* opened fire at 20,000 yards and radioed her position to Cunningham and Nicholson. The British destroyers had not yet spotted Collins' ships, but they could make out the welcome sight of *Sydney's* gun flashes.

The *Sydney* was concealed in some low-lying fog, so the Italians' first warning of her presence came when shells began to fall to port of the *Bande Nere*. From what Casardi could make out, he identified the new ships as possibly two light cruisers of the *Leander* or larger *Southampton* type. By 8:32am he had altered course to the south-east, firing at the gun flashes with his ships' after turrets, holding this course for 10 minutes while Nicholson's force made another 180° turn back towards the enemy and the *Sydney* tried to keep all her guns in play by remaining broadside-on. With the *Sydney* finally in sight of Nicholson's force, Collins detached the *Havock* to join the other destroyers and ordered them to make a torpedo attack.

Collins had now positively identified his opponents as two light cruisers. The Italian gunnery was 'fairly' accurate, with a few straddles, but most of their salvoes at first fell short, and then over the target, whilst yet again Casardi reported the British salvoes as tight and precise. First blood was drawn by the *Sydney* at 8.35am when she hit the *Bande Nere* near the base of her after funnel, causing eight casualties.

At 8.40am the Italian cruisers turned away and steered south, then south-west, to avoid being trapped between the enemy to the north and the coast of Crete to the south, endeavouring, as Casardi said, to draw 'the enemy formation towards waters free of any land restrictions'. By turning away and leading the enemy in a chase, he also had the option of launching torpedoes back at their line. By 8.58am his ships were in line abreast heading south-west.

During the run to the south, the British ships had been in line abreast chasing the Italians, the *Sydney* only able to fire her two forward turrets at a range of 18,000 yards and increasing. While the British destroyers may have been faster than Casardi's ships, there was no question that the *Sydney* was slower than them, although later in the action the *Bande Nere* had to temporarily shut down one boiler and dropped to 29 knots. But when the Italians turned to the south-west, the range began to narrow and both sides were occasionally able to bring their full broadsides into play. The *Sydney* shifted her fire between the two enemy ships depending on which was less obscured by smoke, concentrating mostly on the rear ship, the *Colleoni*. The destroyers came into range of the *Colleoni* at 8.49am and opened fire, but the Italian smokescreen affected their shooting.

At 9.15am Collins finally turned to bring his rear turrets to bear, which was followed 3 minutes later by the Italian ships turning further west away from Crete. At 9:21am the *Sydney* was hit for the only time in the action, by one shell that caused minor damage to one of her funnels, wounding one man, but at 9:24am she hit the *Bartolomeo Colleoni*, jamming her rudder so she steamed straight ahead, unable to manouevre. Immediately she was hit again twice by 6in shells from the Australian cruiser, first on her lightly-protected bridge, killing many, and then in the boiler room, which brought her to a stop and also disabled her main armament ammunition hoists. She could only fire her secondary 4in guns on manual control as the British closed in. By 9:30am she had 'become smothered in the large and smaller splashes of cruiser and destroyer shells', hit repeatedly – at least seven times – and 'was reduced to a wreck'. Her mortally wounded commander, Captain Umberto Novaro, gave the order to abandon ship. Virtually all the shells had penetrated her thin armour and burst inside the ship, so from the outside she appeared almost undamaged.[6] The *Hyperion* now closed to about 7500 yards and fired three torpedoes, all of which missed. The *Ilex* then hit her with one torpedo just forward of 'A' turret, blowing off 30 feet of her bows, another torpedo from *Hyperion* hit amidships and she sank at 9.59am (*Havock* has been incorrectly credited with this in the past). The destroyers picked up 545 survivors, of which 51 were wounded, including Captain Novaro who later died (he was awarded the *Medaglia d'Oro*). A further 7 men were picked up by a Greek freighter, trying to swim to Crete, but 121 men were lost.

The *Sydney*, *Hero*, and *Hasty* continued in pursuit of the *Bande Nere*, which had circled back to see if she could help the doomed *Colleoni*. Seeing that her position was hopeless, Casardi sped on to the south with the British in pursuit. The *Sydney* scored another hit at 9:58am, penetrating the *Bande Nere's* quarterdeck, wounding twelve and killing four. But with the range gradually increasing and with the *Sydney's* forward turrets down to their last shells, Collins called off the pursuit at 10:37am and headed for Alexandria at low speed to allow the rest of the force to catch up.

The *Bande Nere* continued south for an hour to make the British think she was bound for Tobruk, and then made for Benghazi, where she arrived safely, steaming on to Tripoli on the 21st. Thinking that she might be at Tobruk, the British moved a squadron of six Swordfish up to Sidi Barrani and made a night attack on the 20th, sinking the old destroyers *Nembo* and *Ostro* and one small freighter. The freighter was hit after one of the low-flying Swordfish had hit her boom with one wheel, lost it, regained control and then successfully launched its torpedo. It landed along with the other five at 5:00am on one wheel![7]

Nicholson's force of three destroyers, packed with rescued Italians, came under attack from four waves of S.79 and S.81 bombers based at Rhodes. A near miss damaged one of *Havock's* boilers, reducing her speed to 24 knots, and wounding both crew and prisoners, but they all made it back to port, and with the destroyers alongside, the *Sydney* entered Alexandria in triumph. Crews of the ships in harbour cheered for 15 minutes and HMAS *Stuart* signalled 'Whacko, *Sydney*'!

Cape Spada was the first clear British daylight gunnery success against a roughly equal force, but there are some discrepancies in the various accounts of the action. Just as some British accounts give the Italian light cruisers a higher speed than the British destroyers, so the thicker armour of the Australian cruiser (a 4in belt and about 2in of deck armour versus 1½in belt and 1in deck armour on the Italian ships) is thought to have made the *Sydney* an 'armoured' cruiser, ignoring the fact that this armour was concentrated over the ship's vitals and much of her was virtually unprotected. Of course, if you cannot hit the target its level of protection is hardly relevant! It has also been argued that while the Italian 6in guns outranged those of the British destroyers at the start of the engagement, the British 4.7in guns had a higher rate of fire. But at long range, with both sides having to wait and spot the fall of shot, it is likely that they were both firing at the same rate. Finally, the claim that the British force was inferior to the Italians is obviously false once the *Sydney* had joined the action. Neither side had any real advantage over the other.[8]

Casardi was too cautious at the start of the action. If he had closed in immediately, his ships might have done better shooting, holding the widely-separated destroyers at a range of about 17,000 yards with their longer-ranged 6in guns. Closing further might have produced better results, but would also have exposed his own ships to enemy fire. By waiting until 8.00am before closing, Casardi lost valuable time, which the British put to good use.

The operation might have been more successful if *Supermarina* had sent a more powerful force, such as four light cruisers, or a pair of the better-protected *Garibaldi* class, perhaps with destroyer support. As Fioravanzo comments, the Battle of Cape Spada was 'the proof of the vulnerability of the six types of "Condottieri"; ships too light and unprotected against the 6in gun which they fought and had to reply to'.[9] Once again, British gunnery was superior. The Italians scored only one hit at long range, while the British hit the enemy at least five times. Mussolini was far from happy with the result, gathering that the action had not gone in 'a very brilliant manner'.[10] The Italians responded to this by keeping up with the increased gunnery exercises instituted after Punta Stilo, while the threat of air attacks of their naval bases lead to the installation of more searchlights and AA guns, as well as anti-torpedo netting.[11]

The British immediately followed this success up by running a convoy to the Aegean which left Alexandria on 21 July, with another making the return trip. The first convoy was supported by a 'demonstration' off the Italian island of Castelorizo on 23 July by the light cruiser *Orion* and the destroyers HMAS *Vampire* and HMAS *Vendetta*, and on 26 July a similar operation covered the returning convoy, this time with two landing ships simulating an invasion. Some starshell was fired but again there was no response from the Italians. Cunningham with the main fleet operated in support south-west of Crete, with the *Eagle* providing the air component.

As the convoy headed south between 27 and 29 July it was attacked several times by S.79s and S.81s from the Dodecanese, but only HMS *Liverpool* was hit, by a bomb which penetrated two decks without exploding. On the 29th, two Gladiators from the *Eagle* intercepted three S.79s at 15,000ft, shooting down one and chasing off the remainder, at the cost of one Gladiator which ran out of fuel.[12] The *Sydney*, now repainted in camouflage pattern and with a new aircraft, suffered bomb splinter damage that yet again wrecked her aircraft and wounded a few of her crew. She was detached in company with the *Orion* to hunt down the Greek tanker *Ermioni*, which was known to be supplying the Italian islands in the Dodecanese. They found her on the evening of 28 July, and after her crew had taken to the lifeboats, *Orion* sank her with gunfire. They were bombed again on their return trip to Alexandria, but without serious damage, and arrived safely, as did the rest of the convoy. The Italians also sucessfully ran convoys to and from Libya. In mid-July two convoys arrived safely in Italian ports from North Africa, while at the end of the month Operation 'TVL' was launched with three convoys heading for Libyan ports, one slow convoy heading for Tripoli at 7½ knots, a faster one making for Benghazi at 16 knots, and a small 10-knot group which hugged the Tunisian coast, bound for Tripoli. All arrived safely, escorted by a force of heavy and light cruisers, destroyers and torpedo-boats.

The British then set out to reinforce the air defences of Malta. The *Argus*, the first flat-top aircraft carrier built, was to fly off twelve Hawker Hurricanes to the beleaguered island, escorted from Gibraltar by Force H. It had been hoped to take advantage of the distraction of Cunningham's convoy operations to carry out Operation 'Hurry', but delays in preparing the Hurricanes meant the *Argus* did not sail from Gibraltar until 31 July, in company with the *Hood*, *Valiant*, *Resolution*, *Ark Royal*, three light cruisers and twelve destroyers. The *Argus* carried two Skuas for this operation, as well as the twelve Hurricanes.[13]

At sea on 1 August, the Hurricane pilots were briefed on their mission, but they said that if they took off from the planned launch point, their planes would never reach Malta. Radio silence was broken to consult with the Admiralty, and this alerted the Italians, who immediately launched air attacks and deployed two lines of submarines. One of the Italian bombers carried *Generale di Brigata* Stefano Cagna, commander of the *Marte* brigade, who had personally participated in the Punta Stilo operations and was known for leading from the front. His was the only Italian aircraft shot down by the Skuas defending the British ships, and he was posthumously awarded the *Medaglia d'Oro*. Interestingly, three of the Italian planes had to land in Vichy Algeria, where they were refuelled and flew back to Sardinia.[14] The *Hood* and *Ark Royal* moved into position to launch an air strike on Port Elmas near Cagliari with nine Swordfish, one of which crashed on take-off. At 6.40am they attacked the nearby airfield, in the face of heavy AA fire, damaging a hangar and two aircraft on the ground, and laid mines in the outer harbour. One plane was forced down and its crew captured, but the rest returned safely.

The *Argus* then moved into position and launched her Hurricanes with the two Skuas, one with a Fleet Air Arm pilot and the other with an RAF pilot assisted by a Royal Marine captain as navigator, to guide them the 380 miles to Malta. After a flight of 2 hours and 20 minutes, they arrived, although one Hurricane crashed performing a silly stunt over Luqa airfield.[15] Force H returned to Gibraltar without incident, arriving safely on 4 August. The British were surprised by the lack of Italian response. The air attacks were limited compared to those at Punta Stilo, and there had been virtually no naval response apart from the ineffective submarine screen.

At the same time two submarines, loaded with supplies, arrived at Malta as reinforcements. On 1 August the British lost their fifth submarine of the war, when HMS *Oswald* was sunk off Cape Spartivento by the destroyer *Vivaldi*, and Cunningham complained to the Admiralty that the old, larger submarines were unsuited to operations in the Mediterranean. The only British submarine success had been by

Lieutenant-Commander M G Rimington of the *Parthian*, who had sunk an Italian submarine, and he would mount an unsucessful attack on a cruiser at the end of August. The arrival of two new 'T' class boats in September improved matters, with three merchant ships and the torpedo-boat *Palestro* being sunk.[16]

There now followed the first overt act of war by Italy against Greece. Cesare Maria De Vecchi, the Italian governor of the Dodecanese Islands, had been stirring up trouble with the Greeks for some time, in the hope of provoking a short and successful war that would benefit his career. *Supermarina* had authorised 'unknown submarine' attacks, as in the Spanish Civil War, against neutral shipping trading with the enemy, and De Vecchi had enthusiastically ordered the submarine *Delfino* to attack the Greek port of Tinos. On 15 August the old cruiser *Helle* was torpedoed by the *Delfino* whilst she was taking part in a religious festival in the harbour at Tinos, killing one and injuring twenty-nine. Two other torpedoes hit the quayside, injuring civilians, one of whom died. The Italians denied all knowledge of the attack, but soon they would start building up their forces in Albania for their ill-fated invasion of Greece.[17]

*   *   *

The *Regia Aeronautica* tried to make its presence felt by conducting a series of long-range bombing missions beginning in July 1940. Malta was regularly attacked, in June alone by 630 planes dropping 170 tons of bombs. The Italians lost two bombers and one fighter in this period, and shot down one Gladiator in reply. Total losses for the first two months of war would climb slowly to three British planes (a Swordfish, a Gladiator, and a Hurricane), and five bombers and three fighters for the Italians. The low Italian losses were in part due to one of the few advantages of their high-altitude bombing technique. By the time the defending fighters could climb to the bombers' altitude, they had often already dropped their payloads and turned for home.[18]

But Malta was not the only target. The first of eight raids on Gibraltar was carried out by three S.82 bombers on 15 July 1940, which covered 2175 miles to drop 4500lbs of bombs. The S.82 was primarily a transport aircraft but could also double as a bomber.[19] The oil refinery at Haifa was bombed seven times between mid-July and the end of September, and by 15 October Alexandria had been attacked eight times. British bases on Cyprus also received attention and the Suez Canal was bombed on 28 August by a force of eight S.81s. Most attacks were carried out at night and at high altitude. In one particularly daring attack, four specially-equipped S.82s travelled 2600 miles to raid the oil refinery on the island of Bahrain in the Persian Gulf, going on to land in Italian East Africa. But overall these small-scale attacks did little real damage.

The early attempts by the *Regia Aeronautica* to attack shipping had proved that their bombing technique was ineffective and also that the bombsight currently in use was 'complex and difficult to handle'. At Punta Stilo it was found that it took so long to release the bombs that the planes had already passed over the targets. Furthermore, the 100kg bombs tended to scatter more than others: more than 500ft when dropped from 3000ft and 900ft when dropped from 9000ft. To remedy this it would be necessary to change the 'irrational' vertical storage of the bombs aboard the aircraft, but the S.79 was a converted commercial aircraft with too short a fuselage for any other way of loading its bombs. The *Regia Aeronautica* had relied on a report from General Pinna addressed to Valle that claimed that the light bombs achieved good effects against ships in most cases.[20]

In an attempt to rectify the problem, the Italians sought to buy the Germans' 'Lofte' type bombsights to replace their overly complicated and ineffective Jozza U.2/U.3, although there was an Italian-manufactured Type CG electric fire-control system which was somewhat better than the Jozza.[21] They also began to develop dive-bombing for anti-shipping attacks to replace their earlier tactics. The first aircraft chosen was the Italian-built twin-engined S.85 which had good air brakes for diving attacks at 45° and 90°, but the aircraft suffered from so many technical problems that the only unit to be equipped with it, the 96th *Bombardamento a tuffo* (Diving Attack Group) based at Pantellaria, had to return its nineteen S.85s to the depot as unusable. The 96th was then re-equipped with Ju87 Stukas, fifty-two of which were bought from Germany on 2 July 1940. A further fifty would be delivered in 1941.[22] Pricolo also bought one Ju88 twin-engined bomber for study, and placed an order for 500kg and 250kg anti-shipping bombs. He also studied German-style fuel tanks.[23]

The 96th went into action with its Ju87s on 2 September, with attacks on shipping and later land targets on Malta, which Arena reports as being effective. A second group, the 97th, was soon formed, but both were then transferred to the Greek front, where the army needed all the support it could get. Eight planes would be lost by the end of the year.[24]

Being more orientated towards support of the army, the *Regia Aeronautica* had to improvise techniques and tactics to meet the anxious requests for air support from *Supermarina*, but the history of rivallry between the two services was the main handicap to genuine co-operation.[25] A perfect example of these 'jealousies, delays, contradictions, lack of professionalism that would have grave consequences on the preparation of the Italian armed forces' was the issue of torpedo bombers. As early as 1923 the *Regia Marina* wanted to employ the torpedo bomber but the project never went beyond the experimental stage, and the *Regia Aeronautica*'s victory in the battle for control of naval aviation in 1928 put an end to such independent developments by the Navy.

Finally, in 1935 agreement was reached between the two services and a training centre for torpedo-bombing was established at Cadimare, but the pilots were never organised into a unit to make use of their skills. According to a navy memo of November 1937, there was an agreement to carry out twenty practice drops of torpedoes from modified S.79s, but it took a year for the first eight to take place. Air Force opposition was due to their championing of high-altitude bombing and their resistance to the expense of torpedoes, but the principal reason could well have been that the Air Force Chief of Staff General Valle feared that torpedo-bomber units might fall under Navy control, a typical inter-service 'turf war'. The Air Force experts set extremely high performance requirements for an air-dropped torpedo, wanting a weapon that could be dropped from over 1000ft at a speed of 500km/h, well in excess of those considered satisfactory by the Germans, probably in order to sabotage the project. In contrast, the Swordfish dropped its torpedo at much lower altitude and at a top speed of 145 knots (it could not even make a speed of 500km/h!). General Valle would later write in his memoirs 'it would be too soon in 1939 to create a torpedo bomber unit because we lacked the main element – the torpedo', but this was largely due to the actions of his own service.[26]

Until the summer of 1940 there was extensive correspondance and prolonged discussions between Badoglio, Valle (and after 10 November 1939 his replacement General Pricolo) and Admiral Cavagnari, until the critical situation at sea finally forced Pricolo to start adapting the S.79 as a torpedo bomber. An example of the sort of arguments taking place between the Services over this issue is shown in this excerpt from the minutes of a meeting held by Badoglio on 18 November 1939:

> . . . *6th point: torpedoes for aeroplanes and torpedo bombers.*
>
> *Badoglio:* . . . we should no longer discuss if the bomb is more effective than the torpedo; these are opinions without any practical confirmation and should be examined from a more realistic point of view. We have had too long of an exchange of letters on this point.
>
> *Cavagnari:* The principle is not on the table but only who pays for it. The Navy holds that this problem has been solved for three years. The Air Force must purchase them.
>
> *Badoglio:* It is not useful to deal here again with the problem of aircraft torpedoes. I want to avoid discussions that would result only in a waste of words. Who pays is always the State. Therefore, we should not become rigid on this question.
>
> *Air Force representative:* The question is already settled. The Air Force was unable to buy thirty torpedoes because the production plants are busy with the order going to Germany.
>
> *Cavagnari:* This is not true.[27]

The first torpedo-bomber unit, the *Reparto Speciale Aerosiluranti* (Special Air Torpedo Unit) was formed at Gorizia on 25 July 1940 and sent hurriedly to North Africa on 10 August. The crews were skilled pilots, but they were still inexperienced in torpedo operations. Only two or three practice attacks against stationary targets had been made, and they still had not worked out the optimum altitude to drop their weapons from. But on the evening of 15 August, five aircraft were sent to attack shipping at Alexandria, armed with torpedoes requisitioned from the 300 weapons ordered by the Germans, as no aerial torpedoes had yet been ordered by the Italians themselves.[28]

Two of the planes succeeded in launching their torpedoes against the light cruiser *Gloucester*, but they were dropped from too high an altitude for a shallow harbour and buried themselves in the sea-bed. The other three were unable to carry out their drops and returned to base. All of the planes were short of fuel and were compelled to land in the desert or close to the airfield at El Adem, with one crew being captured by a British patrol. This improvised attack was a failure, but it did encourage Cunningham to improve his defences against such low-level attacks, erecting masts on the breakwater at Alexandria and putting up kites to serve as barrage balloons.[29] Pricolo later wrote that this attack had not been carried out too soon, and the real problem had been that the target was at the extreme range of the aircraft, but the lack of an effective torpedo-bomber force was one of the bitter consequences of the rivalry between the Italian Air Force and Navy extending back through the entire history of the Fascist Regime.[30] Later, the handful of improvised S.79 torpedo-bombers would achieve better results than many of the high-level bombing attacks. It was not until 28 October 1940 that the first torpedo training unit (*Nucleo Addestramento Siluranti*) was formed at Gorizia under the command of Lieutenant-Colonel Carlo Unia, who would write the history of Italian torpedo-bombers after the war.[31]

* * *

In August 1940, Italian naval transport operations were primarily small convoys on the Libyan coast, running between Tripoli and Benghazi. The few convoys between Libya and Italy were usually quite small (two merchant ships being typical) and escorted by a single torpedo-boat. The bulk of the reinforcements for Graziani's army had already arrived for his September offensive into Egypt and/or were being shifted forward from Tripoli.

The Royal Navy gave support to their army on the morning of 17 August, by bombarding Bardia and Fort Capuzzo on the Libyan border for 22 minutes. *Warspite*, *Ramillies*, and *Malaya*, supported by the heavy cruiser *Kent* and three destroyer flotillas, participated in this operation, with air cover from *Eagle*'s fighters operating from land bases, which shot down four and damaged eight of the twenty-six S.79s that attacked the fleet. Although later air reconnaissance indicated Fort Capuzzo had been damaged, Cunningham concluded that the Italians' 'skill in dispersing stores and transport over wide areas' meant future bombardments would bear little fruit.[32]

British plans to extend their attacks beyond Tobruk and into the Gulf of Bomba near Derna, using a combination of destroyers and three Swordfish from the *Eagle*, operating again from a land base, would destroy the first attempt by the Italians to use their *Maiali* SLCs (human torpedoes) against British capital ships at Alexandria. ULTRA was not a factor in this success, aerial photographic reconnaissance providing the 'up-to-date information that was required'.[33]

Operation GA 1, as the attack was code-named, was set for midnight on 25 August, the targets being two battleships and the *Eagle*. On 16 August the submarine *Iride*, commanded by Francesco Brunetti, which had been detached from the 14th Flotilla at La Spezia in July for 'special means attacks' under the direct command of *Supermarina*, sailed from Messina for the Gulf of Bomba on the North African coast, 38 miles west of Tobruk. There she was to take aboard the SLCs from the torpedo-boat *Calipso*, and both vessels would be refuelled by the merchant ship *Monte Gargano*, which for this operation was the flagship of Rear-Admiral Bruno Brivonesi, the naval commander in Libya. The Gulf of Bomba was chosen for the rendezvous for its isolation, and also because it was close to the target. At this time the SLCs were transported fixed to the hull of the submarine, not in waterproof canisters as later, which limited the *Iride* to a diving depth of 100ft.

At noon on 22 August, the SLCs had been loaded aboard the *Iride* and the crews were being transferred when three Swordfish came into the attack at low level, the centre aircraft commanded by Captain Oliver 'Ollie' Patch of the Royal Marines. The Italian ships had been sighted the day before by aircraft attacking the nearby seaplane base.[34] The *Iride* was under way, about to make a test dive with the *maiali* aboard. Unable to dive in only 50ft of water, Brunetti ordered full speed ahead and turned head-on towards the approaching aircraft, opening fire with machine-guns at a range of 1000 yards, after the Swordfish had come down to only 200ft. Two crewmen were killed and several more wounded by return fire from two of the aircraft as they passed, while Patch dropped his torpedo about 160 yards from the *Iride*, which 'crashed straight into the bows of the submarine and exploded'. As the submarine sank, fourteen men on deck managed to get clear, including Captain Elios Toschi, one of the original 'Gamma men' (frogmen) and one of the inventors of the *maiali*. Meanwhile the other two Swordfish attacked the *Calipso* and the *Monte Gargano*, missing the former and sinking the latter, making it a most successful day for the old 'Stringbags', all of which returned safely to base.

There were still survivors trapped in the wreck of the *Iride*, and diving equipment was rushed from Tobruk for rescue operations lasting 20 hours, with the well-known divers Captain Teseo Tesei and Luigi Durand de La Penne rescuing seven men, one of whom later died from his injuries. Borghese blamed the failure of this operation on the decision of Rear-Admiral Conte de Courten, commander of special operations, to deploy the *maiali* before they were ready,[35] but Captain Mario Giorgini wrote after the war that Courten had spoken during a visit to the 'special means attacks' base at Bocca di Serchio of the urgent need to reduce British naval forces after the failure of the submarines and the *Regia Aeronautica* to do so, which explains why the SLCs were rushed into service.[36] This was a terrible start for the SLCs, and the failure of the *Gondar* in September would delay the vital impact they were later to have.

The British attacked the Gulf of Bomba again the following night. Early in the morning of 23 August, the destroyers HMAS *Stuart*, *Waterhen*, *Diamond*, *Juno* and *Ilex* sailed from Alexandria, with the *Sydney* leaving later to give distant support, while the 625-ton gunboat *Ladybird*, built in 1915 and armed with two 6in guns, left Mersa Matruh for an attack on Bardia. After detaching the *Waterhen* to support the little gunboat, the remaining destroyers carried out a night bombardment of the seaplane base in the Gulf of Bomba, which inflicted little damage. Meanwhile the *Ladybird* had been making her way quietly up the coast to Bardia, and then steamed straight for the harbour entrance. The Italian coastal batteries failed to hit her as she entered the harbour itself. There were no ships in port for her to attack, but she bombarded shore installations at point-blank range, safe from the Italian batteries which faced seaward. She then steamed out of the harbour at her top speed of 14 knots, covered by smoke and gunfire from the *Waterhen*. The Italian guns again failed to hit her, and all ships involved returned safely to Alexandria on the 24th.

* * *

The British now launched Operation 'HATS' ('Hands Across The Sea'), the first of their major reinforcements of their forces in the Eastern Mediterranean, which was to provide Cunningham with some of the units he had requested after Punta Stilo.[37] Force F left Gibraltar on 29 August, consisting of the modernised battleship *Valiant*, the new and powerful armoured aircraft carrier *Illustrious* with twenty-two Swordfish and twelve fighters, four of which were Fulmars, the flagship of Rear-Admiral A L St G Lyster, Flag Officer commanding aircraft carriers in the Mediterranean, and two AA cruisers, the *Coventry* and *Calcutta*, all four of which were equipped with air-search radar. Protecting it was Somerville's Force H with his flagship the battlecruiser *Renown*, the *Ark Royal*, the light cruiser *Sheffield*, and twelve destroyers. Consideration was given to including up to four fast transports (capable of 16 knots) in this operation, carrying tanks to General Wavell's Western Desert Force (later the 8th Army), but it was decided inside to send them via the Cape, escorted by the cruisers *York* and *Ajax*, arriving at Suez on 24 September. Cunningham's fleet was sailing west from Alexandria, with the *Warspite*, *Malaya*, *Eagle*, one heavy and four light cruisers and thirteen destroyers covering a convoy of two transports and a tanker for Malta, which arrived safely on 2 September.

In response the Italians sortied from Taranto on 31 August with four of their five battleships, including the new *Littorio* and *Vittorio Veneto*, supported by thirteen cruisers and thirty-nine destroyers. Despite some losses, Campioni's fleet was stronger than it had been in June and better trained, 'in magnificent condition as to effectiveness, readiness for action, and fighting spirit'.[38]

Yet again Italian reconnaissance in this operation was limited. Neither their submarines nor aircraft provided sufficient information quickly enough for the fleet to be able to intervene, although this was partly due to the terrible weather at the time, with men being washed overboard from the destroyers. The Italian fleet retired to the north during the night of the 31st, heading south again the next morning, but the hoped-for contact with the British fleet did not happen, although at dusk they were about 90 miles away from Cunningham. In fact, they were unaware of the transfer of Force F until the ships were sighted in Alexandria harbour and it was thought they had arrived via the Red Sea.

Somerville successfully escorted Force F as far as Sardinia, launching two minor air raids on Port Elmas, and then retired on Gibraltar. His force suffered two air attacks on the way, during which the radar-equipped *Sheffield* warned the *Ark Royal* of approaching aircraft. The carrier did not respond to the first warning, but after being heavily bombed, fighters were put up at the first hint of the second. After this operation, a group of *Ark Royal*'s officers went to the *Sheffield* to study this newfangled invention, and Somerville later personally thanked the cruiser's radar personnel for their services.[39] Radar had the added advantage of negating the Italians' tactic of attacking out of the sun, they being unaware of the fact that the British had it.[40]

Force F rendezvoused with Cunningham's fleet south of Sicily, while Italian air attacks damaged the Polish destroyer *Garland* of Force H, and one of the transports, which still reached Valletta. Cunningham's fleet was also attacked, but without result, and three S.79s were shot down. This operation also saw the first attacks by

Italian Ju87s against British ships. Fifteen aircraft participated, but without result or losses, despite the inflated claims of both sides.

The carrier aircraft were particularly effective in shooting down Italian reconnaissance planes, the *Ark Royal*'s taking care of two on 31 August alone, a problem soon to be further compounded for the Italians by the British use of radar to vector fighters in on their targets. In July alone the Italians had averaged forty-three reconnaissance missions a day, flying a total of 19,000 miles, so obviously strenuous efforts were being made, but the two main aircraft used, the Cant Z501 (which Vice-Admiral Odoardo Somigli referred to as 'an archaeological artefact') and the newly introduced Cant Z506 were both inadequate, being slower than the British carrier fighters. The Italians' attempts to build an aircraft carrier, and to operate catapult-launched fighters from warships would be part of their inadequate response to this problem.

After calling at Malta to drop off much-needed supplies and AA guns, Cunningham returned to Alexandria, splitting his fleet into two groups passing to the north and south of Crete, attacking airfields and naval bases in the Dodecanese on the way. One *MAS* boat that attempted to counter-attack was sunk by the destroyer *Ilex*. Rhodes was attacked by aircraft from the two carriers, destroying or damaging a total of thirteen Italian aircraft for the loss of four Swordfish.

Mussolini was 'enraged' by the fleet's failure to close with the British and gave Cavagnari a direct order to 'engage without fail at the next opportunity', but he was unaware of the problems the Navy had with reconnaissance and the telling failure of the submarines to make contact with the enemy.[41] The Italian fleet sortied again on 6 September, this time with all five battleships, when Force H left Gibraltar and heading into the Western Mediterranean. But this was just a feint prior to an operation in the Atlantic, and the fleet returned to base when Somerville's ships reversed course and passed through the Straits of Gibraltar.

* * *

September also saw renewed activity by the Vichy French, which once again developed into open conflict with the British. On 9 September a squadron consisting of the modern light cruisers *Georges Leygues*, *Gloire* and *Montcalm*, and the 'super-destroyers' *L'Audacieux*, *Le Fantasque* and *Le Malin* sailed from Toulon in an operation to recover Gabon, which had gone over to the Free French. Slipping past Gibraltar, they reached Dakar on the 14th. They failed to re-take Gabon, and, shadowed by British ships, retired to Casablanca.

The station commander at Gibraltar, Vice-Admiral Dudley North, would be replaced as a result of the French ships' escape from the Mediterranean.[42] On 23 September the British and the Free French launched an unsuccessful attack on Dakar. The Vichy then retaliated with two air raids on Gibraltar, the first on the 24th with forty planes, and the second the next day with over a hundred. Little damage was done, although a trawler was sunk, a few buildings damaged and two bombs just missed the *Renown*. Four destroyers also sortied into the Straits, firing a few rounds at a British destroyer but causing no damage. Relations quickly settled down to their previous level, and on the 27th a Vichy convoy passed Gibraltar without interference. The successful defence of Dakar had done much to boost Vichy morale, particularly that of its navy.

* * *

At the start of Marshal Graziani's offensive into Egypt, which would have him reach Sidi Barrani by 17 September, the Royal Navy conducted a series of daring operations in support of their land forces. On 16 September a force consisting of the *Valiant*, *Illustrious*, the heavy cruiser *Kent*, the AA cruisers *Coventry* and *Calcutta*, and seven destroyers left Alexandria to attack Benghazi, the deepest British raid into Italian waters to date. That night the *Illustrious*'s aircraft successfully attacked the harbour with torpedoes, sinking two merchant ships and the destroyer *Borea*, and laid mines, which sank the destroyer *Aquilone* (which was later partially salvaged). On the return trip to Alexandria the *Kent* was detached with two destroyers to attack Bardia. The cruiser was attacked by one of the new Italian S.79 torpedo-bombers, and was hit in the stern, damaging her propellers and bringing her to a dead stop. Thirty-two men were killed in this first successful attack by Italian torpedo aircraft, and the *Kent* had to be towed back to Alexandria for extensive repairs. A series of bombardments by destroyers and the Inshore Squadron, made up of the monitor *Terror* and three small gunboats similar to the *Ladybird*, were then conducted against the seaward flank of Graziani's army, disrupting its operations and forcing it further inland, but all these ships would be lost by 1941 except the gunboat *Aphis*.

It had been decided that Malta needed more troops in case of an Italian invasion, and so the large light cruisers *Liverpool* and *Gloucester* were detailed to transport 2000 troops to the island, on 28 September in Operation 'MB 5'. Supported by Cunningham's fleet, with two battleships, the *Illustrious*, three cruisers and eleven destroyers. It was located by Italian air reconnaissance on 29 September and Campioni's larger fleet sortied against it, with five battleships, seven heavy and four light cruisers, and twenty-three destroyers. Yet again, there was no contact, the British seeking to deliver their troops to Malta, not fight the Italian fleet, while Campioni's main concern was to protect the Italian coast and Benghazi from attack, and the weather again hampered air reconnaissance. Admiral Iachino later argued that the cruisers could have been deployed in a traditional scouting line to locate the British.[43] On the British Fleet's return to Alexandria, the cruisers *Orion* and *Sydney* were detached for another brief bombardment of the island of Stampalia in the Dodecanese, which they carried out successfully. ULTRA intercepts had given the British details of Italian submarine dispositions, leading to the sinking of the *Berillo* off Libya by two British destroyers on 2 October.

However, on 30 September, the Italians suffered another grievous loss in their attempts to employ their SLCs against British ships at Alexandria. The submarine *Gondar*, commanded by the *Iride*'s former captain Brunetti, sailed from Messina on the 23rd with the *maiali* aboard, this time in new watertight casings that allowed the submarine transporting them to dive to 300ft. The attack was cancelled when it was learnt that the fleet was at sea, and the *Gondar* was returning to Tobruk when she was detected by the destroyer HMAS *Stuart*. The *Stuart* had been with Cunningham's fleet when engine problems forced her to return to Alexandria early, so it was quite by chance that she ran across the *Gondar* on the evening of the 29th. At 10:20pm she launched her first depth charge attack and hunted the Italian submarine throughout the night. By dawn, the *Stuart* had been joined by a Sunderland flying boat and an ASW trawler, while the air was running out aboard the *Gondar* and she was taking on water. A last depth charge attack forced her to the surface, where she came under fire from the *Stuart* and the Sunderland. Her crew abandoned ship and she sank at 9.50am. Her valuable cargo was lost, and Elios Toschi was among those captured, but the British did not learn what the *Gondar*'s target had been nor the weapon she was to use.[44]

Another SLC operation against Gibraltar by the submarine *Scire*, commanded by Borghese, was cancelled at the same time, once it was learnt that Force H was in the Atlantic, but Borghese would make another attempt at the end of October. On the evening of 29-30 October, he brought the submarine into Algeciras Bay, hugging the Spanish coast. Because of the complex currents, Borghese decided to approach near the mouth of the Guararranque River, so when the SLCs were released, they would have a gentle current carrying them toward the entrance of Gibraltar harbour.[45]

Having confirmed the presence of British battleships in the harbour, Borghese assigned targets and launched three of the two-man *maiali* to attack. One was commanded by De La Penne, and another by Tesei, one of the original designers. The *Scire* now retraced her route out of the bay and headed back to Italy, at one point remaining submerged for 40 hours.

All three SLCs were in less then perfect condition when removed from their casings, with a range of technical problems including faulty compasses and breathing gear. De La Penne's *maiali* was discovered approaching on the surface and depth-charged. Too damaged to continue, he and his crewmate swam to Algeciras, met up with an Italian agent and later returned to Italy. Tesei's crew had numerous problems with their craft and it had to be abandoned near the harbour entrance, but they too returned to Italy via Spain. It was probably this one that was recovered by the British and would inspire them to design and build their own equivalent, the 'Chariot'. The third crew got their pig to within 75 yards of the *Barham* when the engine gave out, and their air was running low. The weapon did explode, but too far from its target to do any damage, and the crew were captured trying to escape through the harbour. The British were now alerted to the existence of this new Italian weapon.

* * *

Mid-October witnessed the Italians introducing a new code and the next British resupply operation to Malta, 'MB6'. This was another major fleet operation, which had one often-overlooked effect on the Italian fleet, forcing them to continue to burn fuel in prodigious amounts, fuel it was difficult for the Axis to replace, unless they could manage to capture large oil fields.[46] 'MB6' had four merchant ships steaming in convoy protected by the two newly-arrived AA cruisers and four destroyers. The covering force was made up of Cunningham on his flagship *Warspite*, three other battleships, both carriers, six cruisers (one being the *York*, armed with just six 8in guns and smaller then most heavy cruisers), and sixteen destroyers.

Again bad weather prevented air reconnaissance locating the convoy, which arrived safely on 11 October, with only the destroyer *Imperial* damaged by a mine. Two Australian destroyers, the *Stuart* and *Vendetta*, were left at Malta to refit, which they did over several weeks, relatively undisturbed by Italian air raids. An Italian airliner early on the 11th sighted the fleet on its way home and the Italians decided to ambush the British fleet at night and sent several units to sea, but the main action would be with torpedo-boats and destroyers. Cunningham was escorting a small convoy of ships from Malta, largely empty, and had established a cruiser line for scouting at night steaming at a speed of 15 knots. The scouting line was a tactic as old as the wooden frigate, but one which was to be largely superseded by aircraft and radar. One of the ships was the light cruiser *Ajax*, a similar ship to the *Sydney*, under the command of Captain E B D McCarthy. Although equipped with radar, it would be of little use in the forthcoming night action, as the Type 279 set she carried was principally for detecting aircraft, and it would anyway be knocked out early on.[47]

Campioni's battlefleet did not sail for this operation as it was thought to be too late, but some light cruisers were placed on alert, and a destroyer flotilla was ordered to operate off Cape Bon in case ships were heading for Gibraltar, which none were. Some *MAS* boats sortied from Augusta in Sicily, but did not sight the enemy. Air units were alerted and all traffic to North Africa was suspended.

But there would be a spirited action involving the three torpedo-boats of the the 1st Torpedo Squadron, the *Airone*, flagship of Captain Alberto Banfi, the *Alcione* and the *Ariel*, each armed with three 3.9in guns and four 17.7in torpedoes. Nearby were four destroyers of the 11th Destroyer Squadron under Captain Carlo Margottini on the *Artigliere*, with the *Geniere, Aviere,* and *Camicia Nera*. Margottini had been the Italian officer responsible for establishing an Italian base on Mallorca during the Spanish Civil War.

The Italian ships were spread out in a long line of bearing with each ship spaced about 4 miles apart. The *Alcione*, steaming at about 17 knots, first sighted the *Ajax* at a range of 19,600 yards, zig-zagging at a speed of 17 knots. Visibility was excellent in the moonlight, and at 1:57am the *Alcione* fired two torpedoes at a range of 1900 yards at the *Ajax*'s port side, both of which missed. She then lost contact with the *Ajax*. The *Airone* was close on the heels of the *Alcione*, sighting the *Ajax* at 1:42am and firing two torpedoes at about 2000 yards 14 minutes later. She then opened fire, and launched two more torpedoes at a range of just under 1000 yards. The *Ajax* had sighted the first torpedo-boat at 1.55am, identified her as a small destroyer, commenced firing and ordered full speed, after the Italian used 'an unknown challenge immediately prior to the first salvo'. All the torpedoes missed, but she was hit three times by the *Airone*'s guns, once amidships 6ft above the waterline, starting a fire, and twice on the bridge superstructure.

The *Ajax* slowed to 25 knots at this stage of the action and 'was kept under constant rudder to avoid torpedo and shell fire'. She ran in and out and with her powerful 6in guns quickly disabled the *Airone*, eventually machine-gunning her decks 'to sweep the upper deck and complete the demoralisation [*sic*] of the enemy crew, who were shouting and many were seen to jump overboard'. The destruction of the *Airone* took about 20 minutes. The *Ajax* fired two torpedoes at her, one of which may have hit. The *Ariel*'s action report is incomplete, but she may have fired one other torpedo without result. The cruiser then chased her down and 'after a few minutes [she] was burning fiercely and stopped'.[48]

The destroyers next joined the action against the fully alert *Ajax*. The *Aviere* was hit on her bow and failed to launch any torpedoes. By 2:18am she was damaged and lost contact. The *Artigliere* then launched a torpedo at the *Ajax*'s starboard side, which missed. The *Ajax* took her under fire, but it was difficult to hit her as she was steaming at a higher speed than the other Italian ships and was zig-zagging. Also the moonlight was fading and the *Ajax*'s guns gave off bright flashes that had a 'blinding effect' on her crew. But the *Ajax* still damaged her severely, hitting her bridge and killing Margottini and silencing her guns, putting her out of action by 2.32am, in just 2 minutes. The *Artigliere* managed to hit *Ajax* with four shells, which knocked out her radar and one 4in gun.[49]

The *Ajax* now thought the two distant ships still in sight were cruisers. The *Camicia Nera* ('Blackshirt') fired two salvos at 5500 yards, receiving two in reply, all of which missed, and she then retreated behind a smokescreen. The *Ajax* then broke off the action, having been ordered to return to the main fleet. She lost thirteen killed and twenty-two wounded in the action, and had fired 342 rounds from her forward 6in guns and 148 from her after turrets. She expended four torpedoes.[50]

The *Camicia Nera* now attempted to tow the disabled *Artigliere* home, but had to cut her loose when the British 3rd Cruiser Squadron came into view at dawn, having been ordered by Cunningham to support the *Ajax*. Although attacked by carrier aircraft, the *Camicia Nera* reached port. The *York* was then detailed to finish off the disabled *Artigliere* after the crew abandoned ship, showing the difficulty of sinking even a stationary ship at close range. She first fired six or seven rounds from a single 8in gun, and missed. She then fired with all six 8in guns at a slow rate of fire, but with little apparent effect. She then fired two 21in Mark VII torpedoes of which the first missed, but the second hit, there was a spectacular explosion and the *Artigliere* sank at about 9:05am on 12 October.

The Italian Navy sent ships out to help bring in the survivors, and both British and Italian accounts speak of the 'great gallantry' of the destroyers' crews. But how could at least seven torpedoes, fired from several different directions, fail to hit? Part of the reason was surely the brilliant conduct of McCarthy during the action. Vice-Admiral Pridham Wippell would later say he handled his 'ship with promptitude, ability and great determination'.[51]

At dawn the *Regia Aeronautica* attacked the British Fleet several times with a total of eighty-four bombers and thirty-eight fighters and did damage the *Eagle* enough for her to miss the upcoming Taranto operation. They lost one Cant Z501 and three S.79s in the attacks, and yet again, seven bombers mistakenly attacked a squadron of

Italian ships. The *Liverpool* was torpedoed in the bow by Italian torpedo-planes on her way back to Alexandria. The British ended the operation with an air attack on Leros on the night of 13-14 October.

Supermarina later undertook an analysis of night actions and looked into several problems. It was noted that Italian warships tended to catch fire as soon as they were hit, and therefore all flammable materials, such as woodwork, were to be removed. The inquiry also considered whether the Royal Navy was in fact using incendiary shells and unexploded shells from later bombardments of Tripoli, Genoa and Valona in Albania were examined, and also looked into employing such incendiary rounds themselves in night actions. Some attention was also paid to the use of searchlights and starshell, often employed by the British in night encounters. *Supermarina* also thought that radar made this easier and wrote that, 'Every progress in this field will be of paramount importance and perhaps the most important element to organise will be to co-ordinate the employment of searchlights and flares shells from the outset of the action'.[52]

* * *

Several other minor operations occurred in October. One distressing incident for the Italians was the accidental sinking of the submarine *Gemma* by the *Tricheco*, which occurred in the approaches to the Aegean on 8 October. The *Gemma* left her patrol area, under orders, on 3 October to take up position between Rhodes and Scarpanto, and the *Tricheco* was returning from patrol to the island of Leros when she spotted her. Due to communication problems, both were unaware of each others' movements. *Supermarina*'s doctrine was to assign strictly defined operational areas to their submarines, unlike the Germans who allowed their boats greater flexibility, accepting the risk of possible 'friendly fire' attacks. The *Trichero* fired two torpedoes and sank the *Gemma* with no survivors, and the use of fixed patrol zones for submarines was to be continued.[53]

Italy also had eight mine-laying submarines of which six were ready for action (three *Foca* class, two *Bragadin* class and the *Micca*), each of which carried between 16 and 36 mines. Two operated off Palestine in mid-October, and one, the *Foca*, was lost on the 14th. Similar problems with the other boats of this class led to their being used mostly for supply missions.[54] Italian destroyers also laid mines off Malta between 7 and 10 October, and the destroyer HMS *Imperial* was damaged by one of these mines on the 11th.[55]

British submarine operations were beginning to bear more fruit, but with continuing losses. In October the *Triton* and the *Regent* each sank two merchant ships, the former off Albania and the latter near La Spezia. On 15 October there occurred an action between two submarines that for many years was shrouded in mystery. The old Italian cruiser submarine *Enrico Toti*'s electric motors had failed, and she was returning to Taranto on the surface when at 1.10am a British submarine was sighted, which opened fire and launched a torpedo which passed near the *Toti*, which returned fire with machine-guns and her 4.7in gun, hitting the enemy submarine on the conning tower. The *Toti* herself was hit at the base of her conning tower, but damage was minor, and at 1.40am the British submarine was seen to sink. For 40 years the British boat was believed to have been the *Rainbow*, but the more recent study of Rastelli and Bagnasco has identified her as HMS *Triad*.[56] The *Rainbow* had in fact been operating off the coast of Albania and was probably rammed and sunk by the merchant ship *Antonietta Costa* at about this time.[57]

Italian submarine losses continued to increase, with the 600-ton *Durbo* lost off Gibraltar on 18 October in a combined attack by two British destroyers and two flying boats. Boarders captured her codebooks and learned of the presence and operation zone of a second submarine, her sister-ship *Lafole*, which was hunted down and sunk two days later. She was rammed by the destroyer *Hotspur*, which damaged her sonar and lost a few knots in speed as a result.

* * *

On 28 October Mussolini took another major step on the road to his and Fascist Italy's defeat by declaring war on Greece. Attacking a mountainous country on the eve of winter with a force inferior in numbers to the enemy was the height of arrogance and a singular failure of military planning. The Italians claimed that Greece had been helping Great Britain, but British 'breaches of Greek neutrality were confined to the occasional use of remote anchorages to refuel short-range warships from naval oilers'.[58]

In 1940 the Greek Navy was small and still suffering from the effects of the *coup d'etat* of 1935 that brought the right-wing army General Ioannis Metaxas to power. Liberal and left-leaning naval officers were purged, and the navy received only two new British-built destroyers, similar to the 'G' class, just before the war. She had six older French-built submarines, and four other destroyers built by the Italians and armed with four 4in guns, as well as miscellaneous small craft, and the ancient armoured cruiser *Averoff*, a near sister of the *San Giorgio*. The *Averoff* would escape to Alexandria and serve as an escort in the Indian Ocean for much of the war.[59]

The navy commander Vice-Admiral Kavvadias would say that Greece entered 'the war with only naval personnel. If it is to be seriously examined it possessed no ships'. It first conducted convoy duties and left the main fighting to the British fleet, which now began to deploy the MNBDO to Suda Bay on Crete. When the Italians first attacked, a battalion earmarked for the defence of Malta had been rushed to Suda Bay since it had both the best anchorage and airfield (at Maleme) on the island. The Greek merchant marine made a great contribution to the Allied war effort. Of her 577 ships, 429 would be lost in the war (thirty-two of which were seized by the Axis), many after 1943 and all around the world, not just in the Mediterranean.

There would now follow one of the most daring and successful British operations of the war, which marked a major turning-point in the fortunes of the Italian Navy.

CHAPTER 8

Taranto Night, and the Role of the Aircraft Carrier in the Mediterranean

I must deplore to not have pursued my intention to build aircraft
carriers; but all the Air Force and the General Staff were against it,
supporting the view that these ships were useless in the Mediterranean.
Now we see who was right.

Benito Mussolini 7 January 1941[1]

For the Italian Navy, the attack on Taranto would be a watershed, equivalent to the early defeats in Greece and the destruction of the 10th Army in Egypt and Libya, and finally burying hopes of a short victorious war. In the aftermath, new men with new strategies would come to the fore, and when this process was completed with the introduction of German air and naval units, the war in the Mediterranean ceased to be Italy's 'parallel war' against the British but became instead part of the wider Axis struggle.

With the arrival of Rear-Admiral Lyster in the Mediterranean at the end of August, planning accelerated for an air attack against Italy's main fleet at one of her major ports. Lyster had served in the Mediterranean before the war and had worked on such a plan, partly to serve as one desperate attempt to knock out the Italian Fleet before 'Mussolini's massive air strength was deployed against' the Royal Navy, but of course the *Regia Aeronautica* would turn out to be less of a threat than had been feared.[2] Lyster originally wanted to attack with both the carriers and thirty Swordfish, but the *Eagle* was still under repair and so could not participate. Code-named Operation 'Judgement', it was to be a night attack, which the British were the most experienced at carrying out from aircraft carriers.[3]

The attack was to be part of a series of operations in early November, including another reinforcement of Cunningham's fleet, Operation 'Coat', and a raid by light forces into the Straits of Taranto. There was also an Aegean-bound convoy leaving Alexandria as well as an important supply convoy heading for Malta (MW3 of five ships with a minimum speed of 11½ knots), covered by four battleships, the *Illustrious*, five cruisers and thirteen destroyers. Leaving Valletta for Alexandria were three empty fast freighters, an Australian destroyer and the monitor *Terror*, which would safely arrive at Suda Bay and later proceed to Alexandria (Bragadin, in his history written after the war, said that the British had to explain to him what transpired during this operation).

Operation 'Coat' was executed by Somerville's Force H, made up of the *Ark Royal*, one cruiser and six destroyers, covering Cunningham's reinforcements, Force F, consisting of the battleship *Barham*, the cruisers *Glasgow* and *Berwick* and three destroyers, with 2150 troops for Malta on board.[4] The Italians deployed a

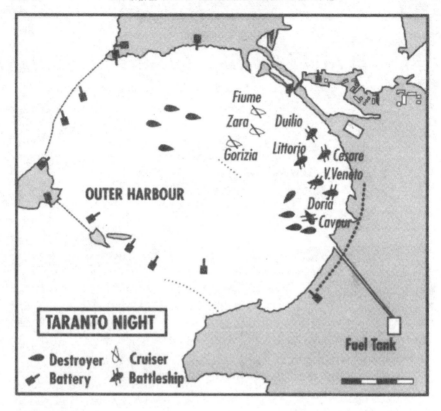

submarine line near Sardinia and a destroyer flotilla off Sicily, but both failed to locate Somerville's ships.

Cunningham's fleet now sent the convoy into Valletta, and steamed to meet with Force F. This force was spotted by the Italian submarines and one, most likely the *Capponi*, fired at least three torpedoes at the *Ramillies*, but missed, although two hits were claimed. During these operations three Swordfish were accidentally lost due to fuel contamination so the strike force was further reduced to twenty-one aircraft.[5]

On 9 November ten S.79 bombers failed to find the British ships due to the weather. The following day fifteen S.79s took off from Sicily to attack the Malta convoy, but only six of them found it and were repulsed by British fighters that hit three S.79s, wounding six men. A further attack in the afternoon was again beaten off by heavy AA fire and the Fulmars, one S.79 being shot down.[6]

Force F now rendezvoused with Cunningham south of Malta on 11 November and part of the fleet entered Valletta to land troops, refuel, and boost the morale of the people of the island by their presence, while Cunningham moved into position for the air attack, unseen by Italian reconnaissance. He detached the *Illustrious* at 6.00pm along with four fast cruisers and four destroyers to run closer in towards Taranto.

The target had been previously reconnoitred by aircraft based on Malta. Three Martin Maryland reconnaissance aircraft had arrived on the island in September, one

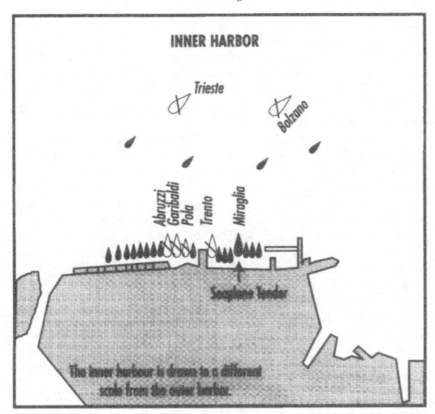

piloted by Commander Adrian Warburton who would go on to an illustrious career. He would earn six gallantry awards (one being an American medal), and once arrived back having flown so low that an Italian ship's radio aerial was caught in his landing gear! The Maryland was faster than the Sunderland flying boat and had a ceiling of 28,500ft, relying only on their speed of 278mph to evade attackers.

On 10 November they had overflown Taranto and reported that five battleships were in port. The sixth, which arrived later that day, was spotted by a patrolling Sunderland. The Italians were well aware of these high altitude reconnaissances, but it was difficult to have planes in the air and in position to attack them, though one Maryland was hit on 7 November, but still escaped. The hundreds of photographs taken over the previous weeks had also been analysed at Cairo to determine what ships and what defences were at each port. High-altitude photographic interpretation was a new science and was about to yield some rich fruit.[7]

Supermarina had chosen Taranto as a base because of its proximity to the British lines of communication through the Mediterranean. The port was under the command of Vice-Admiral Riccardi. While the Italian army, entrusted with coast defence (manned by Blackshirt units), preferred the fleet to be based at Naples, the Navy wanted to be in striking distance of Malta and would require less fuel to reach the enemy. Every decision that Italy would make in the war would be partly influenced by fuel considerations, and this influence would become stronger as the war continued and stocks ran ever lower.

Taranto had an inner and outer harbour, connected by a narrow channel. The outer harbour had two breakwaters and a third submerged breakwater that connected with a small island to protect the port. The inner harbour was relatively safe from torpedo attack because of its small size and shallow waters, and therefore most damage would be done in the deeper outer harbour.

The port's anti-aircraft defences were made up of twenty-two searchlights, approximately 200 machine-guns, and twenty-one batteries of 102mm guns (several on rafts located in the harbour). The Italians had no radar, though there were a number of airphonic listening posts, but these rarely gave much advance warning of approaching aircraft, and the Germans later reported that a lack of training lead to poor co-ordination between the guns and searchlights. Ninety barrage balloons had recently been deployed, but many had been damaged in a storm and only twenty-seven were up on the night of the 11th. Photographic reconnaissance had accurately identified these balloons and measures had been planned to counteract them. All the reconnaissance flights had alerted the Italians and the ships' AA guns were kept permanently manned at night.

For the outer harbour, 12,800m of anti-torpedo netting was required. Of this, only 4200m had been deployed while a further additional 2900m was available but had not been set, as the admirals and captains felt that having to get the nets in and out made entering and leaving harbour too time-consuming. However, since the netting extended only to the depth of the ships' draught, it offered no protection against the British torpedoes with their Duplex magnetic detonators, which exploded the warhead underneath the ship rather than against its side. This would also negate much of the benefits of the ships' Pugliese underwater protection system. Although the Duplex detonators could be unreliable, they worked well enough that night.

Twenty-one Swordfish would be used in the raid. Despite the carrier approaching to within only 170 miles of the target, each aircraft still had to be fitted with an extra 60-gallon fuel tank in place of the third crew member. The hardy Swordfish was far from being a modern aitcraft, but as we have seen, it was good at its job. Part of the reason for this was that it was extremely stable and could fly at very low speeds, which is a great advantage in making landings at night on a pitching carrier deck, and it could also out-turn the Cr42 fighter.

Between 11-19 November, the moon was favourable for an attack, and the ships on the night would be silhouetted in the moonlight. To further illuminate the target, the two of the first wave of twelve planes carried four 250lb bombs and sixteen reliable Brock parachute flares. Six carried Mark XII 18in torpedoes, while the remaining four each carried six bombs. This wave was the largest as it would have the advantage of surprise. The bombers were to go after ships in the inner harbour, where torpedoes would be ineffective, or the seaplane base, in part to act as a diversion for the torpedo planes' attack on the battleships in the outer harbour. The only exact orders for the attack were given to the aircraft carrying the flares. They were to drop their flares between the moon and the Italian battleships to help silhouette them for the attacking Swordfish.

They had to launch the torpedoes at least 300 yards from the enemy ships for the detonator to arm, and from an altitude of not more than 150ft, so the torpedoes would not bury themselves in the harbour bottom. The torpedoes were set to run at a depth of 33ft (below the torpedo nets), in a harbour that averaged 49ft in depth. Not an easy task at night, under fire, with barrage balloons and after a maximum range flight. The second wave, coming in from a different direction, had six aircraft with torpedoes, and three with bombs, two of which also carried flares and would go in an hour later, against a fully-alerted enemy.

At 7.45pm the *Illustrious* increased speed to 28 knots and prepared to launch the first wave. Cunningham had signalled to Lyster and the carrier, 'Good luck, then, to your lads in their enterprise, their success may well have a most important bearing on the course of the war in the Mediterranean'. Lyster simply said to his men, 'Go to it, and good luck'. Vice-Admiral Schofield later wrote;

> Then, just as eight bells struck in muffled tones over the ship's broadcasting system, the last of the twelve Swordfish came up the forward lift and was ranged beside the other eleven. The warning klaxons were sounded, engines were switched on, Pilots and Observers, now clad in bulky Sidcot suits and Mae Wests, clambered into their aircraft and fastened their parachute harness with the help of the fitters. Engines were revved up, oil pressures checked and the reading of the many dials in the cockpit scanned by practised eyes . . . A green light flashed from Flying Control, the fitters and riggers, lying prone on the deck, whipped away the holding chocks and one by one the pilots opened their throttles, causing their aircraft to speed along the flight deck, now outlined in fairy lights, and up into the surrounding darkness.

Twice already that evening the Taranto garrison had sounded the air raid sirens and one AA gun briefly opened up, in false alarms probably due to the distant engines of a Sunderland patrolling off the harbour, though one of the Swordfish arrived early at the harbour and loitered outside waiting for the remainder of the wave to arrive, which may have been responsible for one of them.

The third alarm at 10:50pm was real and the first Italian batteries opened up on the south-west corner of the harbour at the attacking British planes approaching at 75 knots and a height of 7500ft. Four planes of the first wave, three bombers and one torpedo-plane, had become separated from the group, so only eight planes began their descent to attack. The weather was clear, with little wind at sea level, though at 8000 feet there was a 10-knot westerly wind. The missing torpedo-bomber now rejoined the wave, and the flare-equipped aircraft now went in, dropping them from 4500ft.

The lead torpedo-bomber launched its payload at the *Conte di Cavour*, the southernmost of the anchored battleships, and was then shot down by the destroyer *Fulmine*, near the heavy cruiser *Gorizia*. The torpedo exploded almost directly under the *Cavour*'s keel, between the bridge and 'B' turret, and she would sink to the bottom of the harbour from this single hit, the most damaging of the raid. The next two dropped their weapons, which missed, and escaped, while the crew of the first Swordfish were captured.[8]

The next Swordfish came in from the north and launched its torpedo 1000 yards from the *Littorio*. It exploded on her starboard bow, doing the most damage of the three torpedoes that hit her that night and she immediately began to take in water and go down by the bow. A second Swordfish, the one that had arrived early, also dropped her weapon from about 400 yards away which exploded against the *Littorio*'s port quarter. The battleship managed to beach herself in the shallow harbour, which would help in her rapid repair.[9] The last Swordfish in the first wave failed to hit the *Littorio* at about 11:15pm. The four bombers attacked the inner harbour but with little effect. One bomb hit the destroyer *Libeccio* but failed to explode, while some minor damage was done to the port's facilities. Several of the bombs that night would fail to explode, possibly due to the low altitude they were dropped from.

The second wave now came into the attack. One plane had been damaged during take-off and so it was already down to eight planes. A second, one of the bombers, had difficulties with the extra fuel tank and had to return to the *Illustrious*. Again the two flare planes got in successfully, and then bombed the fuel tanks, starting a small fire. The five torpedo-planes now attacked, being greeted by intense AA fire. The first dropped down through the flak, and launched its torpedo from a height of 30ft and 700 yards away from the *Littorio* which was hit a third time, again on the starboard side near the bow. To complicate future salvage operations, an unexploded torpedo would later be found in the mud near her. The next plane was shot down by the *Gorizia*. A torpedo was later found in the harbour with its head crushed, but otherwise complete and is thought to have come from this aircraft. The last three planes all launched their torpedoes, but only one hit. The successful plane made a descending loop as it approached the outer harbour, thus avoiding much of the AA fire, and launched her torpedo 800 yards from the *Caio Duilio*. This hit below 'B' turret, 29½ft below the waterline on the starboard side, and she beached herself to avoid further flooding. The damaged Swordfish back on the *Illustrious* had been repaired in twenty minutes, and the crew pleaded to go in with their wave, and their wish was granted. Arriving late, they bombed the inner harbour from 500ft, hitting the heavy cruiser *Trento*, but again the bomb failed to explode. Two other destroyers were slightly damaged by near misses during the attack. The anti-aircraft defences fired a total of 13,489 rounds of all calibres that night, and claimed six aircraft shot down.

By 1:00am on 12 November the *Illustrious* was in position to recover her aircraft. The first were picked up on radar at 1.12am and by 3.00am all the surviving aircraft were back aboard. Only two had been lost, far less than had been expected. The pilots were unsure of the damage they had caused and made only modest claims, but aerial reconnaissance the next day revealed the three damaged battleships, left behind when the remaining three had sailed to Naples. Most of the cruisers and many of the smaller vessels also left Taranto for other ports.

The attack had done substantial damage. The *Cavour* suffered seventeen dead and a hole that was 36ft by 22ft in size. Unfortunately she sank in deep water, causing extensive water damage. Although she was refloated and moved to Trieste in December 1941, repairs would not be complete by the 1943 Armistice. She was out of the war. The *Littorio* had lost thirty-two dead, and had three holes in her side, one being 50ft by 32ft, the second 40ft by 30ft while the one near her stern was only 22ft by 5ft, but she would be back in service by 9 March 1941. The *Duilio* had a hole

36ft by 22ft in her side, but had lost only three men. She would be serviceable again by 15 May 1941. The Italian fleet had suffered a major blow, and its previous high morale 'dropped below zero' for a time.

The British considered a second attack the following night, but rejected it as too risky due to poor weather. When one Swordfish pilot was asked about a second raid, he had replied 'After all, they only asked the Light Brigade to do it once!'. This would be the last major air attack by British carrier planes against an Italian harbour, future ones being by land-based aircraft.

According to British accounts, three Cant Z reconnaissance planes were shot down on the 12th and the British ships were not reported. But according to the Italian Air Force history they were two Cant Z506s, while another Cant Z was shot down on the 9th, after it had signalled the presence of Force H. Then twenty S.79s from Sardinia attacked the British ships claiming some hits and two planes shot down, eighteen of them receiving hits and suffering three dead and eight wounded.[10]

On the return of the *Illustrious* to the main fleet, Cunningham signalled, '*Illustrious* manoeuvre well executed'. Churchill would say shortly after in the House of Commons, 'As a result of a determined and highly successful attack, which reflects the greatest honour on the Fleet Air Arm, only three Italian battleships remain effective . . . [the] result affects decisively the balance of naval power in the Mediterranean, and also carries with it reactions upon the naval situation in every quarter of the globe'. It also aided the Greek cause by bolstering their confidence and removing the immediate threat of the Italian fleet from the Aegean. In all, the attack was brilliantly conceived and brilliantly executed.

There has been speculation on how far Taranto Night influenced the Japanese in their plan to attack the American fleet at Pearl Harbor. A Japanese attaché, Takoshi Naito, arrived from Berlin shortly after the attack and visited Taranto, while a report was made to Admiral Yamamoto in Kagoshima.[11] In May 1941, Vice-Admiral Iachino was visited by a Japanese military mission at Taranto on board the *Littorio*, and he had several discussions with them, asking especially about Japanese carrier tactics. This sentence in Iachino's book is quite interesting: '. . . the Japanese mission was very difficult and gave us little helpful information, but they posed many questions about the night air attack of 11 November, of which they wanted from the eyewitnesses all possible details.'[12]

The first German report on the action simply passed on the news coming from the Italian Navy, adding the comment: 'A black day for the Italian Navy!' Some days later, the German naval attaché criticised the 'complete defensive attitude of the Italian Naval command' which had handed the British the initiative. Without a change in this stance, disaster threatened on land fronts such as Greece and North Africa.[13]

The German War Diary then described the attack and emphasised its results as 'decisive', but this emphasis was then deleted, showing the impression it made upon the German High Command, which on 14 November ordered improvements to the protection of German ships in harbour. The possible strategic consequences would be complete freedom for the British to reinforce their positions in the Mediterranean and Middle East, to transfer ships to the Atlantic now the Italian threat was reduced, and it also placed the Italian offensive in Egypt in jeopardy.[14]

But the British had not finished yet. In conjunction with the Taranto attack they had sent Force X, consisting of the light cruisers *Orion* (flagship of Vice-Admiral Pridham-Wippell who had relieved Tovey, now bound for the Home Fleet), *Ajax*, and HMAS *Sydney* with the big 'Tribal' class destroyers *Nubian* and *Mohawk* on a raid in the Straits of Otranto against the Italian convoys carrying troops and supplies to Albania for the war with Greece. Indeed, from October 1940 the Italian Navy's principal mission became supplying the armies in North Africa and Greece, marking a shift away from the strategy of the decisive naval battle.[15]

Force X was detached from the main fleet on the afternoon of the 11th, and sped towards the Straits. In the early evening they steamed northward off Corfu at 25 knots, slowing to 20 knots as they arrived off the Albanian coast. The sea was calm and the moon about three-quarters full. Force X had just reached the northern limit of their patrol and had reversed course to return to Cunningham's fleet when at 1:15am they sighted a darkened Italian convoy with four merchant ships being escorted by the ancient torpedo-boat *Nicola Fabrizi*, armed with four 4in guns and four 17.7in torpedo tubes, and the auxiliary cruiser *Ramb III*, with four 4.7in guns, which the British identified as a destroyer. Both escorts were on each flank of the four merchant ships proceeding in a north-westerly direction, with the *Ramb III* on the far side from the approaching enemy. Force X was deployed with the cruisers in a column with the *Orion* leading and the *Sydney* in the rear with about 800 yards between each ship. The *Nubian* was about 2.5km to the west of the column, and the *Mohawk* to the east.

The *Mohawk* first sighted the convoy at 1:15am, notified the *Nubian* and immediately closed on the *Fabrizi* and opened fire at 1:27am, hitting her on the fourth salvo at a range of 4000 yards. The British also fired starshell to illuminate the Italians. The *Orion* also engaged the *Fabrizi* with her 4in guns, while she fired two torpedoes and her main armament at the third ship which was hit by one torpedo and began sinking. She fired thirty-one salvoes, mostly from her forward guns at this target. She shifted her fire to the rear merchant ship at about 5300 yards range and it was quickly set on fire and after the crew abandoned ship, it was torpedoed and sunk.

The next two cruisers fired on the two lead merchant ships, with the *Ajax* firing a torpedo that missed. The *Sydney* began firing at 7000 yards when the *Mohawk* first opened fire. The *Fabrizi* did fire torpedoes of which one passed astern of the *Sydney*, in a vain attempt to protect her convoy from the overwhelming British force, and she too would be severely damaged. The merchant ships had all turned away from the enemy, but damage to the remaining two was too great, and all would be lost that night. The *Fabrizi* made smoke and although engaged by several of the British ships, managed to limp away to safety, while the *Ramb III*, having fired nineteen salvoes, escaped undamaged. The *Fabrizi* lost eleven killed and seventeen wounded. Two other torpedo-boats later arrived and rescued survivors from the merchant ships, but a further thirty-six men had died in the action. The merchant ships lost totalled 16,938 tons. Force X broke off the action at 1:53am and headed back towards Cunningham's fleet at 28 knots, having suffered no damage or casualties. At the time they did not realise they had sunk all four freighters, thinking one got away. As was typical with wartime propaganda, the British announced that the escort had 'adopted the curious defence tactics of making off at full speed', which was certainly untrue of the *Fabrizi*.[16] As a result of this attack, the Italians were forced to reschedule their convoys so they sailed during the day, and increase the escorts to three torpedo-boats and an auxiliary cruiser for every four merchant ships. Pairs of submarines would also operate in the Straits of Otranto for several months.[17]

Cunningham's force now retired on Alexandria and Italian air reconnaissance failed to locate it until 13 November, losing three planes to the *Illustrious*'s fighters on the 12th. That night, the attack on Taranto was followed up by a raid by four recently-arrived Wellington bombers from Malta. Little damage was done and the aircraft all flew on safely to land in Egypt.

* * *

Italy's failure to adopt the aircraft carrier before the war, to rapidly pursue the conversion of merchant ships to carriers once the war had started and to develop a powerful naval air arm were important contributing factors to her defeat in the Mediterranean naval war. This cannot be solely blamed on Mussolini, as the leaders of the Navy and Air Force themselves were also culpable.

Italy, in the centre of the Mediterranean and with many island possessions, was considered by many of these commanders as an 'aircraft carrier' itself. The 'Admirals Report of 1921' had opposed building aircraft carriers, especially in the cash-strapped postwar environment with major naval cutbacks, arguing that air bases up and down the Italian coast would solve the problem. In 1936 Admiral Giuseppe Fioravanzo stated that Italy 'constituted in its entirety a great base of air-sea operations aimed toward the heart of *mare nostrum*, with appendices in the Aegean, Libya, [and] East Africa'. The view that the Mediterranean was an inland sea, not a broad ocean, meant that an aircraft carrier was less valuable there than elsewhere.

This decision must be viewed in the context of other nation's attitudes. For example, the Imperial Japanese Navy was the most air-orientated navy of the inter-war period, yet in 1938 its fleet commander refused to travel by aircraft. They likewise viewed their mandate islands in the Pacific as 'unsinkable carriers'. It has also been argued that if the attack on Pearl Harbor had not effectively neutralised the American battleship force, the development of fast carrier task forces, so valuable for the Allies in the Pacific, would have been much slower, due to the 'battleship admirals' still retaining their dominant position, as they did in most navies, although the US Navy had done much to develop carrier aviation in the 1930s.[18] So by no means can we say that Italy's position was unusual when placed in context with other nations or that the use of an aircraft carrier in a confined sea was viewed as having real value.[19]

Therefore, the utility of aircraft carriers to Italy was downplayed, especially when compared to the battleship. The dominance of the battleship was due to several factors, with 'institutional conservatism' certainly being one of them. But it must also be remembered that carrier aviation was still in its infancy in the 1920s and

1930s when these decisions were being made. The aircraft available were short-ranged, unable to operate at night or in bad weather, and the carriers of the time could not accommodate sufficient aircraft to overcome enemy defences and obtain decisive results. They were also slow to deploy; by the time a flight was launched and assembled for an attack, enemy ships could be on the horizon bearing down on the carrier. The new AA weapons being developed were thought to be an effective deterrent, and finally the small torpedo-bombers could only carry smaller torpedoes. The standard airborne torpedo in 1939 was the 18in type, weighing 1000lbs less than the standard 21in ship-launched weapon. These drawbacks helped keep the battleship a powerful and effective weapon, far less vulnerable to air attack than smaller, less well-protected ships, with powerful AA armament and modern underwater protection systems offering excellent defence against the lighter airborne torpedoes.[20] But at the start of the war the Italians were the only major power not to have carriers or any plans to build them. Even the Soviet Union envisaged building two carriers in the 3rd Five-Year Plan of 1938. So why was this?

In the literature of the period, there were articles which debated alternatives to the battleship, but these alternatives were not adopted, for a variety of reasons.[21] Firstly, for most of the inter-war period Italy had regarded France as her most likely enemy, with Great Britain neutral or possibly even an ally. In the Western Mediterranean, where such a war would be fought, there were many islands with airfields from which the *Regia Aeronautica* could operate. In these circumstances it was difficult to justify spending the limited resources available to the navy on aircraft carriers, instead of the seemingly more valuable battleships, which could decide control of the Mediterranean. Battleships also carried the most weight at the international naval conferences.

There had been earlier proposals for building aircraft carriers, following the Italian Navy's experiences with seaplane tenders and small floatplanes operated from conventional warships in the First World War. The 1922 Washington Treaty allowed Italy 60,000 tons for carrier construction, and consideration was given to converting the superdreadnought *Francesco Caracciolo*, as was done with the French *Béarn* and the US *Lexington*. In the late 1920s a merchant ship was converted into the seaplane tender *Giuseppe Miraglia*, which spent the Second World War as a training and experimental ship. The Italian Official History of The Second World War summarises this question in one and half pages. It first discusses the role of Italy's popular Grand Admiral and then Navy Minister Thaon di Revel. On 10 December 1924 he advocated building carriers to Parliament, and it was viewed purely as a budgetary problem, saying he lacked the money to build such a large ship at that time. He would later resign, in part due to the navy losing much of her air arm to the new *Regia Aeronautica*.[22] In 1924 the idea was shelved due to a combination of the Washington Treaty, shortage of funds and opposition from the admirals who felt that the need to turn into the wind to launch aircraft would affect fleet operations.

A later study in 1934 also came out against building a carrier, though the reasons were not clear. Cordon, in his article, suggests that the budget was still a problem, that it was thought that battleships should be built with what funds were available, and Mussolini opposed them.[23] The Official Naval History also brings up Admiral Cavagnari who proposed building a carrier in December 1935, but it was axed by Mussolini the following summer, along with new battleship contruction, because of the cost and 'raw material shortages'. It then goes on to quote Cavagnari's speech in which he argued that the development of aircraft meant that large numbers of land-based aircraft could swamp an enemy fleet, contrasting with the handful of planes that a carrier could put up. The author, Giuseppe Fioravanzo, concludes that Cavagnari did not properly consider that carrier aircraft could intervene more rapidly in naval engagements.[24]

During the Abyssinian war the Navy suggested the construction of two or three aircraft carriers to support distant operations, as part of their aim of becoming an 'oceanic' rather than a purely Mediterranean navy. It was planned to convert the passenger ships *Roma* and *Augustus*, but these plans were dropped after the war again due to cost and the time it would take to convert them.

The famous naval officer, writer and advocate of naval aviation, Vice-Admiral Romeo Bernotti, head of the *Istituto di Guerra Marittima* (Naval War Institute) wrote in his memorandum entitled *Fondamenti di politica navale* of 1927 (published after the war in his *Memoirs*) that the carrier was not a valuable warship for the Italian Navy. But he later changed his view and in the same memoirs he states that during a meeting of the Committee of Admirals in mid-December 1935 that the Navy was all pro-carrier, while Mussolini refused to proceed with one.[25] After the war, the Navy always complained about the lack of aircraft carriers. One of the authors was present at a dinner when this sentiment was expressed by Rear-Admiral Galuppini, who served on a light cruiser during the war. More often than not, the British air reconnaissance kept them under observation and vulnerable, while nearby Allied ships were not sighted by Italian aircraft.

The historian Alberto Santoni challenges the view that Mussolini was responsible for preventing carrier construction and suggests that he was told they were luxuries by the Navy. Santoni reviews minutes of various meetings in the 1930s in which Mussolini goes along with the recommendations of the Admirals not to build carriers. In August 1936 the office of naval construction asked Cavagnari what kind of carriers they should plan for, and the reply was 'NO!!'. Rear-Admiral Sansonetti also wrote in *Brassey's Naval Annual* that there was no need for aircraft carriers given Italy's numerous airfields, and Vice-Admiral Angelo Iachino, shortly to take over the fleet from Campioni, wrote in the 1938 edition of *Almanacco Navale* that carriers were not needed. *Capitano di Vascello* Uberto Degli Uberti wrote the popular contemporary book *La Marina da Guerra* and based his negative view on the carrier on other naval writers in *Rivista Marittima* (the magazine of the Italian Navy) stating that the decision not to built them was a wise one, because the vulnerability of a ship with a large flight deck and the fact that Italy was a carrier itself. Santoni concludes;

Unfortunately the time wasted because of objections from the Navy as well as changes in the meantime to the original conversion project, did not allow for the carrier *Aquila* to be completed before the Italian armistice on 8th September 1943. After the war a tale was invented: Italian naval officers did not admit their blunders and maintained the story that the aircraft carrier had never been built because of Mussolini's insensitivity and the Air Force's jealousy.[26]

Another contemporary historian, Giorgio Giorgerini, reassessed the question, stating that the navy deserved much of the responsibility in the decision not to build the carriers. On other hand, he did express the opinion that such a ship would have been helpful, but not decisive, because the role of the Italian Navy was mainly one of defence of the traffic in the Central Mediterranean supplying North Africa.[27]

But the Navy also lacked aircraft. The *Regia Aeronautica* exercised a virtual monopoly over military aircraft after 1928, and was committed to a doctrine of strategic bombing and a large fighter force. Italo Balbo, the air commander and considered by some before his death in the opening days of the war as Mussolini's successor, wanted to see the army and naval air branches reduced and the *Regia Aeronautica* increased in size and take over many of their tasks. He declared to Vice-Admiral Bernotti that 'you want aircraft carriers, but we shall not let you build them'. This part of the battle may not have been that hard for Balbo to win, as the senior officers of the Italian Navy did not view the air arm as very important. He also wanted to halt battleship construction, but in this he failed.[28]

The *Regia Aeronautica* was closely linked with the Fascist regime. Douhet, who had invented the doctrine of strategic bombing, had joined the Party in 1919, and the Fascist Poet Gabriele D'Annunzio served (at the age of 52) in the air force during the First World War, flying missions over Pola, Cattaro and Vienna. Both were heroes to many Italians and Italian Fascists, and the regime embraced the aircraft as a weapon system that embodied its philosophy.[29]

So when Balbo met with representatives of the Italian Navy on 27 January 1928, to settle the question of the auxiliary air forces, he had the advantage of being at the head of the most 'Fascist' of the Services. He made it clear that fighter and bomber units would remain under the control of the *Regia Aeronautica* because of the offensive and defensive (including coast defense) roles for those units. In war, air units would be released to either the army or the navy. Bernotti told Balbo that training directly with the fleet would be desirable, but it was not properly followed up. Balbo did concede that torpedo bombers, which had been used by Italy in the First World War, should be developed from the Navy's long range reconnaissance planes, but Bernotti replied that the Navy had developed her air arm for anti-submarine warfare and reconnaissance. Therefore, the Navy would now have to depend on Balbo's promises and the efforts of his successors for air support. The result of this 'co-operation' would be seen with the poor performance of the *Regia Aeronautica* at Punta Stilo and other actions. The failure of the Air Force to give proper support to the Navy was its main failure in the Second World War. What was needed was either a substantial air arm under naval control, or effective co-operation between the two Services, neither of which the Italians had. The result was that the Italian Air Force 'starved the navy of maritime reconnaissance aircraft, and steadfastly refused Cavagnari's requests to form aerial torpedo units'. By late 1940 the employment of the S.79 as a torpedo bomber, essentially a stop-gap measure, had been forced by the demands of the war in the Mediterranean and the failure of high-altitude bombing to achieve substantial results. Sadkovich argues that this lack of a naval land-based air arm was the main handicap in Italy's attempt to win air superiority over the Mediterranean.[30]

As we have seen, the British carrier asserted its importance in several engagements in 1940, and would continue to do so into 1941, most notably at Matapan. The ability to put fighters up over the fleet to shoot down or drive away enemy reconnaissance aircraft and launch damaging air strikes was vital. Taranto marked the high point, but all major operations had a carrier present, or the British wished they had, especially in 1942.[31] Sadkovich argues that Britain suffered heavy carrier losses, with the *Ark Royal* and *Eagle* sunk, the *Illustrious* and *Furious* heavily damaged, and three others slightly damaged, and that long-range torpedo bombers operating from Malta could have done the same damage at Taranto. But neither Britain nor Italy had such aircraft at the beginning of the war. One or two carriers, for reconnaissance, fighter cover or air strikes, would have been a useful addition to the Italian Fleet.

In response to the successes of the British carriers, on 7 January 1941 Mussolini ordered the navy to convert the passenger ship *Roma* into the 28-30 knot aircraft carrier *Aquila*. It was to carry a unique air wing entirely consisting of up to fifty-one modified Re2001 fighters. In 1942 the smaller *Augustus* was also approved for conversion into the *Sparviero*, to carry thirty-five fighters, and two further conversions were planned. The *Regia Aeronautica* said that they lacked the aircraft for use on the carrier but that they would provide them as soon as possible, while the Navy sent a memorandum saying that there were many problems with the project, principally cost and various technical problems, including the development of the elevators, catapults and arrester gear for the aircraft and the need to study turbulence created by the island superstructure. Furthermore, there were no planes with folding wings (easier to stow below and allowing more to be carried) and it would take two years to develop them. The Navy also pointed to the similar problems the Germans were having building their own carrier, the *Graf Zeppelin*. All these objections lead to the suspension of the project later that same month![32]

On 21 June 1941, three months after the disaster at Matapan, the Air Force and Navy met and decided to proceed with the conversion of the *Aquila*. *Comando Supremo* issued a memorandum on 14 August 1941 stating that work had started on July 15 and would last ten months. They also developed catapult-launched Re2000 fighters to be carried aboard conventional warships. In May 1942 the first Re2000 was so launched from the *Giuseppe Miraglia* in the Gulf of Taranto, and from September of that year they would be carried aboard the *Littorio* class battleships. Admiral Riccardi clearly wanted aircraft carriers and repeatedly pushed for their development, even commissioning a study of the conversion of the heavy cruiser *Bolzano* to a small carrier. She would have had all her heavy guns removed and carry twelve Re2001s to be catapulted off the bow, and would be armed with ten 90mm and twenty 37mm AA guns. A similar conversion was considered in January 1943 for the ex-French cruiser *Foch*, captured when Toulon fell to the Axis.[33]

But the *Aquila* would not be ready by 8 September 1943. As late as 20 February 1942 the builders Ansaldo had not submitted its list of raw materials required for the ship's completion to the war production office! However, even if the ship had been completed and had employed fixed-wing aircraft, experiments had shown that the

Aquila could launch the Re2001 but not recover it. The fighters, once launched, would either have had to fly to a land base or ditch. Italy lacked the planes for a carrier, having no suitable torpedo or bomber aircraft, although a fighters-only carrier would have doubled the range of fighter cover for the fleet, and it would have taken approximately 9 months to build a carrier for such a limited role.[34] Even the choice of planes became a problem as FIAT did not want to work on any Reggiane-built planes. The jealousy of the various corporations over orders and the failure to co-ordinate plane manufacturers was a notorious problem throughout the war for Italy.[35]

The Germans did provide some technical assistance to an Italian naval mission in October-November 1941, supplying parts from their second carrier under construction, including two catapults and five sets of arrester gear, as well as plans of other components. A second mission led by Captain Freri worked at the Luftwaffe's War Experience Training Centre between 6-15 March 1942.[36]

In September 1942 the building of a second carrier was still defined as an 'imperious necessity', not only for the war in the Mediterranean, but also for employment in the ocean(!).[37] A final memorandum of the Naval General Staff on 17 July 1943 said that it would still take 6 months of work and 1500 workers to complete the *Aquila*. It would be far too late.[38]

The basic problem for Italy in the development of the aircraft carrier was that by the time the war arrived it was too late and she lacked the will to see the effort through. With her limited industrial base and inefficient wartime mobilisation, she simply could not produce new designs in the quantities required to fight a modern war with Great Britain and her allies. If the Germans had provided more equipment sooner, the Italian armed forces would have been more effective, particularly in the air, but it is hardly surprising that the Germans gave their own forces priority for their limited output of modern equipment.

But if a carrier had been available to the Italian Navy in 1941, what would have been the result? Would a carrier have helped in the primary mission of escorting convoys to North Africa? A converted passenger ship certainly would have been vulnerable with its unarmoured deck and poor internal subdivision, but if it had arrived on the scene about the time of Pearl Harbor, the situation in the central and eastern Mediterranean would have been much changed.

The British had suffered terrible losses in 1941 and early 1942 including the *Ark Royal*, *Barham*, *Prince of Wales*, *Repulse*, and even the tiny carrier *Hermes*. Two battleships were crippled at Alexandria by the *maiali*. There were no carriers in the Mediterranean except for Force H which also had to be available for service in the Atlantic. One needs to only look at the number of Allied carriers involved in Operation 'Torch' or the invasion of Sicily or Salerno to see the need for them.[39]

The *Aquila* in early 1942 would have offered immediate, direct fighter protection to the Italian fleet and could have driven off Allied air reconnaissance, boosting the fleet's morale, even with aircraft that had to land at shore bases. She might have also widened the operating area of the Italian Navy, but this would still have been very limited by the shortage of fuel. Although the *Aquila* would have been a prime target and possibly quickly lost, she should still have been a priority for construction.

CHAPTER 9

The Battle of Cape Spartivento, 28 November 1940

With the triumph of the Greek Army over the invaders of its
homeland, the Royal Navy's strike at Taranto (equivalent in effect to a
decisive victory in a great sea fight), and now this epic advance against
heavy numerical odds by O'Connor's British Empire forces, fortune
filled the sails of the Allied cause in the Mediterranean theatre and
wafted it on waves of hope into 1941.

Correlli Barnett[1]

Directly after Operation 'Judgement' came another attempt to deliver Hurricanes to Malta from the old *Argus*. For Operation 'White', as it was codenamed, Somerville sortied from Gibraltar with the *Renown*, the *Ark Royal*, two cruisers and eight destroyers on 15 November 1940. The Italians deployed three submarines to intercept Force H, but they failed to locate it. However, the Italian Fleet also came out from Naples against Somerville, with two of the battleships undamaged in the Taranto attack, three heavy cruisers and accompanying destroyers. When it became known that the Italian Fleet was out, Somerville was forced to launch the Hurricanes from the *Argus* further away from Malta than had been planned.[2]

The operation would therefore end in tragedy for the two flights of six Hurricanes, each lead by a single Skua as before. They might have still made it, as there was a margin for error, but the first flight took too long in getting off, and a head wind came up, costing both fuel and time, while the second flight would suffer from faulty navigation. Two of the six Hurricanes in the first group failed to reach Malta, and crashed due to lack of fuel, though one pilot was rescued.[3] But the second flight became 'hopelessly lost' and the guiding Skua's radio could transmit but not receive. All the Hurricanes crashed into the sea and their pilots were lost, while the Skua crash-landed on a beach near Syracuse in Sicily. The official inquiry was kept secret and blamed the aircrews, but the British learned from this disaster and in the future these operations, with rare exceptions, were better arranged. On Malta, it was always considered a tragic failure, and Churchill would later say, 'Never again would the margin be cut so thin'.[4] More importantly, the fact that the Italian Fleet had sortied and was prepared to intercept Somerville's force had he been running a convoy to Alexandria instead of flying-off aircraft to Malta showed that its spirit had not been broken by the Taranto attack, and Somerville would be aware of this in the next action.[5] Covered by the return of Force H from Operation 'White', the light cruiser *Newcastle* delivered 200 RAF personnel and vital aircraft supplies to Malta, arriving on 19 November, while four British cruisers also ran 4000 troops to Piraeus without encountering opposition. During October, November and into mid-December, Italy continued to run a few small convoys between Palermo and North Africa, usually escorted by a single torpedo-boat. Many one and two-ship convoys operated between North African ports, and Allied opposition to these operations was negligible, although this situation would change in the New Year.[6]

The next surface action was the Battle of Cape Spartivento, known to the Italians as the Battle of Cape Teulada, a classic chase action off the western coast of Sardinia. Again, the Italian Fleet did not decline battle, but like the British they wanted it on their own terms and ultimately the battle was indecisive.[7] The British had been considering running a convoy through the Mediterranean, and with the damage to the Italian Fleet and the power of their aircraft carriers, it was decided to do it. Three fast (16-knot) merchant ships were used, two carrying supplies for Malta while the third was to go on to Alexandria. The destroyer *Hotspur* was on her way to Malta for repairs to her bow after ramming the Italian submarine *Lafole*, and also joined the convoy, which was accompanied by four of the new 'Flower' class corvettes. Originally designed for operations in the Atlantic, these 1100-ton escorts were built primarily in merchant yards, armed with one 4in gun and depth charges and sonar for anti-submarine operations and could make 16 knots. A total of about 700 of these and related classes would be ordered during the war. These four were equipped with sweeps to counteract the new German magnetic mine, which, it would be discovered, reduced their speed to only 14 knots.[8]

This operation, codenamed 'Collar', would also present an opportunity to bring the *Newcastle* west from Malta, along with the slow battleship *Ramillies* and the *Berwick* – the latter needed for duty in the Atlantic. These ships would form Force D, and would be supported by the AA cruiser *Coventry* and four destroyers, which after escorting these ships west, would then accompany the merchant ships back to Malta. Two of the big 'Town' class light cruisers at Gibraltar, the *Manchester* and *Southampton*, would also be packed with 1370 RAF personnel between them, along with a handful of soldiers, bound for Egypt. These were the ground crews necessary for the aircraft flying the so-called 'Takoradi Route', a series of airfields stretching through Central Africa, many of which were in Free French territory, maintaining an air route between the South Atlantic and Egypt. Somerville's Force H covered the convoy with the *Renown*, the *Ark Royal*, the cruisers *Sheffield* and *Despatch*, and nine destroyers.[9]

Cunningham was running a convoy to Suda Bay covered by his slower warships including the *Ramillies* and *Eagle*, while the remainder of his force, built around the faster *Warspite*, *Valiant*, and *Illustrious* followed two days later. On the way the *Illustrious* raided Leros on the 26th, losing one Fulmar and doing some minor damage. Five empty merchant ships left Malta and headed for Alexandria, where they arrived safely. But Cunningham also had a role for the *Eagle*, which headed southwest and launched an air raid on Tripoli on the 26th as a diversion.

The Italians reacted quickly to this operation, in part because of their excellent intelligence of activities at Gibraltar, sending their fleet to sea with orders to engage Force H if conditions were favourable. They were hoping to intercept a convoy, but the presence of a carrier indicated that their battleships might be threatened by a repeat of the Taranto attack. However, they did not sight the convoy and therefore thought that the operation was another attempt to reinforce Cunningham. Peter Smith comments that 'In this it will be seen that, yet again, the Italians were badly served by their aerial reconnaissance units and were left much in the dark subsequently'.[10] A submarine line was established to the south of Sardinia and two submarines stationed off Malta would make two unsuccessful attacks on Cunningham's fleet. Air operations against his forces were very limited, with only three torpedo planes mading an attack against the convoy near Crete, scoring no hits.

On 27 and 28 November, the Italians attacked Malta several times, once with six Ju87s escorted by sixteen Cr42s. In various dogfights with Fulmars from the *Illustrious* and Hurricanes over Malta, the Italians lost two S.79s and at least two fighters with only one Fulmar damaged. One Blenheim flying into Malta from Gibraltar was attacked by a trio of Vichy French fighters on the 28th but escaped, although a second Blenheim was not so lucky the following day.

The main Italian operation was the sortie of Campioni's fleet from Naples with the battleships *Vittiorio Veneto* and *Giulio Cesare*. The cruiser force was commanded by Vice-Admiral Iachino with three of the *Zara* class heavy cruisers, and a total of eleven destroyers accompanied the heavy units. A further three heavy cruisers and three destroyers from Messina under Vice-Admiral Sansonetti rendezvoused with Campioni's fleet off the southern tip of Sardinia, while several small units of torpedo-boats and *MAS* were deployed in the same area for possible night attacks. It was planned to have the main fleet assembled south of Sardinia by dawn on the 27th, so there would be a full day for combat. The *Regia Aeronautica* would be heavily involved in this action as it took place close to airfields on Sardinia. A *gruppo* of Cr42 fighters was assigned to defend the fleet, while S.79s were to conduct bombing missions and a *gruppo* of Cant Z506s provided reconnaissance. Campioni was under orders to remain within range of his fighter cover from Sardinia and bases near Cagliari, for protection against British air attacks.

As Force D headed to Gibraltar on the night of 27-28 November, it was spotted by the torpedo-boat *Sirio*, part of a scouting line of light vessels, just after midnight. She fired torpedoes at long range, but failed to hit. Although some sources say the *Sirio*'s attack went unnoticed, the British were in fact aware of it. The *Sirio*'s initial report said only that seven enemy ships had been sighted, but later reports added details and *Supermarina* was now aware that at least one British battleship and six other units were passing through the Sicilian Straits, which would influence their assessments of British strength as they sought battle with Force H.

Campioni did not receive reconnaissance reports from his aircraft immediately that morning, one Cant Z506 having been shot down by a Fulmar from the *Ark Royal* at 7.55am, and he ordered the launch of Ro43s from his ships, and one from the *Bolzano* sighted Force H at 10.15am, but not the convoy it was covering. Several more aircraft would be launched in the course of the morning, and they did provide some valuable information. Campioni decided to head south and engage, requesting air support. His aim was to intercept one or other of the British forces before they could join up. He received some very limited fighter support from Sardinia to cover his fleet, and as usual, it was late in arriving. Somerville likewise was not in an easy position. First, he had not yet joined up with Force D and secondly, the slow speed of the four 'Flower' class corvettes had forced him to detach them and order them to proceed independently. Finally, he had inexperienced aircrews on the *Ark Royal* which had to provide his main reconnaissance and strike aircraft. Even with help from aircraft from Malta, he still had little information on the Italians' position. At this point Campioni was heading south by south-west at 16 knots still undetected by the British in the hopes of intercepting Force H before it was joined by Force D approaching from the east. Force H, with Somerville on the *Renown*, accompanied by the *Ark Royal*, *Sheffield*, and five destroyers, lay between the rest of his force covering the convoy and the approaching Italian fleet. The *Renown*'s engines were giving trouble and she was 2 knots slower than her normal top speed of 29 knots. Somerville had launched reconnaissance aircraft and protecting fighters that morning, and one of the scouting Swordfish had found the Italian fleet at 9:06am but her radio report was not picked up by Force H, which had meanwhile turned back towards the convoy to protect it from possible air attacks, heading away from the approaching Italians.

By 9:56am Somerville was at the rear of the convoy, when the returning Swordfish confirmed the presence of five cruisers and five destroyers. Although these ships had not been positively identified and might have been Force D, Somerville assumed they were hostile and ordered all his ships to increase speed. The *Ark Royal* was ordered to launch a strike and was detached for independent manoeuvring with two destroyers, while the light cruiser *Despatch*, the *Hotspur*, and two other destroyers covered the convoy. All other ships, the battlecruiser, the three big 'Town' class light cruisers (two filled with 'passengers'), and five destroyers prepared to engage the enemy.

As Campioni drew closer, with the enemy just over the horizon to the south, he received the sighting report from the *Bolzano*'s aircraft, the number of ships reported leading him to think it was the same force contacted by the *Sirio* in the Sicilian Straits the previous night. At 11.00am he ordered his fleet, which was now heading to the east, to turn south-southeast towards the enemy, with the cruisers in the van. His force was in three divisions, two of heavy cruisers and one made up of the two battleships. By now Somerville's scouts had relayed enough information so that he now had an accurate picture of the Italian fleet and he had reported his situation to Malta. Force D was now only 34 miles away from Somerville, and Campioni had already lost the race to intercept the British while their forces were still divided, but he was as yet unaware of this.

Supermarina now signalled Campioni to keep looking for the enemy until noon, probing south with the cruiser divisions, and then to return to base unless the enemy was located, and also gave him fuller details of the *Sirio*'s sighting of Force D. Campioni modified this by also advancing with his battleships. Iachino's heavy cruisers, led by the *Pola*, were to the northwest and closest to the enemy, while the division led by Sansonetti on the *Trieste* was to the northeast, and Campioni and his two battleships were to the east. Of course, during this entire redeployment, Campioni was under constant observation by a Swordfish as his covering fighters still had not arrived from their bases on Sardinia.

Force D now arrived, and Somerville immediately ordered the *Berwick* and *Newcastle* to join the other three cruisers and continued to head north by northeast, thinking the Italians were on the run, and intending to cut them off from their bases. The cruisers were under the command of Vice-Admiral L E Holland. As the destroyers from Force D joined up, one, HMS *Defender*, came close enough to the flagship for Somerville to wave to his son who was serving aboard her.

Somerville's next information on the enemy came from a Sunderland out of Malta that reported the enemy cruisers but not the battleships, and its report was incomplete, leading Somerville to think that the Italians were working around his flank and might have an opportunity to get at the *Ark Royal* or the convoy. Therefore he altered course to the north, away from cutting the Italians off.

It was at this point that Campioni's reconnaissance aircraft supplied him with two items of information. The *Gorizia*'s scout plane sighted a battleship and four destroyers at 11.52am while a *Regia Aeronautica* bomber had sighted the convoy for the first time at 11.10am and made an accurate report, giving its speed as 16 knots, although Campioni did not receive this report until 11.55am. This lead him to conclude that he was facing two, possibly three, British battleships and the *Ark Royal*, and thus outnumbered, he felt he had to retreat, having failed to intercept the British before their two forces joined. *Supermarina* likewise ordered him to return to port, the presence of the carrier being decisive. However, Somerville believed that the Italian commander did not know he had joined with Force D and that he could cut him off, unless Campioni '(retired) at once at high speed'.

As Campioni concentrated his fleet for the return home, an engine failure aboard the destroyer *Lanciere*, escort to the *Trieste*, caused her to fall behind the main force. At 12:15pm she sighted ships approaching bow on from astern. The distant *Renown* sighted enemy smoke at the same time. The main Italian elements were deployed as follows: the *Pola* group (the *Pola*, *Gorizia*, and *Fiume*) and destroyers were to the northeast and closest to the enemy in line ahead at 28 knots. The *Fiume* was also having engine difficulties and would end up being closest to the enemy as she lagged behind the rest of her division. The division led by Sansonetti in his flagship *Trieste* was about 8km to the northwest making 25 knots – this force was further to the west then the *Pola* group and was waiting for its destroyers to catch up. Sansonetti would shortly re-deploy to line abreast and would be to the north of Iachino. His division had misunderstood an earlier manoeuvre and in the confusion the *Trieste* had ended up being sandwiched between the *Bolzano* in the van and the *Trento* in the rear. Campioni and his two battleships and destroyer escort were 24,000m to the northeast also steaming at 25 knots.

Despite Campioni's order at 12.07pm, 'Do not, repeat, not, engage in battle', the Italian heavy cruisers of the *Pola* division opened fire at 12.20pm on the approaching five British cruisers, which were in line abreast, at a range of 22,000 yards. Their order from east to west was *Berwick*, *Manchester*, *Newcastle*, *Southampton*, and *Sheffield* and they were steaming at about 30 knots. Sansonetti's 3rd Division joined in at a range of about 21,500 yards and straddles were quickly achieved on both the *Manchester* and the *Berwick*. Some of the cruisers' floatplanes were also catapulted to spot the fall of shot. At 12.22pm the *Berwick* was hit on 'Y' turret by a shell which

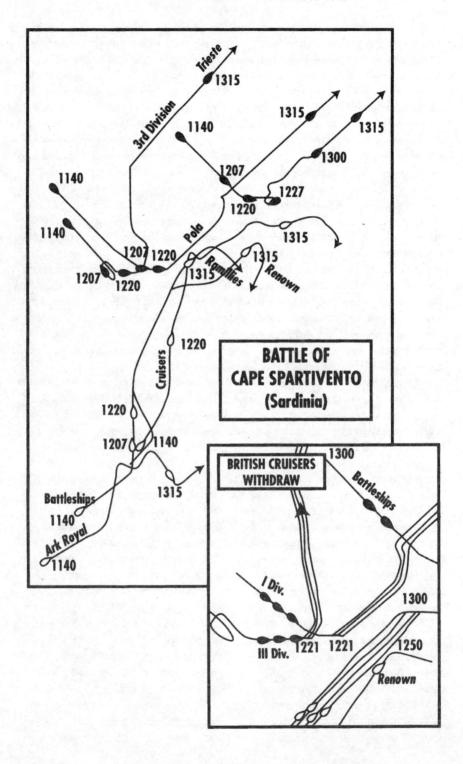

BATTLE OF
CAPE SPARTIVENTO
(Sardinia)

BRITISH CRUISERS
WITHDRAW

penetrated the armour and knocked out both guns. Casualties were heavy and one rating later wrote, 'They say war is glamorous, but I was there when they opened up "Y" turret, and I don't want to see the like again'.

The action mostly involved the cruisers in a running fight, with the ranges dropping down to a low of 17,000 yards for the lame *Fiume* and 18,000 yards for the rearmost ship of the 3rd Division, the *Trento*. Gunfire was heavy until 12.42pm when it became more intermittent, in part because of the returning air strike from the *Ark Royal* passing near the Italian heavy cruisers. It built up again towards 1.00pm, but the range opened to 26,000 yards, which was beyond the range of even the Italian heavy cruisers, as they increased speed, the *Pola* getting up to 34 knots in this stage of the action.

The *Manchester*, loaded down with extra passengers, had several near misses, with the shells falling 100 yards off either the bow or stern. Yet again the Italian salvoes were not lined up properly on the target. Only the *Berwick* with her 8in guns was actually in range, but the 6in cruisers kept up a lively fire, even though they were often out of range. As in previous actions, the high rate of fire of their guns meant that they expended large amounts of ammunition in this battle. At 12.35pm the *Berwick* was hit again on the stern by a cruiser from the 3rd Division, as the *Pola* division passed out of range, but no casualties were suffered.

Both the *Renown* and *Ramillies* steamed as fast as they could towards the developing action, but only the former came into action, opening fire at 12.24pm at a range of 26,500 yards and would fire a total of eighty-six shells from her 15in guns. The *Ramillies* fired two distant salvoes but was out of range. With her top speed of only 20⁷/₁₀ knots there was no way she could get into this running action. Meanwhile, Campioni completed a loop with his battleships to let the cruisers close with his force and at 12.37pm again requested air support from Sardinia.

Every ship in any navy has her own personality, largely a reflection of her crew. One ship, the *Sheffield*, on this day flew for the first time a special oversized battle ensign sewn by the 'Ladies of Sheffield'. It was saved for surface actions like this. Also, her Walrus seaplane was damaged when launched in the action by the blast of her own guns. This earned the aircraft the name 'Spotter of Spartivento' which was engraved on her fuselage after the action.[11]

The *Ark Royal* had launched eleven Swordfish which entered the action only slowly due to their low speed, combined with that of the retiring Italian fleet. They eventually attacked Campioni's two battleships at about 12.40pm after they had completed their loop, claiming one hit, but in fact all torpedoes missed. Several did fire their machine-guns at the Italian battleships, escaping any serious damage.

The British cruisers concentrated their fire on the *Fiume* and *Trento*. Fortunately for the *Fiume*, she early on requested a smokescreen and thus avoided being hit. The *Fiume* fired 210 rounds in this action, the most of all the Italian ships engaged. All three crusiers of Iachino's division fired over 100 rounds, while the *Bolzano* only fired twenty-seven because of the *Trento* masking her guns. The *Southampton* then switched her fire to a closer destroyer, the *Lanciere*, one of three covering Sansonetti's division. She was hit by a 6in shell at 12.40pm, and was 'deluged' by many near misses. She would head away from the British fleet on a northerly course, partially crippled. She managed to restore power to one of her engines and make 23 knots. Escorted by her two companions, she escaped destruction, a second 6in shell passing clean through her at 12.45pm, failing to explode, while a third fell right alongside her but likewise failed to go off. She came to a halt again, but was towed back to Cagliari by her sister-ship the *Ascari*, covered by aircraft from Sardinia.

It was at about 1.00pm that the two Italian battleships came into action against the pursuing British cruisers. The *Vittorio Veneto* opened fire at the extreme range of 29,000 yards, the *Cesare* joining in when the range dropped to 26,000 yards and after 10 minutes, the British cruisers began to retire, the battleships ceasing fire at 1.15pm. Campioni decided not to pursue the enemy as he had received neither the promised fighter or bomber support, and he was faced by an enemy aircraft carrier.

Somerville wanted to re-concentrate his fleet and while he was doing this at 1.26pm Sansonetti requested to return and support the *Lanciere*, which was approved by Iachino, his immediate superior within signalling range. Iachino's cruisers were later attacked by a second wave of seven Swordfish, which again failed to hit and suffered two aircraft slightly damaged, and the 3rd Cruiser Divison was attacked by seven Skuas with 500lb bombs later in the afternoon, but with no result, although the Skuas did manage to shoot down one Ro43, probably from the *Vittorio Veneto*, for the carrier planes' only success of the day.

At 1.35pm Somerville received reports of a crippled enemy cruiser, which was in fact the *Lanciere*, but decided to cover the convoy rather than run it down. But this decision would bring Churchill's wrath down on Somerville's head, as he thought he was not aggressive enough. Before Somerville could return to Gibraltar and make a report, there was a Board of Inquiry on its way out to review his conduct.

Campioni's ships returned safely to port the following day, but Somerville still had to run the convoy through and that afternoon was attacked by the *Regia Aeronautica*. The first attack took place just after 2.00pm by ten S.79s, escorted by five Cr42s. The *Ark Royal* had seven Fulmars up, which were guided in to intercept by the *Sheffield*'s radar. One Italian fighter was shot down, and the high-altitude bombing only scored near-misses. The next wave of ten S.79s came in at 4.45pm with no escort. Nine of the ten would be damaged, two seriously, by the Fulmars and AA fire. Again the *Ark Royal* was surrounded by near-misses, but escaped unscathed. That night the fleet safely passed the convoy through the straits to Malta and Force H returned to Gibraltar.

As for the Board of Inquiry, it was quickly apparent that the vast majority of the officers of the fleet strongly supported Somerville and felt that he was certainly an aggressive fighting admiral. Cunningham also did not approve of Churchill's treatment of Somerville, and said so. Therefore, even though Rear-Admiral Sir Henry Harwood, the victor of the Battle of the River Plate, had already been chosen as his successor, the Board found in favour of Somerville. But there was a different fate in store for Campioni. He would shortly be relieved and given a command in the Dodecanese, where his future actions would bring about his execution.

This battle showed that the Italian strategy now required that the *Regia Aeronautica* keep fighters over the fleet to protect it both from British torpedo-planes and their reconnaissance aircraft, and this need to provide air cover would give rise to both the proposed conversion of the *Aquila* to a carrier equipped only with fighters, and mounting catapult-launched fighters on other warships.

*   *   *

It was at this point that Churchill put forward one of his many schemes for an operation in the Mediterranean. He wanted Cunningham to help in a combined operation, codenamed Operation 'Workshop', to take the tiny Italian island of Pantelleria in the Narrows between Tunisia and Sicily as a base to strengthen British control in the Central Mediterranean, under the command of the elderly Admiral Sir Roger Keyes, a hero of the First World War. Cunningham opposed this as Pantelleria had neither water nor a harbour, and it would have to be supplied by a fleet that already had to supply Malta and in waters 'more or less dominated' by the Italians. Even Admiral Pound did not support this move, as it also left Keyes in command at his retired rank of 'Admiral of the Fleet'.[12]

A series of attacks now followed in support of operations in Greece. On 28 November, four destroyers of the 5th Flotilla, consisting of three *Navigatori* class with eight 4.7in guns and the First World War era *Augusto Riboty* armed with eight 4in guns, bombarded Greek positions on the mainland northeast of Corfu. Covered by two torpedo-boats, they fired 1600 shells of all calibres. The same ships launched another bombardment raid on 18 December, against the Greek lines 30 miles north of the Corfu channel, this time with two light crusiers adding the weight of their 6in guns. Both sides were busily shipping men and munitions to the Greek front. The Italians were especially concerned about the deteriorating situation of their army and reinforcements poured through the ports and airfields of Albania throughout the winter, and the first direct German assistance to her ally would be the arrival of Ju52 transport planes in southern Italy on 10 December to help ferry supplies to Albania. Stiffening Italian resistance, as well as the harsh winter conditions in the Albanian mountains, slowed the Greek advance, and in the air the Italians were particularly active. Despite British reinforcements, Allied daylight raids on the Albanian ports had to be quickly abandoned due to mounting losses. However, increasing Italian air raids on Greek cities brought about reprisal raids against cities in southern Italy, which although on a relatively small scale, did affect civilian morale. The war was obviously not going as well as they had been lead to expect.[13]

The British and Greeks also deployed submarines off the Albanian coast, the British sinking two merchant ships and damaging the 6040-ton *Olimpia*. They lost the *Triton*, most likely to two torpedo-boats and three *MAS* boats, while the *Regulus* was sunk by a mine off Taranto. The Greek submarine *Proteus* sank the nearly empty passenger liner *Sardegna*, transporting troops from the front, but was herself rammed and sunk by the torpedo-boat *Antares*. Two other Greek submarines sank three more ships before the end of the year.[14]

*   *   *

In December 1940 there was a major shake-up in the Italian high command. But it was now that some major housecleaning in the Italian Navy and Italian Air Force took place. It began with Mussolini's dismissal of Marshal Badoglio on 1 December and his replacement by his long-time opponent General Ugo Cavallero. A small man, who had a reputation as something of an intellectual as well as a soldier, Cavallero had fallen from grace in the 1930s over accusations of corruption in his involvement with Ansaldo, but he was adept at the industrial management that this war demanded.[15] Six days later, Cavagnari was also replaced as Undersecretary of the Navy and Chief of Staff, which was greeted with some rejoicing in the navy, ratings at Messina cheering when they heard the news. Many of the disasters of the opening months of the war were blamed on him. Giuseppe Grotto recalled that Cavagnari was generally regarded as incompetant.[16] Mussolini personally chose Admiral Arturo Riccardi as his replacement. Formerly commander of the 1st Battle Squadron, he had been in command of naval forces in the invasion of Albania in 1939 and earlier commanded at Taranto. A supporter of the Fascist regime, he was not an innovator in naval doctrine. Campioni was also replaced as fleet commander by Admiral Iachino, and the fleet was also reorganised, bringing all the major ships together. Vice-Admiral Bruto Brivonesi commanded the three available battleships in the 5th Division, while the *Zara* class heavy cruisers remained in the 1st Division under Vice-Admiral Cattaneo and the three remaining heavy cruisers were in Sansonetti's 3rd Divison. Two light cruisers, the *Bande Nere* and *Armando Diaz* and two destroyers were taken under the direct control of *Supermarina*. Previously, on 15 November Pricolo was also relieved from command of the *Regia Aeronautica*, but this may not have been entirely due to the poor performance of the Air Force. He had been in conflict with industrial interests and Cavallero.[17]

* * *

With the military reverses suffered by Fascist Italy in the summer and autumn of 1940, those officers and politicians who had not wanted to enter the war in June, or had expected a short war, began to look at the possibility of overthrowing Mussolini and making peace with the British, helped by the fact that there were anti-fascist Italians abroad, like Count Sforza and Gaetano Salvemini, and that the home front seemed to be on the point of collapse.[18] If exploited this could have helped the British policy that was aimed at cutting Italy away from Germany. In early 1941, the British considered forming a Free Italian Army from among the large number of Italian prisoners captured during O'Connor's campaign in Libya, but the unexpected continued success of the British offensive meant that any such 'Garibaldi Legion' would mean that Libya would remain in Italian hands after the war. The lack of any leader equivalent to De Gaulle and poor results from POW interrogations meant that this policy was abandoned and the British shifted to supporting the Senussi tribes. The Foreign Office adopted a punitive attitude to Italy which was to continue even after the Armistice, an attitude passed on to the SOE and the Ministry of Information.[19] In any case, Rommel's surprise offensive in February 1941 deprived the British of the territory to form any 'Free Cyrenaica'.

Evidence of low morale in Italy began to reach the Foreign Office from several sources and there were also messages from the Italian 'peace party', including the politicians Ciano, De Vecchi and De Bono, and Badoglio and Cavagnari among the military.[20] The fact that Mussolini was ultimately compelled to ask for Hitler's help to save Italy from defeat and preserve his own regime, caused the failure of the peace contacts. Although the 'peace party' continued to plot behind the scenes to overthrow Mussolini, there were few practical results.[21] Secret contacts would be resumed later at the end of 1942 when the war was going very badly for Italy, but the last act was to be the secret armistice signed at Cassibile.[22]

The proposed 'Free Cyrenaica' movement could have played a significant role if the Italian fleet had sailed to North African ports and surrendered to the British. Such a possibility came to light in November when Countess Amelie Posse, a refugee from Czechoslovakia, asked her friend, the Press Attaché at the British Embassy in Stockholm, if the British were interested in buying the Italian navy.[23] Such a move was suggested to the Countess by her friend J H Walter, who had aided her escape when Czechoslovakia was invaded. He was already in contact with the Italian Navy attempting to buy warships for the Swedish Navy and was short of money having lost his income when his business had been taken over by the Swedish government. The Press Attaché passed this on to the Naval Attaché Captain Henry Dehnam who was instructed by the Admiralty and Foreign Office to proceed. The contact with the Swedish was made by an Italian whose name was not revealed.[24]

Walter wanted to visit Italy in January 1941 because he needed evidence of his dealings with the Italian Admiralty in a case against the Swedish government, which refused to pay him his commission for buying four destroyers, which the British had seized when *en route* to Sweden at the outbreak of war with Italy. He claimed he was in contact with Admiral Cavagnari and the submarine commander Rear-Admiral Angelo Parona, and that they were worried about German intervention in Italy and their pressure to take control of the fleet, and that they would rather surrender it to the Allies or scuttle it than let that happen. The British proposed to give the entire Italian fleet free passage to a Allied port but at this point the Foreign Office's enquiries about Walter led to contact with his adversaries and probably a leak to German Intelligence. Nevertheless, Walter succeeded in travelling to Italy via Russia and returned reporting that the Italians wanted to be paid in US dollars for each ship surrendered or scuttled. For example, a battleship was worth $300,000, a heavy cruiser $60,000, and a torpedo-boat $15,000. At any rate, Walter himself received an advance payment of 50,000 Swedish krona for his role as go-between.

The file was shown to Churchill who authorised the continuation of the affair, but Walter was unable to travel to Italy again after the German invasion of Russia, although Cavagnari's successor, Admiral Riccardi, did share his views about the Germans. The British did propose setting up a secure means of communication with the Italians, but nothing more is known of this. Among the Italians named in an anti-fascist plot were Badoglio, Grandi and Cavagnari.[25] Things came to a halt when Walter was arrested by the Swedish secret police, just after having received his money in Dehnam's flat in Stockholm, and was sentenced to one year's imprisonment for espionage, which was doubled after his failed attempt to appeal against the sentence. He was freed in 1943 but by then the Fascist fleet was in its last days. Walter was arrested when enquiries made about him by Lieutenant-Colonel Cordeaux of Naval Intelligence aroused the suspicions of the secret police, and in turn those of the *Abwehr*, who had good contacts with their Swedish counterparts. As Tennant concluded in his article, it is difficult to say if Walter was taking the British for a ride, or if the Italians were actually prepared to do this, or if it was all part of a great game of deception to divide the Axis allies. It all does sound quite bizarre, and the prices asked for the ships seem far too low.[26]

However, it does shed some light on feelings in the Italian Navy, and the names of the plotters given by Walter surfaced several more times in the course of the war. For example, both Marshals Badoglio and Caviglia were named in a War Office memo relating to talks with the British Embassy in Berne at about this time. Moreover, there are also other indications that the Navy plotted against Mussolini, including the rumour that one resistance radio station operated aboard a warship in Livorno harbour.[27]

* * *

Back in the Mediterranean, the Royal Navy established four special units to support the Western Desert Force under the command of General Wavell in its offensive which began on 7 December 1940. Under Rear-Admiral H B Rawlings, it was known as the Inshore Squadron and was to co-operate with the Army by conducting operations, usually bombardments, on the Italian sea flank. Units assigned to it would vary between missions. Force A was built around the First World War monitor *Terror*, recently stationed at Suda Bay, which was armed with twin 15in guns, and three Chinese river gunboats, the *Ladybird*, *Aphis*, and *Gnat*. Force B, under Captain H M L Waller of the Australian Navy, consisted of the old destroyers *Vampire*, *Vendetta*, *Voyager* and *Waterhen*. They were fast, and would reinforce Force A from 'time to time'. Force C consisted of the battleships *Barham* and *Malaya*, while Force D was made up of the *Eagle* and her supporting ships. The Inshore Squadron would conduct numerous operations on this sea flank, and would also bring up supplies from Alexandria. While initially small scale, it would grow as the fighting continued, and would only be severely curtailed with the arrival of the *Luftwaffe*.

The Italians deployed three submarines against this force, and the *Neghelli* did succeed in torpedoing the AA cruiser *Coventry* on 13 December but she was easily patched up. She approached what she thought was a 'Town' class cruiser, and at 8.36pm launched a spread of four torpedoes – three 21in and one 17.7in. One hit far forward on the bow, but the damage would be easily repaired by filling the damaged compartments with concrete! The Italians lost another submarine, the *Naiade*, on 14 December in these operations to the destroyers *Hereward* and *Hyperion*.

Italy had two types of torpedoes in the Second World War, the 21 in (553mm) and the 17.7in (450mm), the former being the most widely used. As well as aboard the older submarines, to save money the smaller torpedo was generally used against small ships and every submarine had two 21 in tubes reduced to 17.7in to launch these torpedoes.[28] Both torpedoes had thermal propulsion, leaving a revealing wake behind them like British torpedoes, and did not have the magnetic detonators used by both the British and the Germans, but had few problems with them. By 1940 only 5 per cent of trial launches were erratic.[29] Their main shortcoming were their warheads, weighing only 595lbs and 375lbs respectively for the 21in and 17.7in against the more powerful 722lbs of the British 21in MkVIII. Italian torpedoes were fast with the later model 21in capable of running at 50 knots for 4000m and the 17.7in at 42 knots for the same range. Longer ranges could be obtained at slower speeds.[30]

Two firms were responsible for torpedo production, Whitehead of Fiume, which had also opened a plant near Livorno in 1937, and the Silurificio Italiano near Naples, but both these firms produced their own designs of each type (in total the Italian Navy had twenty-three different types of torpedo in service), and plans to build only four standard types at both companies were abandoned on the outbreak of war.

* * *

On the eve of the next major British supply operation, three air attacks were carried out on Naples, which was in range of Malta, and was now the main base of the Italian fleet. In one of these three on 14 December, the heavy cruiser *Pola* was hit in her bows, suffering flooding in her boiler room and thirteen killed and thirty-three wounded. This brought about the transfer of the fleet to Maddalena and Cagliari in Sardinia, out of range of British aircraft.

The British planned two operations: MC2, a re-supply mission to Malta, and MC3, an attack into the Straits of Otranto. Four freighters, under close escort from four destroyers and the battleship *Malaya* headed for Malta from Alexandria on 16 December. The convoy arrived safely and the *Malaya* proceeded on towards Gibraltar with two empty merchant ships and three destroyers, one of which, the *Hyperion*, was mined passing through the Narrows and had to be scuttled.[31]

Cunningham with the main force first launched air attacks on airfields in the Dodecanese from the *Illustrious* but poor weather there hampered operations (snow covered the mountains of Greece and came down almost to sea level), so therefore Cunningham detached the carrier with an escort to operate in the central Mediterranean for the next stage. The battleships *Valiant* and *Warspite* ran towards the Adriatic and on the night of 18-19 December bombarded the port of Valona, firing mostly at the airfield. One hundred 15in rounds brought the war home to that city. The 7th Cruiser Squadron, consisting of three light cruisers and three destroyers, had been patrolling in the Straits of Otranto, but were unable to locate any enemy shipping in the bad weather, and rejoined Cunningham's ships after the bombardment. He then took the *Warspite*, with an escort, into Valletta and inspected the harbour from the 20th to the 22nd, before rejoining the fleet and heading back to Alexandria, arriving there for Christmas. While touring the port large crowds had turned out and sang 'God Save the King' and 'Rule Britannia'.

The *Illustrious* had enjoyed some success while detached. A small convoy of three ships escorted by the torpedo-boat *Vega* was sighted on 21 December, bound for

Tripoli. Attacked by nine Swordfish, two merchant ships totalling 9000 tons were sunk, while the other two ships escaped.[32] However, the Italians were able to successfully transport large numbers of men and supplies to Libya that month and into the New Year, including several large troop convoys built around several passenger ships escorted by destroyers and on one occasion two light cruisers, just before and after the British operations. A total of thirty-six merchant ships were sent to Libya during December and three of them were lost, as well as the torpedo-boat *Cairoli* which was sunk by a mine in the afternoon of 23 December. With the New Year there were some additional operations before Germany made her presence felt. British submarines sunk four merchant ships in early January, while the Free French submarine *Narval* was sunk by the torpedo-boat *Clio* on the 9th.

As 1940 came to a close, Nazi Germany was sending reinforcements to help her faltering ally. Plans were afoot for military action against Greece when spring came, and later in Yugoslavia as well. But it would be German air power that would tip the scales in the naval war in the Mediterranean. The Allies had thus far more than held their own at sea and in the air. Both sides had suffered losses, but on the whole Italian losses had been higher. More importantly, the Royal Navy had been able to supply Malta, run convoys to Greece, and control both ends of the Mediterranean. For Italy it was no longer 'Italy's War' but the 'Axis' War' to win. She had now realised her areas of weakness. Could she learn from these and recover? As we will see, she could improve in some areas but not all.

CHAPTER 10

The Arrival of the X Fliegerkorps, December 1940

If we do win, the best we could be in the future is one of the
several minor members of the Germanized Europe.
Alberto Pirelli[1]

O n the eve of the arrival of the German Air Force in the Mediterranean, Great
Britain continued to improve her position. Submarine operations continued
through the winter and into the spring, with the British now achieving greater success
as the 10th Submarine Flotilla began regular patrols. The vulnerable larger British
submarines had been withdrawn, although not before almost 500 seamen had been
lost, and they were replaced by the smaller, more modern 'U' class boats. At 540 tons
and 195ft long, they were ideally suited to the shallow Mediterranean coastal waters.
Armed with four bow tubes and eight torpedoes, and a small deck gun, they had a
crew of 33 men. Eight would be based on Malta, operating from various harbours, and
at this time were to be employed primarily on the Axis convoy route between Trapani
in Sicily and Tripoli. One of the most successful British submarine captains was
Lieutenant Commander M D Wanklyn who would receive the Victoria Cross for his
actions commanding the *Upholder*. On her first war patrol the *Upholder* damaged the
German freighter *Duisburg* off the Tunisian coast.[2]

The British had also improved their supply situation. Work on building up
docking facilities along the Suez canal and adjacent waters had proceeded rapidly,
and there was even a small supply route directly to Palestine from the tiny port of
Aqaba. Furthermore, the number of aircraft using the Takoradi route across Africa
was increasing. British forces, especially in the air, were still under-strength, particularly on Malta, but Allied strength would increase as the war continued.

On Malta, only the land forces approached full strength, with six battalions on the
island out of the required seven. Numbers would increase in 1941 and into 1942,
thanks to the arrival of additional British forces and the raising of four Maltese
battalions under the Conscription Law of 22 February 1941, although this law was
not well received by the Maltese who were offended that they were paid less than
the British soldiers. As one Maltese later stated, 'Once again the British found a way
to remind us of our inferior worth'.[3] But the long association of the Royal Navy
with the island meant it still had a special place in the hearts of many Maltese. By
July 1940, the British had ceased regarding Malta as untenable and the reinforcement and resupply operations detailed earlier got under way. Literally hundreds of
aircraft would fight over this tiny island, and forces based there would strike
damaging blows against the enemy. The Italian air attacks on Malta during 1940 had
been for the most part high-altitude bombing attacks against military installations

with less than 100 civilian casualties, and many people had returned to the crowded downtown areas of Valletta and even to places near the harbour. The Italian fleet was referred to by the Maltese as 'the Phantom Fleet', as so little was seen of it.[4]

*   *   *

It was rumoured that the Vichy French battleships *Jean Bart* and *Richelieu* were to be transferred to the Mediterranean from Casablanca and Dakar respectively that winter. It was during this period that a *rapprochement* with Vichy was again attempted, including Churchill's suggestion of sending six divisions to French North Africa to help defend against Axis encroachment.[5] This would all come to nothing, as would trying to establish a 'third force' in French politics under Weygand. It is hard to see how Britain could have brought Vichy around as there had been so many clashes between the two powers after the 22 June 1940 Armistice, particularly Mers-el-Kebir. Eventually the Allies would play the American card in dealing with Vichy France. As one historian has stated, '. . . it was Britain, not the United States, which supported de Gaulle, and British, not American guns which sounded at Oran'.[6] One result of all the fruitless secret negotiations with Vichy and Weygand was that De Gaulle's stock slowly continued to climb. He had rejected peace with the Axis from the start and his movement was gaining momentum. However, attempts to undermine De Gaulle's position by factions within various Allied governments were to continue up to the fall of Vichy, which may explain some of his later resentment of the British and Americans.

*   *   *

Beginning in November and throughout the winter, the RAF would send planes to help the Greeks. Blenheims, Wellingtons, Gladiators, and even obsolescent Fairey Battles would clash with the Italians over Albania and even the Italian ports of Bari and Brindisi, and suffer losses. The Greek Air Force during this period would suffer losses on a 1:1 ratio with the more numerous *Regia Aeronautica*. Indeed, it was only in the air that the Italians were not outnumbered in their ill-advised invasion of Greece.[7]

Increasingly disturbing news from the Mediterranean began to reach the German High Command in late 1940. While various war plans, including ones against the USSR, were being considered, Mussolini's fortunes as a warlord were dropping like a stone. Not only had the Italians missed the opportunity to carry out the expected series of successful operations against Alexandria, Malta and other British bases, but soon Germany's ally was on the brink of disaster, having refused any assistance.[8] The unsuccessful invasion of Greece on 28 October, the attack on Taranto, and the disasters suffered by Graziani's Army in the desert after the advance to Sidi Barrani, were milestones on the road to failure of the last Fascist war. This was a shock for the German military and political leadership, who regarded the Italian failure in the Mediterranean with a mixture of 'dismay, rage, contempt, fear and secret satisfaction'.[9]

Faced with this situation, Hitler's first reaction was that the Italians had to find their own way to solve the problem and on 12 November he cancelled the planned help to North Africa, but there the worst had yet to come. When it did, he was compelled to help Italy in order to keep her in the war and secure his southern flank, and particularly the Rumanian oil fields, vital for the war with the Soviet Union. Although the Italians had not notified their ally in advance of the attack on Greece, the Germans were not surprised as it had been rumoured in Berlin for some time. It was the fact of growing German influence in Rumania (ten divisons of 'military advisors' were stationed there) which caused Mussolini to send his troops into Greece in order to forestall any possible German moves and maintain Italian influence in the region.

The most serious consequence for Hitler of the invasion of Greece was the immediate occupation of Crete by the British on the day of the attack, since bombers based on Crete could attack the vital Rumanian oilfields. Indeed, there had been plans to strike at German oil supplies since the earliest days of the war, when there had been discussions with the French about bombing the Russian oilfields in the Caucasus, which were supplying the Germans under the terms of the Nazi-Soviet Pact of 1939.

The first meeting between the Axis powers after the attack on Greece took place at Innsbruck on 14-15 November. Badoglio met with Keitel, the OKW Chief of Staff, and tried to blame Mussolini for the disaster in Greece, which would cost him his post of Chief of the General Staff. In the meeting, Badoglio tried to find out what the state of German-Soviet relations was, following the recent meeting with the Soviet Foreign Minister Molotov, but Keitel was evasive, explaining the withdrawl of German divisions from France as a measure to protect them from British air attacks.

For his part, Keitel first explained that Germany had not informed Italy in advance of the invasion of Norway since at that time Italy had not been at war, a very different situation than when Greece had been attacked. He then wanted to discuss German and Italian spheres of influence in the Mediterranean and the Atlantic. The Germans particularly wanted a share in the control of French shipping to North Africa, hitherto controlled by the Italians alone. An attack on Gibraltar, Operation 'Felix' (see below), was also discussed but without the involvement of Italian units and Badoglio raised no objections. He welcomed the offer of help from the *Luftwaffe* when the offensive in North Africa was resumed, but said that it would not be required until the capture of Mersa Matruh closer to the Nile, which the Italians foresaw for December. The situation in the Mediterranean was not yet so bad as to require large-scale German intervention, except in the Balkans, where he asked for support via Bulgaria against Greece.

Count Ciano later had two rather difficult meetings with Hitler in Salzburg on 18 and 20 November. The German dictator needed to take steps to prevent any further British successes in the Mediterranean, but he avoided commenting openly on Italian failures, encouraging them to put pressure on General Franco to join the Axis and enter the war. This was all part of Hitler's plan to win support from Italy, Vichy France and Spain by promising them all war prizes at each other's expense.

However, there were those in the *Kriegsmarine*, for example Grand Admiral Raeder himself, who having seen the war with Britain come to something of a standstill, saw the Mediterranean theatre as the one in which Britain could be brought to her knees, by cutting off oil supplies from the Middle East and threatening her communications with India. As Petersen has written, 'for Raeder the

Mediterranean exerted an almost overwhelming fascination'. It is difficult to assess the chance the Germans had to win the war in the Mediterranean, as opposed to a strategy of attacking Russia, but it was a vital factor in the German intervention in the region, which had the effect of delaying Italy's surrender.[10]

It was difficult for the Italians and Germans to wage war in coalition, as although they did have a military alliance, there had been no pre-war planning for joint operations. The first regular meetings were held in the winter of 1941-42 to deal with the shipping problems to Africa and there was no formal organisation, simply the goodwill of numerous officers to keep things going. A joint commission for the attack on Malta was established in the spring of 1942, but by then it was too late.

The entire German intervention in North Africa may have had a profound effect on the approaching war with the Soviet Union which is sometimes overlooked. The German Quartermaster-General, General Wagner reported on 11 February 1941 on the effect of sending units to North Africa (Operation 'Sunflower') on Barbarossa. The transport required for the two divisions being sent was equivalent to the transport space required for the entire 12th and 17th Armies in the Soviet Union, and this does not take into account the fuel used for ships and aircraft in the Mediterranean theatre.[11]

The first manifestation of the ending of the 'Parallel War' and the birth of the Axis War in the Mediterranean was the arrival of fifty-three Ju52 transport planes at Foggia in Apulia on 8-9 December to help move troops and supplies to Albania in the war against Greece.[12] This was followed by the transfer of the *X Fliegerkorps* from Norway to Sicily for operations against Malta and the British Mediterranean Fleet. Pricolo's request for German Stukas for the Greek front was refused on the grounds that Germany was not at war with Greece. It was a mixed unit of fighters (initially the twin-engined Me110) and bombers, which specialised in anti-shipping operations, commanded by Lieutenant-General Hans Ferdinand Geisler, who established his headquarters at the Hotel San Domenico in the scenic Sicilian town of Taormina. By mid-December over half of its aircraft had arrived in Sicily.[13]

Although the Me110 was inferior to the single-engined Me109 in air combat, it had longer range and although outclassed by the Hurricane, it could hold its own against British carrier fighters. The bomber force was made up of the Ju88 that was used initially for high-altitude bombing, but was later employed for glider-bombing and reconnaissance as well as a torpedo-bomber, where it equalled the S.79 in inflicting damage. It was even used to provide air cover for convoys and the fleet, as it was the only plane with sufficient range available, showing how desperate the Axis were to get aircraft over their ships.

But the principal weapon at this early stage was the Ju87 Stuka dive-bomber. Although short-ranged, it could deliver a devastating blow. To defeat it, it either had to be intercepted by fighters before it reached the target, or shot down or driven off by massive and effective close-range AA batteries, which were an area of weakness aboard British ships. As early as 1936, Admiral W W Fisher had recognised that British warships had no effective defences against dive-bombers. This was the reason many British ships fitted captured Italian 20mm and 37mm AA guns, or had their AA batteries augmented when undergoing refits at home.[14] Mussolini also asked for German naval assistance, primarily submarines, motor torpedo-boats, and minesweepers.

* * *

In the first week of January 1941, the British mounted Operation 'Excess', an important convoy from Gibraltar made up of four fast merchant ships, one of which, the 11,000-ton *Essex* was bound for Malta with a cargo of seed potatoes, twelve crated Hurricanes and 4000 tons of ammunition, while the others were to proceed on to Greece.[15] The convoy was to be covered by Force H which would rendezvous with Cunningham's fleet from Alexandria. The close escort of this included the new radar-equipped light cruiser *Bonaventure* of the *Dido* class and four destroyers, which carried 400 troops and airmen between them bound for Malta. The convoy departed on 6 January (first with a feint into the Atlantic), with Force H heading out the following day.

Force B under Rear-Admiral E de F Renouf, made up of the cruisers *Gloucester* and *Southampton* (carrying 500 troops and airmen for Malta) escorted by two destroyers, departed from Alexandria for Malta the same day. They arrived there safely on the 8th, leaving a few hours later to reinforce the escort of the approaching convoy. Somerville wanted one of Cunningham's battleships so that he would have three to face the Italian fleet if it came out. Cunningham gave him the cruisers instead. With the exit of the cruisers, two convoys of merchant ships at Malta also headed to sea. As Somerville neared Malta he pushed the *Ark Royal* ahead to fly off six Swordfish all of which landed safely on the island. He then fell back on the convoy as it continued eastwards.[16]

The first air attack on Force H came from ten S.79s which attacked the *Malaya*. Two were shot down by one of the *Ark Royal*'s Fulmars which had Somerville's nephew aboard as navigator. One of the crews was rescued by an escorting destroyer. The other eight made an accurate bombing run but the *Malaya* suffered no hits as the bombs all landed just ahead of her. A later attack by fifteen Cr42s, carrying only two 50kg bombs each, was ineffective, but the carrier's Skuas were unable to intercept them. Cunningham's fleet met the convoy on the evening of the 9th and continued on to Malta, while Force H retired on Gibraltar. Cunningham had with him the *Warspite*, *Valiant*, *Illustrious* and seven destroyers. The Mediterranean fleet's cruisers were in the Aegean.

The Italians were under-strength at this time. Their main fleet did not sortie against this convoy (though some cruisers and destroyers took up defensive positions in the Straits of Otranto and elsewhere), and her air strength had been siphoned off to Africa and Greece to replace losses. They did deploy five submarines, of which two fired torpedoes but all missed. They had sent out two torpedo-boats, the *Circe* and *Vega* which at dawn on 10 January were off Pantelleria when they sighted the *Bonaventure* and the destroyer *Hereward* at a range of 7000m. Though heavily outgunned, they closed to 5000m and fired seven torpedoes, all of which failed to hit. The *Vega* was shot to pieces and sunk, while the *Circe* escaped. In the coming actions in the next few days, the *Bonaventure* would fire off 75 per cent of her 5.25in ammunition, which caused problems for her as the 5.25in gun was a new weapon and ammunition for it was scarce in the Mediterranean.[17]

At this point, Cunningham began to suffer problems. First the destroyer *Gallant* was mined and although she was towed to Malta, she would never be rebuilt. To cover her, Cunningham had to detach several ships, including the *Bonaventure* which with her powerful AA armament helped keep attacking S.79s at a distance when dropping their torpedoes.

The *Illustrious*'s aircraft had damaged an enemy reconnaissance plane that morning, and she had five Fulmars up when two S.79s came in low, under her radar. The Fulmars dropped down to intercept, and while failing to destroy them, their torpedoes passed astern of the *Valiant*. But then the carrier's radar picked up a large force of planes approaching, at high altitude. This was the *X Fliegerkorps* with eighteen He111s and forty-three Ju87s escorted by ten Me110s. The first group of five Fulmars were now low on fuel and ammunition and had to fly to Malta. Four more flew off the *Illustrious* and struggled to gain altitude to protect the ship as the attack began at a little past noon. She was operating between the two battleships at the time, and it was argued by some on board that it might have been better if she had been operating independently to the south of the convoy, thus putting her further away from the airfields on Sicily.[18]

Approximately thirty Stukas were involved in the attack on the *Illustrious*. Diving from 12,000ft, they released their bombs at 2000ft and hit her five times (one failing to explode) with one near miss that damaged her steering gear and caused some flooding. One bomb hit a lowered elevator, causing tremendous damage in the hangar and heavy casualties among the aircraft maintenance crews. Nine Swordfish and five Fulmars were destroyed. Lieutenant-Commander Hubert Treseder of the *Sheffield* said; 'The Italians were brave men, their high-level bombing attacks were good, but the German dive-bombers were lethal, their pilots superbly trained. Nobody who has heard the attacking scream of a Stuka will ever forget it'. Cunningham would later write that 'We could not but admire the skill and precision of it all. The attacks were pressed home to point blank range, and, as they pulled out their dives, some of them were seen to fly along the flight deck of *Illustrious* below the level of her funnel'.[19] Although her 3in armoured flightdeck was penetrated in this attack, the careful stowing of aircraft and ammunition aboard prevented the fires that were responsible for the loss of many carriers in the Pacific War. The armoured decks of the *Illustrious* class were designed to be proof against 500lb semi-armour-piercing bombs, and in the Pacific would offer good protection against Kamikaze attacks.[20] Her Fulmars landed in Malta to refuel and rearm, and immediately flew back to help the damaged carrier make port.

Further air attacks followed. A flight of seven S.79s were frustrated by the intense AA fire, but at 4.00pm six Italian Stukas from the 96th *Bombardamento a tuffo* hit with one 500kg bomb and had two near misses. Fourteen German Stukas then attacked the *Valiant* and *Janus* without hitting, and one Stuka was shot down by Fulmars. Finally fourteen He111s attacked of which only eight found the target and none hit. One hundred and twenty-six men would be killed and ninety-one wounded before the *Illustrious* saw Alexandria again. Five German Stukas would be lost over two days of operations.[21]

One more disaster was in store for the British. The cruisers *Southampton* and *Gloucester*, returning to the fleet, were surprised by He111s attacking from out of the sun owing to their lack of radar. The *Gloucester* was hit once by a 250kg bomb that failed to explode after penetrating five decks and the *Southampton* was hit at least twice and so heavily damaged that she had to be abandoned and was sunk by three torpedoes fired by the light cruiser *Orion* which arrived after receiving their distress signals.[22] As a result of these losses, Cunningham was forced to abandon his planned operations against Italian supply shipping.[23]

* * *

When the *Illustrious* arrived at Malta at 10.00pm on 10 January, she was immediately taken into the dockyard and repairs to her hull proceeded rapidly. The Axis air forces did not return immediately due to a shortage of bombs, but soon she was under furious attacks led by the Stukas. The Maltese would call this the '*Illustrious* Blitz' and it saw the first serious damage to the city of Valletta. On 16 January it began with ten Mc2002s with an escort of ten Cr42s teaming up with twenty Me110s escorting forty-four German Stukas. During these attacks bombs of up to 1000kg were used, although it took the Stukas with their heavy loads nearly an hour to reach an altitude of 11,000ft. Another heavy attack followed the next day, but work continued on the *Illustrious* around the clock. One benefit of the attacks was the bombs exploding in the harbour brought up an incredible number of dead fish which the population gathered up, cooked and ate with gusto.[24]

The final major attack on the 19th again failed to damage the carrier. Both sides had aircraft shot down, including one Cr42 being downed by an Me110! A British Fulmar pilot later lamented over how he was shot down that day. He wrote; 'The poor old Fulmar had problems gaining height and in gaining speed against the Ju88s. My aircraft was hit – I think, of all degrading things, by a Ju87 – which stopped the engine some miles . . . south-east of Malta'. It was also on this day that the first Spitfire arrived on Malta, a Photographic Reconnaissance Unit aircraft, which was not expected on the island at all.[25]

The *Essex* was hit by one bomb that 'dropped neatly down the ship's funnel' into the engine room, killing fifteen and injuring twenty-three of the crew, but not setting off the 400 tons of ammunition still remaining on board. This slowness in unloading supplies would be a chronic problem at Malta which would come to a head in the summer of 1942.[26]

During these attacks, Lieutenant Micallef Trigona, an officer of the 3rd Light AA Regiment stationed near the harbour entrance, found that the German Stukas flew out of the harbour after dropping their bombs at such low level that his 40mm Bofors guns could not depress low enough to hit them. Consequently, he had the depression rails removed, so he could have the battery fire on the next wave. Although he was able to fire on the retreating Stukas, some of the Bofor shells hit the bastion of Fort St Angelo and one of the lighthouses on the breakwater![27] For four days heated air battles raged over the island, with the Axis losing more aircraft than the British, and the harbour suffering terrible damage, but finally the *Illustrious* was able to steam to Alexandria at 24 knots arriving safely on 25 January.[28]

* * *

During these first joint attacks on Malta, there were some examples of good co-operation between the Germans and the *Regia Aeronautica*, when the attacking Ju88s and Stukas had to be escorted by Italian Mc200 and Cr42 fighters as there were insufficient numbers of Me110s. General Geisler praised the Cr42s for carrying out their operations 'perfectly'. But at the same time the *X Fliegerkorps* had numerous problems, mostly relating to the airfield facilities, the need to build roads, and to properly disperse their aircraft on the ground. Especially at Catania the planes were parked too close together and suffered losses in the nightly raids by Wellington bombers. The OKW liaison officer General von Rintelen requested greater freedom of action for his forces, so that every action did not have to be cleared by Rome first.

The basic problem was that Fascist Italy never fully mobilised for war, and on the Home Front peacetime conditions still prevailed. This is in contrast to the First World War, when the full mobilisation of society was a major factor in the success of war production which largely overcame that of Austria-Hungary, whereas in this war, the land for the expanded Catania airbase still had not been requisitioned on the eve of the armistice in 1943![29] General Heinrich von Vietinghoff, the last German commander in Italy, wrote in his memoirs that when the Germans came to build coastal defences, it was common for enraged local farmers to turn up demanding an explanation, as if Italy was still at peace.[30]

The British did launch some air raids of their own at this time. Wellingtons continued to hit Axis bases, and Naples was a prime target as a key base for convoys to North Africa. The port's AA defences had consequently been upgraded with the addition of smoke generators to cover the ships in harbour, but during a night raid on 8-9 January they were not efficient enough as the battleship *Giulio Cesare* was near-missed by three bombs which opened leaks and killed five men and wounded twenty more. She would move to La Spezia for 20 days of repairs along with Italy's one undamaged battleship the *Vittorio Veneto*.[31]

Malta later came under air attack again because of the movement of General Erwin Rommel's 5th Light Division and 15th *Panzer* Division to North Africa. The forces on Malta had to be suppressed to ensure the safe passage of the convoys. At the end of January they also began mining the Suez Canal, which impeded traffic and several ships were lost. In February two large convoys successfully ran from Naples to Tripoli with Italian troops and supplies, and in the first convoy the lead elements of the *Afrika Korps*. This convoy had to have a short lay-over in Palermo because Force H was at sea, conducting a bombardment of Genoa. After an earlier failure in an attack on a major hydroelectric dam in Sardinia, Somerville was ordered to bombard Genoa as the Admiralty feared that an expedition to seize the Balearic Islands was about to be mounted from there. The Italians thought this operation was another convoy to Malta and prepared their forces accordingly.[32]

The Italians had an early report of carrier planes near the Balearics, and sortied from La Spezia with three battleships (the *Vittorio Veneto*, *Andrea Doria*, and *Cesare*) and eight destroyers. They would be joined by the three heavy cruisers of the 3rd Division and two more destroyers from Messina. The main Italian fleet steamed along the west coast of Corsica, bound for Cape Falcone on the north-west coast of Sardinia near the Straits of Bonifacio, the cruisers launching two floatplanes to search for Force H along the west coast of the island (the aircraft later landed at Cagliari). Meanwhile the British were approaching Genoa, arriving on the morning of the 9th, as the Italian fleet sped south along the Corsican coast.

The *Malaya*, *Renown*, and *Sheffield* shelled the harbour, while the *Ark Royal* provided three Swordfish for spotting, while sixteen others ineffectively attacked an oil refinery at Leghorn and mined La Spezia harbour. The *Malaya* concentrated on the docks, while the other two ships bombarded the Ansaldo shipyard and the marshalling yard. The *Sheffield* fired 782 high-explosive shells and the two capital ships fired off 273 15in and 400 4.5in shells. The Italian coastal batteries only opened fire after 20 minutes, having first thought it was an air raid and also having difficulty seeing the enemy in the early morning mist.[33] Four merchant ships and one training vessel were sunk, and eighteen others were damaged. There were 144 people killed (Italian propaganda down-played casualties to 72) and there was damage to the city itself. One Swordfish was shot down.

Iachino immediately turned his fleet in an attempt to cut the British off. During the pursuit, two land-based reconnaissance planes were shot down by the *Ark Royal*'s fighters and the Italian Fleet mistakenly chased a French convoy for a time. The *Trieste* launched an aircraft that passed close to the course of the British Fleet but failed to locate it. Therefore due to poor visibility and the usual problems with aerial reconnaissance, Force H escaped. The Italians also returned to port safely.

Italy suffered another loss on 25 February, when the light cruiser *Armando Diaz* was torpedoed by the submarine *Upright*. She and a sister-ship were covering a vital troop convoy of three large passenger ships bound from Naples to Tripoli. Two days previously the *Upright* had sunk a 9600-ton tanker, and in the early morning of the 25th was on the surface when the *Armando Diaz* and her destroyer escort was sighted. She was torpedoed, her magazine exploded and she sank in 6 minutes off the Tunisian coast. There were only 133 survivors out of her crew of 633.[34] But this was the only serious loss as two other large convoys successfully made the crossing to North Africa. All nineteen ships arrived safely and gave Rommel means to roll over the British front line in Libya. More convoys arrived in early March, and Tobruk would soon be under siege, with the Axis armies on the borders of Egypt.

* * *

Several options for naval operations involving the Axis powers or just Germany alone were discussed at this time. One was the transfer of U-boats to the Mediterranean, which would come in September 1941. Once through the perilous Straits of Gibraltar, they did well in the Mediterranean, and would be responsible for some of the greatest submarine successes of the war.

The suspension of Operation 'Felix', the proposed German attack on Gibraltar, on 10 January 1941 marked another of the 'might have beens' of the Mediterranean war.[35] Spanish intervention on the side of the Axis was briefly mooted in early 1941. Hitler was unable to persuade Franco to enter the war, though it is possible that if Great Britain appeared to be collapsing he might have come in of his own accord. However, the rumoured arrangements between Spain and Italy if they had joined the war were untrue. Ciano had claimed that Italy had the right to use the Balearics and other unnamed Spanish bases in event of war. This was not true and no such agreement had ever been made.[36]

The plan for the capture of Gibraltar originated just after the fall of France in June 1940, with General Alfred Jodl, Chief of the German Army Operations Staff, already contemplating such an operation. By July Hitler was discussing the possibility of an attack on this last British outpost on the continent with the Italians, and serious planning got under way. Gibraltar is essentially a spit of land leading to a mountain, with a small harbour on one side, facing the Spanish town of Algeciras, 3 miles long and at no point as much as a mile wide. During the war the British constructed 40km of tunnels, the spoil from the diggings being used to build an airfield that could handle up to 600 aircraft by the time of Operation 'Torch' in 1942. The Rock was heavily fortified, well garrisoned, and many of the civilian population were evacuated to safer areas in Africa.[37]

German reconnaissance had been considerable. *Abwehr* officers had observed Gibraltar from across the frontier and from Spanish airliners flying nearby. The *Luftwaffe* also used a special squadron for photographic reconnaissance overflights. It was thought that the British had ninety-eight landward-facing guns and fifty AA guns. One *Abwehr* officer boarded the Spanish 2100-ton gunboat-minelayer *Jupiter* at Algeciras which cruised just outside of territorial waters observing the fortress. The vessel was shadowed by a British plane, and when it came near the battlecruiser *Renown* the officer jokingly suggested to her captain that he fire on her! Another took photographs of the Rock from a house of ill-repute, with the woman in the foreground. Being fairly obvious as to the premises from which the pictures were taken, his superiors asked some awkward questions!

Early plans for an airborne assault with gliders and paratroops were abandoned because of the difficult wind conditions around Gibraltar, as was any idea of a surprise attack. The assault force changed and matured as planning proceeded, to the point where German troops practised assaults on Gibraltar look-a-likes, and to where only the word of command was needed to launch the operation.

Operation 'Felix' was to be under the overall command of Field-Marshal Walter von Reichenau. The assault force would be two regiments in strength, one a mountain regiment, the other the elite *Grossdeutschland* infantry regiment, supported by two combat engineer and one construction engineer battalions. There were special mine units also involved, as well as the 'Goliath' remote controlled mobile mines, and smoke units to camouflage the attack. Supporting the attack against Gibraltar would be some additional units in north and south Spain. The motorised division *SS Totenkopf* was one unit, and the 4th *Panzer* another. Additional units would be made available if needed, primarily if Portugal had to be invaded.[38] The main force for the attack would be artillery. A total of 164 guns could be used, the maximum that could be deployed in positions that would not be exposed to destructive counter-battery fire. The Navy would contribute some powerful coast-defence batteries, some of which were to be emplaced after the capture of Gibraltar to cover the Straits. Otherwise the naval component was small, with only some submarines forming a screen off the Rock. Admiral Raeder strongly supported the attack and in December 1940 informed Hitler that this submarine line would be in place and ready. He also hoped for a future submarine base on Spain's Atlantic coast. The *Luftwaffe*'s contribution would, however, have been substantial. It would begin with a special assault against the Royal Navy, with Ju88 medium bombers flying from bases near the French border with Spain and landing at Spanish airfields. Ju87 dive-bombers would arrive on the fourth or fifth day of the attack, after rapidly deploying to airfields in southern Spain, to begin pounding the Rock itself. The plans called for 800 planes, 3000 support vehicles, and AA units to help in the assault and protect the air bases. Once the British navy was chased from Gibraltar (which was thought to require several days because of the heavy AA defences), the ground assault would begin.

It would open with an artillery barrage, using literally tens of thousands of shells. When the defences sufficiently reduced, the land assault would begin, covered by smoke. Also standing by for special operations was the *Abwehr's* elite *Brandenburg* regiment which with Spanish troops would be used to defend against any possible British sortie against the artillery batteries ringing the north end of Gibraltar.

But the basic problem lay with Spain and Franco. The indifferent Spanish railways and the British intelligence network made a surprise attack, after travelling the length of Spain, impossible. Spain was also receiving hundreds of thousands of tons of food from Canada, which led Franco to demand a long list of requirements from Germany – food, arms, etc, before Spain could enter the war. Germany, which could not even fully motorise its own army, decided not to pay the price, postponing the attack on 10 January 1941.

Later, Mussolini was asked to try to persuade Franco, but he also failed. It was at this meeting on the Italian Riviera on 12 February 1941, that Franco added French Morocco to his price for entering the war and insisted that Spanish troops would have to lead the attack on Gibraltar. With Spain's continued intransigence, and with the date for Operation 'Barbarossa' getting closer and closer, the attack on Gibraltar became less and less feasible. Alternatives would be put forward as late as 1943, but the moment had passed.

The failure to take Gibraltar was one of Hitler's greatest mistakes – Goering would declare it was the greatest strategic error. What would have been the consequences of Operation 'Felix'? Firstly, it would have been doubtful that the *X Fliegerkorps'* attacks against the Mediterranean Fleet and Malta that winter would have occurred. With such a heavy commitment by the *Luftwaffe* against Gibraltar, it is unlikely it would have been sent to Sicily. Similarly, the air raids on Britain at that time would have been much reduced with so many German aircraft in southern Europe.

But the loss of Gibraltar would have meant the British would have been unable to operate in the Western Mediterranean apart from an occasional swift raid by surface ships or submarines, thus freeing-up Axis sea communications. Raeder, who strongly supported this effort, saw it as stabilising the entire deteriorating Italian position in the Mediterranean. Malta would have been more difficult to supply, as Axis forces would have been able to concentrate against the sole remaining route from Alexandria, and the island might consequently have faced an airborne invasion instead of Crete. The fall of Gibraltar would have allowed the Axis to plan for the capture of Suez, which would have meant the collapse of the whole Allied position. The invasion of Syria in the summer of 1941 would have been more problematic as well.

For Spain it would have meant the loss of her colonies, and particularly the Canary Islands. There were some German schemes to reinforce those islands, but some were impractical – one idea was to send 150mm guns by surface ship from Hamburg, which was an idea quickly discarded in the face of the Royal Navy! Some air units and submarines could have been deployed there, but they could have been easily captured by the British if Spain had declared war. But it would have been relatively easy to ship guns to Spanish Morocco, which Germany planned to do, and Vichy North Africa would have received a boost. However, Franco's reluctance to become involved, and the high price he set for that involvement, spelt the end for the attack on Gibraltar.

*   *   *

As the Axis armies advanced back across Libya to the Egyptian frontier in February and March 1941, the recaptured ports had to be put back into service. Damage to facilities varied from base to base, but they were rapidly repaired, Benghazi being back in use 9 days after being reoccupied.[39] Cunningham said that besieged Tobruk could be supplied by sea, and over the next few months ships would run in and out of that port at night, often hugging the coast, and keep it supplied. But he later said;

> Had I been gifted with second sight and been able to foresee the long tale of ships lost and damaged in supplying the fortress, I very much doubt if I should have been so confident in saying that it could be done.[40]

The monitor *Terror*, longtime member of the Inshore Squadron, was the next victim of the *Luftwaffe*. She had augmented her AA armament by adding seven captured Italian 20mm guns, but this was not to be enough to save her. She had arrived at Benghazi on 17 February, '. . . but was damaged after repeated attacks, and Admiral Cunningham ordered her to steam for Tobruk on 22nd February'. Her captain had reported to Cunningham that 'I consider it only a matter of time before the ship receives a direct hit'.[41]

She was near-missed at Benghazi on 22 February which started leaks, but caused no casualties. She was then damaged by two acoustic mines laid by an He111 on leaving port that night. Still leaking the next morning, she was then further damaged by three 'very near misses' from five Ju88s that had attacked just after her escort of a lone Hurricane had to return to base. They attacked at an angle which kept her from bringing more than a small part of her AA armament to bear. Slowly settling, she finally sank near Derna on the morning of the 24th. She had been escorted by an old minesweeper, the *Fareham*, and the new corvette *Salvia*, which rescued her crew, who had miraculously suffered no losses. On the same day, the destroyer *Dainty* was lost near Tobruk to He111s. Other small craft would be sunk in the coming days, but the Inshore Squadron continued to operate along the coast that winter.[42]

The end of February also saw two battalions brought into Malta by three cruisers on 21 February, and the passing out of a small convoy. All arrived safely back at Alexandria. It would not be until 10 March that the aircraft carrier *Formidable* arrived at Alexandria to replace the *Illustrious*, after passing through the Suez Canal, now partially blocked by wrecks courtesy of mines laid by the *Luftwaffe*. She would be of vital help in the coming British operations in the eastern Mediterranean.

CHAPTER 11

The Battle of Matapan, 28 March 1941

[In a night action] instant and momentous decisions have to be made in
a matter of seconds. With fast-moving ships at close quarters and the
roar of heavy gunfire, clear thinking is not easy.

Admiral Cunningham[1]

On the eve of the Battle of Matapan, the Italians enjoyed one success against the British Mediterranean Fleet using another of their special weapons systems introduced at the time of the Abyssinian War. Developed from weapons used with some success against the Austro-Hungarian Navy in the First World War, the *Motoscafo Turismo* (*MT*) was a small speedboat packed with explosives, with a single crewman steering from the rear of the boat. As he approached his target he would escape in a small liferaft and the boat would crash into the target and explode. There were three models, with modifications, of this weapon.[2] The *MT*s were operated by the *I Flottiglia MAS*, lead by Commander Vittorio Moccagatta. On 15 March, just before their first successful operation, this unit formally received the name under which it would become famous, the *X MAS*. Their distinctive shoulder patch carried a skull at the top clutching a rose between its teeth.

In December 1940 two torpedo-boats, the *Dardo* and *Strale*, had transported eight of these *MT*s from Augusta to the island of Leros. Then on the night of 25-26 March 1941 the torpedo-boats *Crispi* and *Sella* carried six of them close to Suda Bay on Crete. They successfully negotiated the harbour entrance and attacked the British ships there. The heavy cruiser *York* was hit twice while the 8324-ton tanker *Pericles* was hit once and sunk. The *York* was wrecked, with her boilers and engine-room flooded and no power to her main guns, and was later claimed as finished off by the Germans in their air attack on Crete in May. Beached, she would be used as an AA platform and her crew was employed on shore. The other three *MT*s missed. All six Italian sailors would survive to be taken prisoner and would be awarded the *Medaglia d'Oro*.[3]

*   *   *

The operation that would lead to the Italian defeat at Matapan was a result of the German desire for a surface naval strike to cut off the Allied armies in Greece, now staring defeat in the face, and they promised the Italians the air reconnaissance they needed. For the Italians it 'also possessed enormous moral value. If we could carry it off successfully, it would give us a tremendous lift. It would show the world that our fighting spirit and courage were the equal to any, that we were ready to take the offensive anywhere, even in waters that till now had been dominated by the British'.[4]

After the intervention of the *X Fliegerkorps* in Sicily the low point of Italian fortunes in the Mediterranean seemed to have passed. Malta was under pressure and the land front in Albania had been stabilised. A major land offensive in March by the Italian armies would fail to break the Greek defence, but tied down the bulk of their army so that the coming German attack would face little resistance. But the Taranto raid had left the Italian fleet with only one modern fast battleship available and moreover based at Naples, far from the central Mediterranean.

The replacement of Cavagnari with Admiral Riccardi seemed to the Germans to have thus far changed little in Italian naval planning, and it was this inaction, and the German criticism of it, that caused Admiral Iachino to urge *Supermarina* to raid Allied shipping to Greece.[5]

Operation 'Gaudo' was planned and carried out after the meeting between high-ranking officers of both navies which took place in the pleasant South-Tirolean town of Merano on 13-14 February 1941 at Grand Admiral Raeder's request. It was the follow-up to the 1939 Friedrichshafen meeting, which the Italians had delayed for some time as they did not want the Germans intruding in their *'guerra parallela'*. But after Taranto and Italy's other recent reverses, Raeder let it be known that a meeting between their two Naval Chiefs of Staffs would be proper. In fact, the meeting had already been planned before Cavagnari was fired. Raeder's intention was to have talks about the 'strategic situation' but also to arrange co-operation between the two navies' headquarters, influencing the Italian Navy towards the German viewpoint and encouraging them to become more active.[6]

At the meeting Admiral Riccardi first presented to Raeder a memorandum which summed up Italian strategic views and was somewhat pessimistic as a result of the loss of the eastern Libyan airfields and the isolation of the Dodecanese islands following British intervention in Greece. This strategic analysis stressed that the Italian Navy could engage the enemy main force, but a defeat would have an enormous effect on it, while a success would not have the same effect on the balance of power between Britain and Italy, because the Royal Navy could replace any losses more easily (Japan was not yet in the war, so little British naval strength had been drawn off to the Far East). Riccardi's memo stated that the British supply shipping was never unescorted and that generally it sailed with considerable forces in support. In his opinion, the only role the Italian Navy could play was to tie down British forces in the Mediterranean, and its main goals were to be aerial surveillance of the enemy, reoccupation of her main bases (particularly Taranto), and the continuation of convoy protection to Libya and Albania. These tasks were considered a priority and explain why Riccardi was taking similar views to his predecessor.

Without mentioning the relationship between the navies and possible collaboration in the Mediterranean, Riccardi presented a list of requests ranging from oil, of which reserves were now almost gone, to anti-aircraft weapons and equipment such as fire control systems. He also made clear that the Navy's air reconnaissance force was too small to cover the Mediterranean and could not provide enough information for operations.[7]

The Germans were also concealing their true intentions somewhat. Admiral Fricke said that the continuing war with Britain need not include an actual invasion of the British Isles, since air and submarine action should be enough to isolate her and bring to surrender, showing that Operation 'Sea Lion' was dead. Fricke did not mention the Mediterranean, thus seeming to go along with the Italian idea of the 'Parallel War'. But behind the scenes the interest of the German Navy in the Mediterranean theatre was strong. Raeder and his staff dreamed of the Third Reich flag flying over Gibraltar, Malta and the Suez Canal. For the moment they thought they could at least establish, in view of Operation 'Marita' (the code-name of the Balkan invasion), a South-East Command (*Admiral Südost*) which would have control over the Italian naval units in the Dodecanese and Aegean. This was intended as a blueprint for future control over operations in the Mediterranean and all the units of the Italian Navy.[8]

The German naval officers at the conference told their counterparts that they hoped for more aggressive action from the Italian Navy and particularly proposed raids by fast battleships. But Riccardi refused the German proposal for two reasons: the shortage of fuel for his major warships and of air cover.[9]

A memorandum of 10 April 1941 gives the fuel situation: 415,000 tons of fuel actually available for employment while 58,000 tons was required for full bunkers for the entire fleet. The importation of oil from Rumania had been suspended, so the navy calculated that they had enough fuel for only 2 months and 20 days of operations. On 5 May this situation was unchanged, with 342,000 tons available giving an operational capability of 2 or at most 3 months. It should, however, be noted that 50,000 tons had already been put aside for 'one year of submarine war'.[10]

Oil was vital for the running of the Axis war machine and allocations of new supplies were largely at Germany's discretion since Italy, with her Albanian colony, could produce only a minuscule amount of oil domestically, the majority of which went to the Navy. The Italian Navy had recognised the danger of this situation, which was brought home to her during the Abyssinian Crisis when an oil embargo had been threatened but not implemented. So by 1 July 1940 1,666,674 tons of oil had been accumulated. Neither the Italian Air Force or the Army had large oil reserves at the start of the war, although aircraft clearly used far less fuel than warships and the largely non-motorised Italian army did not create much of a drain on supplies.[11]

Italy never received her full requirement for oil during the war, nor what she was promised by Germany. In 1938 18 per cent of her imported fuel came from other European nations, primarily Rumania. The rest came from Mexico, the United States, Venezuela, and the Dutch East Indies, which would be lost when the blockade began. Although Italy would misrepresent the true situation to the Germans when it suited her needs, her reserves would steadily decline throughout the war. By 31 December 1940 after the extensive naval operations of the first six months of the war, her fuel reserves were down to 1,011,133 tons. Italy was due to receive 80,000 tons of fuel per month in 1941 but it was not enough. In January the Navy consumed 133,000 tons of fuel oil while the bombardment of Genoa by Force H in early February 1941 alone caused the fleet to expend 35,000 tons of fuel in its fruitless pursuit of the enemy.

After the war many Italian authors have stressed this point in order to explain the lack of initiative shown by the navy Chiefs of Staff and commanders.[12] But on the other hand, it has sometimes been written that the Italians typically hid large quantities of fuel during the war. The German Navy always believed the Italians asked for more than they really needed.[13] But the German report after the occupation of Italy following the armistice of 8 September 1943 shows that the amount of oil left was very low, only 17,000 tons, while at the end of August 1943 the amount was 66,000 tons of which 23,000 tons was in the ships' tanks. The report concluded 'the suspicion that the Italian Navy was asking for too much oil and had massed an overly large reserve with what was supplied, is therefore numerically not proved'.[14]

By the end of 1941 Italy would have reserves of only 142,318 tons. This fuel crisis and the demands of shipping to Libya in 1942 would cause Germany to double the allocation of fuel to Italy. Still, on a quarterly basis, Italy consumed less and less naval fuel oil as the war continued, and had less to consume. She ended the war in September 1943 with 58,750 tons of fuel available.[15] According to Admiral Weichold of the *Marinkommando Italien*, the Italian fleet could not have reacted to the 'Torch' landings in North Africa because the major ships were without fuel and the reserve was only 11,260 tons. The German Navy wanted to check why the Italian Navy needed 80,000 tons of fuel per month and in March 1942 stationed an officer in Italy to report on the use of oil by the Italians. It was discovered that the fuel was not made directly available to the Navy, which had to request it from the Supreme Command and AGIP, the main Italian oil company, which was responsible for distributing fuel to all sectors of the war effort. Therefore, the Germans wanted to supply their oil, reduced to 54,000 tons monthly, directly to the Navy but this was refused. Then Weichold arranged for the Italian Navy to receive the oil directly from Rumania.[16]

The Italian Navy had to rely on German help to stay afloat and for operations of minor vessels and escorting the convoys to North Africa and the Aegean. Her fuel reserve on 1 April 1943 was 49,000 tons and they foresaw using at least 50,000 tons. In the final months of the war, the need was partly decreasing: 39,500 tons in May and 52,000 tons in June, leaving 58,000 tons on July 1943. Of course the loss of Tunisia had decreased fuel consumption.[17]

At the beginning of the war the Italian Navy had massed a strategic oil reserve of 1,666,674 tons as of 1 July, compared to the 500,000 tons which the German Navy had available in September 1939. During the war she received (in tons):

1940	1941	1942	1943	Total[18]
15,109	254,393	630,700	403,126	1,303,328

The recent studies on the Italian Navy and the naval war in the Mediterranean stress that the fuel supply was not as vital a factor in restricting fleet operations as had been claimed. One historian has recently written 'In any case, the oil was not a decisive factor in the limitation of the activity of the battle fleet: all the times it was decided to go at sea, the fleet sailed'. But, as we have shown, Italian naval operations were greatly reduced after the first 6 months of war, so while it might be stated that when the Italian fleet went to sea, it did have fuel, there were times when it might have gone to sea but did not because the enemy operation was thought to be one that could not be responded to and the fuel situation restricted activities.[19]

* * *

On the eve of Matapan, the fleet commander Vice-Admiral Iachino was one among the Italian sea officers frustrated by the cautious attitude of *Supermarina* and already convinced of the necessity of active operations against the British. At the end of February he proposed a raid with a fast battleship and three cruisers on the supply route between Benghazi and Greece, which Admiral Weichold strongly supported. Riccardi stated that there was no longer any shipping running to and from Benghazi, which was dominated by German bombers, and therefore such a raid would be useless, and furthermore the Commonwealth shipping to Greece had already been halted. But a plan of this kind had already been developed at *Supermarina* against shipping in the Eastern Mediterranean.[20]

In fact, a few days later the convoys for Operation 'Lustre', the aid to Greece decided by the British Cabinet at the beginning of March, began in order to bring 58,364 Commonwealth troops to Greece. At the same time plans were laid down to establish a motor torpedo boat base in the Dodecanese, seizing the island of Kastelorizo (Castelrosso) close to the Turkish coast. At this time Malta had her last flying boat evacuated to Alexandria as the air attacks were too heavy.[21]

The attempted occupation of Kastelorizo, Operation 'Abstention', was carried out between 25-28 February 1941 with the landing of 200 commandos supported by the destroyers *Decoy* and *Hereward*, the submarine *Parthian* and the gunboat *Ladybird*. The armed yacht *Rosaura* would land a company of Sherwood Foresters the next day. The landing in the first hours of the 25th began in confusion and provoked an Italian response. At first only fifty men landed, then the attack proceeded and the Italian garrison of thirty-five men surrendered after having lost six dead and seven wounded, while the remainder of the commandos came ashore. But the *Regia Aeronautica* intervened, damaging the *Ladybird* for the loss of two bombers. At 9.00pm the torpedo boat *Lupo* appeared off the island and opened fire. On the 27th the Italians landed reinforcements consisting of 250 soldiers and 80 sailors covered by the destroyers *Crispi* and *Sella*, the torpedo-boats *Lupo* and *Lince* and *MAS 541* and *MAS 546*, with air support. This was just before a British squadron consisting of the cruisers *Perth* and *Bonaventure*, and the destroyers *Decoy*, *Hero*, *Hasty* and *Jaguar* arrived from Alexandria just before midnight. The British began to land the Sherwood Foresters, but soon the situation appeared difficult and the island was abandoned. Both sides made use of torpedoes but there were no hits. The British failed to conquer the island due largely to the quick reaction by Vice-Admiral Luigi Bianchieri, but they did gain the valuable booty of the Italian Y-I cipher book and twelve prisoners, for the loss of three killed, eleven wounded and twenty-seven missing. The Italians lost eight killed, eleven wounded and ten missing.[22]

Because of these British activities, the exchange of letters between Weichold and Riccardi become more heated. Riccardi replied to the renewed German proposal by writing that Taranto was still unusable as a naval base and he still had only one fast battleship. Plans to transfer an Italian cruiser to the Atlantic, or a German cruiser to the Mediterranean, were discussed but never implemented because of the difficulty of getting past Gibraltar in either direction. But now Weichold was ready to help Italy by sending one cruiser into the Atlantic to act as a diversion, and at one point the Germans considered forcing the Straits of Gibraltar with the battlecruisers *Scharnhorst* and *Gneisenau* to raise the Italians' offensive spirit.[23]

Coming under pressure from both Iachino and the Germans, *Supermarina* finally approved the operation on 16 March. It would be carried out by one battleship, eight cruisers and seventeen destroyers which would act in a pincer movement south of Crete to intercept the British convoys, as had already been planned. It was often supposed in previous works on the Battle of Matapan that the decision to launch the operation was encouraged by the fact that two *X Fliegerkorps* planes had reported that the British Mediterranean Fleet had few battleships available. But as we will see, this was not the case.

Vice-Admiral Iachino was informed of the decision to carry out the raid the same day, exploiting the element of surprise, since the operation would be carried out far beyond the line Iachino himself had supposed (Benghazi-Greece). This would require a more complex system of air cover and reconnaissance, so support was requested from both the *X Fliegerkorps* and the Italian Air Force in the Aegean. But it is clear from looking at the map that the Eastern Mediterranean was completely under the control of British forces, since Cyrenaica with its important airfields was in their hands.

The reasons why *Supermarina* ultimately took this decision after the misfortunes of the previous year were summarised in a letter from the Deputy Chief of Staff of the Navy, Admiral Campioni, to the liaison officer in Berlin Admiral Giotto Maraghini. They were (i) the volume of shipping between Egypt and Greece; (ii) the need to allow the Navy to go into action; and (iii) the pressure from the Germans.[24]

Significantly, it was the air support, perhaps the most vital component of the entire operation, that was planned without a clear view of the situation and seemingly at the last moment. It was another example of lack of co-operation between the Services and one of the main factors contributing to the eventual disaster. First, on the 24th, Riccardi assured Iachino that he could rely on the support of the Aegean-based *Regia Aeronautica*. He had spoken the previous evening with an air force officer and also asked for help from the Germans, without informing the Italian Air Force, which resulted in complaints that the proper chain of command was not being followed.

The day of the operation, 28 March, was 'X Day'. General Geisler promised air reconnaissance on X-2 and X-1 in the operational area. Air cover for the ships was also planned during X Day itself, from 2 hours after dawn until 2 hours before twilight, but this would mean that the North African convoys would be without protection, for which he needed Goering's permission, which was given. Other air activity planned consisted of reconnaissance of the British harbours of Suda Bay and Alexandria on X-1 and X-2, but not for X Day itself, when only 'armed reconnaissance' in the area south of Crete would be provided. Iachino felt better when he learned that German fighters would escort his ships on X Day, but Major A A Fontana, a member of his staff and chief of air operations for the fleet noted the limits of German cover eastwards and that the Italian Aegean Air Command would provide only 'armed reconnaissance', a rather vague term which gave no clear indication of what sort of support the fleet could expect.

On the 25th, the day before the commencement of Operation 'Gaudo', Iachino asked *Supermarina* for clarification of this important point. The meeting between the Navy and the Air Force, with representatives of the *X Fliegerkorps* present, took place only on the 26th, and the resulting agreement was not communicated to Iachino.[25] The agreement assured escort by *X Fliegerkorps* fighters on X-1 and X day within the limits of time already mentioned, and the reconnaissance of the Suda and Alexandria on the mornings of X-2 and X-1. In the afternoon of both days it would be the duty of the *Regia Aeronautica* to carry out such reconnaissance, while the Aegean Air Command's 'armed reconnaissance' became 'offensive reconnaissance' and fighter cover was promised between 7.00am and 9.00am on the 28th, only 2 hours.[26]

At this time, ULTRA was intercepting and reading *Luftwaffe* signals and practically all those of the Italian armed forces, and *Kriegsmarine* radio traffic was also being partly deciphered by British cryptanalysts, and signals intelligence was to prove vital in alerting the British to the Italians' plans.[27] The breach in security had not come from *Supermarina* itself. On 23 March Iachino had received his operational orders from them by wire, and he in turn passed his orders to his subordinate commanders by special courier, apart from the orders sent to Vice-Admiral Sansonetti of the 3rd Division by wire at 8.00am on 24 March, but there is no evidence that this signal, No. 10356, was intercepted. However, on 24 and 26 March, the orders for the Aegean Air Command from *Comando Supremo* were transmitted by radio via the Italian Navy's Enigma machine. *Supermarina* could not, of course, issue orders to the Air Force itself, and the orders were signed by General Alfredo Guzzoni of the Supreme Command. This caused some puzzlement among the British cryptanalysts, who could not understand why an army general was signing orders sent by the navy.[28] This was the only area of weakness, where the signals were intercepted, and from them the British learnt that 28 March was 'X Day', though it is not clear whether the orders sent to the submarines *Galatea*, *Dagabur*, *Ambra*, *Nereide* and *Ascianghi*, to deploy into ambush positions for this operation, were also intercepted.

But this was not all. Since the *Luftwaffe* code was easily read by ULTRA, messages concerning a possible landing operation on the Libyan coast were disclosed and Cunningham put his ships on alert. Then the orders for the transfer of air units from North Africa to Sicily for 'special operations' added to those sent to the Italian Aegean Air Command. Cunningham concluded that the Italians were preparing a surface operation against 'Lustre', and had therefore issued appropriate orders to his fleet before the Italians had even left port![29]

The Italians of course had their own signals intelligence assets. On the *Vittorio Veneto*, Iachino had embarked a cryptanalyst section under the command of Commander Eliseo Porta to intercept and decode messages exchanged between British aircraft and their bases. Furthermore, a team of *X Fliegerkorps* officers (Captain Withus and Lieutenant Moser with four signal specialists) was also aboard the flagship to help maintain contact with the expected escort of German fighters.[30]

At 8.30pm on 26 March the *Vittorio Veneto* sailed from Naples, hoisting the flag of Vice-Admiral Iachino, escorted by four destroyers of the 10th Flotilla, *Maestrale*, *Libeccio*, *Scirocco* and *Grecale*. Half-an-hour later the 8th Cruiser Division under the command of Rear-Admiral Antonio Legnani aboard the *Abruzzi* set off from Brindisi with the *Garibaldi* and the destroyers *Da Recco* and *Pessagno* of the 16th Flotilla, and at 11.00pm the 1st Cruiser Division (*Pola*, *Zara*, *Fiume*) sailed from Taranto commanded by Vice-Admiral Carlo Cattaneo, whose flagship was the ill-fated *Zara*. The cruisers were escorted by the 9th Destroyer Flotilla with the *Alfieri*, *Gioberti*, *Carducci* and *Oriani*.[31] On the following day, the 27th, the 3rd Cruiser Division (*Trento*, *Bolzano* and *Trieste*), left Messina at 5.30am under Vice-Admiral Sansonetti, embarked on the *Trieste*. Escort was provided by the 12th (*Corazziere*, *Carabiniere* and *Ascari*) and 13th (*Granatiere*, *Fuciliere*, *Bersagliere* and *Alpino*) Destroyer Flotillas. A total of one battleship, eight cruisers and seventeen destroyers were at sea, showing that despite the fuel shortage, the Italians would send the fleet to sea when needed.

Meanwhile, at 1.00am on the 27th, the 7th Cruiser Division, known as Force B, under the command of Vice-Admiral Pridham-Wippell, sailed from Piraeus heading for the waters south of Crete. The force comprised the light cruisers *Orion* (flagship), *Ajax*, *Gloucester* and HMAS *Perth* with the destroyers *Hereward* and HMAS *Vendetta*. They were ordered to rendezvous with the destroyers *Ilex* and *Hasty* from Suda Bay at 6.30am off the island of Gaudo, 10 miles south of the western coast of Crete in the Ionian Sea.

At 6.00am on the 27th the *Vittorio Veneto* met the ships coming from Messina and her escort was taken up by the destroyers of the 13th Flotilla. The four destroyers of the 10th Flotilla were then sent to Messina to refuel and stand by in case of necessity. Examining the information available to Iachino, he should have already cancelled the operation following the discovery by *X Fliegerkorps* that in Alexandria there were three British battleships operational, instead of the one previously supposed, following an inaccurate report on 17 March from two German He111s claiming that they had each torpedoed a battleship the previous day. Earlier reconnaissance at Alexandria had seemed to confirm that two battleships were indeed damaged, which led the Germans to increase the pressure on the Italians to take advantage of what appeared to be an extremely favourable situation. But this was uncertain, as General Geisler pointed out in the meeting with the Italians on the 26th. The report that there may have been three battleships at Alexandria was received by *Supermarina* on the afternoon of the 26th, but Iachino later claimed in his memoirs that it was never passed on to him. However, the decision to go to sea had already been taken on the 16th, a day before the inaccurate report arrived. In any case, as the German official history says, it had little significance: 'In the final analysis, the question whether the British Mediterranean Fleet had one battleship ready for action, or three, had no effect on the result of the operation'.[32]

More important were the signals intercepted by the Italians on the 27th. At 12.35am a Sunderland flying boat of 230 Squadron RAF spotted Iachino's cruiser force and radioed his base, the message being intercepted and read by *Supermarina*'s cryptanalysts. Due to bad weather the flying boat was unable to keep the enemy ships under observation and also lost radio contact with his base. For the same reasons the *Luftwaffe*'s Me110 fighters were unable to locate the Italian fleet, costing it its air cover. That evening Iachino was informed of the signals sent by the British flying boat and of the British reaction, since Malta relayed the message to other Mediterranean radio stations and Alexandria asked several times for the Sunderland to supply further information on the enemy.

Further information was gleaned from the interceptions decrypted by Porta's team aboard the flagship. At 10.20am they informed Iachino that the aircraft carrier *Formidable* was at sea. At this point, having lost the advantage of surprise, failure of the operation become not only possible, but probable. As a result, at 2.10pm Iachino ordered his forces to turn to a course of 150° (south by south-east) 1 hour in advance of the time given his written orders to limit their exposure to British air and surface attacks in the Aegean. At 4.00pm Iachino's position became even more worrying, when a long message from Cunningham to the various other commands, among them the 7th Cruiser Division at Suda Bay and destroyers already at sea, was intercepted by the Italians. Although they could not actually read it, its length made it obvious that it was an important operational order alerting a wide range of naval and air forces against them.

This was indeed the case. Admiral Cunningham had ordered Pridham-Wippell to recall all merchant ships in the Aegean to port and at 6.30am also ordered for the 7th Division to sail to join the Mediterranean Fleet coming from Alexandria after gathering up the destroyers. The only convoy at sea at that time was AG.9, composed of six merchant ships escorted by the AA cruiser *Calcutta* and the destroyers *Juno, Defender* and *Jaguar*. It was ordered to sail on the 26th and head towards Piraeus until sunset on the 27th and then reverse course back to Alexandria. As always, in this return voyage its codename would change to GA.9.[33]

At 10.30pm and 11.22pm Iachino received two messages, one from the *X Fliegerkorps* and the second from *Supermarina*, confirming that photographs taken that morning revealed three British battleships anchored at Alexandria. That evening a conference was held at the Italian Navy headquarters, during which it was concluded that it was no longer possible to carry out the mission as planned, since there were no British convoys at sea for the fleet to attack and more importantly the element of surprise had been lost. Nevertheless, *Supermarina* accepted the suggestion of *Comando Supremo* to continue the operation in the waters south of Crete, avoiding the foray into the Aegean since the Air Force in the region said it had too few fighters to give effective air cover.

Riccardi knew that British naval forces were at sea but it was supposed that they were limited to a cruiser division, because at midday the Mediterranean Fleet was still anchored at Alexandria. Concentrating their forces south of Crete would have given the Italians superiority over the British. But by the evening of the 27th there were numerous indications that the Mediterranean Fleet was at sea: signals from the intelligence service, reports from the *X Fliegerkorps*, and from Berlin a report that Vice-Admiral Cunningham had sailed with the *Formidable*, accompanied by at least one battleship, but probably by three.

Indeed, the *Formidable* had sailed at 3.15pm, embarking her aircraft from Dekheima airfield, a couple of miles from the harbour. They were thirteen Fulmars of 803 and 806 Squadrons and ten Albacores and four Swordfish of 826 and 829 Squadrons. In order to deceive any Axis agents watching the port, that afternoon Cunningham went ashore with his golf clubs and an (empty) suitcase, to give the impression that he intended to spend the night ashore. He slipped back aboard the *Warspite* after dark.[34]

Despite all this, *Supermarina* had to continue the operation after all the pressure from the Germans and Iachino himself, and the fact that German support had been arranged after complex discussions and it was therefore difficult just to give up, although the operation was now without an objective. The Italian Fleet wanted to fight just to show they could, counting on their superior speed to disengage from the Mediterranean Fleet if it was at sea.[35]

At 7.00pm, after a long discussion with his staff, Cunningham sailed from Alexandria with three battleships as Force A. He was joined during the night by the *Formidable*, escorted by the four destroyers of the 14th Flotilla (*Jervis, Janus, Nubian* and *Mohawk*) and Force C (HMAS *Stuart, Greyhound, Griffin, Hotspur* and *Havock*). While leaving the harbour the *Warspite* passed a mud bank which clogged her condensers and temporarily slowed the ship to about 20 knots, resulting in Force A missing its rendezvous with Pridham-Wippell's ships the following morning. As mentioned above, four Italian submarines had been deployed near the exit routes from Alexandria but the British force was not sighted. Only the *Ambra*, commanded by Commander Mario Arillo, at 2.45am and 5.11am on the 28th heard some engine noises but no ships were sighted and, as ordered, did not break radio silence.

At 6.35am on the 28th the *Vittorio Veneto*'s Ro43 reported the presence of Pridham-Wippell's Force B with four cruisers and four destroyers about 45 miles away, steering south-east at 18 knots. The Italian ships were divided into three squadrons all steaming south off the western coast of Crete. Five minutes previously the cryptanalysts had intercepted a signal from a British flying boat reporting to an aircraft-carrier. That morning the sea was calm and the weather was clear, but bad weather in the Kaso Straits meant that the fifteen Cr42s of the 162nd Squadron of the Aegean Command that took off in five patrols were unable to find the ships they were supposed to escort, apart from three planes that were at the limit of their endurance and could accompany the Italian fleet for only 10 minutes. Another patrol of two S.79s of the 68th Squadron were able to provide some cover between 7.10am and 8.15am. The Aegean Air Command had a total of only eighteen Cr42s, eight S.81s and twelve S.79s ready for action, and should have been reinforced in order to accomplish its role in this operation.[36]

At 8.00am Sansonetti's 3rd Cruiser Division (three heavy cruisers and three destroyers) sighted Pridham-Wippell's four light cruisers and four destroyers at an estimated range of 27,000m. Until 8.12am, when the Italians opened fire, the range was very difficult to judge: the fire control officers thought it was 22,000m. The only rangefinder working properly in this first phase of the battle was the *Bolzano*'s, which was new, while the other heavy cruisers had to rely on older equipment which should have been replaced.

Both sides had major forces to their rear and could attempt to lure the enemy onto them, but against his instructions Sansonetti immediately pursued the British cruisers as they retired eastwards, being out-ranged but not outgunned (having thirty-six 6in guns to the Italians' twenty-four 8in). The only British cruiser to return fire was the *Gloucester* which fired three salvos that fell short. Fortunately, she had recovered her best speed of 30+ knots by then, as the previous day she could only make 24 knots.[37]

Iachino was following on *Vittorio Veneto* at 28 knots and suspected the British manoeuvre to be a trap, and therefore he urged Sansonetti to halt the pursuit at 8.55am. Sansonetti obeyed and the British turned to follow and observe the manoeuvres of the Italian fleet. Five minutes later Iachino received a sighting report from a nearby S.81 of one British carrier with two battleships, nine cruisers and fourteen destroyers but it turned out that this was mistaken, the ships being the Italians' own. From intercepted British messages the Italians got the impression that Force B was unaware of the presence of the *Vittorio Veneto* some miles behind Sansonetti, although Pridham-Wippell had been informed at 8.54am that a plane from the *Formidable* had spotted three enemy battleships and was therefore prepared for this dangerous eventuality, and Iachino concluded that he could trap the British ships between his battleship and the 3rd Division, beginning this manoeuvre at 9.45am against the advice of his Chief of Staff.

An officer was on the bridge of the *Orion* eating a sandwich, when he turned to a member of Pridham-Wippell's staff and remarked, 'What's that battleship over there? I thought ours were miles away'. At 10.55am the *Orion* radioed that an unknown enemy ship (a report later amplified to two battleships) had been sighted and 30 seconds later the *Vittorio Veneto* opened fire with her six forward 15in guns and held her targets under fire for 23 minutes, concentrating on the *Gloucester* once the *Orion* was covered by a smokescreen. The cruiser did a little salvo-chasing to help throw off the Italian fire. Some shells fell near HMAS *Perth*, and her Captain later wrote 'Brrrrrp went her broadside. "That's not 8-inch," said someone … Halfway through the turn the salvo fell. It was terrific. I'd no idea 15-inch splashes looked so big when they meant business'.[38] Sansonetti turned back to join the fight, but Force B reacted immediately by turning back to a southern course and making smoke, increasing speed to about 30 knots. The inaccuracy of the Italian gunnery, coupled with poor visibility, meant they missed their chance for decisive success that day.[39]

In this first half-hour of the battle, the *Trieste* fired 132 shells, the *Trento* 204 plus 10 high-explosive (HE) shells, and the *Bolzano* 189. All three ships suffered breakdowns in the electrical equipment for loading and training their guns, and had to resort to manual controls. *Vittorio Veneto* fired 94 rounds in 29 salvos, opening fire at an estimated range of 23,000m, which Pridham-Wippell thought was about 12 miles. For the first 10 minutes the battleship's salvoes overshot the *Orion*, but then became more accurate and the cruiser was slightly damaged by a near-miss. She was saved by a smokescreen and the Italian battleship held her fire for 3 minutes, resuming at the *Gloucester* which came under accurate fire but was not hit, while the destroyer *Hasty* tried to aid with smoke. The action report stated that the extreme range meant that the fall of shot could not be accurately spotted, and finally fire ceased as the range increased still further. The *Vittorio Veneto* also had mechanical problems: 'A' turret failed to fire seven shells, and 'B' and 'X' turrets had two misfires each, but the gunnery report concluded that the performance of their equipment was 'was very good, except for the usual shell stoppages'.[40] According to some sources 'the 15in salvos of the *Vittorio Veneto*, although well aimed, were as always too much dispersed in length'. One Swordfish pilot who witnessed to engagement later wrote, 'The battleship was also doing some good shooting at our cruisers and appeared to be straddling them frequently. I suspect that the only reason that they did not score any direct hits was that the spread of their individual salvoes was too large'.[41]

Cunningham was about 90 miles south-east of Force B when he was informed at 7.39am of the presence of the Italian cruisers, sighted by one of *Formidable*'s aircraft and this was confirmed by the *Orion* at 8.27am. Consequently he ordered his ships to increase speed to 22 knots, the maximum allowed by the *Warspite*, but in any case barely two knots short of his fastest battleship *Valiant*'s top speed. At 9.05am a plane from the *Formidable* sighted other enemy ships north of the cruisers pursuing Force B. Cunningham was aware that Italian battleships had been spotted, but was still not sure of numbers, and he prepared a strike force from the carrier of six Albacore torpedo-bombers of 826 Squadron and two Fulmars of 803 Squadron and at 9.25am he asked also for 201 Group in Greece to send flying boats to help locate the enemy fleet.

While Cunningham was not as air-minded as Somerville, for example, who was a flyer himself, Taranto Night had made him realise the great potential of aircraft carriers, although '(like) most of his contemporaries on both sides of the Atlantic, he believed that the job of the carrier was to find the enemy fleet, then slow it down enough so that the big guns could come up and sink it. This is essentially how he used his aircraft in Mediterranean actions, . . .'. This certainly was the way he gained many of his successes, but such tactics may in part have been forced upon him by the lack of aircraft carriers and modern aircraft reducing the effectiveness of his carrier strikes.[42]

The critical situation of Force B compelled Cunningham to launch his air strike at 9.38am, earlier than he had planned. They sighted the *Vittorio Veneto* with her escorting destroyers at 10.58am and attacked her at 11.27am, providentially relieving Force B. Met by AA fire from the Italian ships, the Albacores aimed for the *Vittorio Veneto* while the two Fulmars engaged two Ju88s of the 1st Strategic Reconnaissance Unit, shooting down one and driving the other off. The lumbering torpedo-bombers had to slowly catch up with the speeding battleship, all the while under fire from her escort. Eventually they reached attack positions and launched their torpedoes from about 2200 yards. It was thought that one torpedo had hit, but all had passed astern of the battleship. The attack forced Iachino to take evasive action and contact was lost with Force B. With the presence of an aircraft carrier now confirmed, he decided to turn north-west for home at 11.40am.

At the same time, roughly 70 miles away, Cunningham sent the *Valiant* with the destroyers *Nubian* and *Mohawk* ahead at 24 knots, but the aircraft had been unable to slow the Italian Fleet down enough for his ships to catch up with them. At 8.45am 815 Squadron based on Crete had been ordered to attack the Italian cruisers engaging Force B with its Swordfish, three of which made an unsucessful attack on the *Bolzano* at 12.05pm. But an attack at 3.20pm by three Albacores and two Swordfish from the *Formidable* supported by three Blenheims from Greece, led by Lieutenant-Commander Dayell-Stead, was far more successful. Dayell-Stead's Albacore, before being shot down, launched a torpedo from about 1000 yards, hitting Iachino's flagship on her port side, damaging her sternmost screw and bringing the ship to a stop at 3.30pm for 6 minutes. She got under way again at only 16 knots, later improving it to 19½ knots, because of the damage to her screw. 'Heavy damage occurred within minutes after the explosion. Some watertight hatches and doors sprung open in the area of the torpedo hit.' She shipped 3500 tons of water. Shortly afterwards a near-miss from a Blenheim caused some further flooding and temporarily disabled the steering gear.[43] Although his fleet had been slowed, Iachino was not overly worried, because at 2.25pm he had received an incorrect sighting report of one battleship and one carrier 80 miles east of his force at 12.15pm, further away than the British actually were. Cunningham now had a chance to catch up with the Italian fleet before dusk.

At 12.30pm Force B had come in sight of Force A and Cunningham's ships could now operate together. He had established a line of two destroyers between the two forces to relay visual signals, thus reducing unnecessary radio traffic. Later in the afternoon, the speed of Cunningham's fleet was helped when the easterly wind dropped. *Formidable* could now fly off her aircraft without having to pull out of the line and turn into the wind, while the rest of the fleet would have to slow down in order to keep together. On this day the *Formidable* would conduct twenty-one separate flight operations, though many were just the launching of a single scout.

Further attacks were made on the Italians by the Blenheims based in Greece later in the afternoon, but without success. Only when the British attacks had ended did the air cover from the *X Fliegerkorps* arrive, ten Me110s that escorted the Italian ships for 50 minutes, beyond the limit of 22°E in the operational agreement with the Germans. Iachino's requests at 4.00pm and 5.00pm for air cover and attacks on the British aircraft carrier were denied because the aircraft would be unable to intervene before dusk. Furthermore, the *Luftwaffe* did not like to engage when British and Italian ships were in close proximity because of problems in ship identification.

At 4.15pm Iachino received a worrying report from the German 1st Strategic Reconnaissance Unit that at 3.15pm a group of three British cruisers had exiting the Antikithera Channel (Cerigotto to the Italians), heading south-west, thus threatening to cut the Italians off from the north-east, but the ships were in fact the destroyers *Juno*, *Defender* and *Jaguar* of Force D sent by Cunningham to patrol the straits north-west of Crete. As a result, Iachino alerted the 1st Division of this potential threat and then issued orders to change the fleet's formation. The damaged battleship was placed in the centre of the fleet with the cruisers of the 1st Division (*Zara*, *Pola* and *Fiume*) and the 9th Destroyer Flotilla to starboard and the 3rd Division (*Trieste*, *Trento* and *Bolzano*) with the 12th Flotilla to port. The *Vittorio Veneto* had the destroyers *Granatiere* and *Fuciliere* ahead of her and the *Bersagliere* and *Alpino* astern, while the two light cruisers of the 8th Division were sent on to Brindisi. This concentration hindered Vice-Admiral Pridham-Wippell maintaining contact with the enemy, but he kept in pursuit, remaining out of visual range.

The Italians had mounted one air attack with two S.79 torpedo-bombers a little before 1.00pm. Before the *Formidable* rejoined the British battleships, two attacked from different angles at very low level, and were not sighted until almost too late. One of them was piloted by the soon to be famous Carlo Emanuele Buscaglia, who reported a battleship, carrier, six cruisers and five destroyers steaming at 18 knots.[44] But Iachino did not receive this report for some time, as it followed the complete chain of command before being passed to the fleet, and the reports he did receive mentioned only that the ships had been sighted, not that they had been attacked. These problems were due to the fact that instructions for communications between the Aegean Air Command and the fleet had only been issued by *Superaereo* on 28 March and did not arrive until after the action. In contrast, the *X Fliegerkorps'* reports were passed directly to the German liaision team aboard the *Vittorio Veneto*, thus allowing far closer co-operation. Not having information of Buscaglia's attack, the generally varied quality of the intelligence reaching Iachino that afternoon seriously affected his asessment of the situation. For example, the Italian radio direction-finding stations at Porto Palo and Borgo Piave detected what was probably the flagship of the Mediterranean Fleet at 110 miles from Tobruk bearing 60°, which led Iachino to believe that the British were about 170 miles south-east of him, again far further away than they actually were.

After Buscaglia's attack, another S.79, piloted by Major Cannaviello of the 34th Bomber Group, was sent against the British ships, which were supposed to be a convoy, attacking at 5.35pm and claiming to have hit a cruiser. His first report only mentioned the possible hit on the cruiser and was not made until an hour after he had returned to base. His second report arrived at *Superaereo* at 8.30pm but was also intercepted three times by *Vittorio Veneto*. This report contained all the relevant information, *ie* position, speed, course of the enemy ships and showed that the supposed 'convoy' was in fact the British fleet. First, there were no convoys in the eastern Mediterranean, which Iachino was aware of, and secondly, it was heading directly towards the Italian fleet, unusual behaviour for a transport convoy! The S.79s of the Aegean Air Command sighted and attacked the British fleet twice during the 28th but this had no effect on the assessment of the situation made by Iachino. His postwar memoirs defended his evaluation of the enemy forces:

> Therefore, when at about 8.00pm *Supermarina* informed us that from radio intercepts resulted that a group of enemy ships was at sea in one point about 75 miles eastwards of the *Vittorio Veneto*, we did think of course that they could be the main Alexandria force, which we supposed to be returning to her base.[45]

Meanwhile Force A was closing on the unaware Italians at their best speed of 21 knots.

At this point, Lieutenant-Commander A S Bolt, aboard the *Warspite*'s spotter plane, made a vital contribution to the eventual destruction of the Italian 1st Cruiser Division in an operation that contrasts starkly with the failings of Italian air reconnaissance. Bolt had been catapulted from the *Warspite* at 12.15pm to maintain a link between Force A and Force B and to 'report generally on the tactical situation as seen from the air'. Cunningham decided to recover the aircraft even though it would slow his pursuit of the Italian fleet, but Bolt's pilot and the crane crew on the *Warspite* worked so well together that he later estimated that the *Warspite* never slowed to less than 18 knots while the plane was being brought aboard. In contrast, the Italian catapult-launched aircraft had to go on to land bases, as their ships could not recover them at all.

After a flight of almost five hours, Bolt saw the 'chaotic plot' of the situation aboard the flagship and decided that he might be able to offer clarification. Force B had reported no visual contact with the Italian fleet for some time, which did not please Cunningham. The wide variety of reports coming from numerous sources, including scout planes (some with inexperienced observers), the aircraft from *Formidable* and bases on Crete, and signals inteligence, created as many questions as they answered.

Bolt later wrote, 'As soon as we were refuelled we were catapulted [at 5.45pm] to clear up the situation caused by conflicting reports about the position, course, speed, composition, and disposition of the enemy fleet'. Bolt sighted the *Vittorio Veneto* at 6.20pm and began reporting at 6.31pm, which helped clarify the situation for Cunningham and allowed Force B to make visual and radar contact with the rearmost ships Italian fleet by 7.15pm. Bolt eventually landed at Suda Bay and would receive a bar to his DSC.

Porta's team aboard the *Vittorio Veneto* intercepted and read a message sent at 6.18pm by Cunningham asking the Swordfish of 815 Squadron based at Maleme to attack the Italian fleet. At 7.28pm six Albacores from the *Formidable* and two Swordfish from Crete sighted the Italian ships, which adopted a new tactic. Iachino ordered the port and starboard columns to make smoke and all ships to turn their searchlights on the attacking aircraft. As twilight descended the ships also put up a tremendous AA barrage – the *Vittorio Veneto* at one point fired a salvo from her main armament at the attacking aircraft. All this broke up the first attack and the torpedo planes had to come in separately.

At 7.58pm one of the aircraft dropped its torpedo 546 yards from the heavy cruiser *Pola*, which had had to stop engines to avoid colliding with the *Fiume* ahead of her and was thus unable to take evasive action. The torpedo hit amidships on the starboard side, flooding five of her boilers and damaging the main steam pipeline, which brought the ship to a dead stop and all electrical power was lost. The escaping steam from the fractured pipe was mistaken for smoke from a fire, and the captain ordered the 4in ammunition in the vicinity of the hit to be thrown overboard to prevent explosions. He then ordered the crew to stand down from action stations and prepare the ship to be taken in tow.[46]

The ship was found to be in no immediate danger of sinking and was able to get under way again around midnight at 6 knots. Only at 8.40pm did her commander ask Iachino to have his ship taken in tow, but he was already aware of the *Pola*'s situation from signals from her sister-ships at 8.15pm.[47]

The British aircraft had therefore scored an excellent hit that brought about an important victory in the war in the Mediterranean. The Italians noted that the British air attacks were well carried out, the planes attacking from the bow and stern where the ships had less AA defence. After the battle it was suggested that the

Italians adopt the German quadruple 20mm AA gun, since this calibre appeared to be more effective than the 37mm used by the Italian ships. The German gun did not have the range of the 37mm, but it was more reliable and had a rate of fire of 400-500 rounds per minute compared to the Italian gun's 120 rounds per minute.[48]

At 6.15pm Cunningham sent a signal with orders for the search for the Italian Fleet that night, but this one was not read by the team aboard the *Vittorio Veneto*, nor by the *Supermarina* cryptanalysts. Cunningham decided to 'form a striking force of eight destroyers under Captain Philip Mack, of the *Jervis*' and at 8.37pm detached it, formed around the 2nd and 14th Destroyer Flotillas, to intercept the damaged battleship, supposed to be on a course of 295° at 13 knots. Mack's force set off at 28 knots bearing 300° toward the slowly retreating enemy, estimated to be only 33 miles ahead.[49]

Cunningham would also continue the pursuit into the night with the main fleet, despite the opinions of his staff officers who did not want the fleet to come into waters covered by Italian air power. Cunningham had his dinner and then decided to press on. But this was also the Admiral who said to Commander Manley Power (later Admiral) when he was appointed to his staff, 'I hate staff officers who agree with me'.[50]

At 5.45pm *Supermarina* had estimated the position of the British fleet flagship as being 75 miles south-east of Iachino, when it was in fact 20 miles closer, but when Iachino was informed of this at 8.05pm, he paid little attention to the fact that the British fleet was probably nearer than supposed in view of his slowed flagship.

This appears confirmed when Iachino a few minutes later, at 8.18pm, instructed Vice-Admiral Cattaneo, commander of the 1st Division, to return and escort the *Pola* with the remainder of his force. But he also warned the *Zara* that at 4.00pm *Supermarina* had informed him that 'one enemy battleship, four heavy cruisers, three light cruisers, twelve destroyers were at 34°05' N and 25°04' E course 30° and high speed'.[51]

There was an exchange of messages between the two commanders and at 9.06pm Cattaneo moved to help the *Pola*. It has always taken for granted that Vice-Admiral Cattaneo agreed to this order, but he did not because the state of fuel of his destroyers. He was therefore forced to have his cruisers in the lead with the destroyers trailing behind, all at the slow speed of 16 knots so the destroyers could conserve fuel.

As pointed out by Santoni,

> to cover the sea space of 67 miles and steam to the point in which the Italian fleet was attacked by air, to look for one or more ships that the British pilots claimed to have hit, it would be necessary for a British 'complex command' [the naval High Command] to travel just a little more than three hours at the probable speed of 20-21 knots. Consequently it would be reasonable to suppose that such an enemy naval group would arrive in the waters where the *Pola* was dead on the water just after 11.00pm. In reality the contact took place after 10.00pm because, as recalled before, the British naval HQ was 20 miles nearer that estimated by Intelligence service of *Supermarina*.[52]

At 8.15pm the radar of the *Ajax*, a surface Type 279, and *Orion*'s fixed Type 286M set picked up a ship about 6 miles to port, dead in the water. Informed of this at 9.11pm, Admiral Cunningham changed course to 280° to close in. Then at 10.10pm the *Valiant's* radar (*Warspite* was not equipped with it) detected a large stationary ship 6 miles ahead, estimated to be 600ft in length, which he suspected was the torpedoed *Vittorio Veneto*, but was in fact the *Pola*. Shortly afterwards HMAS *Stuart* sighted Cattaneo's approaching squadron.

Force A sped toward the *Pola*, turning 40° to port, when suddenly three other vessels appeared on radar at 10.25pm at about 4000 yards, followed by three more. Before these ships were identified, Cunningham ordered his battleships to turn towards the enemy, not normally a recommended manoeuvre at night. They were sighted by Cunningham's Chief of Staff, Commodore John Edelsten, and were correctly identified as *Zara* class cruisers.[53]

At about 10.20pm the Italians had also spotted some ships but they were thought to be Italians, so one or two red recognition flares were fired, but there was no reply. Their 8in guns were still trained fore and aft and lacked anti-flash powder – they were totally unprepared for what was about to befall them.

Cunningham immediately ordered a course of 280° and to form line ahead, towards the enemy ships. As he approached at 20 knots, he led with the *Warspite*, followed by the *Valiant*, *Formidable*, and *Barham*. A mile to starboard were the destroyers *Stuart* (still under the command of Captain Waller) and *Havock*, while a mile to port were the *Greyhound* and *Griffin*. This put the disabled *Pola* somewhat to port of the British and between them and the other Italian ships. The *Formidable* turned out of the line shortly before the action opened.

The second ship of Cattaneo's divison, the *Fiume*, was the first to be illuminated by the *Greyhound*'s, searchlights and became the first target. As the battleships moved into line ahead and opened fire, they also switched on their searchlights. At 10.27pm the *Warspite* opened fire on the *Fiume* at about 3800 yards, quickly followed by the other battleships. The first 15in salvo from the *Warspite* was of six shells, five of which were seen to hit the target. A second main-battery salvo followed as her 6in secondary batteries joined in. As the first shells hit, the gunnery officer was heard to exclaim, as if surprised, 'Good Lord! We've hit her!' She fired a total of fourteen 15in shells (two salvoes) and sixteen 6in shells in four salvoes and then switched targets to the *Zara*, which received four 15in salvoes and four 6in salvoes of sixteen shells, the range having dropped to about 3000 yards. The total number of 15in shells she fired was between twenty and twenty-six. She then fired one 15in salvo (six shells) and two 6in salvoes (eight shells) at the *Alfieri* which was seen to be turning towards her, and hits were probably scored. Finally, a second destroyer appeared in the distance to port, and received one 6in salvo, which fortunately missed as she was HMS *Havock* closing in on the enemy! *Warspite* then turned and led the battleline away.

Valiant first opened fire on the *Fiume* at 4000 yards with one 15in salvo of four shells and seven 4.5in salvoes totalling some seventy rounds. She then shifted fire to the *Zara* and fired five more 15in salvoes (thirty-five shells), and hits were seen. She probably also fired five 4.5in salvoes totalling fifty shells and then ceased fire.[54]

The *Barham* first trained her guns on the *Pola* and continued to aim on her as Cunningham brought the battle line around to attack Cattaneo's approaching squadron. As she shifted her guns to the new enemy, the *Warspite* illuminated the *Fiume* and a cruiser ahead of her and so the *Barham*'s gunnery officer switched targets to the *Zara*. After two partial salvoes of only seven 15in shells the *Zara* turned away and was thought to have sunk, so *Barham* shifted her fire to the unfortunate *Fiume* which now received three more 15in salvoes of fourteen shells, and six 6in salvoes totalling thirty-four shells, and then ceased fire.

The Italians were completely surprised by the British fire, as recalled by Commander Guidi of the *Fiume*:

> The first two shots hit the stern, one between X and Y turrets and another more to the stern, toward the point where I was. I was wounded, but the sailors and the boatswain that were speaking with me disappeared and I did not ever again see them. Between the two turrets raised a high flame. The stern deck remained strongly hunchbacked. Most of the sailors at the stern were dead and there were cries from the severely wounded. In the meanwhile the ship was clearly heeling to starboard.[55]

Only the Italian destroyers astern of the cruisers counterattacked. One of them, the *Alfieri*, launched torpedoes, but at 10.31pm the British battleships made a 90° turn away from them, after only 4½ minutes of fire. The 15in salvos had completely shattered the Italian cruisers, transforming them into 'nothing but glowing torches and on fire from stem to stern'. The *Fiume* sank rapidly but the *Zara* remained afloat for some time, until scuttling charges were detonated, although she was helped on her way by torpedoes and gunfire from the *Stuart*. Admiral Cattaneo was alive after the initial action with the battleships, but died when his ship went down.[56] The *Formidable* had turned out of the line to starboard to keep clear of gunfire but the *Warspite* mistakenly trained her guns on her – Cunningham personally stopped her from firing. At 10.28pm Iachino saw the flashes of the big guns 45 miles astern and finally realised how near the British battleships were to him.

Now the British battleships turned away to starboard and left the four destroyers to finish off the wrecked enemy ships. Having seen the gun flashes on this moonless night, the executive officer of the *Pola*, Commander Brengola, asked permission to clear for action with the secondary batteries and this was done, but De Pisa ordered boiler No. 8 turned off. It had been restarted but produced too much smoke. About at 11.15pm Captain De Pisa gave the order to abandon ship, having found that there were almost no 4in ammunition, much of which had either been used or thrown overboard earlier.

While the ship was being abandoned, the *Havock* sighted her and opened fire, setting her on fire. Some sailors jumped into the sea, but others who had left the ship came back on board again due the cold water. *Havock* reported first that she had attacked a battleship, but then she corrected the report saying that it was a heavy cruiser, but she had already expended all her torpedoes. At 1.40am the *Greyhound* and *Griffin* arrived and picked up many survivors. Later at 3.25am Captain Mack's *Jervis* arrived and went alongside the *Pola*, rescuing the remaining 257 crew and taking several Breda machine-guns to augment her AA defences. Both the *Jervis* and *Nubian* then launched a torpedo and the *Pola* finally sank at 4.10am.[57]

Later that morning, two of the crew of the *Jervis* approached an Italian sailor who was off by himself. They tried to open up a conversation when 'imagine our surprise when he suddenly blurted out in broad American: 'I'm f..k..g fed up with this war!' It turned out he was visiting his homeland when war broke out and had been drafted into the Navy![58]

The small-ship actions that night were confused, but can be summarised as follows. The damaged *Alfieri* was near the *Pola*, and the *Stuart*, after coming upon the crippled *Pola*, saw her stopped, on fire and listing heavily. She capsized and sank some time after midnight. While the *Stuart* was thus engaged, an Italian destroyer almost collided with her, racing past her to starboard less than 150 yards away. She was fired upon by the *Stuart* but missed and it was likely the target was the *Carducci*, which did not return fire because the *Stuart* was firing Breda gun tracers and may have been mistaken for an Italian ship.[59] The *Carducci* was then attacked by the *Havock* which fired four torpedoes, and hit her with one at 11:15pm. *Havock* then took her under fire and, ablaze and sinking, she went down 15 minutes later. The *Oriani* and *Gioberti* both escaped that night.

Captain Mack's destroyers, having no radar, had missed the *Vittorio Veneto* having passed astern of the Italian ships some miles to the south.[60] Also Admiral Pridham-Wippell, not being in contact with the Italians, was ordered to disengage in order to avoid accidental clashes with Mack's destroyers on that moonless night, planning to rendezvous in the morning.

The destroyers rescued a total of 905 men, breaking off when German planes appeared. A further 110 were rescued by Greek destroyers. Losses were high as the slow hospital ship *Gradisca* only reached the scene on 31 March, too late to save more than 160 men in 6 days of searching. The Italian Navy lost a total of 2303 dead and 1411 prisoners at Matapan.

The British destroyers rejoined the fleet at 7.00am, and Cunningham's ships turned for Alexandria, coming under air attack only once on the way and suffering no damage. The *Vittorio Veneto* would be under repair until August 1941.[61]

The papers of the Italian commision of inquiry into the battle and the loss of the cruisers reveal that Iachino was wrong to send the other ships back and Admiral Cattaneo had not agreed with this decision, as has previously been thought, in part because the fuel status of his destroyers, which, as Chirico has recently argued, would not allow them to manoeuvre properly to provide a screen for the larger ships.[62] In other words, if Iachino had abandoned the crippled *Pola*, he would have lost only one ship instead of five, and what was a tactical defeat would not have been turned into a national disaster.[63]

For many years the surprise at Matapan was suspected to be the result of treason. Commander Brengola, who was First Officer of the *Pola*, once rescued and aboard the *Jervis*, had the chance to read an order of the day signed by Admiral Cunningham and addressed to officers and sailors of the Royal Navy which foresaw the coming battle posted on a wardroom bulkhead. The order was dated on the same day, 26 March, on which Brengola was suddenly recalled to his ship for a mission which turned out to be Operation 'Gaudo'. The obvious conclusion was that the Italian Fleet had been betrayed.[64]

A traitor was also commonly held responsible for giving the British information on the North African convoys, which were often attacked with great precision. The

Germans suspected an Italian, Rommel actually making direct accusations against Italian naval officers, and *vice versa*, suspicions which the British encouraged, for example in Operation 'Crusader' and during the battle of Alam Halfa.[65] But when the role of ULTRA in decrypting Italian Navy and *Luftwaffe* messages was revealed, the truth was known and explained why the British were so well informed about the Italian operation. Its role must not, however, be overemphasised. In 1941 it still had many problems to overcome, and the British success at Matapan owed just as much to good interpretation of the information ULTRA made available, and to Cunningham's excellent instincts. But it was nonetheless a vital advantage for the British.[66]

Radar also played a part, since the visibility on that moonless night was only 2½ miles. The report written after the battle stressed the 'high degree of effectiveness reached by the British naval units in the night gunfire'. It was mainly attributed to radar, which allowed them 'to prepare their weapons to begin immediately the fire action as soon as the enemy was sighted'. One important result of this action was that the Italians were now aware the British ships had radar, which they had not known previously.[67] A complex series of factors led to the Matapan disaster, one of which was the tendency of Iachino to take risks beyond his capabilities. All the others were due the generally inferior technology of the Italian fleet, which entered the war far behind the Royal Navy in equipment, training and resources.

The Chief of the German Navy Liaison Command commented that the result of the operation, although the details were still not available, showed that the command of the Italian Navy had not grasped the situation and how to deal with it. The best solution would be for a German officer to take overall command of a combined fleet. This would be difficult, and high-level intervention would be better. In his view the exchange of officers for common experience, as recently happened in the Aegean sector, would also be helpful.[68]

On 7 April 1941, Vice Admiral Fioravanzo, later historian of the Italian Navy, wrote in one memorandum:

> The night's events happened because, lacking every experience for a case of this kind, the Commander in Chief did not take the responsibility to abandon the ship [*Pola*], nor did the air reconnaissance of the day allow him to guess how near the enemy force was. The intervention of *Supermarina* to free him of this responsibility, ordering him to abandon the *Pola*, came, unfortunately, too late . . .[69]

CHAPTER 12

The Invasion of Crete, May 1941

Stick it out. Navy must not let Army down.
No enemy forces must reach Crete by sea.

Admiral Cunningham[1]

V ichy France enjoyed a rare success on 30 March 1941 when they successfully ran a convoy of six ships escorted by the destroyer *Simoun* through the Straits of Gibraltar to Oran. It was thought to be carrying war material, primarily rubber from Indo-China (although this had already been off-loaded at Casablanca) and the cruiser *Sheffield* and four destroyers tried to intercept it, but the coastal batteries forced the British to retire after a brief exchange of fire. The French retaliated with five minor air attacks on the *Sheffield*'s squadron and several near misses shook up the cruiser and a destroyer, but no serious damage resulted, and the ships anchored safely at midnight.[2]

The Italian submarine *Ambra* was preparing to return to base after the Matapan operatiom when she sighted a convoy of two freighters, escorted by the AA cruiser *Bonaventure* and three destroyers, off Alexandria. The *Bonaventure*, steaming at 16½ knots, was torpedoed from a range of 2200 yards and sank quickly with the loss of 138 lives. HMAS *Stuart* made sonar contact and attacked the *Ambra* seven times but failed to destroy her.

More ominous for the Allies was the shifting of elements of the *X Fliegerkorps* east and the deployment of more German air assets to the Balkans for the operation against Greece. Preparations for German intervention, together with her minor Balkan allies, against Greece was approaching. One early event was the air attack on a British convoy bound for Greece when over a period of 2 days, Ju88s operating from Italy sank three freighters totalling 21,155 tons. Earlier in March there had been some losses, and the invasion of Greece and Yugoslavia would begin on 6 April, involving nearly 1000 Axis aircraft.

* * *

On 3 April Force H successfully carried out Operation 'Winch', flying in twelve of the first Hurricane Mark IIs to Malta. One was badly damaged on landing but they were very welcome, along with two more Skuas. These new Hurricanes were faster, had heavier armament and could be fitted with extra fuel tanks for longer range.

On the eve of the Greek débâcle, the British had decided that something more had to be done about the Axis supply line between Italy and Libya. Cunningham now felt that the air threat at Malta was receding with the Axis losses and the shifting of German air resources away from the island, and so he ordered the 14th Destroyer Flotilla under Captain Mack of the *Jervis* to Malta from Suda Bay. Mack, as with many British officers, was something of a character, but certainly looked the part of a captain – including snakes tattooed up his arms and wrapped around his chest! Stationed at Valletta, it would be the first Allied surface force to attack Axis convoys at night, arriving at dawn on 11 April. The other destroyers were the *Janus*, with six 4.7in guns and the big *Nubian* and *Mohawk* of the 'Tribal' class, with eight 4.7in guns each. All except the *Jervis* were equipped with radar.[3]

The plan for attacking convoys was to have good intelligence on a convoy, and plot its course for interception off the Tunisian coast, ideally in the area of Kerkenah Bank near Sfax, so the British destroyers would come upon the convoy in the middle of the night as it was starting to head out into deeper water for the run into Tripoli. It would also put the British force farthest away from Axis aircraft operating from either Africa or Europe. However, to arrive there in good time, the Malta force would have to leave and arrive back at Valletta in daylight. The Italians soon became aware that Mack's ships were at Malta, and this in part was the reason why the first two Allied forays failed to find their target convoys.

Their first success came on 15 April when a Maryland reconnaissance plane sighted a convoy of four small German freighters, three with approximately 3000 soldiers on board and the fourth, along with an Italian freighter the *Sabaudia*, carrying ammunition, plodding south at 8 knots. Flagship of the escort was the *Navigatori* class destroyer *Tarigo* armed with six 4.7in guns, commanded by Captain Piero Di Cristofaro, leading the two smaller destroyers *Lampo* and *Baleno*. The Maryland, darting in and out of the heavy cloud cover, shadowed the convoy, and was later relieved by a second aircraft. Their reports aided Mack in his approach to battle, as did radio traffic from the convoy that was intercepted by radio operators aboard his ships.

Mack was steaming from Malta at 26 knots with the *Jervis* in the lead, followed by the *Janus*, *Nubian* and *Mohawk*. Meanwhile, Cristofaro was aware he was being shadowed and had requested air support, but due to bad weather, only one S.79 got airborne and it failed to find Mack. All hands were at battle stations, but the wind was high and visibility poor. As Mack approached the coast he zigzagged and slowed to 20 knots, looking for the convoy where he expected to find it, but had no luck. Finally, after almost an hour of searching, at 1.58am on 16 April, the *Nubian*'s radar picked up the convoy at a range of about 12,000 yards and further out to sea than the British. Therefore, Mack would be approaching it from the rear and from a direction they would least expect. The crescent moon was on the leeside of the convoy, illuminating the convoy and hiding his force.[4]

The convoy was deployed as shown opposite. The British trained their torpedoes to port and began approaching the wing of the convoy where the *Baleno* was closest to Mack. Finally, at 2.20am and at a range of 2400 yards, the *Jervis* opened fire to port with her main armament and her AA guns. Two minutes later the *Janus* joined in, using her radar to direct her gunnery and the *Baleno* was soon seriously damaged, her captain and all her officers killed or wounded early in the action. Left in a sinking condition, her crew managed to run her aground on a sandbank, but she would be a total loss. The *Nubian* was now firing on the *Sabaudia* which caught fire on the third salvo. She was then hit by a torpedo from the *Janus* and the

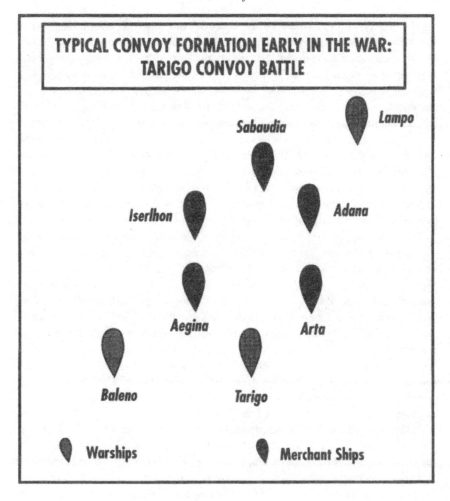

TYPICAL CONVOY FORMATION EARLY IN THE WAR: TARIGO CONVOY BATTLE

Lampo

Sabaudia

Iserlhon

Adana

Aegina

Arta

Baleno

Tarigo

Warships

Merchant Ships

ammunition-laden ship exploded, sending a pillar of water and debris 2000ft in the air and fragments, some weighing as much as 20lbs, rained down on the nearby *Jervis*.

The battle was a confused melee with 'ranges which varied from 50 yards to 2000'. All the transports would be sunk, although one of the German freighters, along with the *Lampo*, managed to ground on the nearby sandbank. The *Tarigo* bravely reversed course and charged the British line, exchanging heavy fire with the *Nubian* at 1000 yards. Now the *Mohawk*, which had passed between the *Tarigo* and *Nubian*, joined with the *Jervis* in firing on the *Tarigo*. Captain Cristofaro lost a leg to a large shell splinter, but continued to con the ship until he died from loss of blood. He would be awarded the *Medaglia d'Oro*. Ensign Ettore Bisagno, the only officer of the *Tarigo* to survive the action, had to assume command. With the ship dead in the water, on fire and sinking, he managed to fire one torpedo and a few minutes later another, whilst still under fire.

The first struck the *Mohawk* on the starboard side at a little after 2.30am, while she was avoiding being rammed by one of the freighters, and about 5 minutes later, as she turned, the second one hit her on the port side. She would settle on a sandbank and would have to be shelled to open her up and allow her to sink to a depth of 7 fathoms. Forty-one of her crew were lost. The surviving British destroyers turned for home at 4.00am and reached Valletta 6 hours later.

The Italians were busily picking up survivors and patching up the *Lampo* which would eventually make port and return to Italy for complete repairs on 8 August. Losses were severe, with only 1271 men out of more than 3000 surviving this massacre and even the one freighter that that had been beached was not saved as the submarine *Upholder* later sent a party on board and blew her up. Vice-Admiral Weichold was of the opinion that the Italians should have sent a light cruiser with the convoy for added protection since they were aware of the threat from surface warships.

A little-known sequel to the destruction of the *Tarigo*'s convoy came when a German reconnaissance aircraft overflew the site and spotted the sunken *Mohawk* in shallow water. It was suspected that her rapid sinking might mean important documents were still on board, so late in April a *X MAS* party of six volunteer frogmen under the command of Commander Eliseo Porta, late of Admiral Iachino's staff, dived on the wreck, despite the turbulent waters and the threat of sharks, in the hope of recovering them. They found a few documents in the muddy waters, but the radar set was too heavy to raise. The documents included a code delivery group that was no longer in use and a map of the minefields at Alexandria, which would be of help in the coming SLC attack. The British later bombed the wreck as they knew the codebooks were still on board and they may have wanted to destroy the radar set.

Later, Giuseppe Guglielmo joined the *X MAS* as a diver and learned of this operation. After the war, in 1952 he was detailed to dive on the *Tarigo* and while doing that visited the wreck of the *Mohawk*. There he found and recovered the rusted but still intact cipher box, which contained the current naval code, and after bringing it up found the by then heavily-damaged papers. It is interesting to speculate what use the Italians would have made of these if they had recovered them back in 1941.[5]

The significance of the destruction of the *Tarigo* convoy was threefold. First, at one blow an entire convoy was effectively destroyed, a striking success which at this stage of the war Allied submarine and air attacks could not achieve. Secondly, the surface ships had shown that they were still a force to be reckoned with, and thirdly it gave notice to the Axis that the relative ease of transport to Libya which they had enjoyed in 1940 and early 1941 was over.

*   *   *

Before turning to the events that were unfolding in the Balkans, the Mediterranean fleet carried out several other operations at this time, including a dangerous attack against the port of Tripoli. It was an operation that Churchill had forced on Cunningham and his original idea was to sink a blockship in the harbour mouth. He had been upset with the first two failed attempts by the 14th Flotilla in finding convoys. Although he did send a message of congratulations after the destruction of the *Tarigo* convoy, he also wrote at the time, 'Yes, brilliantly redeemed. But what about the next [convoy]?'.[6] He wanted to block the harbour of Tripoli with the old First World War battleship *Centurion*, now a target ship, but Cunningham pointed out that she was too slow to cover the distance between Malta and Tripoli in daylight. On 16 April Churchill then proposed using the *Barham*, but Cunningham did not want to lose the ship and a still considerable crew on something so prone to failure as sinking such a large ship in waters that in places were only 2ft below the keel.

Therefore, Cunningham recommended a bombardment by the main fleet in lieu of the blocking operation. The fleet consisted of two forces, one made up of the trio of battleships that had been at Matapan and their escorts, and a second force built around the *Formidable*. The fleet left Alexandria on 18 April, ostensibly to escort the transport *Breconshire* to Malta and bring out four empty merchant ships and it successfully covered these convoys.[7]

After arriving at Valletta, Cunningham reorganised the fleet and combined with part of Mack's force to create the following:

- Convoy: four freighters, the AA cruiser *Calcutta* and the new *Dido* class cruiser *Phoebe* with the *Nubian*, carrying survivors from the *Mohawk*, and the refitted destroyer *Diamond* (soon to be lost on 27 April).
- The three battleships, the light cruiser *Gloucester* and the destroyers *Jervis*, *Janus*, *Juno*, and *Jaguar* acting as an anti-submarine screen.
- The *Formidable* accompanied by the light cruisers *Orion* (flagship of Vice-Admiral Pridham-Wippell), *Perth* and *Ajax* with four destroyers.
- Four destroyers, the *Hotspur*, *Hero*, *Havock* and *Hasty* employing their mine-sweeping gear ('A' to 'H' class destroyers were built with limited minesweeping capability), out ahead of the battleships to sweep the approachs to Tripoli.

The force then raced towards Tripoli on the night of 20-21 April where it was to rendezvous with the submarine *Truant* to establish a firing point for a night bombardment. She was to act as a marker 4 miles off the port. The four heavy ships passed around the *Truant* like a ship would steam around a buoy, and then at 5.00am opened fire at a range of about 7 miles. For 45 minutes the port was shelled by the three battleships, the light cruiser and Mack's four destroyers with 15in, 6in and 4.7in salvoes. The *Gloucester* was there primarily for counter-battery fire. The *Formidable*'s planes joined in, dropping bombs, spotting the fall of shot, and also assessing damage. Lieutenant H H H Mulleneux of the *Jervis* later wrote:

> The party was started by the RAF and FAA who bombed the place. This was highly spectacular with guns firing, bombs dropping, flares and best of the bright red and green tracers from the 'Wop' close range AA guns . . . . [At 5.00am] more flares were dropped and more guns went off including the 15 inch from the battleships which are always a fine sight at night.[8]

The shore batteries replied but only after a 20-minute delay and failed to hit any of the British ships. The following day there was no retaliation by the Axis air forces and the only damage done to the attackers was when a mine exploded near the *Valiant*, doing only minor damage. This lack of effective retaliation must have been in part due to the Greek and Maltese operations involving large numbers of the available Axis aircraft and the fact that the attack was a complete surprise.[9]

At the time the damage was thought to be greater than it was, and most sources even today give varied figures. The torpedo-boat *Partenope* was slightly damaged but her commander was killed. A guard boat was sunk along with two freighters and another damaged. The port was also considerably damaged in the attack including the docks, an air force depot, two hospitals, two barracks and the provincial administrator's residence. Fifty-five died of whom 19 were military personnel (eight Italians) and 126 wounded of which 35 were military. Ironically, the explosion of an ammunition ship in the harbour on 3 May would cause greater damage than the bombardment.[10]

The bombardment of Tripoli was a major effort (a 5-day operation), that Cunningham thought could equally well have been accomplished by a heavy bomber squadron. Churchill later wanted to base a battleship at Malta to attack convoys, although Cunningham wanted to know how it was to be resupplied with fuel from an island under siege!

On 27 April Force H conducted an operation that would send reinforcements to Cunningham. Operation 'Dunlop' had the *Argus* fly off twenty-four Hurricanes of which twenty-three arrived at Malta after a 3 hour and 20 minute flight, with three Fulmars from the *Ark Royal* guiding them.[11] By now the *Luftwaffe* was operating Me109s from Sicily and one of their famous aces, Lieutenant Joachim Muncheberg, was making a career of shooting down RAF planes, getting a mammoth Sunderland on this day. His unit, never numbering more than nine Me109s, had arrived in February. Muncheberg had 23 kills when he arrived and would go on to be credited with 135 victories before being shot down over Tunisia by an American-piloted Spitfire on 23 March 1943.[12]

Breaking off from Force H to join Cunningham was the new light cruiser *Dido*, the fast minelayer *Abdiel* and the 5th Destroyer Flotilla commanded by Lord Mountbatten in the *Kelly* and consisting of five other modern destroyers. Mountbatten would take over the duties of Captain Mack at Malta, whose three destroyers, after sinking a naval auxiliary off Lampedusa Island about midnight on the 23rd, would leave for Alexandria with the *Dido* and *Abdiel*. Cunningham had sent the light cruiser *Gloucester* to Valletta to reinforce Malta as the Italians were now sending cruisers to give distant support to their convoys plying between Trapani and Tripoli, and this strong squadron became Force K.

Force K was quickly gutted when the destroyer *Jersey*, returning from an operation, hit a newly-laid magnetic mine on 2 May and sank at the harbour entrance, temporarily blocking it. The *Gloucester* and the destroyers *Kipling* and *Kashmir* were outside the harbour and therefore sped off to join Force H at Gibraltar. The *Jersey* was quickly blown up but there were no vessels capable of sweeping for magnetic mines at Malta. The remainder of Force K was sealed in.

Between the fall of Greece and the airborne assault on Crete was the valuable 'Tiger' convoy. The first part of the operation was the dispatch from Gibraltar of thirteen long-range twin-engined Beaufighters to Malta to help give air cover for the convoy, but they would stay on and conduct very effective anti-shipping operations.[13] On 5 May Force H left Gibraltar and passed into the Atlantic, this time to rendezvous with a very special convoy. Coming from Great Britain was the modernised battleship *Queen Elizabeth*, sister ship to the *Warspite*, which was also equipped with radar. Attached was a fast convoy heavily laden with tanks and Hurricanes bound for Wavell to be used in an abortive attempt to relieve Tobruk. Additional reinforcements for Cunningham were the *Gloucester*, the new light cruisers *Naiad* of the *Dido* class (carrying the flag of Rear-Admiral E L S King), the *Fiji*, and four destroyers. The 8500-ton *Fiji* was a brand new cruiser based on the earlier 'Town' class, armed with twelve 6in guns, eight 4in AA and capable of 30 knots.

The convoy passed through the Straits of Gibraltar on the evening of 5-6 May while two others (the slow one consisting of two tankers) left Alexandria bound for Malta. Covering them was Admiral Cunningham with the bulk of the fleet. He did have time to detach the *Ajax* and three destroyers which raced to Benghazi and bombarded it on the night of 7-8 May at close range and sinking two small steamers, one of which was carrying explosives and blew up violently.

By 8 May both forces had been located by Axis reconnaissance, but the Italian fleet's deployment of four cruisers and five destroyers from Palermo was too late. Air attacks by both German and Italian aircraft failed to score any significant hits, although the destroyer *Fortune* of Force H was hit and reduced to a speed of 8 knots on the return journey to Gibraltar. One transport of the 'Tiger' convoy was mined and sunk, and another damaged, but this ship would arrive safely at Alexandria with the others. Unfortunately, an accident with a 4.5in gun aboard the battlecruiser *Renown* killed six men and wounded another twenty-six.

After the harbour mouth had been swept for magnetic mines by the specially-equipped corvette *Gloxinia*, the two convoys from Alexandria arrived safely at Valletta. The five destroyers of Force K, finally freed from their confinement, raced off to Benghazi and bombarded it on the night of 10-11 May. Some of the 'K' class ships had been fitted with a single 4in AA gun and these were used to fire starshell to illuminate the target during the bombardment. By the 12th all ships had returned safely, after experiencing the first dive-bombing performed by moonlight! By 21 May they had left for operations off Crete and once again Malta was left without a surface strike force.[14] But by then the full force of German might had been brought to bear in the eastern Mediterranean, with devastating results.

*   *   *

Just before the German declaration of war on Greece, there was a coup in hitherto pro-Axis Yugoslavia and the new government decided to stand firm against the Germans and Italians. With his forces poised on the Greek border, Hitler was furious and ordered an invasion of Yugoslavia, which would be quickly overrun.

The role played by the Yugoslavian Navy was minimal, but does need to be examined. It was created after the First World War and was established with eight modern and four older torpedo-boats of the former Austro-Hungarian Navy. This was smaller than requested by the newly-formed government but Italian opposition to there being any other viable naval force in the Adriatic prevented them receiving more ships. An example of this opposition was the sinking of the Austro-Hungarian dreadnought *Viribus Unitis* on 1 November 1918 in a clandestine operation by two

Italian officers using a delayed-action mine. Despite later claims by Italian historians that the battleship was still in Austro-Hungarian service, she had in fact already been handed over to the 'Southern Slav Council' and renamed *Jugoslavija*.[15]

The Yugoslavian Navy was not strong, but did contain some modern units, mostly purchased from foreign yards due to her weak economy. She had the ancient cruiser *Dalmacija*, purchased in 1929, which was the former German *Niobe* launched in 1899, and the powerful British-built flotilla leader *Dubrovnik*, which would be captured and renamed *Premuda* by the Italians. She was an example of some of the interesting supply problems this small navy had, with her 'main guns from Czechoslovakia, Swedish AA guns, British torpedo armament, a gunnery fire control system from the Netherlands, and Belgian communications equipment'.[16] Three other destroyers rounded out the flotilla (*Beograd*, *Ljubljana* and *Zagreb*), and there were four submarines, the British-built *Hrabri* and *Nebojsa* and the rather more effective French-built *Smeli* and *Osvietnik*. Two of the three destroyers were raised by the Italians after they were scuttled, the *Ljubljana* entering service as the *Lubiana*, to be later lost escorting a convoy to Tunisia, while the *Beogard* was renamed the *Sebenico*.[17] Of her eight 61-ton German-built E-boats, two would escape to Alexandria and continue the war from there while the remainder were taken into Italian service after the country was overrun. During the interwar years the Yugoslavian Navy forged strong ties with the Czech Skoda works for her armament. In spite of very limited budgets, some ships were added to the Yugoslavian Navy and some of the older ships received new, or more often rebuilt, guns. For example, at least four of the six small *Galeb* class minelayers had rebuilt 83.5mm AA guns, instead of the often listed 90mm guns from the First World War. With the exception of some small-calibre AA weapons, Skoda would go on to supply all the navy's guns.[18]

Ground operations against Yugoslavia began on 5 April, and advanced rapidly everywhere, led by devastating air attacks by the *Luftwaffe*. The navy did not offer any resistance, and one of the older submarines escaped with some other minor craft. The captain of the *Zagreb* blew his ship up at the cost of his own life, but Italy did gain a small addition to her fighting force. Virtually all of Yugoslavia's small merchant marine escaped.

*   *   *

Now it was Greece's turn. From 6 to 29 April the Axis, led by Germany's brilliantly-commanded army, overran the Greek mainland. The opening hours of the invasion brought a terrible disaster to the Allies at Piraeus, the port of Athens. The harbour was crowded with shipping and one vessel, the 7529-ton *Clan Fraser* was unloading on the evening of the 6th, and still had 250 tons of high explosives on board. Other cargo still had to be moved in order to get to the explosives when the *Luftwaffe* attacked the port with twenty Ju88s flying from Sicily, followed by eleven He111s. The *Clan Fraser* was hit three times and caught fire, with some of her crew killed. Another ship, the 7100-ton *City of Roubaix*, also laden with explosives bound for Turkey, also caught fire. At 3.15am first the *Clan Fraser* and then the *Roubaix* 'blew up with a vast explosion and resultant fireball' that engulfed nearby vessels, sinking another small British freighter, one Maltese ship, eleven small Greek freighters, as well as a tug and other small craft, for a total of 41,789 tons of shipping destroyed. Windows in Athens were broken by the blast, and it was heard 150 miles away. The damage to the harbour's quays was considerable.[19]

Over the next 2 weeks only a few ships were lost to the *Luftwaffe*, but when the evacuation of British and Commonwealth troops from the Greek mainland began on the night of 25-26 April, losses would soar. Cunningham is supposed to have said, during the discussions before the evacuation, 'It takes two years to build a warship; it takes two hundred to build a naval tradition', but according to Sir Michael Culme-Seymour, he actually said, 'It takes two years to build a battleship: it would take two hundred to rebuild the Commonwealth' if the troops had been abandoned. In total 50,672 troops were evacuated from Greece by sea, while another 500, mosdy RAF personnel, flew out.[20]

Even though all the evacuating ships were to have left by 3.00am so they would be well out to sea by dawn to avoid air attacks, several were lost. Between 24 April and 1 May the British lost two destroyers, the *Diamond* and *Wryneck*, which were unfortunately loaded with troops, and also four British freighters, three Dutch ships, and twenty-three Greek ships. In the entire Greek and Cretan campaigns, over 360,000 tons of shipping would be lost.[21] The Greek Navy would also suffer terribly. Two modern destroyers and two older destroyers were sunk, while another, the modern *Vasilefs Georgios I* would be trapped in Piraeus and sunk on the 20th. She would be salvaged by the Germans and would become their first large warship in the Mediterranean, renamed *Hermes*. Also lost were the two demilitarised predreadnoughts *Kilkis* (ex-*Mississippi*) and *Lemnos* (ex-*Idaho*) sold to Greece by the United States in 1914.

* * *

Soon after the defeat in Greece would come the invasion of Crete. There were numerous Allied troops on the island but much of their heavy equipment had been lost during the evacuation of Greece. Furthermore, the *Luftwaffe* still had overwhelming air superiority, some units now having been deployed to bases in the Dodecanese Islands. It was decided to mount an airborne invasion, with German paratroops seizing an airfield to allow elements of the 5th and 6th Mountain Divisions to be brought in by aircraft. The lighter equipment of the Mountain Divisions made them better suited to air transportation than regular Infantry Divisions. The German General Staff wanted to use these troops against Malta but Goering wanted to attack Crete, since it was larger and the defenders could not react as quickly to the landings as they could on Malta. Hitler made the final decision for the invasion of Crete, saying 'There will be time for Malta', being concerned about the threat of air attacks from Crete on the Rumanian oil fields.[22] If an attempt on Malta had been made in early 1941 it would most likely have failed. The island had a smaller garrison than Crete, but were much better equipped than the 'refugees' from the Greek campaign and had far more AA weaponry, and the Italian amphibious capability was a shadow of what it would become in 1942. Additionally, the Royal Navy was stronger in 1941 and the Italian Navy's battleship force was mostly still under repair.

The Italian Navy was not involved in these operations for several reasons. Still cautious after the heavy losses at Matapan, they were introducing new night-fighting techniques and evaluating three new German-supplied 'Dete' radar sets and learning their capabilities as a result of their defeat. Furthermore, *Supermarina* had also ordered the fleet to remain within 100km of air bases in order to ensure sufficient fighter cover.[23]

There were some changes in command for the British fleet as well. Cunningham would now remain ashore, the battlfleet being commanded by Vice-Admiral Pridham-Wippell in his flagship the radar-equipped *Queen Elizabeth*. The fleet now had two cruiser squadrons, the 15th under Rear-Admiral King with his flag in the *Naiad* and the 7th under Rear-Admiral Rawlings in the *Orion*. Just before this Air Marshal Longmore had been replaced by Arthur Tedder.

The troops on Crete were commanded by Lieutenant-General Bernard Freyberg. Although an ULTRA intercept had warned him of a coming German attack, he was also under orders to not inform anyone on his staff of this intelligence! And as with any new tool, there was some doubt as to its true value and significance. His greatest weakness was the absence of any viable air support. The RAF had simply been wiped out in this part of the Mediterranean.[24]

The Mediterranean Fleet would be involved in several operations during the battle for Crete. Some reinforcements were brought in at night during the early part of the fighting, and forces patrolled off the coast to destroy or prevent the landing of seaborne troops, and the battlefleet had to stand ready in case the Italian fleet intervened. Later of course they were involved in the evacuation of troops, at heavy cost.

Seaborne reinforcements were vital for reinforcing the air assault on Crete and there were to be three convoys, rendezvousing initially at Milos to proceed to Crete to land at different places along the coast. The failure to bring through two convoys of small craft would be a major factor in the heavy fighting on Crete and the massive casualties suffered by the airborne forces.

Cunningham rotated two squadrons of two battleships each to the west of Crete in case the Italian battlefleet decided to sortie, while two cruiser squadrons led by King and Rear-Admiral I G Glennie (who had replaced Rawlings who was temporarily commanding one of the battleship squadrons) would operate at night to the north of Crete. Night operations were forced on Cunningham because of the critical shortage of air support, the RAF being non-existant and even the *Formidable*'s air wing being very much under-strength. King's Force C consisted of the light cruisers *Naiad*, HMAS *Perth*, *Calcutta*, *Calcutta* and *Carlisle*, and the destroyers *Kandahar*, *Kingston* and *Nubian*, while Force D under Glennie had the cruisers *Dido*, *Ajax* and *Orion* and the destroyers *Janus*, *Kimberley*, *Hasty* and *Hereward*.[25]

On the night of 21 May, the 1st *Caique* Squadron of about twenty small coasting craft carrying 2331 German troops to Crete, escorted by the lone torpedo-boat *Lupo* under Commander C C Mimbelli, was approaching Cape Spada at 5 knots, when Admiral Glennie's squadron attacked. The *Lupo* launched two torpedoes and opened fire, but was herself hit by eighteen 6in rounds, losing two men killed and twenty-six wounded. Ten of the caiques were sunk, but a prompt sea and air rescue effort meant that only 297 men were lost.[26]

It was the turn of Admiral King's Force C next. Earlier, it had been attacked by six *MAS* boats in the Kaso Straits, but neither side had suffered any damage. But King had continued to patrol later into the morning than would prove prudent. The 2nd *Caique* Squadron of about thirty boats was under the protection of the torpedo

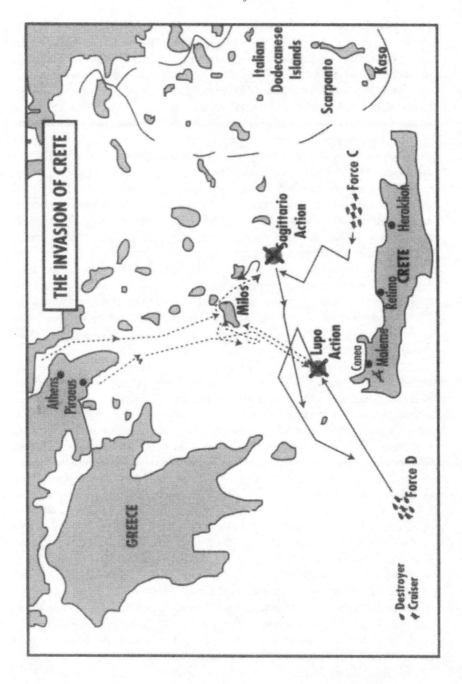

boat *Sagittario* under Lieutenant Giuseppe Cigala Fulgosi. As it neared the north coast of Crete near Retimo on the morning of the 22nd, a stray caique was discovered by the *Perth* at 8:30am and was sunk. King continued to search, although he was hampered by the AA cruiser *Carlisle* which could only make 21 knots.[27]

Force C had been under constant air attack since dawn and as Pack has written, 'every minute took his force closer [to enemy airfields]. Every attack resulted in further massive expenditure of ammunition'. So as King looked for more enemy ships he was subjected to intensifying air attacks. At 9.59am the *Sagittario* sighted King's smoke at a range of 18,000m. By 10:06am the range was down to 8000m and the *Sagittario*, which had been making smoke to cover the convoy, charged the British and fired torpedoes. She was heavily engaged with the *Naiad* and *Perth*, and the three destroyers were moving in to attack the convoy, when King ordered them to break off the action. The *Sagittario* did later suffer some mistaken air attacks by the Germans, but she was not damaged. Later when the grateful German mountain troops found Fulgosi in port they carried him shoulder-high!

King's decision to retire has always been controversial. Although he did force the convoy to abandon its attempt to land at Heraklion, the Germans suffered very few casualties, and Force C was about to take tremendous punishment as it withdrew. The convoy was there for the taking and had the British closed with the enemy, it might have offered them some protection from air attacks. Cunningham later disapproved of King's decision.

The first Axis forces to land on Crete by sea would be a small Italian force from the Dodecanese which did not arrive until late in the battle, but the island fell with the successful though costly seizure of Maleme airfield, which allowed mountain troops to be flown in and reinforce the bridgehead created by the paratroops. Ironically, a coast defense battery, Y battery, could have been traversed to fire on Maleme airfield while the Germans were landing their Ju52s, but orders were never given to shell the airport, although requests were made. The guns' primary duty was to defeat a seaborne invasion.[28]

The Axis air forces inflicted terrible losses on the Royal Navy during the invasion of Crete. Three cruisers (*Gloucester*, *Fiji* and *Calcutta*) and six destroyers (*Juno*, *Greyhound*, *Kelly*, *Kashimir*, *Imperial* and *Hereward*) were sunk, and the battleships *Warspite*, *Barham* and *Valiant* along with the *Formidable* would be damaged as well as the cruisers *Ajax*, *Naiad*, *Perth*, *Orion*, *Dido* and *Carlisle* and seven other destroyers. Naval dead were 1828 with another 183 wounded. Most of these losses were due to the *Luftwaffe*, but Italian S.84s from bases in the Dodecanese bombed and sank the *Imperial* and damaged the *Ajax* on 28 May.[29]

At the end of the battle, 16,500 men had been evacuated from Crete while 15,300 had been killed, wounded, or captured, including 2000 naval personnel. The Germans also came frighteningly close to discovering the secret of ULTRA. They were aware that the British had known the invasion was coming, and a German intelligence unit actually found the first page of an ULTRA message once Crete had fallen but failed to make the connection. They eventually concluded that Greek Intelligence had discovered their plans and passed them on to the British.[30]

During the night of 21 May the fast minelayer *Abdiel* had laid 150 mines off the coast of Greece, which later that month cost the Italians the torpedo-boat *Curtatone*

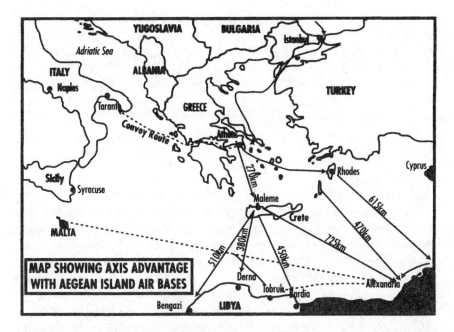

and the old destroyer *Carlo Mirabello*. That minefield also accounted for a small gunboat and two 7000-ton German freighters. Other Italian losses at this time include the torpedo-boat *Pleiadi* which was accidentally damaged by an out-of-control Cant Z.506 off Tobruk and later while being salvaged in October would be destroyed by the RAF. Also, Wanklyn on the *Upholder* won his VC by sinking the 17,879-ton passenger ship *Conte Rosso* under difficult conditions on 24 May. Efficient rescue operations saved 1680 of the 2500 troops struggling in the water.

It has been alleged that some British crews were near mutiny by the losses and incessant attacks by the *Luftwaffe*. Cunningham himself may have been almost thrown into the sea by the crew upon boarding one cruiser. Apparently it had been 'badly mauled' during the early summer of 1941 and he made a comment like 'I see you've been peppered a bit'. 'The sailors drawn up on the quarterdeck broke ranks and were narrowly prevented from throwing him into the harbour.'[31]

This may be in part due to the tremendous efforts made and losses suffered by the Royal Navy in the battle for Crete. Cunningham had been forced to relieve several officers, including the captain of one ship, and blamed it on the enemy air force. In one signal sent to the Admiralty he had commented 'There is no hiding the fact that in our battle with the German Air Force we have been badly battered. No anti-aircraft fire will deal with the simultaneous attacks of ten or twenty aircraft'. Cunningham went on to say in a message of 3 May that 'We'll hold on somehow I'm sure but this air superiority is the devil.'[32]

Despite this disastrous campaign, Churchill could point out quite fairly on the first anniversary of Italy's declaration of war on 10 June the situation was better for the British than it had been in 1940. The AOI was being conquered, Malta was holding out, the fleet had been reinforced and the Italians had suffered considerable losses.

CHAPTER 13

Operation 'Halberd', September 1941

We have to face the possibility of invasion.
Malta is immeasurably more capable of resisting attacks than was Crete.
Lt-General Sir William Dobbie[1]

Vichy France remained a factor in the Mediterranean theatre in 1941 in several ways. The first three months of that year saw 108 French ships pass Gibraltar on their way into Marseilles and other French ports, of which only eight were seized by the Allies. The United States was also attempting to bring Vichy into the Allied camp by diplomatic means, avoiding the sort of 'strong-arm' tactics the British had been using. This included food exports to French North Africa, which Britain objected to, although in fact very little food from America ever reached Vichy.[2]

But all attempts to win over Vichy to the Allied cause were hampered by Germany's continuing successes, such as the conquest of the Balkans in late spring 1941 and the invasion of Russia, which all strengthened the collaborationist factions within the French government. The Allies were further alarmed by the appointment of Admiral Darlan as Foreign Minister in February, who inclined towards helping the Germans in order to secure a better place for France in the European New Order.[3]

The situation came to a head in May when the Iraqi leader Raschid Ali sought to join the Axis and requested material support. Both Germany and Italy sent limited supplies of equipment and air units to fight there, moving some through Vichy-controlled Syria with Darlan's permission. Therefore, the British decided to rid themselves of the threat posed by Vichy Syria by launching an invasion. Such an operation had in fact been planned before the Iraq situation had developed, Syria having been seen as a potential Axis target after the fall of Greece. The Free French also saw the potential of liberating Syria, though most of the Vichy troops there would not look upon the Free French or the Allies as 'liberators'.[4]

On the eve of the attack, Force H sent in more aircraft to Malta in Operation 'Rocket', between 5-7 June, in which forty-two Hurricanes were led in by Blenheims from Gibraltar. One of the Blenheims, on its return flight to Gibraltar, detoured over Mers-el-Kebir to determine whether the *Dunkerque* was operational before the Syrian invasion. The new Hurricanes stayed at Malta, while the newly-arrived pilots exchanged them for the older Mk. 1s and flew them on to Mersa Matruh.[5]

In June the Allies invaded Syria in Operation 'Exporter', with Australian troops driving up the coast towards Beirut. The Axis powers offered air support, but the Vichy government declined it, not wanting foreign forces fighting in Syria, especially if it should be lost. However, the Armistice Commission did permit Vichy to reinforce their garrison there. But such forces could only come by sea, neither Vichy, nor indeed the Axis with Barbarossa about to begin, having sufficient air transport to move substantial reinforcements.[6]

Vichy had the 'super destroyers' *Valmy* and *Guepard*, along with three submarines, based at Beirut under the command of Rear-Admiral Pierre Gouton, and a substantial air force. Deployed against them was King's 15th Cruiser Squadron (Force B) made up of the *Phoebe*, *Ajax*, the AA cruiser *Coventry*, the landing ship *Glengyle* and eight destroyers. The *Glengyle*, a 10,000-ton converted merchant ship, attempted to land commandoes at the start of the invasion but bad weather prevented her.[7]

On 9 June the French destroyers under Captain Gervais de Lafond steamed south and bombarded advanced Allied positions on the Litani River, expending about sixty rounds. King's Force B had one destroyer stationed inshore covering the advance, with the cruisers standing out to sea, while the remaining three destroyers carried out an anti-submarine sweep 4 miles off the coast. The French destroyers were first sighted by the destroyer *Janus*, in the anti-submarine sweep, which moved to engage them.

The French opened fire at a range of 17,000 yards and after 8 minutes of firing damaged the *Janus* with five shells, the green dye in the shells from the *Guepard* apparently tinting her captain's beard! The *Janus* had twelve men killed (mostly among the bridge crew) and seventeen wounded and would require repairs to her boilers in South Africa. The *Jackal* was hit once but suffered no casualties and only minor damage. The range had dropped to 11,000 yards when the destroyers *Iris* and *Hotspur* arrived, covering the damaged *Janus* with a smokescreen, and with the British cruisers approaching the French retired, leaving the *Janus* to be towed into Haifa by the *Kimberley*.[8] The same day the Vichy submarine *Caiman* fired a torpedo at the *Ajax* which only just missed, and the French also mounted air raids on British-held Cyprus, but little damage resulted from these small-scale attacks.

In the following days the Allied force was reinforced with additional ships, including the light cruiser HMNZS *Leander* and the old destroyer *Stuart*. All these light forces ranged up and down the coast, often operating near the front lines for shore bombardment duties and being attacked by Italian, German and French aircraft. The two French destroyers would mount forays down the coast to interfere with operations, dashing back to Beirut at the sight of superior forces. Another skirmish with this enterprising French duo took place on 14 June. The captain of the *Leander*, Captain R H Bevan RN, was in temporary command of Force B, which consisted of the *Coventry* and four destroyers and was patrolling off the coast in the afternoon when the *Griffin* sighted the French about 15 miles away. The *Leander* set of in pursuit at 28 knots with two of the destroyers, while the other two destroyers stayed with the *Coventry* which had a maximum speed of only 24 knots. Bevan wanted to keep away from the shore batteries at Beirut and outside of the range of the French destroyers and therefore tried to fight at a range of 20,000 yards but the speedy French destroyers outran him and safely made harbour.

On 15 June all of Force B was off the coast hunting for the 'super destroyer' *Chevalier Paul* which was bound for Syria carrying ammunition from France. While searching, the destroyer *Isis* was damaged by German Ju88s and her sister-ship *Ilex* by Vichy aircraft. The *Chevalier Paul* was sunk on the 16th by Swordfish operating from Cyprus, although the majority of the crew was rescued and she shot down one attacker. Later, a troopship trying to reach Beirut by steaming along the Turkish coast was sunk on 4 July by Albacores also based on Cyprus. The *Vauquelin*, another of the big destroyers, managed to get through with supplies, arriving in Beirut on the 21st but was hit with six bombs by attacking Blenheims the next day and lost five killed and seventeen wounded.[9]

Another action took place on the night of 23 June, when the *Guepard* and *Valmy* were out from Beirut and were caught and engaged by the *Leander* and *Naiad* supported by the destroyers *Jaguar*, *Kingston* and *Nizam*. The destroyers were providing an anti-submarine screen when the *Naiad* sighted the two French ships at 5000 yards. They opened fire and torpedoes were launched, but the only damage was a 6in shell hit on the *Guepard*. Again, the French used their superior speed to escape to the shelter of a shore battery. Two days later, the British had more success when the submarine *Parthian* sank the French submarine *Souffleur* off Beirut.

During this campaign ULTRA began to play a larger role. The *Luftwaffe* transmitted messages detailing French air reinforcements bound for Syria from North Africa and also German air attack plans were being regularly intercepted and thus warning the British of impending attacks. On 27 June a series of intercepts indicated that the French were about to send one battleship, four cruisers and four to six destroyers loaded with supplies and reinforcements from Toulon, which were to be covered by the *Luftwaffe* as they made their way through the Mediterranean. This was Darlan's plan and he would have committed the *Strasbourg* and additional surface forces to 'secure the approaches to Beirut' but fortunately for the Allied cause this operation was called off on 2 July, because of opposition within the Vichy government.[10]

The bitter fighting in Syria ended any possibility for rapprochement with Vichy for the moment and further strengthened De Gaulle's credentials as leader of the Free French, but once Syria had fallen, he was unhappy at being left out of the negotiations with the Vichy High Commissioner of Syria, General Henri Dentz, for an armistice. The British promise of independence for Syria and Lebanon also angered him, as it was something that should have come from a French government. The French ships in Syria returned to Toulon after the armistice there.

In July, August, and later in November 1941, the Vichy French were also involved in negotiations with the Germans to allow passage of supplies and troops through Tunisia to the Axis front in North Africa. This would be in the main denied, though Vichy did transfer a small quantity of supplies and twenty heavy guns to the Axis from Tunisia. Throughout the war some supplies to the Axis would originate from French North African ports.[11]

* * *

In July British forces on Cyprus were reinforced to deter any possible German attack. Various warships, including the *Leander* and the fast minelayer *Latona*, brought troops into Famagusta from Egypt.

A pre-war Italian propaganda photograph showing co-operation between the battlefleet and seaplanes. However, during the war the problems the Italian Navy had in co-ordinating air support with the *Regia Aeronautica* would be one of their major handicaps. (Vittorio Tagliabue collection)

Major units of the British Mediterranean Fleet at sea. From foreground the battleship *Warspite*, the aircraft carrier *Illustrious* and the battleships *Resolution* and *Royal Sovereign*. (Imperial War Museum: A11790)

The launch of the Italian battleship *Littorio* at Genoa on 22 August 1937. (Ansaldo Archive No.25582)

A 15in gun of the type which armed the three *Littorio* class battleships *Littorio*, *Vittorio Veneto* and *Roma*, in the Ansaldo plant. (Ansalso Archive No. 28266)

(*Below*) The *Littorio* undergoing machinery trials in 1939, during which she made 31.3 knots. (Ansaldo Archive No. 31959)

Admiral Andrew B Cunningham (1883–1963), Commander-in-Chief of the British Mediterranean Fleet 1939–1943. (Imperial War Museum: A9760)

(*Below*) Italian escort destroyer of the *Orsa* class, in the 1941 camoflague pattern. These four ships would see extensive convoy duty during the war, and two would remain to serve in the postwar Italian Navy. (Carlo Pecchi collection)

Campioni's battleships *Conte de Cavour* and *Guilio Cesare* open fire at the Battle of Punta Stilo, 9 July 1940. (Alberto Cuneo collection)

A tightly-grouped salvo from HMAS *Sydney* lands near the *Bartolomeo Colleoni* at the Battle of Cape Spada, 19 July 1940. This photograph was taken from the *Bande Nere* at about 8.40am. Italian warships suffered from excessive salvo-spread throughout the war. (Dr Achille Rastelli collection)

Italian *Alpini* (mountain troops) arriving in Albania to reinforce the Greek front in late 1940. (Carlo Pecchi collection)

RAF aerial reconnaissance photograph taken after the attack on Taranto 11–12 November 1950. This shows the inner harbour and the two damaged heavy cruisers. (Imperial War Museum: CM164)

This photograph shows the battleship *Caio Duilio* beached in the outer harbour at Taranto after being hit by a single torpedo. Note the large amount of oil lost. It would be 6 months before she returned to service. (Imperial War Museum: CM.162)

Assisted by two destroyers, the badly-damaged tanker *Ohio* limps into Valletta harbour. The arrival of her cargo of fuel oil meant that 'Pedestal' was a strategic success for the Allies, despite the heavy casualties suffered. (Imperial War Museum: A11262)

The British battleship *Nelson* photographed during Operation 'Pedestal'. Note the floatplane on 'C' turret. (Dr Achille Rastelli collection)

Italian *MAS* boats escorting a convoy. On the night of 12–13 August 1942, boats of this type caused heavy losses among the ships of the 'Pedestal' convoy. (Carlo Pecchi collection)

British submarines and motor-torpedo boats in harbour in Malta. Striking forces based here had a decisive impact on Axis transport convoys to North Africa, making support for the besieged island a vital part of British strategy in the Mediterranean War. (Imperial War Museum: A14960)

German troops and equipment being landed at a North African port. (Carlo Pecchi collection)

An American air attack on the Italian naval base at La Spezia on 5 June 1943. The battleship in the foreground is the *Roma*, and in the background is the heavy cruiser *Bolzano*. (Dr Achille Rastelli collection)

A view from a landing craft carrying British troops to Taranto during Operation 'Slapstick', 9 September 1943. (Imperial War Museum: A19320)

Signal flags announcing Italy's surrender to the convoy *en route* to the landings at Salerno, 8 September 1943. (Imperial War Museum: MEM 427)

The final moments of the *Roma*, when her magazine exploded after being hit by a German FX-1400 glider bomb, at 3.53pm on 9 September 1943.
(Dr Achille Rastelli collection)

Rather than surrender to the Allies, the cruiser *Attilio Regolo* and the destroyers *Carabiniere*, *Mitragliere* and *Fuciliere*, led by Captain Marini, sailed to the Balearics and were interned at Port Mahon after the Armistice.
(Alberto Cuneo collection)

At this time British submarine and air attacks were becoming more effective against the convoy routes to Libya and the effects of long-term attrition were beginning to be felt. Harrassing attacks were also carried out against Italian coastal railways, but the diversion of effort from attacking the convoys was felt to be unproductive and such attacks were soon halted.

On 5 July at 6.45pm the submarine *Torbay* torpedoed the Italian sub *Jantina* in the Aegean and she quickly sank, while the next day there was an unusual battle off Benghazi in which the *Triumph* first torpedoed a 500-ton freighter plying between Tripoli and Benghazi and then surfaced to engage the escorting gunboat *Dante De Lutti* with her deck gun, damaging her so severely that she became a total loss. Also this summer the first of eventually three modern Dutch submarines began operating in the Mediterranean from Gibraltar as part of the 8th Submarine Flotilla, along with two large British subs, *Clyde* and *Severn*, which had been modified to carry 120 tons of cargo and were used to run supplies to Malta. The Dutch boats were numbered with an 'O' prefix, designating them as being for service in home waters (colonial service boats had a 'K' prefix). The trio would be credited with twenty-one ships totalling 66,300 tons and the German *U-95*. The *O-24* bagged her first victim when she attacked a lone transport, first missing with torpedoes and surfacing to use her deck gun to good effect before finally torpedoing and sinking the 7000-ton ship. These submarines would be transferred to the Indian Ocean in 1942. At Alexandria the 1st Submarine Flotilla was formed with five Greek and twelve British boats, mostly new, modern boats. More 'S' and 'T' class submarines were also starting to operate in the Mediterranean. One British shipyard was turning out a new 'S' class boat every 6 weeks for 'several years', a very good record for war-battered Britain.[12]

* * *

As elements of the *X Fliegerkorps* were transferred to Africa and Greece, the pressure on Malta was reduced, as only the *Regia Aeronautica* was now carrying out air raids on the island and as a result air and naval forces based there became more effective. But the dramatic air assault on Crete had brought home to the people of Malta that their island could be invaded in the same way. After the problems Force K had had with magnetic mines, Malta now had a small minesweeping force of four 'Flower' class corvettes based there. Malta's Blenheims attacked one Italian convoy on 3 June and sank two merchant ships in low-level attacks with delayed-action bombs. However, the flight commander's aircraft in the second wave was caught in the explosion of one of the lead aircraft's bombs and was destroyed.[13]

Between 13-15 June there was another successful flying-off of aircraft to Malta from Force H, Operation 'Tracer'. Both the *Ark Royal* and the new carrier *Victorious*, both of which had been involved in the hunt for the *Bismarck*, took part. Forty-three arrived and several flew on to North Africa. They had been guided in by four Hudsons from Gibraltar. Yet again, there was no real Axis attempt to intercept what was becoming a routine operation. At the end of the month, the old carrier *Furious* performed a similar task in Operation 'Railway', flying-off aircraft on 26 and 28 June.

But the *Luftwaffe* was still causing heavy casualties among the forces trying to keep besieged Tobruk supplied. The destroyers HMAS *Waterhen* and *Defender* were sunk in June and July respectively, as well as other smaller craft. By the end of the year twenty-seven warships and four merchant ships had been sunk on this route and a further twenty-seven warships and six merchant ships damaged.

The British now mounted a major convoy operation to bring supplies and reinforcements to Malta, Operation 'Substance', including two anti-aircraft regiments (one light and one heavy) and thirty field guns, in order to strengthen the island against any possible airborne assault, taking advantage of the relative lull in air attacks.[14] Six freighters and the troop transport *Leinster* would be covered by Force H, reinforced by warships from the Home Fleet. In addition, the Mediterranean Fleet would carry out a diversion in the west, and eight submarines were to be deployed near Italian naval bases. The RAF would also bomb Naples and airfields on Sicily to help disrupt enemy operations.

Somerville's Force H consisted of the *Renown* and *Ark Royal* and eight older destroyers. The *Ark Royal* had twenty-one Fulmars on board, as well as seven Swordfish as reinforcements for Malta. His fleet was augmented by the slow battleship *Nelson*, armed with nine 16in guns, two 'Town' class light cruisers *Edinburgh* (flagship of Rear-Admiral E N Syfret) and *Manchester*, the smaller *Arethusa*, the fast minelayer *Manxman*, and eight destroyers.

The operation began badly when the *Leinster* ran aground on 21 July and had to return to port, but this was more than made up for when *Supermarina* decided this was a flying-off operation and the fleet stayed in port. Only aircraft and light forces would be used against this convoy. Furthermore, at this time the air bases on Sardinia were virtually out of torpedoes.[15]

On the 22nd the *Renown* and HMAS *Nestor* were just missed by torpedoes from the submarine *Diaspro*. On the same day, Adrian Warburton had overflown Taranto in his Maryland to see what the Italian ships there were up to. On the return flight he sighted a Cant Z506 and attacked it! His turret gunner shot it down and got a photograph of the wreckage.[16]

The next day the main convoy was located by the Italians and it was attacked by nine S.79 torpedo-bombers at low level while five Cant Z1007 bombed from high altitude. Four Fulmars already in the air were quickly reinforced by seven more from the *Ark Royal*. Some attacked the S.79s head-on, shooting down one and damaging several others, but three Fulmars were lost to return fire. Five Fulmars then climbed to intercept the bombers, but could not reach them before they dropped their bombs, although their attack was ineffective.[17] The scattered S.79s pressed home their attack and one hit the *Manchester* but was itself shot down. The *Manchester* would be under repair for 9 months. A later attack by two S.79s hit the destroyer *Fearless* and damaged her so severely that she had to be scuttled. Thirty-five of her crew were killed in the attack.[18] Several dogfights and air attacks followed, with one bomb near-missing the destroyer *Firedrake* and forcing her to be towed back to Gibraltar. The new long-range Beaufighters operating from Malta gave good support to the convoy and both the Italians and British lost a few aircraft on the 23rd.

That night *MAS 532* and *MAS 533* torpedoed the freighter *Sydney Star* and escaped. This was after they had been detected by the destroyer *Cossack*'s radar as they were approaching. The *Cossack* engaged, and at one point a *MAS* boat passed only 100 yards astern of her. But the convoy got through. Seven unloaded freighters slipped out of Malta, and proceeded to Gibraltar, although one was torpedoed in an air attack. By the end of the operation twelve Fulmars had been lost, but only two crews were killed.[19]

After the arrival of the convoy in Malta, the Italians decided to mount an air reconnaissance operation to see what was in the harbour and also gather information for a planned attack by the *X MAS* on Valletta. Therefore on 25 July a lone Cant Z1007 was sent out in mid-morning, with forty-seven MC200 fighters escorting it! Twenty-two Hurricanes took off to intercept. In the ensuing dogfight the Cant was shot down along with two fighters for no loss, although the Italians claimed seven Hurricanes shot down. It was shortly after this that the Italians switched to flying camera-equipped MC200 planes over Malta at high altitude, with much better results.

The audacious direct attack on Valletta Harbour by the *X MAS* followed almost immediately.[20] Commander Vittorio Moccagatta had approached within 2 miles of the harbour entrance on two previous occasions to prove that it could be done, and would be aboard *MAS 452* during the attack. On the night of 25-26 July the sloop *Diana* approached Valletta along with *MAS 451* and *MAS 452* from Augusta. Between them they were carrying nine MTs, a MTS, a MTL and two SLCs. One of the SLCs was to attack the submarine base at Marsamxett while the other, commanded by Teseo Tesei, was to blow up the harbour boom so that the MTs could then race in and attack the shipping lying in the harbour. The MTS and MTL were to act in support. Italian air raids on Valletta that night were also arranged, to drop flares and also have their engine noise muffle the sound of the MTs' engines, though this did not work as well as planned.

But yet again ULTRA had cost the *X MAS* the element of surprise. A Special Liaison Unit for ULTRA reports had recently been established at Malta and had alerted the garrison of a seaborne attack, and in Italian literature it would become known as the 'Glorious Failure'. The state of alert was only heightened when the *Diana* was picked up on radar.[21]

One of the SLCs was found to be defective so it was not sent in. Teseo Tesei then took the other SLC and headed for the boom. It is not certain what happened but his craft exploded, failing to breach the boom, and no wreckage was ever recovered. Tesei had written a letter to his parents saying that he would die on the breakwater to set an example for others of how to give their life for Italy. The first two MTs then charged the boom, the first failing to explode after the pilot baled out. The second one hit, with the pilot still on board, and exploded, but only succeeded in bringing down part of the bridge and blocking the harbour entrance further. Then the shore batteries opened up on the remaining seven craft and all were quickly destroyed or captured. Maltese civilians ran to the ancient fortress bastions surrounding Valletta.

Searchlights from Forts St Elmo and Ricasoli were illuminating a wide expanse of the open sea and caught in that web of light was a tiny object moving fast trying to avoid the red tracer shells that were darting at it from the belching guns in the forts. The boat exploded, and the searchlight and guns found another one with the same result.[22]

Despite the arrangements made for the escape of the crews, it was obvious to all concerned that the chances of survival in such operations were very low, and the *X MAS* was to all intents and purposes a suicide unit. Yet there were men to do it, which leaves no doubt of their courage and dedication.[23]

At dawn the *MAS* boats, the MTS and the MTL were hunted down by Hurricanes and sunk (except for *MAS 452* which was only damaged, although Commander Moccagatta was killed) before Italian fighter cover could arrive. One Hurricane was later shot down, for the loss of two MC200s. The second SLC had finally been repaired but its crew would later be captured as well that morning. Only the *Diana* escaped destruction.[24] The pilot of the shot-down Hurricane, Denis Winton, swam to the drifting *MAS 452* and climbed aboard, finding eight dead Italians in it. After 6 hours, a Swordfish floatplane arrived, took it in tow and brought it into Valletta.

* * *

The submarine campaign against Italian communications to North Africa continued with the sinking of the 11,398-ton liner *Esperia* by the submarine *Unique* off Tripoli on 20 August. Of the 1170 troops aboard, 1139 were rescued. The British in turn lost the submarine *P32* to a mine off Tripoli on 19 August, and the Italian torpedo-boat *Partenope* sank the *P33* off Pantelleria 4 days later.

On 22 August, Force H launched Operation 'Mincemeat'. The fast minelayer *Manxman* was disguised as a French steamer and ordered to lay mines off Leghorn, deploying seventy moored and seventy magnetic mines. She would be covered by a reduced Force H, consisting of just the *Nelson*, *Ark Royal* and five destroyers. *Supermarina* thought another convoy was coming and so ordered Iachino to sea with the two fast battleships, all four remaining heavy cruisers and ten destroyers, deploying between Sicily and Sardinia within range of land-based air cover. This was also the first operation where Iachino had a direct radio link with the *Regia Aeronautica*.[25] Three light cruisers and five destroyers were also sent to Cape St Bon to intercept any convoy passing through at night. But they found nothing, as Force H was far to the north and there was no convoy anyway. *Ark Royal* launched a minor air raid against northern Sardinia but by the 26th Force H was back at Gibraltar. The only real success of the British operation was the torpedoing of the heavy cruiser *Bolzano* by the submarine *Triumph*, putting the Italian ship out of action for 11 months.[26] Between 8 and 14 September Force H conducted two ferrying operations of Hurricanes to Malta (Operations 'Status I' and 'II'). Fifty-nine out of sixty aircraft reached the island and Italian submarines failed to make contact with Force H.

In early September, ULTRA handed a major success to the British submarines operating against the Italian supply lines, decoding a signal giving the route of a major troop convoy consisting of three large passenger liners. This allowed Malta to deploy four submarines in two lines to intercept it. The first line of a single submarine was deployed to sight the convoy at sunrise on 18 September, while the second line would be in a position to make a night attack, spread over 10 miles with Wanklyn's *Upholder* in the centre. *Upholder* skilfully approached the convoy, which was escorted by five destroyers, with just the conning tower above the surface, and launched four torpedoes at the two liners *Oceania* (19,475 tons) and *Neptunia* (19,507 tons), hitting both. The *Neptunia* was fatally damaged but the *Oceania* was only stopped, with her propellers destroyed. The *Upholder* did not come under attack immediately, as the third liner had headed away at high speed and the escorts were busy rescuing survivors from the sinking *Neptunia*, so she then dove, reloaded, had to dive deep when attacked by one of the escorts, and then passed under the stricken *Oceania*. She then took up an attack position and torpedoed her twice more, just as another British submarine was coming in to attack as well. Of the 5518 troops aboard only 384 were drowned, but all their equipment was lost. After this the remaining large liners were temporarily taken off the African route.[27]

* * *

The *X MAS* achieved its first success with the SLCs at Gibraltar on the night of 19-20 September. Borghese, commanding the *Scire*, approached Gibraltar and successfully launched three 'pigs'. Their primary targets were warships, but only one of the SLCs managed to penetrate the inner harbour where they were moored. The British were on the alert, with launches patrolling the harbour and periodically dropping depth charges, and one SLC was pursued by a patrol boat, with another shaken up by a random depth charge attack. During the raid, as the explosives went off at intervals, Somerville ordered that all 'ships in harbour . . . to close all watertight doors and to raise steam'.[28]

But all three SLCs were successful. The small tanker *Fiona Shell* and the naval tanker *Denbydale* were sunk and the 10,893-ton freighter *Durham* severely damaged and had to be beached. The SLC that attacked the *Durham* had initially attached their charge to another ship, but it was found to be of Italian registry and they had shifted to another target. Significantly, the *Denbydale* was in the inner harbour. The SLC that sank her had been intending to attack the *Ark Royal*, but the carrier was too far back in the harbour, and as dawn was approaching, the SLC's crewmen decided to attack a tanker in the hope that it might start a large oil fire on the water, but the explosion broke the *Denbydale*'s back and she sank quickly, without any fire being started. All three crews escaped.[29]

* * *

At the end of September, the British launched Operation 'Halberd', the largest resupply effort to Malta of the war so far, taking advantage of recent air reinforcements to the island.[30] The convoy consisted of nine freighters carrying both military equipment and supplies for Malta's civilian population, a total load of 81,000 tons. Somerville, to establish his intentions with the Admiralty and ultimately Churchill, wrote 'I do not intend to fall into the trap of being led away from [the] convoy by an enemy who has the means and desire to avoid action and whose object may well be the reduction of convoy escort in order to facilitate air and submarine attack'. Force H already had the *Nelson* and waited until the Home Fleet could detach her sister-ship *Rodney* and the new battleship *Prince of Wales* before mounting the operation. Five cruisers and eighteen destroyers were assembled to escort the convoy, along with the *Ark Royal* to providing air cover.

The following ships were involved in the operation:

- Group II: *Prince of Wales* (Vice-Admiral A T B Curteis) and *Rodney*, the cruisers *Kenya* and *Edinburgh* of the 10th Cruiser Squadron, the cruisers *Sheffield* and *Euryalus* of the 18th Cruiser Squadron, and the 13th Destroyer Flotilla consisting of the *Duncan, Gurkha, Legion, Lance, Lively, Oribi, Isaac Sweers* (Dutch), *Piorun* (Polish), *Garland* (Polish), *Fury, Farndale* and *Heythrop*.
- Covering Group (I) of Force H with the *Nelson, Ark Royal*, the light cruiser *Hermione*, the 4th Destroyer Flotilla (*Cossack, Zulu, Foresight* and *Forester*) and the 19th Destroyer Flotilla (*Laforey* and *Lightning*).
- The convoy was made up of the *Breconshire, Clan MacDonald, Clan Ferguson, Ajax, Imperial Star, City of Lincoln, Rowallan Castle, Dunedin Star* and *City of Calcutta*.

The warships were to be divided in two forces. Force X under Rear-Admiral H M Burrough, comprising all the cruisers and some destroyers, were to provide close escort to the convoy. Force H under Vice-Admiral Somerville, with the three battleships *Rodney, Nelson* and *Prince of Wales*, the *Ark Royal* and the remaining destroyers, formed a covering force, providing a screen for the convoy until it reached the Sicilian Narrows. When the *Ark Royal* turned back to Gibraltar, air cover would be provided from Malta, which had received twenty-seven long-range fighters (twenty-two Beaufighters and five Blenheims). Malta's aircraft also carried out attacks on enemy airfields, and Somerville later wrote '. . . the bombing and machine gunning of enemy aerodromes in Sicily and Sardinia undoubtedly reduced to a considerable extent the scale of air attack which the enemy intended to launch'.[31] Nine submarines were deployed to ambush any Italian warships sent to intercept the convoy: the *Unbeaten* and *Ursula* were south of the Straits of Messina, with the the *Utmost* and *Upright* to the north, the *Urge, Trusty, Upholder* and the Polish *Sokol* were off the northwest coast of Sicily and the Dutch *O-21* was stationed near Cape Carbonara in the Gulf of Cagliari. As always, the Mediterranean Fleet would create a diversion in the eastern Mediterranean, making heavy radio traffic in order to fool the *Luftwaffe* into suspecting a large-scale operation was underway. At the same time, a complex manoeuvre was carried out at Gibraltar to deceive any Axis spies watching the harbour.

At 6.15pm on 24 September the *Nelson* headed west out of Gibraltar escorted by the destroyers *Piorun, Garland* and *Isaac Sweers*, after Somerville had shifted his flag to the *Rodney*, in order to give the impression that she had been replaced and was now being redeployed to the Atlantic. But the *Nelson* turned back at dusk and steamed eastwards to join up with the force that had sailed at 11.00pm with *Ark Royal, Rodney*, the cruiser *Hermione* and the destroyers *Duncan, Foresight, Forester, Lively, Zulu, Gurkha, Legion* and *Lance*, at 7.30am on the 25th. Half-an-hour later

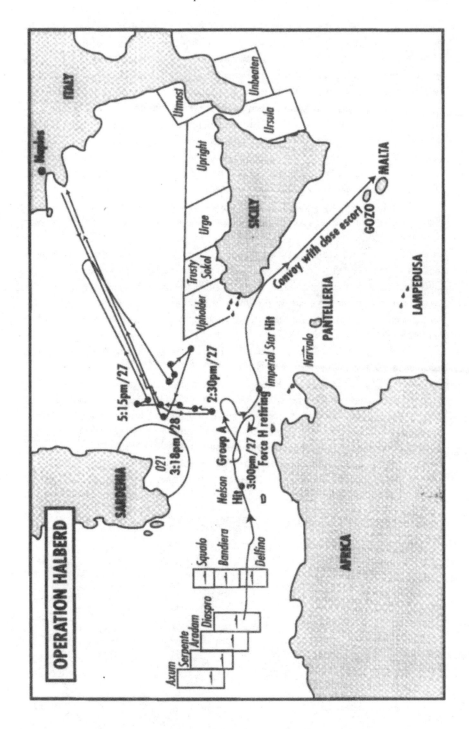

OPERATION HALBERD

they rendezvoused with Convoy WS11X which had sailed from England with fourteen merchant ships, five heading for Gibraltar and nine to make up the 'Halberd' convoy to Malta. The Gibraltar ships were escorted in by the corvettes *Jonquil*, *Spurea* and *Azalea*, while the remainder sailed on to Malta in two groups. When the ships met Force H, the transports followed a route south of the Balearics hoping to avoid civil ships and aircraft. Moreover, by employing two groups, they might make the enemy think that only Force H was at sea. That morning the *Ark Royal* begun to use her twenty-seven Fulmars of 807 and 808 Squadrons to provide air cover for the convoy. The weather was clear and fine, and when Italian air reconnaissance sighted the convoy on the afternoon of the 25th, the distant escort closed up to provide more protection.

The Italians were aware from the outset that the *Rodney* and *Nelson* were operating together and suspected a bombardment operation against the Italian coast, following Borghese's *X MAS* attack on Gibraltar. They had also detected activity at Alexandria and the presence of cruisers and light forces in the eastern Mediterranean, but crucially they had not yet spotted the transport ships heading for Malta. Submarines were therefore deployed to ambush the British ships, the *Axum*, *Serpente*, *Aradam* and *Diaspro* east of the Balearics, and the *Squalo*, *Bandiera* and *Delfino* south-west of Sardinia. Another three Italian submarines, *Dandolo*, *Adua* and *Turchese*, were already stationed south-southwest of Ibiza and the *Narvalo* was off Cape St Bon. Five submarines, *Beilul*, *Da Procida*, *H-1*, *H-4* and *H-6*, were sent to protect the Ligurian coast on the night of the 27th.[32]

The 8th Cruiser Division at Palermo (the light cruisers *Attendolo* and *Duca delgi Abruzzi*) was ordered to La Maddalena, instead of Taranto as originally planned, ready to intervene. From Taranto the cruiser *Trieste* was sent to reinforce the 3rd Cruiser Division (the heavy cruisers *Trento* and *Gorizia*) with the 12th Destroyer Flotilla. The battleships of the 5th Division, *Doria*, *Duilio* and *Cesare*, were ordered to stand by for possible commitment from Taranto. Arrangements were made with the *Regia Aeronautica* for air cover of the ships and attacks into the Gulf of Genoa. From the morning of the 26th, aircraft conducted reconnaissance in the western Mediterranean.

AIRCRAFT AVAILABLE 26 SEPTEMBER 1941

SARDINIA

Base	Aircraft	Total Available	Operational
Decimomannu	S.84	29	19
	S.79	4	4
Elmas	S.79	14	13
	Cant Z.501	6	3
	Cant Z.506	9	6
Alghero	Cant Z1007	21	12
Monserrato	Cr42	35	29
	MC200	5	4
	G.50	26	15
Olbia	Cant Z501	10	7
	Cant Z506	8	5
TOTAL		134	117

SICILY

Base	Aircraft	Total Available	Operational
Chinisia	Cant Z1007	9	8
Trapani	Cant Z1007	11	6
	Ju87	20	12
	Cr42	28	16
	MC200	9	3
	Re2000	11	3
Sciacca	S.79	21	9
Catania	BR.20	18	9
	Cr42	15	9
	MC200	67	47
Gerbini	BR.20	15	6
	S.84	5	3
	S.79	6	5
Comiso	MC202	28	28
Gela	MC200	24	15
	Cr42	8	5
Syracuse	Cant Z506	6	3
Augusta	Cant Z506	11	8
	Cant Z501	17	15
Stagnone	Cant Z501	12	7
TOTAL		341	217

A further thirty-two MC200s would be flown in to Sardinia from the mainland on the 27th. Approximately 60 per cent of the available aircraft were actually operational.

During 'Halberd', Sardinia would deploy twenty-six torpedo-bombers and fifty fighters (thirty MC200s and twenty Cr42s), and Sicily three torpedo-bombers, nine Italian Ju87s, and twenty-four high-level bombers with eighteen fighters (three Re2000s and the rest MC200s). Several sources, including the official historian Giuseppe Santoro, state the units that participated in the action and not the number available. Now this, especially in relationship to air units based on Sicily, is due to other activities, where air raids and actions against Malta were constant fare. This is a key element that needs to be reviewed whenever evaluating what air units were or were not available for a particular action.

Force H was first sighted at 9.32am on the 26th by a Cant Z506 of the 287th Squadron and later by other aircraft, all giving varying strength estimates. The aircraft carrier was identified as the *Furious* and this led *Supermarina* to conclude that, since the *Ark Royal* had been seen leaving Gibraltar, there were two carriers in the Mediterranean, with the *Furious* perhaps flying-off planes to Malta while the other attacked Genoa. Admiral Riccardi ordered the fleet to concentrate off Asinara in Sardinia, just south-west of Maddalena, putting it in a position to attack any British forces in the Gulf of Genoa or attacking Sardinia on the 27th, but also able to respond if the British were operating further south. But orders telephoned to the fleet commander Admiral Iachino at 11.00pm on the 25th stated 'the order of Riccardi is not to engage unless in decisive superiority of forces', which would have

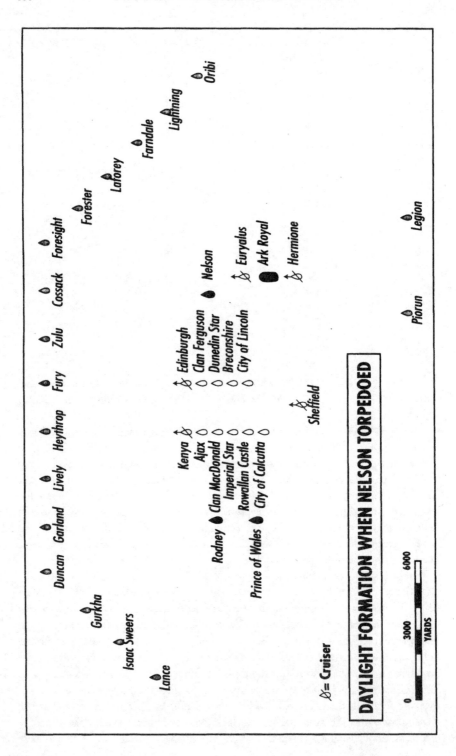

Lance

Isaac Sweers

Gurkha

Duncan Garland Lively Heythrop Fury Zulu Cossack Foresight

Forester

Laforey

Farndale

Lightning

Oribi

Kenya ⌀
Ajax ○
Clan MacDonald ○
Imperial Star ○
Rowallan Castle ○
City of Calcutta ○

Rodney ● Clan MacDonald
Prince of Wales ●

Sheffield ⌀

Edinburgh ⌀
Clan Ferguson ○
Dunedin Star ○
Breconshire ○
City of Lincoln ○

Nelson ●

Euryalus ⌀
Ark Royal
Hermione ⌀

Piorun

Legion

⌀ = Cruiser

DAYLIGHT FORMATION WHEN NELSON TORPEDOED

0   3000   6000
YARDS

a decisive effect on Iachino's actions during this operation. At 1.02am on 27th the 9th Naval Division consisting of the *Littorio* (Iachino's flagship) and *Vittorio Veneto* (flying the flag of Rear-Admiral Carlo Bergamini) sailed from Naples at 20 knots, escorted by the destroyers *Granatiere*, *Fuciliere*, *Bersagliere* and *Gioberti* of the 13th Flotilla, and *Da Recco*, *Pessagno* and *Folgore* of the 16th, heading for the concentration point off Sardinia.

Meanwhile, at midday a message arrived from the Italian Armistice Commission in France reporting that an Italian officer aboard a French mail plane had sighted a fleet of twenty-three ships, many of them transports, 80 miles north-north-east of Algiers. Also, the British aircraft carrier was positively identified as the *Ark Royal*. It was now clear that no forces were directed against Genoa and *Supermarina* reacted by ordering Iachino to change course in order to arrive at a point 50 miles east of Cape Carbonara (the south-eastern tip of Sardinia) by noon next day, requesting that he confirm receipt of the message. The Italian commander at Messina was instructed to concentrate his light vessels (two torpedo boats and eight *MAS* boats) in the Sicilian Strait, while the *Regia Aeronautica* was asked to transfer the fighter squadrons to Sardinia. Five torpedo-bombers with ten torpedoes were also transferred as reinforcements.

At 7.10am on 27 September the two British naval groups had merged into one which steamed towards Malta in the formation shown opposite.

Although between 8.00am and 11.00am the carrier had launched sixteen Fulmars in four patrols, they failed to intercept the Italian reconnaissance aircraft, one of which had reported sighting the *Ark Royal*, a battleship, two cruisers and four destroyers on a course of 90° at 8.10am, and later at 10.45am another Cant Z506 gave a more detailed report. The fleet's speed of 16 knots was noted, confirming the presence of a convoy.

At 10.40am Iachino was joined by the cruisers of the 3rd Division, *Trento*, *Trieste* and *Gorizia* under Rear-Admiral Bruno Brivonesi, escorted by the 12th Destroyer Flotilla (*Corazziere*, *Carabiniere*, *Ascari* and *Lanciere*), which were ordered to take up position 10km ahead of the battleships. An hour later the *Littorio* launched an Ro.43 for reconnaissance, and at 11.48am further reinforcements arrived with the 8th Cruiser Division (*Abruzzi* and *Attendolo*) commanded by Rear-Admiral Giuseppe Lombardi, with three destroyers of the 10th Flotilla (*Maestrale*, *Grecale* and *Scirocco*). The assembled fleet was inferior to the British in gun-power, but much superior in speed. The *Nelson* and the *Rodney* could only make 23 knots to the *Littorio*'s 30 knots.

The first problem on the Axis side arose when the thirty-one MC200s of the 52nd Wing, which were to provide air cover for the fleet, did not arrive in Sardinia until 12.35am on the 27th, leaving Iachino with only six aircraft of the 24th Group as escort, since the other twenty Cr42 fighters had been detached to escort the torpedo-bombers. Furthermore, the air escort for the fleet was not to fly further than 100km from its bases.

At 12.00 noon, on the basis of incorrect reconnaissance reports and the *Regia Aeronautica*'s assurances of good air support, Riccardi gave Iachino 'freedom of action', because he thought he faced only one British battleship and would enjoy a fighter escort. Iachino asked the fighters to be in position at 2.00pm 53 miles south of Cape Carbonara, and the Air Force in Sardinia was also ordered to attack the British ships.

After some confusion on take-off, the twenty-eight torpedo bombers (a mixed group of S.79s and S.84s) and an escort of twenty Cr42s headed off in misty and cloudy conditions. The sky cleared just as they launched their attacks between 1.00pm and 1.30pm, meeting heavy AA fire and the Fulmars which had been alerted by radar that had picked up the approaching aircraft 30 miles away. Seven torpedo-bombers and one Cr42 were lost, but the *Nelson* was hit by a torpedo dropped from 450 yards away.[33] Somerville later wrote,

> Three of the aircraft pressed on through the barrage of the starboard wing destroyers, and carried out a most determined attack on *Nelson*, who was swinging to starboard to comb the tracks. One aircraft dropped its torpedo about 450 yards . . . on *Nelson*'s starboard bow, passing over the ship at about 200 ft height . . . . The track of the torpedo was not seen until about 150 yards dead ahead of the ship, which had been steadied on a course which proved to be the exact reciprocal of the torpedo. No avoiding action was possible and a second or two after the bubbles disappeared from sight there was a large 'crump', the ship whipped considerably and a column of water rose approximately 15-20 ft high above the forecastle deck port side.[34]

Another account of the attack stated that:

> Meanwhile, though, *Nelson*, in turning towards the bow attack with the object who very gallantly closed almost to point-blank range through heavy fire. In so doing, he ran the gauntlet not only of the merchant ships' fire but also that of *Prince of Wales* and [the *Sheffield*]. The Italians passed so close that I could see the crew plainly, bent over their instruments as if urging their machine to greater speed. They must have sensed that they had only seconds to live. *Prince of Wales*' pom-poms were roaring away, and close-range armament, which should have done better, appeared to chip bits off the aircraft's rear as she went past. To make certain, one of our Fulmars flashed down on her tail; a moment later an ominous splash astern from *finis* to a brave effort.[35]

The *Nelson* was slowed to 15 knots and down by the bows, but would remain in position in the convoy, although she would be out of any offensive action against the Italian fleet if it should arrive. Later, in port the crew would have to off-load 19 tons of rotting beef from one of the storerooms damaged by the torpedo! Another torpedo bomber was shot down 1000 yards from the *Ark Royal*, which was now escorted by two *Dido* class cruisers, the *Euryalus* and *Hermione*, which provided heavier AA protection than the two destroyers she used to operate with. Unfortunately two Fulmars were accidentally shot down by British AA – one by the *Prince of Wales* and the other by the *Rodney* – and a Swordfish returning from a scouting flight was badly shot up by the Italian fighters.[36]

At 1.00pm Iachino changed course from 240° to 210° and ordered the *Vittorio Veneto* and *Trento* each to launch a seaplane. Then at 2.00pm he ordered 'clear for action', with the cruisers leading the two battleships, the *Littorio* ahead of the *Vittorio Veneto* and the destroyers to port. Another Ro43 was then launched by the

Abruzzi, but at 2.30pm Iachino ordered a turn back to the north, explaining in his report that he wanted to wait until the weather improved. Visibility was better to the north, and the promised air cover had not yet arrived, while his fleet had been shadowed by a British scout plane from Malta since 1.07pm. At 2.30pm the fleet was 85 miles away from the air base at Cagliari and only about 40 miles from the enemy, and Iachino realised the fighters were not going to find him in the overcast conditions, a dangerous situation in the presence of an enemy aircraft carrier. The attacking aircraft had not yet correctly reported the strength of the British fleet and Iachino still thought he only faced one battleship. The seaplanes launched earlier had done little to cast any light on the situation, the *Littorio*'s aircraft making a particularly confusing report. At 3.30pm additional reports began to come in and some fighters did arrive, which were welcome as the reconnaissance aircraft from the *Ark Royal* were shadowing the fleet from 3.15pm until 5.50pm. But unfortunately the first squadron of Cr42s that arrived over the Italian fleet was fired upon and its commander shot down by a destroyer. Later in the operation, ten MC200s ran out of fuel and had to ditch, with two pilots being lost. At 4.50pm Iachino felt he was now far enough from the aircraft carrier and slowed to 20 knots, turning south again a little later to be able to exploit any successes by the aircraft. Iachino was informed at 3.34pm and again at 4.27pm of substantial damage to several of the British ships (although only the *Nelson* had actually been hit).

Somerville did detach the *Prince of Wales*, the *Rodney*, the cruisers *Sheffield* and *Edinburgh* and six destroyers under the command of Vice-Admiral Curteis at 3.30pm '. . . to close and drive off the enemy . . .' to the north-east, but they were recalled at 5.00pm without making contact, and had rejoined the convoy by 6.30pm.[37] Twelve Swordfish and four Fulmars were launched from the *Ark Royal* at 3.40pm but did not find the Italian fleet, because Iachino was retreating to the north at that time. However, at 5.00pm Iachino received a message from *Supermarina* saying there was only one enemy battleship, and he responded by heading south again to try to find the British convoy, but he could not now make contact before dusk, so he turned east at 6.12pm, slowing to 18 knots.

The exchange of messages between Iachino and *Supermarina* shows that he was first invited to exploit the possibility of attacking the convoy since the claims of the aircraft crews were quite high (and incorrect). But later he was instructed to spend the night in the Tyrrhenian Sea to be ready to attack the British convoy in the morning, preventing him heading south. This would mean that in the morning the British fleet and convoy would be well to the east, and no engagement would be possible.

Mattesini in his study notes that:

1. In reporting to Mussolini, Riccardi said that the Italian fleet did not engage because there were two battleships of the *Nelson* class and an aircraft carrier present, plus six cruisers. Mattesini notes that Riccardi did not stress the aircraft carrier to *Il Duce*, which was more important than the presence of the battleships, which had not been reported until Iachino had already turned north.
2. Iachino was restricted by orders that only allowed him to fight in conditions of clear superiority, including air superiority. In Mattesini's opinion, Iachino was too inclined to stick to the letter of his instructions.

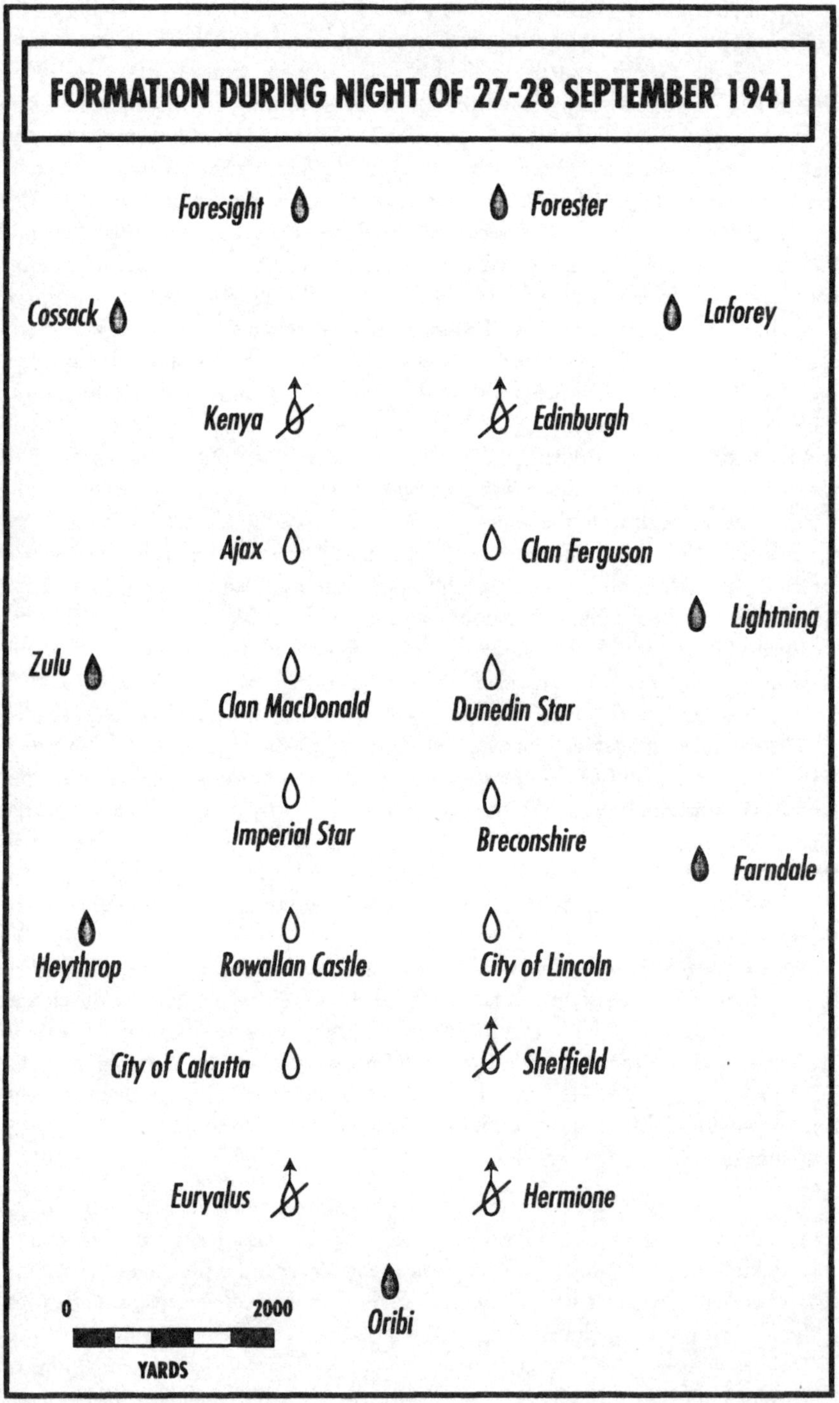

FORMATION DURING NIGHT OF 27-28 SEPTEMBER 1941

Foresight 🜂   🜂 Forester

Cossack 🜂   🜂 Laforey

Kenya ⚡   ⚡ Edinburgh

Ajax ◌   ◌ Clan Ferguson

🜂 Lightning

Zulu 🜂

◌   ◌
Clan MacDonald   Dunedin Star

◌   ◌
Imperial Star   Breconshire

🜂 Farndale

🜂   ◌   ◌
Heythrop   Rowallan Castle   City of Lincoln

City of Calcutta ◌   ⚡ Sheffield

Euryalus ⚡   ⚡ Hermione

0   2000
YARDS

🜂
Oribi

3. The *Regia Aeronautica* reported having employed fifty-three airplanes as escort, thirty-two from Sardinia and twenty-one from Sicily. Some took off having been given an incorrect position for the fleet, and so many were unable to locate it. Four patrols did find the ships, a total of seventeen aircraft (nine MC200s from Sardinia, five Cr.42s and three Re2000s from Sicily) providing sporadic air cover from 3.20pm, again after Iachino had turned northwards. On the other hand, the Sardinian Air Command considered the heavy losses suffered by the torpedo-bombers an 'unjustified sacrifice of the air force' which the Navy failed to exploit.

4. Neither Mattesini nor we consider the squadron detached under Curteis superior to Iachino's fleet, being at best equal if the aircraft from the *Ark Royal* are taken into account.

Mattesini writes that, from the actions of the Italian fleet, it appears that 'the hidden, if not the actual reason for the raid of the fleet was planned with the traditional concept of the 'fleet in being". That is, to show the fleet and to draw the British onto the air force and submarine ambushes near the Italian coasts. MacGregor Knox wrote that Iachino 'wandered about indecisively'.[38] After the losses at Matapan and the presence of British air power, in our view Iachino was being conservative as well as just obeying orders, and that he should have taken the chance and sought battle, having a powerful force, while the British were tied down by the convoy.

That night, Somerville turned back and Force X was detached to take the convoy in. With the fleet in night formation, it was attacked by small numbers of torpedo-bombers, one hitting the 12,427-ton *Imperial Star* which later had to be scuttled. *MAS* boats were also sent out, but failed to find the convoy. The cruiser *Hermione* was detached to bombard Pantelleria so the airfield there would be out of action in the morning, but her bombardment was entirely ineffective.

The next day the convoy arrived safely at Malta with 50,000 tons of supplies. Three unladen merchant ships slipped out to head east and would arrive safely at Alexandria. As Force H retired it was attacked by three submarines, one of which, the *Adua*, launched an unsuccessful attack and was sunk by the destroyers *Gurkha* and *Legion*. The Allied submarines also failed to find any targets, though the *Utmost* did attack some cruisers near Naples but failed to score any hits and was almost rammed by one of the escorting destroyers. The fleet's retirement to Gibraltar was uneventful except for the *Prince of Wales* shooting down another Fulmar.[39] The merchant ship *Empire Guillemot* had also arrived at Valletta on 19 September having escaped Axis surveillance thanks to the fact she disguised herself with Spanish, French and Italian flags.

Churchill sent a message of congratulation for this operation and knighted Somerville a second time. Cunningham would send a message to Somerville, which older men will most appreciate, 'Fancy, twice a knight at your age'!

CHAPTER 14

The Balance Shifts, December 1941

> . . . the underwater teams, on the night of 19 December 1941, carried
> out their most superlative undertaking – one that has become legendary
> not only because of its perfect execution but also because of the way its
> consequences affected the conduct of the war in the Mediterranean.
>
> *Commander Bragadin*[1]

As autumn turned into winter in 1941, the situation in the Mediterranean seemed to be stabilising. Germany's main forces were engaged in Russia and the Mediterranean was therefore something of a sideshow for them, although the siege of Tobruk continued. Great Britain continued to build up her land forces in the theatre but two earlier offensives in the Western Desert, 'Brevity' and 'Battleaxe', had failed. Malta was reasonably well supplied and plans were being made to send a new surface strike force to the island. ULTRA was providing more complete information more quickly, especially now that the Italian 'C38' code was being read.[2] In early October, it provided the route of the Italian 'Guilia' convoy of five merchant ships. Once reconnaissance planes from Malta had 'found' the convoy, air attacks over 11-15 October sank three of the ships, in a scenario that was to be repeated many times in the next 19 months.[3]

In September, the Germans decided to transfer six U-boats to the Mediterranean to help their ally in Operation 'Goeben'. Between 24 September and 5 October all would successfully make the dangerous passage past Gibraltar and would shortly be operating in the eastern Mediterranean, based at Salamis in the Aegean. This had been a controversial decision. Although the U-boats did sterling service for the Axis in the Mediterranean, they still had fewer targets than if they had been in the Atlantic, and Admiral Doenitz had opposed the transfer as he wanted the maximum number of units in what he considered to be the decisive theatre.[4] After entering the Mediterranean the U-boats switched to a different Enigma code (*Sud*), which could not immediately be read by ULTRA, becoming 'lost' submarines. The command would be known at *Fuehrer der U-Boote, Italien*, or FdU-Italy.[5]

One of the first successes of the German submarines was the rescue of forty-two sailors from the sub-chaser *Albatros* sunk by the submarine *Upright* on 27 September near Messina. Their first offensive operations were to shut down the supply line to Tobruk. This meant they would be operating in shallow and unfamiliar waters, and they faced a further problem in that they had to spend long periods of time submerged because of the longer days and heavy Allied air activity. Prolonged periods of time underwater caused the air pressure in the hull to adversely affect the torpedo mechanisms, causing them to run too deep. But in spite of this, they began inflicting some immediate losses among the smaller vessels operating there, including the torpedoing of the gunboat *Gnat* on 21 October which was beached as a total loss. But this was only the beginning.

A second group of submarines was dispatched, the 'Arnauld' group of four boats. Two of these, *U-81* (Lieutenant-Commander Friedrich Guggenberger) and *U-205* passed through the Straits of Gibraltar during the night of 11-12 November and almost immediately enjoyed a stupendous success. They engaged Force H and both of their initial attacks failed, but on the afternoon of 13 November the *U-81* fired four torpedoes at long range at the *Ark Royal* and the battleship *Malaya*. Guggenberger would later report both ships hit, with the battleship damaged, but this was not true. His one hit on the *Ark Royal* killed only one man but it was amidships and flooded her boiler room. Despite frantic efforts to tow her to Gibraltar, she eventually capsized and sank. Six Italian subs deployed in the western Mediterranean failed to find any targets.[6] Two more U-boats were sent out in mid-November, but one was quickly lost to a British submarine trap involving a corvette, the *Marigold*, with the new Type 271 radar. The Germans now had nine submarines in the Mediterranean.

* * *

In early November another disaster befell an Italian convoy carrying supplies for the planned Axis attack on Tobruk. On 19 October a re-formed Force K had returned to Malta, commanded by Captain W G Agnew, and initially consisted of two of the smaller British light cruisers, the *Aurora* (flagship) and *Penelope*, armed with six 6in guns, eight 4in AA and six 21in torpedo tubes, and two 'L' class destroyers, the *Lance* and *Lively*, which unlike the rest of their class were armed with eight 4in DP guns in four twin turrets rather than the usual 4.7in guns, which made them much better AA platforms. They also carried eight 21in torpedo tubes. Force K intended to carry out its operations at night, so all the ships were equipped with radar, and the cruisers had been among the first to receive a improved and more powerful type of searchlight.

The question of large versus small cruisers is an interesting one. Given the strained British budgets of the interwar years, they were quite a good deal.

> The Admiralty's policy in the 1930s of building small cruisers and so gaining in overall numbers of ships certainly paid handsomely during the war years. For service in the Mediterranean, the small ship excelled. In night surface actions, they could deliver almost the firepower of a heavy cruiser, and yet were handled like destroyers. What the small cruisers lacked was the ability to receive the large amounts of equipment which the changing scene demanded, and which technology could give.

A further disadvantage of the smaller ships was that they were unable to absorb as much damage, particularly underwater damage, as larger vessels.[7]

Force K was also helped by all the different elements of British Intelligence. As ever, ULTRA was vital in the coming attack on the Italian convoy 'Beta', better known by the name of the largest of two German merchant ships in it, '*Duisburg*', but air reconnaissance still played an important role. Adrian Warburton, now dubbed 'King of the Mediterranean', continued to fly out of Malta, and he later operated a Spitfire rigged for air reconnaissance and photography and he spotted one of the first so-called 'Battleship Convoys'. It was aerial reconnaissance that would confirm in the new year the building of additional runway space on Sicily for the gliders to be employed in the planned invasion of Malta. They also became so familiar with Naples harbour, where many of the Libya-bound convoys sailed from, that the quay they loaded at became known as 'Rommel's Quay'. Depending on the state of loading, a good estimation of departure time could be made, usually to confirm what ULTRA had revealed.[8]

The Italians were aware that Force K was at Malta and so sent a powerful covering force along with a strong close escort to get this convoy through. The convoy consisted of the German steamers *Duisburg* and *San Marco*, the Italian steamer *Sagitta*, the motor ships *Rina Corradoi* and *Maria* and the tankers *Minatit-land* and *Conte di Misurata*, with a total displacement of 39,839 tons, carrying 172 Italian and 217 German vehicles, 34,473 tons of munitions; and 17,281 tons of fuel, as well as 145 Italian soldiers, 78 Germans spread among several ships, and 21 civilian passengers on the *Sagitta*. The convoy was routed to the east of Malta, not down the Tunisian coast. This route was used a great deal when the Libyan airfields were largely in Axis hands.[9]

The *Scorta Diretta* (Direct Escort) under Captain Ugo Bisciani was made up of the destroyers *Maestrale* (flag), *Fulmine*, *Euro*, *Grecale*, *Libeccio* and *Oriani*, while the *Scorta a Distanza* (Distant Escort) was under the command of Rear-Admiral Bruno Brivonesi on board the heavy cruiser *Trieste* with the *Trento* and the modern destroyers *Granatiere*, *Fuciliere*, *Bersagliere*, and *Alpino*. The submarines *Delfino* and *Settembrini* were acting in support. Both admirals would be removed from command after this action. The convoy sailed for Tripoli on 8 November.

Brivonesi had several problems. The Distant Escort had to proceed at a speed of 16 knots and zig-zagging, while the convoy plodded along at 9 knots. But unless the Distant Escort made contact with an enemy force, they were of little value, and the British had the initiative. Furthermore, both Brivonesi and *Supermarina* believed that a surface attack on a dark night was virtually impossible unless the enemy knew their exact route and course, and so only prepared for a night air attack. This view is only understandable if one takes into account the Italians' lack of experience in night combat and their failure to appreciate the full capabilities of radar. They were basing their conclusions on their own capabilities, not those of the enemy.

As Agnew approached the convoy at 28 knots on the night of 8 November, north-east of Malta, he led with his flagship the *Aurora* followed by the *Lance* then the *Penelope*, and the *Lively* bringing up the rear. There was a bit of moon out in the east so he approached the convoy with the enemy convoy between his force and the moon. His orders were to engage the nearest escorts first, then shift fire to the merchant vessels, and engage additional escorts if they appeared. He had adopted a simple line ahead as it was a compact formation and allowed all ships full freedom to fire torpedoes. In contrast, the Italians fired no torpedoes in this action, for fear of hitting their own ships.

Just after midnight the *Aurora* sighted the convoy and slowed to 20 knots, while she manoeuvred into position. The British did not employ illumination and the gun crews were ordered to fire steadily, not rapidly, as accuracy was vital. As they made their final approach they detected other vessels, thought to be merchant ships and destroyers, about 6 miles away – this was the Distant Escort. Force K's attack signal at 12.47am was picked up by the *Trieste* but the *Lively* jammed her radio, preventing her alerting the convoy. As Sadkovich has written, 'as a result, when Force K opened fire around 00.58 at ranges of 5200 to 3000 yards, the only ships expecting an attack were over 17,000 meters to the rear'.[10]

The British opened fire at 12.57am, using radar, with the *Aurora* firing her 6in guns at the *Grecale*, scoring hits with her first three salvoes. The *Lance* fired on a nearby merchant ship, along with the *Aurora*'s 4in batteries, while the *Penelope* engaged the *Maestrale*, again hitting with her first salvoes. The *Lively* opened fire on the merchant ships 3 minutes later. The Italian's initial reaction was to believe they were under air attack, and the radio aboard *Maestrale*, flagship of the Direct Escort, was knocked out almost immediately. The *Euro*, on the starboard side of the convoy and closest to the enemy, was hit several times at a range of 3000 yards but most of the shells passed through the ship without exploding, although she did suffer casualties. She did not return fire as her crew feared the firing ships were Italian! The *Fulmine* tried to close and fire torpedoes but was quickly disabled, sinking later. The other destroyers of the Direct Escort began to make smoke, but it was too little too late, and they drew off some distance to the east.

Meanwhile, the Distant Escort was not sure what was happening, also thinking an air attack was taking place, and as late as 1.13am they informed *Supermarina* that they were probably under attack from torpedo-bombers. They then made their most important error, steaming towards where Force K had been initially sighted, rather than estimating where a much faster force would now be, and therefore were unable to come into action. They did spot Force K at a range of about about 8700 yards and at 1.08am the *Trento* fired off some starshell. The two heavy cruisers did open fire but the British were unaware of this. As Peter Smith and Edwin Walker have put it, '. . . confusion reigned throughout the Italian command'.[11]

Between 1.10am and 1.25am the British pounded the merchant ships with guns and torpedoes, the convoy making little if any attempt to scatter. The escorting destroyers on the port side of the convoy, along with the *Maestrale* and *Euro*, had drawn off over 10 miles to the east, formed up as a unit and then returned to fire ineffective salvoes, being fired on and chased off again by the British. Brivonesi's command sighted the British again and they fired a total of 207 8in shells, obtaining some straddles. But, unable to spot the British amid the burning and exploding merchant ships, he turned north at 24 knots, hoping to cut them of, but never made contact again.

A few partial salvoes landed near the British ships as they completed the destruction of the convoy, but there was only some splinter damage to the *Lively*. By 1.40am firing had ceased, and the British were on their way home after this 'Turkey Shoot' that must be compared to the Allied disaster at Savo Island for being one-sided. All the merchant ships and the *Fulmine* were sunk, while the next morning Wanklyn's *Upholder* torpedoed and sank the destroyer *Libeccio* which was picking up some of the 704 survivors.[12]

The Germans had some strong comments about the action. Admiral Löwisch, the German naval attaché, was quite clear: the Italians' night combat training was primitive, writing that out of 150 training exercises on the German cruiser *Leipzig* he had conducted 130 at night. The capital ships also lacked special night-combat equipment, such as low-light rangefinders. In the torpedo-boats they lacked night control fire to open fire beyond 10,000 yards.[13] Admiral Weichold of the German naval command in Italy, wrote to Berlin that it was insufficient training in the use of weapons which led to the disaster, coupled with Brivonesi's incompetence.

With hindsight, the Italians should have planned better tactics if attacked by surface forces. Firstly, the merchant ships should have be told to either scatter or turn away from the enemy, as the *Tarigo* convoy had done, rather than just hold their course and be shot to pieces. Secondly, the destroyers on the port wing should not have drawn off, but aggressively counterattacked with torpedoes even at the risk of hitting friendly ships. Thirdly, the Distant Escort should have anticipated where Force K would be rather than just heading for the first sighting. Finally, Brivonesi should have brought the British to battle as they retired. As a result of this disaster, all convoys sailing to Tripoli were temporarily suspended, although those to Benghazi continued. Brivonesi was court-martialed for the poor handling of his squadron, but on 5 June 1942 he was reinstated by Mussolini and assigned the Sardinian command. Bisciani was removed from command for not attacking during 46 minutes of combat.

* * *

The Commonwealth victory in North Africa brought about by Operation 'Crusader' which began on 18 November and lasted into December was a true combined operation by the various Allied nations and all the service branches, driving the Axis back and relieving Tobruk. The Royal Navy's contribution in attacking the vital convoys supplying Axis troops was of paramount importance.[14]

Just before 'Crusader', the carriers *Argus* and *Ark Royal* flew off thirty-seven Hurricanes for Malta in Operation 'Perpetual', with a further seven Blenheims flying in from Gibraltar. All but three of the aircraft arrived safely, one of the Hurricanes having the *Argus*'s flag tangled round its tail! Italian torpedo-bombers scored a minor success in November, sinking two large empty freighters heading west from Malta. But getting supplies and men to the Axis forces in North Africa was critical. On 20-22 November two small convoys arrived but both the *Trieste* and the light cruiser *Duca De Abruzzi* were torpedoed, the former by a submarine and the latter by an aircraft. While neither sank, they made port with difficulty and would be under repair for some time.

Just before midnight on the 23rd, Force K sailed to intercept two freighters from Greece escorted by the torpedo-boats *Lupo* (Commander Mimbelli) and *Cassiopea*. The Italians knew that Force K was at sea and convoys were ordered to head for port, but this one did not receive these orders because of the excellent radio jamming by the two destroyers of Force K. Despite this being a daylight action with the *Luftwaffe* overhead, both freighters were sunk, although the *Lupo* launched a torpedo attack against the cruiser *Penelope*. Churchill had wanted the Mediterranean Fleet to sail in support of Force K, although it was without an aircraft carrier.

Therefore, the fleet sortied as Force A of three battleships and eight destroyers, and Force B of five cruisers and four destroyers. Near Bardia on 25 November, the *U-331* under Lieutenant von Tiesenhuasen penetrated the destroyer screen and fired a spread of torpedoes of which three hit the *Barham*. She sank in 3 minutes as her magazines exploded and the captain and 861 sailors died, although Vice-Admiral Pridham-Wippell and 450 others were saved. The *U-331* immediately dove to the incredible depth of 820ft and survived to report hitting 'something big'. The British did not immediately announce this loss.

With the British offensive in full swing and the supply lines to Rommel under heavy attack, Hitler decided to have the *Kriegsmarine* give full support to the North African convoys, and more U-boats were transferred to the Mediterranean as a result. In the last week of November ten boats were heading for the Straits of Gibraltar. In the first group of five, all got through, but two were soon sunk. The *U-95* was torpedoed and sunk by the Dutch submarine *O-21* off the Spanish coast on 28 November, two days after passing Gibraltar, while the Italian torpedo-boat *Orione* rammed and sank the *U-557* on 16 December in a case of mistaken identity. The captain of the *Orione* could only later say that it had not looked like an Italian submarine. Two days prior to her loss, the *U-557* had attacked the cruiser *Galatea* off Alexandria after the Italian submarine *Dagabur* had fired torpedoes at her, and is usually credited with sinking her.[15]

The next five U-boats failed to get into the Mediterranean, being either sunk or damaged on the way there or in the Straits of Gibraltar itself. British anti-submarine precautions at Gibraltar had been strengthened, including radar-equipped Swordfish that could attack U-boats at night. Their first success would be the sinking of *U-451* on 21 December, one of a further group of nine U-boats sent to the Mediterranean after the relief of Tobruk, only three of which made it through.

Germany also sent reinforcements for the *Luftwaffe* in the Mediterranean. The onset of winter on the Russian Front meant that the *II Fliegerkorps* could be ordered to Sicily on 10 November. Field Marshal Albert Kesselring, called 'Smiling Al' by the Allies, had been appointed overall commander of German forces in the Mediterranean theatre, arriving in Rome on 28 November. The *II Fliegerkorps*, or *Luftflotte 2*, was under Lieutenant-General Bruno Loerzer and consisted of a typical mix of Ju87 Stuka and Ju88 bombers, and Me110 and the improved Me109F fighters. The first units to arrive in Sicily were the I/2nd Night Fighter Wing and the 606th Coastal Troops, equipped with Ju88s and under command of 'Air Commander Sicily' Colonel Roth. The strengthening of the *Luftwaffe* in Sicily would threaten the surface forces based at Malta, as well as tightening the blockade of the island itself.[16] At the same time facilities for 30,000 men were under construction in Sicily and additional AA batteries were sent to Naples to help defend the port. At the beginning of December the *II Fliegerkorps* began to arrive in Sicily but it was too late to help starve off defeat in Operation 'Crusader' for the Axis. On 22 December a massive attack would be launched against Malta with 200 aircraft. In 5 weeks the U-boats, the *Luftwaffe* and the Italian Navy's SLCs regained control of the Central Mediterranean, denying it to Commonwealth shipping. With the Axis convoy route secured, Rommel was able to launch a counter-offensive that took him as far east as the Gazala Line near Tobruk.[17]

But for most of December the British kept up the pressure on the Axis convoys. A reinforced Force K, now including the light cruisers *Ajax* and *Neptune* and the destroyers *Kimberley* and *Kingston*, under the command of Rear-Admiral Rawlings, sortied on 30 November. They divided into two forces, Force B made up of the new ships, and Force K, without the *Lance*. The Italians were running several small convoys to Benghazi and Tripoli, deploying three distant covering forces, one of which included the battleship *Caio Duilio*, making this the first of the so-called 'battleship convoys'. These convoys were mostly recalled and British aircraft sank or damaged several of the freighters involved. One ship, the 10,540-ton tanker *Irido Mantovani* was damaged and brought to a stop. The *Navagatori* class destroyer *Alvise da Mosto* took her in tow towards Tripoli. Force K was in the area and spotted three aircraft circling in the distance. Approaching to investigate, they found three Italian Cr42s circling the crippled tanker. The *Da Mosto* dropped her tow and attempted to cover her charge with a smokescreen, as the *Aurora* came straight on, and opened fire at about 16,000 yards at 6.01pm on 1 December. The *Penelope* and *Lively* formed a line parallel to the enemy. The *Da Mosto* fired on the *Lively* and missed, launched a torpedo at the *Aurora* that also missed, and was then turning to fire more torpedoes when both cruisers hit her with 6in shells at 6.09pm. Both Italian ships were then quickly sunk, although most of the crew of the *Da Mosto* would be rescued the following day by torpedo-boats from Tripoli. On 15 December the 6311-ton *Sebastiano Venier* was sunk by the submarines *Porpoise* and *Torbay*. She was returning from Tripoli with 2000 prisoners of war aboard. In inclement weather an Italian hospital ship would rescue most, but 309 prisoners and 11 Italian soldiers died. ULTRA had reported the ship and her route but not her cargo. ULTRA and its role in the fate of prisoners would come to a head in 1942.[18]

Tobruk was relieved on 8 December 1941, the day after Pearl Harbor. The newly arrived Rear-Admiral Vian with the cruisers *Naiad*, *Euryalus* and *Galatea*, and Captain Mack's 14th Destroyer Flotilla sortied against Derna between the 8th and 11th, but while returning to port the destroyer *Jackal* was badly damaged by Italian torpedo-bombers. Philip Vian, another of Britain's great admirals, had first requested the command of a destroyer flotilla upon making captain in 1935 so as to see action against Italy if the Abyssinian Crisis developed into war. He now came to command the 15th Cruiser Squadron that would shortly be the main component of the Mediterranean Fleet.

But yet another disaster was about to strike the Italian Navy. It had decided to supply Libya using fast light cruisers, destroyers, and three of the *Orsa* class escorts loaded with drums of fuel. The smaller ships and the light cruiser *Cadorna*, loaded with fuel (the destroyer *Zeno* was so thick with fumes that the crew was forced to wear gas masks), made several trips to Benghazi and Derna in November and early December, the *Cadorna* returning to Italy with 900 prisoners. It was somewhat ironic that one destroyer, the *Da Noli*, delivered 70 tons of fuel to Libya, using up 200 tons to steam there and back.[19]

Rear-Admiral Antonio Toscano, commanding the 4th Division of the *Condottiere* class light cruisers *Da Barbiano* and *Di Giussano*, with their sister-ship *Bande Nere*, was now ordered to proceed to Tripoli loaded with 950 tons of various fuels in drums and 900 tons of supplies on each cruiser. The *Regia Aeronautica* was to offer some air cover close to the coast of Sicily, and four *MAS* boats from Pantelleria were to provide escort when within range. Nevertheless, Toscano considered the mission 'half suicidal' packed as his ships were with highly flammable fuel. His force first left Palermo on 9 December and had got about halfway between Tunisia and Sicily, when air reconnaissance from Malta sighted it and on the 10th it was attacked by torpedo-planes, so it returned to Palermo. They sailed again at 6pm on the 12th, leaving the *Bande Nere* behind with engine trouble, the torpedo-boat *Cigno* providing escort (her sister-ship the *Climene* was to accompany her but she also had mechanical problems and was left behind).

Meanwhile, the fate of Toscano and 919 other sailors was approaching from Gibraltar. With the entry of Japan into the war and the withdrawal of the RAN's destroyers from the Mediterranean, it had been decided to send four destroyers from Force H to reinforce Cunningham's fleet. Two big 'Tribals', the *Sikh* (flagship of Commander G H Stokes) and *Maori*, joined the *Legion* and the Dutch *Isaac Sweers*, and were steaming east, hugging the French North African coast to avoid minefields. They was sighted by Vichy French ships which alerted Italian forces of their presence, and they were also spotted by a Cant Z1007. At a speed of 20 knots for Stokes' squadron the Italians calculated that Toscano's force would avoid the British destroyers.

But Stokes received word of Toscano's ships and increased speed to try to intercept it. This was in part due good intelligence as ULTRA had alerted the British on the 12th to the entire Italian convoy situation in the Central Mediterranean, even supplying the speed of Toscano's force (22 knots). Force K did not sortie against Toscano because fuel supplies at Malta were low. As Toscano's force proceeded south towards the Tunisian coast, a Wellington reconnaissance aircraft flew along the route given by ULTRA and sighted it. Near Cape Bon on the Tunisian coast, Toscano's force, steaming at 23 knots, turned 180° to the north at 3.20am on 13 December. This placed the *Cigno*, which had been leading the column, about 2000m astern of the cruisers. At this moment the Allied destroyers appeared from around the point. They had earlier seen the Italian signalling lamps at some distance, and so Stokes hugged the coast to help hide his ships with the high land mass behind them. He was surprised to see that the Italian ships had turned and were heading on an opposite course, offering a perfect target for a torpedo attack. What followed was just over 2 minutes of hell for the Italian cruisers.

At 3.23am the *Sikh* fired a spread of four torpedoes from 1500 yards at 3.23am at the *Da Barbiano*. Two minutes later Toscano had just sighted the four destroyers and was about to order open fire, when the cry from below was 'Torpedoes! Torpedoes!' – 300m away. Stokes' attack was devastating as two torpedoes split open her hull – one hitting near 'A' turret – and flames broke out from the fuel stored on deck. A third one would hit later, completing the devastation. The *Di Giussano's* captain ordered 30 knots and quickly fired three salvoes which sailed over the Allied destroyers, but it was too late for her also. The *Sikh* had opened fire on her, quickly followed by the *Maori* and the *Sweers*, while one torpedo from *Legion* hit. At 3.27am a large explosion occurred amidships. The *Sweers* account stated that '... she attacked the second Italian and scored several hits. The second Italian cruiser was enveloped in flames and began to sink'. The chief engineer informed the captain that the situation in the engine rooms was 'desperate'. The *Legion* now hit the *Di Giussano* with a second torpedo while the combined gun and machine-gun fire completed the destruction of the Italian cruisers. These flaming coffins lit up the sky as the fuel fed the flames both in the ships and on the water. The *Cigno* raced north to support the cruisers but was not much involved in this action which ended so quickly. She suffered some machine-gun damage, most likely from the *Sweers*, which fired at least one torpedo that may have passed beneath her, and several salvoes. She would later rescue almost 500 men, while under air attack and another 145 would be picked up by other ships which arrived later.[20]

Stokes' squadron reached Malta the next day and was cheered by the ships of Force K, as the Dutch National Anthem was played by the ships' bands to celebrate the presence of the *Isaac Sweers*. Stokes would justly receive the CB for this action. The Italians blamed Toscano's unfortunate 180° turn, apparently ordered to throw off enemy aircraft. But at his speed, with the enemy already following him, they would still have been able to attack him from the rear, sheltered by the Tunisian coast, if he had made the turn or not.

* * *

Between 13-19 December the Italians mounted Convoy Operation M41, which would involve the entire fleet, including four battleships. The aim was to run eight freighters to North Africa, but two were promptly sunk by the *Upright* while on their way to the assembly point at Taranto on 13 December. The next day, the Italians suffered a further loss when the *Urge* hit the *Vittorio Veneto* with a single torpedo. While she safely made Taranto, she would be under repair for 4 months. At this point the Italians cancelled the operation, recalling all ships to port.

But the British were at sea escorting the freighter *Breconshire* from Alexandria to Malta. It was covered by Vian's *Naiad*, *Euryalus* and *Carlisle* supported by eight destroyers, while Force K under Agnew with the newly arrived destroyers of Stokes's command came out from Malta to meet it, the forces rendezvousing at 8.00am on 17 December in the Central Mediterranean. The Italians had immediately ordered another convoy operation, M42, to sea. Iachino had with him the battleships *Littorio*, *Cesare*, and *Doria*, the heavy cruisers *Goriȥia* and *Trento*, and ten destroyers, due to an erroneous reconnaissance report that had two British battleships based at Valetta. Four freighters were at sea, three in a convoy escorted by six destroyers that had left Taranto on the afternoon of the 16th, and the other by a destroyer and a torpedo-boat. Another covering force was also at sea, consisting of the battleship *Duilio*, two light cruisers and three destroyers under Vice-Admiral Bergamini. The coming action would be called the First Battle of the Sirte.[21]

Iachino was between Vian's force and the main convoy, which was east of Malta. The *Breconshire* had been disguised as a battleship and early Italian air reconnaissance reported her as such. Additional reports were also received from Ju52s flying from Greece carrying troops to Africa. Though only one had been sighted, Iachino had to assume that all three British battleships were at sea and that the entire force

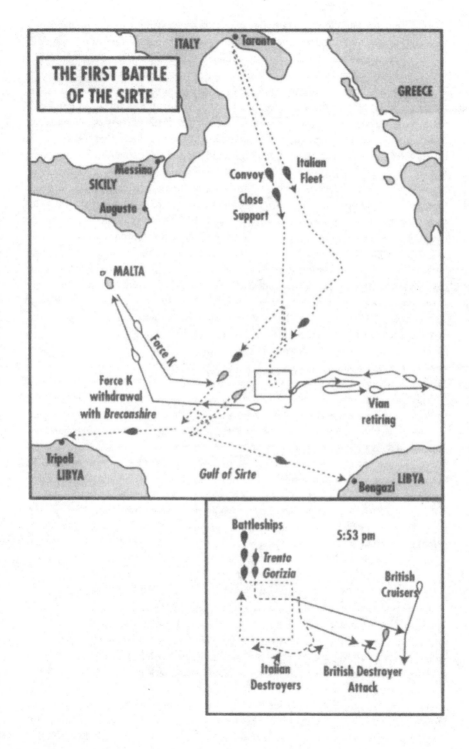

THE FIRST BATTLE OF THE SIRTE

ITALY

Taranto

GREECE

Messina

SICILY

Augusta

Convoy

Italian Fleet

Close Support

MALTA

Force K

Force K withdrawal with *Breconshire*

Vian retiring

Tripoli LIBYA

Gulf of Sirte

Bengazi LIBYA

Battleships

5:53 pm

Trento
Gorizia

British Cruisers

Italian Destroyers

British Destroyer Attack

was hunting for his convoy. The first report reached him at about 10.30am and indicated that the British fleet was 160 miles south and slightly east of his position. Iachino increased speed to 22 knots at 11.30am and to 24 knots 18 minutes later, which was the maximum the *Duilio* could make (her hull needed cleaning).

Vian, meanwhile, was aware of Iachino's approaching force from his own air reconnaissance early in the afternoon. He turned away to the south, so as to protect the *Breconshire*, being also aware that there were other Italian forces at sea which he had received no reports on. Iachino had launched two floatplanes that found Vian's force, and hovered in the distance making steady reports. Vian certainly must have wished he had a carrier at this point. But Iachino, based on his reconnaissance reports, felt he would be too late to engage Vian by the time he could reach him and therefore had slowed his fleet and ordered it to concentrate. The British had been under air attack all day, and the AA fire from Vian's ships was spotted by Iachino's fleet, which increased speed back to 24 knots and prepared for action.

Sunset was approaching when the *Naiad* reported the enemy in sight. The Italians opened fire at the extreme range of 32,000m, which dropped to 22,000m. Vian detached the destroyers *Decoy* and *Havock*, and later Force K, to protect the *Breconshire*, which headed south. The Italian fire was 'very accurate', with several British ships being straddled, and the cruisers turned away while the destroyers made smoke and advanced on Iachino, who countered by ordering his destroyers to repel them. Mack took his destroyers boldly forward, but was almost immediately ordered to retire on the main force. One midshipman on the *Jervis* later recalled 'the 15in shells sounded like motor buses going overhead'.[22]

And so as night fell, Iachino withdrew and Vian, as ordered by Cunningham, did not try to force a night engagement. The destroyer *Kipling* suffered minor damage and one man was killed by a shell splinter. The next morning, Force K took the *Breconshire* into Malta while Vian's ships retired to Alexandria.[23] Force K quickly refuelled and headed out to sea again to try to intercept the convoy near Tripoli on the evening of the 18th, but unfortunately it ran into a minefield laid by the Italians. The *Neptune* and *Kandahar* were lost and the *Aurora* was badly damaged, while the *Penelope* was slightly damaged. Force K had been crippled. While attempts would be made into the New Year to keep Force K functioning, it would achieve only some minor successes and would eventually be chased from Malta along with the submarines stationed there.[24]

*   *   *

While the arrival of the German U-boats in the Mediterranean had a dramatic impact on the balance of power at sea, especially with the sinking of the *Ark Royal* and *Barham*, Italy was poised to make her greatest contribution in the sea war, delivered by Borghese and his SLCs. The crews had been intensively trained in night operations in harbour for Operation EA 3, the attack on Alexandria, and the men were very fit.[25]

Borghese brought the submarine *Scire* in towards Alexandria on the night of 18 December, having received word from Athens that both the *Queen Elizabeth* and *Valiant* were in the harbour. Maps recovered from the wreck of the *Mohawk* helped

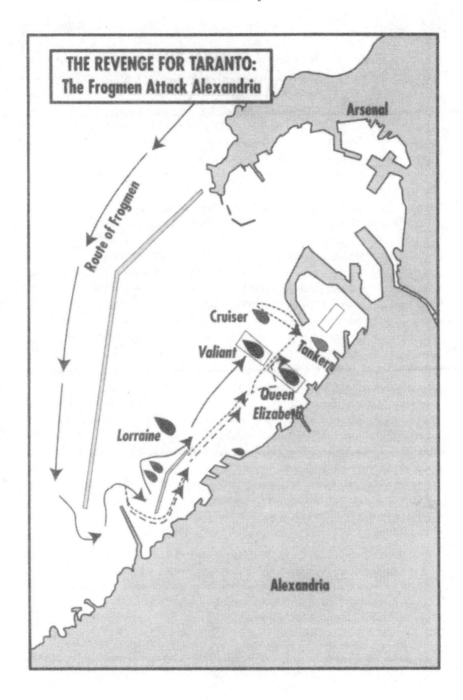

THE REVENGE FOR TARANTO:
The Frogmen Attack Alexandria

Route of Frogmen

Arsenal

Cruiser

Valiant

Tankers

Queen
Elizabeth

Lorraine

Alexandria

in the approach. Borghese came to within 1.3 miles of the mole, then surfaced with just the conning tower above the water so he could pop out of the hatch and look around. Three SLCs were launched, one piloted by Lieutenant-Commander Durand de la Penne, a veteran of the Gibraltar attack, as Vian's ships returned to Alexandria after the First Battle of the Sirte, and would enter the harbour with them, one SLC nearly being colliding with a destroyer.

At 3.25am on the 19th there was a report from the *Valiant* that '. . . two foreigners had been found on her bow buoy'. They were questioned and then locked up down below aboard the *Valiant*, and warnings were issued of the presence of 'human torpedoes' in the harbour. Various ships tried to pass lines underneath their hulls to locate the weapons, and the *Queen Elizabeth* did snag an obstruction, possibly the SLC, but was unable to do anything about it.[26]

At 5.50am the Italian officer aboard *Valiant*, de la Penne, warned a British officer that there would soon be an explosion. He refused to give other details and was left below. At 5.58am the first charge detonated, sinking the Norwegian oiler *Sagona* and damaging the bow of the destroyer *Jervis* nearby. This was followed at 6.05am by an explosion under the *Valiant* that had her crew up from down below and all watertight doors closed. There were no casualties but her forward main magazine and shell room were flooded along with other compartments. Eighty feet of her underside was damaged. Eleven minutes later the *Queen Elizabeth* suffered the same fate. Her A, B and X boiler rooms were flooded and she lost all power and light. Both battleships settled on the harbour bottom. The last two British battleships in the eastern Mediterranean had been 'Tarantoed'.

Within 48 hours the other two teams were prisoners. After the success of this operation, de la Penne freely provided many of the details of the operation, including their flight from Rome to Leros, the embarking on a submarine, and a complete story of how the operation unfolded at a tactical level in the harbour. Some have called this treason although today a warship of the Italian Navy is named after him.

London had warned the Mediterranean Fleet of such just an attempt, and Cunningham had issued an alert. There were stepped-up attempts at protection including the dropping of 5lb depth charges in the harbour, but to no avail. Cunningham later wrote that

> . . . that as the possibility of attack was expected the defences were on the alert, but that protection must not rely on the comparatively out-of-date methods of lookouts, boats and nets. Warning of approach by modern scientific methods is essential. Some method of neutralising [sic] a charge once it has been placed is important, in this instance there was three hours warning.[27]

At the time of the successful attack against the *Valiant* and *Queen Elizabeth* the port commander, Rear-Admiral G H Cresswell, in charge of the defences of Alexandria was 'not up to his job'. He had not been relieved earlier by Cunningham as he had been in his class at Dartmouth.[28]

The *Scire* had crept back out and after 39 hours submerged, surfaced and set a course back to Leros. The results of the attack would not be immediately known, but details would slip out in the coming weeks. The balance of power at sea had shifted.

CHAPTER 15

The Axis Gain the Upper Hand, Spring 1942

> Malta had assumed decisive importance as a strategic key-point, and my
> primary objective at the beginning was to safeguard our supply lines by
> smoking out that hornets' nest.
>
> *Field Marshal Kesselring*[1]

The beginning of 1942 marked a significant point in the war in the Mediterranean, as throughout the year the American presence in the theatre would be growing. Although warships would not be stationed there for many months, units of the US Army Air Corps were sent out in increasing numbers. Furthermore, the output of Italian war industry had peaked in 1941. Tank production was now in decline, plane production was static, and for the most part only small warships were being pushed to completion, as the blockade, the poorly-coordinated war economy, and the toll of the war itself all had their effect.

On 14-15 January 1942 another meeting took place between the German and Italian navies in the famous Alpine town of Garsmisch. The main issue was Malta, which had been having a serious impact on Axis shipping to North Africa. The talks between Raeder and Riccardi (who received the Iron Cross on this occasion) were quite open and cordial, and they settled the course of the naval war for 1942.[2]

The Germans promised to reinforce the Aegean sector, where they were in command, with eighteen launches, thirty-six trawlers and four E-boats. Twenty-four MFPs, 1100-ton vessels, would be built in Italian yards for coastal transport because shipping capacity both in the Mediterranean and the Black Sea had been greatly reduced by all the losses. The Germans suspected that the slow pace of building in the Italian yards was the result of an intention to save shipping for after the war.

Submarine operations would also be increased in the eastern Mediterranean, and Raeder promised to maintain an average of twenty-four U-boats in the Mediterranean. He also asked Riccardi to maintain Italian submarines in the Atlantic. Riccardi had been thinking of recalling them, but he agreed with Raeder and in fact ordered two more boats of the *Cagni* class to the Atlantic as reinforcements. The Italians also consented to the Germans commissioning the captured Greek destroyer *Vasiliev Georgios I* into their navy as *ZG3* (also known as *Hermes*).[3]

It was jointly decided to intensify the blockade of Malta by laying mines around the island and between Sicily and Tunisia, with the Germans providing additional supplies of mines for this, to help ensure the security of the North African convoys, the *Kriegsmarine*'s principal mission in the Mediterranean. The references to the Malta problem were somewhat optimistic: the Italian Navy's report stated that both allies agreed that Malta should be neutralised by the air force, mines and 'stealth means', but that occupation 'should follow . . . in the case there was a favourable situation', which seems to justify speculation as to how serious *Comando Supremo* and the Italian Navy were about plans to invade the islands.[4] They also discussed the deployment of Italian submarines and light forces in the Black Sea against Russia, which took place, and the Italian Navy made three ships available to the Germans there in support of the coming Spring Offensive on the Eastern front.[5]

The Italians made several requests for equipment, including a supply of engines for landing craft to be used in any invasion of Malta, and then put on the table the serious problem of oil for the navy, which was impossible to solve, except by the capture of enemy oil fields. General Thomas of the *Wehrmacht*'s War Economy Office stated bluntly to Raeder that the Italians could not receive any more fuel, but Raeder avoided alienating the Italians with such news, preferring instead to have the *Kriegsmarine* help the Italians out from its own supplies and those from the Rumanian oilfields, with Hitler's permission.[6] Some points remained unresolved, such as relations with Vichy France, which Raeder saw as a possible ally preferable to Italy, and the overall question of control in the Mediterranean, which the Germans wanted despite their limited forces deployed there.

After the successes of the combined effort of the German and Italian air forces and navies in late 1941, Raeder felt the strategic situation was good enough to try and convince Hitler to give priority to the Mediterranean theatre. One month after Garmisch, Raeder had a meeting with Hitler and proposed to push as soon as possible against Egypt, pointing out that the British had to rely on 40,000 men of the Egyptian Army to control the rear areas, and wanted Hitler to put pressure on Mussolini for this. Nevertheless, Hitler thought he had his last chance to bring the Soviet Union to its knees with a summer offensive against the industrial basin of the Donez and the Caucasian oilfields.[7] After the Garmisch talks Raeder wrote a long report in which he noted among other things that the most important problem, after oil, was transport and new shipbuilding in the Mediterranean. Riccardi explained that the procurement of transport ships for the war effort ran into difficulties from the Transport Ministry. The problem was that the requisitioning of ships was hindered by the *Duce* himself. Therefore, Raeder wanted Hitler to put pressure on Mussolini.

Regarding the building of new transport ships, the German Navy announced that twenty would be built in Italian yards and the first ten would be paid for by cancelling Italy's debts to Germany. Of the other ten ships, five would be given to the Italian Navy and the remaining five would again be paid for by cancelling the debt. Ricarrdi would check this possibility and reported that for the important issue of tanker construction, there were four 2000-ton, one 1000-ton and one 600-ton tankers in the yards. But the basic problems were neither solved, nor properly addressed at Garmisch: the shortage of fuel seriously restricted the operations of both navies, and shipbuilding capacity was not sufficient to replace losses of warships and particularly merchant ships which were being sunk by the Allies in increasing numbers.

On 25 January, General Marras, Italian liaision officer to the German High Command, met with the General Walimont of the OKW. There were many subjects to discuss, including the problems of the three badly-equipped Italian divisions on the Eastern Front. Marras also asked on behalf of *Comando Supremo* for the Germans to increase the number of E-boats they were committing to the Mediterranean to twenty and to reinforce the *Luftwaffe*. Also, he made clear that a general common plan for 1942 should be laid down. The agreement between the German and Italian navies was very limited. The talks between the chief representatives were more diplomatic than productive of actual firm commitments. Warlimont commented that 'in case this would be needed, the related proposals would be submitted at the right moment'.[8]

In the first 6 months of 1942, the supply situation to North Africa did improve. Italy, with help from Germany, successfully transported 474 Italian and 331 German tanks to North Africa.[9]

* * *

January also saw changes in command on both sides. On 10 January 1942, Vice-Admiral E N Syfret replaced Somerville, who was to command the fleet facing Japan in the Indian Ocean, while two days later Vice-Admiral Carlo Bergamini hoisted his flag in the *Duilio*, flagship of the 5th Battle Squadron made up of the three modernized battleships. Part of the reason for this promotion was that he had developed a tactical system for capital ships to be part of a convoy, providing additional protection. In early 1942 it would be common practice to have a battleship as part of the direct escort of a convoy, with the distant escort made up of light cruisers. These 'Battleship Convoys' gave Rommel the reinforcements and supplies to push the 8th Army back to the Gazala line and recapture Benghazi, which the Allies held for only a short time, and later to launch the May offensive that would culminate in the fall of Tobruk and the invasion of Egypt by the *Afrika Korps*.

The first of these convoy operations began on 3 January and was codenamed M.43. Conducted much like the previous M.42, it involved three separate convoys, all of which arrived safely at Tripoli. This formula would be repeated several times through the winter and into the spring. These operations were made easier as the striking forces on Malta were gradually reduced by the *Luftwaffe*. The intensifying air attacks forced the surface warships to leave the island in April and the submarines were redeployed to Alexandria soon after. On 14 April Wanklyn and the *Upholder* would be lost on their twenty-fifth patrol, probably being sunk by the Italian escort *Pegaso*.[10]

A second convoy also got through successfully later in the month, although Swordfish torpedo-bombers sank the 13,098-ton passenger ship *Victoria* had been pressed into service as a troopship on 23 January. She was carrying 1125 troops (405 were Germans) and 44 tons of various supplies. The three other ships in the convoy reached Tripoli safely, with a cargo including forty-six Italian and fifty-one German tanks and 118 Italian and 153 German motor vehicles. A fourth ship turned back due to engineering problems after leaving Naples and went to Messina. Both *Luftwaffe* and *Regia Aeronautica* units regularly provided air cover for these operations.[11] Bergamini was providing cover with the *Duilio* and four destroyers, while the

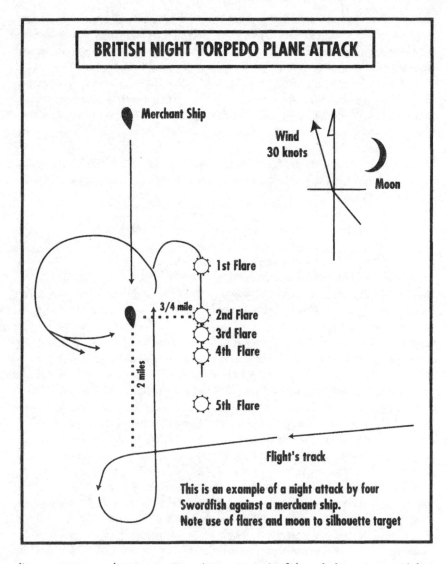

BRITISH NIGHT TORPEDO PLANE ATTACK

Merchant Ship

Wind
30 knots

Moon

1st Flare

3/4 mile

2nd Flare

3rd Flare

4th Flare

2 miles

5th Flare

Flight's track

This is an example of a night attack by four
Swordfish against a merchant ship.
Note use of flares and moon to silhouette target

distant escort was the *Gruppo Aosta* (*Aosta* Group) of three light cruisers and four
destroyers under Rear-Admiral de Courten. The direct escort consisted of six
destroyers, a torpedo-boat, and the *Orsa*.

   There have been various accounts of the loss of the *Victoria* and what cargo she
was carrying. There were only thirty attack aircraft left on Malta for this operation,
a mixture of Swordfish, Albacores, Wellingtons, and Blenheims. But at this time the
British still controlled the airfields near Benghazi, and it would be aircraft from the
mainland which would largely account for the *Victoria*.[12] A radar-equipped Wellington (nicknamed 'Goofington') from Malta located the convoy, on the night of
22-23rd January. Two British-crewed Flying Fortresses (an early version of the
B-17) based at Fuka in Egypt were dispatched to attack it, but bombing achieved

nothing. However, at 5.30pm on the 23rd three Beauforts operating from a base near Benghazi hit the *Victoria* with one torpedo, but the ship did not seem too badly damaged, although she was slowed. Waving off two of the escorting destroyers, she continued on to Tripoli.

Air cover for the convoy was provided by Ju88s, which were largely ineffective in offering protection from British aircraft that continued to snipe at the convoy in small raids, although one shot down a Blenheim that had attacked the *Duilio* group. Then five Albacores from North Africa attacked, and while one was damaged by a Ju88 and another shot down by AA fire, another torpedo hit the *Victoria* and she finally sank just after 7.00pm. Later a lone Wellington, after missing with bombs, came down to 500ft and strafed the escorts but neither the plane nor the ships were damaged. Of the 1455 passengers and crew aboard the *Victoria*, 1046 were rescued.[13]

The British use of aircraft to attack shipping was significant throughout the war, but became increasingly effective in 1941. Torpedo-armed Swordfish would regularly go out on 'Rat Hunts' to sink enemy ships. Night attacks became far more deadly when radar-equipped aircraft came into service, the first two Swordfish thus fitted arriving at Malta in late July 1941. A common tactic in night attacks was for one aircraft to drop flares behind the ships to be attacked, while the rest would approach from the other side to drop their torpedoes at short range from the slow-moving targets.[14] That winter also saw regular raids by Wellingtons on Tripoli, which did little serious damage but disrupted operations nonetheless. But all these raids from Malta would decline as the year continued, with the increasing pressure of the *II Fliegerkorps* on the island.

* * *

The Axis forces in the Mediterranean finally began to make use of radar in 1942, beginning with the German establishment of a radar station at Syracuse against British air raids. The *Regia Aeronautica* had developed radio-interception equipment to an advanced level, but still lagged behind in the area of radar.[15] Radar was a vitally important device in the aero-naval war in the Mediterranean, not only for detecting ships and aircraft beyond visual range or in poor visibilty, but also for gunnery control, fighter direction and navigation, and it was a major feature of the technological gap between the British and Italian forces.[16]

Britain's first operational naval radar was the Type 79Y, with a wavelength of 7.5m, first mounted on the battleship *Rodney* and the cruiser *Sheffield*, which took part in the 1939 Combined Fleet Exercises, where the radar proved useful but also somewhat unreliable. The set's wavelength needed to be reduced and the transmission power boosted. A month before the outbreak of war, the British gave the highest priority on the production of radar to fit some thirty ships, especially AA cruisers, because the Type 79 was principally an air-search set.[17]

The equipment was improved and renamed Type 279 during 1940. Forty additional sets were on order but these were not sufficient, since the Royal Navy also needed a surface-search capability, and therefore the multi-function Type 281 was developed. This was tested in July 1940, a month after Italy's declaration of war, and in August was fitted aboard the cruiser *Dido* while thirty-six more sets were ordered. Meanwhile, the *Carlisle*, which had been converted to an AA cruiser, had been fitted with an army anti-aircraft Type 280 set (3.6m wavelength) at the end of 1939 and had been sent to Malta in February 1940. At the same time, the Type 282 fire-control radar was developed, giving rise to a whole family of 50cm wavelength equipment. Two hundred sets were ordered in April 1940 after successful trials at the Gunnery School. It should be noted that in radar production the British had to rely heavily on American industry, especially for parts.[18]

For many years Italian naval historians claimed that the Italian Navy fought 'blind by night and short-sighted by day', but this was an exaggerated view. Although there is no official account of radar development in Italy, the official history of the Italian Navy contains some information on the story, which can be summarized as follows.[19]

In 1936 the Navy appointed Professor Ugo Tiberio of the *Regio Istituto di Elettrocomunicazioni* at the Naval Academy at Leghorn to study radar (called '*radiolocalizzatore*' or RDL/RDT). A prototype set was developed before the war, but the navy did not approve it until sets with 70cm pulse wavelengths were introduced in 1939-40. Professor Tiberio also said that the delay was due to the need to chose the right type of pulse radar, which explains why Italy entered the war with no operational radar at all.

In September 1941, after the Battle of Matapan, it was decided to install a radar of the 'DeTe' type, supplied by the *Kriegsmarine*, on the destroyer *Legionario*, then under construction, while a petty officer and five ratings were sent to Germany in October for training as radar operators. The equipment was not fitted until March 1942, leading to claims that the Germans were keeping radar technology from their ally.[20] But this was not so, as just before Italy's declaration of war, Raeder himself had ordered the sharing of radar technology. By the end of June 1940, a Italian mission lead by Lieutenant-Colonel Savino had inspected the Freya type of radar and reported to *Supermarina*. A request for two DeTe sets was then made, but it took a long time for them to be delivered.[21]

The Italian Navy's position has recently been reasessed by new studies. Castioni notes that after Taranto Night, the Italian Navy still wanted to build barrages of infra-red transmitters, instead of developing the radar prototypes they already had. He points out that scientific research in Italy between the wars made good progress, citing for example the SAFAR company's experiments with colour TV in 1939, but the outbreak of the war interrupted any further development. Radar research was also well-advanced, thanks to Professor Tiberio and engineers such as Del Vecchio. But the conservatism of the navy made it impossible to have the radar produced and mounted on warships, even though by the end of 1939 they had two rather good experimental models (EC3 and EC3bis) in their depot. Somewhat similar is the experience of the *Regia Aeronautica*, which bought the patent of the French SFR radar mounted on the big transatlantic liner *Normandie* (developed to detect icebergs), but then the experiments stopped in 1939. Interestingly enough, the navy also sent out several missions of officers to gather information on the state of radar research in other countries. This lead to a visit by British naval officers, really of naval intelligence, showing a false infra-red transmitter to their Italian colleagues, while they tried to find out what the Italian Navy was doing with radar.[22] Castioni goes further, saying that the types of radar built in Italy after 1941 were of good quality even in comparison to the British ones, as shown by trials made at Malta after the armistice.[23] At the end of 1940 the Italians suspected that the British had radar, but supposed that it would be base on infra-red technology. Finally they confirmed the existence of British radar from reports in the British press!

In February 1941 the *Regia Aeronautica* noticed that the newly-arrived *X Fliegerkorps* requested power cables for Freya radar sets at the Comiso and Catania airfields, while the German AA batteries used an air-detection system for fire-direction, while Matapan and the analysis of British radio traffic afterwards gave new impetus to the radar question. The following month the German promised to supply a DeTe radar, but only on condition of strict secrecy. The delivery could take place at the beginning of 1943. At the same time the Italians' own research made good progress and in April 1941 the first two prototype sets were ready, the first being mounted on the old torpedo-boat *Giacinto Carani* for a few days for tests and the second later on Iachino's flagship the *Littorio*. The results were not encouraging and the *Littorio*'s radar had to be changed, while the one on the *Carini* was not tested because the ship was too busy on escort duties, which seems a very strange approach to what was seen as a vital issue. By August 1941 the landed set from the *Carini* replaced the unit from the *Littorio*.

Nevertheless, a first order of fifty units was given to SAFAR, the lead company of five that were to produce it. Meanwhile the Germans seemed ready to supply the first radar set and a meeting took place at Bremen, whilst within the Italian Navy there was much discussion over which ship would receive it. Iachino wanted a destroyer and therefore it was assigned to the *Legionario*. Meanwhile the *Regia Aeronautica* also turned to the Germans for radar, asking for five Freya and ten Würzburg sets.[24]

In early March 1942 the first seven Würzburg L40 sets arrived, and were positioned for protection of the largest cities and in southern Sardinia, and made available to the other services. Of course this involved some problems, because the personnel had to be trained in Germany and in Italy and a general organisation had to be settled on. By May 1942 the first Freya set was deployed on the island of Lampedusa.

Italian industry promised to supply the first two EC3ter *Gufo* (Owl) sets in February 1942. On 9 August 1942, while the biggest Allied convoy of the war was about to enter the Mare Nostrum, Cavallero held a meeting centered on the question of range direction finders (known as Ra.Ri from *Radiodetector-telemetri*). But the Italian-produced radar seemed unlikely to arrive in good time, so the Italians had to rely on German help, especially after Iachino's report that the Italian radar still had problems. The first DeTe set was duly fitted on the *Legionario* and tested in the spring of 1942, and on 4 May Iachino reported enthusiastically on its performance.[25] The first *Gufo* set was mounted in September 1942 on the battleship *Littorio*, and the Italian Navy ordered a further fifty, but only thirteen seem to have been delivered before the Armistice.

It seems that the frequent disasters suffered by the convoys to North Africa caused the increase in interest in radar, but progess was slow. Moreover, the Italian Navy began to grasp that night combat was also affected by the quality of optical equipment (in which they were much inferior to the Germans) and by levels of training.[26]

But the German naval staff and especially Admiral Weichold were not particularly helpful in the supply of DeTe sets. Riccardi had to approach his German counterpart directly to obtain a few sets, which were sent only after much delay. By January 1943 the first four Fu.Mo31 model DeTe sets had arrived and were mounted on the destroyers *Malocello* and *Oriani* and on the torpedo-boats *Ardimentoso* and *Procione*. Another two, out of the forty-three requested, arrived in March and were installed aboard the destroyers *Alpino* and *Bombardiere*. By June 1943 a further twelve Wurzburg D radars and twenty Freya sets had been supplied.[27] The German Navy would also supply the Metox Fu.Mb71 radar detector to the Italians, to give warning of the enemy. But the delivery of the Metox, which is reported starting from the spring 1941, really only began from the end of June 1943 at the rate of twenty per month. Yet, according to other sources the first five sets arrived in Italy in October 1942 and were mounted on destroyers and torpedo-boats escorting the Tunisian convoys.[28]

In 1943 radar began to appear in some numbers in the Italian armed forces, while the Germans had their own equipment. An additional twenty *Gufo* sets were ordered in April 1943, while several Freya sets were set up to protect the cities and the bases on the Upper Tyrrhenian Sea. By the end of the war the number of *Gufo*s ordered had reached 100, but at the end of May 1943, Bergamini, the new fleet commander, reported that they were far from satisfactory. Moreover, the problem was not so much the production of equipment, but the shortage of trained personnel to use it.

The *Regia Aeronautica* enjoyed a better relationship with its German counterpart and received thirty-four 'Volpe' and eleven Freya sets by 6 May 1943.[29] On the other hand the German Navy was less obliging towards its ally. The Italian Navy got five Würzburg L40 sets for coastal surveillance from the *Regia Aeronautica* (which in turn had received them from the *Luftwaffe*). A total of twenty sets were mounted on ships, but mostly only when the war was already lost. A DeTe set was also mounted on the torpedo-boat *Aliseo*, while the *Gufo* radars were installed on the battleships *Littorio* (two sets), *Vittorio Veneto* and *Roma*, the cruisers *Scipione Africano*, *Attilio Regolo*, *Montecuccoli* and *Eugenio di Savoia*, and the destroyers *Carabiniere*, *Dardo*, *Fuciliere*, *Pancaldo*, and *Velite*. At the end of the war Italy developed two interesting prototypes of advanced radars which were later captured by the Germans.

The coastal defence radars in Italy on the eve of the landings in Sicily were manned mainly by the Germans, who controlled fifty of the eighty-six sets, while the Italian Navy controlled only two Löwe L40 type sets near Trapani. According to the circular order SM59S, issued in 1935 and again in 1938, the wireless centre of *Supermarina* was connected to *Superaereo*. The procedure foresaw that the requests for air support would be pass through *Supermarina* and then to *Superaereo*, but in conditions of great urgency, *Supermarina* could contact the relevant air base directly.[30] It should be noted that little use was made of short-wave signals in the

Italian Navy, forcing the ships to communicate with ciphered messages via regular wireless, increasing chances of interception and breach of security.

Santoni observed that in the Second World War radar was something of an obsession with the *Regia Marina*, but it should be noted that although important, it did not solve all the problems of night actions. For example the Imperial Japanese Navy was able to fight and win a number of night battles (Kula Gulf, Tassafaronga, Vella Lavella, etc) without radar and against an opponent with the best radar available at the time. But the Japanese were probably the best-trained for night combat, while the Italians may have been the worst, certainly far below the Germans and the British. The Italian Navy's resistance to radar both before and during the war, and its consequent failure to invest money in its development, cost Italy dear.[31]

* * *

But to return to the war. Vian's forces successfully ran one ship, the *Glengyle*, into Malta on 8 January, and brought out the *Breconshire* which likewise safely reached Alexandria. On the 25th, the *Glengyle* and one other empty ship came out while the *Breconshire* made her seventh run into Malta. During the winter of 1941-42 the Italians carried out forty-six trips by submarines carrying fuel to North Africa, mostly to besieged Bardia. Two were lost in these operations, the *Ammirglio Saint-Bon* being sunk by the *Upholder* on the night of 5/6 January, while the *Caracciolo* was sunk off Bardia by the 'Hunt' class destroyer *Farndale*.

Both the Germans and the British now had fast attack craft operating in the Mediterranean. The Germans had sent two flotillas of E-boats, and one, the 3rd, was based at the town of Porto Empedocie near Agrigento in Sicily. One of their first operations was the laying of mines off Valletta on 15 January. The British had had some small craft operating in the Mediterranean since before the war, either Motor Torpedo Boats (MTBs) or Motor Gunboats (MGBs). The British were latecomers to building this type of vessel and at the beginning of the war had been handicapped by the lack of a suitable engine, eventually having to make use of American-built engines for many of their boats. The MTBs were of two types, the short boat (under 100ft in length) and the long boat, usually a Fairmile 'D' type which was 115ft long and displaced 120 tons. They would, under normal conditions, receive a major engine tune-up every 200 to 300 hours. A type peculiar to the British was the MGB, simply an MTB without the torpedoes and with an increased gun armament, either a 2pdr or an old 6pdr, developed to counter the E-boats which were armed with very effective 20mm guns.[32] Many were used in the English Channel, operating against German coastal convoys. Because of the need to transport them out to the Mediterranean and their limited numbers, they saw most service in the Mediterranean after the surrender of the Italians.

The few boats stationed in the eastern Mediterranean were based at Alexandria and Tobruk, and ran small amounts of supplies and key personnel into that besieged fortress during 1942, and also ferried agents to the Greek islands, mostly Crete. One squadron of early Vosper boats were so ineffective at long-range operations that they were largely harbour-bound or capable of only short-range forays. Combat tactics were quite simple: close the enemy and either fire torpedoes or fire on the enemy escorts if you commanded a MGB, with gunnery range being 500 yards or less. They were most vulnerable to aircraft in daylight, especially as many British boats lacked AA armament. After two motor launches, *ML129* and *ML132*, were attacked and sunk by Italian aircraft whilst on their way from Gibraltar to Malta, small craft were packed on freighters and sent to Alexandria via the Cape.

* * *

Malta had received some naval reinforcements including the *Dido* class light cruiser *Cleopatra* and a destroyer. On 11 January the *Cleopatra* was damaged by a near-miss that killed eight of her crew. The following night at about midnight the big 'Tribal' class destroyer *Maori* was sunk by Ju88s. The bomb burst in her engine room and the ensuing fire caused her to explode at 2.10am, though the loss of life was fortunately small as only a skeleton crew was on board.[33]

The next major effort to supply Malta was Operation MF.5. Two small convoys totalling three merchant ships left Alexandria on 12 February, with Vian providing a distant escort of three light cruisers and eight destroyers. Eight Beaufighters were flown in to Malta to help provide air cover but overshot the island. The lead pilot realised something was wrong when he approached Sicily and saw Me109s taking off from an airfield! The planes succeeded in turning around and landing at Malta.[34]

The two small convoys joined up after arriving near Tobruk, but air attacks had already damaged one of the merchant ships which limped into the harbour. Over the next two days German aircraft sank the other two merchant ships, though four empty freighters did make it out of Malta with Force K escorting it some of the way. All the freighters and three of Force K's destroyers safely reached Alexandria.

Bergamini had sortied to intercept the convoy with the *Duilio*, two heavy cruisers, two light cruisers and eleven destroyers, but the only result was that one of the destroyers, the *Carabiniere*, was damaged by a torpedo from the *P36*. The escorts dropped 225 depth charges but failed to sink her. The *Duilio* had returned to Taranto (she sailed at 6.40pm and was back by 7.55pm) when *Supermarina* realised no British battleships were at sea and with her slower speed she would hold back the strike force. On the 14th, the *P36* was involved in an unfortunate incident of war. A small convoy from Tripoli had been attacked by aircraft and one ship, the *Ariosto*, had been damaged. That night the *P36* attacked her and sank her, but she was carrying 294 prisoners of whom 132 died. ULTRA had reported the presence of prisoners aboard her, but it is unlikely the *P36* could have received the message before her attack.[35]

In February, the first attempt to fly-off Spitfires to Malta took place, Operation 'Spotter'. The Spitfires could only be flown off from carriers whose lifts could accommodate their wingspan, and they also required extra fuel tanks for long-range flights. Force H sortied on 27 February, but had to return to port without launching the aircraft because the tanks were improperly prepared. In addition, the Spitfires' cannon were not working correctly and it turned out that they had never been tested before being sent to the Mediterranean![36]

However, another attempt was made using the carriers *Argus* and *Eagle* on 7 March. The *Argus* had Fulmars providing air cover and radar-equipped Swordfish for anti-submarine operations. A repeat of Operation 'Spotter', this attempt was successful in getting off fifteen Spitfires which were guided in by eight Blenheims that flew from Gibraltar.[37]

In Operations 'Picket I' and 'II' on 21 and 29 March respectively, the *Eagle* flew off nine and then seven Spitfires in the two operations. The Italian submarine *Mocenigo* launched three torpedoes at the *Argus* which was again providing fighter cover, but failed to hit. A decision was made at this time to have the Spitfires and Hurricanes concentrate only on German bombers and ignore the Me109s. The Spitfire could only break even in losses with it and that was not good enough given the desperate supply situation. The Hurricane could not compete against the Me109F.[38]

The Malta air forces had scored a magnificent success early in March. Warburton, 'the eyes of Malta', now flying a Beaufighter, had overflown Palermo on 2 March and spotted three heavily-laden freighters, probably bound for Tripoli. Therefore a raid by Wellingtons was planned. Ten went in that night. The Italian smoke screen did not hide the targets, and early in the raid the German merchant ship *Cuma* was hit. She was loaded with fuel and ammunition and was soon ablaze. Other bombers arriving later had a better view of the target, and a second German freighter was soon hit and quickly sunk. Other ships were damaged, including the Italian freighter *Securitas* and the torpedo-boat *Partenope*, whose commander was killed. The Wellingtons returned to Malta, with one being lost on landing, and six of them refuelled and flew back to attack yet again. No fighters attacked them and AA fire was reported to have been 'fairly light and inaccurate'.[39] Over the next two days the *Cuma* burned and finally exploded, sinking the *Securitas* and heavily damaging the destroyer *Freccia* and four small merchant ships. Many other ships suffered minor damage, including a torpedo-boat and three more destroyers. Casualties numbered 14 killed and 210 wounded.[40]

Axis convoys to North Africa continued, and at the end of one operation, V 5, a false report was made that an Italian cruiser had been torpedoed. Vian reacted by heading to sea with a mixed force of cruisers and destroyers to finish it off, joining up with the *Cleopatra* and the destroyer *Kingston* from Malta. On his return to harbour on 11 March, his flagship *Naiad* was torpedoed by the *U-565* and sunk, with the loss of eighty-two lives.

The British scored another series of successes against Italian submarines when on three days, 14, 16 and 17 March, three different 'U'-class submarines sank three Italian boats. Throughout the spring Allied submarines were busy up and down the Mediterranean, but they also suffered losses in the process. Specialised operations would be implemented as well, such as in early June involving Greek and British submarines in the Aegean sinking a dozen small caiques by gunfire.[41]

CHAPTER 16

The Second Battle of the Sirte, 22 March 1942

I saw only one full broadside. Her 15-inch shells made a great
mushroom of flame but her 6-inch secondary armament one could not
see because of their flashless propellent. The splashes from the 15-inch
seemed immense, their ranging appeared good, but the spread was bad.

View from the destroyer Legion[1]

By late spring 1942, supplying Malta from the west was deemed impossible and with the retreat to the Gazala line before Tobruk by the Allies and the loss of airbases in Libya between Derna and Benghazi, it was now proving increasingly difficult from the east.[2] The island was suffering from the increasing bombing campaign unleashed by the Axis powers, especially since the arrival of the *II Fliegerkorps*, and was short of supply, because of strong Axis opposition to the convoys. Moreover, the bombing campaign redoubled in intensity after 15 March.[3]

On 20 March 1942, a date chosen for the state of the moon, Convoy MW.10 of four merchant ships (*Clan Campbell*, *Pampas*, the Norwegian *Talabot* and the Fleet Auxiliary *Breconshire*) sailed from Alexandria to supply Malta with fuel and food. It was escorted by the 15th Cruiser Squadron consisting of the light crusiers *Cleopatra* (flagship), *Dido* and *Euryalus*, the AA cruiser *Carlisle* for close escort, the 14th Destroyer Flotilla (*Jervis*, *Kipling*, *Kelvin* and *Kingston*), the 22nd Destroyer Flotilla (*Sikh*, *Hero*, *Lively*, *Havock*, *Hasty*, and *Zulu*) and 5th Destroyer Flotilla made up of the small 'Hunt' class destroyers *Southwold*, *Beaufort*, *Dulverton*, *Hurworth*, *Avon Vale*, *Eridge* and *Heythrop*. Force K would join up from Malta consisting of the light cruiser *Penelope* and the destroyer *Legion*.[4]

The 'Hunt' class destroyers displaced only 1050 tons, could make 25 knots, and were armed with six 4in guns but lacked torpedoes. They were sent ahead on the 19th in order to sweep the convoy route for enemy submarines and to refuel at Tobruk before rejoining the formation, since they only had limited range. Of the seven started that sailed, the *Heythrop* was hit by a torpedo from *U-652* and was towed toward Tobruk but sank on the way, while another had to have its propeller cleaned before she could rejoin Vian's ships. Vian hoisted his flag in the newly-commissioned cruiser *Cleopatra*, describing the convoy as 'a desperate measure'.[5] Captain A L Poland had replaced Mack, having been in charge of the Inshore Squadron, based ashore, either at Mersa Matruh or Tobruk.

Cunningham had also sent out the submarine *Proteus* from Alexandria, which patrolled the approaches to Taranto with *P36* and *Upholder* from Malta, while the *Unbeaten* and *P34*, also from Malta, were to watch the Straits of Messina. The plan was to reach Malta at dawn on the day D+3, to avoid exposing the convoy to air attack during daylight hours in the most dangerous area. The weather was change-able at that time and Vian had to wait until he was sure of good conditions before sailing. At the same time the convoy sailed from Alexandria on 20 March, the remnants of Force K, the light cruiser *Penelope* and the destroyer *Legion*, left Malta to rendezvous with it.

The Axis came under additional pressure because on the same day, Force H sailed from Gibraltar as part of Operation 'Picket I' (see Chapter 15) with the battleship *Malaya*, two carriers (*Argus* and *Eagle*), the light cruiser *Hermione* and nine destroyers to fly-off reinforcing aircraft to Malta. This was the first move that the Axis were aware of, thanks to their intelligence at Gibraltar.[6] Therefore the air forces were alerted for operations in the Western Mediterranean, while the 8th Army and the Desert Air Force launched other diversionary operations draw the enemy's attention away from the Eastern Mediterranean. However, no Italian naval units were committed against Force H.

At 2.20pm on the 21st the Italian submarine *Platino* patrolling south of Crete heard engine noise from the convoy approaching from Alexandria and sighted the ships at 5.05pm, reporting one light cruiser, four destroyers and three merchant ships. Other Axis submarines were on patrol in the Eastern Mediterranean, the Italian *Galatea* and *Onice*, and the German *U-73*, *U-205* and *U-431*.

The reaction of *Supermarina* that evening is interesting. The strategic assessment was correct, since the aim of the convoy operation was understood. The possibility of other cruisers being present was taken into account (confirmed by a report at 6.30pm from the *Onice*), while reports from air reconnaissance over Malta suggested the possibility an imminent supply operation and the consequent sailing of ships from Valletta. Therefore, orders were issued to activate the *Gorizia* Group at Messina composed of the heavy cruisers *Gorizia* and *Trento*, the light cruiser *Bande Nere* and the 13th Destroyer Flotilla (*Alpino*, *Bersagliere*, *Fuciliere* and *Lanciere*), under the command of Rear-Admiral Parona. These ships rendezvoused next morning with Admiral Iachino who hoisted his flag in the *Littorio* escorted by the *Ascari*, *Aviere*, *Oriani* and *Grecale* of the 11th Destroyer Flotilla, which had steamed south from Taranto to meet Parona's ships.[7] Meanwhile, air reconnaissance kept Force H under observation until it turned back toward Gibraltar during the night of 22-23 March.[8]

Iachino's force moved south-east to intercept the British convoy. Vian was informed by submarine *P36*, which was patrolling the Gulf of Taranto, that the Italian ships were at sea steaming south at an estimated speed of 23 knots. Iachino knew that this time he had two advantages. First, the Mediterranean Fleet was without battleships after the sinking of the *Barham* and the successful *maiali* attack on Alexandria, and secondly, the Italians could rely on good air cover.

On 22 March Vian's principal concern was the higher speed of the Italian ships, as his convoy could only make approximately 11½ knots and the enemy could be in position in the afternoon to intercept it before it could reach Malta. If he turned south, he could delay this encounter, but it would also delay the convoy's arrival at Malta. The arrival of air cover from the island was vital. He did make a small turn to the south and also hoped that the increasing south-east wind would delay the Italian warships. A severe storm was building. Vian joined up with Force K from Malta at 8.00am.

The British ships began to come under air attack at 9.30am, an hour after their fighter escort had left, but these early attacks did no damage. The first four Ju88s were unable to find the convoy due to cloud cover. Then at 9.35am five Italian S.79 torpedo-bombers from Libya attacked, one of them being shot down, but they dropped their weapons at too great a range to have any effect, and at 11.07am four more also failed to hit.

But Iachino's force was now nearing the convoy. Vian decided to confront him and had formed his fleet into six divisions. One was made up of the AA cruiser *Carlisle* and the destroyer *Avon Vale* and was to make smoke, while the other 'Hunt' class ship guarded the transports. During the first phase of the coming action these two ships would have a minor collision while manoeuvring to lay smoke and avoid bombs. The other cruisers and destroyers were to engage the enemy with guns and torpedoes, making smoke screen at an angle at the same time, reversing course 'in time to attack with torpedoes'.[9] The other five divisions were the 14th Destroyer Flotilla, Force K reinforced by the *Dido*, the destroyers *Sikh*, *Hero*, *Havock* and *Lively*, the destroyers *Zulu* and *Hasty*, and the remaining two cruisers.

At 2.10pm Captain Bush of the *Euryalus* reported enemy in sight to the north (incorrectly reporting three battleships), which triggered Vian's signal to make smoke and to head north forming line ahead by divisions, while the convoy was diverted to the south-west, but it could not hold this course for long because of the delay it would cause in reaching Malta before daylight the next day.[10]

Contact had occurred earlier than Vian had expected, but the Italian ships were the cruisers and destroyers of Rear-Admiral Parona, which had sailed from Messina undetected by the British, and could have been there sooner, taking the convoy by surprise, if the strong south-east gale had not held them to 22 knots instead of their best speed of 30 knots. The Italian ships were about 14 nautical miles away when first sighted, but did not themselves sight the British until 2.26pm at a range of 23,000m. They had already been ordered to clear for action at 12.40pm, after the *Trento's* seaplane made its report. The wind was blowing to the north-west, towards the Italian fleet, so the British smoke would interfere with their gunnery.

Parona was surprised by the smokescreen laid so quickly by the British, and after 3 minutes he turned north, while Vian ordered a turn to the east and realised that the enemy ships were cruisers and not battleships as first thought. Meanwhile Parona turned to starboard several times, making a complete circle without trying to attack the British, and only ordered 'open fire' when his ships had completed this circle at about 2.56pm. The exchange of fire had little result as the range was extreme and each side had difficulty seeing through the smoke, although the *Bande Nere* straddled the *Cleopatra* and *Euryalus*. Between 3.04pm and 3.09pm Parona steamed west, but then turned north. At 3.15pm the Italians broke off the action, and Vian signalled to Cunningham 'Enemy driven off. Iachino was later critical of Parona's conduct.

Vian steamed back towards the convoy, which had been heading south-southwest and had been under air attack, suffering no damage, but had expended 60 per cent of its 4in ammunition. He had barely regained the convoy when the *Zulu* sighted the Italian fleet again at 4.37pm. Parona's cruisers were in the lead, with the *Littorio* in the rear. Iachino's intention was to steam to the south-west and cut Vian off from Malta as well as getting downwind of the immense smoke screens being made by the British. Vian's forces continually advanced and fell back, feinting and threatening, for the remainder of the afternoon, as the range slowly closed. Even Vian had difficulty making out the enemy in the thick smoke, and three times shifted forces to the east, *ie* away from the enemy threatening the convoy, because he was unsure whether enemy ships were also working around to the east.

At 4.43pm the *Cleopatra* and *Euryalus* were engaging Parona's squadron when the *Bande Nere* hit the flagship at a range of just under 20,000 yards. This knocked out the radio and killed fifteen men. Another man was killed and some minor damage done by near misses. The *Littorio* now had an opening in the smoke and splinters from a 15in shell hit the *Euryalus*. The *Cleopatra* was now firing her forward three turrets against the Italian ships, and her rear two turrets at the aircraft attacking her and the convoy!

Captain McCall of the *Dido* later recalled;

> Outside the smoke screen, visibility was good. Time and time again we dashed out to sight the enemy and fire a few salvoes. When the enemy shells got too close, we retreated under the blanket, altering course as soon as we were unobserved, to mislead the enemy.

Vian had detached one of the divisions, Poland's 14th Flotilla, to assist the convoy and he had taken his own division to the east at this point, so it was left to Captain St. J A Micklethwait's division of the 22nd Flotilla, led by Micklethwait's flagship the *Sikh*, to keep up the pressure on the Italians. At about 5.00pm he led his destroyers forward, and engaged the Italian cruisers for 6 minutes until the *Littorio* hove in view. As he fell back, at 5.20pm, the *Havock* was hit by splinters from a 15in shell that killed seven men and wounded nine, and flooded one boiler, causing her to be detached to help the convoy.

Micklethwait gallantly came on again at 5.40pm and opened fire on the *Littoriol* He straddled the battleship but did not hit her. The *Sikh* herself was straddled in return, and not wanting to be sunk with all his torpedoes aboard, Micklethwait fired off two, but at long range and they failed to hit.

The climax of the battle was now approaching. The convoy was only 11 miles from the *Littorio*, well within range of her guns, but invisible in the heavy smoke. Vian massed his forces and, using a jury-rigged radio, coordinated an attack through the smoke to support Micklethwait and drive the Italians back.

Vian attacked with cruisers through the smoke at 6.02pm, firing torpedoes at the *Littorio* at a range of six and half miles, and saw her make smoke and disappear. The *Littorio* was the only Italian ship hit in this action, and it was now as Poland's division of four destroyers and the *Legion* was to the south-east of the closing Italian fleet. He had been under orders to cover the convoy, but interpreted a garbled signal from the *Cleopatra* as an order to help Micklethwaite. At 6.34pm his five destroyers attacked the *Littorio* at 28 knots, which was followed by the three cruisers in line ahead, at 6.34pm. The range was dropping rapidly (a mile every 2 minutes) and this may have contributed to the 'erratic' firing of the Italians. Vian and his cruisers were also firing from further to the east and at longer range.

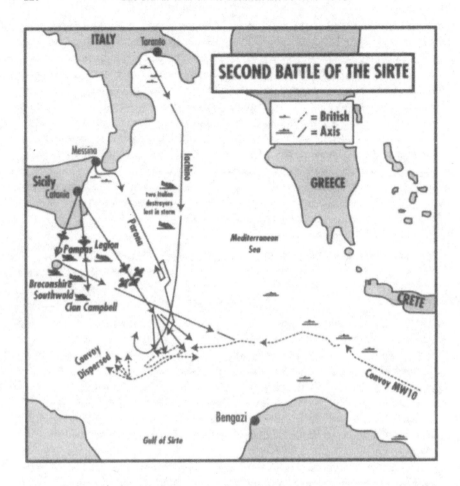

When Poland was about 5000 yards from the enemy, he turned and launched torpedoes. A total of twenty-three would be launched at the Italian fleet (the *Kelvin* had fired two earlier at longer range). The only hit on an Italian ship took place at 6.51pm, a 4.7in shell on the *Littorio*, doing little damage. The *Kingston* was then hit by a 15in shell that passed right through the ship, starting a small fire and wrecking some of the light AA guns, killing fourteen and wounding twenty. She would be temporarily stopped by damage to her engine-room.[11] Micklethwait also launched some torpedoes from his division, but at longer range. The *Lively* was hit by 15in splinters and suffered some minor flooding. The Italian fleet, ordered by *Supermarina* to avoid night combat, turned away and headed north in a rising sea. The last shot was fired at 6.56pm. After 2 hours of smoke screens and the menace of torpedo attacks the Italian ships were still far from doing any damage to the convoy.

The convoy would arrive the following day but not under the cover of night, having all been ordered to make best speed to Malta with whatever escort could be managed, while Vian retired on Alexandria. The *Talabot* and the *Pampas* both safely made Valletta, arriving mid-morning on the 23rd, the *Pampas* having been hit by two bombs that both failed to explode. The *Breconshire* was damaged by three bombs dropped from Me109s and was stopped just short of the island. As the gale increased, the *Penelope* was unable to take her in tow, and so she anchored near Marsa Scirocco, Malta's other smaller port. The *Clan Campbell*, the slowest ship in the convoy, was not so lucky and was sunk before making harbour. The destroyer *Legion* was damaged by near-misses and had to be beached at Marsa Scirocco, where she was later sunk, and the *Southwold* was lost to a mine.

The ships that arrived were nevertheless heavily bombed and on 24 and 25 March the fighters at Malta, both Hurricanes and Spitfires, were partly successful in checking the *II Fliegerkorps'* onslaught. However, on the 26th the Axis planes sank the *Pampas* and caused a dangerous fire aboard the *Talabot*, both anchored in the Grand Harbour, while the *Breconshire*, already damaged and towed to Marsa Scirocco was sunk on the 27th after 4 days of continual attacks. The *Talabot* still had ammunition on board as she burned and it fell to the torpedo officer of the *Penelope*, Lieutenant Dennis Copperwheat, to place demolition charges to sink her. The heat was so intense that the charges had to be placed on the outside of the ship, and after the area was cleared, Copperwheat exploded the charges from only 40 yards away. He was injured but survived.[12] But 5000 tons of the 26,000 tons of supplies that had been loaded at Alexandria were disembarked and gave some relief to the besieged garrison. A further 1522 tons were salvaged from the wrecks.

Iachino also had bad luck after the battle. Due the severe weather, the destroyers *Lanciere* and *Scirocco* sank with the loss of 453 men – only 18 survived – and the *Trento* received heavy damage trying to assist them. The *Bande Nere* was also damaged in the storm and while trying to make port for repairs would be sunk on 1 April by the submarine *Urge*. But for the British, the heavy losses of merchant ships proved the near-impossibility of getting convoys through to Malta at this time.

According to Iachino's after-action report, the errors which plagued the battle off Calabria were no more; the many aircraft that passed over the Italian ships to attack the British 'never made errors in recognition'. Also signals performance was judged good. More complex was the question of fire control and gunnery, which suffered several problems during the battle. Ammunition expenditure was as follows: *Littorio* 181 15in, 445 6in, 21 90mm; *Gorizia* 226 8in, 67 4in; *Trento* 355 8in, 20 4in; *Bande Nere* 112 6in; and *Aviere* 84 120mm.[13] The British cruisers fired off between 1600 and 1700 rounds and the destroyers 1300.[14]

It is quite interesting to note the observations made after the battle about the quality of the gunnery of both sides. In the Italian gunnery report the British fire was

> . . . always quick and intense: often it was all concentrated on the *Littorio*, and then it was a true boiling of water pillars around this ship. However, it could be said that only a small number of enemy salvos were concentrated, and sometimes the salvos appearing good were short shots of a cruiser and long ones of another. This explains why, although the enemy salvos were very concentrated (always 5-6 shots in 100-150 meters), no hit was scored on the *Littorio*.[15]

It was noted that the British had fired near the smokescreen and that their fire was hampered by the very bad weather, and sometimes by their own smoke. According to the Italians, British fire was nevertheless 'aimed by the destroyers on the basis of the falling points, which evidently was possible, by the better quality of the optical instruments of the British ships'.

The main problem of the Italian fire was the weather. One 15in gun barrel burst on the *Littorio*, and the optical range-finders were put out of service or difficult to use due the penetration of salt water inside them, rendering them useless. The water also caused the malfunctioning of the electrical system aboard the battleship, disabling one 15in turret and putting another out of action for 15 minutes. After the battle there was a meeting on board the *Littorio* in order to urge the shipbuilding industry to solve the many problems suffered during battle in bad weather, in direct criticism of the suppliers of the *Regia Marina*. After the experiences of another ship in rough weather in February and of the *Littorio* on 22-23 March, it was written that 'it can be affirmed that it is absolutely necessary that *in design of new ships the total waterproofing must be foreseen and care given to its perfection*'.[16]

CHAPTER 17

C3: The Proposed Invasion of Malta, 1942

Right through the spring they turned such a blitz upon Malta as no
other island or city (until then) had seen in the war. . . . Malta became
the most bombed place on earth.

Alan Morehead[1]

I t would have been difficult for the Axis to seize Malta in 1941. Indeed, a
Kriegsmarine memorandum of July 1941 said that an attack was not considered
possible and that a year of preparation was needed. That year had now passed.[2]

1942 saw steps made to prepare for the invasion but several times it surfaces in the
documents that there were differing opinions within the German military about the
Malta operation, as there were within the Italian high command and the navy.
Riccardi had said at the Garmisch conference that the operation would be carried
out 'whenever there would be favourable conditions', frequently taken to mean that
the Italians did not want to take the British base.

Several minutes of meetings of the Italian Supreme Command suggest that the
Malta problem was exasperating Italian commanders. As the navy pointed out, 'At
least 80% of the losses of our navy and merchant ships are caused by the fact that
Malta is in enemy hands'.[3]

It should be remembered that the Kesselring's memo to the Italians on the causes of
the shipping losses proposed more air attacks on Malta and Gibraltar. *Supermarina*
agreed, commenting that 'Neutralizing the island would be, as has already been
shown, a very easy solution to the ocean traffic problem, and every threat of enemy
action in the Mediterranean would automatically be minimized'.[4] But this could only
be achieved by an invasion. It could have taken place in early to mid-1942, with the
balance in the Mediterranean having shifted towards the Axis powers, but the many
German senior officers who did not want the operation (ranging from Hitler to
Rommel and many in the navy) had the upper hand, and furthermore the only
partially-convinced Cavallero preferred to agree with Mussolini.[5]

Malta played a vital role in Axis strategy for the war in the Mediterranean in
spring and summer 1942. The Axis plan called for Rommel's Italo-German army to
advance and capture Tobruk, while a tight air blockade was maintained on Malta.
Once Tobruk fell, and the Allied airbases nearby had been pushed back out of
range, the island would be invaded by both air and sea.[6] There were many air
attacks throughout the spring and the island was heavily pounded. By early April all
surface ships had either been evacuated from Malta or sunk. The cruiser *Penelope*
escaped but had so many small holes in her that she was nicknamed 'HMS Pepper-
pot'. By the middle of the month what was left of the 10th Submarine Flotilla was
ordered from the island too and would not return until the end of July.[7]

On 15 April King George VI awarded the island the George Cross 'to honour her brave people'. Certainly many on the island were proud to see the people of Malta so recognised, but as the siege wore on there was some dissent on the island. Graffitti appeared that said 'Hobz, mux George Cross' ('Bread, not George Cross').[8] The Governor, Lieutenant General Dobbie, who was disappointed to learn that no convoys to Malta would be attempted in either April or May due to the worldwide naval situation, was considering surrendering the island. Others in the Maltese government wanted to soldier on and informed Churchill of the situation, and consequently in early May Dobbie was removed and replaced by General Lord Gort, who had most recently been in command of Gibraltar. A winner of the Victoria Cross, Gort was a good choice and a fighter.[9]

There had been one major operation flying-off Spitfires to Malta in April (Operation 'Calendar'). Force W, built around the American aircraft carrier USS *Wasp*, had sailed from Britain for the Mediterranean and on 20 April, with eleven Grummam F4F Wildcat fighters overhead providing cover, it successfully launched forty-seven Spitfires of which all but one arrived.[10] They were immediately pounced upon by the *Luftwaffe* on arrival and by the end of the month only seven remained. The next attempt was more successful. On 9 May 1942, in Operation 'Bowery', sixty-four fighters were flown off from the carriers *Wasp* and *Eagle* and only three failed to reach the island. It would after this operation that Churchill would write to Roosevelt, 'Who says a wasp can't sting twice'.[11]

During the first half of 1942, there were twenty small shipments of supplies made to Malta by submarines carrying cargoes consisting of medical supplies, aviation fuel, powdered milk and letters (the Maltese called these visits 'the Magic Carpet Service'), and six runs by the large, fast minelayers *Manxman* and *Welshman*. The *Manxman* on at least one occasion disguised herself as the French large destroyer *Le Tigre*. But it would be the *Welshman* that arrived on the 9th with smoke canisters which were used the following day to cover the arrival of the new Spitfires.

Careful plans had been made to disperse and then refuel the newly-arrived Spitfires, which paid off as few were lost as quickly as during Operation 'Calendar'. There then followed a terrible battle over the island. Both sides suffered, but the important point was that the British were contesting Axis air superiority over Malta, and would continue to do so from then on.

The American correspondent Jack Belden later wrote that the people of Malta were cheered by the sight of numerous parachutes falling into the sea around the island, assuming these were Axis pilots bailing out, but they did not realize that the Ju88s that were attacking were dropping mines on parachutes![12] Axis air attacks did not end with this, and from 10 May on there were large-scale air battles over the island. The Germans were being sent elsewhere and the Italian high-level bombers had returned. The local population felt that a turning point had been reached. One civilian later said that:

> It was a comforting sight to look up and see the 'black crows', as we called them. It was like being visited by old friends. We felt that our prayers had been answered. God had sent back the Italians.[13]

So how did the plans for the invasion of Malta develop? In early 1942 the main call for the capture of Malta came from Mussolini himself, who ordered the military to put together plans for an invasion (codenamed 'Operation C3'). Both Hitler and Admiral Raeder agreed with the general idea. The fall of Malta would help in the capture of Egypt, which would allow a junction of forces with a German drive south from the Caucasus, and an eventual link-up with the Japanese in India.

The Italian planners quickly discovered they would need German help in two areas to take Malta. First, they needed the *Luftwaffe*, recognising that the Me109f was a decisive weapon in the struggle. The first *Luftwaffe* contribution for Operation C3 ('Operation Hercules' to the Germans) would be their *II Fliegerkorps* along with elements of the *X Fliegerkorps* and *Fliegerführer Afrika* (the German air command in North Africa) plus additional forces from one fighter and two bomber groups. The Italian contribution was to be slightly larger. The figures were:

Aircraft Type	Italian	German
Bomber	270	216
Fighters	222	189
Torpedo Bombers	36	–
Ground Attack	168	27
Transports	170	216
Rescue Planes	24	18
Large Gliders	–	27*
Totals	840	693
Grand Total:		1533

*at least a dozen, and possibly all twenty-seven, of these gliders were to be the huge 'Gigant' model.

The second German contribution was to be parachute units and the transports, mostly Ju52s, to get them to Malta. The famed *7th Fallschirmjaeger* (paratroop) division under General Kurt Student, together with the Italian *Folgore* (Lightning) paratroop division, would form the core of the airborne assault. The Italian parachutists were reputed to be 'living for the invasion', but Student felt, even though they were certainly highly motivated, they lacked some of the equipment needed for such an operation, but the presence of the German paratroops would make up for this and that the invasion would be successful.[14]

In the months prior to the proposed invasion, the German and Italian paratroops spent time training together. General Bernhard Ramcke, commander of a German parachute battalion, who was a strong believer in co-operation between the Axis forces, was very important in this period. His battalion was based near the training area of the *Folgore* division and spent a great deal of time working with his Italian counterparts, but it is an exaggeration to say that the *Foglore* division was trained by the Germans.

The final invasion plan called for a three-week preparation phase, during which the island was to be softened up by an all-out air attack. The first week was to see the Axis regain air supremacy over Malta. During the following week, the attackers would concentrate on neutralising defensive ground positions (rocky Malta had numerous rock and/or concrete pillboxes scattered throughout the island, many still visible today), while in the third week, air attacks would be concentrated specifically against the British AA defences around planned drop sites. This was to avoid the kind of fiasco that had taken place near Maleme airfield on Crete, where one intact Allied AA battery had inflicted heavy losses on the Ju52s attempting to land there.

'Y-Hour' was set at 1:30am. Just before that, however, one battalion of German paratroopers (under the command of the famous Colonel von der Heydte, who would later lead the last German paratroop drop during the Battle of the Bulge in 1944), was to land in gliders to ensure the destruction of any remaining AA batteries around the main landing zone. Although such a move might alert the defenders, it was considered worth the risk to save casualties.

The initial German landing force was to be two regiments of paratroopers, with four gun sections. The Italian contingent was to be one regiment (three battalions) of the *Folgore* and one company of 47mm AT guns. A second wave of equal size, but with more support elements such as engineers, would land at the end of the first day, after the transport planes had returned to base and been reloaded.

The paratroop landing area was to have been on the west side of the island, and was selected for two reasons. First, it was to allow the paratroopers to clear and then protect the amphibious beachhead area. Secondly, the paratroopers were to seize an airfield as quickly as possible, so that the Italian air-transportable *La Spezia* division and more supplies could be brought in if transport were available. The *La Spezia* division was playing the role of the German mountain divisions in the Crete operation.[15]

What options were available for an amphibious assault? A direct attack on the north or east coasts of the island faced many old but nonetheless powerful coast defense batteries. Many dated back to the 19th century, but against slow transports they would have been able to inflict heavy losses.[16] This left the extreme west coast, beyond St Paul's Bay, which would have been the easiest landing area but also the furthest from Valletta. An advance from this position would have met virtually no coast defense or AA batteries but would have to cross the old 19th century Victoria Lines, a series of four forts connected by entrenchments, which could have slowed down the Axis advance.

The west beach was also near two airfields – the large one at Luqa, and a smaller one at Hal Far. It was behind the Victoria Lines, and the AA (and shore batteries) on the West Beach were negligible. Some have argued that the west beach would be difficult to land on, but one of the authors has visited this area twice and confirmed the Italian opinion that it was practicable. While it is an ascending slope, there are, on a day without very rough seas, numerous landing places – though no real beaches. The shore is formed of sloping rock rising, in some places, steeply from the water's edge. While by no means a sheer wall, the high ground does dominate the landing zone, which is why it was vital for the paratroops to secure the heights overlooking the beach. Attard argues that the invasion of Malta would have been difficult. He points out that the lack of AA was important for the fall of Crete, but there the airfields were the initial objective. On Malta, however, the paratroops were principally being employed to secure the beachhead, so that the invading troops could march inland and seize an airbase in conjunction with the airborne forces.

Wherever possible, Italian aircraft were to attack separately from their *Luftwaffe* counterparts to avoid confusion and duplication of effort. From Y+3 hours and 30 minutes to Y+6 hours, there were to be in the words of the official German planning document, '… attacks in successive waves by the German Air Force in continuous support of the paratroops'.

The Italians were to assist in the capture of the first airfield by committing the *Regia Aeronautical* 1st Assault Battalion (400 men). A follow-up force of 800 men from the *Loreto* Battalion of combat engineers were to prepare the captured field to receive supplies and reinforcements as quickly as possible, while also fighting alongside the 1st Assault Battalion. The proposed airdrop sites had also been selected to keep away from the numerous small fields surrounded by stone walls that covered much of the island. The western end had less agricultural land then either the north or east sections of the island.

While all this was being undertaken, a 300-man Italian *nuotatori* (swimmers) commando unit drawn from the *San Marco* marines and supported by Italian destroyers, German Seibel ferries armed with 88mm guns and aircraft from both air forces would attempt to capture Fort Benghasua at Marsa Scirocco Bay, a fishing harbour on the east side of the island which was used from time to time by British submarines and other vessels during the war, and which formed a critical part in the plans to land supplies and heavy artillery in the follow-up to the initial landings. At the same time, a second group of 300 naval paratroops, also from the *San Marco* Regiment, would attempt to drop directly into Fort St Lucian, a 16th-century fort modernised by the British in the 1860s, which was situated on a small peninsula jutting into the middle of Marsa Scirocco Bay. This would have been a daring operation, and possibly one that would ultimately have failed. As a cover for all of this, during the afternoon of Y-Day, Italian planes were to release 220 dummy parachutes, with twenty real commandos mixed among them, across the northern part of Malta, in an attempt to confuse the British.

Shortly before midnight, the first amphibious units were to begin landing, while the force bound for Gozo was to move into position for an assault in the morning. Comino, the small unoccupied island between the two, was to be occupied after Gozo fell. Night operations are always hazardous, and this would have been a dangerous time for the invasion and could have led to problems or even total failure.

But the naval operations would have been decisive. The plan called for the Italian fleet to be positioned southwest of Malta, to support diversions at three points on the island, one on the south-west coast and two on the north coast. It was also to provide fire support against positions along the Victoria Lines, but its main role was to escort the invasion convoy to the island and intercept any British naval units approaching from Alexandria or Gibraltar. The covering fleet would consist of the battleships *Vittorio Veneto*, *Littorio* (if available), *Duilio*, and *Doria*, four heavy cruisers, eight light cruisers and twenty-one destroyers under the command of Vice-Admiral Iachino. He would be supported by twenty-five torpedo-boats and many *MAS* boats operating in the Sicilian Channel under the command of Rear-Admiral Angelo Parona. The two *Littorios* were under the command of Rear-Admiral Guiseppe Fioravanzo, who would go on to write the official history of the battlefleet after the war.

The actual invasion fleet would be under Vice-Admiral Vittorio Tur who had been heavily involved in the training of the specialized units of the *San Marco* regiment. His flagship would have been the destroyer-escort *Procione*. Her three sister-ships of the *Orsa* class would be present, along with ten destroyers and six torpedo-boats, for escort and fire-support for the invasion, the sloop *Diana*, nine *MAS* boats, three patrol boats, twelve minesweepers, and a German E-boat flotilla and a German minesweeping flotilla.

Support ships for the invasion force consisted of ten ships of between 800 and 1100 tons, twenty-five trawlers, three cistern ships, two oilers, ten tugs, and two hospital ships. The actual invasion craft were made up of both Italian and German ships. The German contribution was forty-six ships and a company of small assault boats numbering eighty-one. The Italians had a mosaic of various ships and boats ranging from light passenger ships and two more transports, to twenty-four speed-boats, thirty-seven motor rafts, two ferry boats adopted for tank transport, etc, for a total of 151 various craft. Construction of some of these specialised craft had been proceeding through the winter and into the spring and some of the troops had practiced landings with them.

Two days were to be allowed to complete the amphibious landings, during which the *Duilio*s would offer the primary shore bombardment support against enemy positions. Although only 200 rounds per battleship were allocated for this, the effect of 12.6in gunfire would have been considerable. Numerous Italian and German submarines would also be deployed for this operation, including one that was to act as a navigation beacon for the transport aircraft carrying the paratroops to Malta. Attard argues that the Italian fleet, sailing under an Axis air umbrella and protecting the invasion convoy, would have suffered attacks by the Royal Navy, aircraft, and from coast defense batteries. The Royal Navy, primarily Force H, could have been a factor, if it came out in force, pushed through the air and undersea obstacles facing it, and arrived in time – all these factors being a question of luck – and might then have hindered or stopped the Italian amphibious force. The fleet at Alexandria was weak at this time and the Italians left it out of their planning. However, the Italians now did have some limited radar capability which would have helped them to defend the convoy, and in a daylight action the four battleships should have been able to hold off the inferior British fleet. With so much Axis air power in the area, and the submarine lines, the British might have suffered serious losses and never arrived to engage the Italian fleet. If the convoy had not made it to Malta, the airborne troops would probably have been wiped out by the numerically superior British garrison, but Force H would have had serious problems in preventing the landings.

Once the convoy arrived, there would have been two landing zones, the main one codenamed 'Famagusta', while a smaller landing was codenamed 'Larnaca'. At 'Famagusta' the first units ashore would have been the Italian *Friuli* and *Livorno* Divisions, with the former advancing on Marsa Scirocco while the latter secured the western flank, while at 'Larnaca' a force of 1900 men, made up of three lightly-armed Blackshirt battalions and three companies of *San Marco* marines, would be landed to secure the south-west entrance of Marsa Scirocco bay, and would have faced a tough fight.

There were two key operations in the invasion. The first was the securing an airfield so that the *La Spezia* Divison could arrive safely, which would probably have been the most difficult immediate objective as not only would the Axis have to secure the defended airfield which was an essentially open space with little cover, but they would also have to secure the area surrounding it, and the British had much more AA available to them on Malta than they had on Crete. The second was the seizure of Marsa Scirocco Bay. Faced with all the special landing forces assaulting the harbour, and then having the *Friuli* Division advancing from the west, it is unlikely the harbour could have been held, as it would have been defended at best by only four battalions, which were spread out all over the eastern sector of the island.

Two more Italian divisions were to follow up the initial landings, with orders to advance on Valetta. As with most Italian divisions, they numbered six battalions each but both were reinforced with two additional battalions of Blackshirts. While Italian medium tanks were eventually to form the main armoured element in the Axis force, it was planned to include twenty German Panzer IIIs. At the meeting between Hitler and Mussolini on 30 April, Hitler had suggested using some captured Soviet heavy tanks in the assault, though nothing came of that. The British fielded about ten tanks, both heavy Matilda IIs and light Vickers Mark VIC tanks. The Matildas were a real threat which the Axis had planned to counter by landing eight Semoventi 75mm Assault Guns in the first wave ashore. They also had nineteen more armed with the inferior 47mm AT gun. Later troops due to arrive at Marsa Scirocco would have had heavy Italian 90mm and 75mm AT/AA guns. There were also over fifty L-3 light tanks, similar to the British Universal Carrier, with the first two divisions to land. The artillery of the *Friuli* and *Livorno* infantry divisions would arrive with the main convoy, as would additional heavy guns consisting of twelve 149mm and twenty-four 105mm field guns, for the reduction of Valletta if the city refused to surrender once surrounded and with its water supply cut off. Even if Valletta's garrison lingered on in defence, Malta would still have been lost to the Allies as a base of operations.

The grand total of the Axis invasion force was 96,000 men, 754 guns, 850 motorcycles, 270 81mm mortars, and 170 tractors for the heavy guns. Facing this were the half-starved British and Maltese defenders. Malta Command numbered eleven British and four Maltese battalions divided into four brigades, a total of 26,000 men, although some of the local farmers would have joined in the fighting, especially during the parachute landings. If the invasion force had got ashore in strength, it would have been difficult for the British to have held the island. Photographs of the time show many British soldiers with their uniforms hanging off them due to starvation.

Attard argues that the number of Spitfires in July were sufficient to have broken up the attacking airborne forces. If the Axis could not gain air superiority over Malta, the invasion would have been much more of an uncertain affair, but the concentrated weight of the Axis air forces on the eve of the assault would most likely have knocked out the remaining RAF fighters.[17] The strike capability of the RAF on the island was minimal, and the coast defences on the western side of Malta were likewise negligible. The main batteries had always been positioned near the harbour entrance and on the stretch of coast immediately to the west. Finally, only one invasion against an island garrison failed in the Second World War, against Wake Island in the Pacific. This starving island would have most likely put up 24 hours of resistance and then surrendered. Field Marshal Kesselring, who was deeply involved in the planning of the operation, later wrote in his memoirs, 'It would have been easy to capture the island'.[18]

Interestingly, the Japanese assisted in planning for this invasion, one of the rare instances where there was co-operation between all the Axis powers. An Admiral Abe attended the Italo-German planning session of 20-23 February 1942, and offered eight observations based on the recent Japanese experience in the Phillipines and Malaya.[19]

1. Careful planning was required.
2. Security for the operation was a paramount consideration.
3. They recommended the use of the Italian *Alpini* mountain troops for the invasion. They would be lightly-equipped and therefore less of a load for the amphibious craft, and also constituted something of an elite force. The Japanese had made good use of mountain troops, especially their lightweight artillery, in their amphibious landings in the early months of the war.
4. Once engaged, objectives had to be taken swiftly through grim determination and by achieving local superiority.
5. The first wave ashore should be infantry, the second machine-gun troops, and the third should contain the artillery.
6. Absolute radio silence needed to be observed and enforced prior to the invasion.
7. The assault force should be assembled together in the same few boats and land as a unit.
8. Heavy air attacks should take place just after the troops were ashore.

They recommended a purely seaborne operation, abandoning the airborne element, and also advised going in at night. They calculated the attack would require three Japanese divisions totalling twenty-three infantry and six artillery battalions. The Japanese and Italians differed on the use of air power in the operation. The Italian plan called for a great deal of independent air activity all around the island, while the Japanese believed it should all be directly controlled by the Navy or Army commanders involved, reflecting the fact that the Japanese did not have an independent air force.

But the invasion was never launched. Hitler had little confidence in the Italian Navy and feared it would let his airborne forces down, and it has been argued that his heart was never really in the plan. But more fundamental was Rommel's success at Gazala and the fall of Tobruk. Rommel wanted to push on immediately into Egypt, and Hitler, followed by Mussolini, agreed with this new plan, which meant that assets, principally aircraft, would not be diverted to the planned invasion of Malta.

Malta held out because the population, by and large, became united against the attacking Axis, as their friends and relations were killed in air raids. It was not unusual for the Maltese to kill Axis pilots who bailed out over the island with pitchforks or large rocks, much as the Cretans did during the German attack in 1941. British troops usually rushed to landing sites to prevent this. Furthermore, supplies were never completely cut off. If a tighter blockade had been maintained, the island might have been forced to surrender through starvation. This entire aspect of food is often overlooked by historians. Supplies from neighbouring Gozo had dried up by July 1942. Throughout the summer the number of goats dwindled (and with them goats' milk for babies) and by August virtually all the goats and pigs were gone. Throughout the summer the horses were kept as well as could be since they supplied most of the transport on petrol-starved Malta, but they too were in a weakened condition and horsemeat for dinner was not unusual. The victory kitchens set up to supply a meal were quickly dubbed 'siege kitchens' by the Maltese.[20] The rocky nature of the island itself helped in the resistance to the attacks, providing materials for defensive positions and shelters. Furthermore, stone-built Valletta did not burn like a city of wooden houses would have.

Finally, one can not forget the presence of Lord Gort. He could be seen riding a bicycle to work and eating the same rations as everyone else. He did all in his power to improve conditions and make them as fair as possible. The Maltese would call him 'Malta's luck'.[21]

So Malta hung on and eventually proved very damaging against Axis convoys attempting to supply Rommel's Italo-German army at El Alamein. Hitler's failure of will in 1942 and Italian poor planning in 1940 allowed this beleaguered fortress to play a vital role in the Second World War. After the success of Operation 'Pedestal', called by the Maltese 'The Santa Marija Convoy', there was a lull in air attacks which saw only a few ineffective air raids in October and new tactics of attacking ships further out to sea. The last Italian raid took place on 23 February 1943, and on 20 June King George VI visited Malta on board the cruiser *Aurora* escorted by four destroyers.

CHAPTER 18

Operation 'Harpoon', June 1942

But for the enemy surface force, both of these ships [the *Kentucky* and *Burdwan*] might have been brought in.

Captain C C Hardy, 21 June 1942[1]

In the summer of 1942, the tide of war turned both in North Africa and in the Mediterranean. Both sides had greatly improved their logistic network, with the Axis able to use Benghazi and the Allies Tobruk. In April the Axis succeeded in transporting 150,389 tons of supplies and equipment to North African ports out of 151,578 tons shipped, as opposed to the 47,588 tons that arrived in March, and in May 86,439 tons out of 93,188 tons arrived. This remarkable improvement was due to the combined Axis effort at sea and in the air.[2]

On 17 March Rommel flew to Führer HQ to argue for the importance of a decisive blow in North Africa. But to Hitler, Africa was only a subsidiary theatre that was kept going largely to keep his weak Italian ally in the war, and also to tie down as many Allied forces as possible to prevent intervention on what he believed to be the decisive Eastern Front. Losses that winter in Russia had been so great that no reinforcements could be sent to Rommel. The *Kriegsmarine* also made proposals, based on their assessment that the Mediterranean could be the decisive theatre of war, by capturing the Suez Canal and Basra, but Hitler refused to follow Raeder's suggestions. Interestingly enough, this assessment of the strategic situation was quite different from those the *Kriegsmarine* had made at the outbreak of war, when the Atlantic was seen as the main theatre.[3]

According to Gerhard Schreiber's research, the *Kriegsmarine* wanted to gain control of the Mediterranean ports and thus influence the command and employment of the Italian Navy, with this control being exercised by the German liaison officers aboard Italian ships, which would 'let the German flag be hoisted not only on transport ships, but also on warships', as some compensation for the German blood spilt in the Mediterranean war. This is partly confirmed by the statements of several Italian admirals that they would sooner scuttle their ships or surrender them to the Allies than have the Germans take control of them.[4]

This was the strategic background against which what was supposed to be the decisive effort of the Axis forces in the Mediterranean was planned. On 29-30 April 1942 Hitler and Mussolini and their respective military staffs met at Klessheim castle near Salzburg in Austria, where the strategy for the coming year was established, with a timetable of operations. The plan foresaw that Rommel's Army in North Africa would attack and defeat the Allied forces at Gazala, while the Italian and German Air Forces would neutralise Malta, and after this first phase and the capture of Tobruk, the invasion of Malta would go ahead. Only once the island had fallen would Rommel be free to continue his offensive towards Suez (codenamed Operation 'Aida'), with his supply lines secured and all the Axis aircraft in the Mediterranean available to support him. But all of Hitler's discussion of these questions was a pure tactical manoeuvre with his allies.[5]

When he went to the Klessheim meeting, he had already decided that the operation against Malta would never pass beyond the planning stage, as he was little inclined toward the Mediterranean overall and towards this operation in particular, doubting that the Italians would give all the naval support required and believing that they would abandon the German paratroops to their fate. This view was challenged by General Ramcke, the man who helped in the training of the Italian paratroops, who thought they were ready for action. On 11 April 1942 Ramcke had made a presentation before Mussolini, Kesselring, Cavallero and a group of selected German and Italian senior officers of all three services on the experience of the seizure of Crete saying that 'the training of the German and Italian paratroops is the same and is sufficient'.[6] However, Rommel supported the Führer, saying that 'the Italian soldier is unable to conquer Malta'.[7] A month before the meeting, a directive sent by the High Command of the *Wehrmacht*, to the German Liaison Officer in Italy, von Rintelen on 27 March, said clearly 'to the Italians it could not be said that they can cease their preparation for Malta'. But the German and Italian paratroops would be a very rapid reserve intended for the African front or for France. It was unlikely that the invasion would proceed, but Italy would continue to prepare for it.[8]

* * *

On the Allied side the strategic situation was influenced by the events occurring in the Pacific, where the need to stop the wave of Japanese conquest drew resources both from the Middle East and the Western Desert. Nevertheless, Churchill put pressure on the commander in the Middle East, General Sir Claude Auchinleck, urging him to assume personal command of the 8th Army in the field and to attack Rommel.[9] But Auchinleck waited for more reinforcements which had to make the long trip around Africa via the Cape, while at the same time the Axis supply situation was very good, thanks to the effective 'neutralisation' of Malta's striking forces.

The British had one success in May when the Italians attempted another attack by the *X MAS* on Alexandria, following-up their successful raid of December 1941. The Italian submarine *Ambra* had crept close to Alexandria on the night of 14 May carrying three *maiali*. Their targets were the large floating dock containing the battleship *Queen Elizabeth* under repair, and the submarine depot ship *Medway*. The 40,000-ton floating dock was the only large one available to the British in the eastern Mediterranean – the nearest alternative was at Durban in South Africa. Two 'pigs' were detailed to attacks the dock which would with luck result in both its destruction and that of the battleship within it. The *Medway* was the mothership for the successful operations by small British submarines which had been the major cause of losses to the Axis supply convoys.

The *Ambra* surfaced near the harbour entrance, released all three 'pigs' and then submerged, temporarily becoming stuck in a sand bank, before returning to her home port of La Spezia. However, ULTRA had alerted the British to the attempt when on 5 May they intercepted an Italian transmission revealing that another attack was to be attempted, even giving the floating dock as the main target. The SLCs failed to get into the harbour due to the currents which forced the *Ambra* to a point too far to the west of the harbour entrance, several searchlights which blinded the crews, star shells, patrol boats, and random depth charge attacks. The six Italian sailors had to abandon their SLCs and swim ashore. Four of them were immediately taken prisoner while the other two would enjoy the freedom of Alexandria for a month before being captured.

That same month the British had tried to repeat their earlier successes by surface warships raiding from Malta against the Axis convoys by sending four destroyers from Alexandria under the command of Captain A L Poland to attack a convoy bound for Benghazi. The four British destroyers, the *Jervis*, *Jackal*, *Kipling*, and *Lively*, all large ships, set off at high speed for the central Mediterranean on the evening of 10 May. German aircraft based on Crete and the Greek mainland sighted them (much of the *II Fliegerkorps* had been shifted to the Eastern Mediterranean after the successful attacks on Malta). The destroyers had tried to steam a middle course so as to avoid Axis aircraft, but unfortunately this drew them away from the long-range Beaufighters which were held in readiness at airfields to support them. The Beaufighters arrived too late. The first attack by eight Ju88s in the early afternoon had them bomb the ships from 3000ft, coming out of the setting sun. They sank the *Lively*, which was the AA destroyer armed with eight 4in guns. Attacks continued all afternoon with one at 8.00pm by ten Ju88s which saw the determined German pilots come down to 1500ft and sink both the *Kipling* and the *Jackal*. Only the *Jervis* succeeded in returning to Alexandria crowded with 630 survivors.

* * *

The two most important tasks for the Royal Navy in the summer of 1942 in the Mediterranean were cutting off Axis supplies and sustaining Malta. Properly supplied, surface ships, submarines and aircraft could all operate from the island against the enemy convoys, but at this time Malta had practically no effect on the supply lines to North Africa, a situation that would continue until resupply by convoy.

The Allies had several advantages in the war at sea over the Axis. Allied naval power overall was greater than their enemies', and they had more warships under construction or completing. The longer the war continued, the stronger the Allies would become. Furthermore, ULTRA allowed them to learn when Axis convoys were sailing and their destination a few days in advance, but they still needed ships in position to exploit this information, and they still needed to defeat the Axis air forces and the escorting ships.

The Royal Navy had one operational battleship in the Mediterranean, the old *Malaya* at Gibraltar. The Gibraltar Force (best known as Force H but that codename was not used that summer) had two carriers available for the upcoming operation, the old *Argus* (nick-named HMS 'Ditty-box') and the *Eagle*. While not the equal of modern carriers, they had experienced crews. The ships' air complement consisted of sixteen Sea Hurricanes and four Fulmars aboard the *Eagle*, and thirteen Swordfish and two Fulmars aboard the *Argus*. The Sea Hurricane was a successful conversion of the land-based aircraft to carrier operations, armed with eight machine guns. When compared to the modern aircraft carried on Japanese carriers, one can see how British carrier forces in the Mediterranean in 1942 were still essentially second-class.[10]

The units of the *Regia Aeronautica* based on Sardinia meant that the British fleet could not operate too close to that island in daylight. Three *Stormos* of bombers were based there, made up of twenty-eight S.79 and thirty-eight S.84 torpedo-bombers, and thirty-three Z1007 and six P108B bombers. All were three-engined aircraft, except for the P108B, which was a four-engined long-range bomber – the Italian 'Flying Fortress' – which occasionally flew night missions against Gibraltar. Italian planes suffered from being slow and lightly armed, as well as being largely made of wood since metal was an expensive item for the Italian war machine. Fighter escort was provided by the 54th *Stormo*, comprising twenty-nine Macchi 200s, thirty-one Cr42s (primarily acting as fighter-bombers) and seventeen G50s (note that in all these cases, not all the planes listed were all actually available for operations at any one time). Although highly manoeuvrable, the Italian fighters lacked both firepower and speed, although the Macchi could fly at 318mph and the G50 could almost touch 300mph. The real advantage the British fighters had was their heavier weaponry, superior to that of any Italian fighter and equal to those of the *II Fliegerkorps*.

The Italian aircraft based on Sicily were primarily used for attacks against Malta. At this time there were 62 Italian multi-engined bombers or torpedo-bombers (but with only 12 torpedoes), 15 Italian-operated Ju87 dive bombers, and 129 fighters, including 36 of the new Macchi 202s and 14 Re 2001s.[11] The sleek Macchi 202 had been introduced in late 1941 but still had only two machine-guns. With its German-designed Daimler Benz engine built in Italy, it could hit a top speed of 373mph. This was a modern fighter capable of holding its own against modern Allied aircraft. The Re2001 also used the same engine but was not quite as fast as the MC202. It did however have four machine-guns and would end up as a night fighter over Italy. It was not as successful as the MC202, as it was a difficult plane to manufacture, and therefore did not have as high a building priority as the MC202. While most of the *Luftwaffe* was in North Africa and the Aegean, some aircraft remained on Sicily, including twenty-seven Me109Fs and twenty-one Ju88s. Their main mission was to prevent Malta from being used as a base for attacks on the convoys. The British tried to have their convoys operate in daylight as they approached the central Mediterranean, making the final run into Malta at night, as a ship crippled close to Malta could suffer devastating attacks from these aircraft.

Facing these forces was a gradually strengthening RAF presence on Malta. That June there was a squadron of anti-submarine Albacores, 6 torpedo-fitted Wellington bombers, and several reconnaissance aircraft on the island, as well as 95 Spitfires (all that remained of the 213 that had reached the island over the past three months), and 5 Beaufighter night-fighters.

Operation 'Harpoon' would be under the overall command of Vice-Admiral Curteis. As well as the battleship *Malaya* and the two carriers, the covering force for the convoy consisted of the cruisers *Kenya* (flagship), *Charybdis* and *Liverpool*, and eight destroyers. The main convoy was made up of five freighters loaded with food and supplies and the oil tanker *Kentucky*, one of a class of fast tankers built for Texaco in 1940. Her US merchant crew would prove unreliable. The close escort under Captain Hardy on board the anti-aircraft cruiser *Cairo* consisted of nine destroyers (one, the *Kujawiak*, being Polish-manned), as well as several small craft including six MLs. During the operation, the fast minelayer *Welshman* was to accompany the convoy until in a position to race ahead at 28 knots, unload valuable ammunition for the aircraft based there and then return to support the convoy during its final approach to Malta.[12] Thirteen submarines were also operating off the Italian coast, and would reap one of the few Allied successes of this operation.

As it steamed east on the morning of 12 June, the convoy faced a powerful Axis naval force, although one partially crippled due to lack of fuel oil. Operation 'Harpoon' was known to the Italians from a 'reliable source', most likely from the intercepts of American radio traffic flowing from their attache Colonel Fellers in Cairo. The Axis had mustered a powerful force to oppose the convoy: twenty-one Italian and six Germans submarines; two light cruisers of the 7th Cruiser Division under Rear-Admiral Alberto Da Zara and two squadrons of destroyers were ready to intercept; and six German E-boats and numerous *MAS* boats would be operating in the narrow straits and off Malta. Twenty-three more Italian submarines were also patrolling throughout the Mediterranean.[13] Only in one area were the Allied forces superior to the Axis forces facing them and that was in destroyers. Attrition of Italian forces had been so heavy, and with so many ships under repair or convoying troops and supplies to North Africa, Greece or the islands, that less than thirty ships could be mustered for duty throughout the Mediterranean.

As the British approached Sardinia, *Supermarina* was not quite convinced that this was the real thing. It shifted some aircraft to Sardinia, but on 13 June it was unable to locate the convoy. The next day the action began. The first attacks by Cr42 fighter-bombers armed with 100kg bombs failed to inflict any major damage, but in the next attack one freighter was torpedoed and sunk and the cruiser *Liverpool* damaged. By 6.00pm the convoy was coming within range of Sicily's airfields. Their first attacks, which now included German planes, were ineffective and both sides had lost many aircraft.[14]

The convoy was now detached from the covering force to proceed on its own. At dawn on 15 June, off Cape Bon near the Italian island of Pantelleria, the convoy encountered Da Zara's squadron which had come from Sardinia via Palermo. It had previously detached two destroyers, the *Gioherti* and *Zeno*, due to engine trouble, but two light cruisers and five destroyers remained. Although De Zara lacked the benefit of radar and was unsure of the makeup of the force he faced, he had a full day before him.

Hardy's dilemma was simple. For every warship he detached from the convoy to fight the Italian squadron, there would be one less ship protecting the convoy from air attacks. He decided to have the five fleet destroyers, led by the *Bedouin*, attempt to hold off the Italian squadron while the *Cairo*, the four 'Hunt' class escorts and the smaller craft remained with the convoy. The *Bedouin*, commanded by Commander B G Scurfield, led the five destroyers in the order given below.

SHIPS ENGAGED IN SURFACE COMBAT

Italian Ships	Standard Disp (tons)	Armament
Cruisers		
Eugenio di Savoia	8997	8 × 6in, 6 × 3.9in, 6 21in TT
Montecuccoli	7550	8 × 6in, 6 × 3.9in, 4 21in TT
Destroyers		
Oriani	1685	4 × 4.7in, 6 × 21in TT
Ascari	1715	4 × 4.in, 6 × 21in TT
Vivaldi	1943	6 × 4.7in, 6 × 21in TT
Malocello	1943	6 × 4.7in, 6 × 21in TT
Premuda*	1880	4 × 5.5in, 6 × 21in TT

*captured Yugoslav destroyer. *Premuda*'s top speed was 31 knots in Italian service as her 'wartime chief engineer Bandiera . . . flogged to her flank speed of only 30 to 31 knots'.[15]

Allied Ships	Displacement (tons)	Armament
Cruiser		
Cairo	4290	8 × 4in
Destroyers		
Bedouin	1854	8 × 4.7in, 4 × 21in TT
Partridge	1540	4 × 4in, 8 × 21in TT
Ithuriel	1370	4 × 4.7in, 10 × 21in TT
Marne	1920	6 × 4.7in, 8 × 21in TT
Matchless	1920	6 × 4.7in, 8 × 21in TT
'Hunt' class escorts		
Blankney	1050	6 × 4in, no torpedoes
Middleton	1050	6 × 4in, no torpedoes
Badsworth	1050	6 × 4in, no torpedoes
Kujawiak	1050	6 × 4in, no torpedoes

Hardy ordered the fleet to make smoke to cover the convoy, but Italian 6in shells straddled the *Cairo* with their second salvo at a range of about 20,000 yards. Da Zara detached two of his slowest and oldest destroyers, the *Vivaldi* and *Malocello* of the 14th Destroyer Squadron, to attempt to attack the slow-moving convoy, while he took his two cruisers and remaining destroyers (of the 10th Destroyer Squadron) to try and keep between it and Malta. The *Vivaldi* and *Malocello* would soon become engaged with the 'Hunts' with the *Vivaldi* being brought to a halt with a hit to her engines after firing two torpedoes, but both ships were now out of the action. Da Zara detached his other destroyers to assist the crippled *Vivaldi* which was towed to Pantellaria for repairs.

Commander Scurfield had led his destroyers forward boldly, perhaps too boldly. The action quickly developed, which might not have been the best thing to do, as Vian had demonstrated at the Second Battle of the Sirte. Ranges would eventually fall to as little as 5000 yards that morning, and the Italian cruisers would expend almost all their high-explosive shells – armour-piercing rounds were somewhat ineffective against unarmoured warships, often passing clean through the target without exploding. The *Bedouin* and *Partridge*, in the lead and closest to the two cruisers, were both quickly disabled. The *Bedouin* was hit twelve times, mostly by 6in shells, though not all of them exploded. By now the convoy was actually heading west, away from Malta and Da Zara's force, and was also under air attack. The three remaining destroyers closed with the cruisers and the *Ithuriel* got to within 8000 yards, inflicting 'light damage' and forcing them to open the range. Even the *Cairo* eventually entered the fray, and was slightly damaged, continuously salvo chasing and maintaining the range to the enemy. One shell penetrated deep into the ship, but failed to explode. Hardy later said that if it had it would have disabled his flagship. In the air, a Ro43 floatplane launched from the *Savoia* was shot down by one of two Beaufighters operating over the convoy. The other Beaufighter chased off two Ju88s, even though its guns were not working! At 7.15am Hardy ordered the three undamaged destroyers to concentrate on the *Cairo*, while Da Zara opened the range, in part due to the heavy smoke, but by 8.22am the Italians were again closing in and threatening the convoy, but neither side achieved any significant results and the action was broken off at 10.00am.

But Hardy had not fully solved the problem facing him. He had been able to keep the surface ships away from the convoy, but the Axis air forces had attacked and attacked hard. In a series of air attacks during the morning, the tanker *Kentucky* and the freighter *Burdwan* were damaged and had to be taken in tow and another freighter sunk, leaving only two undamaged merchant ships in the convoy, reducing its speed to 6 knots. At 11.42am Hardy decided to scuttle the two crippled ships and proceed to Malta with the remaining two freighters which could make 14 knots. The *Bedouin* and *Partridge* were going to join the convoy when Da Zara reappeared and fired on the *Hebe* and hit her as she was leaving the crippled *Kentucky*. Hardy turned back with the *Cairo* and three destroyers, but did not engage the Italian squadron, which then attacked the *Bedouin* and *Partridge*. The *Partridge*, which could only make a maximum of 18 knots, tried to defend the *Bedouin* and was under fire for an hour, but an S.79, one of those led by Buscaglia, torpedoed the *Bedouin*, although it was shot down in the process. The *Partridge* now kept watch on the Italian squadron as it rescued the crew of the *Bedouin*. Twenty-eight men were lost from the *Bedouin* and the *Partridge* returned to Gibraltar.

The convoy sailed into a minefield that sank the Polish 'Hunt' escort, caused further losses and generally disrupted the entire operation. Hardy's only consolation was that he was now joined by the returning *Welshman* who could offer some additional AA support, and so his battered fleet limped into Valletta that night. On the 16th, the *Cairo* and four destroyers (two being 'Hunts') left Malta and steamed for Gibraltar, and though attacked, arrived safely. The two freighters had brought in 15,000 tons of supplies but the shortage of oil was becoming critical.

Clearly this was an Axis victory and a tactical victory for the Italian Navy. Part of the convoy did get through to Malta, but the British suffered far heavier losses than the Italians and Mussolini would later personally present medals to Da Zara and some of his men for their efforts. It would be the only squadron-sized surface naval victory of the war for Italy.

* * *

In conjunction with 'Harpoon' was an attempt by the new Admiral who had replaced Cunningham at Alexandria, Sir Henry Harwood of River Plate fame, to run a large convoy to Malta, codenamed Operation 'Vigorous', made up of eleven merchant ships protected by a close escort of 'Hunts' and small craft, including towed MTBs. Vian had a covering force of the 15th Cruiser Squadron of six light cruisers and had two big 'Town' class cruisers from the 4th Cruiser Squadron which had come through the Suez Canal for this operation. With escorting destroyers, Vian's force was much stronger than that he had had at the Second Battle of the Sine.

Essentially, Harwood, new to his position and based ashore at Alexandria, dithered when air attacks began against the convoy and the Italian fleet built around the *Vittorio Veneto* and *Littorio* sortied from Taranto. On 12 June one freighter was lost to German planes operating from Crete and on the 14th another had engine trouble, headed for Tobruk and was sunk. Rough weather forced the MTBs to return to Alexandria, one being lost on the way. That afternoon more planes sank one freighter and damaged another. That night, six E-boats operating from Derna under Lieutenant Wuppermann attacked the convoy. The *S60*, *S54*, *S55*, *S56*, *S58*, and *S59* were one of the smaller classes of *Schnellboote*, designed for theatres requiring smaller craft. While the Mediterranean really did not fall into that category, they were easier to transport there than the larger boats.

Built in 1940-41, these 107ft boats displaced over 100 tons when fully laden. Powered by three Daimler 16-cylinder engines, each generating 1320hp, they could make 36 knots in colder climates. In the warmer Mediterranean speeds of about 30 knots were the best obtained. They were armed with two torpedoes and two 20mm cannon, and had a crew of 16. The 'mosquito fleet' concept was that small, fast craft like the *S60*s could control the waters along the coast, near coastal trade routes, and in confined waters – like those around Sicily or along the North African coast. Unfortunately, for this doctrine to work, it required large numbers of these craft, and not the few that Italy and Germany had so far produced. It also required relatively calm seas, as in heavy weather they had to remain in port. The Italian *MAS* boats were stationed elsewhere in Sicily and on the island of Pantelleria. That night the E-boats hit and damaged the cruiser *Newcastle* and the destroyer *Hasty* was sunk by the *S55*. Later, the other big cruiser, the *Birmingham*, would be near missed and damaged by air attack. These attacks reduced Vian's ability to fight the approaching Italian fleet.

Harwood had reversed the course of the convoy twice, in part as he knew that Iachino would intercept the convoy on its present course on the morning of the 15th. Finally he gave Vian a free hand on the 15th and Vian kept the convoy on course back to Alexandria with the two Italian battleships only 100 miles away. Iachino had been attacked by submarines and aircraft, and a combination of the two had sunk the heavy cruiser *Trento*. The *Littorio*, Iachino's flagship, was hit by a 500lb bomb from a B24 Liberator of the US Army Air Corps.[16] Finally, as the fleet was returning to Taranto, a Wellington scored a torpedo hit on the bow of the *Littorio* and the combined damage put her out of action for 3 months. As Vian retreated he lost another destroyer, the *Airedale*, and then the *Nestor* to air attacks, and finally, the light cruiser *Hermoine* with eighty-eight men to the *U-205*. As the official history says, 'There is little to be said in summing up this disappointing operation'. The Italian fleet could not be stopped by Allied air power and submarines alone, and the escort could not take on the Italian fleet and fight the convoy through.[17]

*   *   *

June would see the fall of Tobruk. At that time there were five MTBs based there, usually operating off the Gulf of Bomba on patrol or landing agents on the coast (these latter operations were referred to as 'False Nose Jobs'). These five, along with two South African minesweepers and numerous small craft, escaped the harbour on 20 June as it was falling to the attacking Germans. The MTBs were fired on by both tanks and mortars in the escape. After reaching Mersa Matruh they went on to Alexandria.[18]

On the eve of the Battle of Gazala and the fall of Tobruk, both sides had plans to employ amphibious attacks. The best known proposal was the *Kampfgruppe Hecker*. It was to land between the Gazala line and Tobruk and act as a blocking force. Numbering just over 500 men (373 being of the Italian 3rd *San Marco* Marine Battalion) it had an element of subterfuge with the 13th company of the 800th *Brandenburger* regiment with commandos who could speak Arabic and English and even included three captured British tanks. It was to sail from Derna and would be protected by S-boats, the *Luftwaffe* and U-boats now operating close to Tobruk with the impending attack, but Rommel decided against the operation. The British had a similar operation in hand with Valentine tanks actually loaded aboard landing barges at the time of Rommel's attack. They were to land near Derna and disrupt the Axis rear areas, linking up with the Long Range Desert Group.[19]

The German 3rd Motor Torpedo Boat Flotilla under Lieutenant-Commander Kemnade operating against the retreating British fleeing Tobruk and sank the South African minesweeper *Parktown* and some small craft. One E-boat would be badly damaged but another captured a 296-ton landing craft.

The Malta resupply operations took place while Rommel was pursuing the badly battered 8th Army to Alamein and some days later Tobruk fell, freeing the way to Egypt for the Axis. But the fact that he wanted to follow his '*Fingerspitzegefühl*' ('gut feeling') and pursue the British caused the dedication of the *Luftwaffe* and *Regia Aeronautica* to the African campaign and thus the ultimate end of the Malta project.

Land operations were also affecting the naval situation in the Mediterranean, when the Axis took Mersa Matruh with its airfield. The Mediterranean Fleet was compelled to leave Alexandria and disperse to ports in the Near East such as Haifa, Port Said and Beirut to avoid the threat from the advanced enemy airfields, now only 160 miles away, but the French squadron at Alexandria remained. During this withdrawal, part of the famous 'Flap', the submarine depot ship *Medway* was torpedoed by the *U-372* and sunk off Port Said on 30 June, taking ninety torpedoes down with her, although forty-seven were later salvaged. The British would undertake several night bombardments of Mersa Matruh over the next few weeks to try to put the small port and airfield out of action. They had some success against submarines, sinking two Italian boats early in the month near Gibraltar. On 29 June, the *Thrasher* sank the Italian sloop *Diana*, the only ship of her type, which had sometimes been called 'Mussolini's Yacht'.

But Malta retained its great value in British strategy: its central position on the Axis supply route and its capability to damage them had to be intact. For this reason the problems with the air defence of the island were solved by sending two waves of Spitfires, thirty-nine in all, launched by the *Eagle* on 15 and 21 July (Operations 'Pinpoint' and 'Insect' respectively). The shortage of aviation fuel was also partly releived by the use of submarines, as the Axis also did, such as *Parthian* and *Clyde*, and the minelayer *Welshman* which brought fuel in from Gibraltar. Finally, the hard work of minesweeping, coupled with the declining Axis air offensive, allowed the British to order the submarines of the 10th Flotilla to Malta again towards the end of July, when at the same time the fighters on the island were numerous enough to allow them to attack the Axis bombers out at sea instead of over the island. In fact, during the forthcoming 'Pedestal' operation there were always serviceable 100 Spitfires, 36 Beaufighters, 30 Beauforts, 3 Wellingtons, 2 B-24 Liberators, 2 Baltimores, 3 Albacores and Swordfish of the Fleet Air Arm at Malta, not counting the reconnaissance aircraft. At the beginning of the operation there were 211 planes at Malta, 141 of them serviceable. The duties of this force were reconnaissance to protect the convoy, attack and destroy the enemy naval forces and protect the convoy from air attack, also by attacking enemy airfields.[20]

At the same time the British closely pursued and attacked the Axis supply shipping, thanks to ULTRA intercepts, as happened during the first day of June 1942 when the Germans hurried forty tanks, forty-nine anti-tank guns and thirty heavy howitzers to the critical front at El Alamein. July 1942 was one of the worst periods for the Axis in North Africa. So not only were the Axis powers suffering from increased attacks, but they also had the strain of additional troops and supplies arriving at the already congested ports and airfields at Tripoli, Benghazi and Tobruk, and furthermore these now had to be transported much further east to the distant El Alamein front, resulting in most of them not arriving until late July or early August. It was only then that the Italian and German infantry was reinforced enough to resist British attacks, generally launched against the weaker Italian units. On 13 August General Montgomery assumed command of the 8th Army, replacing Auchinleck, and retained the plan to defend the Alam Halfa positions, beginning to reorganise the army for this decisive battle.

In the Mediterranean the Allies were experiencing a high point in the convoy battle. On the one hand the arrival in Africa of Axis reinforcements during July and August and of new units such as the German 164th Divison, the Italian *Pistoia* Infantry Division and the Ramcke and *Folgore* paratroops was causing more supply consumption than could be brought to the front by the Axis supply system, and on other hand the Allied offensive against supply routes in the Central and Eastern Mediterranean began to show an increasing superiority in the air. By the time of late summer 1942 the attacks on Axis shipping were delivered not only from Malta, but also from Egypt, because the supply route along the coasts and the light vessel coastal traffic were stretched and exposed all along the coast of North Africa.

CHAPTER 19

Operation 'Pedestal', August 1942

Having arrived in Malta to that tumultuous welcome into Grand
Harbour, well you'd have to be a pretty hardened case not to think we
did a good job and there's a thousand thankful that we did it, you can't
help feeling perhaps a sense of pride that you were there to have done
that work, but you wouldn't volunteer for it and you wouldn't want to
go through the experience again.

A sailor on the 'Pedestal' Convoy[1]

Forces were now being assembled for the largest Allied operation in the
Mediterranean to date. The Admiralty in London thought that another resupply convoy to Malta was vital to keep control of this important base and to continue offensive operations against the Axis supply routes, which were now extremely long and more vulnerable to attack. Operation 'Pedestal' or 'Middle August' as the Axis called the resulting battle, could also be called the last victory of the Axis in the aero-naval war in the Mediterranean.[2]

The decision to mount another convoy operation was difficult to take because of the high degree of risk, as the 'Harpoon' convoy in June had shown. But Churchill overrode any doubts when he wrote to the First Sea Lord, Admiral Sir Dudley Pound, stating that the possession of Malta was of paramount importance to the defence of the Middle East. At the same time, on 25 July, the decision to invade French North Africa was taken, and events were set in train for Operation 'Torch' which would see two American and one combined British and American force land at various points along the coast from the Atlantic to Algeria to take the Axis armies on two fronts.

Initially, two convoys were planned for this operation, one from Gibraltar and another from Alexandria, but the fact that until the Battle of El Alamein the Axis controlled the entire North African coast made the 'bomb alley' between Crete and Africa too dangerous, and thus only the eastbound convoy went ahead. This had to pass within range of the Axis bases on Sardinia and Sicily for some 400 miles until it could reach Malta, and therefore the operation had to be carried out on moonless nights. It took about 30 hours to cover this distance if the merchant ships could make 13 knots. As the tanker *Ohio* which was to participate in the convoy was not ready in July, the operation was planned for the middle of August, and codenamed 'Pedestal'.

The British decision to take the risk should be seen also against the strategic background that took into account two other factors: the outcome of the PQ17 Arctic convoy operation and the influence of the battle of Midway. Both released forces for the Mediterranean, since the Arctic convoys were suspended for some time after the disaster of PQ17, and after the Japanese defeat at Midway the Indian

Ocean theatre was less threatened. For this reason, the convoy could assemble a total of fourteen transports, and enjoy the escort of warships taken from three different theatres: the Home Fleet, which supplied the light cruisers *Nigeria*, *Kenya*, *Manchester* and *Sirius* with two destroyer flotillas and also recalled the battleships *Nelson* and *Rodney* from Freetown. Force H was reinforce by the Eastern Fleet which sent the new carrier *Indomitable* with the light cruiser *Phoebe* and the destroyers *Laforey*, *Lookout* and *Lighting*. This ensured that 'Pedestal' would not suffer the earlier problem of weak escorts: this would be the most powerful escort force ever formed by the Royal Navy in the Mediterranean.

The naval component, Force Z, was under the command of Vice-Admiral E Neville Syfret (who was also in command of the whole convoy – codenamed Force F) and was formed around the battleships *Nelson* (flagship) and *Rodney*, with the carriers *Indomitable*, *Eagle* and *Victorious*. The carriers had a total of 100 aircraft and were commanded by Rear-Admiral Lyster, now returned to the Mediterranean, on board the *Victorious*. The aircraft were distributed as follows:

- *Indomitable*: ten Martlet fighters (the British version of the American Wildcat) of 806 Squadron, twenty-four Sea Hurricanes of 800 and 880 Squadrons and fourteen Albacores of 827 and 831 Squadrons.
- *Victorious*: sixteen Fulmars of 809 and 884 Squadrons, six Sea Hurricanes of 885 Squadron and fourteen Albacores of 817 and 832 Squadrons.
- *Eagle*: sixteen Sea Hurricanes of 801 and 813 Squadrons.

Another aircraft carrier, the *Furious*, would take the opportunity of such a huge force of ships being at sea to reinforce Malta with forty Spitfires before returning to Gibraltar with an escort of eight destroyers. Her mission was codenamed 'Bellows'. At the same time, the two empty freighters from 'Harpoon' would leave Malta to return to Gibraltar with the patched-up *Badsworth* and *Matchless*, as Operation 'Ascendant'. They reached their destination safely, after a brief exchange of gunfire with the Italian destroyer *Malocello*, which was laying mines of Cape St Bon. The Italian ship used false French recognition lights to fool the British into breaking off the action.

The Axis air attacks would face a strong defence from the three AA cruisers *Sirius*, *Phoebe* and *Charybdis*, armed with 5.25in DP guns, and fifteen destroyers of the escort. Force Z was to escort the convoy as far as the Skerki Channel and then turn back to Gibraltar, handing over the convoy to Force X under the command of Rear-Admiral H M Burrough who flew his flag in the light cruiser *Nigeria*, leading the cruisers *Kenya* and *Manchester*, the AA cruiser *Cairo*, and eleven destroyers. It was planned to refuel this force from two oilers and one tug escorted by four corvettes. This force was to escort the fourteen merchant ships to Malta, including the American tanker *Ohio* carrying 12,000 tons of oil, which was one of three American transport ships in the convoy.

Several submarines were also committed to the operation in order to counter possible movements by Italian surface forces: the *Unbroken* was patrolling off Milazzo in the Lipari islands, and the *Safari* off Palermo, while the *Una* was to land an Army commando near Catania. The *Uproar*, *Ultimatum*, and *United* of the 10th

Flotilla and the *Unruffled*, *Utmost* and *P222* of the 8th Flotilla from Gibraltar were deployed as a screen south of Pantelleria, instructed to stay on the surface until they were spotted by enemy air reconnaissance to draw the attention of the enemy fleet to them.[3]

The total of 85,000 tons of supplies were loaded in such a way that every ship had a mixed cargo so that the loss of one ship would not mean that all of one particular item went down with her. Besides the *Ohio* with a British crew, there two other American merchant ships, the *Santa Elisa* (8379 tons) and *Almeria Lykes* (7773 tons). The other freighters were British: *Rochester Castle* (7795 tons), *Deucalion* (7516 tons), *Clan Ferguson* (7347 tons), *Empire Hope* (12,688 tons), *Wairangi* (12,436 tons), *Waimarama* (12,843 tons), *Port Chalmers* (8535 tons), *Dorset* (10,624 tons), *Melbourne Star* (12,806 tons), *Brisbane Star* (12,791 tons) and *Glenorchy* (8982 tons).

The Mediterranean Fleet also had a part in the plan, to draw Axis attention to the Eastern basin with another force escorting a dummy convoy, and deploying some submarines to check the Italian warships in case they sortied against the convoy. This operation, codenamed 'MG3', consisted of four merchant ships from Haifa and Port Said escorted by Sir Philip Vian's force of five cruisers, thirteen destroyers and two more escort ships. This would be supported by a submarine patrolling off Navarino, where the 8th Italian (light) Cruiser Division was based, and two more west-south-west of Crete.

When the convoy passed through the Straits of Gibraltar on 10 August, it was spotted by the Italian agents at Algesiras who reported to Rome. The Axis high command decided to counter this move employing aircraft and light forces such as submarines, MTBs and a couple of cruiser divisions one from Cagliari, the other from Messina, and for them to rendezvous mid-way between Sicily and Sardinia. Eight submarines were set up to ambush in the Mediterranean (and five in the Atlantic).

The battleships were not committed to the operation because of the shortage of fuel. But oil 'consumption was really 50,000 tons for the Navy' wrote Cavallero in his diary, but unfortunately he did not explain in how much time this amount was consumed, leaving us some doubt about the question if the battleships were not committed for other reasons. A recent history of the Italian Navy in the Second World War seems to confirm that oil was sometimes an excuse to avoid committing the battlefleet. Clearly though, fuel was a vital consideration.[4]

At that time the situation in Egypt was fairly calm, with only local artillery and patrol activities at the front, while in the Mediterranean ships and aircraft had a lot to do to transport supplies to Rommel's troops. On 9 August no Italian aircraft took off from Greece for Africa, simply because there was insufficient fuel available.

At first there was some uncertainty about the Allied objective. Cavallero believed in a possible landing in North Africa (perhaps Libya), while Admiral Sansonetti thought it was a flying-off operation for Malta. In any case orders were issued on the 11th alerting the *Regia Aeronautica* to launch reconnaissance aircraft and to prepare the light vessels and submarines necessary to check the Allied threat. Cavallero cancelled a trip to Africa because he foresaw 'an air-naval battle' in the 'days of 14-15th in the Mediterranean'. Riccardi's report of the 11th was reasonably correct: the magnitude of the Allied naval forces at sea was impressive, but the objective remained unclear as it seemed too large for a Malta convoy.

In fact, on the 9th Admiral Riccardi reported during a meeting at the Italian Supreme Command that the traffic in the Eastern Mediterranean had been suspended because there were 'three submarines that we are chasing'. In turn this would cause delay in the shipping of aviation fuel and the halting of the air transport of men to Africa.[5]

Meanwhile Allied air raids hit airfields in Sardinia, Decimomannu and Elmas, destroying five torpedo bombers and one bomber, while three other torpedo-bombers were damaged. Peculiar air activity, bombing, reconnaissance and dropping of flares, was detected by the Axis during the night of 12-13 August, and also the six commandos mentioned previously landed near Catania and were captured.

As soon as the convoy was sighted, it was shadowed by reconnaissance planes, and eighteen Italian and two German submarines were deployed to ambush the convoy, raising the total of Italian submarines on patrol in the Mediterranean to twenty-six. Five of them were deployed in the area between Algiers and the Balearics, with the German *U-73* and *U-331*. Another group of eleven was deployed between Cape Bon and Sicily, while the *Asteria* was stationed west of Malta.

The *Uarsciek*, one of the Italian submarines of the first screen the British convoy would encounter, which was positioned to the north-west of the rest of her group, sighted the British ships at about 4.30am, spotting a carrier and a battleship. The submarine was on the surface and approached the enemy, launched three torpedoes, and then dived to escape the hunt which followed. Her commander was sure he had hit the carrier, but he had not. After evading the British ships, at 9.36am the submarine surfaced, with no ships in sight, and radioed her sighting report. On the evening of the 11th a German Ju88 had carried out a photographic reconnaissance of the convoy and although detected on radar, it was flying too high to be reached either by the battleships' AA barrage or the carriers' fighters. The Italian submarines were ordered to form three screens through which the Allied ships had to pass, initially to spot them and if possible to attack.

* * *

The meetings which took place at *Comando Supremo* on the 12th are significant for what took place during the forthcoming battle, particularly for the deployment of the battlefleet. At 8.30am Kesselring informed the Italians that the *Luftwaffe* could not provide air cover for the naval forces, as they were already busy with bomber escort, and suggested laying mines on the route of the convoy. A minefield had already been laid and the Italian Navy considered it well placed. The discussions around the table between the chiefs of staff of the navy, Riccardi, and air force, Fougier, showed the different and uncertain views of the Italian commanders about this operation. Fougier thought the eastern force would be the most important part of the Allied operation, but Admiral Sansonetti correctly saw the main threat as coming from the west, especially fearing an air attack on Sardinia from the carriers. It is clear from the outset that the lack of air support from the *Luftwaffe* for the ships was one factor that hindered the employment of the main Italian fleet. Also the shifting of the light cruiser *Attendolo* from Naples with an escort of two destroyers to the base at Navarino was submitted to Mussolini by Cavallero, but during this action the ships would instead be used to reinforce Parona's squadron of heavy cruisers at Messina.

In the afternoon meeting Cavallero asked Admiral Riccardi if the employment of the naval forces was feasible taking into account the risks, who replied that it was not convenient to deploy the battlefleet. Fougier said that this was just Field Marshall Kesselring's opinion. Cavallero said that the risk was not from the enemy's naval forces, but from their air force as Malta was quite effective at that time. Therefore, Cavallero recommended that the Navy should not commit large surface forces without adequate air cover.

Admiral Riccardi agreed and said that the risk was too great. He added that the navy was in crisis 'due to the lack of oil'. Besides the fact Cavallero thought, too optimistically, that in 4 months the Italian Navy could rely on the captured oilfields in the Caucasus for her needs, it seems that the Riccardi's final argument is the same one later often used to explain the fleet not being employed, which other chiefs of staff and senior officers may have thought was just an excuse. But these exchanges suggest that the balance of forces in the air at this time was such that Kesselring was also of this opinion.[6] The Italian Navy's final plan was for the submarines to attack the convoy in the area between Algiers and the Balearics, while between Cape Bon and Pantelleria the MTBs would attack. Finally, the cruisers of the 3rd and 7th Division would engage the already weakened convoy.

The state of readiness of the *Regia Aeronautica* can be guessed by her Chief of Staff General Fougier's speech at the meeting at 10.05am when he said that 'we have forty modern fighters and bombers', but then the bulk of the bombers and torpedo-bombers would follow. 'Fourteen Macchi 202 should clean the sky'. This seems a tiny force to 'clean the sky' with but Fougier was relying on radio-controlled 'bombers with two 1000kg bombs which . . . will crash on board the [aircraft carrier]'. This was a new weapon, but one which perhaps had not been fully tested, as will be seen below.[7] Despite the fact that during the 11th Fougier was able to rush 101 planes from bases on the Italian mainland to Sardinia and Sicily, bringing the total available up to 247, *Superaereo* decided not to launch any attacks until the following day, while the Germans prepared a hasty attack for that evening.[8]

*   *   *

By now the British force was within the Axis submarine ambush area. During the morning of 11 August the commander of the *U-73*, *Kapitänleutnant* Helmut Rosenbaum, brought his submarine to periscope depth and at around 8.00am spotted enemy ships but was unable to get within range to attack. Following this first formation there was another one composed of merchant ships, with an aircraft carrier (the *Eagle*) bringing up the rear. Rosenbaum was able to bring his boat to within 400 yards of the carrier, launched four torpedoes, and then dived deep. At 1.15pm the *Eagle* was hit by all four torpedoes and it took just 8 minutes for her to sink. Many of the crew realised what was happening immediately and jumped into the sea. The destroyers *Lookout* and *Laforey* with the tug *Jaunty* immediately assisted the sinking ship and managed to rescue 929 men of her 1160 crew, including the captain. Four of her Hurricanes were in the air and were ordered to land on the other two carriers.

This was a bad start to the operation, with some 20 per cent of the air support lost and also the German submarine was able to escape, since it was not picked up by the escorts' sonar. The boat had to pass between two destroyers to approach the *Eagle*, and it was speculated that stratification of thermal layers in the water hindered the operation of the sonar and allowed Rosenbaum's escape. The loss of the *Eagle* put the convoy on the alert for submarines and there were frequent alarms at possible sightings.

However, the Italian submarine *Dagabur* was less fortunate. She was on the surface when she was detected at 12.54am on the 12th by the Type 271 radar of the destroyer *Wolverine* (Lieutenant-Commander Gretton) at a range of 4900 yards. This destroyer was one of those escorting the *Furious* and had been detached with the *Keppel*, *Malcolm*, *Venomous* and *Wrestler* for anti-submarine work after the sinking of the *Eagle*. The *Wolverine* closed at high speed, sighting the submarine at 700 yards, increased speed to 27 knots and rammed her, sinking the *Dagabur* immediately. Her crew had probably been taken by surprise and sighted the destroyer too late to react, but as there were no survivors, this is only conjecture.[9]

The *Wolverine* was also damaged and had to return to Gibraltar, where she arrived the day after the *Furious*, which has launched her aircraft beginning at 11.29am, 584 miles from Malta and then turned westwards. Thirty-eight were launched and all but one, which landed on the *Indomitable* due to mechanical problems, arrived safely at Malta. Operation 'Burrows' was therefore successfully accomplished. The *Furious*'s change of course was reported to the Germans by a reconnaissance aircraft at 7.55pm on the 11th. The Axis commanders suspected the *Furious* was the carrier the *Uarsciek* had supposedly hit, because she was put in dry-dock as if she had been damaged, but she soon left port again for other operations.

At 2.30pm the convoy's radar picked up an approaching aircraft: it was a Ju88 which carried out a photographic reconnaissance mission without being intercepted by the Hurricanes which were escorting the fleet, since it was flying too high. The Ju88 was one of the ten aircraft of the 122nd Strategic Reconnaissance Group which had been following the convoy since 10.10am.

The first air attack came in later, when the convoy was some 200 miles from Sardinia, consisting of three He111s and twenty-seven Ju88s attacking simultaneously from different directions. The former went in low with their torpedoes, while the Ju88s launched a shallow diving attack in the twilight, which helped them, but the AA fire from the convoy was highly effective, with two Ju88s shot down with no damage to the convoy. However, the British fighters returning to their carriers were also mistakenly fired upon by their own ships and some were damaged.

No night attacks were launched at this stage, as they were to come when the convoy was passing through the Sicilian Straits. But the following day the convoy was in an area dominated by enemy airfields and close to the Axis naval bases. At 6.20am the first enemy aircraft were picked up on radar. Ten minutes later, after four Sea Hurricanes and Fulmars from the two carriers had been launched to hold off the enemy reconnaissance planes, every plane fit for combat was prepared for takeoff. Again the Ju88s on reconnaissance were too high and too fast to be intercepted, which meant that the convoy was kept under constant surveillance, both in the air and at sea, as the Italian submarines were maintaining contact as long as possible with the slow-moving convoy. *Comando Supremo* and German High Command South were therefore receiving sufficient information to determine the Allies' intentions and how they could be attacked.

Just after 9.00am nineteen Ju88s of the LG1 attacked but they were intercepted by the fleet fighters 25 miles out and four of them were shot down. Another two were shot down by AA fire from destroyers, according to the British. German sources state a total of five were shot down and two more lost due to mechanical failure over Sardinia.[10] The Ju88s did little damage in turn, but their pilots made the usual optimistic claims.

Returning from an attack on Sardinia, some Beaufighters sighted the 7th Italian Naval Division (Da Zara's light cruisers) at sea, alerting the British to their presence. The convoy was well protected by the fighters of the carriers, which succeeded in shooting down three Italian reconnaissance planes.

It was attacked again around midday by three waves of Italian aeroplanes from Sardinia, totalling ten S.84 bombers of the 38th Group of the 32nd Wing and eight Cr42s of the 24th Fighter Group employed as bombers, escorted by fourteen Mc202s. Five minutes later a mass of forty torpedo bombers attacked from two directions: to starboard, nine S.79s and ten S.84s escorted by fourteen Re2001s, and to port, twenty-one S.79s escorted by twelve Re2001s. Their targets were the merchant ships at the centre of the British formation.

The third wave was made up of a pair of Re2001s of the Special Section which were supposed to have been armed with a new 630kg low-altitude armour-piercing bomb, but these were not ready in time and they carried anti-personnel bombs instead, and a specially-equipped S.79 loaded with a 1000kg bomb and radio-controlled by Brigadier-General Ferdinando Raffaelli from a specially-equipped Cant Z1007. However, the remote-controlled aircraft, which was intended to crash into an aircraft carrier, malfunctioned and flew straight ahead until it crashed in Algeria. These special aircraft were to be escorted by five G50s of the 24th Fighter Group but only two managed to join the mission.

Another special weapon employed in this attack was the Motobomba FFF torpedo, equipping the first ten S.84s. These were 50cm electric torpedoes which followed a circular course when dropped, the circle getting gradually larger. They weighed 350kg, of which 120kg was the warhead. In this attack they were dropped some 2000 yards from the target ships, which were able to evade them, and no hits were scored.

The torpedo-bomber wave had been delayed for 15 minutes because of a shortage of maintenance personnel to prepare the Re2001 fighters that were to accompany them. Mechanical problems meant that only thirty-one planes took off, and they met a heavy AA barrage from the British ships. Those that got within range of the transport ships failed to hit any of them thanks to violent evasive manoeuvres. The two Re2001s were able to approach the *Victorious* as they were mistaken for a pair of returning Hurricanes. Both bombs hit the carrier, one killing six and wounding two, while the other bounced off the deck and exploded over the water.

Between the second and the third Italian waves, thirty-seven German Ju88s of KG54 and KG77 coming from the bases at Catania and Comiso in Sicily rendezvoused with twenty-one Me109s over Elmas after having blinded Malta's radar with countermeasures, and attacked the convoy. Five bombers had to abort the mission due mechanical problems. Without loss, the Germans got through the four Fulmars on patrol and hit the merchant *Decaulion* which slowed down so much that she was ordered to leave the convoy and proceed along the North African coast escorted by the destroyer *Bramham*.

Never before had the Axis air forces used so many aircraft (117 Italian and 58 German) for so little result. Two bombers, one torpedo-bomber and a fighter had been lost for only one ineffective hit on the *Victorious*. Although the special weapons and the Re2001s' bombs had failed, the fact that many of the attacking pilots had released their weapons too soon in the face of heavy AA fire explained the lack of success. However, the Sardinian-based aircraft of the *Regia Aeronautica* were re-fuelled and prepared for another attack, while the German reconnaissance aircraft and one Cant Z1007bis maintained contact with the convoy.

The submarines had also attempted to attack the convoy, but the destroyer screen was hard to penetrate. Two Italian submarines were easily located and attacked. The *Giada* was intercepted on the surface at 9.30am while trying to approach a group of warships detected on her hydrophones (probably the *Furious*). She was attacked by a Sunderland flying boat causing serious damage, so that she could not dive and headed for the nearest Spanish port on the surface. At 1.34pm she was attacked by another Sunderland of 202 Squadron, but shot it down and was able to reach Valencia, with casualties of one dead and eight wounded, but the boat was still out of this operation.

At 4.49pm the *Cobalto* was discovered by the destroyer *Ithuriel* to the north-east and immediately attacked with depth charges. The first pattern hit the submarine which was at periscope depth, forcing it to surface where it was hit by gunfire and then rammed. At 5.02pm the submarine sank after the captain of the *Ithuriel* tried to send two sailors aboard the submarine. Two Italian and two British seamen were lost when she suddenly went down. Furthermore the ramming had badly damaged the *Ithuriel* which was slowed to 20 knots and had her sonar knocked out.[11] A few minutes later the *Avorio* was discovered taking up position to attack the convoy and was driven off by the escorting destroyers. The anti-submarine defence was working well, but there were a lot of false alarms, probably due to 'ghost' sonar contacts in the warm waters of the Mediterranean. On the suggestion of Rear-Admiral Burrough, Admiral Syfret ordered two destroyers on each side of the convoy to drop a couple of depth charges every 10 minutes to deter enemy submarines.

Force F was about to enter the Italian submarines' 'C' ambush area and shortly after 4.00pm the destroyer *Pathfinder* picked up the *Granito* on sonar, attacking it immediately with five depth-charges which did not damage the submarine but kept it at a distance. But the escorts could not remain in the area to hunt the submarine indefinitely, and the *Pathfinder* and the *Zetland*, which had come to assist, soon had to rejoin the convoy.

At 4.30pm the *Emo* got into attack position 2200 yards from a carrier but a course-change by Force F forced her commander Giuseppe Franco to switch targets. He launched four torpedoes and then dived, but the convoy had changed course again and the destroyer *Tartar* raised the alarm, having seen the torpedo tracks while the *Lookout* raced toward a spotted periscope, which was not the *Emo*, but the *Avorio* which was manoeuvring to attack and was forced to dive. The *Lookout*'s attack caused no damage but prevented the submarine firing any torpedoes, and at 5.40pm the *Lookout* rejoined the convoy. The *Dandolo* was equally unlucky, being detected and attacked on her approach, the resultant damage forcing her to return to base.

* * *

Another air attack was launched in the afternoon by eight Italian Cr42s acting as dive-bombers escorted by nine Re2001s of the 362nd Squadron. One Re2001 was shot down by a Martlet of 806 Squadron from the *Indomitable*. Nine S.79s escorted by MC202s also took off at 4.45pm from Decimomannu but their mission was aborted because they could not find the convoy.

The air attacks from Sardinia were now finished with very little result, the British ships having put up a very effective defence. The convoy was now entering the area chosen by *Superaereo* for attacks from Sicily, that is east of the 10th parallel where the attacking bombers could enjoy fighter escort. The plan involved 105 aircraft attacking in three waves but there were problems with the fighter support. The Re2001s of the 2nd Fighter Group which had escorted the aircraft attacking from Sardinia could not be employed again the same day as they had landed in Sardinia and were to move to Sicily the next day, the 13th. The final plan saw the torpedo- and dive-bombers moved to Pantelleria in order to ensure them the escort of the MC202s of the 51st Fighter Wing, as it had proved difficult in the past to co-ordinate different flights of aircraft coming from different bases.

While four aircraft took off to locate the British convoy, the Italians experienced further problems which again reduced the number of aircraft available for the attack. Four out of thirteen Ju87s of the 102nd Group could not participate because they did not have the supplementary long-range fuel tanks, and six S.84s were unable to load their torpedoes. Meanwhile three Fulmars from the *Victorious* shot down Captain Giuseppe Mollo's S.79 on a reconnaissance mission, but a Cant Z1007 was able to maintain contact with the British and give reliable information on the course, speed and position of the convoy. The *II Fliegerkorps* in Sicily was also preparing its attacks and arrangements were made with the Italians to co-ordinate their attacks, which were however always carried out independently. The Germans had transferred the 1st Group of 3rd Stuka Wing from Trapani in Sicily to Elmas, and at 5.30pm twenty Ju87s escorted by Me109s took off heading south.

The Italian Ju87s of the 102nd Dive Attack Group arrived over the convoy in conditions of poor visibility but suddenly at 6.35pm the clouds parted and revealed the convoy in all its glory. The aircraft of the two carriers were ready to engage the enemy who had been detected on radar 40 miles away. Three Martlets, twelve Hurricanes and six Fulmars were already in the air and when the attack came both carriers were launching four more planes each. But the attackers had a strong fighter escort of high-quality aircraft, MC202s and Me109s. This time the attacks of the dive-bombers and the torpedo-bombers were properly timed, the latter approaching the convoy at 1200 feet in three waves while the Ju87s were diving. Nevertheless, the only hit scored by the Stukas was on the *Rodney*, but the 500kg bomb slipped off 'X' turret and exploded in the sea. The heavy AA fire shot down one Ju87 and another was shot down by a Hurricane. But while the ships were evading the torpedo bombers, another wave of Ju87s, the Germans of the 3rd Stuka Wing, came in at 9000 feet. They attacked the *Indomitable* from out of the sun and hit her twice, killing fifty and wounding fifty-nine, seriously damaging the ship which was on fire and lost speed. Three of the 1000kg bombs near-missed (one very close alongside) and two hit the flightdeck, which was rendered unserviceable. The carrier was assisted by the cruiser *Charybdis* and by the destroyers *Lookout, Lighting* and *Somali*. The attacking S.79s met heavy AA fire and only twelve were able to drop their torpedoes, again too far out, from 3000 yards. Only the destroyer *Foresight* was hit but not sunk and was towed back to Gibraltar by the *Tartar*.

The damage to the *Indomitable* were not enough to stop her, and she signalled at 7.27pm that she could make 17 knots. By 8.30pm she had got up to 28½ knots, but the damage to her flight deck meant she was effectively out of action. Her aircraft had to land on the *Victorious* and the commander of the carriers, Admiral Lyster, had to order the planes that could not be accommodated thrown overboard. The last Axis attack was carried out by twelve S.79s and twenty-eight Ju87s, losing two Ju87s, while other planes were damaged. After landing at Pantelleria the Axis aircraft were attacked at 8.45pm by three Beaufighters which started a fire in a German fuel depot, destroyed a Ju52, damaged two S.79s and one S.84 and killed one Italian Stuka pilot caught on the landing strip.

The result of the day was that little damage was inflicted by the Axis, and that mostly by the Germans, although the pilots claimed to have scored many hits. Admiral Syfret estimated optimistically that thirty-nine planes had been shot down, but only eighteen Axis aircraft did not return: nine Ju88s, two S.79s, three Cant Z1007s, two Ju87s and two Re2001s.

The British side had lost one carrier and had another put out of action, greatly reducing the convoy's air cover. Seven fighters had been shot down (three Fulmars, three Hurricanes and one Martlet), and after the loss of the *Eagle* with sixteen aircraft and the fact that forty-seven more were unemployable aboard the *Indomitable*, the fighter force of the convoy was reduced to eight Hurricanes, three Martlets and ten Fulmars, just when the covering Force Z was about to leave the convoy and take station out of range of air attacks from Sardinia. This was planned for 7.15pm, but Admiral Syfret decided to bring it forward to 6.55pm, to get the damaged *Indomitable* out of danger as soon as possible. Problems with the *Rodney*'s boilers reduced the speed of Force Z to 18 knots, but in any case Syfret was confident that the convoy could reach Malta, because no surface or air attacks were thought likely that night.

Barely 40 minutes after Force Z turned back a German reconnaissance aircraft reported it to the Axis high commands. Burrough had now the dangerous job of bringing the convoy through the remaining 250 miles of narrow seas between Africa and Sicily to Malta. No air cover was available because the Fulmars had been heavily engaged by the Axis attacks and of the four committed to the escort to Malta, one was shot down by a Me109, and another was damaged. Soon six Beaufighters of 248 Squadron from Malta took over this duty.

It was necessary to change formation and the thirteen transport ships (the damaged *Decaulion* remained behind with the *Bramham*) formed two columns, each lead by a cruiser, with another cruiser in the centre, while the ten destroyers of Force X surrounded the convoy. The starboard column had the *Kenya* leading and the *Manchester* sixth back astern of some freighters; while the port one was headed by the *Nigeria* and had the AA cruiser *Cairo* in the middle.

As night fell, the Axis forces launched a series of dangerous attacks. The convoy was changing formation again as it entered the Skerki Banks, where five Italian submarines were waiting, and at 7.38pm the *Dessie* fired four torpedoes at a transport from 2000 yards and dived to 130ft. Her commander Lieutenant-Commander Renato Scandola heard two explosions and was sure he had scored hits, but in fact the torpedoes were from the submarine *Axum*, which had sighted the convoy at the same time and launched four torpedoes at 7.55pm, when the change in formation had put a large number of targets in front of the submarine. After evading Lieutenant-Commander Renato Ferrini heard three explosions, and in fact his torpedoes hit the *Nigeria*, *Cairo* and *Ohio*. Burrough's flagship had to return to Gibraltar at 14 knots escorted by the *Bicester*, *Derwent* and *Wilton*, while the admiral shifted his flag to the destroyer *Ashanti*. She lost fifty-two killed. The *Cairo* was so badly damaged that she had to be sunk with torpedoes and gunfire, while aboard the *Ohio* the resultant fire was soon extinguished and she was able to get under way again at 7 knots, with a 23ft × 26ft hole in her side.[12]

The situation was bad because four destroyers had had to be detached to assist the *Nigeria* and the *Cairo*, which were the only warships equipped with the radio equipment to guide in the fighters from Malta. Admiral Syfret, when he had been informed of what had occurred, detached the *Charybdis* escorted by the two big 'Tribal' class destroyers *Eskimo* and *Somali*, to join the convoy, as she also had the necessary equipment.

At 8.35pm an unexpected air attack was detected on radar. The Beaufighters were recalled and were fortunate not to be shot down by 'friendly fire' from the ships. The KG54 and KG77 had committed thirty Ju88s along with seven He111 torpedo bombers of the 6/KG26 with the tiny escort of six Me110s of the 6/ZG26. Burrough ordered the *Penn* to make smoke but this was not enough. Although the sun had been down for 25 minutes, the German attack, to which the British could not reply with the same firepower as before, was deadly. At the end of the 30-minute assault, the *Brisbane Star* was dead in the water, the *Clan Ferguson* was a blazing wreck, the

Rochester Castle was damaged and the *Empire Hope* had to be sunk by the destroyer *Penn* after her crew was taken off. The same fate befell the isolated *Deucalion* which was attacked by two Hel111s and torpedoed, the crew being rescued by the destroyer *Bramham* which gave the *coup de grace* to the ship. Three ships were thus lost, while the *Brisbane Star* was able to continue at only 5 knots.

The German aircraft were still attacking the convoy when at 9.05pm the Italian submarine *Alagi* fired her four forward torpedo tubes at the *Kenya*. The tracks were sighted by the *Port Chalmers* and by the *Kenya*, which turned sharply, avoiding three of them, but the fourth hit her on the starboard side aft. The cruiser was saved by her strong construction and was able to keep her place in the line with the *Manchester*, the only undamaged cruiser in Force X. When the *Alagi* surfaced, her commander reported seeing a long line of burning ships.

The torpedoing of the *Kenya* had increased the confusion in the convoy. The ships were scattered and the fact that *Ashanti* and *Pathfinder* were detailed to assist the two damaged cruisers meant that the merchant ships were without protection and some of them might well have turned back to Gibraltar. The *Ohio* was dangerously close to the burning *Clan Ferguson* and could have caught fire herself, or been torpedoed by a submarine, but when the Italian *Bronzo* arrived on the scene, she only finished off the *Clan Ferguson.*

The convoy had never taken up the formation Rear-Admiral Burrough had planned, and at 11.56pm passed Cape Bon with the ships still scattered, entering another danger area, where Axis MTBs were lying in wait for them. These were the German 3rd Squadron (*S59, S58, S30* and *S36*), and the Italian 18th *MAS* (*MAS 556, MAS 560, MAS 562* and *MAS 557*), 2nd *MS* (*MS 16, MS 22, MS 23, MS 25* and *MS 26*) and 20th *MAS* (*MAS 552, MAS 553, MAS 554* and *MAS 564*).[13]

The 18th *MAS* had sailed from Trapani and was on station south-east of Pantelleria. When the convoy approached it was spotted on radar but thereafter attacked the leading warships, which opened fire to starboard and manouevred to evade the torpedoes that were launched but scored no hits. The Italians then preferred to shift their attention to the merchant ships astern because of the firepower of the escort ships.

The German *S58 and S59* sighted the head of the convoy at 12.20am and attacked but came under heavy fire which damaged the *S58*. While *S58* was able to return to Port Empedocle, the *S59* attacked what appeared to be a merchant ship 5 miles north-east of Cape Bon and claimed to have hit her target, but according to the British sources, no ships were hit in that area. The Allied ships were also in danger because the lighthouse at Cape Bon was revealing their position some 10 miles from the coast.

A little later, at 1.02am on the 13th, south of Kelibia near Ras Mustafa the Italian *MS 16* and *MS 22* of the 2nd Squadron, also sighted the convoy and attacked it but initially the former failed to hit the targets. But then both vessels attacked the *Manchester* at very close range, and she was hit by a torpedo from each of them. Damage was serious: her boilers, fuel tanks and magazines were flooded and the ship was listing at 12°, but counter flooding reduced this to 5°. The merchant ships astern of her, *Waimarama, Almeria Lykers* and *Glenorchy* did their best to avoid colliding with her and scattered, losing contact with each other. The *Glenorchy* sighted a MTB and fired upon it, claiming to have seen it explode, but no Axis boats were lost to gunfire on this dramatic night. All efforts of the *Manchester*'s commander and of the crew to get her under way failed, and therefore she had to be abandoned, later being scuttled by her crew. The two Italian *MAS* ran aground on the Tunisian coast.[14]

The *S59* tried to make contact again with the convoy but lost it after 20 minutes. Meanwhile *MS 31* under Lieutenant-Commander Antonio Calvani arrived on the scene having picked up signals from *MS 22* and at 2.15am launched two torpedoes at the illuminated *Glenorchy* (a searchlight was trained on her) from 750 yards and hit her on the starboard side, flooding her engine rooms and leaving her dead in the water, and she had to be abandoned. In contrast the *MS 26* received a warm welcome from the escorts: after an attack on what was thought to be a cruiser, the *Pathfinder* illuminated the MTB and opened fire. She sought shelter in a minefield near the coast and the *Pathfinder* was alerted to the presence of other light vessels, among them the *MS 31* which having fired its torpedoes was maintaining contact with the convoy to guide other boats in. *MS 23* and *MS 25* found the British ships alerted and were held off by intense defensive fire. At 2.20am the *Kenya* turned south-east to pass Pantelleria and found some other transports which had passed through the minefield to reduce the distance to Malta, which was 180 miles away.

It was 2.40am when the reinforcements from Force Z (*Charybdis*, *Somali* and *Eskimo*) arrived at the head of the convoy, bringing their powerful arament to help the battered warships as they entered the ambush area of a section of the 3rd German and 20th Italian MTB squadrons. Their first task was to assist the *Manchester* but all they could do was take off her crew.

The *S30* and *S36* has sighted the convoy at 2.20am and moved in to attack. The former, under the command of Lieutenant-Commander Horst Weber, penetrated among the British ships and at 3.14am, launched two torpedoes at a transport. The boat remained in the area but was targeted by the escort and had to escape at high speed. The *S36* attacked a destroyer and, both torpedoes having missed, launched another at what may have been the *Almeria Lykes* from 650 yards, seeing it hit the target amidships. She had to retreat immediately because of the reaction of the escorts.[15] *MAS 552* appeared to starboard and was fired upon by the *Kenya*, but succeeded in launching a torpedo that hit the *Wairangi* aft, and just after 4.00am she also had to be abandoned. At 3.40am *MAS 554* (Lieutenant-Commander Marco Calcagno) attacked the *Almeria Lykes* which was following the *Somali*, his target being lit up by six flares. Two torpedoes were launched from 550 yards, one of which hit on the port bow. Fortunately her cargo of ammunition did not explode, but yet again another merchant ship was crippled.

The 20th *MAS* were less aggressive, their commander displaying little initiative. Nevertheless, one of his vessels, *MAS 557* under Midshipman Battista Cafiero, found the *Santa Elisa* at 4.40am which had passed through the minefields. The *MAS* attacked the merchant but her noisy main engines had alerted the target's crew who put up a spirited defence. After one failed attack, Cafiero returned to attack on the other side and scored a hit which was fatal because the *Santa Elisa* was carrying aviation fuel. A pillar of flame 500ft high shot up from the burning ship, from which twenty-eight survivors were rescued by the destroyers *Penn* and *Bramham*.

This was certainly another success for the Axis, but many times the MTBs' attacks were unsuccessful, such as the *MAS 564* which launched a torpedo at 5.00am at the *Rochester Castle* but missed, as did the *S30*. The *MAS 564* repeated her attack from the starboard side and one torpedo hit the *Rochester Castle*, but the ship was well built, her bulkheads held and she could still make 13 knots although she was down by the bow. The *MS 31* was one of the last to try to attack before daylight. At 5.15am, being without torpedoes, she dropped depth charges near a transport in an attempt to damage it but failed and was chased off by a destroyer. The success of the light vessels that night was helped by the confined waters and the confusion among the convoy, exacerbated by the damage the *Axum's* initial attack had done to the escorts. Certainly the young commanders of the motor torpedo boats had displayed a high degree of initiative (apart from those of the 20th Squadron).

*   *   *

The convoy could have been completely destroyed if the Italian fleet had decisively attacked the remaining ships. However, the fact that on the evening of the 11th the Beaufighters returning from their attacks on the Sardinian airfields had sighted the cruisers of the 7th Division en route from Cagliari affected their plans. This report was the first hard information the British received on the movements of the Italian surface units.

The two light cruisers of the 7th Division had sailed from Cagliari at 8.10pm on the 11th, escorted by the destroyers *Maestrale*, *Oriani* and *Gioberti*. They were to rendezvous with the *Attendolo* from Naples in the middle of the Tyrrhenian Sea. In the early hours of the 12th the *Trieste* left Genoa and sped to Naples accompanied by the *Fuciliere* and the torpedo-boat *Ardito*. She would later join Parona's 3rd Cruiser Division, bringing it up to three heavy cruisers and one light cruiser plus escorting destroyers.

Admiral Parona's 3rd Division, comprising the heavy cruisers *Gorizia* and *Bolzano*, escorted by six destroyers, left Messina. He would later be joined by the *Trieste* and the *Attendolo*. Parona was supposed to leave early on the morning of the 12th, but a signal from the *U-83* of Lieutenant Commander Hans Werner Kraus brought the news that an enemy formation of four cruisers and ten destroyers was near Crete.

Meanwhile, the Mediterranean fleet was working to help the convoy at least indirectly, mounting Operation 'MG4', a bombardment of Rhodes, carried out by the light cruisers *Arethusa* and *Cleopatra* and four destroyers, all of which returned to base. In fact 'MG4' had no real effect on Axis strategy, as there were no alterations in the deployment of Axis forces in the eastern Mediterranean.

The *U-83* gave the first information of these ships being at sea and this was confirmed by a signal intercepted from a Sunderland. Furthermore, from air reconnaissance reports from Malta, it seemed that the British were making smoke over the harbour to hide a couple of cruisers which had arrived there, but it later appeared more likely that they were concealing warships sailing west to meet the convoy. *Supermarina* suspected a possible 'eastern' phase of the operation, since the eighteen merchant ships reported to be in the convoy were too many for Malta alone.

In this confused situation, the sailing of Parona's 3rd Division was delayed, until things became clearer. It was possible that the British threat from the east would make it necessary to reinforce Rear-Admiral De Courten's weak 8th Division at Navarino. Moreover, during the day it was announced that no fighter escort would be available for the ships and this complicated the strategic problem. The *II Fliegerkorps* preferred to employ their 50 fighters to escort their 170 bombers in the climax of the battle against the convoy rather than support the Italian Navy, which had requested 80 fighters as air cover. Nor could the Italian Air Force easily supply such a number of aeroplanes, having assigned only thirty fighters, eighteen of which were Cr42s, to the operation.

During the 12th the Italian cruisers and destroyers rendezvoused 60 miles north of Ustica, an island north of Palermo, and headed south in two squadrons, although some ships were short of fuel, while two torpedo-boats, *Climene* and *Centauro*, were patrolling the route to protect the cruisers. British aircraft from Malta conducted surveillance over the Italian ports and probable points of passage, and a Spitfire noted that the 3rd Division was no longer in port. Later at 6.54pm a Baltimore sighted the Italian ships just as they joined up. Back at Malta, Air Vice-Marshal Park was not too worried until the convoy and the escorts suffered the losses and damage already described. In this situation, Force X could not easily oppose the Italian warships, and therefore he ordered five Wellingtons to look for the Italian ships while holding fifteen Beauforts equipped with torpedoes and the same number of Beaufighters as long-range escorts on standby to strike against the Italians.

On 12 August the meetings of the German and Italian senior officers were mostly spent dealing with the surface forces of the Italian Navy and on possible air cover. In the end, for various reasons it was decided not to proceed with the operation, but Mussolini was not of this opinion until the heavy damage to the cruisers (see below) settled the question. There was still some concern that 'Pedestal' was for an invasion of Libya. The Italian Navy did not want to risk its ships within the radius of Malta's aircraft but two destroyers, *Pigafetta* and *Da Veranano*, were sent from Piraeus to Navarino and two submarines from Libya took up ambush positions north of Cyrenaica.

During the night the 7th and 3rd Cruiser Divisions steamed south towards Pantelleria where they would receive further orders. *Supermarina* was aware that the ships had been discovered and finally obtained an escort of forty-five fighters. Mussolini was eager to see the Navy's guns in action and was afraid of a possible landing in Libya meeting no opposition.

While the British shadowed the Italian ships all night, they were picked up on the *Legionario's*, radar, the only Italian ship in the formation which had it, which made this the first occasion Italian radar had detected surface ships. The Germans intercepted a British signal mentioning an air attack against the Italian squadron and both the *Bronzo* and *Alagi* signalled to the three British warships coming to help the convoy (the *Charyhdis* group), thinking they were Italian. What the Italian Navy did not want in any case was a night combat south of Pantelleria, and therefore at 11.50pm *Supermarina* recalled the ships, Parona turning back at 12.28am on the 13th.

The morning of the 13th was marked by continuous attacks by Axis aircraft. Six He111 torpedo-bombers scored no hits, but a lone Ju88 hit the already wrecked *Santa Elisa* with a 500kg bomb, setting her on fire. A Wellington located the returning Italian cruisers at 1.56am and signalled the fact to Malta, where Park ordered an air attack by two Albacores and one radar-equipped Swordfish, and passed the information on to the submarines *Safari* and *Unbroken*.

The *Unbroken* under Lieutenant-Commander Alistair Mars took up an ambush position after having been informed of the presence of the Italian ships and sighted them at 7.25am. Among the successful British submarine commanders of the Second World War, Mars of the *Unbroken* could claim an impressive record and this would be his most striking success. The light cruiser *Attendolo*, the heavy cruisers *Bolzano*, *Gorizia* and *Trieste* escorted by eight destroyers, two of which equipped with sonar, were steaming north with an air escort of two Cant Z506 seaplanes. They were passing between the island of Filicudi and Panarea at 20 knots when they encountered the *Unbroken*.[16]

Captain Mars had been waiting since the 10th in his patrol position 2 miles north of Capo Milazzo lighthouse. The submarine had been chased but had suffered no damage. Mars decided to shift his ambush position by 30 miles to a point 12 miles from Stromboli, and here in the morning of the 13th he first heard and then could see the Italian warships approaching. After having calculated their course, he took up position to attack, as the cruisers drew nearer. Mars made good use of the periscope, raising it for very short periods to avoid to be detected by the destroyers and especially by the two seaplanes.

When he was in position he launched four torpedoes at the Italian cruisers after a short delay, as three destroyers passed less than 1000 yards from the submarine, but they were pursuing numerous possible contacts, then ordered 'Eighty feet!'. As Mars noted, he could have launched using sonar only but it was much better to fire at a visual target.

Two minutes and fifteen seconds later an explosion was heard, and 15 seconds after that another. It was a moment of great happiness and great danger for Mars and his men. He then dove to 120ft and rigged for silent running. In 45 minutes the Italians dropped 105 depth charges, but they were set for too shallow a depth to cause damage to the submarine, although Mars could tell they were in the right position.[17]

At 8.05am the Italian cruisers had slowed to 18 knots to allow the *Gorizia* to launch a seaplane and a few minutes later the destroyer *Fuciliere* sighted a submarine to port, firing a machine-gun at the periscope at 450 yards. The *Gorizia* and *Bolzano* sighted the torpedo tracks, the former turning sharply and avoiding them, but for the *Bolzano* it was too late, and she was hit just as she began to turn. The *Attendolo* had not sighted the torpedoes or received the *Fuciliere*'s alert and began to take evasive action only when the *Bolzano* was hit, but again too late as she was also hit a few seconds later. The destroyers *Fuciliere* and *Camicia Nera* began to slow to hunt the submarine. The *Fuciliere* was equipped with sonar but at her previous speed of

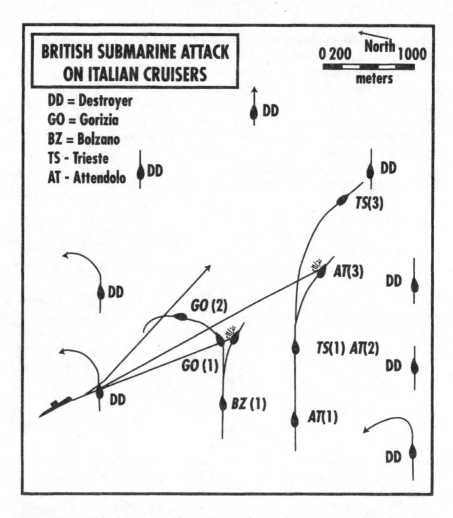

BRITISH SUBMARINE ATTACK ON ITALIAN CRUISERS

DD = Destroyer
GO = Gorizia
BZ = Bolzano
TS - Trieste
AT - Attendolo

about 20 knots had been unable to locate the *Unbroken*. Two other destroyers escorted the *Gorizia* and *Trieste* on to Messina, while the remaining five remained with the two badly-damaged cruisers, occasionally launching depth charges as a precaution. The *Fuciliere* only picked up the submarine on sonar at 8.45am but as we have seen, the depth charges were incorrectly set. Mars, an experienced commander, later said, 'the Italians were not as efficient as our own side in the use of Sonar', although they had experienced hydrophone operators.

The torpedo blew open 82ft of the *Attendolo*'s bow, but the rest of the hull resisted any additional damage. At first the ship had to be towed to Messina due to the wrecked bow, but when this fell off the cruiser could make 5 knots, escorted by the *Grecale* and *Ascari*, later joined by the *Freccia*. She arrived at Messina at 6.54pm, incredibly having suffered no fatalities. The *Bolzano* was hit amidships, flooding six engine-rooms and a magazine as well as starting a fire, although the ship was not in immediate danger of sinking. Therefore, the commander of the 11th Destroyer

Flotilla was ordered to tow the cruiser aground on the island of Panarea near Stromboli. The cruiser burned until the next day, covered by *Regia Aeronautica* fighters. She was worked on there for a month and then towed to Naples. In the evening, 'after ten unbroken hours of silent misery' the *Unbroken* surfaced and made contact with Malta, and she was recalled.

Supermarina made several observations following this action. In first place, the route taken by the naval force was influenced by the fact the *Unbroken* had already been sighted in her original patrol area, and Mars's estimation of the ships' new course gave him the advantage of surprise. He was also helped by the fact that the cruisers were not zig-zagging, contrary to orders, and had slowed to only 18 knots. The two destroyers equipped with sonar were unable to pick up the submarine for some time, probably because of the disturbing movements of the destroyers and the explosions of the depth charges. *Supermarina* also assumed that the *Unbroken* had not been damaged because the Italian depth charges were not powerful enough.[18]

*   *   *

Meanwhile, air attacks against the convoy continued. At 7.17am the convoy consisted, according to the Axis reconnaissance, of four transport ships, which was correct (*Rochester Castle*, *Waimarama*, *Melbourne Star* and *Ohio*), two cruisers (*Charybdis* and *Kenya*) and seven destroyers but there were also the *Ashanti*, *Icarus*, *Intrepid*, *Fury* and *Ledbury* as protection. Behind this main group, following at some distance were the *Dorset* and *Port Chalmers*, with the destroyers *Penn* and *Bramham*, while the *Eskimo* and *Somali* were further west. In the Hammamet Gulf was the damaged *Brisbane Star* and some submarines were stationed south of Pantelleria (*Utmost*, *Unruffled*, *Ultimatum*, *United*, *Uproar* and *P222*), but they did not sight any Italian ships.

Twenty-six Ju88s then took off in several formations and later at 9.15am an additional sixteen Ju87s escorted by eight Me109s and eight Me110s also started to attack the convoy. A group of ten Ju88s of II/LG1 attacked and scored some near misses on the *Ohio*, and sunk the *Waimarama*, one plane being caught in the explosion of the ship. At 9.23am eight Italian Ju87s of the 102nd Group escorted by ten MC202s of the 20th Fighter Group (both had had one aircraft abort the mission due to mechanical breakdown) attacked. A Stuka was then shot down, crashing into the side of the *Ohio*, and another was lost to AA fire. One Spitfire was also shot down, according to the British by friendly fire and to the Italians by one of the MC202s. The *Rochester Castle* was damaged by a near miss from a German Ju88 while the *Dorset* was hit by the Stukas of the I/StG3 and had to be abandoned. Two Ju87s and one Me109 were shot down, the British losing one Beaufighter. The *Port Chalmers* was also damaged, but when five S.79 torpedo-bombers escorted by fourteen MC202s attacked at 11.25am, the one torpedo that did hit was caught in the *Port Chalmers'* torpedo netting. One S.79 was shot down by a Spitfire after the attack. In the evening fourteen German Ju87s launched another attack and finished off the damaged *Dorset*. But the long-range Spitfire cover from Malta was becoming hour by hour too much for the Axis, and eighteen Ju88s which took off at 11.00am with only three fighters as escort were recalled for this reason.

The surviving ships arrived at Malta at different times. First the *Melbourne Star*, *Port Chalmers* and *Rochester Castle* were met by four minesweepers and seven motor minesweepers from Malta and escorted in, arriving at 6.18pm. Incredibly enough, the *Ohio* was still afloat although she was dangerously low in the water. Her 11,500 tons of fuel were too important to lose and every effort was made to tow her to Malta where she arrived with the *Penn* and the minesweeper *Rye* after several further air attacks had damaged her again. The last to arrive was the *Brisbane Star* which came in alone after being attacked by a couple of Italian S.79s of the 254th Squadron, but the torpedoes malfunctioned. She continued to navigate along the coast of French North Africa and was lucky that the *MAS* boats were unable to find her. The *Ledbury* was attacked also but succeeded in shooting down both the S.79s. Finally, the Germans suffered some casualties attacking the ships and also some friendly fire incidents occurred. For example the *Alagi* was attacked by three Ju88s but was fortunately undamaged. A total of 32,000 tons of supplies reached Malta, enough for 2 months' operations by the submarines and aircraft based there.

At 4.00pm on 13 August the escort ships of Force X turned back to Gibraltar. They were the cruisers *Charybdis* and *Kenya*, plus the destroyers *Ashanti*, *Intrepid*, *Fury*, *Icarus* and *Pathfinder*. The fact that the *II Fliegerkorps* devoted all their efforts against this force played a part in the safe arrival of the surviving transports at Malta. Thirty-five Ju88s and thirteen Ju87s attacked the warships without result, apart from some damage caused to the *Kenya* by a near miss, and losing one Ju88 and one Ju87. Fifteen Italian bombers and twenty torpedo-bombers likewise attacked without result. In the afternoon Force X was joined by Force Z. During the day there were further attacks by Axis planes, submarines and light craft, but there were no further losses, apart from the damaged destroyer *Foresight* which had to be scuttled by the *Tartar* when she could no longer navigate. The last ships to enter Gibraltar were the *Eskimo* and *Somali* at 5.30am on 15 August, carrying the survivors of the *Manchester*.

* * *

It has been said that 'Pedestal' was the last victory by the Axis in the Mediterranean, although only in tactical terms, because, strategically, the arrival of the heavily-damaged tanker *Ohio* was a major success and justified the decision to field such a powerful naval force. Allied losses were very heavy and the low percentage of shipping that actually arrived made the operation a failure in general terms. But the arrival of the aviation fuel allowed the Malta striking forces to become more powerful as they continued their harassment of the Axis shipping which was now more vulnerable given the longer distances it had to travel. At the same time the operation began, the Axis had to suspend at once all transport shipping in the Mediterranean. But this was not completely done, as shown from the meetings held by the Chief of General Staff of the Italian Supreme Command with the German officers like Rintelen, Kesselring, Wenninger, etc. Part of the reason for suspending the flow of supplies was the sinking on the 12th of the transport *Ogaden* near Derna by the British submarine *Porpoise*.[19]

Figures for the supplies delivered to North Africa in the critical months of July and August (literally the 'hottest' for the soldiers at the front) show that only 11,661 tons were lost out of 274,337 tons shipped in July and 45,668 tons out of 253,005 tons in August. But further analysis reveals that the Allies were mainly targeting tankers, which were carefully tracked by Bletchey Park. Thanks to the air offensive Malta was not operating against Axis shipping until the end of July, and therefore only two transports were sunk by submarine in that period. Air attacks were also hindered by the fuel shortage and the fact that most Axis convoys were too far east for Malta's planes. After the arrival of the *Ohio*, the submarines returned and the island began to recover its effectiveness. Coupled with the arrival of the Spitfires launched from the *Furious*, this allowed a major effort against Axis shipping lanes. On 15 August the freighter *Lerici* was sunk by the *Porpoise* and on 17th the 8000-ton freighter *Pilo* was also sent to the bottom by air attack. More serious for the Italians in Africa was the sinking of the tanker *Poẓarica* on the 21st.[20] What then happened to Rommel's offensive against the Alam-Halfa position at the end of August is well known but to some extent the seeds of that failure lay in the strategic success of Operation 'Pedestal', at least where fuel supply is concerned. Although Rommel stressed the lack of fuel and the fact that the promised tankers did not arrive as the reason for the defeat, the fuel in fact did arrive but too far from the front line. The German High Command gave Allied air superiority as the main reason for the failure of the offensive.[21]

Losses during the convoy battle were high on both sides, mainly aircraft for the Axis. The *II Fliegerkorps* reported employing 650 aircraft between 11-14 August, losing 18 and claiming 12 enemy planes shot down.[22] The Axis lost a total of sixty-two aircraft, of which forty-two were Italian and nineteen were German, including the aircraft destroyed on the ground and those shot down erroneously by friendly fire. The Allied AA fire and fighters shot down forty-two aircraft of which twenty-six were Italian and sixteen German, against an estimate of seventy-four made by the British. Claims by the Italians and German pilots were also too high. Naval losses were limited to two submarines sunk and two cruisers heavily damaged for the Italians, while the Germans had the *S58* badly damaged.[23]

For the Allies it was a dearly-bought victory, since not only nine transport ships were sunk (another one was sunk at Malta after unloading), but also several warships were lost or heavily damaged. Aircraft losses were comparatively low, since only thirteen were lost by the Fleet Air Arm in combat and another sixteen when the *Eagle* went down, while the RAF lost six (one Beaufighter and five Spitfires), plus a Sunderland shot down by the *Giada*.[24]

The Axis commands commented on the results in various ways. The best known are the boasting propaganda declarations, but the views of the commanders at the time, while interesting, are not always accurate as they did not have full information. As the *Kriegsmarine* report on the action says: 'Evidence is not complete and is often contradictory, therefore we cannot gain a clear and unequivocal picture.'[25] The Germans considered the arrival of the four transports and the tanker as 'unsatisfactory'. The supplies would help Malta for a while, but they noted that the reactivating of the island as an offensive base would cause 'notable disturbance' to the Axis supply route in 'perhaps [the] decisive phase of the struggle for North Africa'.[26] *Supermarina* concurred with this assessment, as did General Santoro, Deputy Chief of Staff of the *Regia Aeronautica*, who wrote that 'the Royal Navy achieved the strategic success to put Malta in the position to make an important contribution to the final phase of the struggle in Egypt'.[27]

One of the consequences of 'Pedestal' was its influence on the planning of Operation 'Torch'. There was some disagreement among the Allies about where to land, since the British and Admiral Cunningham in particular supported a plan to land east of Algiers and proceed directly to seize Tunisia. Early occupation was the main objective of the British strategy, to prevent the Axis powers retaining contol of the North African shoreline. But a different view was held by the Americans, and General Eisenhower, appointed Commander-in-Chief of the Expeditionary Force, cancelled the landings east of Algiers.[28] The heavy losses suffered by the naval forces during 'Pedestal' appeared to confirm the American view that to launch a landing directly against Algeria and Tunisia was too great a risk to take.[29]

*   *   *

Of course it was hard for Italy to replace any of her losses, either of merchant ships or warships, losses which would continue to increase. During the Second World War Italy's yards were able to produce the following warships: in 1940 only two battleships, one small ship and fifteen MTBs were completed, and in 1941 the only significant production was seven submarines, four of which were ocean-going, six midget subs and twenty-six MTBs. In 1942 the first six anti-submarine escort corvettes were finally commissioned, along with ten torpedo-boats built for the same purpose. Another battleship was completed (*Roma*), plus one light cruiser and five destroyers, while the submarine losses were partly made up for with twelve new boats. Fifty-three MTBs were also built.[30] Of the ships laid down for 1943, the majority were light vessels: thirty-six submarines, sixteen midget submarines (a total of seventy-two were planned) and seventy-seven motor torpedo boats. Before the armistice in 1943 two light cruisers, five escort torpedo-boats, one torpedo-boat, twenty-three corvettes, ten submarines, six midget submarines and thirty-four MTBs were commissioned.[31]

Many difficulties were faced in completing these ships, and to build some merchant ships to replace the heavy losses on the 'Route of Death' to Tunisia. This was due to the problems of distributing raw materials as much as to the actual shortage of those materials themselves, and also the shortage of skilled workers, of which there were 48,242 in September 1942, the yards needing at least 1500–2000 more. Of these, 10,932 of them were working on building new merchant ships. One of the problems was the continuous need for repairs to both warships and transports, and 11,660 skilled workers had to be assigned to this.[32] To make matters worse, the yards were unable to prevent their workers being conscripted into the armed forces, which further slowed output. The German opinion was that the Italians showed the 'strongest reluctance to employ their shipping', and they thought the Italians were 'plainly sparing Italian shipping for the time after the war when there would be a shortage of transports'.[33] Merchant ship construction was likewise a problem of workers and raw materials according to various sources. Forty-five transports were in the yards in March 1941, and of these about thirty should have been ready by the end of the year, while another nineteen, and twenty-one tankers had to laid down in the 1942 but the yards still lacked raw materials for all required construction.[34]

For 1943 the Italian navy foresaw a considerable increase in the building of cargo ships: 124 steel-built, but also thirty concrete-built and 144 wooden ones. According to Agostino Rocca, the chief manager of Ansaldo, production of these ships could have been increased threefold if types had been standardised and the number of ships in each order increased.[35]

The Italian Navy also laid down a new class of improved destroyers, though none would be more than 20 per cent complete by the Armistice. The 'Comandanti Medaglia d'Oro' class were to be improved 'Soldatis', the last pre-war class, named after commanders killed in action who had been awarded the Medaglia d'Oro.[36] It is interesting to note the direction the Italian Navy was heading with this design. Most significant was the main armament, 5.3in guns with 45° elevation, thus making them a limited DP weapon, in single mounts. The first group (of eight and the most advanced in construction) would have four, the second series (eight to be begun in 1943) five. They were slightly larger than their predecessors, with a standard displacement of 2100 tons, Gufo radar and a complement of 277 officers and men. Torpedo armament would be two triple mounts with the standard 21in torpedo. The AA armament was also interesting. The first group had twelve single mount 37mm Breda cannon (not the usual dual mount). The second series was to receive two improved quadruple 37mm mounts and two quadruple 20mm mounts, probably with German guns. The concentration of the AA armament allowed for a fifth 5.3in gun.

Another project that the Italian Navy had under development in 1942 was the 'Avviso Scorta 450', known as 'AS 450'. Based on the successful *Gabbiano* class corvette, this handsome design called for an increase in size to 1120 tons normal load displacement, three single 4.7in guns, a substantial anti-submarine armament, and two 17.7in torpedo-tubes. With a speed of just 24 knots, it was clearly designed for escort work. But the decline of Axis, and particularly Italian, fortunes in the war, meant that this project was never undertaken. But it does prove the recognition of the need for escort ships in the Mediterranean.[37] Both sides had to spend more and more effort on anti-submarine warfare as the war continued.

CHAPTER 20

Submarine Warfare in the Mediterranean: August–December 1942

Communications intelligence was also decisive in North Africa, . . .
was it a coincidence that the flow of information correlated well with
the successes and failures of the two sides?

Daniel R Headrick[1]

August ended with Operation 'Baritone', the reason why the *Furious* had entered dry dock upon her return to Gibraltar after Operation 'Burrows'. On 17 August the carrier sailed with Force H to just south of the Balearics and launched thirty-two Spitfires for Malta, twenty-nine of which arrived, although one crashed on landing. To give a sense of the Allied, and particularly Commonwealth, nature of the war, of thirty-one pilots in this operation whose nationality is recorded, two were US citizens, one was a Rhodesian, one an Australian, three were New Zealanders, and six were Canadian. The remainder were British.[2]

On 4 September, the Italian torpedo-boat *Polluce* was damaged in an air attack near Tobruk and sank when her magazine exploded. As the Axis tried to move supplies to small desert ports like Tobruk and Bardia, closer to the front, it placed them once again closer to the bases of the RAF and the American AAFMTO (Army Air Forces, Mediterranean Theatre of Operations). As larger numbers of more capable long-range aircraft became available to the Allies, the threat to Fascist Italy from the air would increase in the final year of Mussolini's war.

The Axis won another victory with the defeat of Operation 'Agreement' on 13-14 September, when the British attempted a combined sea and land attack on Tobruk, which has been described as the Mediterranean equivalent of the ill-fated Dieppe raid. The Long Range Desert Group (LRDG) was to cross 1500 miles of desert and attack Tobruk from the rear as commandos poured ashore from a flotilla of small ships led by two big 'Tribal' class destroyers, the *Sikh* and the *Zulu*. Also operating with this force were seventeen MTBs carrying 200 troops between them. LRDG units were also raiding targets elsewhere in the rear as far as Benghazi, combined with RAF operations, which would also be unsuccessful.

The MTBs were part of Force C, which was accompanied by three motor launches, which was to enter the harbour after it was captured to help in the demolition of the port. The 700-mile trip was uneventful, except that one MTB had to drop out due to engine trouble. However, in the approach to Tobruk the MTBs became scattered and their poor station-keeping later came in for criticism. An initial landing to secure the coastal defences at the tiny port of Mersa Sciausc just east of Tobruk did succeed in capturing one battery, but by then the garrison was alerted and put up such strong resistance, that as the small craft approached to land the Royal Marines, the two destroyers had to come in close to provide gunnery support on the east side of Tobruk, where the *Sikh* was disabled by the tremendous volume of fire put out by the Italian and German batteries, particularly a battery of 88mm AA guns commanded by a Lt. Wegener. The unarmoured destroyer took heavy damage as shrapnel tore holes through her. After 3 hours the *Sikh* capsized and sank, after a failed attempt by the *Zulu*, which was also damaged, to take the crippled ship in tow. The Italian *San Marco* battalion, late of *Kampfgruppe Hecker* took part in the battle and was later renamed battalion 'Tobruk' for its sterling service.

The Italians then sent up MC.200s armed with small under-wing bombs which effectively attacked some of the small landing craft being used by the British in this attack, while German Ju88s damaged the old AA cruiser *Coventry* so severely that she had to be scuttled by the *Zulu*, which herself sank after repeated attacks while being towed back to Alexandria. Five MTBs and two of the motor launches were also lost, four to air attacks and the rest to gunfire from Mersa Sciausc. This operation was a complete disaster for the British, with 576 prisoners being taken as well.[3]

At Alexandria after the 'Flap' were, among other warships, twenty-eight MTBs, almost exclusively American-built PT boats. Some were later sent north to Cyprus and Lebanon for anti-submarine work, as Alexandria was too far away for these short-ranged craft to patrol those waters, even with extra fuel tanks.[4] Later, during the pursuit of the *Afrika Korps* west the MTBs would operate off the coast at night, often firing tracer and dropping smoke floats to confuse the Axis forces, as well as occasionally shooting-up the odd truck moving along the coast roads. Their base also had to relocate frequently, following behind the advance of the 8th Army.

* * *

At this time, the only German destroyer in the Mediterranean, the ex-Greek *Hermes* (*ZG3*), was involved in a number of convoys to Tobruk that suffered almost no losses, because they had not operated on a rigid timetable that had been radioed to the ships involved, thus preventing British interception. It was not unusual for senior Italian destroyer captains to subordinate themselves to the Germans to avoid rigid *Supermarina* procedures.[5]

During the war, the British did lose a large number of submarines to the Italians, despite their lack of radar and weak depth charges. Ben Bryant would later write,

> The reason why our losses of submarines were so heavy was that the shipping was never far from the shore, and surface and air support could be concentrated. And always there were the undersea menaces, the opposing submarines, to which I accorded considerable respect, and mines, which were an ever-present danger.

Furthermore, the coastal waters, where there were targets, were shallow and it was harder to escape once discovered.[6]

For example, the commander of the submarine *Safari* liked to lurk near the Italian coastline and use his deck gun to sink enemy freighters. In one action in the summer of 1942 he attacked a freighter at dusk and scored several hits, but instead of abandoning ship as expected, the crew rallied and returned fire with their ship's own gun, a coastal battery joining in also. The combination of the two chased the submarine off and saved the freighter.[7]

Another example of a successful ASW action is that involving the British submarine *Thorn*, under the command of Lieutenant-Commander Norfolk, which sailed from Haifa on 21 July 1942 to patrol off Tobruk until 6 August and thereafter to the south of Crete. She sank the 5322-ton merchant ship *Monviso* on 3 August and then proceeded to the Matapan area. In the afternoon of 6 August the freighter *Istria* sailed from Benghazi for Piraeus escorted by the *Pegaso*, one of the *Orsa* class escort destroyers. She had undergone an extensive refit in early 1942, where she was equipped with a German sonar set and returned to service in the second half of April after a period of training.[8]

At 12.55am on the 7th the *Pegaso* was alerted by a Ju88 escorting the convoy that it had sighted and fired on a periscope, which the destroyer was also able to spot. The periscope was very quickly spotted on the port side of the convoy and two minutes later disappeared, but the *Pegaso* had reached the point and picked up a clear sonar contact 1600 metres ahead. The *Pegaso* attacked seven times with depth charges between 12.58am and 1.47pm, never losing contact, and believed the submarine to have been sunk, seeing oil and air bubbles coming to the surface. There were no survivors from the *Thorn*.

This action was a clear example of co-operation with the air force, and the *Pegaso*'s report made a few interesting observations. The *Thorn*'s periscope was exposed too long during the manoeuvre into attack position (unlike Captain Mars's during his attack on the Italian cruisers). The commander of the *Pegaso* could only conclude that something had gone wrong aboard the submarine for the periscope to be left up so long. The evasive manoeuvres by the *Thorn* appeared to be good, but she appeared to have been damaged in the first attack, as oil was seen, and she was slowed down. After the sixth attack she may have been trying to surface, but failed.

It should also be noted that the *Pegaso*'s crew was an experienced one. Although they had only just completed training with their new sonar, they had escorted numerous convoys in the past. On 14 April 1942, while escorting a convoy to Tripoli, she chased and sank what may have been the *Upholder*, and engaged the *Turbulent* on 4 July while escorting three transports to Benghazi. The submarine war in the Mediterranean was quite different from that in the Atlantic. The shallower waters meant that submarines at periscope depth could be spotted by aircraft which could guide in surface forces.

The British began the war with fifty-eight submarines (or fifty-two and eighteen under construction according to some sources), of which ten were stationed in the Mediterranean. Compared with the Italian fleet of 113 operational submarines, they were always few in number but they distinguished themselves throughout the war. The Mediterranean was also the only theatre in which there were plenty of targets available for British submarines, while for the Axis the Atlantic was more target-rich, with more merchant vessels under less heavy escort than in the Mediterranean.[9]

The Italian submarines were of two types, seventy-seven coastal and thirty-eight 'oceanic' type, of which thirty-six of the latter were operational at the outbreak of war. Two more oceanic submarines were being completed and six more under construction, as well as six coastal boats.[10] In general terms these vessels were well-built, no more than 10 years old, safe and with good sea-keeping capabilities.

Tactical employment resembled a re-fighting of the First World War in the Adriatic rather than a campaign against the world's foremost navy. Of course, the boats were built for that kind of war. It is difficult to list the different types of submarines of the Italian fleet, because they were built over a period of 10 years in response to various events. After the Abyssinian Crisis, Italy laid down eight new classes of submarine, of which six were for employment in the Atlantic (one of minelayers) and only one of coastal submarines. According to some authors, the vessels built in this period were generally worse than those built previously, particularly the *Brin* and *Liuzzi* classes, tending to be mechanically unreliable and poor seaboats.[11]

A total of 172 submarines were commissioned in the Italian Navy during the Second World War of which 90 were lost. Most were lost before the surrender of Fascist Italy, a high figure compared to the 75 lost by the Royal Navy, 45 of them in the Mediterranean, out of the 215 which served during the war. Two, *Axum* and *Settembrini*, were lost after the Armistice, fighting on the Allied side. In the first month of war, the Italians had eighty-four submarines available for operations, of which fifty-five were sent on patrol, the largest number the Italians ever had at sea at one time. Losses were heavy, with six boats sunk and twelve damaged in June alone. In the Red Sea, the capture by the British of the codebooks and secret orders from the *Galilei* on 11 June 1940 led to the sinking of the *Torricelli* on the 23rd and the *Galvani* the next day.[12]

The losses could have been due to poor training and the surprise effect of British anti-submarine equipment, while the lack of success of their own attacks may have been partly because of their tendency to fire only a few torpedoes, often only two, and at too great a range. Tactical employment was to assign an ambush area to a submarine that had to remain in that area where of course the enemy could assume their presence, such as off Alexandria and Gibraltar. The other kind of deployment was to form a extended line in which the submarines had about 30 miles between them, too great a distance to allow proper coverage of the area.

After these first unexpected losses, *Supermarina* ordered only twenty-six vessels out on patrol while the rest remained in port. In the first 7 months of the war, the average number of submarines at sea would be twenty-seven. Until then, noted *Supermarina*, Italian submarine losses were following damage or breakdowns that forced the vessels to the surface under the enemy's guns. 'In this way many lives were saved, but throughout the war this happened only in the *Regia Marina*'.[13] This lead also to more captures of documents and codebooks as in case of the *Durbo*, sunk on 18 October 1940, after the British were able to board her. As a consequence 2 days later the submarine *Lafole* was also sunk. Wireless interception and ULTRA played its part in submarine losses, and would lead to the loss of several Italian submarines during the war.

In any case, after the first bad experiences, losses began to slow down to ten vessels per trimester, thanks to the fact that the number of submarines at sea dropped by half and the commanders became more experienced. However, the Italian shipbuilding industry could not make good even these reduced losses

Faults in the design of Italian submarines began to be shown as well. In his analysis of the Italian submarines from a technical point of view, Turrini argued that these faults were over-emphasised by numerous authors and that in reality they were on average of good quality, compared to those of other navies. Great technical improvements had been made in the inter-war years and if they had 'poor effectiveness' the causes 'had to be traced to the different exploitation made of the experiences taken as starting point for all during the First World War'. The Italian Navy's submarines did sink more merchant ships than the Japanese and Russian submarine fleets during the war.[14]

But Turrini, in pleading 'the extraordinary commitment of the technicians, the dedication of the crews, the far-sightedness of a Navy Staff which was able to built more than a hundred vessels' seems to avoid the fact that after the first months of the war steps had to taken to modify Italian submarines. These changes included:

- reduction of the time required to dive, which was around 60 seconds,
- reduction of the size of the conning tower, which was easily spotted by radar on the surface,
- reduction of noise in underwater movement,
- use of electric torpedoes, eliminating wakes,
- reducing of air bubbles when torpedoes launched,
- installing electrically-driven mechanical fire control systems for torpedo launching.[15]

The poor fire control systems were partly responsible for the lack of success the submarines had. It was calculated that only 14 per cent of torpedoes hit the target, a very poor performance. The causes varied from errors in torpedo and target speed estimates and therefore in the angle of firing, to variations in the torpedo gyros, all of which were exacerbated when the torpedoes were fired at too long a range. Torpedo launching controls was ordered from the Germans but were not fitted before the end of the war.[16]

The reasons for the few hits scored by Italian torpedoes were:

- too often torpedoes were launched too far from the target,
- poor quality control in torpedo manufacture meant no two torpedoes ran alike,
- inability to automatically calculate impact angle.

Furthermore, the wakes of the torpedoes frequently alerted the targets, allowing them to take evasive action. From 1942 the Italian submarines began to employ the German G7e torpedo which was not propelled with warm air and left little wake. They also exploded under the target, causing greater damage

In any event, attacks could only take place when targets had been spotted, and this seems to have been another shortcoming of Italian submarines. *Supermarina* issued tactical directives for operations, instructing the submarines to attack during the day while submerged, tracking the target with hydrophones, in order to avoid air attack. A less rigidly-defined patrol area was allowed, however, as the submarines often had to shift position by up to 100 miles in a day. In the opinion of an experienced British submarine commander, the air threat was overestimated by the Italian submarines, and the 'listening' watch resulted in very few targets being located and attacked.[17]

The losses suffered by the Italians in the first months of the war can be compared with those suffered by the British in the same period. By the end of May 1940, nine submarines of the 'O' and 'P' classes, plus two minelayers, were concentrated at Alexandria for the expected outbreak of war with Italy. By the beginning of August five of them had been lost, three being 'O' class boats. Like many Italian submarines they were too large for Mediterranean operations and took too long to dive, at least 40 seconds (but the Italians took nearer 60 seconds), and the tired crews and inexperienced commanders also played apart. But soon the arrival at Gibraltar of smaller boats of the 'U' and 'T' classes reduced losses and increased the number of successes, helped by the fact that Italian ASW techniques did not really improve until the end of 1941.[18]

In 1929-30 the Italians had conducted unsuccessful trials with a French-built sonar, but in 1937 rumours reached the navy staff that foreign countries had had better results. This lead to the mounting in 1939 of a domestically-produced sonar, the Safar P600, on the corvette *Albatros*, and the same company was selected to produce two types of submarine sonar, the Safar MC 3000 and GC 3000, which began to appear towards the end of 1942. Since production of the Safar P600 was also very slow – sets would not start being delivered until early 1942 – the navy turned to the Germans for help and at the end of 1941 received 40 German-built sets. Thus the introduction of sonar took place only after 20 months of war and there appears to have been very little training, as all anti-submarine units had on average only 1.5 opportunities to launch depth charges.[19] The torpedo-boats *Lince*, *Castore*, *Orsa* and *Sagittario* begun to operate in December 1941 patrolling the Taranto gulf with the *Gino Nais* and *Pasman*, two small merchant ships equipped with sonar and depth charges. They did not sink any British submarines but helped to keep them out of the patrolled area. The installation of sonar began to increase in May 1942 with sixteen more ships so equipped; by the end of 1942 52 sets had been installed and the total for the war period was 101.[20]

The British 'T' and 'U' classes were built shortly before the war and only three vessels of each type were operational at the outbreak of the conflict. The 'U' class were small and relatively slow, and had considerable success in the Mediterranean. The early boats of this class did not have welded hulls and therefore could not dive as deep as the 'S' and 'T' classes, but later the use of different steel and welding increased maximum depth from 200ft to 300ft. However, some of the improvements made to these boats during the war were similar to those made by the Italians, including:

- silencing of machinery (particularly the 'U' class),
- reduction of diving times,
- installation of freon air conditioning.[21]

During the war they sank 493 merchant ships, totalling 1,524,000grt, 26 per cent of the total Axis merchant shipping sunk in the Mediterranean, and 169 warships.

Italian submarines operating in the Atlantic, based at Bordeaux, enjoyed some success against the less well escorted merchant traffic, sinking 600,000 tons for the loss of sixteen boats. But when the Germans entered the Mediterranean in September 1941 the contrast between the two submarine forces' results could not have been greater. The German U-boats would sink 476,383 tons of Allied shipping up until the Italian armistice compare to 39,337 tons sunk by Italian submarines in the same period.[22]

There was little actual direct co-operation between the Axis powers in the Mediterranean, and perhaps least of all between the two navies (the air co-operation was much better), but the deployment of Italian submarines in the Atlantic was an exception to this rule, to the extent that in 1943 the *Kriegsmarine* gave seven U-boats to the Italians for Atlantic operations, but the Armistice came before they entered service.

On their first visit to the Italian submarine base at Bordeaux, *Kriegsmarine* officers made a number of technical and tactical observations. The Italian submarines appeared 'very large with enormous towers and with the periscope container visible at long distances although good for increasing the periscope height'. They were astonished that the Italians had done so little to reduce the visibility of their boats from the air. Tactically, 'there is a lack of tactical ideas and of tactical training of the submarines' officers, although they are very dynamic and good willing'. The preparation of the submarine service was generally inadequate by the German standards but they thought the goodwill of the allies could overcome these shortcomings.[23]

In 1943 the tactical instructions for the Italian submarines still foresaw patrolling during daylight hours at a depth of 40-50m using hydrophones (now often of better quality supplied by the Germans) in order to avoid being spotted by aircraft, although some use of the periscope was now envisaged. When a ship had been detected the submarine would go to periscope depth and possibly surface to follow the target at full surface speed without being limited to a specific patrol area. At night the submarine had to patrol on the surface and to dive when radar impulses were detected. Although no Italian submarines were equipped with radar themselves, from the second half of 1942 some received Metox Fu.Mb 1 radar detectors from the Germans. Two fore and two aft torpedo tubes would be open for rapid torpedo firing if the tactical situation required it.[24] But their employment in the first weeks of 1943 showed that these submarines were not up to the job. The escorts were usually able to prevent them closing with the targets, attacks having to be carried out at up to 2000 yards, and the submarines were lucky if they could escape pursuit by air and sea.

In a memorandum of March 1943, *Supermarina* looked back at the submarine war in the Mediterranean and predicted that in the future operations had to be restricted in order to avoid suffering losses that would condemn the fleet to destruction. Thirty-six submarines were operational at that point, of which ten were in the Atlantic. The new strategy would be to reserve the existing vessels to be used in large-scale operations like the attack on the 'Pedestal' convoy in August 1942.[25]

Toward the end of Italy's war the gap between the capabilities of her submarines and Allied ASW assets was hopelessly wide, resulting by 1943 in the rising losses that prevented them being a real threat either in the Mediterranean or elsewhere. By this time the boats at Bordeaux were no longer considered fit for combat operations and had been reduced to transport duties. The Allied forces covering the landings in Sicily inflicted severe punishment on the Italian submarines. In a few days seven were sunk, while others were severely damaged, like the *Dandolo* after she torpedoed the cruiser *Cleopatra*.[26]

*   *   *

The British pulled off a brilliant coup against a German submarine, the *U-559*, on 30 October 1942. Five destroyers and RAF aircraft cornered her in the Eastern Mediterranean and forced her to the surface. As the crew tried to scuttle their boat (seven men were lost), a specially-trained unit from the destroyer *Petard* raced on board and charged down to the wireless and cipher room. There they attempted to secure the German 'M-4' cipher machine. In this they failed, and two British sailors went down with the submarine, but they did secure vital documents that allowed Bletchley Park to break an important code ('Triton') on 13 December.

There is one tragedy that needs to be discussed before we turn to the final defeat of the Axis in North Africa. In the course of the war hospital ships were accidentally bombed and torpedoed, but also, as we have already seen twice, some Allied prisoners of war, of various nationalities, were killed in British submarine attacks, almost certainly by accident. However, on 9 October 1942 the *Loreto* was reported by ULTRA to be leaving Tripoli and that it would '. . . transport 350 POWs'. Four days later, she was sunk by the *Unruffled*. On the night of 14 November the *Sahib* sank the *Scillin* and about 800 prisoners died. Santoni could discover no ULTRA alert on this ship and Hinsley does not discuss it. But Santoni did find a witness to this.[27]

A long unsigned report in the PRO dated 20 November 1942 is titled 'Italian Ships Transportation POWs'. It notes that both the *Loreto* and *Scillin* had been discovered by ULTRA and that they were carrying prisoners. The *Scillin* ULTRA alert came on 13 November. The report then recommends that this stop and gives details of twenty-nine ships that had been known in the past to carry prisoners on board. The question that has arisen is, did the British deliberately sink these two ships so as to protect the secret of ULTRA? The authors believe that this is more a case of inefficiency than a plot or conspiracy. But it is interesting to note that no British historian that the authors are aware of have tackled this subject directly, and that an Italian historian was the one to uncover this. This remains an uncomfortable topic in the Commonwealth as well. The *Nino Bixio* was carrying 2921 'Empire soldiers', and with another unmarked prisoner ship, had departed Benghazi for Brindisi on 16 August 1942. On the 17th, the *Turbulent*, out of Alexandria, torpedoed her twice. She managed to make Navarino Bay with 432 dead, many Indian, though 117 were New Zealanders.[28]

CHAPTER 21

Operation 'Torch', November 1942

Why has so little been written about the Navy?
Anyone would think the army beat Hitler singlehandedly.
How do people think the army even landed in Europe?
Admiral John Lesslie Hall[1]

For the Allies, control of all the North African coast would mean the eastern Mediterranean would be more secure and Malta could be supplied more easily. Furthermore, it would make it easier to run convoys through the Mediterranean, thus avoiding the long route around the Cape. It would also open up Italy and her islands for possible invasion and potentially bolster the people of France and further depress Italian morale. Finally, if the French did come over to the Allies, there were upwards of 120,000 trained though poorly-equipped troops available in North Africa.[2]

One of the other motives for the invasion was simply the need to do something to help the Soviet Union in her struggle with Germany. Stalin was not only demanding supplies, but a Second Front. After a series of convoluted negotiations between the two main western Allies, it was finally decided to land on the Atlantic coast of Morocco, and at Oran and Algiers on the Mediterranean coast of Algeria.

It was proposed to land further east as well, attacking Tunisia directly, which in hindsight should have been done with the winter rains approaching which would have slowed down movement to the east by the invaders. But it was decided not to do this, primarily due to the threat to a slow-moving fleet of crowded transports from Axis forces based in Sardinia and Sicily. Bone was substituted as it was out of range of most Axis aircraft. There were also plans to invade Sicily directly, Operation 'Whipcord', but this too was decided against, as the nearest base for this would be Malta and it would be dependant on Allied control of Libya, which did not look likely in the summer of 1942.[3]

The overall commander of this coalition operation was the newly-appointed American General Dwight D Eisenhower. While not the most brilliant commander of the war, he got along well with Churchill and his fellow British commanders. The commander of the naval forces was our old friend Cunningham. Initially, the air and land commands were not unified. This arrangement would prove unsatisfactory and as the fighting continued over the next few months an overall army and air force commander would be appointed, who in this period would be British. The concept of a unified commander for coalition forces and also for unifying the army and navy came largely from the American General George Marshall. He had originally suggested it for the fighting in South-East Asia (ABDA) where General Wavell was given command.[4]

A key aspect of the invasion of French North Africa, Operation 'Torch', was that it was to be an essentially American operation, with the bulk of the land forces being

American, as there was less bad feeling towards them from the French. The British, of course, were very unpopular with Vichy thanks to Mers-el-Kebir and the recent conquest of Madagascar, which had finished only a few months before 'Torch' was due to begin. The American government had maintained a relatively friendly relationship with Vichy, and had some contacts with local French forces, both Free French and Vichy, in North Africa.[5]

It was always envisioned that this invasion would coincide with an operation at the other end of the African coast, now to be in Egypt before El Alamein. There, the British 8th Army under Montgomery was preparing to throw the Axis army out of Egypt and back into Libya in the autumn of 1942. The decisive battles fought there would result in a victory for the 8th Army which would begin a drive to the west which would not end until the Mareth line on the Libyan/Tunisian border was reached. This was all being helped by the Allied submarines and air forces operating against Rommel's supply lines, with ULTRA intercepts allowing concentration on tankers, many of which failed to make it to North Africa.

While the American Office of Strategic Services (OSS) was active in French North Africa, and French officers were involved in the plotting to bring Vichy North Africa over to the Allies, senior officers, such as for example the naval commanders at Casablanca and Algiers, were not involved. This would result in much of the early fighting between the Allies and Vichy forces at the time of the invasion.[6] The OSS was the American counterpart of the British Special Operations Executive (SOE) that carried out clandestine and intelligence-gathering operations in occupied Europe. Led by William 'Wild Bill' Donovan, its first major operations were in French North Africa where it was involved in watching the French modern battleship *Jean Bart* at Casablanca and in aiding the Allied invasion. It was also involved in watching Spanish operations in Spain and Spanish Morocco, though with much more success in the latter than the former.[7]

In Corsica it ran a model operation. After the fall of Vichy in November 1942, the island was occupied by the Italians who by December had over 25,000 men on the island, provoking resentment among the inhabitants, so the OSS decided to send a team there. The modern French submarine *Casabianca* was one of the few ships to escape from Toulon when it was seized by the Germans, and was used to carry OSS personnel to Corsica. The first success was an OSS radio team which began sending messages on 25 December 1942 from north of Ajaccio.[8]

US PT-boats would later run a team to Sardinia in July 1943, but they was quickly captured by the Italians. Later OSS operations would be carried out in Sicily during the invasion and at Salerno. Donovan himself landed at Salerno, which was highly dangerous as if he had been captured and forced to talk, he could have revealed many secrets to the Axis and was one reason why the British did not on the whole trust OSS operations in Europe.[9]

* * *

Comando Supremo and the *Luftwaffe* knew something was coming, but they along with Vichy were fooled. However, the French were still ready to oppose any attacks on their territory. They were aware of the shipping build-up at Gibraltar, and Darlan was of the opinion that it might be aimed at Dakar, while the local French naval commander thought it was for an invasion of Sicily, Sardinia, or even possibly Libya. He did however place his coast defence units on alert.[10] Furthermore, Spain ordered partial mobilisation during the build-up for 'Torch'.[11]

The *Furious* was attached to the main covering force, a considerably-augmented Force H under Vice-Admiral Syfret, stationed closest to the Italian fleet to the east with the battlecruiser *Renown*, and the battleships *Rodney*, *Nelson*, and *Duke of York*, a new ship of the *King George V* class. They were supported by the carriers *Victorious* (flagship of Rear-Admiral Lyster) and *Formidable*. In total, for the entire operation off the three main invasion areas near Casablanca, Oran, and Algiers, there were a total of five fleet carriers (including the USS *Ranger* and the tiny *Argus*) and seven escort carriers, four of which were American. The inexperience of the American flight crews aboard the carriers lead to heavy accidental losses. The green crews on the *Santee* lost twenty-one out of thirty-one planes of which only one was 'possibly' due to combat.[12]

The majority of the French people throughout the world supported the Free French and therefore De Gaulle, as much as the British and American leaders might have disliked it. Also in the background was Admiral Darlan, who had reassessed Germany's chances of victory and had been maintaining back-channel contacts with the Allies throughout 1942. At the time of the invasion he happened to be in Algiers visiting his son who was ill with polio. He initially ordered resistance, but once he realised the scale of the landings, he ordered a cease-fire beginning at Algiers. The Allies, particularly the Americans, wanted to negotiate with him, as they hoped he would order the French fleet to join him in North Africa from Toulon. On this point, Churchill had told Cunningham 'Kiss Darlan's stern if you have to, but get the French Navy'.[13]

Darlan had anticipated a negotiated entrance of American or Allied forces but when Robert D Murphy, Roosevelt's diplomatic representative in North Africa, informed Darlan personally that troops were coming ashore on the 8th (and that a small number of Free French resistance fighters controlled parts of Algiers), he was very upset. He told Murphy 'I have known for a long time that the British are stupid, but I always believed Americans were more intelligent. Apparently you have the same genius as the British for making massive blunders!'[14]

There were several factors that Darlan had to take into account in responding to the Allied landings. Was this going to be an attack on the scale of, say, Dakar or Dieppe, which would be defeated, and what would the reaction of Petain and the Vichy regime be? In the opening hours of 'Torch' he did receive an offer from the Germans to send aircraft to Algeria, which he declined, although he did give permission for the *Luftwaffe* to attack Allied ships off the coast of French North Africa (which they would have done with or without his approval).[15]

On 12 November, after a period of confused negotiations and some actual fighting (particularly at Casablanca), French North Africa joined the Allies, rather than just remaining neutral, apart from Tunisia, where Axis units had quickly moved in, despite Petain's orders for continued resistance. Ironically, since French North Africa was led by Darlan, it was still technically Vichy and Free French prisoners remained in custody for up to a month after the surrender.[16] Admiral Cunningham had been of great help during the negotiations with Darlan. His liaision officer had been well received, as Darlan remembered Cunningham's diplomatic handling of the disarmament of Admiral Godfroy's squadron at Alexandria, which had been accomplished without bloodshed, unlike at Oran.[17] Cunningham wanted to land at Bizerte and rally the French there. Admiral Esteva, after the war and while in prison for helping the Axis, said that he would have joined the Allies if he had more troops available to him than just the garrison.[18]

However, the Axis powers reacted very quickly to the Allied invasion and rapidly overran most of Tunisia. Furthermore, Allied interdiction of the supply lines from Italy to Tunis, Bizerte and minor Tunisian ports and airfields was slow to develop. But Hinsley may have the best view of it:

> It was the Germans who won the race; and neither the distance from Algiers to Tunis nor the delay in reaching an accommodation with the French would have been of much moment if the Allies had succeeded in limiting its scale and effect . . . The Germans intervened with a rapidity and a determination in excess of what the Allies had allowed for.[19]

Let us turn now to some of the actual fighting that went on during the invasion. Although outside the Mediterranean, the invasion of Morocco by 35,000 troops under General Patton was an integral part of Operation 'Torch' and must be briefly discussed. The American Admiral in overall command in the Mediterranean was Vice-Admiral Hewitt, with 51-year old Rear-Admiral John Lesslie Hall under him in direct command of the Moroccan invasion. This was only the second large-scale American amphibious operation, the first having been at Guadalcanal, and the first involving Army and Allied units. Many important lessons were learned here for future operations. For example, the assault was made at night, which would never be attempted again because of the confusion that resulted.[20]

Patton and Hall became friends while preparing for the invasion and after one debacle during a practice landing in Chesapeake Bay, the general remarked 'Never in history has the Navy landed an army at the planned time and place. If you land us anywhere within fifty miles of Fedala and within one week of D-Day, I'll go ahead and win.'[21]

The Morocco invasion force of over 100 ships left Norfolk, Virginia on 24 October, while the forces for Oran and Algiers sailed from Britain. Facing them at Casablanca, the vital port city of Morocco, was a French squadron built around the still-incomplete battleship *Jean Bart*. The first troops came ashore at Fedala, just north of Casablanca, and although initial surprise was achieved, the Vichy forces resisted and shore batteries opened fire. The American flagship, the heavy cruiser *Augusta*, therefore signalled 'Play Ball' – the order to return fire and disable the Vichy guns and warships. At Fedala, the *Augusta* launched her four spotter planes and quickly forced the shore batteries there to cease fire. The Vichy forces attempted two sorties against the invasion force. The *Augusta* and *Brooklyn* engaged them, and this would be the last time that the flagship of an invasion fleet, the communications centre for the operation, would be risked so close to the action. The *Augusta* had several near-misses but the French were repulsed with heavy losses.

Later, on 8 November the battleship *Massachusetts* approached the harbour of Casablanca with the heavy cruisers *Tuscaloosa* and *Wichita* and four destroyers. After one of the shore batteries opened up on the Americans, the battleship's guns roared back at the *Jean Bart* at a range of about 24,000 yards. The engagment between these two ships has produced several conflicting accounts, but it appears that while the *Massachusetts* was near-missed a few times, the stationary *Jean Bart* suffered five direct hits as well as damaging near-misses. The harbour was also damaged in the exchange of fire. Two of the hits were duds, the fuses having been disabled by the oblique angle at which the shells had struck the target, although one did jam the only functioning turret. The French were able to free the turret by cutting away the armour jamming it. Two days later, as the landings at Casablanca began, the *Augusta* was unexpectedly straddled by fire from the *Jean Bart*, which Admiral Hewitt thought had been abandoned following attacks by dive-bombers. Hewitt had pressed on with the landing without fully studying air reconnaissance photographs taken by aircraft from the carrier *Ranger*.

The landings showed up the need for better training for amphibious operations and also for better control of naval fire support, which would improve with time. It also pointed out that the American 8in and 16in armour piercing rounds were often duds, while their high explosive shells were more dependable.[22] Patton would later write: 'The performance of the Navy in this fleet, particularly Admirals Hewitt and Hall, has been of the highest order. I am amazed at their efficiency, and I am delighted at the whole-hearted spirit of co-operation they have evinced.'[23] Importantly, although three transports were sunk over the coming days by U-boats, Casablanca harbour was cleared and prepared for a major follow-up convoy which arrived on 18 November.

At both Algiers and Oran there was an attempt to seize the ports by a *coup de main*, warships landing small assault forces. Howver, at Oran both ships were lost and about 300 men were killed or captured. The most resistance at Algiers centred around the attempt to land a US army assault force in the harbour. Two destroyers, HMS *Broke* and HMS *Malcolm*, raced into the port and were quickly brought under fire. The *Malcolm* turned back, but the *Broke* successfully landed her troops, suffering twenty-two hits and sank the next day. The two shore batteries responsible were knocked out by Allied air support. The assault battalion lost fifteen men and the two British destroyers lost nine, while the French had about seventy killed. The cruisers *Sheffield* and *Bermuda* had been detached to attack a small French fort, which surrendered without a shot being fired, but on their return to the fleet they came under attack from Italian bombers. Although there were several near-misses, neither ship was hit.

The successful capture of Algiers was followed by two smaller operations to seize the ports of Bougie and Bone to the east. On the evening of the 10th three fast troopships with a light escort led by the *Sheffield* and *Bermuda* under Rear-Admiral C H J Harcourt headed east to seize Bougie. On the following night a similar force was sent off to Bone, a further 40 miles to the east. Bougie was taken on the 11th without resistance. As one British writer commented, 'the undistinguished harbour accommodated a few small and shabby freighters, native fishing boats, a coastal brigantine, a rusting water-boat, and several French naval launches whose crews stared unemotionally'. Harcourt withdrew towards Algiers as the troops were disembarking, but in a later air raid, all three of the big transports (all at least 10,000 tons or more) were sunk by German aircraft.

Almost fifty Axis submarines operated in the Mediterranean or off the Atlantic coasts of Spain and Morocco in an attempt to hamper the landings. From 7 to 17 November a series of attacks, combined with aircraft, failed to do sufficient damage to prevent the invasion. The Dutch destroyer *Isaac Sweers* was sunk on 13 November, while *U-331* was sunk 4 days later, her captain Lieutenant-Commander von Tiesenhausen surviving.

It was also at this time that the legendary Royal Navy diver Lionel Phillip 'Buster' Crabb arrived at Gibraltar, to help counter the SLC attacks. He also helped perfect the British 'Chariots', based on the SLC. After the war he made Commander and mysteriously 'died in April 1956 at the time of a goodwill mission by Krushchev and Bulganin on board the Russian cruiser *Ordzhonikidze*'. Crabb dived to examine the ship and never resurfaced. A headless corpse was later claimed to be him, but there was much doubt about this at the time. It was claimed he had been captured and there were reports later that he was seen training Soviet frogmen in the Black Sea. A Russian merchant skipper who made these claims turned up dead on 8 May 1968.

British 'Chariots' would have one success against the Italians before the Armistice. On 3 January 1943 the submarines *Thunderbolt* and *Trooper* crept close to Palermo and released attack teams. The light cruiser *Ulpio Traiano*, completing for sea, was heavily damaged and was a total loss. The freighter *Viminale* was also damaged. The X MAS was also conducting operations, the *Ambra* under Mario Arillo launching an attack against Algiers on 12 December 1942 that badly damaged four freighters.

The French fleet at Toulon had an opportunity to flee the port, and was invited to steam to Mers-el-Kebir, but Vice-Admiral Jean de Laborde would not take orders from Darlan, only from the Vichy government. Therefore, instead of joining the Allies it scuttled itself on 27 November, possibly in part due the 'deep scars left by the British attack on French ships at Mers-el Kebir'.[24] The scuttling was very successful though some light warships were pressed into Axis service before the Italian Armistice. In the following months work crews went aboard the larger ships to salvage steel from the wrecks.

If El Alamein was the decisive land battle in the Mediterranean, then the latter stages of the Tunisian campaign broke the Axis war effort and destroyed any chance of Italian resistance to the Allies in Italy itself. For the Italian Navy the convoys between Italy and the Tunisian ports would become the 'Route of Death' for convoys and the ships protecting them as they plied between Sicily and the Tunisian ports. Malta again became an effective raiding base, with strong forces acting in support from North African ports, but the principal danger was the powerful Allied air forces now based well within range of the convoy routes.

In this period, the Americans used the twin-engined P38 Lightning fighter for much of their air reconnaissance in the Mediterranean. It had good range, but could not operate at the high altitudes usual for this sort of work, and losses mounted as a result. The 3rd Reconnaissance Group lost 25 per cent of its strength during the North African campaign.[25]

* * *

The first US naval unit to serve in the Mediterranean was MTB Squadron 15, which consisted of eighteen boats, three more than the usual complement of a squadron. The first boats arrived at Gibraltar on 13 April 1943 and after being unloaded and prepared, were sent on to Oran. By 27 April they had arrived at the forward Algerian port of Bone where they joined the British coastal forces which had already been there for several weeks, operating MGBs and MTBs, including several US-built lend-lease PT-boats. The US boats were fitted with radar, and it is interesting to note that these 77ft-boats had radar when there were less than two dozen sets in the entire Italian navy by the time of the Armistice! The boats first saw action in early May, but their nightly patrols did not achieve any decisive results, and on one occasion they came under friendly fire from a British destroyer. The British thought the American boats were overloaded and thus sluggish in action, but the fact that they also operated the same type of craft eased maintenance problems, the Americans being quite relaxed about sharing parts.[26]

The British coastal forces had been present in the Mediterranean for some time. As the front line of the 8th Army moved west, they moved further west as well, several eventually ending up at Malta. But they were still out of range of the Tunisian convoy routes, and their patrols off the Sicilian ports and Pantellaria during the winter of 1942-43 had failed to yield targets. However, by January Bone was available as a base, and the MTBs had their first success on the night of 19-20 January off Tripoli, which was about to fall to the advancing 8th Army. The Italians had been running some small convoys in and out of Tripoli right up to the end, also using four submarines to ferry ammunition, of which two would be lost. On the night of 19-20 January the submarine *Santorre Santarosa* was being towed out of Tripoli by tugs when she was ambushed by British MTBs. She was torpedoed and ran aground, a total loss. During another operation off Tripoli in January, the British MTBs passed right through a formation of *MAS* boats – with both sides being so surprised that neither opened fire.[27]

At this time the Germans were employing two new types of transports, the 143-ton Siebel ferry originally planned to be used in Operation 'Sealion' and the larger MFP of 200 tons (there were three types, A, B, and C). A larger 280-ton type was later introduced. These ships were slow, but armed with numerous 40mm and 20mm AA guns and being flat-bottomed were virtually invulnerable to torpedoes. As British strength in coastal forces increased, with the new Fairmile D type boats becoming more numerous, their torpedoes were modified to run at a depth of only 2ft, to be effective against these shallow-draft transports.

From the end of March to 28 April 1943 there were a series of Axis supply convoys run to Tunisia which landed 2800 troops, 18,690 tons of supplies and 353 guns and vehicles. The Allies, using submarines, MTBs, warships, and aircraft managed to sink and damage numerous ships while suffering some losses in return.

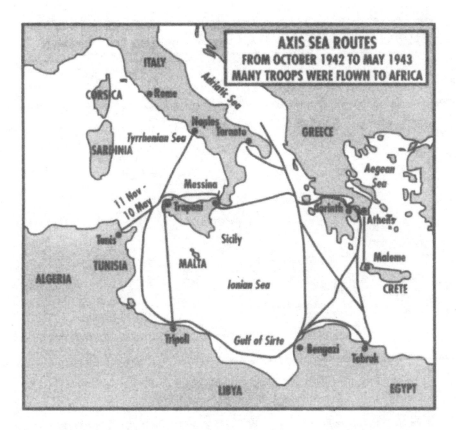

On 1 April a convoy of three merchant ships, escorted by four torpedo-boats, one of the new Italian corvettes and three small German submarine chasers, was attacked first by aircraft, which torpedoed one of the transports, the other two being sunk by MTBs for no loss.[28] On the night of 27-28 April the Italian torpedo-boat *Sagittario* sank *MTB 639* when she and two others attacked her convoy, but the steamer she was escorting was later sunk by Allied aircraft. The crew of the MTB were rescued, while the *Sagittario* shot down a Liberator bomber, picked up some of its crew and made it safely to Tunis.[29]

Other surface forces were committed against the Tunisian convoys. On 27 November 1942 Cunningham had ordered the revival of Force K at Malta, under Rear-Admiral A J Power with three *Dido* class cruisers (*Cleopatra* as flagship) and four destroyers. Force Q was also established at Bone under Rear-Admiral Harcourt with the cruisers *Aurora*, *Argonaut* and *Sirius* and the destroyers *Quentin* and *Quiberon*, which in January 1943 would become frequent targets of Axis air raids. On the night of 1-2 December Force Q slipped out of Bone just after sunset and headed for the Narrows between Tunisia and Sicily. Soon after midnight, having skirted minefields, and with supporting aircraft dropping flares, Force Q made radar contact with a convoy, moving to attack about 60 miles to the north-east of Bizerta.[30]

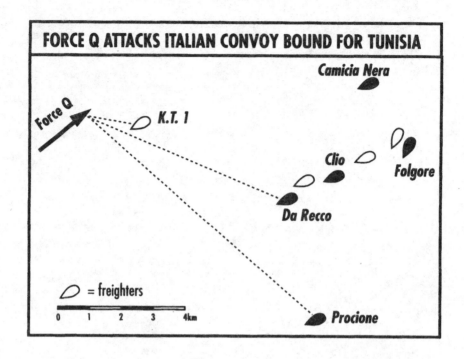

FORCE Q ATTACKS ITALIAN CONVOY BOUND FOR TUNISIA

Four convoys had been at sea, and when it was learnt that a British force was in the area, two had been recalled and a third redirected to Pantellaria. But Convoy H remained on course, consisting of three Italian transports and the German 7800-ton military transport *KT 1*, escorted by the destroyers *Da Recco* (Captain Aldo Cocchia), *Folgore* and *Camicia Nera* and the torpedo-boats *Clio* and *Procione*. Three of the transports had come from Palermo, while the other had joined up from Trapani.[31]

As Force Q approached at about 20 knots it came upon the somewhat disorganised convoy at about 12.37am and opened fire on the *KT 1* at a range of 1500 yards. Harcourt adopted Agnew's tactic from the *Duisburg* convoy and looped around the transports which had turned and were steaming slowly towards Sicily. The Italians conducted a spirited defence, with two of the destroyers launching torpedoes at the attacking British, but the convoy was quickly overwhelmed. Only one Italian transport was left when Force Q retired on Bone at 1.30am, but it would have to be scuttled. The *Folgore* was also sunk, and the *Da Recco* and *Procione* damaged, with the *Da Recco* having to be towed back to Sicily. Force Q was virtually undamaged, although the *Quentin* was sunk by German aircraft the following day and on 10 December the *Argonaut* would lose most of her bow to a torpedo from the submarine *Mocenigo*. On 2 December the torpedo-boat *Lupo* was rescuing survivors from another convoy when she was attacked by the four destroyers of Force K and sunk.

*   *   *

On 4 December 1942 the US 9th Air Force carried out its first attack against the Italian Navy in port, with an attack on Naples. The 7th Division suffered serious losees with the light cruiser *Attendolo* sunk and the *Montecuccoli* badly damaged, while the *Savoia* and four destroyers were slightly damaged. To sum up the question of the inability of the *Regia Aeronautica* to control (at least) the Central Mediterranean from the beginning of the war, we shall summarise some of the latest research on the development of this service.

Between the wars the *Regia Aeronautica*'s self-image was of a highly-modern and well-developed force, with skilled pilots who had frequently shown their abilities both in combat and in aerobatic displays. At the beginning of the war these aircraft and their pilots, which the British had been so concerned about, performed poorly, not only the Cr42 biplanes, but also the new MC200 and G50 fighters. The reason for this was often claimed to be inferior engines, but this forgets that US fighters such as the Hellcat, Wildcat and Thunderbolt had engines of similar design. But the Wildcat developed 1200hp against barely 500hp of the Macchi Mc200 and this lack of satisfactory engines (and high octane fuel) meant that the armament of the planes had to be limited to only two machine-guns forward-firing in the fuselage. To mount weapons on the wings would have required them to be heavier, further slowing the plane, and the Italians suffered from faulty wing design, the result of the 'hero-designer' system which prevented them ever forming proper design teams.

It is true that General Valle acquired the DB 601 engine patent instead of leaving it to some important aircraft builder and it is possible that this was the reason why he was sacked soon after and then routinely blamed for every problem the *Regia Aeronautica* had. The first aircraft to be fitted with a German engine was the MC202, the first good fighter the Italians had, apart from the armament. Later, only on the eve of the Armistice, the DB605 engine was mounted in the Mc205 Veltro. It was too late, as it was to fit (receive-only) radios and sand filters in 1942. It is surprising to think that Italy had held Libya since the Italo-Turkish war of 1911, yet apparently did not think to fit sand filters to its aircrafts' engines until 31 years later.

The absence of radios, the general shortage of fuel, and the fact that training was geared more to individual flying ability than squadron combat, meant that there was little night or winter flying, and flying on instruments was likewise neglected, the principal reason for the failure of 48 per cent of the Italian aircraft sent to Belgium to participate in the Battle of Britain to return to base. The majority of the bombers sent there were the infamous BR20, which may also have contributed to the losses. This poorly-designed aircraft suffered frequent engine failures and such a high level of vibration that rivets were shaken out of the wings. The S.79 therefore had to be the workhorse of the *Regia Aeronautica*, and also take up the improvised role of torpedo-bomber, which grew increasingly difficult as the war progressed and more advanced enemy aircraft and heavier AA defences came into service.

The story of General Valle and the DB601 engine suggests that the air under-secretary was far too much in the pocket of the aircraft industry, which may partly explain why the Cr42 biplane continued in production until the Armistice and useless aircraft such as the Caproni Ca312 reconnaissance plane were ordered in large numbers. Old construction methods were still practised and therefore the MC202 required 4000 hours to produce while any German fighter could be completed in about 500.[32]

* * *

On 13 March 1943 the British submarine *Thunderbolt* was lost off Sicily while attacking a Tunisia-bound convoy escorted by the torpedo-boat *Libra*, and damaged a 3100-ton freighter badly enough that when Sicily was later evacuated it remained behind as a wreck. However, the *Libra* counterattacked for over 2 hours, keeping the submarine down and reporting her position, and then returned to the convoy. The corvette *Cicogna* then left Trapani to take over the pursuit. The *Thunderbolt*, thinking the coast was clear, had come up to periscope depth, but the *Cicogna* sighted the periscope and attacked her. She was lost with all hands, and her wreck has been recently located.[33]

The heavy cruiser *Trieste* was sunk by US bombers and capsized off La Maddalena on 10 April. She would later be salvaged by the Spanish after the war and towed to Ferrol. When she capsized, fuel had covered her engine parts and protected her from the seawater, so it was proposed to convert her to an aircraft carrier, but this was not done and the Spanish later took possession of a carrier lent by the Americans. The *Gorizia* was also damaged in the same attack.

Italy's merchant marine had suffered heavy losses during the war and new production had not nearly kept up with the rate of attrition. However, with the occupation of Vichy France, some new ships had been acquired and by 31 December 1942 Italy had 1,452,000 tons of shipping still available.[34] Many of the Axis troops transported to Africa in these final months would go by air, while their seaborne-equipment might arrive or might be sunk below them. The best remaining troops in Italy (such as those earmarked for the abortive Malta invasion) were hustled off to North Africa, to the ultimate mass surrender in May 1943, where more prisoners would be taken than at Stalingrad. Of 2.68 million tons of cargo shipped to North Africa during the war, 83 per cent arrived safely. The percentage had also increased as the war went on.[35] As a result, Italian units in Sicily were found to be equipped with old French tanks captured in 1940, or only small amounts of the best Italian equipment, such as the Semovente 90mm self-propelled gun. All the best troops and (mediocre) equipment had been shipped to North Africa and lost there. Germany and Italy would have been better served after winter set in in 1942-43 to have evacuated Tunisia and fought on in Sicily, but Hitler's decision to fight on, endorsed by Mussolini, had been taken.

With the fall of Tunisia only a matter of days away, Cunningham ordered the fleet to 'Sink, burn and destroy. Let nothing pass'. During May the patrolling MTBs captured sundry Axis soldiers trying to get to Sicily in all sorts of makeshift craft. On the evening of the 12th, three boats had picked up a total of 117 Axis prisoners including several German paratroopers armed with sub-machine-guns. It had been difficult finding weapons for all the sailors and some had been acquired from the prisoners. Suddenly one of the MTB captains heard the familiar burst of one of the German guns and whipped around to see what had happened. He was quickly assured by a stoker who said, 'It's all right, sir; he's only showing me how it works'![36]

On 13 May General Alexander could signal Churchill, 'Sir, it is my duty to report that the Tunisian campaign is over. All enemy resistance has ceased. We are masters of the North African shores.'

CHAPTER 22

The Invasion of Sicily, July 1943

Ain't that the goddamdest thing you ever saw?
The goddam navy. The good old navy.
Jesus, there ain't nothin' like navy guns.
Unknown G.I. as support ships opened up on attacking Germans during the
fighting on Sicily[1]

The surrender of the Axis troops at Tunis on 13 May 1943 marked an important turning-point in the war in the Mediterranean. If the Allies did invade Italy, which now seemed certain, German's ally would soon be out of the war. Therefore Hitler had ordered the formation of an Army Group command under Rommel before the fall of Tunis to formulate a response if the Italians surrendered. These measures were already in draft form by 21 May, planning for the German occupation of the Italian peninsula and Italian-occupied France under the codename 'Alarich'. The parallel takeover in the Balkans was codenamed 'Konstantin'.[2]

However, when the war in Africa came to an end, Mussolini still seemed to be trusted by the King. Dino Grandi, one of the leading men in Fascist Italy and former Ambassador to Britain in the early 1930s, received the impression from conversations with Victor Emmanuel III that the king assumed the Italian Army was much better than it was in reality, and did not really appreciate the size of the Allied war machine.[3] Grandi was well regarded by the British as a possible successor to Mussolini, while other people, both Fascists and anti-Fascists, were not. As the military situation worsened, several people attempted to extend peace feelers to the Allies, as had happened in 1940 following the defeats in Africa and Greece and Taranto Night. German intervention had kept Italy in the war then, but with the collapse of Axis fortunes in Africa in 1942, there now seemed little for the Italians to hope for.

These approaches came from both from Fascist and anti-Fascist individuals, an example of the latter being Emilio Lussu, who fought in the First World War in the famous Sardinian Brigade *Sassari* and wrote his memoirs, *Sardinian Brigade*, in exile. He proposed to organise guerrilla activity against the Fascist regime in Sardinia, asking only that Italy's territorial integrity be respected but the Allies did not support him. These feelers had little effect as Britain's attitude toward Italy was becoming increasingly rigid. From the outbreak of the war the main British intention was to put 'the weakest link' of the Axis out of the war either by military defeat or internal collapse. In almost all circumstances the Foreign Office replied to Italian approaches that only unconditional surrender would be accepted.[4]

At least from the beginning of 1942, well in advance of the Casablanca announcement of January 1943, this was the official British position, although Churchill himself was rather more flexible, considering the possibility of a separate peace with

Italy and saw the danger of a German takeover. A similar view had been held by the US State Department, but after the Axis military disasters in the autumn of 1942, the US switched to demanding unconditional surrender. At the Casablanca Conference in January 1943 it was decided to invade Sicily, giving priority to Mediterranean operations over the war with Japan. The attack on Sicily was an operation the British had planned already in 1941, codenamed 'Influx', and for them proceeding with it was the fulfillment of a previously-planned strategy, while for the Americans it was more of a compromise with British plans.

The British heavily influenced the Casablanca Conference, in large part because they were prepared at staff level to present papers and simply persuaded the Americans, who did not have a large staff with them and were less prepared to argue against the British proposals that this was the course to take. There were even some British 'dirty tricks' to the extent that that one of the chief advisors to the US Army Chief of Staff General Marshall, Brigadier-General Albert C Wedemeyer, had his office bugged so when British officers were present he could secretly record the conversation, so it could not be later misconstrued or misquoted![5]

Although the United States left Mediterranean affairs to the British, Eisenhower's HQ suggested to the Foreign Office, which had reserved to itself any contact with the Italians, Fascist and anti-Fascist, to modify their propaganda in a way favourable to the Italians. After some discussion this was done on the eve of the landing in Sicily, and leaflets dropped over the island stated that the war was against Mussolini and the Germans, not the Italian people. Intelligence received from the Balkans by both Britain and the United States confirmed that morale was very low in the Italian Army, following the defeat at Tunis and particularly among inactive units and those in touch with the civilian population who had really had enough of the war, and surrender was very likely, although some, including Montgomery, thought that they might fight harder for their own homeland. In the event the majority of the Italian army, wretchedly armed, would put up only limited resistance.

The plan for 'Husky', as the Sicilian invasion was called, foresaw the employment of a new Army Group, the 15th, formed from Montgomery's desert-hardened 8th Army and the US 1st Armoured Corps under Patton. Cunningham was in command of the combined naval forces, and the several Allied air commands were grouped under Headquarters Mediterranean Allied Air Forces under Air Chief Marshal Tedder, controlling 146 American and 121 British squadrons.

The naval operation was complex. Some of the forces had to come from England or even America and therefore had to run the gauntlet of the U-boats in the Atlantic. All the ports along the North African coast, from small fishing villages to the newly-cleared port of Bizerte, were crowded with shipping preparing for the invasion. Finally the Allies had to worry about enemy submarines, aircraft, and MTBs. Five 'Spitkit' convoys brought the vast majority of the landing-craft required for the invasion of Sicily, and other supplies which were 'distributed among various harbours, small and large, along the Barbary Coast'.[6]

The US warships furthest east were the PT boats which had quickly established a base at Bizerte by mid-May 1943, which would be the principal base for the 'Husky' landing-craft. The port had been badly damaged both by Allied bombing and then

Axis demolitions, and required extensive repairs and clearing before it could be fully used. The British were operating four squadrons of MTBs from Malta, one consisting of US lend-lease PT boats, and soon Allied coastal forces were operating in the Straits off Tunisia, landing OSS agents in Sardinia at the end of June, and even sneaking into Palermo harbour on the night of 9-10 June, but withdrawing safely when they found no suitable targets.[7]

Of course, the Italian fleet was one area of uncertainty and the fact that Allied intelligence was having difficulty reading the high-grade cipher in use at the time made discovering its intentions difficult. The six battleships, two heavy cruisers and nine light cruisers were distributed from Taranto to La Spezia and could intervene against the landing force, which therefore had to have a powerful naval escort. Cunningham was concerned about the Italian fleet and said 'If they should ever slip through the Allies' cordon and get mixed up in a convoy, they could be a jolly nuisance'. He still had considerable respect for the fast, modern ships of the Italian Navy, which was why the new battleships *Howe* and *King George V* were sent to the Mediterranean.[8] The Allies mustered six battleships, the carriers *Formidable* and *Indomitable*, two AA cruisers, and fifteen other cruisers. The United States cruisers were organised into Cruiser Division Eight under Rear-Admiral Lyal A Davidson, consisting of the *Philadelphia*, *Savannah*, and *Boise*, and Cruiser Division Thirteen under Rear-Admiral Laurence T DuBose with the *Birmingham* and *Brooklyn*. All five were large light cruisers armed either with fifteen or twelve of probably the fastest-firing 6in gun then in existance. There were also forty-eight American destroyers, more than Italy had operational at this stage of the war. Both admirals Hewitt and Hall were no longer on warships but had established themselves on attack transports which would keep their important communication functions safe from surface combat and were roomy enough to accommodate their large staff. However, these improvisations were still not true command ships, able to adequately house a full headquarters staff and all its functions, and also offer sufficient protection against enemy attack.

Supporting this force both during and after the landings was the British monitor *Abercrombie*, laid down in 1940 and armed with two 15in guns from the First World War. Built to modern design concepts (her armour protection was modelled on that of the *King George V* class and her deck was protected by 3in of armour), she would give valuable service here and later at Salerno as the flagship of Rear-Admiral Davidson. Vice-Admiral Hewitt would later write that Davidson became a leading expert in gunfire support operations and a 'tower of strength to his Fleet Commander'. The *Abercrombie* would carry into battle a team of American officers who would prove invaluable in the coming days as a 'US Shore Fire Control Party'. During the initial invasion she would be called upon to fire 30,000 yards inland, a range the American cruisers could not match.[9]

The first step for the invasion of Sicily, once the decision had been taken, was for extensive mapping of the island, carried out by air photo-reconnaissance units operating from Malta and Algiers. The legendary Adrian Warburton would be posted to the American group of Lightnings stationed at Malta as a liaison officer.[10] ULTRA was able to read the *Luftwaffe*'s codes, allowing close monitoring of

German air activity, although this was more difficult with the Italians. Finally, a well organised plan called Operation 'Mincemeat' succeeded in partially deceiving the Axis powers about the objective of the future Allied landings in Europe. In May the body of a British officer with documents giving his identity as 'Major Martin' was found washed up on the Spanish coast with a case of false documents giving the objective of the landings as Greece and Sardinia, which were passed to the Germans who considered them genuine. ULTRA reports revealed the success of this deception on 14 May, and the news was passed to Churchill who was attending the 'Trident' conference in Washington.[11] But it should be noted that the Axis command in Italy did not 'swallow' Mincemeat completely and also according to some witnesses Hitler was not as convinced by 'Major Martin' as Canaris was. Several other intelligence sources were favouring different targets. For example, on 19 May the Germans received information that preparations were in progress to attack Pantelleria, while another report of Italian provenance, classified and not totally reliable, predicted landings in Sardinia, Corsica and Southern France. Interestingly, most reports were dealing with Allied preparations in Libya and French North Africa rather than the Eastern Mediterranean.[12] Later, on 7 June, a commando unit of forty men aboard *MBT65*, *MBT268* and *MBT313* was sunk near Lampedusa, some being captured, while the following day leaflets were dropped on Pantelleria asking the garrison to surrender.

A German intelligence assessment of 19 May estimated that a major landing operation was possible in the eastern Mediterranean only after the transports in French North Africa became available.[13] In fact, the minutes of the meeting between the German and Italian senior officers show that Sicily, Sardinia and Corsica were all given reinforcements. The Italian Chief of the General Staff General Ambrosio, who had replaced Marshall Ugo Cavallero, was with Mussolini when the visiting Grand Admiral Doenitz said that Sicily and Sardinia needed to be reinforced at once, and on 2 July, a few days before the landing, there was this conversation:

> *General Ambrosio*: In any case the [enemy] deployment is mainly against Sicily.
> *Fieldmarshall Kesselring*: Something also against Sardinia.
> *Admiral Sansonetti*: Really from Bizerta it is possible to attack Sardinia.
> *General Ambrosio*: A point that gives more weight to the supposed attack against Sicily are the heavy bombardment operations against Sicily now in progress. Moreover we know that at Malta there are many forces.

Before the invasion of Sicily the Allies wanted to secure the island of Pantelleria and its smaller neighbours Lampedusa and Linosa to prevent them becoming a base for enemy aircraft, since they could operate about 100 planes, Eisenhower wanting the airfields for the Allies' own use as well as the port in the north-west corner of the island which could be used as a base. Tedder and Cunningham both supported this decision though General Alexander opposed it, fearing the attack would fail.[14]

The attack was preceded by massive air raids carried out by the US 9th Army Air Force and Northwest African RAF starting on 8 May as it appeared that the island could be neutralised from the air, followed up by bombardment raids by British cruisers.[15] On the night of 5 June, the US 15th PT Boat Squadron circled the island to assess the state of the defences, and witnessed the air attacks in progress. On only a single day, the anniversary of Italy's entry into the war on 10 June, some 1400 tons of bombs were dropped on this one small island.

On the day of the landings, 11 June, five British cruisers, eight destroyers and the little gunboat *Aphis* took care of the surviving coastal batteries. Eisenhower and Cunningham were aboard the *Aurora* observing the operation. Finally, while US and British MTBs screened towards the north (some PT-boats coming under Axis air attack), a brigade element of the 1st British Infantry Division landed unopposed. The first white flag had appeared at 11.25am before the troops were ashore but the bombardment of the batteries continued until 11.45am. Then Rear-Admiral Gino Pavesi, having lost only 139 men out of the garrison of 11,657, surrendered the island. The tiny harbour had been devastated by the bombing. Lampedusa and Linosa fell shortly afterwards.

However, the surrender of Pantelleria cannot be put down solely to the effects of bombing reducing a strong position; the messages exchanged between Pavesi and senior officers in Rome still leaves something to explain. Pavesi surrendered before receiving permission and prevented well-prepared demolitions from taking place. According to De Felice, Mussolini was influenced by Pavesi's reports of casualties among the civilian population and authorised the surrender, but later Mussolini called Pavesi 'the first in chronological order of the traitor Admirals'. It is interesting that General Ambrosio waited until *after* the surrender before submitting a memo to Mussolini stating that Pavesi was underestimating the defensive capability of the island, that there was no shortage of water and casualties were quite low.[16] Although the Allied ships had been discovered by German reconnaissance which alerted *Comando Supremo* which passed the information on to *Supermarina*, they in turn did not communicate this important news to Admiral Pavesi! Moreover, Pavesi began to consider surrendering because he said he could not supply water to both the defenders and the civilian population, but the Germans at the signal station reported that this was rather surprising. *Comando Supremo* was informed of this and ordered some torpedo-boats to bring water to the island.[17]

From the quite detailed reconstruction of events made by Santoni, Mussolini's message ordering surrender at 12.00am and suggesting also to declare it was due the water supply problem passed through *Comando Supremo* and *Supermarina* who changed their tone after Pavesi had surrendered. Moreover, a telephone conversation between Air Force General Santoro, deputy Chief of Staff and General Monti of the Air Force Command in Sicily concerning the order not the destroy the hangar seems to be a bit unusual:

> *Santoro*: I do not understand why they don't want to destroy the hangar.
> *Monti*: Oh! Excellency . . . to let it remain . . . There is no other explanation.

When Monti learned of Pavesi's order not to destroy the hangar, he ordered his men at Pantelleria to destroy it, but when he asked confirmation of this order from Santoro and *Comando Supremo* he never received a reply.

The fall of Lampedusa proceeded similarly, the capitulation coming at 4.00pm on the 12th after heavy air and naval bombardment, despite the island's successful repulse of the commando landings on the 6th. But the commander there, Captain Bernardini, decided to surrender after picking-up *Supermarina*'s signal authorising the surrender of Pantellaria.

* * *

On the night of 10 July an Allied force totalling 2590 ships and 180,000 men began to land along the coasts of Sicily. Having earlier passed through heavy seas, many of the men aboard were seasick. The first landings were made in the dark and as they approached, Italian searchlights knifed out of the darkness. 'Going from one ship to another, the light paused at each one'.[18]

Vice-Admiral Bertram H Ramsay commanded the ships transporting the British force making a landing on the eastern coast, while the force landing near Gela in the west was under Vice-Admiral Hewitt with Rear-Admiral Hall in charge of the landings themselves, assisted by two battalions of Seabees (US Navy construction units).

The main resistance came from General Hans Hube's 14th Armoured Corps and some Italian units which retreated on three lines of resistance to the north-eastern corner of the island. The Axis air and naval response to the invasion was only on a small scale. The Allies had launched a 6-week bombing campaign against enemy air bases, beginning before the fall of Tunis, to achieve air superiority for the invasion. Air and naval targets in Sardinia, southern Italy and Sicily were attacked, as well as communications infrastructure to hinder the flow of supplies to Sicily. Strategic bombing raids on the industrial centres of northern Italy also further lowered civilian morale.[19] Furthermore, the aircraft which remained not only had to provide support for the fleet, but also for the ground forces fighting in Sicily. Attrition was heavy for both the *Luftwaffe* and the *Regia Aeronautica*. According to Allied figures, their air forces carried out 42,227 missions, losing 250 planes, while the Germans lost 323. The *II Luftflotte* had 578 serviceable aircraft on 11 May and 593 on 10 July, but only after reinforcements had been sent from Germany.[20] According to official data the Italians had 620 planes in Central and Southern Italy, but ony 40-60 per cent of these were operational, including a squadron equipped with eight Piaggio P108 four-engined bombers. The Germans had partially accepted Italian requests for new aircraft for the *Regia Aeronautica* since Italian industry was unable to replace glorious but now obsolete planes like the S.79 torpedo-bomber, and therefore Kesselring transferred twelve Ju87s and some thirty Me109s. Meanwhile fifty-two bomber crews were sent to Germany to be trained on the Ju88. Recent research has revealed that the *Regia Aeronautica* had a total of 930 combat aircraft in Italy on 9 July 1943, of which 449 were serviceable.[21] Further problems stemmed from the Axis powers' failure to establish any kind of co-operation between the two air forces, at both tactical and command level, problems exacerbated by language difficulties which hindered the development of common procedures and tactics. Italian aircraft were still short of radios, and jealousy between the two sides also contributed. On the eve on the invasion of Sicily, the Germans made a concerted attempt to take control of the *Regia Aeronautica*, with the formation of a separate command for the *II Luftflotte* under *Generalfeldmarschall* Wolfgang von Richtofen, which Goering had done also because he thought Kesselring was overworked as both overall commander of German forces and air force commander.

The Axis air forces put up the most resistance to the invasion and some Allied ships were lost, including the US destroyer *Maddox* sunk by dive-bombers while on anti-submarine partol on 10 July, and the destruction of the ammunition ship *Robert Rowan* the next day in a spectacular explosion. In all, the Americans had three ships sunk and five damaged.[22]

The Allied air forces were rather ineffective at this stage of the operation, largely because of the absence of the escort carriers used in Operation 'Torch' and later at Salerno. Land-based fighters were within range of the landings, but because of the flight time required, they could not operate over the fleet for large parts of the day. Furthermore, many of the available aircraft were tied up attacking roads and bridges inland to prevent Axis counterattacks. While losses were not crippling, only a few landing ships and freighters being lost or damaged, the troops on the beachhead did suffer from air attacks. The greatest problem in this invasion would be co-ordinating air support, particularly that provided by the Americans, which would lead to unnecessary losses and much recrimination after the battle.[23]

The American beachhead near Gela was counter-attacked by the *Hermann-Goering* and the Italian *Livorno* divisions. There were several tense moments, but it was largely naval gunfire from the light cruisers that ultimately helped to throw back the enemy attacks. In the course of supporting the ground troops the *Savannah* had three of her four spotter floatplanes shot down.[24] The effectiveness of the naval gunfire here was a factor of range. During the Moroccan landings fire support had been conducted at long range and from fast-moving ships, while on the first two days at Gela Rear-Admiral Hall specifically ordered the ships to close in. The cruisers were firing at ranges as short as 3100 yards, while the destroyers came as close as 1200 yards.[25]

As the advancing land forces overran Axis airfields, they were taken over for Allied use and within 2 weeks of the landings there were thirty-seven fighter and fighter-bomber squadrons based on Sicily. Together with aircraft from Tunisia and Malta, these launched a round-the-clock assault against ports and airfields in south-ern Italy. The Sicilian Straits between Messina and Reggio were heavily bombed, both cities being largely reduced to rubble, but this was not able to prevent the successful evacuation of Axis forces from Sicily in August.

*   *   *

In this final stage of the war, it was more difficult than ever to explain the cautious attitude of the Italian Navy to the Germans. But both the naval commanders and the Italian politicians were aware that the fleet would be an important bargaining chip in any armistice negotiations. In fact, the OSS had prepared a secret plan called the 'McGregor Project' to transfer the Italian Navy to the Allies with the help of Italian naval officers, which Vice-Admiral Raffaele De Courten, Deputy Chief of Staff of the Navy, was aware of. The Italians deployed only light forces and submarines against the invasion, fearing that the use of the capital ships without sufficient air cover would be disasterous in the face of Allied air superiority.

On 12 July Doenitz, who had a poor opinion of the Italian Navy, asked Riccardi to move the battleships south to be ready to intervene against the Allied fleet anchored off the south coast of Sicily, but he replied that in view of the air and naval superiority of the Allies such an operation would be impossible. Riccardi was particularly hurt by Doenitz's reported comment to Hitler that if they were rid of *Supermarina* the situation would improve. There were 'fighting Admirals' among the high command, like Manfredi and Legnani, but Riccardi also refused to deploy lighter vessels because he wanted to reserve them for escorting the capital ships when they did sail, which Doenitz said would never happen. He could do little other than send signals to Riccardi urging him to go to sea with his ships and fight, to which Riccardi replied that he would submit the issue to the *Duce*. Hitler was sure that these requests never reached Mussolini.[26] Doenitz wrote again arguing that it would be better to send the capital ships against the Allied invasion fleet than to leave them in port to be destroyed by air attack, and that light forces and submarines should be used to attack the Allied supply lines by night. Richthofen would say that the Italian fleet would not seek battle 'to save its honour'.[27] It is interesting to note that in the minutes of the meetings Riccardi attended at *Comando Supremo* there are frequently no records of his having said anything. On 2 August, Riccardi explained in a memo to *Comando Supremo* and the Germans the reasons why the fleet could not intervene and concluded that only fast cruisers could act, besides of course MTBs and submarines, although *Supermarina* said these would have little success. In any case Sicily was now under Allied control.[28]

*   *   *

As a diversion to the main landings, the new British battleships *King George V* and *Howe* steamed up the west coast of Sicily on the night of 11-12 July and bombarded Favignana in the Trapani islands, while the cruisers *Dido* and *Sirius* bombarded the nearby port of Marsala.

Early on 17 July the *Warspite* and *Valiant* were in Marsa Scirocco Harbour at Malta when they were both ordered, with their escorts, to head for Sicily. The *Valiant* had become entangled in the anti-submarine netting and was forced to remain behind while the *Warspite* raced off and fired fifty-seven rounds against Axis artillery near Catania.[29]

On 17 July the Allies were advancing toward the straits of Messina facing increasing resistance mostly from the Germans. That day there was also a minor encounter between the brand new light cruiser *Scipione Africano* and four British MTBs (*260*, *313*, *315* and *316*). The cruiser was ordered to Taranto where there were no fast cruisers, starting from La Spezia on the 15th and reaching Naples in the evening, shadowed by a British seaplane, and there embarked an air liaison team and Metox equipment. She sailed again at 6.15pm on 16 July and reached the Messina Straits just after 2.00am on the 17th the where she sighted four British MTBs apparently stationary (waiting in silence for E-boats to attack), increased speed to 30 knots and opened fire. The MTBs attacked from two directions, the *260* and *313* from astern and *315* and *316* to starboard, in a set attack formation against warships. The first two launched their torpedoes which missed, while *MTB 316* was hit and blew up with all hands.[30] The *Scipione* then came under fire from German and Italian coastal batteries on both sides of the Straits, and despite making recognition signals she suffered light damage, two men being wounded. At 9.46am she reached Taranto, saved by her high speed and powerful armament.

We have already commented on the tendency of Italian naval guns to have too wide a salvo-spread, but this does not apply to all ships, particularly the cruisers and destroyers. The separate propellant charges for the heavy-calibre battleship guns often varied in weight, preventing consistent performance of the guns, whereas the fixed ammunition of guns of less than 8in calibre did not suffer from this problem.

The human factor must also be kept in mind when considering this problem, which was added to by the fact that the Italians wanted to exploit the superior range of their guns over the British, and therefore Italian cruisers opened fire at ranges between 18,000 and 20,000 metres, at a high rate of fire, making the gunnery officer's task even more difficult. First, he had the difficult job of evaluating the target's course and speed from its silhouette and bow wave. Then, as a former fire control officer, Commander Nesi, wrote:

> Here the training which could give different results from marksman to marksman, because no man is the same of another man, but the results could be appreciated if the training is constant and the marksman maintained the control of his nerves, concentrating at the utmost on those little triangles which try to evade the contact with the other little triangle while he is performing the procedure called 'coincidence'.[31]

He is referring to the fire control system used by the Italian Navy where the gunnery officer had to line up two triangles in the field of view of his rangefinder. There was also the problem of difference in the training of the rangefinder and the larger, more sluggish turrets themselves, which also contibuted to salvo spread. Cruisers fired in the following sequence: the forward guns would fire first, then the stern guns after correction, and then the forward guns again followed by further correction, and then either the stern guns again or the full broadside, this third salvo being generally on target. The procedure was different on the battleships, where all the main turrets fired full salvos.

* * *

Palermo fell to the Allies on 23 July and PT boats quickly established a base there. They captured the staff of the Italian admiral commanding the harbour making off in a small boat, along with some isolated Germans, and sank two escaping ships. Overloaded as they were, these PT boats could only make 27-28 knots at this time.

The British MTBs had developed a new tactic which benefited them now. They had realised that for a half an hour after sunset they could see fairly well from their low lying craft, while they themselves were hard to spot, starshell being useless against them in these conditions. Therefore on the night of 12 July a patrol from the 24th Flotilla crept into the Straits of Messina. The *U-561* surfaced in what she thought were safe waters, only to be torpedoed and sunk by *MTB81* at a range of only 80-100 yards. Another U-boat managed to crash-dive and escape, after another attacking MTB had two misfires.[32] Just as the Americans moved their PT-boats forward to Palermo, the British were also on the move, first operating from a mobile support base at Syracuse, but moving rapidly on when Augusta fell, and were soon engaged in aggressive patrols against enemy shipping and shore batteries.

At the end of July the Italian fleet was ordered into action against the Allies, to at least give the impression to the Germans that 'something' was being done. But this never happened and on 25 July Mussolini was deposed by the Grand Council of Fascism and then arrested on the orders of the King. The new Prime Minister, Marshall Badoglio, wanted to end the war, but also wanted to avoid confirming German suspicions about his intentions. Therefore two bombardment missions against Palermo were planned.[33] For security reasons the orders were transmitted to the 7th Crusier Division at La Spezia from *Supermarina*. The light cruisers *Montecuccoli* and *Eugenio di Savoia* were first to steam to La Maddalena at 25 knots, and then to Palermo to attack the transports there. The *Luftwaffe* was also asked to carry out an air raid at the same time. It was a moonless night.

The 7th Division left La Spezia under the command of Rear-Admiral Romeo Oliva at 7.55pm on 4 August and reached La Maddalena at 10.00am on the 5th, after having detected an Allied seaplane and a submarine with the Metox equipment supplied by the Germans. That same evening the two cruisers sailed separately (at 5.43pm and 7.18pm), zig-zagging at 26 knots towards Ustica island, with two fighters providing air cover until 8.30pm, and a corvette for ASW escort. During the night two torpedo tracks were sighted and evasive manoeuvres taken. Ustica was sighted at 4.00am on the 6th, and 20 minutes later small craft were spotted to starboard, while the Metox gear warned that a land-based radar had picked up the two ships. The *Montecuccoli* opened fire and turned away to the port, followed at 4.31am by the *Eugenio di Savoia* while *Supermarina* was informed of the situation. The cruisers had been discovered 34 miles from their objective, about an hour's sailing, and with the element of surprise lost, they returned to Naples and then to La Spezia.

Supermarina had already prepared plans for another raid against the same target. In fact, while the 7th Division was still at sea, the cruisers of the 8th Division under Rear-Admiral Giuseppe Fioravanzo, based at Genoa, were likewise ordered to bombard Palermo. The two light cruisers were the *Garibaldi* (which had some mechanical problems) and the *Duca d'Aosta*, which sailed at 8.10pm on 6 August, the operational orders being read at sea. They reached La Maddalena as planned on the morning of the 7th, and after an exchange of signals with *Supermarina* and the *Garibaldi* had taken on supplies, sailed at 6.35pm. They then had to wait at sea for a boat bringing a top-secret message, but it failed to arrive.

After they had resumed their course, the German wireless interception team aboard received a message from a German reconnaissance aircraft at 2.30am on the 8th, reporting a sighting of three large Allied ships at 1.45am, half-way between Palermo and Ustica. The division kept going, but visibility worsened and as neither of his ships had radar, Fioravanzo feared he might be ambushed. Therefore at 3.07am he radioed that he would turn for home unless ordered otherwise. For the moment, however, he continued south and received a report that four slow ships, possibly a convoy, had been spotted near Cape San Vito between Trapani and

Palermo. At 4.00pm the cruisers turned back, and *Supermarina* was informed of this 21 minutes later, replying that the mission should continue if they had not already changed course, but it was too late. Fioravanzo was already on his way home, receiving a continuous fighter escort from 8.23am, while the destroyers *Legionario* and *Carabiniere* accompanied them from Sardinia to La Spezia. The following day the squadron sailed to Genoa escorted by the destroyers *Mitragliere*, *Gioberti* and *Carabiniere*, with fighter cover and a Cant Z506 for anti-submarine patrol but at 6.24pm four torpedoes fired at the *Garibaldi* were sighted. The cruiser managed to avoid them but two hit the *Gioberti* which sank shortly afterwards. This successful attack had been carried out by the British submarine *Simoom*.

Despite their lack of success, these two operations nonetheless showed that *Supermarina* was still capable of mounting offensive actions even at the end of the war and also now had the means and necessary experience to organise and co-ordinate air cover (including German aircraft), and the naval high command seems to have shown some determination. But it was too late. The *Garibaldi* had problems with her main fuel pumps and had to use the reserve ones, but this produced an enormous amount of smoke at her best speed of 29½ knots (really 28 knots because of fouling, for a ship that had been designed for 35 knots and could normally make 32 knots).

Both admirals' decisions to turn back were justified because ULTRA had followed the transfer of the cruisers and was aware of their objective, denying them the vital advantage of surprise. The 'three large Allied ships' reported to Fioravanzo were the American cruisers *Philadelphia* and *Savannah* escorted by the destroyers *Rowan* and *Rhind* which were with the four merchant ships. After the war these two failed operations were violently criticised, but in view of the situation the decisions of the commanders were justified, since they would probably have had to face superior forces and be caught by surprise.[34]

* * *

Several minor actions took place during the Sicilian campaign, mostly involving E-boats and *MAS*, sometimes transporting *X MAS* frogmen or landing commandoes behind the Allied lines. Two *MAS* were sunk by air attack in harbour at Termini Imerese in the afternoon of 15 July and on the evening of 3 August *MS 66* was sunk by escorting American destroyers while attacking a convoy near Cape Orlando. In the same action *MS 63* had her bows shot away but was able to reach Messina with the assistance of *MS 21*.

While numerous Axis submarines were deployed against the invasion, they had only minor effects. The Italians had over a dozen submarines off Sicily, and six of them were lost in the first 8 days of the campaign, the first being the *Flutto* which was sunk by British MTBs on 11 July, north-east of Catania. The following day the *Bronzo* was captured when she surfaced among Allied ships off Augusta, her commander mistakenly thinking the fortress was still in Italian hands and the ships were friendly. On the 13th two submarines were sunk, the *Nereide* off Augusta by the British destroyers *Echo* and *Ilex*, while the *Acciaio* was torpedoed by the submarine *Unruly* north of the Straits of Messina. The same happened 2 days later to the *Remo*, torpedoed by the *United* while en route from Taranto to Naples, and the *Micca* was sunk by the submarine *Trooper* on 29 July. However, on 16 July the *Dandolo* had been able to torpedo the light cruiser *Cleopatra* off Augusta and escape the anti-submarine hunt that followed. Other boats made several attacks against Allied shipping, but without success. The German submarines likewise had little effect as they had already been on patrol off the North African ports since 22 June. They sunk eight merchant ships (and four small sailing vessels), for the loss of three boats, and on 23 June the *U-407* torpedoed and damaged the new light cruiser HMS *Newfoundland.*

Throughout this period the *X MAS* was active, and trying out refined tactics. Operating from the interned tanker *Olterra* in Algeciras, they had sunk three freighters at Gibraltar on the night of 7-8 May, and in a series of attacks between 30 June and 1 August against Alessandretta, three merchant ships were sunk and one damaged. From 30 June to 1 August there were three individual successes at Gibraltar against merchant ships that were sunk, and a fourth that was damaged.

*   *   *

There has been much controversy over the fall of Augusta and Syracuse in the south-east corner of Sicily on 12 July. In their advance on Messina the 8th Army met increasing resistance after having taken the Catania plain, where there were a large number of airfields and a major naval fortress, Augusta-Syracuse. This fortress was well garrisoned with a battalion of sailors, an air force battalion and a coastal regiment. The six main batteries (two 15in, two 8in, two 190mm/45, and fourteen 6in guns) were manned by units of the 7th Milmart Legion, the coastal defence organisation of the MVSN (Blackshirts). There were a further eleven 4in and thirty 3in DP guns and thirty-six dedicated 3in AA guns. There was also an armoured train and two armed pontoons.

Two and a half hours before the Allied landing, the commander of the fortress, Rear-Admiral Priamo Leonardi, issued orders through his Chief of Staff to the deputy commander of the 7th Milmart Legion to prepare to destroy the guns, but he did not carry out this order, believing it would be bad for his men's morale. However, 2 hours later the order came again, this time in writing and 30 minutes afetr that the first indications oi Allied airborne landings came, with the capture of some paratroops, including a chaplain. The fortress also began to come under air attack.[35]

The paratroops seized the Ponte Grande bridge on the Anapo river, holding it until the afternoon when the British 17th Infantry Brigade arrived. Meanwhile, early in the morning oi the 10th, the Milmart Legion commander finally issued the order to prepare demolitions to all his batteries. During the night two SAS groups and the 3rd Commando had occupied four batteries in the Maddalena peninsula, while a little later units of the 5th Infantry Division began to land. Later that morning orders arrived for the destruction of the batteries, as did reports of large-scale amphibious and airborne landings. The German 3rd S-Boat Flotilla evacuated the port, after destroying their shore installations, reinforcing the notion that the entire fortress should be abandoned. Many of the garrison were native to the area and were beginning to think that 'the game was lost and that no resistance could change the

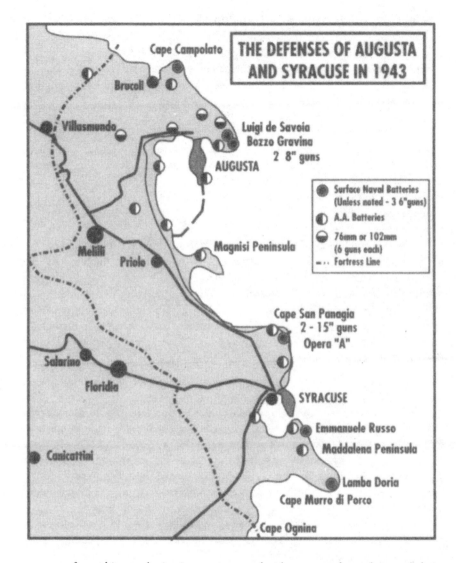

THE DEFENSES OF AUGUSTA AND SYRACUSE IN 1943

Cape Campolato

Brucoli

Villasmundo

Luigi de Savoia
Bozzo Gravina
2 8" guns

AUGUSTA

Surface Naval Batteries
(Unless noted - 3 6"guns)

A.A. Batteries

76mm or 102mm
(6 guns each)

Fortress Line

Melilli

Priolo

Magnisi Peninsula

Cape San Panagia
2 - 15" guns
Opera "A"

Salarino

Floridia

SYRACUSE

Emmanuele Russo

Maddalena Peninsula

Canicattini

Lamba Doria

Cape Murro di Porco

Cape Ognina

outcome; from this standpoint it was easy to decide to save themselves and their families (often nearby) who were under the same threat', since everything pointed to the end.[36] Therefore by nightfall most of the batteries and other installations, such as the pontoons and the radio station, had been blown up, without the defenders having seen a single Allied soldier. At 9.00pm the British entered Syracuse and attempts by four *ad hoc* combat groups from the Napoli Division and the German *Kampfgruppe Schmalz* to drive them out failed.[37]

In any case the overland advance toward Augusta was stopped and the fortress was seized 2 days later from the sea when British ships tried three times to enter the port but were faced by some German guns. The remainder of the fortress was destroyed and the fourth attempt made by three destroyers, three gunboats and the merchant ship *Ulster Monarch* succeeded in landing three companies of the 1st Special Raiding Squadron, at the cost of only two killed and eight wounded. No attempt had been made to demolish the port installations and these were captured intact. The Allies were stopped on the Catania plain by stubborn German resistance, to which the remnants of the Napoli Division contributed. But decisive political events would bring the Sicilian campaign to a quick end.

In attempts to turn the Germans' right flank on the north coast of Sicily as they steadily fell back towards Messina, the Allies used amphibious landings. Palermo was to be the base of operations, but it had to be cleared first as there were about fifty vessels sunk in the harbour and Allied bombing and Axis demolitions had done serious damage to the shore installations.[38] Using LSTs based at Palermo, the army landed a reinforced battalion on the sea flank of the 29th Panzergrenadier Division, which succeeded in holding its position despite a strong counterattack on 8 August that cost the Germans dearly.

The second amphibious landing on 10 August by 650 men at Brolo would carry a higher price tag due to heavy counterattacks (and accidental bombing by the USAAF which knocked out four artillery pieces). The US Navy supplied critical gunfire support, aided by the presence of a navy spotter with the landing force. While unable to stop the 29th's retreat, the force held its position and inflicted about as many casualties as it took – about 200 men. If these landings had been carried out on a larger scale, they might have resulted in the 29th being cut off, bringing about a decisive Axis defeat in Sicily.[39]

*   *   *

The Axis evacuation of Sicily was truly a remarkable feat. On 16 March 1943 Doenitz had appointed Rear-Admiral Friedrich Ruge to oversee German convoys to Tunisia, and on 18 May he was made commander of the German Navy in Italy. Although he had only a small number of ships under his control, this appointment was the means by which Captain Gustav von Liebenstein was sent to Sicily as the Sea Transport Leader for the Straits of Messina, thus ensuring that the evacuation of German troops from Sicily would be a German-controlled operation.[40]

When von Liebenstein took command on May 28 he discovered that the situation was not good. The ports had been repeatedly attacked from the beginning of the war and the ferry between Messina and Reggio had suffered severe damage. In 1943 Messina alone had had over 2000 tons of bombs dropped on it, although as these had mostly been aimed at the port facilities and only eleven ships had been sunk in the harbour. He also found that all three German armed services were operating their own sea-transport system, largely without reference to each other. By bringing all the available craft, approximately sixty vessels, under a unified command von Liebenstein rapidly increased the volume of men and material that could be shipped each day. He increased the number of routes and landing places in order both to increase the volume of traffic and confuse Allied air attacks, and instituted the first 'roll-on/roll-off' ferry system for vehicles, doing away with the laborious and time-consuming loading and unloading that had hitherto been necessary. The German Army had re-organised and strengthened the AA defences, and the coastal batteries had likewise been reinforced against any naval attack. The Italians of course had their own ferry system, which also improved as the end in Sicily drew near. Rear-Admiral Pietro Barone would command the Italian ships employed, which also operated from the ancient port of Taormina, south of Messina. The Italians would lose seventeen small ships during the evacuation. All of these factors would combine to bring about the successful evacuation of Sicily.

It was codenamed Operation 'Lehrgang' (a course of instruction) and planned well in advance to avoid a repeat of the terrible losses suffered in Tunisia. Between 1 and 17 August, in spite of Allied air raids, the Germans were able to evacuate 54,723 troops (some wounded), 9789 vehicles, and many tons of supplies, while the Italian Navy got off approximately 62,000 men and 227 vehicles. Ironically, the last unit to be evacuated was an eight-man Italian patrol in a German assault boat.

The Royal Navy threw in its MTBs against the evacuation ships and all the serviceable boats at Malta, thirty-two out of a total of forty-seven, were in action. On the night of 15-16 August, *MTB 665* was sunk by shore batteries, and in all four boats would be lost during the Sicilian campaign.[41] By the 17th Allied guns were trading fire across the Straits of Messina with Axis guns on the far side.

* * *

The successful Allied invasion of Sicily was the final event that brought about the fall of Mussolini on 25 July, when the Grand Council of Fascism voted the 'Order of the Day Grandi' against the *Duce* who resigned and was then arrested on the orders of the King, Marshal Pietro Badoglio replacing him as Prime Minister. But this was only the last act in an ongoing crisis within the Italian political and military establishment, which began with the sacking of Cavallero as Chief of the General Staff, probably because of his behind-the-scenes plotting against Mussolini. Both the House of Savoy and the military were contemplating deposing *Il Duce*, but had delayed acting because the King had hoped that Mussolini might be able to influence Hitler to make peace with Russia, and also prevent German reprisals when Italy left the war.[42]

The Germans responded to the change of leadership by accelerating their plans for a takeover. In Operation 'Schwarz', 20,000 paratroops concentrated around Rome under General Student would have staged a coup, but opposition from within the German high command lead to its cancellation. On 28 July, the planned takeovers of Italy, the Balkans and Italian-occupied France were unified into one operation codenamed 'Achse', and at the end of August the German ambassador von Mackensen was replaced by Rudolf Rahn, and General Rudolph Toussaint replaced Enno von Rintelen as liaision officer at *Comando Supremo*. The Germans intended to hold the Italian peninsula if the government surrendered, not only in order to keep the war away from Germany's borders for as long as possible, but also because it would finally allow them to exploit the agricultural and industrial wealth of northern Italy without hinderance, the loss of their eastern territories to the advancing Russians making Italian resources all the more necessary for the German war machine. The importance of northern Italy is shown by the fact that the *Waffenamt* (the German army weapons office) calculated that of the 1 billion lire-worth of orders had been placed in Italy, only 70 million-worth had been placed south of the Appenines. They began to evacuate plants and material north, 'saving' for example the 88mm AA guns at Naples.[43]

The Germans sent ten divisions to Italy as a reaction to the coup, without asking permission from the Badoglio government. This was a show of force. Although the Germans claimed these units were to help their ally, they stayed in the north of Italy and did not move south to where any future fighting would be. The Italians, unable to do much about this even if they had wanted to, did nothing in response. The Italian Government tried to deal with the Allies without previous agreement with the Germans, which they could obviously never have obtained, for the reasons given above. The Germans were preparing for Italy's defection, redeploying and re-organising units to increase their presence in the peninsula and also remove German units from Italian control. These redeployments confirmed their interest in the Po Valley, where a power-ful group of divisions under Army Group B was based, far from the front line in Sicily and Calabria, commanded by Rommel who seems to have been appointed largely for his hostility towards the Italians. Reflecting on this move by Germany, *Comando Supremo* at one point thought that the large number of German troops in the north meant that they would not fight for southern or central Italy in case of an armistice and Allied landings, hoping that only the Po valley would suffer German occupation. But the Army Chief of Staff, General Roatta, made a more accurate assessment of German intentions and expected them to seize as much territory as they could.[44]

Although there had been those in Italy who had wanted peace since the disasters of 1940, the first real moves towards an Italian surrender came on 31 July 1943, at a meeting between the King, Badoglio, the Foreign Minister Guariglia, the House of Savoy Minister Acquarone, and the Chief of the General Staff Ambrosio. The rump of the Fascist Party that had deposed Mussolini was brushed aside, and it was decided to send several secret missions to open contacts with the Allies, and General Giuseppe Castellano left on 12 August to negotiate an armistice. The final decision was taken on the evening of 1 September, which was followed by the signing of the so-called 'short military armistice' at Cassibile by General Castellano on behalf of Badoglio 2 days later.[45] On the same day Allied troops landed in Calabria which the 7th Italian Army and the German 10th Army were defending. Under continuous air attacks and naval bombardment the defenders did not deploy on the beaches which meant that the landings were unopposed. On the evening of the 3rd the Chief of Staff of the 7th Italian Army tried to get German support for a counterattack, but the Germans replied that forces could not be shifted to Calabria, while a decisive attack was expected 'in more dangerous places like Apulia and Naples'.[46]

On 5 September a Major Marchesi, who had accompanied Castellano, returned to Rome bearing some important documents, including the text of the so-called 'long armistice' and a memo with the instructions for the fleet. The Italians supposed the armistice would be announced on the 12th but they were not sure of this. Although the Allies knew the Italians would not actually join with them, they hoped they would at least take some action against the Germans that would make the proposed landings in the Naples/Salerno area easier, while it was also planned to land an airborne divison at Rome. But Badoglio and the military soon realised they could not make preparations for this without alerting the Germans, who also controlled the AA batteries at the airfields near Rome. The Allies realised this only on 7 September, when General Maxwell Taylor and Colonel William T Gardiner left Palermo at 2.00am aboard a British PT boat and met an Italian corvette near Ustica, and arrived in Rome that evening. They found only General Carboni and Major Marchesi to deal with, as Ambrosio, the Chief of the General Staff, was inexplicably at Turin. As at Caporetto, Badoglio was sleeping and General Taylor insisted in seeing him, requiring that the old Marshal send a message to the Allies cancelling the airborne landings as he could not guarantee contol of the airfields.

As has been said, the Italian fleet was the 'trump card' in any armistice. During his negotiations with the Allies in Lisbon, Castellano had tried to avoid the humiliation of the fleet having to surrender in Allied ports, hoping that it could be concentrated instead at La Maddalena in Sardinia. But the Allies rejected this, as the fleet was too important, and the instructions Marchesi had brought for the fleet were for the ships at La Spezia to proceed to Bone, while those at Taranto and the Adriatic ports were to surrender at Malta.[47]

But these instructions were passed to Admiral De Courten only on 6 September with the so-called 'Dick memorandum', named for the Chief of Staff of the Mediterranean Fleet, and he protested against this measure. Ambrosio, trying to calm him, said that there was no problem about the fleet going to La Maddalena with the Navy and the King. Incredibly enough, Ambrosio hoped to obtain this from the Allies and sent instructions to this end to Castellano on the same day. At the same time De Courten was asked to send two torpedo-boats to Ustica to pick up two 'British officers' and bring them to Rome.[48]

De Courten had been informed of the peace manoeuvres on the 3rd at the latest, and may indeed have known of them since the end of August, which should have warned him about the stage the talks had reached. On the same day he received 'Promemoria No.1' from *Comando Supremo* stating what the fleet had to do in case of a German occupation of Italy. He was to leave port in case of alarm and if necessary scuttle his ships, but he was also authorised to pursue offensive action against German naval units. Up until the last moment De Courten continued to act as if he was preparing for a last heroic battle with the Allies, no mention being made of the armistice negotiations to his subordinates, or at the meeting with his admirals the following day when they were verbally briefed on 'Promemoria No.1', which nonetheless clearly envisaged action against the Germans.[49]

On the morning of the 8th, De Courten ordered Admiral Bergamini to be ready to sail with the fleet and engage the enemy in the Tyrrhenian Sea; Bergamini replied that the fleet was ready for the last sacrifice. The senior sea-going officer of the Navy was therefore unaware that the armistice had already been signed, but as Aga Rossi has written, the Navy was ready to fight or to scuttle in port. That the fleet could have scuttled is confirmed by a note made by General Rossi of *Comando Supremo* in documents he was bringing to the Allies on September 8. In order to delay the armistice announcement, and to wait for the German reaction, without taking the initiative against the former ally. In Rossi's words 'It's in our interest that the fleet co-operate. Do not force her into the mainland ports. She'll be scuttled. It's better to steam for Sardinia'.[50]

CHAPTER 23

Operations 'Avalanche' and 'Achse', September 1943

Be pleased to inform Their Lordships that the
Italian battle fleet now
lies at anchor under the guns of the fortress at Malta.

Admiral Cunningham 11 September 1943[1]

U p until the actual announcement of the armistice, events are relatively easy to follow, but after that the situation becomes less clear, as all three Italian armed services produced their own accounts of the events of 8 September 1943.[2]

The date of the announcement was decided by the Allies and General Taylor had warned the Italians the night before. Furthermore, Kesselring's HQ at Frascati was bombed on the morning of the 8th and the Italians knew that this was a sign the armistice was imminent. The Navy's proposal to intern itself at Sardinia was rejected by General Eisenhower, who also refused Badoglio's request to delay the announcement, which was to take place at 6.30pm. This reached Badoglio just after 5.00pm and from that moment on the old Marshal appeared to be paralysed by indecision. Clearly the situation was too much for him. A meeting with the King was therefore held, resulting in a decision to announce the concluded armistice, but not without difficulty. There was still a strong body of opinion in favour of continuing the war as Germany's ally, but Major Marchesi, who had been with Castellano at the signing of the surrender document, was able to convince the meeting of the reality of the situation. We now know that ULTRA allowed the Allies to discover the state of German preparations in case of the Italian surrender, which helps in assessing their attitude to events between 3-8 September. As early as 29 July, Hitler had obtained evidence of Italian contacts with the Allies from SS Intelligence which had intercepted an intercontinental telephone call between Churchill and Roosevelt.[3] Meanwhile the Germans' fears of another landing were confirmed: on the 7th aerial reconnaissance sighted a convoy north of Palermo heading north-east. The following day the orders for the execution of Operation 'Achse' were issued *before* the announcement of the armistice.[4]

The armistice between the Kingdom of Italy and the Allied nations announced on 8 September by Marshall Badoglio would be more of a surprise to the Italian forces than to the Germans, who were aware in general terms what had been going on, while Badoglio and the chiefs of staff never distributed 'Memoria 44' to Italian units and decided against any action against the Germans. The orders sent on the night of the 8th were for the troops to defend their positions if attacked by the Germans, but not to initiate hostilities. Rome was also abandoned, the forces there retreating on Tivoli, which can be seen as a move to cover the escape of the King, who could not embark for Sardinia from Ostia as planned, as the Germans were in control of the beach. Furthermore, leaving Rome undefended would make it easier for the Germans to withdraw north as the Italians hoped they would, without any fighting.

Even if the Italians had a few more days before the announcement of the armistice, it is doubtful much more could have been done to prevent the German takeover. After three catastrophic years of war, the level of effectiveness remaining was rather low. Furthermore, neither the military commanders nor the politicians planned for any direct action against the Germans, and the presence throughout the Italian military of liaision officers and German units which had taken place during the war meant that the Germans had a high degree of actual control already. An example of this is given by a note which appeared in the war diary of the OKW reporting a breach in security of the armistice thanks to a source inside the Italian staff.[5]

Badoglio's government could also not depend on a consistent reaction throughout the armed forces, and as a result the orders issued by *Comando Supremo* and the respective services' staffs were somewhat vague and came too late. Loyalty to an ally and fear of German reprisals also played their part. As Aga Rossi has written; 'It seems impossible to establish the attitude of the top-ranking military, but certainly there was a strong faction opposed to a change of side and in favour of continuing the war and the alliance'.[6]

But the main point is that Badoglio and the military hoped that Germans would retreat north of Rome as a result of the Allied landings. There is at least one eyewitness source that confirms that this was the German intention until the morning of the 9th, but soon Kesselring realised he could hold a good part of southern Italy despite the Italian military defection and the Allied landings at Salerno, although the fear of further landings was not dispelled.[7]

* * *

Allied strategy called for a British crossing at Messina to seize Taranto, while an Allied force landed at Salerno – Operation 'Avalanche', with the ultimate goal of capturing Naples and its port. In the preparations for this operation, the Americans placed heavy emphasis on naval gunfire support for the invasion force.[8]

The Salerno landings were the most northerly operation carried out by the Allies, as to go further north would have placed them out of range of land-based air support, and carrier aircraft and naval gunfire could not do the job by themselves. Unlike during 'Husky' the Allied fleet now included four escort carriers, and one light fleet carrier, the *Unicorn*, under Rear-Admiral Vian, to protect the troop convoys. There would be no preliminary naval bombardment in order to keep the advantage of surprise. Although very different from what was common practice in the Pacific, Rear-Admiral Hall, who would be landing General Clark's 5th Army, agreed to this as he thought a night bombardment would be ineffective anyway.

The preparations for the invasion suffered from their own problems. Some disruption and losses were caused by a number of Axis air raids on the port of Bizerte. Rear-Admiral Hall also had to stop the USAAF loading a supply of 250lb and 500lb bombs aboard one of the transports in the initial wave, in the expection of the early capture of airfields, as he did not want a repeat of the explosion of the *Robert Rowan*. The bombs were brought up safely in a later convoy.

Hall's command consisted of 142 ships, while the total force bound for Salerno numbered 600 ships. The force left the North African ports, and as it neared Salerno, it picked up additional ships from Sicilian ports. Initial gunfire support was limited as the area was being cleared of mines, and because of the intense German resistance, Hall ordered some of the landing craft be armed with machine-guns, to give fire support of some sort. Eventually the light cruisers *Philadelphia* and *Savannah* with two destroyers were able to come into action. The *Abercrombie* gave important gunfire support, assisted by a USN spotter plane, along with a Dutch gunboat.

The *Savannah* was particularly successful at Salerno, at one point engaging German tanks at 17,450 yards using a spotter plane. But her luck would run out here. On 11 September, while German FW-190 fighters created a diversion by making low-level attacks against the harbour, Dornier 217 bombers got into position to launch their FX-1400 armour-piercing guided bombs. One just missed the squadron flagship *Philadelphia*, while another hit the *Savannah* which was moving at about 15 knots. It was the largest bomb ever to hit a US warship in the Second World War. It 'hit the roof of the no.3 turret [C turret], passed down the barbette, and exploded in the midst of the magazines . . . the explosion blew a large hole in the bottom, to port, and opened a seam in the port shell just below the armour belt. The inrush of water doused the magazine fire before it could endanger the ship, although no. 3 turret was entirely wiped out . . . In all, 152 feet of the ship was flooded, owing in part to severe blast, wrecked bulkheads, and sprung watertight doors'.[9] Despite having more than 100 of her crew killed, the *Savannah* was able to bring the damage under control and was able to limp off to Malta under her own power for emergency repairs.[10]

The FX-1400 glider-bomb had a 600lb warhead, and when dropped from 12,000 to 19,000ft could be radio-controlled by the parent aircraft. The weapon had been tested before in the Mediterranean, including an ineffective attack on Malta in mid-1943. It was not that successful a weapon as the launching aircraft had to approach the target slowly and on a fairly straight course, thus making it an easy target for either AA or a defending fighter.[11] Interestingly, Germany bought more than 2000 FFF Italian-produced motorbombs. The first 100 were exchanged with the same number of P500 rocket-accelerated bombs (or Fritz) given to the Italians for mutual testing.[12]

Later the British light cruiser *Uganda* was also hit by a FX-1400 in her bows, which exploded under her after passing through the armoured deck. Sixteen men were killed, and she shipped 1300 tons of water, putting her out of action as well. On 16 September, the *Warspite* would be seriously damaged by one of these new weapons. After the surrender of the Italian fleet, the *Warspite* and *Valiant* headed west, but were shortly recalled to the Salerno beachhead to supply vital fire support, which they performed as well as ever. On the afternoon of the 16th, the *Warspite* was engaging some German fighters and failed to spot bombers launching three FX-1400s, of which one would hit and another would near-miss. The one that hit dove down through the decks, making an entry hole 5½ft square, to the boiler rooms where it exploded. Five of the six boilers were knocked out, and one would never be repaired. The near-miss distorted the hull next to where it hit. Two turrets were also knocked out – one for the remainder of the war. She limped away from the beach powered by the one remaining boiler, which also eventually failed. Towed to Malta, she would arrive there on the 19th having shipped 5000 tons of water and with a 4° list.

All this attention from the *Luftwaffe* was due to the excellent support that the warships gave to the land forces. The volume of gunfire was truly tremendous, far greater than in 'Husky' or 'Torch'. The American cruisers fired off so much 6in ammunition that all the local reserves were depleted and a supply ship had to rush off to Malta to recover the shells left on board the crippled *Savannah*. Naval gunfire played a key role in defeating the German counterattacks against the beachead.[13]

As the fighting at Salerno continued, the Germans were taking over much of Italy. Although the operation to disarm Italian troops had variations according to local conditions, it had some common traits, such as detailed preparation and quick and determined execution. The success of 'Achse', the early surrender of Rome and the cautious approach of the Allies to the new situation all encouraged the Germans to pursue Kesselring's plan to extend their control over southern Italy as well, which he thought he could hold even with the relatively few troops he had available.

The announcement of the Armistice had triggered the sending of the codeword 'Achse' at about 8.00pm on 8 September. As well as the disarming of Italian units, the plan called for the occupation of a defensive position in the Apennines along the line Pisa-Arezzo-Pesaro, the garrisoning of the Apennine and Alpine passes and the abandonment of Corsica and Sardinia. However, the two commanders in Italy, Rommel as commander of Army Group B and Kesselring as Supreme Commander South (OB Süd), disagreeded on the timing and speed of the retreat from southern Italy, a vital question for the exploitation of the country's resources. While the operation was in progress the *Wehrmacht* High Command did not make a decision about the line of defence to adopt in Italy, as they thought that the Allies would prefer to invade the Balkans rather than fight their way up the mountainous Italian peninsula.

Italian resistance to the Germans, as happened in Corsica, was initiated by local commanders and although there were examples of stubborn and effective defence, the Italians were generally outclassed.[14] The achievement of complete surprise, plus the determination and on occasions violence used in its execution, added to the structural weakness of the Italian armed forces led to the greatest disaster in modern Italian military history, and what has been called the 'last victory of the German *Wehrmacht*'.[15]

* * *

The sometimes violent arguments within Italian historiography about the events of 8 September 1943 cannot be gone into fully here. Suffice it to say that it has been a politically-motivated debate, and most personal accounts were largely self-justification, seeking to avoid blame or throw it on to others. The recently published memoires of Admiral Raffaele De Courten throw some light on the actions of the Italian Navy, which is our principal interest. On 5 September De Courten had ordered two destroyers, the *Da Noli* and *Vivaldi*, to be ready on the morning of the 9th in order to take the King and the Court to La Maddalena. But as we have already mentioned, the beach was occupied by the Germans and the King had to go to Pescara on the Adriatic coast to embark for Apulia where the Italians were gaining control of the situation.

The two destroyers sailed for La Maddalena anyway, intending to attack German shipping transferring troops between Corsica and Sardinia. Passing into the Straits of Bonafacio they were fired on and hit by the now German-manned coastal batteries and 88mm flak guns. Both were damaged, and then at 5.50pm on the 9th, the *Da Noli* hit a mine, split in half and sank, 228 of her 287 crew being lost, including her captain. The *Vivaldi* made it through the Straits, although reduced to 10 knots due to damage, but that night she came under air attack, a near-miss bringing her to a dead stop, and her captain ordered the ship scuttled. A nearby squadron consisting of the new light cruiser *Regolo* and three destroyers rescued all but forty of her crew.[16]

Although the Navy has often been described as being pro-British, it was not ready to surrender while it still had ships ready for action. Therefore, when the armistice was announced the Admirals carefully explained to their men that to follow the armistice conditions would be of great help in improving the treatment of the losers by the victors. As the British already suspected, in several ships the sailors wanted to scuttle them rather than give them up to the enemy without a fight, and in some cases there were mutinies.

On board his flagship, the battleship *Roma*, Admiral Bergamini was in a difficult situation because the fleet had only recently been prepared to fight and therefore he held a conference to explain that the navy had to follow orders even when these were morally difficult to carry out. He promised that the ships were not being surrendered, nor would they have to lower the flag.

The ships of the Tyrrhenian Sea fleet were instructed to return to port, then to steam to La Maddalena and wait there for further orders. An exception to this were the ships of the 5th Division at Taranto which were ordered to go directly to Malta. The fleet was en route for La Maddalena when Admiral Bergamini was ordered instead to head for Bone in Algeria, because La Maddalena had been occupied by the Germans. While Bergamini was changing course German aircraft attacked the ships with FX-1400 glider-bombs. One of them hit the *Roma*, which sank with the loss of almost all her 1325 crew. With the Italians thinking that the approaching planes were friendly, and lacking adequate air cover, the attack was quite likely to succeed.

The battleship *Roma* was built in the yards of Cantieri Riuniti dell'Adriatico at Trieste, launched on 9 June 1940 and completed two years later. She displaced 46,215 tons and had a top speed of 30 knots. Her wartime career was limited. She was sent to Taranto in August 1942 as part of the 9th Division and carried out gunnery exercises. On 13 December she moved to Naples and La Spezia to avoid the increasingly heavy Allied air attacks. During air raids on La Spezia on 5 and 23 June she was damaged and sent to Genoa for repairs, returning in time to sail with the fleet on 9 September. As recalled by an eye-witness, who was aboard the cruiser *Regolo*:

> A few planes, 5 or 6, scattered, about 5000 meters high, the battleships turn left, we do the same, I see clearly the aeroplane above us launching a source of light which falls from the aircraft at high speed leaving a smoky white tail, the bomb falls into the sea

very near to the *Italia* . . . I do not understand why the ships do not scatter as ordered by the fighting regulations. While we steam on this course another plane drops his bomb, which is similar to the other already fallen, and this one seems aiming at us. We turn right at full power, but bomb is aimed at the *Roma*. We follow it falling with our hearts in our mouths. It falls on the deck of the battleship on the starboard side, aft of the last 90mm turret. A modest flame with little smoke, it seems that the bomb had caused little damage, but we are evidently wrong because the *Roma* heels considerably to the starboard and slows.[17]

Later it seemed to Notarbartolo that the *Roma* was hit again. In any case, after a few minutes:

At 3.53pm our attention is drawn to the *Roma*, which was clearly on fire, and after some moments an enormous, terrible yellow-red flame bursts out and envelopes all the bow part of the beautiful ship, while a gigantic pillar of smoke climbs up to several hundred of meters in the air and thousands of pieces of iron blown up now continue to fall in the sea.[18]

In fact, the *Roma* broke in half and sank very quickly. The first bomb exploded under the keel, acting like a magnetic mine and jammed two screws, reducing her speed to 16 knots. The second bomb hit the ship between the conning tower and 'B' turret, setting off the magazine and sinking the ship. Only 622 men were picked up and of these 26 died later of their injuries. Bergamini died in the attack.

After that, the fleet sailed for Malta, Rear-Admiral Romeo Oliva taking command. Many thought they had been attacked by Allied aircraft. The ships were not scuttled and although some were lost, most went to Malta after being assured by *Supermarina* in Rome, which had not been disbanded like the Army command, that the fleet would continue to fly the Italian flag and would not be demilitarised. Some ships, however, went elsewhere. After the sinking of the *Roma* the destroyers *Carabiniere*, *Mitragliere* and *Fuciliere* along with the crusier *Attilio Regolo* sailed to the Balearic islands and were interned there. The commander of this group, Captain Marini, after having finished rescuing the survivors from the *Roma*, wanted to take them to an Italian base. He was thinking that the fleet would be directed to La Spezia, and he wanted to go to Elba or Leghorn but after having intercepted messages clarifying the armistice situation, he decided to go to the Balearics.

The other important squadron was at Taranto, comprising the two old battleships *Duilio* and *Doria* of the 5th Division which were the bulk of a detached squadron of the battle fleet under command of Vice-Admiral Da Zara, whose flagship was the *Duilio*. The squadron also comprised the light cruisers *Cadorna* and *Pompeo Magno*, and the destroyer *Da Recco*. Da Zara received orders on the 8th for the armistice and returning from the meeting in Rome in the evening of the same day, he sent for his commanders with whom on the following day he discussed the armistice and what they would have to do. The majority were inclined to scuttle their ships but an order arrived instructing them to head for Malta and this caused some more discussion, after which all but Rear-Admiral Giovanni Galati (who had been decorated for his performance during 'Harpoon', and whose career was ended by his refusal), obeyed the orders which promised that the ships would not be handed over to the Allies. At 5.00pm they sailed for Malta and were met by British warships along the way after being attacked by four German planes which caused no damage.

The battleship *Giulio Cesare* of the 5th Division had been detached to Pola in the Adriatic with a reduced crew for repairs when the news of the armistice reached the ships. Her commander, Commander Vittore Carminati, gave orders to sail but without explaining where the ship was going. She had to load heavy ammunition which she did not have aboard while undergoing repairs. She was then instructed to go to Cattaro because she had not enough oil to go further. On the way the seaplane carrier *Miraglia* joined with her as she steamed south. But the crew did not want to give up the ship. So the petty officers, with the encouragement of three officers, unsatisfied by the commander who kept the truth from them, took up arms in order to scuttle the ship. But the captain assured the mutineers that the ship would not be given up to a foreign power, and that he would scuttle her 'one hundred meters deep' if otherwise. The *Cesare* then headed for Taranto, attacked on the way by German aircraft. She then put into Cattaro, which she shortly departed and steamed to Taranto. Here she was refuelled and at 2.00pm on 12 September she set off for Malta, where she arrived on the morning of the 13th, having been met on the way by her old enemy the *Warspite*. After the war there was a commission of inquiry into the mutiny on the *Cesare*, but the Navy preferred to close the story with a year's suspension from the service for the three officers involved, a penalty which was thereafter nullified.[19]

* * *

On 10 September the British 12th Cruiser Squadron of four light cruisers commanded by Commodore Agnew, who had destroyed the *Duisburg* convoy, along with the fast minelayer *Abdiel* and the American cruiser *Boise*, which had last seen action in the Dutch East Indies against the Japanese, transported British airborne troops to seize Taranto. Arriving at Taranto for the improvised Operation 'Slapstick', they successfully seized this valuable harbour (and later nearby Bari and Brindisi on the Adriatic), but lost the *Abdeil* with heavy loss of life to a mine.

This was due to two escaping E-boats, the *S54* and *S61*, accompanied by a MFP loaded with Germans. Theirs is quite a story. Led by Lieutenant Klaus Degenhard Schmidt on the *S54*, they escaped from Taranto on the night of the Italian surrender, laying mines as they left. Then, heading up the Adriatic, they made a short stop at Dubrovnik which probably prevented them from intercepting the battleship *Guilio Cesare* that was steaming south from Pola on her way to Malta. They then attacked and sank the Italian auxiliary gunboat *Aurora*. On 11 September off Venice they attacked the destroyer *Sella*, which they torpedoed twice and sank, and captured a troopship with several hundred soldiers aboard. Finally, they entered Venice at 7.00pm that day where they helped compel the Italian naval commander to surrender to the Germans![20]

* * *

The Italian decision to not defend Rome was apparently taken in the early hours of 9 September, when the Royal Court decided to leave Rome with Badoglio. The retreat on Tivoli of the Italian divisions that defended Rome was therefore ordered by Roatta to General Giacomo Carboni, commander of the mobile corps, which comprised the armoured and motorised divisions. At 3.30pm on 10 September an agreement was signed by Colonel Leandro Giaccone, Chief of Staff of the *Centauro* division, for the Italians and by General Siegfried Westphal, Chief of the Operation Office of German South Command, for the Germans, put to an end the battle for Rome. The Italians did not want Rome to become a battleground, while the Germans preferred that Rome as an open city would remain a crucial node of communications free from Allied interference. The reasons why Rome was not defended further become the object of legal proceedings mainly against Carboni and Roatta, because the Inquiry Commission established in 1944 could not prosecute the House of Savoy and the senior officers who negotiated and signed the Armistice. Thus any prosecution was limited to the 'failure to defend Rome', and this unsolved question gave rise to a wide critical domestic literature. It seems in other words that the problem was not the armistice, the disbanding of the armed forces and the German occupation but rather if General Carboni was or was not the principal responsible party, if not the only one, for the disaster.[21]

The conclusion of the agreement, quickly violated by Kesselring, partly solved the urgent problems that the Germans had in central Italy. They had to act against the Allied forces at Salerno and build up a front against them. The Italian surrender freed important forces that could be used for this, and Rome was now available for the free transit of supplies.[22] The German strategic situation developed well in the first two days from the armistice and already with the agreement of Rome, Kesselring could hold on. The beginning of the German occupation in Italy was possible thanks to the successful disarmament of Italian troops and the effective defence against the Allies. This happened according the secret directives issued by Hitler personally on 11 September 1943, which divided Italian territory into operation zones and other actions which assured the rapid conduct of this operation.[23]

Although the main capital ships of the fleet and others reached Malta and Bone, or were interned in the Balearics, many other ships either had to scuttle or chose to do so, and some fell into German hands. The Germans sunk, captured or damaged 386 warships totalling of 292,771 tons, while another 199 warships were captured in the yards adding another 210,653 tons to the haul. The merchant ships suffered heavily, with 1214 of them, totalling 976,902 tons, remaining in German hands.

In other cases the order to surrender was simply ignored and the sailors either disbanded or joined the Germans, which is what the *X MAS* did, under the command of Prince Valerio Borghese, who negotiated an agreement directly with the Third Reich, as Mussolini's Social Republic had not yet been formed. The details of the agreement signed by Borghese and *Korvettenkapitän* Max Berninghaus, commander of the Ligurian coast, is printed in several books based on what the witnesses remember, and recently by Borgogna:

1. The *X MAS* Flotilla is a complex unit of the Italian Navy fully independent in logistics, organisation, disciplinary and administrative fields.
2. It is an ally of the German armed forces with the same duties and rights.
3. It flys the Italian flag.

4. It is acknowledged to her members that they may use any weapon.
5. She is allowed to recover and equip with Italian flag and crew, the Italian vessels found in Italian ports: the operative employment is under control of the German Navy.
6. Commander Borghese is the acknowledged commander with the rights and duties of this appointment.[24]

This agreement took place mainly because Borghese was what in the past would be called a 'condottiero' (mercenary) and the Germans agreed because they needed to co-operate with the 'secret weapons' of the *X MAS*, which had achieved more during the war than the surface squadrons. Later, at the end of September, Borghese travelled to Germany to report to Doenitz and finally met Mussolini. German documents mention also that Commander Grossi, in charge of the Atlantic submarine base at Betasom, also joined with the Germans to continue the war.[25]

*   *   *

Admiral Inigo Campioni, who had commanded at Punto Stilo, now commanded the Dodecanese Islands in the summer and autumn of 1943. There were a total of 37,000 Italian personnel there, though many were in support units and were not fighting troops. The Aegean was an area that the British and Greek governments wanted to take. Churchill had always looked upon the Aegean as an area of importance.

The fall of Fascist Italy, along with the terrible losses suffered by Germany in Tunisia and in Russia lead General Sir Alan Brooke, Chief of the Imperial General Staff, and his Director of Military Operations, General John Kennedy, to consider in September that pressure needed to be applied in the Balkans as well as in Italy. Nazi Germany might collapse as a result, much as Imperial Germany had in 1918.[26] Much of the reasoning for a presence in the Aegean came from the need to liberate occupied Greek territory. But other advantages would accrue, such as the defence of shipping in the Eastern Mediterranean, support for Turkey and encouragement of her entry into the war on the Allied side, and the memory of what had happened at Salonika in 1918. That had begun the collapse of the Central Powers and it might happen again.

The Allies had set aside two British divisions to support Turkey in case of attack, had been practising an invasion of Rhodes with units on Cyprus and even had secretly prepared airfields in Turkey in anticipation of their entry into the war. The Turks, who would eventually join the Allies but not until 1945, were concerned with keeping open a sea route in the Aegean, which the Germans would continue to dominate if they moved quickly against the Italian islands.[27]

Rhodes was targeted along with Crete, though the latter was assumed to require large forces to capture it. This would be Operation 'Accolade'. With the imminent surrender of Fascist Italy, it was viewed as a potentially easy operation. While the results of this is beyond the scope of our book, events transpired that are part of the end of the war for Fascist Italy. The *Cuneo* division was stationed on several of the Aegean islands, while the core of the Dodecanese Islands was held by the *Regina* infantry division. Several resourceful British operatives, on their own initiative, went to Samos and met with the commander of the *Cuneo* division, but were not properly supported.[28] The island of Leros became a target for both sides. Rear-Admiral Luigi Mascherpa commanded there and would turn the base over to British officers at the time of the armistice. But the Germans counterattacked and with speed and cunning seized the island before the slower-moving Allies could react. Mascherpa would be captured by the Germans and was executed by firing squad on 15 May 1944.

One of the fundamental problems facing the British in any operation in the Aegean was the distances involved. With bases in North Africa or from Cyprus, it was too far for single-engine fighters to operate from their bases in North Africa and Cyprus, and the twin-engined fighters such as the Lightening and the Beaufighter were either in too short supply or outclassed by the Me109s based on several Aegean islands, the Germans had effective air superiority. Yet, for a moment, audacious actions by a few men, supported by Greek guerrillas had secured the islands of Leros and Samos, 20,000 troops, and a sea area of 5000 square miles, only to lose it to the closer and quicker Germans.

General Scaroina of the *Regina* division was captured early on, and Vice-Admiral Campioni, when he learned that the British could not arrive until 15 September, surrendered on 11 September. Not immediately going over to the Germans cost him his life, as he was executed at Parma on 24 May 1944, one of two Italian admirals to be executed, and would be posthumously awarded the *Medaglia d'Oro* in November 1947.

*   *   *

On 29 September 1943 Badoglio signed the 'Long Armistice' during a meeting with Eisenhower and kept it secret from the other members of the government. Its terms were only published in November 1945, after the end of the war. This was because Eisenhower accepted Badoglio's request to not publish the harsh conditions it contained and the consequences to Italy. The main element was that according to the peace treaty signed at Paris on 10 February 1947, the Italian Navy was almost completely ceded to the Allies, with 65,000 tons left to Italy to patrol her long coasts.

As an epilogue to this, in 1949 the old battleship *Royal Sovereign*, loaned to the Russians in August 1941, was returned to the Royal Navy. At the same time, the Italian battleship *Giulio Cesare*, veteran of the action off Calabria, was ceded to the Soviet Union as reparations for war damages. She was renamed *Novorossisk* and was based at Sevastopol. On 29 October 1955 she blew up with the loss of 544 men out of a crew of 1576. It was supposed that there was a German mine still active in the harbour. But in 1991-92, at the time of *glasnost*, articles appeared in Russian magazines like *Morskoi Sbornik* and *Sovershenno Secretno* which revealed that the *Novorossisk* was not lost to a mine, but either due to an explosive charge hidden inside the hull and detonated by veterans of the *X MAS* led by Borghese, or an attack like that conducted against Alexandria in December 1941. There was no definitive assessment of the cause of the 150 square meter wide hole after she was raised in March 1956 and late scrapped. The *Kerch*, also a war reparations light cruiser from Italy, may have also had an explosive charge placed on her that was discovered and removed. This may have been the last act of the Fascist War.[29]

CHAPTER 24

Conclusions

The importance of the Mediterranean as the jugular vein of the British Empire is indubitable. It should be remembered that the need to protect this supply line was one of the factors why the Russian Empire had been fought by the Turks, French and Sardinians, as well the British, in the previous century. This strategic concept could still be seen when the Allies accepted the surrender of the German forces in Italy in order to reach Trieste as soon as possible to prevent that port being made available to the Russians by Tito, who by this time had turned to the Soviet Union.[1]

Mussolini clearly understood in his 'oceanic' speech that the key points for control of the Mediterranean were Suez, Gibraltar and Malta, which were regularly scheduled for capture in Axis documents during the war, but quite astonishingly plans to seize all these objectives were not made from the outset with clear agreement between both Axis powers. This was contributed to both by Hitler's world view and Mussolini's desire to fight (or perhaps not fight) a parallel war alongside Germany but keeping his own strategy and objectives with his limited capabilities.

The post-war view of the war in the Mediterranean is similar both in Great Britain and in Italy. The Italians always claimed, both during and after the war, that the Germans made a strategic 'error' of paramount importance by not committing enough forces to the southern flank. In Britain, as noted by Lewin, 'For the greater part of the war there were few weeks when the Mediterranean was not in the mind of the British public', and after the war, the bulk of war histories concerned the Mediterranean, where the basis of the British strategy was to fight the Axis in a forward position to protect the vital Middle East and especially the Persian Gulf, without which the war could not have continued.[2]

Nevertheless, at the beginning of the war, British strategic analysis considered the Atlantic supply lanes decisive for national survival. In a memorandum written by Admiral Sir Percy Noble to the Admiralty, the Mediterranean was not considered the decisive theatre. He reasoned that the experience of the previous war had proved the danger posed by only a small number of enemy submarines and therefore the Italians' 100 modern submarines with trained crews, plus the unknown capabilities of the *Regia Aeronautica*, would compel all naval units to retire on Gibraltar. Noble's picture was what Italy should have done: a war launched without a formal declaration, massive air attacks, comprehensive mine-laying in the waters between Sicily and Africa (but the Tunisian coasts would be in Allied hands since the war would very probably see France siding with Great Britain), and finally acting very aggressively with the large number of submarines available. This was indeed a very pessimistic forecast.

At the outbreak of the war both Germany and Italy were aware that for Great Britain to continue war against Germany and Italy, the decisive sector would be the lines of communication with the United States and the Dominions.[3] We have already discussed elsewhere Hitler's plan for winning his ideological war against the Soviet Union to create an empire in the East and reach an agreement with Great Britain on the basis of the 'Teilung der Welt' ('Division of the World'). Several speculations about Hitler's errors are therefore put forward, observing that from September 1940 onwards the Raeder began to propose to Hitler the displacement of the 'Schwerpunkt' to the Mediterranean. These suggestions were made by most military leaders of the Third Reich opposed to the Russian campaign thirteen times between Italy's entry into the war and the beginning of Operation 'Barbarossa'.[4] The first occasion was on 30 June 1940 when General Jodl mentioned the Mediterranean for the first time as a secondary theatre of war, but Hitler refused direct involvement there, and the last was on 6 June 1941 when Raeder again put forward his plans. Of course these proposals were made after Italy had joined the war: before that date the German naval command was suspicious, refusing to help Italy because there were no reason to supply technical advantages to the Italians which might pass these on to the enemy. 'Of course this would be different if the Italians enter actively on our side in the war'.[5]

However, it should be noted that many strategic options proposed to Hitler by military leaders were particularly stressed in postwar accounts, to create the image of the generals and admirals who would have been able to win the war if only Hitler had listened to them, and were often had not been intended as a strategic alternative to the Russian invasion. For example, Jodl regarded the Mediterranean as a second-ary theatre where he did not want a direct commitment of the *Wehrmacht*. Further-more Hitler himself also twice offered limited help to Alfieri and Ciano on 1 and 7 July 1940.[6] Raeder's opinion, presented to Hitler, was not ruling out the Russian campaign, but only suggesting its delay. Furthermore, those who claimed that Hitler made the wrong choice tend to overlook 'that Hitler looked for the vital space for National Socialist Germany not in the Near East or in Africa, but in European Russia'.[7]

Certainly the German Navy, after the abandonment of Operation 'Sealion', had reconsidered its plans, but this did not apply to all the senior officers. Looking back to pre-war naval strategy, it is well known that before the war there were different points of view in the 'Marineleitung', to use Schreiber's word for the German Navy. There was a difference of opinion between Dönitz who favoured the U-boat as the principal weapon against merchant shipping and the Naval High Command which planned raids on the shipping lanes with surface ships. Therefore the navy's U-boats were not ready for a war with Great Britain, also partly because after the 1935 Naval Treaty Britain was not considered an enemy, at least until 1938. This led to a compromise and the building of big ships, which could be used to raid shipping. Then in May 1938 a 'Denkscrift' (memo) was issued considering Britain as a possible enemy.[8]

In March 1939 the alliance with Italy was seen as a chance to menace the British fleet with a link to Africa via Malta and land operations by the Italians to seize Gibraltar and Suez. The German Naval Command was surprised by the outbreak of the war in 1939 because they had been told to plan for war in 1943-45, and as a first consequence, the Z Plan for naval rearmament which had been approved on 29

January 1939 was dropped. By October 1939 the attempt to enter the Mediterranean with three U-Boats had failed. The main point which caused talks to break down between the Italian and German navies was the fact Italy refused to give support to German U-boat war in the Mediterranean at that time.[9] As commander of the submarine forces Dönitz thought that only 'the sinking of the British merchant ships' would bring about a 'decisive success against Britain'. In a book interview Admiral Cunningham is quoted thus: 'He [Dönitz] always realised that the Atlantic was the one theatre in which a German victory could be gained and he thus constantly opposed diversions to the Mediterranean'.[10]

After the conquest of Denmark and Norway, although the German Naval Command still had a 'Utopian' building plan for the future, immediate necessity forced then to try and increase U-boat production. Furthermore, the failure of the fall of France to force Great Britain to surrender, and the indefinite suspension of 'Sealion', meant a new strategy was needed. Therefore the German Naval Command begun to look south and to see in the British position at Suez as the door to the oilfields in the Persian Gulf with which the Axis could come nearer to victory. In Hitler's view the 1942 offensive in southern Russia was the last chance to bring the Soviet Union to its knees and to force an agreement with Great Britain. Between 30 August and 5 September a strategy was formulated that planned the expulsion of the Royal Navy from the Mediterranean, the occupation of French North Africa and Casablanca and Dakar. From there they would launch the main stroke against Britain's jugular vein with the help of Italian warships.[11] We should remember that the fact the German Naval Command began to think to a maritime encirclement of Britain was also helped by the proposals of the Italian Navy, which in the days after the Punta Stilo action proposed collaboration. But the encounter off Calabria also proved to the Germans that the Italian Navy was unable to cut British communications across the Mediterranean.

An Italian Navy memorandum of 24 July 1940 proposed collaboration. But the strategies of the two navies were so different that no common strategic plan could exist. The one exception to the general lack of direct co-operation between the Axis powers was the deployment of Italian submarines in the Atlantic. After the Italian disasters in autumn 1940, on 14 November Raeder again proposed his strategy to reach a decision in the war by neutralising British forces in the Mediterranean. This could be 'the important premise for the success of a direct war at sea against Britain'. At this point, seeing that the Italian conduct of war at sea was miserable, the German Naval Command thought that they should leave operational control to them.[12]

The main question here is whether the Axis could in fact have won the war by seizing the Suez Canal as Raeder expected. This was of course only a starting point to seize the Iranian oilfields for their own use and to deny them to Great Britain. The Caucasian oil fields would have been more useful, but there would have been problems getting the damaged fields back into production, and although they would have given the Third Reich much greater resources, Britain would still have had her source of supply and the war would have continued.[13] The seizure of the oilfields in the Middle East would in any case left the British Empire able to fight on because the key routes were the routes from the United States and from the Commonwealth. As noted in the interesting article by Klaus Schmider, Britain had already taken steps to replace the oil coming from that area in order to avoid a disaster in case of an Axis advance across the Nile.[14] Of course German strategic options in 1942 were different from those in 1940. There was no longer the possibility to fight either against the Soviet Union or against Britain, but only to try the last chance against the Soviets.

One Italian Admiral upon surrendering was asked if the Navy had done a poor job in the war. His reply was 'No one can play chess blindfolded. We never knew where the Allied Navy was. But the Allies knew the exact position of every unit of our fleet at all times.' While exaggerated, this says a great deal about the Fascist War with the Allies in the Mediterranean.[15] In writing this book we came to certain conclusions about the war in the Mediterranean. Certainly it evolved and changed. New equipment and new tactics changed the course of the war. It is also interesting to see what each side lost in the war in the Mediterranean.

The Italian Navy and Italian Air Force sank the following major enemy warships. Units marked in parenthesis are those sunk by air attack.

7 cruisers
15 destroyers (7)
34 submarines (2)
1 sloop (1)
2 corvettes (1)

The German Navy and Air Force to September 1943 (not including Italian ships sunk at or after the armistice) sank the following:

1 battleship
2 aircraft carriers
8 cruisers (5)
40 destroyers (26)
8 submarines (4)
1 monitor (1)
3 sloops (2)
3 corvettes (2)[16]

The Royal Navy losses included the *Barham, Eagle, Ark Royal,* fourteen cruisers, two AA ships, two fast minelayers, forty-four destroyers, forty-one submarines and over 100 other vessels. Nor does this total include ships that were severely damaged such as the battleships *Queen Elizabeth* and *Valiant.*

Italian naval losses were heavy: 339 ships of all types were lost in the Mediterranean and an additional fifty-four outside. The major warships were as follows in the Mediterranean only:

11 cruisers
37 destroyers
39 torpedo-boats
65 submarines[17]

Another key point is that Italy's war economy failed, and failed in two ways. First it never fully mobilised. For example, much of the steel production went to strategic industries for future economic growth after the war and for Italy's drive for self-sufficiency and not for immediate war production needs. Secondly, it never produced the modern weapons of war needed, largely due to poor and obsolescent design. Another important element is that the individual was meaningful. The various outcomes of battles often time hinged on the decision of one or two key individuals whose decision sometimes cast a long shadow over a portion of the globe.

Also, more pre-war planning and preparation around the *X MAS* and the creation of a more powerful air force that could project its power into at least the Central Mediterranean would have made a vital difference. That this was not done was a failure of the Naval and Air Force High Commands, and ultimately Mussolini. But the one thing about the war in the Mediterranean and specifically the Italian Navy and the Italian Air Force in the Second World War that we want the reader to take away after setting this book down can be summed up in one word: training. If the Italian Navy was a 'Fair Weather' navy and if their Air Force was an extension of First World War 'acrobatic combat' then solid and realistic training in the inter-war period would have revealed the need for improved techniques. Range-finding optics, heavier bombs, torpedo and dive-bombers, submarines that could dive more quickly and all the other aspects of a powerful war machine were found wanting. The need for training, training both before and during the war, was paramount and one of the greatest advantages the Royal Navy enjoyed over the Italians. A unit must work extensively with the weapons of war before it has to use them for real and the cost of this must be assumed to be part of the cost of waging war. If the Italian Navy had not built two or three light warships and had instead invested that money into intensive training exercises in all types of weather, and under all sorts of conditions, the course of the war might have been quite different. The High Command of the *Regia Marina* and *Regia Aeronautica*, and ultimately Mussolini, failed to create a powerful war machine which was within their means to do so. They failed the pilots and sailors that fought the war, ironically for the benefit of the Free World.

Notes

Chapter 1

[1] Attributed.

[2] Pratt, Lawrence R, *East of Malta, West of Suez* (Cambridge 1975), pp40, 127; Mack Smith, Denis, *Mussolini's Roman Empire* (New York 1976), pp33-34, 139; and Sullivan, Brian in Millett, Alan R and Williamson, Murray (eds), *Military Effectiveness* (Winchester 1998), Vol II, p175.

[3] Pratt, op cit, pp5-16. Ferdinando Minniti is preparing a book on Italian pre-war planning. The earliest Italian war plans after the First World War were against Yugoslavia, with plans to seize Corsica from France formulated in 1926. A war with both France and Great Britain was considered in January 1938 but not confirmed until a year later.

[4] Both the German and Italian goal was to be equal with France's navy by treaty. This was of course a theoretical goal, since both remained behind France in tonnage. Britain did not offer a formal continental commitment to France until February 1939. See Bernardi, Giovanni, *Il disarmo navale fra le due guerre mondiali (1919-1939)* (Rome 1975), p263; Schreiber, Gerhard, 'Die Rolle Frankreichsim strategischen und operativen Denken der Deutschen Marine', in Hildebrand, Klaus, and Werner, Karl Ferdinand (eds), *Deutschland und Frankreich 1936-1939* (Munich 1981), pp167-213; and Deist, Wilhelm, *The Wehrmacht and German Rearmament* (Basingstoke 1981), p77.

[5] Dissertation by Perett, William Gregory, 'French Naval Policy and Foreign Affairs, 1930-1939' (Stanford University 1977), pp22-23, 168.

[6] Young, Robert J, *In Command of France* (London 1978), pi04; and Sullivan, Brian R, 'The Italian-Ethiopian War' in Ion, A Hamish, and Errington, E J, *Great Powers and Little Wars* (Westport, 1993) and Salerno, Reynolds M, 'The French Navy and the Appeasement of Italy 1937-9', *The English Historical Review* Vol CXI I, No 445 (February 1997), pp69-70.

[7] Pratt, op cit, pp16-19, Young, op cit, pp91-92, 103-104, and Robert A. Doughty in Williamson, Murray, and others (eds), *The Making of Strategy* (Cambridge 1994), pp478-479.

[8] Roskill, Stephen, *Naval Policy Between the Wars* (Annapolis 1976), Vol II pp251, 322.

[9] Salerno, Reynolds M, *The Mediterranean Triangle* (UMI 1997). His basic argument is that Britain tried to keep the Mediterranean quiet by appeasing Italy.

[10] Chatfield papers 16 September 1935, as given in Pratt, op cit, p24-26. Dissertation by Brian R Sullivan, 'A Thirst for Glory' (Columbia University 1981), p414. Italy's ambassador to London added supporting intelligence to this conclusion. This was never done.

For further information on German assistance to Italy in this period, see Petersen, Jens, *Hitler e Mussolini. La Difficile Alleanza* (Bari 1975).

[11] Raeder, Erich, *My Life* (Annapolis 1960), p225.

[12] Rahn, Werner, *Reichsmarine und Landesverteidigung 1919-1928* (München 1976), pp188-189; Schreiber, Gerhard, *Revisionismus und Weltmachtstreben. Marineführung und Deutsch-italienische Bezehungen 1919-1944* (Stuttgart 1978) pp59, 63.

[13] Kehrig, Manfred, *Die Wiedereinrichtung des deutschen militärischen Attachédienstes nach dem Ersten Welthrieg (1919-1933)* (Boppard am Rhein 1966), p92 n95, 'The good relations between the *Reichsmarine* and the *Regia Marina* were again confirmed to me by Adm. Doenitz …'. The *Luftwaffe* ace Adolf Galland received training in Italy and wore an Italian uniform!

[14] On the general anti-republican and anti-democratic feelings of the military in the Weimar republic, see Carsten, F H, *The Reichswehr and Politics 1918 to 1933* (Oxford 1966).

[15] Marder, Arthur J, *From Dardanelles to Oran* (London 1974), pp66-73; and Sullivan, Brian R, 'A Deal with the Devil: Italian Military Intelligence under the Fascist Regime, 1922-1943' (unpublished) *passim*. ASDIC stood for 'Allied Submarine Detection Investigation Committee'. It was renamed sonar in 1943 and will be so called hereafter. As to the Nile, see Cunningham, Andrew, *A Sailor's Odyssey* (New York 1951), p176.

[16] Salerno, *The Mediterranean Triangle*, pp50-51.

[17] Knox, MacGregor, *Mussolini Unleashed* (New York 1982), pp6, 8. Also see Sullivan, 'A Thirst for Glory', pp554-580.

[18] Clerici, Carlo Alfredo, *Le Difese Costiere Italiane Nelle Due Guerre Mondiali* (Parma 1996), *passim*.

[19] Morewood, Steven, 'The Chiefs of Staff, the 'men on the spot' and the Italo-Abyssinian emergency, 1935-36' in Richardson, Dick and Stone, Glyn (eds), *Decisions and Diplomacy* (London 1995), p95

[20] Ireland, Bernard, *War in the Mediterranean* (London 1993) p14; Knox, op cit, pl6; and Marder, op cit, p81.

[21] Borghese, J Valerio, *Sea Devils* (Chicago 1954), pp12-16. The few test weapons were put in storage and in 1938 Commander Paolo Aloisi, commanding the First Light Flotilla, brought them out. In July 1939 Vice-Admiral Il-debrando Goiran, commanding the Upper Tyrrenhian District, was formally ordered to carry out 'experiments and tests concerned with the perfecting of the said weapons'.

[22] Schreiber, Gerhard, *Germany and the Second World War* (Oxford 1995) Vol III, pp80-82; and Mack Smith, op cit, ppl74-175.

[23] Sullivan, 'A Thirst for Glory', pp371, 429 and 'A Deal with the Devil', p18.

[24] Marder, op cit, pp64-104.

[25] Young, op cit, pp112-113.

[26] Pratt, op cit , pp93, 104-105.

[27] Ibid, p184

[28] Roskill, op cit, p326. The sterling conversion is as of 1935. Roskill really does not address the fact that Italy's naval budget was that of a 'poor man's Great Power'. Everything Italy did in the inter-war period, and indeed during the war itself, was on a shoestring. It should, however, be noted that with the possible exception of Japan and the Soviet Union, Italy had the lowest labour costs of any of the major powers.

Chapter 2

[1] Roskill, *Naval Policy between the Wars*, Vol II, p389.

[2] Pratt, op cit, pp42, 133. Darlan was considered anti-British during the war, but he had sought talks concerning the Mediterranean naval situation and Italy before the war, and then later saw his fleet suffer attacks by the British in 1940. He was rebuffed over co-operation with the Loyalists during the Spanish Civil War – Pratt wonders if this was why Darlan was an Anglophobe – see Funk, Arthur Layton, *The Politics of Torch* (Lawrence, Kansas 1974), pp22-26 and also Hood, Ronald Chalmers III, *Royal Republicans* (Baton Rouge 1985), *passim* and especially pp96-97, 179, who points out that French naval officers as a group were anti-British, and that Darlan resented that the 1930 London Naval Conference was convened in the Trafalgar room! According to Salerno, Darlan was also quite upset with the British appeasement of Italy during the Spanish Civil War. On the British side, Admiral Dudley Pound once remarked that the French Navy wasn't worth a 'hatful of crabs'!

[3] Pratt, op cit, pp164, 170 and Salerno, Reynolds M, 'The French Navy and the Appeasement of Italy 1937-9', *The English Historical Review* Vol CXII, No 445 (1997), p66-73. The British Cabinet authorised air and army discussions in February 1938.

[4] Sullivan, Brian R, 'Fascist Italy's Military Involvement in the Spanish Civil War', *The Journal of Military History*, Vol 59, No 4 (1995), pp713-715, and Frank, Willard C, Jr, 'Naval Operations in the Spanish Civil War, 1936-1939', *Naval War College Review* (January-February 1984), pp24-25. At one point the bulk of the Republican Navy returned to port and the two small ships left to contain the Nationalist were too weak to stop the convoy, which was supported by the Italian Air Force.

[5] Frank, 'Naval Operations in the Spanish Civil War, 1936-1939' pp34-35, and Frank, Willard C, 'German Clandestine Submarine Warfare' in Roberts, William R, and Sweetman, Jack (eds), *New Interpretations in Naval History – 9th Naval History Symposium* (Annapolis 1990).

[6] Frank, 'Naval Operations in the Spanish Civil War, 1936-1939', p37, and Bargoni, Franco, *L'impegno Navale Italiano durante La Guerra Civile Spagnola (1936-1939)* (Rome 1992), pp142-146. There were four brief and ineffective port bombardments by submarines in this period and possibly two small ships sunk – see Frank, 'German Clandestine Submarine Warfare', p118.

[7] Frank, 'Naval Operations in the Spanish Civil War, 1936-1939', pp29-31 and Bargoni, op cit, pp266-271.

[8] Bargoni, op cit, pp185-186 and Brian R Sullivan's foreword to the forthcoming translation and reprinting of Romeo Bernotti's *Fundamentals of Naval Tactics and Fundamentals of Naval Strategy* from the Naval Institute Press.

A picture of the minor damage appears in Bargoni, Franco, *Orizzonte Mare* (Rome 1979), Vol A6, p43.

[9] Salerno, *The Mediterranean Triangle*, p141.

[10] Sullivan, 'Fascist Italy's Military Involvement in the Spanish Civil War', p716 and Bargoni, *L'impegno Navale Italiano durante La Guerra Civile Spagnola*, pp280-330. This Italian response was due to Franco's complaining of the approach of a Soviet convoy of five ships loaded down with military supplies for the Republicans. It did not exist.

[11] The *Sanchez Barcaiztegui* class took its name from a hero in an 1866 action with Peru off Callao and this class did somewhat resemble the *Havock*. Bargoni, *L'impegno Navale Italiano durante La Guerra Civile Spagnola*, pp309-310 and Letter to Admiralty dated 4 September 1937. HMS *Basilisk* also used her sonar against an enemy submarine on 3 October 1937 and also lost contact. See Poland, Rear-Admiral E N, *The Torpedomen* (London 1993), p248.

[12] Roskill, *Naval Policy Between the Wars*, Vol II, pp62-63, 383-386, Sullivan, 'Fascist Italy's Military Involvement in the Spanish Civil War', pp715-716, and Salerno, The *Mediterranean Triangle*, p141. The Italians were also assigned a sector!

[13] Frank, Willard C, Jr, 'Misperceptions and Incidents at Sea: The *Deutschland* and *Leipzig* Crisis, 1937', *Naval War College Review* (Spring 1990), p32. It would be interesting to see a thorough study of these attacks, which we assume were unintentional. Italy would not be the only power whose air force misidentified warships – early in the war the *Luftwaffe* attacked and sank some of their own destroyers operating off Borkum in the North Sea. See Groener, Erich, *German Warships* (London 1990), Vol 1, p200.

[14] Frank, 'Misperceptions and Incidents at Sea', pp31-45. Corrects Pratt, op cit, pp72-73 and concludes that the Republican government did not deliberately attack a German warship. For the damage to HMS *Hunter*, see March, Edgar J, *British Destroyers* (London 1966), p312.

[15] Sullivan, 'Fascist Italy's Military Involvement in the Spanish Civil War', p716; Bargoni, *L'impegno Navale Italiano durante La Guerra Civile Spagnola*, p722 and final quote from Pedriali, Ferdinando, *Guerra di Spagna e Aviazione Italiana* (Rome 1992), p305. It should be noted that various sources give different figures for shipping losses, but clearly the air campaign against shipping had many successes. The *Jaime I* was lost due to a 'terrible' internal explosion on 17 June 1937 but the myth that Italian bombs helped destroy her aided the officers of the *Regia Aeronautica* to further justify their position against the Navy.

[16] Sullivan, 'Fascist Italy's Military Involvement in the Spanish Civil War', pp722-724. Italy would spend between 8 and 9 billion Lire in this war, money that might have been better spent on her rearmament programmme – though the possibility of a Soviet-oriented state on the French border and commanding the Western Mediterranean in 1940-1942 is a provocative concept. Italy shipped 764 aircraft to Spain – 377 Cr32 fighters alone.

[17] Two boats of the same class, the *Galileo Ferraris* and *Galileo Galilei*, and two smaller 680-ton boats, the *Iride* and *Onice* were transferred to Nationalist service as 'Legionary submarines' but kept their Italian officers and crew. They performed a total of thirteen missions, conducted five unsuccessful attacks and would soon return to Italian service: Bargoni, *L'impegno Navale Italiano durante La Guerra Civile Spagnola*, pp340-341.

[18] Roskill, *Naval Policy Between the Wars*, Vol II, p371.

[19] Ireland, *War in the Mediterranean*, p13.

[20] Roskill, *Naval Policy Between the Wars*, Vol II, p388; March, *British Destroyers*, p381; and Young, *In Command of France*, p135.

Chapter 3

[1] Pratt, *East of Malta, West of Suez*, p84.

[2] Ibid.

[3] Ibid, pp111-112.

[4] Ibid, pp117, 129. Pound thought a slow convoy passing through the Mediterranean would be 'suicidal'.

[5] Letter from Reynolds M Salerno to authors dated 12 August 1997.

[6] Pratt, op cit, pp159-160. See also Salerno, *The Mediterranean Triangle*, pp324-327. Italy immediately began improving the roads to the Greek border and planned to seize Corfu and attack Greece itself. The Greek intelligence service alerted the French and British governments to this.

[7] Salerno, op cit, p221.

[8] Toscano, Mario, *The Origins of the Pact of Steel* (Baltimore 1967), pp224, 256. The Italians viewed a war with France as being mostly fought in North Africa as the Alpine frontier was thought to be too strong for either side to break through.

[9] William Gregory Perett's dissertation 'French Naval Policy and Foreign Affairs, 1930-1939' (Stanford University 1977), p428 and unpublished article (1988) by Alessandro Massignani on the Friedrichshafen meeting. An earlier meeting had taken place in April between Raeder and the Italian Vice-Admiral Silvio Salza and Rear-Admiral Raffaele Conte de Courten. Cavagnari was surprised to learn that the German naval plans called for operations only in the Baltic and North Seas with no plans for operations in the Atlantic. This would mean more naval pressure on Italy. De Courten would later play several key roles in the war. See Salerno, op cit, pp344-348.

[10] Quoted in Salerno, Reynolds M, 'The French Navy and the Appeasement of Italy 1937-9', *The English Historical Review* (February 1997), p98.

[11] Quoted in Young, *In Command of France*, p194 and Salerno, 'The French Navy and the Appeasement of Italy 1937-39', p86.

[12] Salerno, *The Mediterranean Triangle*, pp195, 498.

[13] Pratt, op cit, pp174-179. It must be noted that much of the main American fleet in 1938-39 was in the Atlantic, due in part to the Czech crisis, and the Pacific was only reinforced later. The authors were unable to discover any other supporting evidence for the connection suggested by Pratt.

[14] Ibid, pp184-185. In return Britain was to base four of her modernised battleships in the Mediterranean. Darlan was concerned that by mid-1940 Italy would have more modern battleships available to her then France; see Salerno, 'The French Navy and the Appeasement of Italy 1937-39', p93.

[15] Quote from Joint Planning subcommittee, 'Plans for Action Against Italy', 12 July 1939 as quoted in Pratt, op cit, p187.

[16] Salerno, *The Mediterranean Triangle*, pp400-429.

[17] Raspin, Angela, *The Italian War Economy 1940-1943* (New York 1986), p100.

[18] Knox, MacGregor, *Military Effectiveness* (Boston 1988) Vol III, p140 for quote and Salerno, *The Mediterranean Triangle*, p385.

[19] Sullivan, Brian, *Military Effectiveness*, Vol II, pp171-172 and Raspin, *The Italian War Economy 1940-1943*, p423. The competition for resources was so strong between the Axis that in 1942 Germany protested to Vichy France about a contract for iron ore that Italy had with an Algerian mining firm, and got Vichy to break the contract! See Raspin, op cit, p261.

[20] Knox, *Mussolini Unleashed*, pp8-16.

[21] Ibid, p23.

[22] Ibid, pp55-57. The commander of the army, Alberto Pariani, was also 'fired' for the incompetent mobilisation of the army.

[23] NARS, T821/144, *Ufficio di Stato maggiore della R. Aeronautica, Situazione giornaliera efficienza bellica velivoli ed equipaggi*, 11 June 1940.

[24] Arena, Nino, *La Regia Aeronautica 1939-1943* (Rome 1981), Vol 1, p169; Greene, Jack, *Mare Nostrum* (Watsonville 1990), p74-75; and Sullivan, Brian, *Military Effectiveness*, Vol II, pp171-172.

[25] See Gerhard Schreiber in *Germany and the Second World War*, Vol III, pp84-85 and compare with Santoro, Giuseppe, *L'aeronautica italiana nella seconda guerra mondiale* (Rome-Esse 1957) Vol 1, pp91-92.

[26] Almost 300 were available at the start of the war and were considered first-line fighters by the Italians; see Angelucci, Enzo, and Matricardi, Paolo, *World War II Aeroplanes* (Verona 1976), Vol I, p205. Only the Cr42 DB (MM 469) was fitted with the 1000hp DB 601A 12-cylinder inverted-'V' liquid-cooled engine. 'This prototype was first flown in early 1941 and, externally, differed considerably from standard Cr42s in having a long pointed nose and ventral radiator. Although capable of a speed of 520 km/h, it was recognised as being inferior to foreseeable opponents and was abandoned'.

[27] *Dimensione cielo caccia assalto* (Rome 1971) Vol 1, p55. Italy over the years has produced numerous colourful small booklets primarily on their naval and air units, and this is one in a series from the publisher Bizzarri by Angelucci and Matricardi, *World War II Aeroplanes*, Vol I *passim* for this section. It should be noted that the French aicraft industry had also not geared up for war and had a very low monthly production rate – much lower then Italy's.

[28] Raspin, *The Italian War Economy*, p325.

[29] Germany also received parts for their 88mm AT/AA gun from Italian industry, among other supplies. The *Luftwaffe* was the largest German purchaser of Italian manufactured goods in the war. See Raspin, op cit, pp334-349.

[30] Thetford, Owen, *British Naval Aircraft* (6th ed London 1991), p139

[31] Gerhard Schreiber in *Germany and the Second World War*, Vol III, p89.

[32] See also Coles, Michael H,'Cunningham and King' in Cogar, William B (ed), *New Interpretations in Naval History: Selected Papers from the Twelfth Naval History Symposium* (Annapolis 1997), p279. He also confirms that the United States naval air service was more advanced than the British Fleet Air Arm.

[33] This question is also discussed in Smithers, A J, *Taranto 1940* (Annapolis 1995), pp43-46. He points out the difficulty of obtaining trained men for maintaining naval aircraft.

[34] James Goldrick in *Doing Naval History* (New Haven, 1994), pp20-21. Range figures are somewhat deceptive. A land-based or carrier-launched plane had to join in a 'wave' and much its fuel would be used up waiting for other planes to join.

[35] Valle, Giuseppe, *Uomini nei cieli. Storia dell'aeronautica italiana* (2nd ed, Rome 1981).

[36] Santoro, *L'aeronautica italiana nella seconda guerra mondiale*, 2 vols, *passim*. As Curami writes, 'No criticisms were ever addressed to the fact, for example, that Santoro has falsified the minute Valle-Pricolo published by Canevari'. Emilio Canevari's two-volume work *La guerra*

italiana. retroscena di una disfatta (Rome, 1948) is best approached with caution, because he sympathized with the Fascist Regime, but at least he published complete documents.

[37] Curami, Andrea, 'Piani e progetti dell'aeronautica italiana 1939-1943', *Italia Contemporanea*, No 187 (June 1992), pp253-254 and Minniti, Fortunato, 'L'industria degli armamenti dal 1940 al 1943: i mercati, le produzioni', in Zamagni, Vera (ed), *Come perdere la guerra e vincere la pace* (Bologna 1997), pp55-148.

[38] Sullivan, Brian R, 'Prisoner in the Mediterranean', pp212-221 in Cogar, William B (ed), *New Interpretations in Naval History – 7th Naval History Symposium* (Wilmington 1988).

[39] Brown, D K, *Warrior to Dreadnought* (London 1997), p180, and Gatchel, Theodore L, *At the Water's Edge* (Annapolis 1996), p142. Gatchel also states that the effect of battleship shells in demoralising and defeating an enemy defence was crucial in the Second World War, see pp214-215.

[40] Sumida, Jon Tetsuro, 'The Best Laid Plans: The Development of British Battle-Fleet Tactics, 1919-1942', *The International History Review*, Vol XIV No 4 (November 1992). To better understand Japanese plans for long-range naval actions see the excellent Evans, David C, and Peattie, Mark R, *Kaigun* (Annapolis 1997), pp238-298.

[41] Greene, *Mare Nostrum*, pp68-69 (Iachino quote from his *Tramonto Di Una Grande Marina*).

[42] Another confirming view is given by Gerhard Schreiber in *Germany and the Second World War*, Vol III, pp87-89.

[43] Sumida, 'The Best Laid Plans: The Development of British Battle-Fleet Tactics, 1919-1942', and Campbell, *Naval Weapons of World War II, passim*. The French were also behind the British in night combat – see Marder, *From the Dardanelles to Oran*, p181. For another view to compare with Sumida, see Jurens, W L, 'The Evolution of Battleship Gunnery in the U.S. Navy, 1920-1945', *Warship International* No 3 (1991), pp240-271.

[44] Garzke, William, and Dulin, Robert, *BATTLESHIPS, Axis and Neutral Battleships in World War II* (Annapolis 1985), pp374-381 and de Toro, Augusto, 'Le Origini Politico-Diplomatiche delle Navi da Battaglia *Littorio* e *Vittorio Veneto*', *Bollettino D'Archivio* (March 1997), pp67-151.

[45] Bagnasco, Ermino, and Grossman, Mark, *Regia Marina; Italian Battleships of World War II* (Missoula 1986), p18.

[46] Campbell, *Naval Weapons of World War Two*, p67 and Fitzsimons, Bernard (ed), *The Illustrated Encyclopaedia of 20th Century Weapons & Warfare* (London 1977), pp401-403.

[47] See Nathan Okun's letter in *Warship International* No 1 (1978) pp67-72. Contains a nice diagram of how the system worked on page 70.

[48] Garzke and Dulin, *BATTLESHIPS*, p374.

[49] Bagnasco and Grossman, *Regia Marina*, pp64-67.

[50] Bargoni, Franco, and Gay, Franco, *Orizzonte Mare* (Rome 1972) Vol I, pp35-36 and Vol II, pp42-43.

[51] Koburger, *The Cyrano Fleet*, p16 states that the French had no ASDIC in 1940, apart from the promised loan of some British trawlers fitted with it. Le Masson, Henri, *The French Navy* (London 1969), 2 vols, indicates some French warships under construction were to be equipped with it.

[52] De la Sierra, Luis, *La Guerra Navale nel Mediterraneo (1940-1943)* (Milan 1987), p23; Couhet, Jean Labayle, *French Warships of World War II* (London 1971) *passim* and Le Masson, *The French Navy*, *passim*.

[53] See Elio Ando in *Warship Special 2, Super Destroyers* (London 1978) pp14-35, and John Jordan in *Warship 1996* (London 1996), p56.

[54] Gay, Franco and Valerio, *The Cruiser Bartolomeo Colleoni* (London, 1987), p6.

[55] The *Navigatori* class ships were called scouts until 1938 when they were reclassified as destroyers. See Ando in *Warship Special 2, Super Destroyers*, pp14-35. Sullivan in *Thirst* mentions the recovered British torpedo.

[56] Lassaque, Jean, *Les C.T. de 2400 tonnes du type Jaguar* (Bourg en Bresse, n.d. 1995?), p113. The *Leopard* was considered for the new gun.

[57] The French were in the process of receiving several sonar sets from the British when the Armistice came. See Guiglini, Jean, 'The 2400-tonners of the French Navy', *Warship International* No 2 (1981), p137 for some details on the planned addition of sonar sets.

[58] Rauber, Vitaliano, *La lotta antisommergibile* (Rome 1978), pp30-35.

[59] Ibid, pp30-35 and p338 Appendix 3. The first use by the *Albatros* was difficult because the sonar was not ready for action at the outbreak of war and needed technical support. Appendix 4 lists with some errors antisubmarine vessels equipped with sonar and the date of fitting. For the sonar supplied by Germany see the memo of the Supreme Command of 10 June 1943, 66 out of 112 requested. See NARS T821 roll 202 IT 1395, 'Materiali forniti o in attesa di fornitura in base ad accordi di scambio alla data del 10 giugno 1943'. Also see Sadkovich, J J, *The Italian Navy in World War II* (Westport 1994), p105. But his essay on the Italian Navy in Sadkovich, J J (ed), *Reevaluating Major Naval Combatants of World War II* (Westport 1990), p135 states only seven carried sonar by mid-1942.

[60] Fock, Harald, *Fast Fighting Boats* (Annapolis 1978), pp154-155.

[61] Bassett, Ronald, *HMS Sheffield* (Annapolis 1988), p7.

[62] Roskill, *Naval Policy Between the Wars*, Vol II, p165. The *Brooklyn* and *Mogami* class were at or over the maximum Treaty displacement of 10,000 tons. The British converted AA 'C' class cruisers would have the best record for destroying enemy aircraft – surpassing the *Dido* class. A total of ninety-seven planes are credited to British cruisers in the war – see Raven, Alan, and Roberts, John, *British Cruisers of World War Two* (Edinburgh 1980), p330.

[63] Roskill, *Naval Policy Between the Wars*, Vol II, p331 and Raven and Roberts, *British Cruisers of World War Two*, pp190-195. No other major power at that time was building cruisers that were this small, but Britain needed greater numbers of cruisers for trade defence, and this was part of the reason for the construction of the *Dido* class.

[64] Brice, Martin A, *The Tribals* (London 1971), *passim*.

[65] Roskill, *Naval Policy between the Wars*, Vol II, pp225-226. Campbell, *Naval Weapons of World War II, passim*. Italian light guns tended to have slower rates of fire compared to those of other combatants (fire cycles of 8-10 seconds versus 5-6 seconds), but this is a disadvantage only at short range – such as in night combat or firing at aircraft at short range.

[66] Fraccaroli, Aldo, *Italian Warships of World War II* (London 1968), pp31, 188-189; and Gay, *The Cruiser Bartolomeo Colleoni*, p9. We have relied heavily on Fraccaroli's fine book for much of the data on Italian warships.

[67] Bagnasco, E, and Rastelli A, *Storia Militare #1* (Parma 1993), pp21-29 and Bagnasco, E, *Le Armi Delle Navi Italiane* (Parma 1978), *passim*.

[68] Gerhard Schreiber in *Germany and the Second World War*, Vol III, p66.

[69] *Military Effectiveness*, Vol III, p142 and Koburger, *The Cyrano Fleet*, p13. Somerville had been taken ill while

C-in-C East Indies but had recovered by the time of his appointment in the Mediterranean. Italy's next two commanders would come directly from service afloat.

[70] Babington-Smith, Constance, *Air Spy: The Story of Photo Intelligence in World War II* (New York 1957), pp8-9. A dummy company was set up in London and used a Lockheed 12A to take colour and black and white photographs in the Mediterranean for the Air Ministry.

[71] Bargoni, *L'impegno Navale Italiano durante La Guerra Civile Spagnola (1936-1939)*, p272.

Chapter 4

[1] Mussolini quoted in Rimanelli, Marco 'The Least of the Powers: Italy's Foreign, Security & Naval Policy in the quest for Mediterranean Pre-Eminence, 1860s-1989' (UMI 1990) Vol. 2, p593.

[2] Schmider, Klaus, 'The Mediterranean in 1940-1941: Crossroads of Lost Opportunities?', *War & Society* Vol 15, No 2 (1997), pp19-41. A contrary view to Schmider is put forward in Weinberg, Gerhard L, *A World at Arms* (Cambridge 1994), pp324-327. The capture of Gibraltar and its possible ramifications is discussed in Chapter 10.

[3] Gerhard Schreiber in *Germany and the Second World War*, Vol III, p91.

[4] Sadkovich, *The Italian Navy in World War II*, pp34-36. Additional shipping was secured after the seizure of Vichy France in November 1942.

[5] Irving, David, *Hitler's War* (New York 1977), Vol I, p140.

[6] Marder, *From Dardanelles to Oran*, pp228-229. Force H was based at Gibraltar so it could operate either in the Atlantic or the Western Mediterranean. It was not always known as Force H, but for convenience we use that term exclusively.

[7] Salerno, 'The French Navy and the Appeasement of Italy 1937-9', pp78-100 and Auphan and Mordal, *The French Navy in World War II*, pp96-103.

[8] Shores, Christopher, *et al*, *Malta: The Spitfire Years* (London, 1991) p24. Because of the radar the air raid sirens would give 4 to 6 minutes warning before an attack.

[9] Attard, Joseph, *The Battle of Malta* (London 1980), pp12-46 gives a somewhat unbalanced, but heroic view of the siege. Pratt, *East of Malta, West of Suez*, p121. The RAF thought that after one day of Italian aerial bombardment Malta's dockyard facilities would be destroyed. For Dobbie see Jellison, *Beseiged*, p162.

[10] Parrish, Michael Woodbine, *Aegean Adventures 1940-1943* (Sussex 1993), p62.

[11] Dear, I C B, and Foot, M R D, *The Oxford Companion to World War II* (New York 1995), p597. Before the war SIM had read much of Britain and the Balkan nations' diplomatic mail. See Knox, *Mussolini Unleashed*, p6. A thorough history of Italian intelligence work in the Second World War has yet to be written.

[12] Hinsley, F H, *British Intelligence in the Second World War* (London 1979), Vol 1, pp191-219.

[13] Bragadin, Marc' Antonio, *The Italian Navy in World War II* (Annapolis 1957), p16.

[14] Spooner, Tony, *Supreme Gallantry* (London 1996), pp46-47. Bragadin claims all cables were cut.

[15] Salerno, *The Mediterranean Triangle*, pp270-271, 507. The lack of adequate planning for taking Malta will become apparent.

[16] Aldo Cocchia, A, *La Difesa Del Trafficao con L'Africa Settentrionale* (Rome 1976, 1977, and 1964 editions used respectively (volume numbered VI, VII, and VIII). Volume VI pp20-23.

[17] Rohwer and Hummelchen, *Chronology of the War at Sea 1939-1945*, pp22-23.

[18] Gill, G Hermon, *The Royal Australian Navy 1939-1942* (Canberra 1957), p167. The capture of the code book helped sink some of the ten submarines as the Italian subs used it until 5 July, see Hinsley, *British Intelligence*, Vol 1, pp208-209.

[19] Playfair, *The Mediterranean and the Middle East*, Vol 1, pp109-114 and Giorgerini, Giorgio, and Nani, Augusto, *Gli Incrociatori Italiani* (Rome 1971), pp360-362. According to the Italian histories, she did not suffer major damage in these attacks, though an attack on 12 June caused a troublesome fire – see *Warship International* No 1 (1972), p96. The RAF in the 1953 edition of their official history claim to have crippled her and that she was then beached, but used as an AA platform afterwards, see Richards, Denis, *The Royal Air Force 1939-1945* (London 1953), Vol 1, p245. Barrie Pitt repeats this error in *The Crucible Of War* (London, 1986), Vol 1, p157. Playfair is a little less clear, though on page 113 assumes the RAF reports were correct and the *San Giorgio* was damaged in the 12 June air attack. Later, when the port was under siege, the Royal Navy did station the destroyers HMAS *Stuart* and *Vampire* off Tobruk in case the *San Giorgio* sortied – see Gill, *The Royal Australian Navy, 1939-1942*, p291.

[20] *Diario Storico del Commando Supremo*, Vol 1, p12, 13 June 1940.

Chapter 5

[1] Marder, *From the Dardanelles to Oran*, p267.

[2] Simpson, Michael, 'Force H and British Strategy in the Western Mediterranean 1939-42', *The Mariner's Mirror*, Vol 83, No 1 (1997), pp63-64. Marder concludes it would have taken 18 months for the Axis to have prepared captured French ships for war. Hitler later considered seizing the fleet as early as January 1941. See Burdick, Charles B, *Germany's Military Strategy and Spain in World War II* (Syracuse 1968), p115.

[3] Our account of Mers-el-Kebir is drawn from Marder, *From the Dardanelles to Oran*, pp179-301; Coutau-Begarie, Herve, and Huan, Claude, *Mers-El-Kebir* (Paris 1994), *passim*; Dumas, Robert, *Les Cuirasses Dunkerque & Strasbourg* (Bourg-en-Bresse 1993), pp69-73; Tute, Warren, *The Deadly Stroke* (New York 1973), *passim*; Garzke, William H, and Dulin, Robert O, Jr, *Battleships – Allied Battleships in World War II* (Annapolis 1980), pp43-54; and Mainini, M R, 'L'attacco Navale Britannico a Mers-el-Kebir E Le Sue Conseguenze Sulle Clausole Armistiziali', *Bollettino D'Archivo* (March 1993), pp227-255. The maps of this action in Playfair are very generalised. We have relied on Marder and Herve Coutau-Begarie and Claude Huan. It should be noted that the *Richelieu* sortied from Dakar, where it had fled to at the time of the fall of France, steaming north, before returning on 26 June. Churchill's fear of this mighty ship fighting alongside the *Bismarck* may have been the trigger for Operation 'Catapult' – see Hines, Calvin W, 'Churchill and the French Dreadnoughts' in Cogar, William B (ed), *New Interpretations in Naval History – 7th Naval History Symposium* (Wilmington 1988), pp264-276.

[4] Marder, *From the Dardanelles to Oran*, p258.

[5] The use of spotting aircraft, which may have contributed to the accuracy of British gunfire, is mentioned in Thompson, Julian, *The War at Sea* (London 1996), p56.

[6] On 3 July she had sortied from Oran and had been fired on by two British light cruisers and the two battleships during the pursuit of the *Strasbourg*.

7 Esteva's report is not mentioned by Somerville in his papers. See Simpson, Michael (ed), *The Somerville Papers* (Aldershot 1995), *passim*.

8 Roskill, Stephen, *Churchill & the Admirals* (London 1977), p131. Cunningham considered the move against the French as reprehensible – an act of 'treachery' against friends. Also see Ollard, *Fisher and Cunningham*, pp88–94.

9 Thomas, *Britain and Vichy*, pp47–48, 67 and Irving, *Hitler's War*, p152. Thomas argues that the British were justified in doing this, especially as France had already violated the original terms of the alliance by asking for a separate armistice with Germany. A blockade of Vichy France was also in force. The policy of 'starve or De Gaulle' did result in much of the French African empire gradually declaring for the Free French.

10 Thomas, *Britain and Vichy*, pp66–67.

11 Ibid, pp1–2. Several uncompleted warships had been evacuated from Metropolitan France. The most important were the battleships *Jean Bart* which made Casablanca, and her sister-ship *Richelieu* which went to Dakar. The French Air Force had also moved many of their modern planes and supplies to North Africa before the Armistice – see Auphan and Mordal, *The French Navy in World War II*, pp99–103

12 Thomas, *Britain and Vichy*, pp54–55. Weygand was sent off to North Africa to command Vichy forces there shortly after the Armistice.

13 Cunningham, *A Sailor's Odyssey*, pp241–242. For a modern argument for pulling out of the Mediterranean see Barnett, Correlli, *Engage the Enemy More Closely* (New York 1991), pp670–671 and Barnett in Rodger, N A M (ed), *Naval Power in the Twentieth Century* (London 1996) pp124–127.

Chapter 6

1 Ollard, *Fisher and Cunningham*, p98. Most English-language accounts refer to this battle as the 'Action off Calabria' (though Peter C Smith calls it the Battle of Calabria in *Action Imminent*, p12), while German and Italian works, including their English translations, refer to it as the Battle of Punta Stilo, as we do here.

2 Cernuschi, Enrico, 'Sparammo meglio di quase tutti: le artiglierie navali italiane negli anni di guerra 1940-1943', *Rivista Marittima* (March 1992).

3 Gill, *The Royal Australian Navy 1939-1942*, Vol I, pp163-166; Cocchia, Aldo, *La Difesa del Traffico* (Rome 1977), Vol 6, pp23-25; and Playfair, *The Mediterranean and the Middle East*, Vol 1, p149. When the Japanese undertook similar operations later in the war, they were better planned and the destroyers were able to use their torpedoes.

4 Playfair, *The Mediterranean and the Middle East*, Vol 1, p150

5 *Diario Storico Comando Supremo*, Vol I, p113, 2 July 1940. The principal source for this section is Mattesini, Francesco, *La Battaglia Di Punta Stilo* (Rome 1990), *passim*. The convoys are listed in Cocchia, *La Difesa Del Traffico con L'Africa Settentrionale*, 3 vols, and also used is Fioravanzo, Giuseppe, *Le Azioni Navali in Mediterraneo* (Rome 1970), Vol I, pp99-154.

6 Smith, *Action Imminent*, *passim*; Mattesini, *La Battaglia Di Punta Stilo*, *passim*; Shores, *Malta: The Hurricane Years 1940-1941*, p28; and Caruana, Joseph, 'I convogli britannici per Malta', *Storia Militare*, No 43 (1997), pp25-33. Almost all sources give only four ships in MS 1 but according to Caruana the *Tweed* also sailed.

7 Sadkovich, *The Italian Navy in World War II*, p57, and Hinsley, *British Intelligence in the Second World War*, Vol

I, p209. A short overview of the story of British intercepts of Italian navy ciphers is on p210 of Hinsley. For the condition of the *Malaya* see Smith, *Action Imminent*, p29.

8 Smith, *Action Imminent*, pp39-41. The *Phoenix* would be lost to Italy's only submarine chaser the *Albatros* off Augusta on 16 July 1940.

9 Cunningham, *A Sailor's Odyssey*, p258, and the *Sydney* story is from Warner, Oliver, *Admiral of the Fleet Lord Cunningham of Hyndhope* (Athens, Ohio 1967), p104.

10 Smith, *Action Imminent*, p43.

11 *Diario Storico Comando Supremo*, Vol I, p 150, 8 July 1940. The message to Campioni from *Supermarina* is in Mattesini, *La battaglia di Punta Stilo*, p32.

12 Mattesini, *La battaglia di Punta Stilo*, p82, n105.

13 Hinsley, *British Intelligence in the Second World War*, Vol 1, pp193-7 and PRO, ADM 223/121 message n 891 of the Operational Intelligence Centre, Malta, 10 July 1940.

14 Only crews of 6in and lighter guns had received any training in night combat before the war. For shell weights it was 1938lb and 1157lb respectively. *Malaya* and *Royal Sovereign* were both armed with 15in Mark I, the *Warspite* had Mark I/N (modified for 30° elevation), see Campbell, *Naval Weapons of World War Two*, pp23-25, 322-324. Italian guns tended to have lower rates of fire then comparable Allied ordnance, but rate of fire was not a critical factor at long ranges.

15 Mattesini in his *La battaglia di Punta Stilo* now holds the view that this was correct, but *Supermarina* was criticised for years afterwards for this decision. For differing views see Iachino, Angelo, *Tramonto di una Grande Marina* (Verona 1962), pp201-205; Knox, *Mussolini Unleashed*, p147; and Smith, *Action Imminent*, p65.

16 Smith, *Action Imminent*, p54.

17 Mattesini, *La battaglia di Punta Stilo*, p52. See also the naval air report published on p198 and Smith, *Action Imminent*, p56-57. Quote is from the latter. Smith mistakes the *Bolzano* for the *Trieste*, the latter being absent from this action.

18 Tullio Marcon, *Storia Militare*, No 9 (June 1994), pp14-27.

19 Smith, *Action Imminent*, pp63-64.

20 Mattesini, *La battaglia di Punta Stilo*, pp55-6. Campioni wrote that he received the message when almost in contact with the enemy. He was to take into account the presence of other ships beside those sighted.

21 Interview by the authors with Giuseppe Grotto who served on board the *Cesare*, who commented on the dirty optical equipment.

22 Cunningham's report is in PRO, ADM 199/1048, n.0112/00212, 29 January 1941, and also published in the Supplement to the *London Gazette* of 28 April 1948. Sadkovich incorrectly states that the *Cesare* was hit twice. AUSSME, I4, bundle 10, 4, Relazione sulle operazioni navali dei giorni 6, 7, 8 e 9 luglio 1940-XVIII (Azione di Punta Stilo) pp30-31. Quote is from Cunningham, *A Sailor's Odyssey*, p262.

23 Mattesini, *La battaglia di Punta Stilo*, pp178-179.

24 Playfair, *The Mediterranean and the Middle East*, Vol I, p153. Cunningham used the same words in his report, and described the smoke tactics as impressive.

25 Hinsley, *British Intelligence in the Second World War*, p209.

26 Knox, *Mussolini Unleashed*, p147, and Santoro, Giuseppe, *L'Aeronautica Italiana nella Seconda Guerra Mondiale*, (2nd edition, Rome 1966), Vol I, pp423-424. Twenty-four Italian planes were damaged.

27 Shores, *Malta: The Hurricane Years, 1940-41*, p30.

[28] March, *British Destroyers*, p293. The loss of the *Escort* varies from source to source, including that she was with Cunningham, but she was actually assigned to Force H. See Simpson (ed), *The Somerville Papers*, p117.

[29] AUSMM, Scontri navali e operazioni di guerra, cartella 4, c/2, 'Promemoria per S.E. il Sottocapo di Stato Maggiore', no date, signed by General F Fasano.

[30] *Warship International* No 4 (1985), pp331-332, and No 2 (1986), p115 and Raven and Roberts, *British Battleships of World War Two* (Annapolis 1976), p221.

[31] Somerville, after being criticised for his conduct of Mers-el-Kebir, thought he would be relieved of command – see Barnett, *Engage the Enemy More Closely*, pp226-227.

[32] Knox's view that Mussolini could not get his admirals to fight after this action seems too strong, as we will shortly see. See Knox, *Mussolini Unleashed*, p287.

[33] Mattesini, *La battaglia di Punta Stilo*, pp245-253.

[34] Respectively in his report to the Admiralty, PRO, ADM199/1048, n. 0112/00212, 29 January 1941, p 2, n 7 and in his memoirs, *A Sailor's Odyssey*, p262.

[35] Santoni, Alberto, *Da Lissa alle Falkland. Storia e politica navale dell'età contemporanea* (Milan 1987), p167; Bagnasco, Erminio, *Le armi delle navi italiane* (Parma 1978), and Santoni, 'Perché le navi italiane in guerra non colpivano in bersaglio', *Rivista Storica* (March 1994), pp36-47. But see also the opposing view in Cernuschi, Enrico, 'Sparammo meglio di quasi tutti: le artiglierie navali italiane negli anni di guerra 1940-1943', *Rivista Marittima* (March 1992), and his reply to Santoni, 'Colpito e occultato?', *Rivista Storica* (July 1994), pp22-33 in which he claims that many minor hits scored by Italian guns were not admitted by the British.

[36] Campbell, *Naval Weapons of World War Two*, pp21, 25, 320-322. The quotation is on p21.

[37] Giorgerini, Giorgio, *Da Matapan al Golfo Persico. La Marina militare italiana dal fascismo alla Repubblica* (Milan 1989), pp395-396 and p456, n13. Unfortunately the author does not explain where these documents were made available to him. See also Iachino, *Il Tramonto di una grande marina*, pp61-2.

[38] Mattesini, *La battaglia di Punta Stilo*, p125, and Campioni's battle report published as document n 36 in the same volume, p188. Bragadin notes that no Italian fighters operated over the fleet during the battle

[39] AUSSME, 14, fasc. 10/9, 'Promemoria sull'attività delle forze navali inglesi' 21 July 1940. The assessment made by Cunningham was similar: he thought that the value of the action was that it showed the 'Italians that their air force and submarines cannot stop our Fleet penetrating into the Central Mediterranean', see his already quoted report p4. During a meeting on 26 January 1939, Cavagnari said the experiments on torpedo aircraft were cancelled and he would not spend any more money. See the minute of the meeting published in Ceva, Lucio, 'Appunti per una storia dello Stato Maggiore generale fino alla vigilia della non belligeranza (giugno 1925-luglio 1939)' Alberto Santoni. *Da Lissa alle Falkland. Storia e politica navale dell'età contemporanea*, (Milan 1987), p167, Erminio Bagnasco. *Le armi delle navi italiane*, (Parma 1978), Alberto Santoni. 'Perché le navi italiane in guerra non colpivano in bersaglio', *Rivista storica*, (March 1994), pp36-47. But see also the opposed view of Cernuschi, Enrico, 'Sparammo meglio di quasi tutti: le artiglierie navali italiane negli anni di guerra 1940-1943', in *Rivista marittima* (March 1992); and his reply to Santoni 'Colpito e occultato?', *Rivista storica* (July 1994), pp22-33 in which he holds that many minor hits scored by Italian naval guns were not admitted by British sources, *Storia Contemporanea* 2 (1979), pp207-254.

[40] Muggeridge (ed), *Ciano's Diary*, pp276-277.

[41] PRO, ADM199/1048, n. 0112/00212, 29 January 1941, part 17: Operation M.A.5 – Bombing summary, AUSSME, 14, bundle 10, 9, 'Promemoria sull'attività delle forze navali inglesi'.

[42] Bundesarchiv-Militärarchiv, RL 9/52, Verbindungsstab zur Italienischen Luftwaffe, Nr. 27/40.23 July 1940 'Übersicht über die Unternehmungen der italienischen Flotte und Luftwaffe vom 6.7. bis 13.7.40', p5. The order is published in Mattesini, *La battaglia di Punta Stilo*, p104, and was received later at 10.40pm. Again Campioni did not change his opinion. Later the War Diary of German Naval Staff recognised this fact on 9 July 1940, see Rahn, Werner, Schreiber, Gerhard, and Maierhofer, Hansjoseph (eds), *Kriegstagebuch der Seekriegsleitung, 1939-1945* (Bonn 1989), Part A, Vol 11, p102, and Bundesarchiv-Militärarchiv – Freinug i. Br. (thereafter BA-MA), RL 9/52, Verbindungsstab zur Italienischen Luftwaffe, Nr. 32/40, 2 August 1940: 'Geleitzugunternehmen Nr. 2 Tripolis', pp2-3.

[43] BA-MA, RM 7/233, Italienische Kriegführung, Verbindungsstab zur Admiralstab der Kgl. ital. Marine, Nr. 70/40 of the 12.7.40: 'Mitteilungen des italienischen Admiralstabes', especially sheets 14 and 15.

[44] Rahn, Schreiber and Maierhofer (eds), *Kriegstagebuch der Seekriegsleitung 19391945*, Part A, Vol 11, p148, 13 July 1940. The possibility of employment of Italian submarines in the Atlantic was discussed on the 18th, see pp202-203, BA-MA, RM 7/233, Italienische Kriegführung, Verbindungsstab zur Admiralstab der Kgl. ital. Marine, Nr. 55/40, 10 July 1940: 'Militärischer Bericht Nr. 2: Operation der italienischen Kriegsmarine zur Überführung eines wichtigen Transportes nach Libyen (Bengasi)'.

[45] Schreiber, Gerhard, 'Sul teatro mediterraneo nella seconda guerra mondiale', *Rivista Marittima* (March 1987), pp77-94. See also Schreiber, 'Italien im Machtpolitischen Kalkül der deutsche Marineführung 1919 bis 1945', QFIAB (1982), Vol 82, pp222-269 and *Revisionismus und Weltmachtstreben. Marineführung und deutsch-italienische Beziehungen 1919 bis 1944* (Stuttgart, DVA, 1987), *Kriegstagebuch der Seekriegsleitung, 1939-1945*, Part A, vol 11, p 219, 19.7.40.

[46] Rahn, Schreiber and Maierhofer (eds), *Kriegstagebuch der Seekriegsleitung, 1939-1945*, Part A, Vol 11, p 148, 13.7.40. The possibility of employment of Italian submarine in the Atlantic were discussed on 18th, see pp202-203, BA-MA, RM 7/233, Italienische Kriegführung, Verbindungsstab zur Admiralstab der Kgl. ital. Marine, Nr. 14/40, 5 July 1940: 'Militärische Bericht Nr. 1. Italienische U-Bootskriegführung', sheet 9.

Chapter 7

[1] Maugeri, Franco, *From the Ashes of Disgrace* (New York 1948), p16. Maugeri's book is quite interesting since because of it he was accused by many of supplying the Allies with convoy sailings and routes, which we now know was due largely to ULTRA and not 'the man at the end of the pier'. See Kesselring, Albert, *Memoirs of Field-Marshal Kesselring* (London 1953), p114 who claims Maugeri was 'responsible . . . [for] the loss of many lives'. For years the Italian version of Maugeri's book was suppressed.

[2] For Cape Spada we have relied on Playfair, *The Mediterranean and the Middle East*, Vol 1, pp156-158; Gill, *The Royal Australian Navy 1939-1942*, Vol I, pp184-196; Sadkovich, *The Italian Navy in World War II*, pp63-67; Fioravanzo, *Le Azioni Navali in Mediterraneo*, Vol 1,

pp160-180; Santoro, *L'Aeronautica Italiana nella Seconda Guerra Mondiale*, Vol I, pp442-447; and Gay, *The Cruiser Bartolomeo Colleoni*, *passim*.

³ See Marcon, Tullio, 'I velivoli catapultabili in guerra (1939-1945)', *Storia militare* No 9 (June 1994), pp14-27, and No 10 (July 1994), pp17-27, especially the first part listing the main launches of seaplanes during various Mediterranean battles.

⁴ There is a picture of the *Bande Nere* in heavy seas showing spray over the bow in a Sea State of 5 in *Dimensione Cielo Caccia Assalto*, Vol 4, p21. Special thanks to Andrew Smith for helping the authors wade through this point.

⁵ A recently published photograph taken from the *Neptune* of the *Warspite* under fire at Punta Stilo shows a dispersed fall of three 12.6in shells, with two of the shells off line astern of her. Also noted in the article was that the salvo was quite dispersed, tending to confirm this problem with Italian fire. See Brescia, Maurizio, '9 Luglio 1940: un 'Punto di Vista' Inglese', *Storia Militare* No 43 (April 1997), pp56.

⁶ Cernuschi, Enrico, 'Colpito e occultato?', *Rivista storica* (July 1994), p28.

⁷ Lowry, Thomas P, *The Attack on Taranto* (Mechanicsburg 1995). A recent book, it makes virtually no use of non-English works.

⁸ For speed see Playfair, Vol 1, p156 and compare with Fraccaroli, *Italian Warships of World War II*, p31 – we think a top speed of 33 knots is probably accurate. For armour see Bragadin, p31 who refers to the *Sydney* as an 'armoured cruiser'. Sadkovich argues that the rapid fire of the British destroyers gave them an advantage, see pp63-64. For alleged Italian superiority see Knox, *Mussolini Unleashed*, p148 and Ollard, *Fisher and Cunningham*, p100. Franco and Valerio Gay on p16 give ranges for the *Sydney* opening fire as far too close. The Mark IX torpedo was carried by all British ships in this action and had a maximum range of 13,500 yards when set for 30 knots (Campbell says 15,000 yards); see Poland, *The Torpedomen*, p104.

⁹ Fioravanzo, *Le Azioni Navali in Mediterraneo*, Vol 1, p177.

¹⁰ Muggeridge (ed), *Ciano's Diary 1939-1943*, p278.

¹¹ Sadkovich, *The Italian Navy in World War II*, p66.

¹² Shores, *Malta: The Hurricane Years 1940-41*, p41.

¹³ Ibid, pp45-50, Rohwer and Hummelchen, *Chronology of the War at Sea 1939-1945*, p30 (who leave out the *Resolution*), and Playfair, *The Mediterranean and the Middle East*, Vol I, pp159-162. Various accounts list two or four cruisers.

¹⁴ Arena, Nino, *La Regia Aeronautica* (Rome 1981), Vol 1, p436, and *Diario Storico Comando Supremo* (Rome 1986), Vol 1, p306. Arena says two wings, but the Diary states two squadrons.

¹⁵ Shores, *Malta: The Hurricane Years 1940-41*, p47.

¹⁶ Cunningham, *A Sailor's Odyssey*, p269. Rimington also launched a daring attack against the old *San Giorgio* in Tobruk harbour but the torpedoes exploded in the mud banks of the harbour. See Rohwer, *Chronology of the War at Sea*. The *Osiris* sank the *Palestro* off Albania.

¹⁷ Knox, *Mussolini Unleashed*, pp173-174. The details of this incident were buried until 1960, and did not 'officially' appear in Italian naval histories until 1972. Contrasting views of the incident appear in *Warship International*, Vol VI, No 2 (1969), pp147-148 and No3 (1971), pp226-229 from, among others, Dr. Peter Brook and Andrew Smith. They culminated in a rather sarcastic letter from Peter C Smith in No 2 (1975), p157.

¹⁸ Sadkovich, *The Italian Navy in World War II*, p73.

¹⁹ Santoro, *L'Aeronautica Italiana nella Seconda Guerra Mondiale*, Vol I, pp377-379; and Sadkovich. *The Italian Navy in World War II*, p67. Italy would lose thirty-five planes over Malta in 1940.

²⁰ Pinna's report is commented on in Arena, *La regia aeronautica*, Vol I, pp82-83. The comment on bomb storage is from Curami, Andrea, 'Tecnologia e modelli di armamento', in Zamagni, Vera (ed), *Come perdere la guerra e vincere la pace* (Bologna 1997), pp149-183.

²¹ De Lorenzo, Giovanni, 'L'Aeronautica in guerra (Primo anno)', in Rainero, R H, and Biagini, A (eds), *L'Italia in guerra. Il primo anno, 1940* (Rome 1991), pp85-132.

²² *Dimensione Cielo Caccia Assalto*, Vol 5, pp16-22.

²³ AUSSME, *Diario storico comando supremo*, 1445/A, Fasc.1, Pricolo to Badoglio, allegato 97.

²⁴ Arena, *La Regia Aeronautica 1939-1943*, Vol 1, pp462ff.

²⁵ See Minniti, Fortunato, '"Il nemico vero". Gli obiettivi dei piani di operazione contro la Gran Bretagna nel contesto etiopico (maggio 1935-maggio 1936)', *Storia contemporanea* XXVI, No 4 (1995), pp575-602, who notes the air force and army war plans utilised the same number of planes. Thus, as Minniti wrote, 'the plans of the Air Force followed the denomination, number, and edition date as those of the army'. See Minniti, Fortunato, 'Gli obiettivi di guerra nella pianificazione operativa (1938-1940)', in Rainero and Biagini (eds), *L'Italia in guerra. Il primo anno 1940*, pp11-17.

²⁶ Giorgerini, Giorgio, *Da Matapan al Golfo Persico. La Marina militare italiana dal fascismo alla Repubblica* (Milan 1989), pp464-6. Valle quote from Valle, Giuseppe, *Uomini nei cieli. Storia dell'aeronautica Italiana* (Rome 1981), p410. In any case it should noted that Valle ordered the preparation of the attachments for torpedoes on some S.79s, as confirmed by evidence in NARS T821/144, IT1222 'Relazione per SE il Capo di Stato Maggiore Generale, 1° semestre 1939', dated 25 August 1939.

²⁷ *Diario Storico Commando Supremo*, Vol 1, Part 2, pp171-172.

²⁸ Casali, Antonio, and Cattaruzza, Marina, *Sotto i mari del mondo. La Whitehead 1875-1990* (Bari 1990), p196. Germany would receive about 1000 torpedoes from Italy in the course of the war.

²⁹ Cunningham, *A Sailor's Odyssey*, p270. Cunningham thought at first that magnetic mines had been dropped. The torpedoes were never recovered.

³⁰ Unia, Carlo, *Storia degli aerosiluranti italiani* (Rome 1974), pp77-81.

³¹ De Lorenzo, 'L'Aeronautica in guerra (Primo anno)', in *L'Italia in guerra. Il primo anno, 1940*, pp85-132.

³² Cunningham, *A Sailor's Odyssey*, p271; Gill, *The Royal Australian Navy 1939-1942*, Vol I, pp206-207 and Santoro, *L'Aeronautica Italiana nella Seconda Guerra Mondiale*, Vol I, pp547-548. Both Cunningham and Rohwer and Hummelchen, *Chronology of the War at Sea 1939-1945*, p31, incorrectly state twelve aircraft were shot down.

³³ Hinsley, *British Intelligence in the Second World War*, Vol I, p211.

³⁴ The loss of the *Iride* is based on Borghese, *Sea Devils*, pp33-35; Spertini, Marco and Bagnasco, Erminio, *I Mezzi D'Assalto della Xth Flottiglia MAS* (Parma 1991), p38; De Risio, Carlo, *I Mezzi D'Assalto* (4th ed, Rome 1992), pp21-39; Bertini, *I sommergibili in Mediterraneo*, pp80-82; Bagnasco and Rastelli, *Sommergibili in guerra*, pp43 and 185; and Newton and Hampshire, *Taranto*, pp65-67. N

³⁵ The 1943 Armistice would see Borghese remain with the Axis, while De Courten would be the chief of Naval

Staff for the Italian fleet that joined the Allies. Their personal enmity may explain Borghese's accusation.

[36] Report of Giorgini, the first commander of the 1st Flotilla *MAS*, is quoted from De Risio, Carlo, *I mezzi d'assalto* (Rome 1994), p22.

[37] The account of 'HATS' relies on Cunningham, *A Sailor's Odyssey*, pp271-273; Shores, *Malta: The Hurricane Years 1940-41*, pp57-60; Gill, *The Royal Australian Navy 1939-1942*, Vol I, pp208-211; Playfair, *The Mediterranean and the Middle East*, Vol I, pp190-192, 201-204; Sadkovich, *The Italian Navy in World War II*, pp81-85; Fioravanzo, *Le Azioni Navali in Mediterraneo*, Vol 1 pp181-191, and Rohwer and Hummelchen, *Chronology of the War at Sea 1939-1945*, p32.

[38] Bragadin, *The Italian Navy in World War II*, p33.

[39] Bassett, *HMS Sheffield*, pp53-54, 72.

[40] Ibid, p73. The *Ark Royal* was never fitted with radar in the course of the war, depending on the *Sheffield*, which, with the *Rodney*, was one of the two ships fitted with each Type 79 radar at the outbreak of war.

[41] Knox, *Mussolini Unleashed*, p149. Badoglio at this time started to move towards the navy's position that a this would be a long war. Some sources have five Italian battleships in the fleet sortie, but the *Cesare* had suffered a condenser problem and remained in port.

[42] Some sources incorrectly give this force as six cruisers. The three destroyers were large ships all of the *Le Fantasque* class with a loaded displacement over 3000 tons each. See Marder, Arthur, *Operation Menace* (Oxford 1976). North's removal was protested by Somerville, which was another mark against him in Churchill's eyes. This would come to a head after the Battle of Spartivento.

[43] Iachino, *Il Tramonto di una grande marina*, pp222-224.

[44] An excellent sequence of three photos of the *Gondar's* sinking appears in Bagnasco, Erminio, and Rastelli, Achille, *Sommergibili in Guerra* (2nd ed, Parma 1994), pp44-45. The Italian prisoners did not disclose their mission or the existence of the SLCs to their captors.

[45] Borghese, *Sea Devils*, pp58-73.

[46] Based on Rohwer and Hummelchen, *Chronology of the War at Sea 1939-1945*, pp37-38; Cunningham, *A Sailor's Odyssey*, pp278-279; Shores, *Malta: The Hurricane Years 1940-41*, pp74-75; Gill, *The Royal Australian Navy 1939-1942*, Vol I, pp224-226; Playfair, *The Mediterranean and the Middle East*, Vol I, pp220-222; De La Sierra, *La Guerra Navale nel Mediterraneo (1940-1943)*, pp118-125; Sadkovich, *The Italian Navy in World War II*, pp88-89; and Fioravanzo, *Le Azioni Navali in Mediterraneo*, Vol 1 pp196-212. For the issue of fuel for the Axis see Antonucci, Michael, 'Blood for Oil', *Command*, No 20 (1993), pp34-41.

[47] Hezlet, *Electronics and Sea Power*, pp195-196.

[48] Quote from the *Ajax* after-action report dated 28 December 1940. The 3.9in gun fired a shell weighing 30.4lbs, the Italian 4.7in shell weight was 51.79lbs, while the British 6in weighed in at 112lbs. The Italian ships were unarmoured.

[49] *Ajax* thought she engaged three, not four destroyers, and suffered additional damage from the blast of her own guns due to prolonged low-angle fire at short ranges.

[50] See also PRO, ADM199/797 39706 with the comments on casualties and damage received by the *Ajax*. Losses are shown as lower in other sources – this is how Captain McCarthy reported them.

[51] PRO, ADM199/797 39706, Pridham-Wippell to CiC, Mediterranean 27 February 1941 accompanying the report of action of HMS *Ajax* on 12 October 1940.

[52] AUSSMM, *Promemoria di Supermarina 1941*, Promemoria No.84 of 27 April 1941: 'Azioni notturne. Munizionamento e modalità di tiro del nemico'.

[53] Bagnasco and Rastelli, *Sommergibili in guerra*, p53. Some sources say 6 October.

[54] See Bertini, *I sommergibili in Mediterraneo*, Vol I, p100, and photographs in Bagnasco and Rastelli, *Sommergibili in guerra*, pp20, 38.

[55] Rohwer and Hummelchen, *Chronology of the War at Sea 1939-1945*, p37 states the *Hyperion* as being sunk by this minefield field, but later (p45) gives her as being sunk by the submarine *Serpente*. See Brown, David, *Warship Losses of World War Two* (London 1995), p40. The Italians give probable credit to the minefields for the losses of both destroyers, since the *Serpente* operated some 240 miles away: see Lupinacci, Pier Filippo, *La guerra di mine* (2nd ed, Rome 1988), pp161-162 and Bertini, *I sommergibili italiani*, tomo I, pp117-118.

[56] Bertini, Marcello, *I sommergibili in Mediterraneo* (Rome 1972), tomo I, p 96; Bagnasco and Rastelli, *Sommergibili in guerra*, p48 and Rohwer, Jürgen, *Allied Submarine Attacks of World War Two, European Theatre of Operations, 1939-1945* (Annapolis 1997), p128.

[57] Bagnasco and Rastelli, *Sommergibili in guerra*, p48.

[58] The Greeks did not expect an Italian attack after 21 October because of the weather but the Greek General Staff told the British military attache that '. . . they were equally convinced that a combined German and Italian attack would be launched in the spring of 1941'. Cruickshank, Charles, *Greece 1940-1941* (Newark 1976), p157. Quote on neutrality breaches from Andrew Smith in *Warship International* No 2 (1975), p158.

[59] Malakkasses, John T, 'The Greek Navy in the Eastern Mediterranean During World War II', and Papastratis, Procopis, 'A Fighting Navy in Exile' in Sweetman, Jack (ed), *New Interpretations in Naval History – 10th Naval History Symposium* (Annapolis 1993). The two new Greek destroyers were armed with German 5in guns, so when one escaped to fight on with the Allies it made procuring additional ammunition for her very difficult!

Chapter 8

[1] Quoted in Curami, Andrea, 'I Riflessi delle Operazioni nello Suiluppo della Regia Aeronautica', in *L'Italia in Guerra, Il Secondo Anno – 1941*, p495.

[2] Newton, Don, and Hampshire, A Cecil, *Taranto* (London 1961), pp12-15.

[3] Taranto is based on Schofield, *The Attack on Taranto*; Shores, *Malta: The Hurricane Years 1940-41*, pp81-88; Rohwer and Hummelchen, *Chronology of the War at Sea 1939-1945*, pp40-41; Playfair, *The Mediterranean and the Middle East*, Vol I, pp235-238; Fioravanzo, *Le Azioni Navali in Mediterraneo*, Vol 1, pp213-257; Santoni, Alberto, 'L'attacco aerosilurante inglese a Taranto', *Rivista Italiana Difesa* (November 1990), pp88-97; Lowry, *The Attack on Taranto, passim*; and Smithers, *Taranto 1940, passim* – the latter is unreliable on details, and Newton and Hampshire are also unreliable on details but provide probably the best-written account.

[4] Schofield says three destroyers, Cunningham six destroyers, while Rohwer and Hummelchen list the *Encounter*, *Greyhound*, *Griffin*, and *Gallant*. The *Encounter* later rejoined Force H.

[5] 'Two heavy explosions were felt which may have been from torpedoes.' PRO, ADM199/797 39706 *Operation MB8 Narrative of Commander in Chief, Mediterranean*.

[6] Santoro, *L'aeronautica italiana nella seconda guerra mondiale*, Vol I, p448. The British point of view is in PRO, ADM199/797 39706, *Operation MB.8, Summary of air attacks*.

[7] The Photo Reconnaissance Unit (PRU) would later receive some specialised Hurricanes which were stationed at Malta and elsewhere in the Mediterranean by 1941 for these operations. With ULTRA producing constant information on convoy sailings, it would be part of the role of reconnaissance planes to find a convoy at sea and allow for an attack by ships or planes while not betraying the ULTRA secret.

[8] Several good photographs, including the hole near her keel, appear in the *Orizzonte Mare* series, *Corazze class conte di cavour*, Vol 1, pp54-60. The prisoners had been roughly handled by dockyard workers before the military rescued them.

[9] Again, the *Orizzonte Mare* series, *Corazze class vittorio veneto*, Vol 3/II, pp82-83 has an excellent diagram showing the extent of damage and final beached trim of the *Littorio*.

[10] Santoro, *L'aeronautica italiana nella seconda guerra mondiale*, Vol I, p448-449.

[11] Herde, Peter, *Pearl Harbor* (Milan 1986), pp400-401.

[12] Iachino, Angelo, *Le due Sirti* (Milano 1953), p68. In Lowry's book he makes a broad comparison to Pearl Harbor – in fact it is subtitled 'Blueprint for Pearl Harbor'.

[13] The report is in BA-MA, RM 7/233 dated 21 November 1940 No. 16742/40), *The War Diary of the German Naval Staff (Skl)*. Baum, Walter, and Weichold, Eberhard, *Der Krieg der 'Achsenmächte' im Mittelmeerraum. Die 'Strategie' der Diktatoren* (Göttingen 1973), p68.

[14] Rahn, Schreiber and Maierhofer (eds), *Kriegstagebuch der Seekriegsleitung, 1939-1945*, Part A, vol 15, notes on date 12, 13 and 14 November 1940.

[15] Ferrante, Ezio, 'Il ruolo della marina italiana nella campagna di Grecia tra strategia logistica e operativa, L'Italia in guerra 1940-1943', in Micheletti, Bruna, and Poggio, Pier Paolo (eds), *Annali della Fondazione Micheletti* (Brescia 1990/91) No 5, pp268.

[16] *East of Malta, West of Suez* (British Admiralty account, 1943) p38.

[17] Sadkovich, *The Italian Navy in World War II*, p94.

[18] Hone, Thomas C, 'Battleships vs. Aircraft Carriers: The Pattern of U.S. Navy Operating Expenditures, 1932-1941', *Military Affairs* (October 1977), pp133-141.

[19] Quote from Sadkovich, James J, 'Aircraft Carriers and the Mediterranean 1940-1943', *Aerospace Historian* (December 1987), pp263-271 and Marco Rimanelli's dissertation 'The Least of the Powers: Italy's foreign, security & naval Policy in the Quest for Mediterranean Pre-Eminence: 1860s-1989' (John Hopkins 1989), p738. Rimanelli points out that in the 1921 report there was no discussion of the aircraft carrier and how it might aid in amphibious operations.

[20] Goldrick, James, 'The Problems of Modern Naval History', in Hattendorf, John B (ed), *Doing Naval History* (Newport 1995), pp20-22 and Campbell, *Naval Weapons of World War Two*, *passim*.

[21] Rimanelli, Marco, 'The Least of the Powers', *passim*.

[22] Polastro, Walter, 'La marina militare italiana nel primo dopguerra (1918-1925)', *Il Risorgimento*, No 3 (1977), pp127-170, and Fioravanzo, Giuseppe, *L'organizzazione della Marina durante il conflitto* (Rome 1973), Vol 1 pp 52-532. This is volume XXI of the series *La marina italiana nella seconda guerra mondiale*. Revel actually handed in his resignation when an army general was proposed as supreme head of the navy (and air force). But he was already upset over the lack of a fleet air arm (land based or carrier) as discussed in De Risio, Carlo, *L'aviazione di marina* (Rome 1995), *passim*.

[23] Cordon, Fulvio, 'Il problema aeronavale italiano', in *Bollettino d'archivio US* June 1991, pp161-176; Sept. 1991, pp147-162; Dec. 1991, pp71-82; March 1992, pp211-234; June 1992, pp199-217; Sept. 1992, pp29-54; Dec. 1992, pp29-52.

[24] Fioravanzo, *L'organizzazione della Marina durante il conflitto*, Vol 1, pp52-53.

[25] For the aircraft carriers, see Bernotti, Romeo, *Cinquant'anni nella Marina militare* (Milan 1971), pp169, 234-5.

[26] Quote from Knox, *Mussolini Unleashed*, pp19-25; Santoni, *Da Lissa alle Falkland*, p169. Sadkovich, 'Aircraft Carriers and the Mediterranean 1940-1943', *Aerospace Historian*, *passim*. Santoni's quote is from Santoni, Alberto, 'Italian Naval Policy from 1930-1941', *Revue Internationale d'Histoire Militaire*, No 73 (1991), p93.

[27] Giorgerini, *Da Matapan al Golfo Persico*, pp420-422, 513-517.

[28] Serge, Claudio G, *Italo Balbo* (Berkeley 1987), pp188-189.

[29] Gat, Azar, 'Futurism, Proto-Fascist Culture and the Sources of Douhetism', *War & Society*, Vol 15, No 1 (May 1997), pp31-51.

[30] Sadkovich, 'Aircraft Carriers and the Mediterranean 1940-1943', *passim*. He points out that the failure to develop torpedo-bombers and dive-bombers for antishipping duties was almost criminal in since in 1935 an Italian Air Force bomb practice witnessed by Bernotti on two stationary ships failed to achieve any hits! Sadkovich, *The Italian Navy in World War II*, p7. Beginning in 1936, 1217 S.79s (*Sparviere*) were built, and originally designed as a high-level bomber capable of bomb loads of between 1100-4400lbs, depending upon the range and engines fitted. This was the plane type used in the bombing of Guernica during the Spanish Civil War. They had been very successful in carrying out raids on Republican ports in 1938 but against stationary shipping. Howson, Gerald, *Aircraft of the Spanish Civil War* (London 1990), pp270-273 and Angelucci, Enzo, and Matricardi, Paolo, *World War II Airplanes* (Chicago 1976), Vol 1, pp198-200. Roskill, *Naval Policy Between the Wars*, Vol II, pp390-91 incorrectly says far fewer ships were sunk.

[31] Vian would suffer at the Second Battle of the Sirte from lack of an adequate air component and it allowed Iachino to maintain air control observing the British. See Ch. 16.

[32] AUSSMM, *Promemoria di Supermarina, Promenmoria No. 16 of 17January.1941*, 'Trasformazione di piroscafi in navi portaerei'. The memoranda proves that the navy was still dragging its feet since it includes the sentence: 'Although we doubt for obvious reasons that the ship could be completed before the end of the conflict, it appears convenient to go ahead with the project to affirm for the future that the carrier must absolutely enter as part of our naval forces'. The Stuka dive-bomber was considered for the carrier force along with the Re2001, which was also envisioned as operating as a fighter-bomber carrying two 360kg or one 600kg bomb.

[33] Bagnasco, Ermino, *La Portaerei Nella Marina Italiana* (Rome 1989), pp46-70.

[34] AUSSME, Diario Cavallero, bundle 1343: Minute of the meeting held on 9 July 1941 between the Chief of Staff of the Royal Air Force and General Sigismondi, general manager of Naval Construction of the Naval Ministry in order to examine the following issue: the opportunity to make use of the studies prepared to transforming the ship *Roma* into an aircraft carrier in order to use the *Roma* as a ship to transport fighter aircraft with a launching deck.

[35] AUSSME, Italian Supreme Command correspondence, H4, bundle 24, 6. Curami, Andrea, 'I riflessi delle oper-

azioni nello sviluppo della Regia aeronautica', in *L'Italia in guerra. Il secondo anno 1941* (Rome 1992), pp493-518. Santoni, Alberto, 'Il Duce e la portaerei Italia', *Storia Illustrata* (Dec. 1984), pp94-102. The materials Ansaldo had still to request for the completion of the *Aquila* were given 'absolute priority' (*precedenza assoluta*) by the Undersecretary for War Production: see AUSSME, H4, bundle 24/6, Carlo Favagrossa to Italian Supreme Command, 20 February 1942. Germany had similar problems with the design of their *Graf Zeppelin*, and according to Andrea Curami *Lufthansa* (at the request of the *Luftwaffe*) had purchased several American aircraft in the 1930s to try to solve this very problem (a strong tail assembly was important for the hook when hitting the restraining wire upon landing). Curami, Andrea, 'I riflessi delle operazioni nello sviluppo della regia aeronautica', pp493-518. It should be noted that General Carlo Favagrossa, in charge of the war economy, in a plea for the job that he had so far accomplished and the question of the *Aquila*, wrote that the Italian Navy had received more than 1,000,000 tons of iron and steel between September 1940 and June 1943. The delays on the completion of the *Aquila* may very well have been in large part due to Ansaldo being unsure of what was required. It may also be that Ansaldo had been fully paid on this job though it was never completed. See also Ciano's Diary for 15 and 18 November 1941.

36 Cernuschi, Enrico, 'Il fattore dimenticato. Las componente aerea imbarcata della Regia Marina 1940-1943', *Rivista marittima* No 2 (February 1994), pp135-150. Freri's report is in Auismm, titolario Aquila npa, bundle 1, Fasc. 1/b

37 AUSSME, I4, bundle 20, Memorandum of the Supreme Command 'Programma R. Marina 1943' dated 9 September 1942.

38 AUSSMM, titolario Aquila npa, bundle 1., fasc. 1/g, Stato Maggiore della Regia Marina to CSM, 17, July 1943. On other hand the production in the yards for the Italian Navy was very limited, as noted by Fortunato Minniti, which lists the pitiful total of seven submarines produced up to 1941 as the only shipping commissioned: 'L'industria delgi armamenti dal 1940 al 1943: I mercati, le produzioni', in Zamagni, Vera (ed), *Come perdere la guerra e vincere la pace* (Bologna 1997), pp55-148. See also German complaints about the length of time to get their submarines repaired in Italy.

39 Playfair, *The Mediterranean and the Middle East*, Vol III, pp123-124.

Chapter 9

1 Barnett, *Engage the Enemy More Closely*, p250.
2 Rohwer and Hummelchen, *Chronology of the War at Sea 1939-1945*, p42; Shores, *Malta: The Hurricane Years 1940-41*, pp86-89; and Playfair, *The Mediterranean and the Middle East*, Vol 1, pp243-244.
3 Smith, *Action Imminent*, pp266-267.
4 Jellison, Charles A, *Besieged* (Hanover 1984), pp69-70.
5 Smith, *Action Imminent*, p267.
6 Cocchia, *La Difesa Del Trafficao con L'Africa Settentrionale*, Vol VI, *passim*.
7 Our account of Cape Spartivento is based on Shores, *Malta: The Hurricane Years 1940-41*, pp93-96; Rohwer and Hummelchen, *Chronology of the War at Sea 1939-1945*, p45; Playfair, *The Mediterranean and the Middle East*, Vol I, pp299-307; Fioravanzo, *Le Azioni Navali in Mediterraneo*, Vol 1, pp258-291; Smith, *Action Imminent*, pp259-324; Sadkovich, *The Italian Navy in World War II*, p95-100; and Bragadin, *The Italian Navy in World War II*, pp49-54.

8 *Selected Papers on British Warship Design in World War II* (London 1983), pp85-126.
9 The *Renown* force was known as Force B during this operation. The *Renown* was suffering from structural problems at this time and was potentially quite vulnerable to underwater damage – see Smith, *Action Imminent*, p263. Somerville kept this secret both from his crews and the Italians.
10 Smith, *Action Imminent*, p272.
11 Bassett, *HMS Sheffield*, pp63-67. As with many books of this genre, it is best to be trusted on British details and not Italian.
12 Ollard, *Fisher and Cunningham*, pp103-105.
13 Knox, *Mussolini Unleashed*, p260.
14 Rohwer, *Allied Submarine Attacks of World War Two, European Theatre of Operations, 1939-1945*, p129
15 Knox, *Mussolini Unleashed*, pp247-248.
16 Ibid, p249. Grotto made his comments in an interview with the authors. The lower deck derisively referred to Cavagnari as 'mingo' for his need to urinate often.
17 Curami, Andrea, *L'italia in Guerra, il secondo anno – 1941* (Rome 1992), pp493-518. Ansaldo had supplied substandard armour plate and other items to the Italian Navy in the 1930s, though proof that Cavallero was involved with this corruption has not been established. See Greene and Massignani, *Rommel's North Africa Campaign* (Combined Books 1994), p14 and Ceva, Lucio, and Curami, Andrea, *Industria bellica anni trenta* (Milan 1992), *passim*.
18 Santoni, *Da Lissa alle Falkland*, pp194-6.
19 Varsori, Antonio, 'Aspetti della politica inglese verso l'Italia', *Nuova Antologia*, No 2147 (1983) pp271-298; Ceva, Lucio, *Africa settentrionale 1940-1943* (Rome 1982), pp171-2.
20 The names are quoted by Santoni on the basis of PRO archival evidence. See his *Da Lissa alle Falkland*, pp195-200.
21 For example Pirelli wrote in his diary that the King sent emissaries to look for new ministers, see Pirelli, *Taccuini 1922-1943*, p290.
22 On Italian peace initiatives from 1940 to 1943 see Varsori, Antonio, 'Italy, Britain and the problem of a separate peace during the Second World War: 1940-1943', *Journal of Italian History* No 8 (1978), pp455-491.
23 Tennant, Peter, 'How We Failed to Buy the Italian Navy', *Intelligence and National Security* Vol 3, No 1 (1988), pp141-161.
24 After Santoni's revelations Denham wrote his memoirs (*Inside the Nazi Ring. A Naval Attaché in Sweden 1940-1945* (New York 1984), pp132-140).
25 Santoni, *Da Lissa alle Falkland*, pp194-205 simplifies the story which appears to be more complex in Tennant's memoir.
26 Tennant, 'How We Failed to Buy the Italian Navy', pp159-60.
27 Ibid.
28 Fioravanzo, *L'organizzazione della marina durante il conflitto*, Vol 1, pp107-113; Bagnasco, Erminio, *Le armi delle navi italiane nella seconda guerra mondiale* (Parma 1978), pp127ff.
29 Salerno, *The Mediterranean Triangle*, p363.
30 Compton-Hall, Richard, 'Torpedoes', in Dear, I C B, and Foot, M R D (eds), *The Oxford Companion to the Second World War* (Oxford 1995), pp1119-21.
31 The loss of the *Hyperion* is usually given as from a mine but the submarine *Serpente* is sometimes given credit – it fired torpedoes at a distant enemy earlier and was not near where the *Hyperion* was lost. See Rohwer and Hummelchen, *Chronology of the War at Sea 1939-1945*, p45.

[32] Some sources state the torpedo-boat *Clio* was present, but Cocchia, *La Difesa Del Trafficao con L'Africa Settentrionale*, Vol VI, pp54-56 has only the *Vega* present.

Chapter 10

[1] Pirelli, Alberto, *Taccuini 1922/1943* (Bologna 1984), p290. Pirelli, of the tyre fortune, was one of the two founders of Italy's synthetic rubber factory that went into large-scale production in mid-1942 primarily for producing tyres.

[2] Allaway, Jim, *Hero of the Upholder* (Shrewbury 1991), pp79-82; and Gardiner, Robert (ed), *Conway's All the World Fighting Ships 1922-1946* (London 1980), p53. The British (and Allied) submarine contribution was substantial. Up to the Armistice Italy lost 2,272,707 tons of merchant shipping or 597 ships over 500 tons and 1278 ships under 500 tons (representing only 81,850 tons). Of this, 6.4 per cent was due to surface ships, a substantial 36.5 per cent to submarines, 33.9 per cent to aircraft, 6 per cent to mines, 9.5 per cent was scuttled, and 7.7 per cent sunk by 'natural or unknown causes'. See Dear and Foot, *The Oxford Companion to World War II*, p598.

[3] Jellison, *Besieged*, pp116-117.

[4] Attard, *The Battle of Malta*, p56.

[5] Garzke and Dulin, *Battleships: Allied Battleships in World War II*, pp91-93. Damage was too extensive to the *Richelieu* after the British attack on her in July to transfer her through the Straits of Gibraltar. Thomas, *Britain and Vichy*, pp72-86. Weygand would later say that if the British had come to North Africa with twenty divisions he would embrace them and if they came with four he would fire on them!

[6] Thomas, *Britain and Vichy*, p91.

[7] Shores, Christopher, and Cull, Brian with Malizia, Nicola, *Air War for Yugoslavia, Greece, and Crete, 1940-1941* (London 1987), *passim*.

[8] It should be noted that Italy asked several times for modern military equipment from the Germans, while refusing the German units that they continued to offer, refusing to supply weapons alone.

[9] Knox, *Mussolini Unleashed*, *passim*. See also Lucio Ceva's review in *Storia contemporanea* XIV, No 2 (1983), pp370-380, and Petersen, Jens, 'L'Afrika Korps', in *Commissione italiana di storia militare. L'Italia in guerra. Il secondo anno 1941* (Rome 1992), pp383-396.

[10] Petersen, 'L'Afrika Korps', p385. Hitler's strategy until the invasion of Russia is well described by Andreas Hillgruber in his *Hitlers Strategie, Politik und Kriegsführung* (Koblenz 1984) and also in 'England's place in Hitler's plan for world domination', *Journal of Contemporary History* IX, No 1 (1974), pp5-22, while the Mediterranean involvement is well treated by Gerhard Schreiber in the third volume of *Das Deutsche Reich und der Zweite Weltkrieg*. For 1942 see Hillgruber's student Reuth, Ralf Georg, *Entscheidung im Mittelmeer. Die südliche Peripherie Europas in der deutschen Strategie des Zweitehn Weltkrieges 1940-1942* (Koblenz, 1985); Ceva, Lucio, 'La strategia militare di Hitler, il Mediterraneo e il pensiero ipotetico', *Storia contemporanea* XVIII, 6 (1987), pp1513-1528, reviewing Hillgruber's book, and in his 'Italia e Grecia 1940-1941. Una guerra a parte', in Micheletti, Bruna, and Poggi, Pier Paolo (eds), *L'Italia in guerra 1940-1945* (Brescia, Annali della Fondazione Luigi Micheletti, n 5, 1990-91), pp185-236, says Raeder, Jodl, Halder and von Rintelen asked Hitler thirteen times between June 1940 and June 1941 to turn the German war effort against the British in the Mediterranean.

[11] Bundesarchiv-Militaerarchiv (BA-MA) in Freiburg, No. 'RH 2/460' discussing 'Sunflower'. Also see Van Creveld, Martin L, *Supplying War* (Cambridge 1977), p185. Ulrich Blennemann was helpful on this point. He is currently pursuing his PhD on the 1942 campaign in the Soviet Union. Part of his argument is that the resources expended in the Mediterranean might have tipped the balance on the side of the Germans. The trucks used in Africa were the equivalent of one third of the trucks for all the Army Groups in the USSR.

[12] Shores and Cull, *Air War for Yugoslavia, Greece, and Crete, 1940-1941*, p51.

[13] The orders of 26 December called for 307 planes to operate from Sicily. One hundred, mostly Ju88s, were to operate from Catania, eighty-four, mostly Ju87s, from Trapani, forty-eight He111s from Comiso, thirty-six Ju52 transports from Reggio on the mainland, and thirty-nine Me110's from Palermo. About two-thirds were serviceable at any one time and it was not until well into 1941 that all were transferred. Twelve Ju88s at Catania were for reconnaissance missions. There were initially no Me109s with the German Air Force, and they are incorrectly cited in several English language sources as being present. See Mattesini, Francesco, *L'attivita aerea italo-tedesca nel Mediterraneo, il contributo del 'X Fliegerkorps'* (Rome 1995), pp308-315.

[14] Roskill, *Naval Policy Between the Wars*, Vol II, p333.

[15] This section is based on Mattesini, L'attivita aerea italotedesca nel Mediterraneo, il contributo del 'X Fliegerkorps'; Santoni, Alberto, and Mattesini, Francesco, *La Partecipazione Tedesca alla guerra aeronavale nel mediterraneo* (Rome 1980); Playfair, *The Mediterranean and the Middle East*, Vols I and II; Shores, *Malta: The Hurricane Years 1940-41*, pp106-138; Boffa, Charles J, *The Illustrious Blitz* (Malta 1995), passim; and Schofield, *The Attack on Taranto*, pp63-76.

[16] Shores, *Malta: The Hurricane Years 1940-41*, p108. The Official History states five Swordfish.

[17] Rudolf Claudus has painted a picture of this action that appears in *Claudus Pittore del Mare* (Rome, 1993), pp102-103. He was a contemporary of Claus Bergen.

[18] Shores, *Malta: the Hurricane Years*, p109.

[19] Bassett, *HMS Sheffield*, p73.

[20] Roskill, *Naval Policy between the Wars*, Vol 2, p224.

[21] Mattesini quotes Captain D W Boyd as stating that the Italian attack was not as well co-ordinated or as determined as the German attack earlier in the day. Most works credit this last hit to the Germans but most do not realise Italian Stukas participated as well. Often, only the heaviest bombs are recorded.

[22] Playfair, *The Mediterranean and the Middle East*, Vol I, pp318-329 has Ju88s instead of He111s. Other sources give Stukas.

[23] Mattesini, *L'attività aerea italo-tedesca nel Mediterraneo*, p48, quoting the Mediterranean Fleet Diary.

[24] Attard, *The Battle of Malta*, p76.

[25] Shores, *Malta: The Hurricane Years 1940-41*, pp124-128; and Sadkovich, *The Italian Navy in World War II*, pp159-160.

[26] Jellison, *Besieged*, p99. Jellison states 4000 tons still on board at time of the hit.

[27] Attard, *The Battle of Malta*, pp66-67.

[28] A replica of her heavily damaged bell was presented to the Malta war museum. She was repaired in Norfolk, Virginia.

[29] Mattesini, *L'attività aerea italo-tedesca nel Mediterraneo*, p67, n19.

[30] BA-MA, RH 19/X-84 'Kriegsende in Italien'.

[31] Bagnasco and Grossman, *Regia Marina; Italian Battleships of World War II*, p71; and Bargoni, Franco, and Gay, Franco, *Orizzonte Mare* (Rome 1972), Vol I, p64.

[32] The bombardment of Genoa is based on Rohwer and Hummelchen, *Chronology of the War at Sea 1939-1945*, p50; Playfair, *The Mediterranean and the Middle East*, Vol I, pp329-332; Fioravanzo, *Le Azioni Navali in Mediterraneo*, Vol 1, pp338-381; and Shores, *Malta: The Hurricane Years 1940-41*, pp144-145.

[33] Bassett, *HMS Sheffield*, pp77-79.

[34] Sadkovich, *The Italian Navy in World War II*, p137, has the *Diaz* not sinking for over 40 minutes. He does point out that there was no surface threat from Malta so why were light cruisers at sea?

[35] The best study – from the German standpoint – is Burdick, *Germany's Military Strategy and Spain in World War II, passim*. Hitler was already planning for Barbarossa and also had concerns with Mussolini's miss-handled invasion of Greece.

[36] Toscano, *The Origins of the Pact of Steel*, p250.

[37] Dear and Foot, *The Oxford Companion to World War II*, pp487-488.

[38] Playfair lists the 3rd Panzer. This unit was placed in reserve after Mussolini refused it before the British offensive in December 1940. Hitler did not want to invade Portugal, but as 'Britain's oldest ally' there were concerns, and he was also worried by possible British reactions.

[39] Bragadin, *The Italian Navy in World War II*, p73.

[40] Ollard, *Fisher and Cunningham*, pp111-112

[41] Playfair, *The Mediterranean and the Middle East*, Vol II, p4; Santoni and Mattesini, *La Partecipazione Tedesca alla Guerra Aeronavale nel Mediterraneo*, pp41-42; and Buxton, Ian, *Big Gun Monitors* (Tynemouth 1978), p134.

[42] Brown, *Warship Losses of World War Two*, p41 states dive-bombers sank the *Dainty*, and Rohwer and Hummelchen, *Chronology of the War at Sea 1939-1945*, p52 has Ju88s. See Mattesini, *L'attività aerea italo-tedesca nel Mediterraneo, il contributo del 'X Fliegerkorps'*, p116.

Chapter 11

[1] Ollard, *Fisher and Cunningham*, pp110-111.

[2] Spertini and Bagnasco, *I Mezzi D'Assalto della Xth Flottiglia MAS*, pp40-43, 67-120. One of these craft is on display at the Malta War Museum at Valletta.

[3] One of the small disputes among some of the studies of this period are over which action the *York* should be awarded to. See Sadkovich, *The Italian Navy in World War II*, pp334-335. It is our view that Italy deserves the credit.

[4] Maugeri, *From the Ashes of Disgrace*, p22.

[5] The literature on the battle of Matapan is quite extensive: Cunningham, *A Sailor's Odyssey*; Barnett, *Engage the Enemy More Closely*, pp333-345; Iachino, Angelo, *La sorpresa di Matapan* (Milan 1957), idem, *Il punto su Matapan* (Milan 1969), and *Tramonto di una grande marina* (Milan 1959); Schreiber, Gerhard, 'Die Seeschlacht von Matapan', *Marineforum* No 50 (1975), p332; Stegemannn, Bernd, 'Die italienisch-deutsche Kriegführung im Mittelmeer und in Afrika', in *Das Deutsche Reich und der Zweite Weltkrieg*, Vol 3: *Der Mittelmeerraum und Südosteuropa. Von der 'non belligeranza' Italiens bis zum Kriegseintritt der Vereinigten Staaten* (Stuttgart 1984), pp599-614; Pack, S W C, *Night Action off Cape Matapan* (London 1972); Seth, Ronald, *Two Fleets Surprised* (London 1962); and recently Mattesini, Francesco, *Il giallo di Matapan. Revisione di giudizi* (Rome 1985) 2 vols (this

takes into account the influence of ULTRA on the battle), and Gillet, Jean-Pierre, 'De Gaudo à Matapan', *Marines. Guerre e Commerce* No 49 (May/June 1997), pp37-44.

[6] Aussmm, Promemoria di Supermarina 1941, Promemoria No. 32: 'Relazioni con la marina germanica su questioni operative'; and Schreiber, Gerhard, *Revisionismus und Weltmachtstreben. Marineführung und deutsch-italienische Beziehungen 1919-1944* (Frankfurt 1978), pp302ff.

[7] Fioravanzo, *Le azioni navali*, Vol IV, pp391-4.

[8] De Toro, Augusto, 'Supermarina, la Seekriegsleitung e i Balcani nella primavera 1941', *RID* (November 1992), pp86-97.

[9] For the meeting at Merano, the second after that at Friedrichshafen, see BA-MA, RM7/233 Italienische Seekriegsleitung; for the Italian view see Fioravanzo, *Le azioni navali*, Vol IV, pp389-398.

[10] AUSSMM, Promemoria di Supermarina 1941, Promemoria No. 72 and AUSSMM, Promemoria di Supermarina 1941, Promemoria No. 93. The document titled 'Scorta di nafta per le navi della R. Marina alla data dell '8/5/41' has the hand-written note: 'Rapporto al Duce 8 maggio 1941-XIX'. Clearly it was brought to Mussolini's attention. Ironically, the memo suggested to negotiate with the Soviet Union (one month before Barbarossa), as a source for imported fuel – a figure of 200,000 tons was mentioned. Also see Sadkovich, *The Italian Navy in World War II*, pp189-191.

[11] This section largely draws on Raspin, *The Italian War Economy 1940-1943*, pp227-245, 414. The fuel consumption of the *Regia Marina* was about the same as that of the the *Kriegsmarine*.

[12] For example Bragadin, Marc'Antonio, *Il dramma della marina italiana (1940-1945)* (Milan 1982), pp16, 319.

[13] BA-MA, RM7/233 'Vorläufige Stellungnahme Ib zur Lagebetrachtung des italienischen Admiralstabe' 29 July 1941, fl202-204, paragraph 7.

[14] Hubatsch, Walter (ed), *Kriegstagebuch des Oberkommandos der Wehrmacht* (Munich 1982), Vol 3, p1080, annotation of 8 September 1943. Between January and August 1943 the Italian Navy received 40,000 tons oil per month from the German Navy and Rumania.

[15] To put this in perspective, in the first quarter of each year, Italy consumed 348,230 tons of fuel in 1941, 180,371 in 1942, and 160,000 tons in 1943.

[16] It is interesting to note that Colonel Arturo Calzavara, responsible for oil at Supreme Command, was brother of one AGIP manager. BA-MA, RM7/233, 'Beitrag 1/Skl.Ig zum Kriegstagebuch des Ob.d.M. Monat November 1942', No242/43 of 19 January 1943.

[17] BA-MA, RM7/233, 'Beitrag 1/Skl.Ig zum Kriegstagebuch des Ob.d.M. Monat April', No1560/43 of 22 May 1943. See the German reports for the war diary of the Naval Command of the 26 June, 26 July and 1 October 1943 in BA-MA, RM7/223.

[18] BA-MA, RM7/233 'Beitrag 1/Skl.Ig zum Kriegstagebuch des Ob.d.M. Monat November 1942', No242/43 of the 19 January 1943, p3.

[19] Giorgerini, *Da Matapan al golfo Persico*, pp520-522.

[20] Santoni, *Il vero traditore*, p72. Mattesini, *Il giallo di Matapan*, Vol 1, p10 states that there was no supply traffic between Egypt and Greece before 'Lustre'. But the British had sent units there the previous November and had to rely only on their supply system due to the lack of local resources. Playfair, *The Mediterranean and the Middle East*, Vol II, p78.

[21] Italian submarines tried to intercept the 'Lustre' convoys but failed to achieve any successes and the *Anfitrite*

was lost to the busy *Greyhound* on 6 March. A bomb hit on one ship killed seven soldiers and wounded fourteen. Numbers shipped vary from source to source. The plan called for '58,000 troops with their mechanical transport, full equipment and stores.', PRO, ADM199/806, 39676: Report Med. 2466/00214/2 of 11 December 1941.

22 Cunningham, *A Sailor's Odyssey*, pp306, 316; Santoni, Alberto, 'L'azione dei commandos britannici contro l'isola di Castelrosso', *Rivista marittima* (March 1980), pp61-71 reproduced in *Il vero traditore*, pp67-71 based on British and Italian documents.

23 Among the several sources quoted, Stegemannn, *Die italienisch-deutsche Kriegführung im Mittelmeer und in Afrika*, p608 notes that at the low point after Taranto both Axis allies wanted to help each other.

24 Mattesini, *Il giallo di Matapan*, I, p17.

25 Ibid, p35.

26 Ibid, p37.

27 Hinsley, Vol I, pp404-5.

28 Hinsley, *British Intelligence in World War Two*, Vol I, p404 made clear the role played by ULTRA in the battle of Matapan ('the first important operation in the Mediterranean to be based on Sigint'); see also Hinsley's introduction to Hinsley, F H, and Stripp, Alan (eds), *Codebreakers. The Inside Story of Bletchley Park* (Oxford, 1993), p3. Mattesini, *Il giallo di Matapan*, I, p22 argues that the *Luftwaffe* messages were not important in the Intelligence analysis of the Italian intentions for 'Gaudo'. This is also stressed by Santoni, 'Lo scontro di Gaudo e la tragica notte di Matapan', *RID* (March 1991), pp86-97, especially pp90-91, but see Ceva, Lucio, 'L'intelligence britannico nella seconda guerra mondiale e la sua influenza sulla strategia e sulle operazioni', *Storia contemporanea* 1 (1982), pp99-122.

29 This is particularly stressed by Fioravanzo, *Le azioni navali*, IV, p408-9 and see Santoni, Alberto, 'La battaglia di Matapan', in *L'italia in guerra. Il secondo anno 1941* (Rome 1992), p422.

30 Santoni, *Il vero traditore*, p74.

31 Cattaneo had been at sea since 1940 in the command of cruisers (including heavy cruisers) until he replaced Iachino. Before that he had been attached to the Navy's General Staff from 1938.

32 This is still the subject of discussion: see Fioravanzo, *Le azioni navali*, IV, p422; Iachino, *Gaudo e Matapan*, p50; and Santoni, 'La battaglia di Matapan', *L'Italia in guerra. Il secondo anno 1941*, p421 and Stegemannn, 'Die italienisch-deutsche Kriegführung im Mittelmeer und in Afrika', in *Das Deutsche Reich und der Zweite Weltkrieg, vol. 3: Der Mittelmeerraum und Südosteuropa. Von der 'non belligeranza' Italiens bis zum Kriegseintritt der Vereinigten Staaten*, p611.

33 The convoys transporting personnel were designated 'AG' and those returning from Piraeus to Alexandria 'GA'. See PRO, ADM199/806, 39676, 'Lustre convoys', enclosure 2 to letter 2466/00214/2 of 11 December 1941.

34 The Albacore was the follow-on to the Swordfish and was slightly improved. A single-engine biplane, it had two machine-guns and a top speed of 163mph.Thetford, Owen, *British Naval Aircraft since 1912* (4th rev ed, London 1978), pp146-151.

35 Mattesini, *Il giallo di Matapan*, p48, quoting a memo of Vice-Admiral Fioravanzo, at that time one of the three most senior officers taking turns of duty at *Supermarina*.

36 Mattesini, *Il giallo di Matapan*, I, pp61, 77.

37 AUSSMM, Scontri navali e operazioni di guerra, bundle 27, A, 'Considerazioni tecniche sul materiale' and bundle 28bis, D, a shortened gunnery report. One destroyer,

the *Vendetta*, had engine problems and was shortly thereafter detached to Alexandria.

38 Thompson, *The War at Sea*, p104.

39 Quote is from Barnett, *Engage the Enemy More Closely*, p336.

40 AUSSMM, Scontri navali e operazioni di guerra, bundle 28bis, D, Gunnery report, p3.

41 Mattesini, *Il giallo di Matapan*, I, p81. This performance is often compared with the *Bismarck*'s in her encounter with the *Hood* and *Prince of Wales*, when the German battleship fired almost the same number of rounds (93) at the same range and scored seven hits. Second quote is from Pack, *Night Action off Cape Matapan*, p44.

42 Coles, Michael H, 'Cunningham and King' in Cogar, *New Interpretations in Naval History: Selected Papers from the Twelfth Naval History Symposium*, p279.

43 Garzke and Dulin, *Battleships – Axis Battleships in World War II*, pp387-388.

44 Unia, *Storia degli aerosiluranti italiani*, p104. Buscaglia says the attack took place at 12:15pm. Mattesini, *Il Giallo di Matapan*, 2, pp120-121 has a very good table showing the number and types of planes and bases which the Italian fleet was attacked from.

45 Iachino, *Gaudo e Matapan*, p178.

46 AUSSMM, Scontri navali e operazioni di guerra, bundle 28, B, CV De Pisa, Appunto per il signor Capo di Stato maggiore, 'CA ro Manlio De Pisa-R Incr. Pola', dated 4 August 1989. This is an updated analysis signed by the historical office of the Italian Navy for the Chief of Staff relating a claim by De Pisa concerning his damaged career. S W C Pack in his excellent study utilising Italian works reports the *Pola* as an 8000-ton cruiser – she weighed in at over 11,000 tons.

47 AUSSMM, Scontri navali e operazioni di guerra, bundle 28, RN Pola, Relazioni reduci, 'Verbale di interrogatorio del tenente di vascello Luigi Tomasuolo già 3° DT della RN Pola'.

48 Campbell, *Naval Weapons of World War Two*, pp258, 345.

49 Cunningham, *A Sailor's Odyssey*, p329; Pack, S W C, *Cunningham. The Commander* (London 1974), p145.

50 Ollard, *Fisher and Cunningham*, p110.

51 AUSSMM, CIS, bundle 5, 'Inchiesta sulla perdita della RN Pola e sul comportamento del suo com/te Capitano di Vascello Manlio De Pisa in tale occasione e in prigionia', p3. On p5 it is also confirmed that the *Pola* commander was unaware about the enemy main force at sea.

52 Santoni, *La battaglia di Matapan*, pp430-1.

53 Much of this section is based on a letter to the authors from Andrew Smith dated 16 August 1996. Some reports (and writers) had the lead ship a light cruiser of the *Bande Nere* class or a destroyer. The approaching Italian force in a line ahead led by the *Zara* and followed in the order *Fiume, Alfieri, Gioberti, Carducci*, and *Oriani*. See Mattesini, *Il Giallo di Matapan*, 2, p144.

54 The number of 4.5in salvoes fired at one or the other heavy cruisers is not certain, but the total number of shells expended was 120 semi-armour piercing 4.5in. As pointed out by Andrew Smith, there are three levels of understanding of the battle. One is obtained by the prisoners who were immediately interviewed after the battle, a second group of Italian survivors who returned immediately to Italy, a third by those as POWs (including those who were picked up by the Greek destroyers after the action) who were interviewed later, as well as the relevant British officers, gunnery officers in particular. The value of the relevant information was also based on officers versus seamen information. The final word on the tactical nuances of this action is still to be written.

[55] AUSSMM, CIS, bundle 3, 'Relazione d'inchiesta sulla perdita dell'incr. *Fiume*'. Evidence of Commander Luigi Guidi.

[56] Cunningham, *A Sailor's Odyssey*, p332.

[57] There have been several references that the crew of the *Pola* were drunk at the time of her loss. See Pack, *Night Action off Cape Matapan*, p98. Italian accounts do not have any indication of this, though some of the crew who jumped overboard earlier, were given brandy (*grappa*) upon being hauled back aboard. The *Pola*'s crew assisted with 'alacrity' in getting the British destroyer alongside to rescue part of the crew, but a few may have broken into spirits at some point.

[58] Connell, G G, *Mediterranean Maelstrom: HMS Jervis and the 14th Flotilla* (London 1987), p90. This account also mentions the drunkenness of the few men left aboard the *Pola* when the *Jervis* came alongside.

[59] Waller's account of this action is somewhat confused as he claims to have engaged more cruisers than were actually there! See Gill, *Royal Australian Navy 1939-1942*, pp313-315.

[60] The question of radar on Mack's force has not been answered adequately for the authors. It may be that his force had radar but his flagship did not.

[61] PRO, ADM199/806: Naval Operations in the Mediterranean: reports 1941, Final report of the Mediterranean Fleet HQ, n. 2466/00214 of 11 December 1941.

[62] Chirico, Giuseppe, *Il sacrificio della prima divisione a capo Matapan* (Naples 1995), pp47-50. See also Aussmm, CIS bundle 6, 'Inchiesta sulla perdita del R. incrociatore Zara'.

[63] It is quite interesting to note that the British battle squadron was surprised by the Italian ships coming to rescue the *Pola*.

[64] ACS, SPD, CR,.T586/12 roll 136 Job 154/155 frames 45538-40. Letter of Intelligence service (Ministero della Difesa nazionale, SID), to Undersecretary of the Navy of 4 January 1944, about naval action at Cape Matapan. In the document Brengola spoke of the destroyer *Lewis*, which was clearly the *Jervis*. Other officers testified to this fact before the Inquiry Commission, see also Aussmm, CIS bundle 6, 'Inchiesta sulla perdita del R. incrociatore Zara', p20. Herein lies one of the subtle poisons produced by ULTRA. The two Axis allies would often assume that the individual who was committing treason was a German if you were Italian or vice-versa. See Greene and Massignani, *Rommel's North Africa Campaign*, pp141,181.

[65] Liddell Hart, B H (ed), *The Rommel Papers* (London 1953), *passim* and Greene and Massignani, *Rommel's North Africa Campaign*, pp178-183.

[66] Santoni, *Il vero traditore*, *passim*; and Hinsley, *British Intelligence in the Second World War*, Vol I, p404.

[67] Howse, Derek, *Radar at Sea. The Royal Navy in World War 2* (Annapolis 1993), pp72-77 and Aussmm, Scontri navali e operazioni di guerra, bundle 28bis, D, Gunnery report, pp8-9. Also see Sumida, Jon Tetsuro, 'The Best Laid Plans: The Development of British Battle-Fleet Tactics, 1919-1942', *The International History Review* Volume XIV No 4, (November 1992). The Italians realised radar was used when they intercepted a British report of a target at 11,000m at about 10.00pm on a dark night. Only radar could have allowed this. See Sadkovich (ed), *Re-evaluating Major Naval Combatants of World War II*, p143.

[68] BA-MA, RM7/233 Italienische Kriegführung, pp160-2, a three-page report of the German Navy's Intelligence Service dated 29 March 1941.

[69] AUSSMM, Scontri navali e operazioni di guerra, bundle 28bis, Promemoria Azione di Capo Matapan (27-28/3/1941), compiled by Admiral Giuseppe Fioravanzo and partly replying to German criticism.

Chapter 12

[1] Cunningham quoted in Pack, S W C, *The Battle for Crete* (London 1973), p14.

[2] Rohwer and Hummelchen, *Chronology of the War at Sea 1939-1945*, pp56-57.

[3] The destruction of the *Tarigo* convoy is based on Smith, Peter C, and Walker, Edwin, *The Battles of the Malta Striking Forces* (London 1974); Playfair, *The Mediterranean and the Middle East*, Vol II, pp53-55; Cocchia, *La Difesa del Traffico*, Vol 6, pp104-112; Marcon, Tullio, 'I cifrari del *Mohawk*', *Storia Militare* No 15 (1994), pp13-20; Connell, *Mediterranean Maelstrom*, pp91-99; and Sadkovich, *The Italian Navy in World War II*, pp138-141. ULTRA did not affect this action, but had been helpful with the second missed convoy of 13 April. It would not be until July that a steamer would be intercepted thanks to ULTRA. Smith and Walker is solid and made good use of Cocchia on the convoy battles and the reader is directed to it for greater detail on these vicious night battles waged over the next 2 years.

[4] A large number of British ships were receiving radar in 1941. By 28 September 1941 193 destroyers had some type of radar. See Howse, *Radar at Sea*, p100.

[5] Marcon, 'I cifrari del *Mohawk*', pp13-20. The article has a drawing of the *Mohawk* on its side in the shallow waters, but incorrectly shows the two torpedo hits on the starboard side.

[6] Roskill, *Churchill & the Admirals*, p182. The *Centurion* would later be used in early 1942 as a dummy battleship at Alexandria to mislead Axis aerial reconnaissance.

[7] Playfair states four light cruisers and Cunningham and Rohwer give three. We base our order of battle on Connell, *Mediterranean Maelstrom*, pp99-100.

[8] Quote is in Connell, *Mediterranean Maelstrom*, pp99-100.

[9] The Italian Air Force official historian Giuseppe Santoro does not even mention the bombardment.

[10] Playfair, The Mediterranean and the Middle East, Vol II, pp110-113. Our source for the damage is *Diario storico del Comando Supremo* (Rome 1989), Vol 3, Tomo 1 notes on 21 and 22 April 1941.

[11] Rohwer and Hummelchen, *Chronology of the War at Sea 1939-1945*, p59; and Shores, *Malta: The Hurricane Years 1940-41*, pp189-191. Rohwer gives twenty Hurricanes.

[12] Held, Werner, and Obermaier, Ernst, *The Luftwaffe in the North African Campaign* (West Chester 1992).

[13] Nesbit, Roy C, *The Armed Rovers* (Shrewsbury 1995) has some interesting stories of their exploits while operating in the Mediterranean. One more arrived 2 days later. The Beaufighter carried a crew of two and was armed with four 20mm cannon and six machine-guns. Their range was a little over 50 per cent greater than a Hurricane equipped with tanks and while not as manoeuvrable as Italian fighters, they were faster than all but the best Italian fighters.

[14] Poolman, Kenneth, *The Kelly* (London 1954), p186.

[15] Greger, Rene, 'Yugoslav Naval Guns and the Birth of the Yugoslav Navy 1918-1941', *Warship International* No 4 (1987), pp242-249; and Breyer, Siegfried, *Battleships and Battle Cruisers 1905-1970* (Garden City 1973), p409.

[16] Vego, Milan, 'The Yugoslav Navy 1918-41', *Warship International* No 4 (1982), pp342-361.

[17] Poggiali, Vito, 'La reale marina jugoslava nel 1941', *Storia Militare* (February 1994), pp32-40. *Storia Militare* No 45, pp52-53 has some nice shots of the raising of the *Ljubljana*. Bragadin (p103) incorrectly states she was not scuttled. The *Sebenico* was seized by the Germans at the time of the Armistice in 1943 and was renamed *TA43*.

[18] Greger, 'Yugoslav Naval Guns and the Birth of the Yugoslav Navy 1918-1941'. The Skoda 120mm (4.7in) gun supplied to three small Yugoslav destroyers actually had a better range then the Italian 120mm, firing to 20,800m at 35° elevation, though several of the Italian mounts could elevate to 45° for a range of 22,000m.

[19] Shores and Cull, *Air War for Yugoslavia, Greece, and Crete, 1940-1941*, pp232-233 has a particularly good English account of this incident and the quote is from that. A photo of the damage can be found in Playfair. Also see Mattesini, *L'attivita aerea italo-tedesca nel Mediterraneo, il contributo del 'X fleigerkorps'*, pp171-173.

[20] Ollard, *Fisher and Cunningham*, pp115 and 118.

[21] Shores and Cull, *Air War for Yugoslavia, Greece, and Crete, 1940-1941*, pp405-407.

[22] MacDonald, Callum, *The Lost Battle* (New York 1993), p60. See Vogelin, Detlef, *Germany and the Second World War*, Vol III, pp552-553 who says that the airbases in the Dodecanese could have neutralised the threat from Crete and the airborne forces could have been used against Malta.

[23] The *Regia Aeronautica* was also involved with the *Luftwaffe* in introducing radar for use at air bases. See Arena, Nino, *La Regia Aeronautica 1939-1943* (Rome 1981), Vol 2, pp627-631 who details the moves towards radar after the British use of it at Matapan.

[24] There are several books on Crete, and a classic that has just been republished is Davin, D M, *CRETE* (Nashville 1997) in the Official History of New Zealand in the Second World War series. MacDonald, *The Lost Battle*, and Pack, *The Battle for Crete*, are both good studies. For the *Lupo* and *Sagittario* see Lupinacci, Pier Filippo, *La Difesa del traffico con l'Albania, la Grecia e l'Egeo* (Rome 1992), pp79-83.

[25] MacDonald, *The Lost Battle*, p237, has Force C a little under strength during the engagement with the 2nd Caique Squadron.

[26] Stories of 4000 drowned mountain troops continue from Churchill's history of the war to works as recent as Barnett, *Engage the Enemy More Closely*, p363.

[27] Pack gives thirty-eight caiques and about 4000 troops.

[28] Parrish, *Aegean Adventures 1940-1943*, pp67-68.

[29] Credit for the sinking of *Imperial* and *Hereward* is another of those small disagreements. The *Hereward* is often credited to Italian attacks (Bradagin and Sadkovich), but it was sunk by German Ju87s. We are basing this on Mattesini and Shores and Cull, *Air War for Yugoslavia, Greece, and Crete, 1940-1941*, pp390-391.

[30] This is discussed in Brian Sullivan's review of MacDonald, *The Lost Battle*.

[31] Ollard, *Fisher and Cunningham*, p119. See also Michael Simpson in Rodger, N A M (ed), *Naval Power in the Twentieth Century*, pp140-141.

[32] First quote from Ollard, *Fisher and Cunningham*, pp118-119 and then p120.

Chapter 13

[1]

[2] Thomas, *Britain and Vichy*, p101.

[3] Darlan's leaning towards Vichy has been questioned by conservative French naval officers after the war. See Auphan, Paul and Mordal, Jacques, *The French Navy in World War II, passim*, particularly the section on Syria. Clearly he was walking a diplomatic tightrope but he knew which way the wind was blowing that summer – towards Berlin.

[4] Playfair, *The Mediterranean and the Middle East*, Vol II, pp200-202.

[5] Shores, *Malta: The Hurricane Years 1940-41*, pp229-230. Rohwer gives only thirty-five Hurricanes.

[6] Warner, Geoffrey, *Iraq and Syria 1941* (Newark 1974), pp122-172.

[7] This section is based on Playfair, *The Mediterranean and Middle East*, Vol II, pp199-222; Auphan, Paul, and Mordal, Jacques, *The French Navy in World War II*, pp198-200; and Waters S D, *The Royal New Zealand Navy* (Wellington 1956), pp111-116.

[8] Connell, *Mediterranean Maelstrom*, pp120-121.

[9] Shores, Christopher, *Dust Clouds in the Middle East* (London 1996) pp232-233.

[10] Hinsley, *British Intelligence in the Second World War*, Vol 1, pp425-427; and Thomas, Martin, 'After Mers-el Kebir', *The English Historical Review* (June 1997), pp657-658.

[11] Thomas, *Britain and Vichy*, pp111, 131. Weygand opposed giving any help to the Axis, and the much shorter sea route to Tunisia instead of Tripoli or Benghazi was denied. He would be relieved of his position in mid-November, and thus the third force that Great Britain sought was removed at a stroke. Britain would later try to create yet another third force at the time of Operation 'Torch'.

[12] *Selected Papers on British Warship Design in World War II* (London 1947 and 1983), p75.

[13] Shore, *Malta: The Hurricane Years 1940-41*, p228.

[14] Playfair, *The Mediterranean and the Middle East*, Vol II, pp266-270.

[15] Sadkovich (ed), *Re-evaluating Major Naval Combatants of World War II*, p145.

[16] Shores, *Malta: The Hurricane Years 1940-41*, pp256-258. Warburton would shoot down several enemy aircraft during his career.

[17] Playfair, *The Mediterranean and the Middle East*, Vol II, pp267 gives a very different account of the air attack and we rely on Shores, *Malta: The Hurricane Years 1940-41*, p257.

[18] Simpson (ed), *The Somerville Papers*, pp286-287.

[19] The men, many needed for the airfields, left behind on the *Leinster* made it to Malta during Operation 'Style' at the end of July that was made up of fast cruisers and destroyers and the *Manxman*. There were now thirteen battalions (three Maltese) on the island and a garrison of 22,000 men with 112 heavy and 118 light AA guns plus 104 field guns of various calibres. Two destroyers bombarded an Italian airfield near Cagliari and the *Hermoine* rammed and sank the submarine *Tambien*.

[20] We use for this raid Spertini and Bagnasco, *I Mezzi D'Assalto della Xth Flottiglia MAS*, pp43-47; Sadkovich, *The Italian Navy in World War II*, pp167-168; Rohwer and Hummelchen, *Chronology of the War At Sea*, p75; Shores, *Malta: The Hurricane Years 1940-41*, pp260-266; and De Risio, *I Mezzi D'Assalto* (4th ed), pp85-101.

[21] Hinsley, *British Intelligence in the Second World War*, Vol 2, pp328-329 states ULTRA had not given any warning. Bennett, Ralph, *Ultra and Mediterranean Strategy 1941-1945* (London 1989) does not discuss the point, but Shores confirms that ULTRA did indeed alert the defences.

[22] Attard, *The Battle of Malta*, p107.

[23] Ibid, p109.

[24] Sadkovich accepts the Italian claim of three Hurricanes shot down. Shores has one only. Moccagatta was replaced by Commander Ernesto Forza in December while Borghese temporarily took command as he had been Moccagatta's deputy.

[25] Sadkovich, *The Italian Navy in World War II*, p168.

[26] Sadkovich states that the battleship *Duilio* was damaged at this time by a submarine attack but we can find no evidence of this.

[27] Allaway, *Hero of the Upholder*, pp126-128.

[28] Simpson (ed), *The Somerville Papers*, p307.

[29] Sadkovich, *The Italian Navy in World War II*, pp180-181 has all three lost and the *Denbydale* at 15,893 tons – she in fact displaced 8145 tons. See O'Neill, Richard, *Suicide Squads* (London 1981), pp217-218.

[30] For 'Halberd' we have relied on Playfair, *The Mediterranean and the Middle East*, Vol II, pp274-275; Rohwer and Hummelchen, *Chronology of the War At Sea*, p88; Sadkovich, *The Italian Navy in World War II*, pp179-182; Francesco Mattesini's excellent article in the December 1990 issue of that treasure trove of information, the quarterly issues of *Bollettino d'archivio dell 'ufficio storico della marina militare* (with colour and B&W photographs); and Fioravanzo, *Le Azioni Navali in Mediterraneo*, Vol 2, pp31-77. Quote is from Barnett, *Engage the Enemy More Closely*, p370.

[31] As quoted by Michael Simpson Rodger (ed), *Naval Power in the Twentieth Century*, p144.

[32] The 'H' class submarine were Canadian-built First World War era submarines of only 342 tons. By 1943 they would be used to train new corvette crews in antisubmarine work.

[33] Somerville thought the short-range AA was often seen firing behind the target plane, but that the screen itself, spread over 6000 yards was effective. Simpson (ed), *The Somerville Papers*, p324.

[34] Bassett, *HMS Sheffield*, p106.

[35] Shores, *Malta: The Hurricane Years 1940-41*, pp296-299. The *Ark Royal* during typical operations would launch six Swordfish at dawn for reconnaissance, two on antisubmarine patrol, and a combat air patrol of a flight of Fulmars.

[36] Many sources give only two destroyers, a figure that seems too low. Somerville gives six destroyers. Simpson (ed), *The Somerville Papers*, p314.

[37] Knox, *Military Effectiveness*, Vol III, p167. Also see Rohwer and Hummelchen, *Chronology of the War At Sea*, p88.

[38] Sadkovich on p182 lists German, Spanish and Italian sources claiming damage to *Rodney*, *Ark Royal*, five cruisers (!) and a merchant ship. He also states that 'Italian subs hit at least two British ships' and has the *Southampton* damaged – although the latter was not present in this action. We could find no evidence for any damage other than that given above.

[39] Bassett, *HMS Sheffield*, p108.

Chapter 14

[1] Bragadin, *The Italian Navy in World War II*, p284.

[2] Rohwer and Hummelchen, *Chronology of the War At Sea*, p91.

[3] Cocchia, *La Difesa del Traffico*, Vol 7, pp17-21.

[4] This is well discussed in Blair, *Hitler's U-Boat War*, Vol 1, *passim* but particularly pp388-389.

[5] Blair, *Hitler's U-Boat War*, p396 and Vause, Jordan, *Wolf* (Annapolis 1997), p124.

[6] The 'Goeben' group had been named after the First World War battlecruiser and the 'Arnaud' group after the First World War submariner Von Arnauld de la Periere. He had been ordered to command the Mediterranean submarines but was killed in a plane crash while flying to Rome.

[7] Raven and Roberts, *British Cruisers of World War Two*, p335. The point about the equal broadsides is that at night range is not a factor – all guns are within range. The weight of broadside, *ie* the number of guns multiplied by the weight of shell, is a calculation that is fundamentally changed at night. Rate of fire for a 6in gun is much higher than an 8in gun, and at night rate of fire is much more important than the ability to fire at a long range – when gunfire is more deliberate. The typical rate of fire for an 8in gun would be four rounds a minute, with Italian 8in guns it was less (3.2 for the early 8in cruisers and 3.8 for the later ones). A British 6in gun could fire between six and eight rounds per minute for short periods of time. Italian 6in guns could fire about five rounds a minute. That is one reason why the American 6in gun was so successful in the war, especially at night, as it could fire ten or more times a minute.

[8] Babington-Smith, *Air Spy: The Story of Photo Intelligence in World War II*, pp134-144. The war movie 'Malta Story' with Alec Guinness is based on the exploits of this unit.

[9] The destruction of the *Duisburg* convoy is drawn from Smith and Walker, *Malta Striking Forces*, pp43-62; Francesco Mattesini in September 1996 and December 1996 *Bollettino D'Archivio* pp77-201 and pp29-153 respectively.

[10] Sadkovich, *The Italian Navy in World War II*, p197.

[11] Smith and Walker, *Malta Striking Forces*, p52.

[12] Also in the area but not participating in the attacks were the submarines *Urge* and *P-34*.

[13] Francesco Mattesini in December 1996 *Bollettino D'Archivio* pp83-85.

[14] See Greene and Massignani, *Rommel's North African Campaign*.

[15] Santoni and Mattesini, *La Partecipazione Tedesca*, p133 and Raven and Roberts, *British Cruisers*, p408 both credit the *U-557* while Clay Blair states it was 'never resolved'. Blair, *Hitler's U-Boat War*, Vol 1, p400. Much of this section is based on Blair.

[16] Santoni and Mattesini, *La Partecipazione Tedesca*, pp145-146 for order of battle. Bernd Stegemann in *Germany and the Second World War*, Vol III, p714.

[17] Gundelach, *Die deutsche Luftwaffe im Mittelmeer*, Vol I, pp347.

[18] Santoni, *Il Vero Traditore*, pp254-255.

[19] The loss of the *Da Barbiano* and *Di Giussano* is drawn from Smith and Walker, *Malta Striking Forces*, pp84-87; Sadkovich, *The Italian Navy in World War II*, pp206-209; Francesco Mattesini in September 1991 'Bollettino D'Archivio' pp51-145 (he has some date errors on British forces – but his study is the most complete); and Bragadin, *The Italian Navy in World War II*, pp142-144. Smith and Walker credit the Italian light cruisers with 37 knots, but that was a faded memory from when they were first built. Now they could exceed 32 knots on a good day, not loaded down as they were. This is another good example of the danger of relying on 'Official' records. Sadkovich gives too high a figure for Italian losses.

[20] Bezemer, *Zij vochten op zeven zeeen*.

[21] The First Battle of the Sirte is based on Sadkovich, *The Italian Navy in World War II*, pp212-216; Rohwer and Hummelchen, *Chronology of the War At Sea*, p107; Bernd Stegemann in *Germany and the Second World War*, Vol III,

pp721-724; and Playfair, *The Mediterranean and the Middle East*, Vol II, pp110-115.

[22] Connell, *Mediterranean Maelstrom*, p143. Quote from Pack, S W C, *The Battle of Sirte* (London 1975) (Sea Battles in Close-Up, 15), p20.

[23] For damage to the *Kipling* see Cernuschi, Enrico, 'Colpito e occultato?', *Rivista storica* (July 1994), pp28.

[24] Spooner claims it was a German minefield – see Spooner, *Supreme Gallantry*, p103 and Rohwer and Hummelchen., Chronology of the War At Sea, p107.

[25] Borghese, *Sea Devils*, pp135-166.

[26] Renato Sicurezza in the December 1991 'Bollettino D'Archivio' pp55-70. His article on the 50th anniversary of the attack contains excerpts from the War Diary and we quote from it.

[27] Bernd Stegemann in *Germany and the Second World War*, Vol III p724 and quote is from Renato Sicurezza in the December 1991 'Bollettino D'Archivio' p61.

[28] Ollard, *Fisher and Cunningham*, p123. It has been argued elsewhere that Cunningham did not want to spend additional money for recommended harbour defense improvements. A more complete account of this action will appear in the author's upcoming *Black Prince of the Commandos: The Life of Junio Valerio Borghese* due out in early 1999.

Chapter 15

[1] Kesselring, *Memoirs of Field-Marshal Kesselring*, p105.

[2] Salewski, *Die deutsche Seekriegsleitung 1935-1945*, Vol II, pp54-57; Santoni, *La partecipazione tedesca*, p185; Gabriele, Mariano, *Operazione C3: Malta* (2nd ed Rome 1990), pp96-98; De Toro, Augusto, 'Il convegno italo-tedesco di Garmisch (14-15 gennaio 1942)', *Storia militare* (December 1993), pp41-47.

[3] Fock, Harald, *Afrika-Zerstörer 'ZG3' Hermes* (Herford 1993).

[4] Quoted by Gabriele, Mariano, 'L'operazione C3 (1942)' in *L'Italia in guerra. Il terzo anno – 1942* (Rome 1993), p409. Santoni, *La partecipazione tedesca*, p185. According to Santoni, Cavallero did not intend seriously to invade Malta.

[5] BA-MA, RM7/235, B.Nr.1.Skl.Ib 1402/42 'Ergebnis der deutsch-italienischen Besprächungen am 14. und 15 January 1942 in Garmisch'.

[6] Salewski, *Die deutsche Seekriegsleitung*, Vol II, p57.

[7] *Lagevorträge des Oberbefehlshabers der Kriegsmarine vor Hitler*, pp355-6.

[8] BA-MA, RM7/233, Stellv.Chef WFSt of 20 January 1942: 'Notiz über Rücksprache mit General Marras am 27. Januar 1942'.

[9] Sadkovich, *The Italian Navy in World War II*, p237.

[10] Barnett, *Engage the Enemy More Closely*, p370; Rohwer and Hummelchen, *Chronology of the War at Sea 1939-1945*, p135; and Allaway, *Hero of the Upholder*, pp162-164. A concise overview of convoys to North Africa and ships sunk can be found in Giorgerini, Giorgio, *La battaglia dei convogli in mediterraneo* (Milan 1977). He points out (p188) that losses were much reduced. Wanklyn's *Upholder* has been thought to been lost to a mine or alternatively to three small German minesweepers, the latter postulated by Rohwer and Hummelchen. But Rohwer in *Allied Submarine Attacks of World War Two*, p155 credits the loss to the *Pegaso*.

[11] Cocchia, *La Difesa del Traffico*, Vol 7, pp227-228.

[12] Ibid, pp227-235; Shores, Christopher, *Malta: The Spitfire Year 1942* (London 1991), pp52-55; Spooner, *Supreme Gallantry*, pp107-110, 321-325; and Poolman, Kenneth,

Night Strike from Malta (London 1980), pp149-157. Poolman incorrectly puts a 'panzer division' on the *Victoria* and claims an escorting destroyer was hit.

[13] Most British sources indicate two hits in the first attack, but Italian sources give just one.

[14] For greater detail see Poolman, *Night Strike from Malta, passim* and for the view of a Beaufort pilot in this high summer there is a recently published contemporary account; Gibbs, Patrick, *Torpedo Leader* (London 1992). Poolman notes the introduction of radar on the island on p75 – it was called ASV – Air to Surface Vessel.

[15] Shores, *Malta: The Spitfire Year 1942*, pp22-24.

[16] 'Radar' is the abbreviation of Radio Detection and Ranging, definition used in the US Navy from 1940. Italians called it RDT '*radiolocalizzatore*' and the Germans '*DeTe Gerät*' and later '*Funkmessgerät*'.

[17] We are relying here on Howse, Derek, *Radar at Sea. The Royal Navy in World War 2* (Annapolis 1993).

[18] Barnett, Correlli, *The Audit of War. The Illusion and Reality of Britain as a Great Nation* (London 1996), Chapter 9, pp159ff.

[19] Bragadin, Marcantonio, *Il dramma della marina italiana 1940-1945* (Milano 1968), p234, quoted by Castioni, Luigi Carillo, 'I radar industriali italiani. Ricerche, ricordi, considerazioni per una loro storia', *Storia contemporanea*, XVIII (1987), pp1221-1265, here p1221.

[20] Fioravanzo, Giuseppe, *L'organizzazione della marina durante il conflitto, tomo II, Evoluzione organica dal 10.6.1940 all'8.9.1943* (Rome 1975), p323, and his *L'organizzazione della marina durante il conflitto, tomo I, Efficienza all'apertura delle ostilità* (Rome 1972), p164. Fioravanzo repeats the accusation against the German Navy highlighting the meeting at Merano between Raeder and Riccardi: *Le azioni navali*, Vol IV, p399: Also Admiral Iachino claimed to be not aware of the state of development of German radar equipment.

[21] *Kriegstagebuch der Seekriegsleitung*, 3 June 1940. See the comments by De Toro, Augusto, 'Il radar tedesco e la marina italiana. Ne fu informata l'11 giugno 1940', RID (April 1990); Giorgerini, *Da Matapan al Golfo Persico*, p518 and Mattesini, Francesco, 'I radiolocalizzatori della Regia Marina', in *Bollettino d'Archivio dell'ufficio storico della marina militare* (September 1995), pp95-198, here 118-119. The paper is in two parts, the second published in the same *Bollettino* (December 1995), pp25-141.

[22] Castioni, *I radar industriali italiani*, pp1231-2.

[23] Ibid, p1224, n9.

[24] The request was passed to the Supreme Command (Cavallero) on 25 September 1941, see Mattesini. 'I radiolocalizzatori della Regia Marina', *Bollettino d'Archivio dell'Ufficio storico della marina militare* (September 1995), p131.

[25] *Diario storico del Comando supremo*, Vol VIII, 1.5.1942-31.8.1942 (Rome 1997), p871, note on 9 August 1942, pp878-9.

[26] A very clear memorandum was written by the weapons service of the Italian Navy on this topic, probably at the beginning of 1942. The document is published by Mattesini as Appendix H in his 'I radiolocalizzatori della Regia Marina'.

[27] NARS T821 roll 202 IT 1395, 'Materiali forniti o in attesa di fornitura in base ad accordi di scambio alla data del 10 giugno 1943'.Comando Supremo to General Warlimont, No 11167 of 27 February 1943, allegato 2. The document is in NARS T821 roll 30, IT 170, 'Richiesta di armi e materiali vari'. Sometime other Italian documents gives different figures for the equipment requested, but match the numbers actually delivered. The requested fig-

ures show in many cases the shortcomings of the Italian economy and sometime an attitude of the high ranking officers to accuse the Germans of providing too little help to their ally. See NARS T821 roll 21, Comando Supremo to von Rintelen 11990 of 5 April 1943, allegato 2. Also forty air radar 'Felino' (Freya) and ninety-four 'Volpe' (Wurzburg) type were requested from the Germans. Also see Bagnasco, *Le Armi Delle Navi Italiane*, pp 178-180 which gives a list that includes those ships that received Allied sets in 1944-45.

[28] For the first date see Giorgerini, *Da Matapan al Golfo Persico*, p518 and NARS T821 roll 202 IT 1395, 'Materiali forniti o in attesa di fornitura in base ad accordi di scambio alia data del 10 giugno 1943'; Mattesini, 'I radiolocalizzatori della Regia Marina', *Bollettino d'Archivio dell'Ufficio storico della marina militare* (December 1995), pp28-29.

[29] NARS, T821 roll 354 Comando supremo, promemoria per il capo di SM generale.

[30] Santoni, Alberto, 'L'elettrotecnica e la radiotelemetria nella Regia Marina', *Rivista marittima* (May 1994), pp51-62, here p53.

[31] De Toro also agrees with this point of view: De Toro, Augusto, 'Il radar tedesco e la marina italiana. Ne fu informata I'll giugno 1940', *RID* (April 1990).

[32] Pope, Dudley, *Flag* 4 (London 1954) *passim;* and Fock, *Fast Fighting Boats 1870-1945*, pp 134-146.

[33] Caruana, Joseph, 'Malta: cimitero di navi', *Storia Militare* No 27 (1995), pp4-15. His 'Cemetery of the Ships' gives a list of all forty Allied ships lost in Valletta or near the island and also notes where they were sunk.

[34] Shores, *Malta: The Spitfire Year 1942*, p82.

[35] Santoni, *Il Vero Traditore*, pp147-149, 256.

[36] Shores, *Malta: The Spitfire Year 1942*, p98; and Lucas, Laddie, *Malta: The Thorn in Rommel's Side* (London 1991), pp56-57.

[37] A sixteenth Spitfire was unserviceable. Shores has eight Blenheims making the flight into Malta, while Rohwer and Hummelchen, *Chronology of War at Sea 1939-1945*, p129 gives seven. Four Beaufighter night fighters also arrived in early March. Shores, *Malta: The Spitfire Year 1942*, pp 106-109.

[38] Lucas, *Malta: The Thorn in Rommel's Side*, pp19-20.

[39] Shores, *Malta: The Spitfire Year 1942*, pp100-101, 679-680.

[40] *Diario Storico Comando Supremo*, Vol VI, Book 1, p617, 3 March 1942.

[41] Rohwer, *Allied Submarine Attacks of World War Two*, pp154, 158.

Chapter 16

[1] Smith, Peter C, *The Great Ships Pass* (Annapolis 1977), p278.

[2] Playfair, *The Mediterranean and the Middle East*, Vol III, pp160-162.

[3] The main accounts of the second battle of the Sirte used here are: Pack, *The Battle of Sirte* (Sea Battles in Close-Up 15); Cunningham, *A Sailor's Odyssey; Le azioni navali in Mediterraneo, Dal 1° aprile 1941 all'8 settembre 1943* (Rome 1972); Santoni, Alberto, *La seconda battaglia navale della Sirte* (Rome 1982); Iachino, Angelo, *Le due Sirti* (Milano 1953); and Vian, Sir Philip, *Action This Day. A War Memoir* (London 1960).

[4] MacGregor Knox reduces the British to one lone light cruiser, see Knox, *Military Effectiveness*, Vol III, p167. Sadkovich puts torpedoes on the 'Hunts' – some 'Hunts' carried torpedoes but this batch did not.

[5] Vian, *Action This Day*, p86.

[6] Rohwer and Hummelchen, *Chronology of the War at Sea 1939-1945*, p130. Some sources incorrectly state eightdestroyers (for example *Le azioni navali in Mediterraneo, Dal 1° aprile 1941 all'8 settembre 1943*, p155. Santoni, Alberto, *La seconda battaglia navale della Sirte* p25).

[7] *Le azioni navali in Mediterraneo, Dal 1° aprile 1941 all'8 settembre 1943*, p155. The *Grecale* would suffer engine problems and would have to return to Taranto.

[8] Playfair, *The Mediterranean and the Middle East*, Vol III, p163.

[9] Quote is from Pack, *The Battle of Sirte*, p41.

[10] The immense amount of smoke put out by the British made it difficult for the Italians to locate the enemy. At one point they were quite close to the convoy but simply could not see it. See Rocca, Gianni, *Fucilate gli Ammiragli* ('Shoot the Admirals') (Milan 1987), p228. Rocca is a journalist who has written several competent if somewhat flamboyant histories of the war.

[11] Some sources give it as an 8in shell.

[12] Poland, *The Torpedomen*, p210.

[13] AUSSMM, Scontri navali e operazioni di guerra, 52, A. Rapporti di missioni: Allegato 1: Relazione sul concorso delle forze aeree, p1.

[14] Barnett, *Engage the Enemy More Closely*, p501.

[15] The 4.7in hit on the railing was ignored.

[16] AUSSMM, Scontri navali e operazioni di guerra. 2, A. Rapporti di missioni. Gunnery report, p4. The italics are in the original document.

Chapter 17

[1] Morehead, Alan, *The Desert War* (London 1965), pp125-126.

[2] BA-MA, RM7/233 'Vorlaufige Stellungnahme lb zur Lagebetrachtung des italienischen Admiralstabe' of 29 July 1941, A202-204.

[3] AUSSME, 14, bundle 20, *Supermarina* study of October 1942 'Il problema del traffico con 1'Africa settentrionale', p2.

[4] AUSSME, 14, bundle 20, Der Oberbefehlshabers Sued to Comando Supremo of 8 September 1942: 'Studie ueber Gründe der aufgetretenen Schiffverluste und daraus folgende notwendige Massnahmenzur Besserung der Nachschubver-haltnisse, and *Supermarina*, Promemoria No92 of 12 September 1942 'Note alio "Studio sulle perdite di naviglio e sulle misure necessarie per migliorare la situazwione dei rifornimenti" presentato dall'OBS al Comando Supremo 1'8 settembre 1942', pp8-9.

[5] See the conclusions of Reuth, Ralf Georg, *Entscheidung im Mittelmeer*, pp206-211.

[6] Our discussion of the planned invasion of Malta is based on Greene and Massignani., 'The Summer of '42: The Proposed Axis Invasion of Malta', *Command Magazine* No 20 (January-February 1993), pp64-71; Lundari, Giuseppe, *I Paracadutisti Italiani 1937/45* (Milan 1989); and Gabriele, Mariano, *Operazione C3: Malta* (Rome, 2nd ed 1990).

[7] Wingate, *The Fighting Tenth*, pp 178-184.

[8] Jellison, *Besieged*, p182.

[9] Ibid, pp213-215.

[10] The one Spitfire that failed to arrive was flown by an American, Sergeant Walcott, who deliberately flew to Algeria and claimed to the Vichy authorities that he was a 'lost civilian pilot in need of repatriation' – it was his way to get out of the war.

[11] Tourist guides to this day tell of a bomb that hit one of the great churches filled with worshipers (Mosta) on the island but did not explode. The guides tell the Italian tourists it was a German one, and *vice versa* to the German tourists!

[12] Attard, *The Battle of Malta*, p184; and Belden, Jack, *Still Time to Die* (New York 1975), p189.

[13] Jellison, *Beseiged*, p205.

[14] The *Folgore* was officially so named in June of 1942 – being the '1st Paratroop Division' before that date. An example of the equipment problems was the AT gun used by the *Folgore*, the inadequate 47mm gun standard in the Italian Army at this time. The Germans fielded nine battalions supported by one battalion of engineers, three companies of assault engineers, and a regiment of light artillery. A full order of battle appears in Greene and Massignani, 'The Summer of '42: The Proposed Axis Invasion of Malta'. There is a great deal of confusion as to who trained it and how strong it was. Tony Spooner in *Supreme Gallantry* as late as 1996 makes the *Folgore* division a regiment (p292).

[15] Most Italian divisions were binary – two regiments, and thus smaller then most other divisions of other nations. The *La Spezia* division consisted of six regular battalions, one motorcycle battalion, and a regiment of arillery – both older 65mm infantry guns and 47mm AT guns – and would later fight with distinction in Tunisia.

[16] Spiteri, Stephen C, *The British Fortifications* (Valletta 1991), *passim*.

[17] Attard, *The Battle of Malta*, pp195-197.

[18] Kesselring. *Memoirs*, p122.

[19] There were several Admiral Abes in the Japanese Navy and we have been unable to determine which one this was.

[20] Belden, *Still Time to Die*, p195.

[21] Ibid, pp191-192

Chapter 18

[1] Supplement to *The London Gazette*, 11 August 1948. It published Hardy's dispatch to the Admiralty.

[2] *La marina italiana nella seconda guerra mondiale*, Vol I: Dati statistici (Rome 1972), p134-5.

[3] According to several of the German naval papers relating the war in the Mediterranean, the Germans did look at postwar influence in the Mediterranean and tried to gain a strategic position, see BA-MA, R7/235.

[4] Schreiber, Gerhard, 'Sul teatro Mediterraneo nella seconda guerra mondiale. Inediti punti di vista della marina germanica del tempo', *Rivista Marittima* (March 1987), pp77-94, a summary of his most important studies on the relations between the two navies: 'Italien im machtpolitischen Kalkül der deutschen Marineführung 1919 bis 1945', *Quellen und Forschungen aus Italienischen Archiven und Bibliotheken* (1982) No 62, pp222-269 and *Revisionismus und Weltmachtstreben. Marineführung und deutsch-italienische Beziehungen 1919-1944* (Stuttgart 1978). Quote from memorandum of the German naval Command 1/Skl I Op a 852/42 of 30 April 1942 in BA-MA RM7/235, 287-8. The reaction of the Italian Navy arose during the talks between Italian Navy officers and the Swedish businessman who was involved with the British Naval Attaché in Stockholm, Dehnam. See Dehnam, *Inside the Nazi Ring*, p133.

[5] On the Klessheim meeting: Montanari, Mario, *Le operazioni in Africa settentrionale*, Vol III: El Alamein (Rome 1989), p133; Hillgruber, Andreas, and Förster, Jürgen, 'Zwei neue Aufzeichnungen über Führerbesprechungen aus dem Jahre 1942', *Militärgeschichtliche Mitteilungen* No 1 (1972), pp109-126; and Greene and Massignani, *Rommel's North African Campaign*, pp145-6.

[6] AUSSME, I4, bundle 37 contains the text of the paper delivered by Ramcke 'Conferenza tenuta al comando supremo l'11 aprile XX alla presenza del Duce e con la

partecipazione dell'ecc. Cavallero e del Feldmaresciallo Kesselring ad ufficiali delle 3 forze armate italiane e germaniche dal generale Ramcke ispettore delle truppe paracadutiste in Germania'.

[7] Rommel's words are referred in von Rintelen's report to OKW of 2 March 1942 which summarises the talks between the Afrika Korps commander and Cavallero. Rommel went on to say that the Italian paratroops would jump but not fight the British for Malta as they were too weak, see BA-MA, RH2/2936, 272-3, 'Aktennotiz über den Besuch des Generaloberts Rommel beim Comando Supremo am 18.3.1942, 18.30 Uhr'. See also Greene and Massignani, *Rommel's North African Campaign, passim*.

[8] BA-MA RM7/235, 'Bemerkungen zu dem Bericht des O.B. Süd vom 21. März 1942', No55578/42 of 27 March 1942.

[9] Connell, *Auchinleck*, p492.

[10] Thetford, *British Naval Aircraft*, p237. About 800 of these conversions were ordered.

[11] Sardinia had only forty-eight aerial torpedoes available. Sadkovich, *The Italian Navy in World War II*, p257.

[12] Smith, Peter, *Pedestal* (London 1970), p40-41

[13] Greene and Massignani, *Rommel's North Africa Campaign*, pp172-173; and Sadkovich, *The Italian Navy in World War II*, pp257-258. Fellers sent extensive reports to Washington and the Italians were able to read the code used.

[14] The Germans lost three and the Italians twenty-five aircraft. The reported losses inflicted on the British were over-inflated. Reports had both carriers, a battleship, and six cruisers damaged or sunk! See Sadkovich, *The Italian Navy in World War II*, p259.

[15] *Warship International* No 4 (1974), p420.

[16] Hammel, Eric, *Air War Europa* (Pacifica Ca. 1994), p48. Hammel implies that the Italian fleet withdrew shortly after this attack but Iachino continued on until he learned that Vian had retired on Alexandria.

[17] Playfair, *The Mediterranean and the Middle East*, Vol III, p313.

[18] Pope, *Flag 4*, pp49-52.

[19] Gary M Helmer in Greene, *Mare Nostrum*, pp34-36 and Massignani and Greene, *Rommel in africa settentrionale*, p123. There were some additions and changes in the Italian edition.

[20] Playfair, *The Mediterranean and the Middle East*, Vol III, p317.

Chapter 19

[1] Quoted by Chris Howard Bailey in *The Mariner's Mirror* Vol 79, No 4 (1993), p440.

[2] Our account of the 'Pedestal' convoy is based mainly on Smith, Peter C, *Pedestal: The Malta Convoy of August 1942* (London 1990); Mattesini, Francesco, *La battaglia aeronavale di mezzo agosto* (Rome 1986); Playfair, *The Mediterranean and the Middle East*, Vol III; Rohwer and Hummelchen, *Chronology of the War at Sea 1939-1945*, p155; Shores, *Malta: The Spitfire Year 1942*, Ch 8; and Fioravanzo, *Le operazioni navali*. The Axis called 'Harpoon' and 'Vigorous' the Battle of 'Middle-June'.

[3] Playfair, *The Mediterranean and the Middle East*, Vol III, pp316-7. The *P222* was an 'S' type submarine. The commandoes were to attack an airfield at Catania – it failed as the field was heavily guarded. See Wingate, *The Fighting Tenth*, pp204-206.

[4] *Diario storico del Comando supremo*, Vol VIII, 1.5.1942-31.8.1942 (Rome 1997), p881, note of 9 August 1942

5 Ibid, p871, note of 8 August 1942. Giorgerini, *Da Matapan al Golfo Persico*, pp520-2: 'Every time it was decided the battle fleet to go at sea, she went'. See the same author's *Uomini sul fondo. Storia del sommergibilismo italiano dalle origini a oggi* (Milan 1994), pp658-9, quoting the diary of Admiral Somigli.

6 *Diario storico del comando supremo*, vol VIII, 1.5.1942-31.8.1942, (Rome 1997), p913, note of 12 August 1942.

7 Ibid, pp909-10.

8 Mattesini, *La battaglia aeronavale di mezzo agosto*, p147.

9 Bertini, M, *I sommergibili in Mediterraneo*, (Rome 1968), Vol II, p64; Santoni and Mattesini, *La partecipazione tedesca*, p238 and Rohwer and Hummelchen, *Chronology of the War at Sea 1939-1945*, p155. Mattesini, *La battaglia aeronavale di mezzo agosto*, p133, mentions the *Colbalto* instead of the *Dagabur*.

10 Santoni and Mattesini, *La partecipazione tedesca*, p238.

11 In 1943 the British would issue an order forbidding the ramming of submarines, as their ships suffered too much damage themselves and other anti-submarine methods were more effective.

12 The epic tale of the *Ohio* is well described in Caruana, Joseph, '*Ohio* Must Get Through', *Warship International* No 4 (1992), pp324-348.

13 On the Italian *MAS* (anti-submarine torpedo boats) and *MS* (motor torpedo boats), see Bagnasco, Erminio, *M.A.S. e mezzi d'assalto di superficie italiani* (3rd ed Rome 1996). The *MS* boats were enlarged versions based on the captured German-built Yugoslav boats. The first batch had been ordered in June 1941.

14 Mattesini, *La battaglia aeronavale di mezzo agosto*, p250-1, and particularly Appendix 20, pp544-6 publishing a *Supermarina* document evaluating the attack of the MTBs.

15 Smith, *Pedestal*, p135. Most accounts now credit *MAS 554*.

16 This section is based on Mars' memoirs: Mars, Alistair, *Unbroken. The Story of a Submarine* (London 1953); Fioravanzo, *Le azioni navali in Mediterraneo. Dal 1° aprile 1941 all'8 settembre 1943* (Volume VI of the Official History of the Italian Navy), p400; and Rauber, *La lotta antisommergibile*, pp224-228.

17 Mars, *Unbroken*, pp117-126.

18 The standard Italian depth charge had an explosive charge of 50 or 100kg, while the standard American early war depth charges (the Mk.6) had 136kg, and the standard British Mk VII 132kg.

19 A selection of the minutes from the German side for the mid-June to mid-August meetings is published in Degli Esposti, Fabio, and Massignani, Alessandro, 'Nuovi documenti sulla guerra nel Mediterraneo nel 1942. La logistica dell'Asse' *Italia contemporanea*, No 203 (June 1996), pp305-331.

20 Greene and Massignani, *Rommel's North African Campaign*, p181

21 Ibid, p214-5; Jori, Gino, 'I rifornimenti dal mare alle forze italo-tedesche attestate sul fronte di El Alamein per la ripresa dell'attacco all'Egitto (2 luglio-2 settembre 1942)', *Rivista Italiana Difesa* No 2 (1986), pp77-85; and Warlimont, Walter, *Im Hauptquartier der deutschen Wehrmacht 39-45. Grundlagen, Formen, Gestalten* (3rd ed, Munich 1978), p264.

22 The German report is published in Mattesini, *La battaglia aeronavale di mezzo agosto*, p549.

23 Ibid, p424, which takes into account six aeroplanes destroyed in 'technical accidents', while Arena, *La regia aeronautica*, Vol III, p438 gives thirty lost in action and seven on the ground for the Italians.

24 Fioravanzo, *Le operazioni navali*, Vol V, p454.

25 BA-MA, RM7/235 'Anschliessende Betrachtung über das englische Geleitzugsunternehmen im Mittelmeer in der Zeit vom 10. bis 15. August 1942' of Marine Kommando Italien, p1. The document has 11 pages.

26 Ibid, p2.

27 This statement is also recorded by the Italian Navy official history, see Fioravanzo, *Le azioni navali*, Vol V, p403.

28 For the plans for 'Torch' and the disagreement for time and place see Matloff, Maurice, and Snell, Edwin M, *Strategic Planning for Coalition Warfare 1941-1942* (Washington DC 1953), pp287ff.

29 Mattesini, *La battaglia aeronavale di mezzo agosto*, pp405ff. Unfortunately Cunningham does not supply any more on this subject in his memoirs.

30 Minniti, Fortunato, 'L'industria degli armamenti dal 1940 al 1943: i mercati, le produzioni', *Come perdere la guerra e vincere la pace*, p110.

31 Minniti, *L'industria degli armamenti dal 1940 al 1943*, p136-137.

32 Aussme, I4, bundle 20, 'Programma R. Marina 1943', 9 September 1942

33 BA-MA, RM7/234, 'Beitrag zur Besprächung Führer – Duce' of August 1941. Interestingly enough, according to this memorandum of the Hitler-Mussolini talks, the capacity of the North African ports was just enough for the time being. Further troops would need a increase in capacity of all Libyan ports. To protect ships from the threat from Malta, it would be sufficient to build more sonar-equipped escorts. Certain very large Atlantic liners were not employed either, as they were awkward for the small North African ports.

34 Minniti, *L'industria degli armamenti dal 1940 al 1943*, p111-112.

35 Ibid, pp137-138

36 Erminio Bagnasco and Enrico Cernuschi, 'Dal maestrale potenziato ai comandanti' in *Storia Militare* No. 52 & 53, pp4-15 and 47-57 respectively.

37 Bagnasco, Erminio, 'Il progetto 'A.S. 450'', *Storia Militare* No 7 (April 1994), pp20-25

Chapter 20

1 Headrick, Daniel R, *The Invisible Weapon* (New York 1991), p229.

2 Shores, *Malta: The Spitfire Year*, p519. Rohwer and Hummelchen, *Chronology of War at Sea 1939-1945*, p157 ignores the one that crash-landed.

3 Santoni and Mattesini, *La Partecipazione Tedesca*, pp255-263, and Sadkovich, *The Italian Navy in World War II*, pp306-307. Sadkovich tends to downplay the German contribution to this action; see also p334, in turn, Playfair, *The Mediterranean and the Middle East*, Vol IV, pp19-23 admits that the raiding force ran into Italian troops other then 'low grade' ones. Also see Pope, *Flag 4*, pp56-61.

4 Pope, *Flag 4*, pp53-55.

5 Rohwer, Jurgen, 'Convoy: The View from the Other Side' in Roberts, William R, and Sweetman, Jack (eds), *New Interpretations in Naval History – 9th Naval History Symposium* (Annapolis 1990), p212.

6 Bryant, Ben, *Submarine Commander* (New York 1980), p156.

7 Ibid, pp158-159.

8 Rauber, *La lotta antisommergibile*, pp215-217, and Rohwer and Hummelchen, *Chronology of the War at Sea*, p156.

9 Kemp, Paul J, *British Submarines in World War Two* (London, 1987) introduction; and Mars, Alistair, *British Submarines at War 1939-1945* (London 1971), p27.

[10] On the Italian submarines, besides the official history by Bertini, Marcello, *Sommergibili in Mediterraneo* (Rome, 1972 and 1992, reprints of 1967 and 1968 eds), 2 vols, (Bertini was a former submarine commander) see also Bagnasco, Erminio, and Rastelli, Achille, *Sommergibili in guerra*. *Centosettantadue battelli italiani nella seconda guerra mondiale* (Parma, 2nd ed. 1994); Flamigni, Antonio, Turrini, Alessandro, and Marcon, Tullio, *Sommergibili italiani*. *Cento anni di vita tra storia e leggenda*, Supplement to *Rivista marittima* (Rome 1990) and Giorgerini, Giorgio, *Uomini sul fondo*. *Storia del sommergibilismo italiano dalle origini a oggi* (Milan 1994).

[11] Bagnasco and Rastelli. *Sommergibili in guerra*, p19.

[12] Santoni, *Il vero traditore*, pp50-52; and Hinsley, *British Intelligence in the Second World War*, pp208-209.

[13] Giorgerini, *Uomini sul fondo*, p245.

[14] Turrini, Alessandro, 'Riflessioni sull'arma subacquea italiana della seconda guerra mondiale', *Bollettino d'archivio USMM* (March 1993), pp7-41, here p41. See also his 'L'arma subacquea italiana nella seconda guerra mondiale', *Rivista marittima* (February 1995), pp93-105.

[15] Bagnasco and Rastelli, *Sommergibili in guerra*, p21. Turrini writes (p25) that the British did not have the same launch control as the Americans and Germans, but did launch large salvoes of torpedoes when available. For the British 'Fruit Machine' see Kemp, *British Submarines in World War Two*, picture 55.

[16] Mochi, Giorgio, 'Le cause di fallimento nei lanci dei siluri italiani durante la seconda guerra mondiale', *Rivista marittima* (November 1990), pp103-110. A memo of the Supreme Command of 10 June 1943 states that sixteen such pieces of equipment had arrived by that date, out of eighty-eight requested. See NARS T821 roll 202 IT 1395, 'Materiali forniti o in attesa di fornitura in base ad accordi di scambio alla data del 10 giugno 1943'.

[17] Mars, *British Submarines at War 1939-1945*, p231. Bertini, *I sommergibili in Mediterraneo*, Vol I, pp73-74 comments that the new tactic was fruitless. The case of the *Anfitrite* is a good example. This vessel was on station in the Kaso Channel on 6 March 1941 and her poor hydrophones did not hear a British convoy coming: she was instead detected by the escorting destroyers and heavily damaged by depth charges. Then she surfaced and was scuttled, the crew being rescued by the British. See Bertini, I, p138.

[18] Mars, *British Submarines at War 1939-1945*, pp80ff.

[19] Rauber, *La lotta antisommergibile*, pp30-35.

[20] Ibid, p338 Appendix 3. Appendix 4 lists with some errors the anti-submarine vessels equipped with sonar and the dates they were so fitted. For the sonar supplied by Germany see the memo of the Supreme Command of the 10 June 1943, sixty-six out of 112 requested. See NARS T821 roll 202 IT 1395, 'Materiali forniti o in attesa di fornitura in base ad accordi di scambio alla data del 10 giugno 1943'.

[21] Ship data is taken from the excellent Brown, D K, *The Design and Construction of British Warships 1939-1945*. *Submarines, Escorts & Coastal Forces* (London 1996) and *Selected Papers on British Warship Design in World War II. From the Transactions of the Royal Institution of Naval Architects* (Annapolis 1983) pp65-82. The Italians comment in fact is that they suffered from too long diving times, see Rauber, *La lotta antisommergibile*, p65. The Italian submarines suffered severely at the outbreak of the war due the old air conditioning based on methyl chloride instead of freon.

[22] Santoni, *La partecipazione tedesca*, p606 table D. An additional 152,218 tons were sunk by the end of the war.

The Italian submarines also had a crow's-nest on some of their submarines for when surfaced. On Bordeaux see Mattesini, Francesco, *Betasom. La guerra negli oceani (1940-1943)* (Rome 1993). The authors are preparing a manuscript on the Italian submarine service in the Battle of the Atlantic.

[23] See *Kriegstagebuch der Seekriegsleitung*, Vol 14, note on 2 October 1940. A translation of the relevant part is published by De Toro, Augusto, 'La costituzione di Betasom nelle relazioni navali italo-tedesche 1939-1940', *Bollettino d'Archivio* (September 1991), pp163-195.

[24] But it must be said that according to the already quoted list of German supplied equipment, only 2 were asked for and supplied by 10 June 1943. Memo of the Supreme Command of 10 June 1943, NARS T821 roll 202 IT 1395, 'Materiali forniti o in attesa di fornitura in base ad accordi di scambio alla data del 10 giugno 1943'.

[25] AUSSMM, Promemoria di Supermarina 1943, promemoria No11 of 4 March 1943: 'Impiego dei sommergibili in Mediterraneo'.

[26] The last Italian submarine sunk was the *Topazio*, sunk on 9 September by an British aircraft. Before the armistice it was the *Velella*, sunk on the 7th by the *Shakespeare*.

[27] Santoni, *Il Vero Traditore*, pp254-258; Greene and Massignani, *Rommel's North Africa Campaign*, pp183-185, and Hinsley, *British Intelligence in the Second World War*, Vol 2, pp734-735. Greene and Massignani incorrectly give the sinking of the *Scillin* as being the 13th.

[28] Edge, Spence, and Henderson, Jim, *No Honour No Glory* (Auckland 1983), pp140-149. Rohwer, *Allied Submarine Attacks*, p161 says that 336 men were killed. Hinsley mentions the *Nino Bixio*'s course and route but not her cargo.

Chapter 21

[1] Godson, Susan H, *Viking of Assault* (Lanham 1982), piii.

[2] Sainsbury, Keith, *The North African Landings 1942* (London 1976), pp21, 43.

[3] Ibid, p129. The British were for the most aggressive landings, while the Americans were more conservative. The American position was influenced by the possibility of Spanish intervention and the belief that Algeria and Tunis would voluntarily join the cause if Morocco was invaded. The British did not trust Vichy and were concerned that Axis troops could quickly occupy Tunisia.

[4] Ibid, pp67-70.

[5] Ibid, pp41-42. Some of the first OSS operations took place here.

[6] Ibid, pp145-146.

[7] Cave Brown, Anthony (ed), *The Secret War Report of the OSS* (New York 1976), pp134-154.

[8] Ibid, pp185-187.

[9] Ibid, pp188-196.

[10] Funk, *The Politics of Torch*, pp194-195; Rohwer and Hummelchen, *Chronology of the War at Sea 1939-1945*, pp174-175; and Bassett, *HMS Sheffield*, pp136-140 (though his usually excellent order of battle contains some errors and omissions).

[11] Dear and Foot, *The Oxford Companion to World War II*, p1034.

[12] Gelb, Norman, *Desperate Venture* (New York 1992), p135. A good order of battle can be found in Playfair, *The Mediterranean and the Middle East*, Vol IV, pp139-140.

[13] Darlan was never a Fascist. As early as 1 August 1941 he had remarked to U S Ambassador Admiral William Leahy 'When you have 3000 tanks, 6000 planes and 500,000 men to bring to Marseilles, let me know. Then we

shall welcome you'. Funk, *The Politics of Torch*, pp24 and 230. Also see p195 that when Darlan was told of the approaching invasion on 6 November, he did not believe the report.

[14] Funk, *The Politics of Torch*, p207.

[15] Ibid, pp220-223 – Funk gives an excellent overview of the confusion in Algiers on the 8th and the role of contending parties in the seizure of this port city.

[16] Thomas, *Britain and Vichy*, pp132-144, 150-53; and Sainsbury, *The North African Landings 1942*, p154. Because of the political confusion existing in North Africa at this time, Algiers was delivered to the Allies largely by the Resistance, whose leaders were then arrested by the Allies!

[17] Ollard, *Fisher and Cunningham*, pp140-141.

[18] Ibid.

[19] Hinsley, *British Intelligence in the Second World War*, p493. Hinsley ignores the fact that a large number of Italians moved by both air and sea (and land from Tripoli) into Tunisia, though German troops and planes were clearly the cutting edge of the seizure.

[20] Funk, *The Politics of Torch*, p213. There were not enough landing craft, they hit the wrong beaches, the offloading of trucks and artillery was poorly handled, troops were formed up in large open areas vulnerable to enemy fire if stronger resistance had been faced, etc. Admiral Hewitt lacks a good biography, in part we suspect because he was not a 'colourful' admiral. He has been described as 'level-headed' and a excellent seaman. He had the additional burden, as so often for many in this theatre, of having to work with both the army and foreign services – though the former could be included with the latter!

[21] Godson, *Viking of Assault*, p35.

[22] Ibid, pp44-45. There was also faulty 14in ammunition aboard the battleships *Texas* and *New York*. This was due to the fuses being the same ones installed in the shells in 1918! To rub salt in the wound, two shells ended up upright in front of the entrance to French naval headquarters. The United States Navy at the time of 'Torch' lacked new heavy-calibre ammunition for her older battleships and was forced to rely on this older ammunition. See Fucquea, David C, 'Task Force One', *Journal of Military History* (October 1997), p720.

[23] Godson, *Viking of Assault*, p42

[24] Sainsbury, *The North African Landings 1942*, p158 (quote) and Funk, *The Politics of Torch*, pp243-245. Sainsbury spells his name de la Borde, Funk as shown. Darlan did rally Dakar to the Free French cause in December.

[25] Babington-Smith, *Air Spy: The Story of Photo Intelligence in World War II*, pp158-162

[26] Bulkley, Robert J, Jr, *At Close Quarters* (Washington 1962), pp278-282 and Pope, *Flag 4* pp66, 79. The British were also quite adept at adding armament to their vessels – quite often captured Italian Breda machine-guns.

[27] Pope, *Flag 4*, p70. Pope says they were German E-boats, but it was more likely to have been Italian *MAS* boats, though the Germans would shortly start operating E-boats between Sicily and Tunisia.

[28] Rohwer and Hummelchen, *Chronology of the War at Sea 1939-1945*, p203 and Pope, *Flag 4*, pp80-81. Pope gives a different date.

[29] Some sources have just the *Sagittario* sinking her, but Pope, *Flag 4*, pp85-87 gives a combination of fire from shore batteries, the *Sagittario*, and German fighters.

[30] ULTRA was so capable they could discover the limits of the Axis minefields, and in at least one case, filled in the gap with their own mines!

[31] We base this on Rohwer and Hummelchen, *Chronology of the War at Sea 1939-1945*, p180; Playfair, *The Mediterra-*

nean and the Middle East, Vol IV, pp205-206, and Fioravanzo, Giuseppe. *La difesa del traffico con l'africa settentrionale* (Rome 1964), Vol VIII, pp146-170. Cocchia, who commanded in this action, is the author of the two previous volumes on convoying to North Africa. Fioravanzo does not assign the *Cleopatra* to Force K.

[32] This is based on the following papers: Ceva, Lucio,. 'Lo sviluppo degli aerei militari in Italia (1938-1940)', *Il Risorgimento* (1/1983), pp26-45; Ceva, Lucio, and Curami, Andrea,. 'Air Army and Aircraft Industry in Italy, 1936-1943' in Boog, Horst (ed), *The Conduct of the Air War in the Second World War. An International Comparison* (New York 1992), pp85-107; Curami, Andrea, 'Piani e progetti della Regia aeronautica 1939-1943', *Italia contemporanea* (1992), p187 and 'Tecnologia e modelli di armamento', in Zamagni, Vera (ed), *Come perdere la guerra e vincere la pace* (Bologna 1997), pp149-183.

[33] Sources disagree on the fate of the *Thunderbolt*. Rohwer and Hummelchen, *Chronology of the War at Sea 1939-1945*, p193 give a different date, while Rohwer, *Allied Submarine Attacks of World War Two*, p180 has the *Libra* sinking her (which is possible, but the Italians credit the *Cicogna*.) See Rauber, *La Lotta Antisommergibile*, pp287-289.

[34] Raspin, *The Italian War Economy 1940-1943*, p386.

[35] Knox, *Military Effectiveness*, Vol III, pp158-159.

[36] Pope, *Flag 4*, p90.

Chapter 22

[1] Belden, *Still Time to Die*, p281.

[2] Hubatsch, Walter (ed), *Hitlers Weisungen für die Kriegsführung* (Koblenz 1983), directive No48b. For the English edition see Trevor Roper, Hugh (ed), *Hitler's War Directives 1939-1945* (London 1964).

[3] Aga Rossi, Elena, *L'inganno reciproco. L'armistizio tra l'Italia e gli angloamericani del settembre 1943* (Rome 1993), p24.

[4] Sir Percy Loraine, quoted in Aga Rossi, Elena, 'Gli Stati Uniti e l'armistizio italiano', in *L'Italia in guerra. Il quarto anno, 1943* (Rome 1994), p196 n4.

[5] D'Este, *Bitter Victory*, pp40-1.

[6] Morison, Samuel Elliot, *History of United States Naval Operations in World War II, Vol II: Operations in North African Waters* (Oxford 1947), p273.

[7] Bulkley, *At Close Quarters*, pp282-284. Bulkley says most PT boats received radar in May, while Morrison gives a later date.

[8] Biddle, *Artist at War*, p120.

[9] H Kent Hewitt, articles in the *US Naval Institute Proceedings* (July 1953), p710 and Buxton, *Big Gun Monitors*, pp145-160.

[10] Babington-Smith, *Air Spy: The Story of Photo Intelligence in World War II*, pp161-165.

[11] Besides the classic Montagu, Ewen, *The Man Who Never Was* (London 1953), see also Cave Brown, Anthony, *Bodyguard of Lies* (New York 1975).

[12] This according to Hitler's stenographer Ludwig Krieger, quoted by Irving, *Hitler's War*, p547 and notes at p823 and BA-MA, RH 19-X/9, pp 6-7: OB Süd Ic Intelligence reports of 21, 23 and 27 May.

[13] 'Feindlagebericht vom 19.5.1943', in Schramm, Percy E (ed), *Kriegstagebuch des Oberkommandos der Wehrmacht*, vol III, 1943, I Part (Munich 1982), pp1432-4. See also Salewski, Michael, *Die deutsche Seekriegsleitung 1935-1945* (Munich 1975) Vol 2, pp360-1 and a letter by Colonel Ernest Zolling, former Chief of intelligence section at OBS, published in Santoni and Mattesini, *La partecipazione tedesca*, p370-1.

14 'Less intelligent than Cavallero. But Ambrosio enjoyed the virtues of clarity of expression, common sense, honesty and Germanophobia.' This and the balanced portrait of the General in a draft of an essay by Brian R Sullivan 'One way out: The Italian Army and Italy's Change of Alliances, 1943', p2. We are very grateful to Dr Sullivan for having been able to read this paper. Also see *I verbali delle riunioni tenute dal capo di SM generale*, Vol IV, p175, meetings of 13 May 1943 held by the *Duce*, p376 and those held by General Ambrosio on 2 July 1943, p175; Santoni and Mattesini, *La partecipazione tedesca*, pp397.

15 Morison, *Operations in North African Waters*, pp275-279.

16 Alegy, Gregory, 'Le operazioni in Tunisia e nell'Italia meridionale: l'aspetto aereo', in *L'Italia in guerra. Il quarto anno 1943* (Rome 1994) pp53-82; Santoni, Alberto, *Le operazioni in Sicilia e in Calabria* (2nd ed Rome 1989). See for example the message of 10 June 1943 to *Supermarina* saying that 'We will not surrender although the situation has become untenable' in NARS, T821/125/186. Santoni, and Mattesini, *La partecipazione tedesca*, p366-7.

17 Santoni and Mattesini, *La partecipazione tedesca*, p364-5.

18 Belden, *Still Time to Die*, p245.

19 Santoni and Mattesini, *La partecipazione tedesca*, p389.

20 Gundelach, *Die deutsche Luftwaffe im Mittelmeer*, Vol II, pp587, 597.

21 Santoro, *L'aeronautica italiana nella seconda guerra mondiale*, Vol II, pp532-3. Santoro's old work is still considered more reliable than the more recent four-volume series by Arena. The crew trained for the Ju88 were chosen for the formation of a mixed German-Italian unit under German control. Santoni, *Le operazioni in Sicilia e in Calabria*, p94. The Italians requested 2000 planes!

22 D'Este, *Bitter Victory*, pp275, 308. This has a dramatic picture of the loss of the *Rowan* on p321.

23 Godson, *Viking of Assault*, pp65-67. One paratrooper assault was routed over the invasion fleet and due to previous Axis air attacks, was fired on and many losses resulted from friendly fire.

24 D'Este, *Bitter Victory*, p304; and Friedman, Norman, *US Cruisers* (Annapolis 1984), p324. The *Boise* also launched and lost spotters – see Godson, *Viking of Assault*, p74.

25 Godson, *Viking of Assault*, p74.

26 *Lagevorträge des Oberbefehlshabers der Kriegsmarine vor Hitler*, p522.

27 Santoni and Mattesini, *La partecipazione tedesca*, pp406-8. Richthofen quoted in Irving, *Hitler's War*, Vol 2, p589.

28 *Supermarina* estimate of the possible operations against the Allies was explained in a memo to Italian Supreme Command on 23 June 1943, No 18969, published in Chief of Historical Office paper: Sicurezza, Renato, 'Le operazioni in Tunisia e nell'Italia meridionale: l'aspetto navale' in *L'Italia in guerra. Il quarto anno 1943*, pp33-51. Since all the period following the fall of Tunis is not satisfactorily worked out in the official history of the Italian Navy, this paper is interesting.

29 Raven and Roberts, *British Battleships of World War Two*, p369.

30 Pope, *Flag 4*, pp121-123 and Fioravanzo, *Le azioni navali*, Vol V, pp471-3 which compares the very different British and Italian versions.

31 The authors are indebted to the designer Sergio Nesi for his kind letter of 4 July 1997 to the authors explaining this issue. He was fire control officer of the cruiser *Montecuccoli* and later joined the *X MAS*. In Italian the term is 'telemetro a coincidenza'.

32 Pope, *Flag 4*, pp111-113.

33 Fioravanzo, *Le azioni navali*, Vol V, pp477-9.

34 Santoni, *Il vero traditore*, p243 and Fioravanzo, *Le azioni navali*, Vol V, p492; H. Kent Hewitt. articles in the US Naval Institute Proceedings July 1953 and April 1955.

35 We rely mainly on the recent Santoni, *Le operazioni iu Sicilia e Calabria*, pp171-198.

36 Marcon, Tullio, 'Le difese costiere della piazzaforte di Augusta-Siracusa negli anni '30-'40', *Storia militare*, 2, (November 1993), pp24-32 with many photographs of the defences, gun enplacements, etc. Marcon also wrote a book devoted to the fortress in the war: *Augusta 1940-43. Cronache della piazzaforte* (Rome 1981).

37 The fact that the Napoli Division Commander was captured lead D'Este, *Bitter Victory*, p310 to consider the that the division fought like the coastal divisions.

38 Morison, Samuel Eliot, *Sicily-Salerno-Anzio* (Boston 1964), p188. The first US naval unit to arrive at the port was the 15th PT boat squadron. There would be two minor skirmishes with German F-lighters and MAS boats at the end of July, which while indecisive, showed the need for a heavier armament than PT-boats carried, and aggressive operations were curtailed. The PT-boats' torpedoes were useless in such an action as minimum depth setting for them was 8 feet – much deeper than the Axis boats' draft.

39 D'Este, *Bitter Victory*, p482.

40 Ibid, pp497-522 and Santoni, *Le Operazioni in Sicilia e in Calabria*, pp74-75, 394-407. Ruge would later write a short history of the German Navy during the war.

41 Pope, *Flag 4*, p127.

42 Sullivan, Brian R, 'One Way Out: The Italian Army and Italy's Change of Alliances 1943' (unpublished paper).

43 There is evidence of this: it could be seen the considerations of Schreiber, Gerhard, *Die italienischen Militärinternierte im deutschen Machtbereich 1943-1945. Verraten, Verachtet, Vergessen* (München 1989) also available in Italian edition with updated bibliography: *I militari italiani internati nei campi di concentramento del Terzo Reich 1943-1945. Traditi, disprezzati, dimenticati* (Rome 1992), p31; by the same author, 'La linea gotica nella strategia tedesca: obiettivi politici e compiti militari', in: Rochat, G, Santarelli, E, and Sorcinelli, P (eds), *Linea Gotica 1944. eserciti, popolazioni, partigiani* (Milan 1986), pp25-67. NARS, series T77, roll 893, frames 5643980 (in the following series roll and frames will be written in this order), memo of Captain von Massenbach about the meeting with Major Ludwig of the Intelligence service of Waffenamt, okh/GenStdH/Att.AbtNr.84/43 del 4.9.1943.

44 Schreiber, *I militari italiani*, p93. see also the annotation of 4 September 1943 in the OKW diary, General Ambrosio had opposed the intention to defend only Northern Italy to the envoy Rudolph Rahn: Mehner, Kurt (ed), *Die Geheime Tageberichte der deutschen Wehrmachtführung im zweiten Weltkrieg 1939-1945* (Osnabrück 1988), Vol 8, p21. According to the annotation of the diary of air force General Wolfram von Richtofen, in Hitler's HQ 'Rommel knows nothing, thank God says nothing, and is just revelling in feelings of revenge against the Italians, whom he hates', quoted by Irving, David, *The Trail of the Fox* (London 1978), p290.

45 On the diplomatic aspects of the armistice now two interesting new studies using British and American archive documents by Aga Rossi, Elena, *Una nazione allo sbando* (Bologna 1993) and *L'inganno reciproco*. For some other unpublished documents see Andrea Curami.

46 BA-MA, RH 20-10/54, war diary of the 10th Army, note on 3 Sept. 1943.

[47] Garland, *Sicily and the Surrender of Italy*, p475

[48] Fioravanzo, Giuseppe, *La marina dall'8 settembre 1943 alla fine del conflitto* (Rome 1971), p9-10; see for this also the De Courten's memoirs: De Courten, Raffaele, *Le memorie dell'ammiraglio De Courten (1943-1946)* (Rome, 1993), pp187ff.

[49] Aga Rossi, Elena, *Una nazione allo sbando. L'armistizio italiano del settembre 1943* (Bologna 1993), pp110-111, n111. See the critical notes of Curami, Andrea, 'Otto settembre 1943. Documenti a margine dell'armistizio', *Italia contemporanea* 201 (1996), pp701-713, who notes how De Courten instructed the admirals for offensive actions against German units without explaining that these would be a reaction to possible German aggression.

[50] The document is published in Aga Rossi, *L'inganno repiproco*, pp349-352. Aga Rossi remembers that De Courten had clearly warned it would be difficult for the fleet to accept surrendering in Allied ports.

Chapter 23

[1] Molony C J C et al, *The Mediterranean and the Middle East*, Vol V, p217.

[2] *Le operazioni delle unità italiane nel settembre-ottobre 1943* (Rome 1975), compiled by Mario Torsiello is the final work of the historical office of the army. Torsiello is also the author of an earlier study, *Settembre 1943* (Milan 1963). The same office published Musco, Ettore, *Gli avvenimenti del settembre 1943 e la difesa di Roma* (Rome 1962). The air force point of view is in Lodi, Angelo, *L'aeronautica italiana nella guerra di liberazione 1943-1945* (Rome 1961). The navy view is in Fioravanzo, Giuseppe, *La marina dall'8 settembre 1943 alla fine del conflitto* (Rome 1962).

[3] Santoni, *Il vero traditore*, pp252-4.

[4] BA-MA, RH 20-10/54, war diary of the 10th Army, notes on 7 and 8 September 1943.

[5] *Geheime Tageberichte*, Vol 8, p43: 'a trusted man listened at a telephonic conversation on 4.9 at the command of the Italian Air Force from which it could be understood that the armistice was signed', annotation of 8 September 1943

[6] Aga Rossi, *Una nazione allo sbando*, p151.

[7] Lieutenant Colonel Dogliani, liaison officer to Kesselring's HQ quoted by Aga Rossi, *Una nazione allo sbando*, p120. BA-MA, RH 20-10/54, war diary of the 10th Army, note on 10 September 1943. The fuel situation was so bad that Kesselring could order a general retreat only with great difficulty. Also the Italian fuel dumps appeared exhausted.

[8] Godson, *Viking of Assault*, p86.

[9] Friedman, *US Cruisers*, p325.

[10] Morris, Eric, *Salerno* (New York 1983), pp230-232.

[11] Campbell, *Naval Weapons of World War Two*, p276

[12] Degli Esposti, Fabio, 'L'industria bellica italiana e le commesse tedesche (1937-43)', *Rivista di storia contemporanea*, 2/3 (1993), pp198-244.

[13] Morris, *Salerno*, p284.

[14] Cfr. BA-MA, rh 26-3/16, ktb 3.Pz.Gren.Division, Ic Nr.446/43 del 22.10.43, Tätigkeitsbericht September 1943.

[15] From a military point of view there are several studies from Italian and German sides. The most complete was written by Schroeder, Joseph, *Italiens Kriegsaustritt 1943. Die deutschen Gegenmaßnahmen im italienischen Raum: Fall Alarich und Achse* (Göttingen-Zürich-Frankfurt a.M., 1969). Schröder's main limit is the treatment of operations for the Italian peninsula and not for the forces outside. Schreiber's book on the introductory part, some 300 pages out of 900, of Gerhard Schreiber's book on the Italian military internees, supplies a general background to the dramatic events of these soldiers, and offers also a balanced analyses of what happened in the days of the Italian surrender to the Allies.

[16] *Warship International*, No 2 (1988), pp203-205.

[17] Incisa della Rocchetta, Agostino, *L'ultima missione della corazzata Roma* (Milan 1978), p153. This book publishes several eyewitnesses accounts and papers from the Inquiry Commission lead by Admiral Iachino.

[18] Ibid, p154.

[19] The Italian Navy official history deals with this episode briefly: Fioravanzo, *La Marina dall'8 settembre alla fine del conflitto*, pp42-3. There are much more details in the article by Botti, Ferruccio, 'L'8 settembre 1943 sulla corazzata Giulio Cesare', *Storia militare*, No 3 (Dec 1993), pp7-14, based on Captain Spotti's recollections.

[20] This adventure is recounted with maps in *Storia Militare* No. 4 by the authors Erminio Bagnasco and Fulvio Petronio, in '*Una Incrediblile 'Crociera di Guerra'* in *Adriatico*', pp11-18.

[21] Text of the agreement in NARS, T/5. Carboni, Giacomo, *L'amistizio e la difesa di Roma. Verità e menzogne*, (Rome, 1945), and the same author's *L'Italia tradita dall'armistizio alla pace* (Rome 1947) and *Le verità di un generale distratto sull'8 settembre* (Rome 1966). Besides the already quoted book of the historical office written by General Musco, his *La verità sull'8 settembre* (Milan 1965) should also be mentioned. The most recent volume from the Historical Office, Torsiello, *Le operazioni . . .* , p120 criticises Carboni in a more balanced way. In the discussion Monti, Paolo, *Roma 1943* (Rome 1945) could also be quoted, a journalistic account of the events which ran to many editions, and Monelli also criticises other personalities involved in the armistice. Reference could also be made to Castellano, Giuseppe, *Come firmai, La guerra continua* (Milan 1963) and *Roma kaput* (Rome 1967), and also Lussu, Emilio (ed. Orru, G G, and Plaisant L M), *La difesa di Roma* (Sassari 1987), pp260ff relating the orders of Roatta or De Stefanis on the morning of the 10th.

[22] Westphal, Siegfried, *The German Army in the West* (London 1951), p151; a different opinion is held by Pinzani, Carlo, 'L'8 settembre 1943: elementi ed ipotesi per un giudizio storico', *Studi storici* XIII n.2 (1972), pp289-337.

[23] Schroeder, *Italiens Kriegsaustritt. Akten zur deutschen Auswertigen Politik*, Serie E, vol.VI, doc311, pp533-535; The Führer order was published by Stuhlpfarrer, Karl, *Die Operationszonen 'Alpenvorland' und 'Adriatisches Küstenland' 1943-1945* (Vienna 1969), Italian edition *Le zone d'operazione Prealpi e Litorale Adriatiche 1943-1945* (Gorizia 1979), pp193-195.

[24] Bordogna (ed), *Junio Valerio Borghese e la X Flottiglia Mas*, pp41-42. See also Bonvicini, Guido, *Decima marinai! Decima Comandante!. La fanteria di marina 1943-1945* (Milan 1988), pp15-17; Lazzero, Ricciotti, *La X Mas. La compagnia di ventura del principe nero* (Milan 1987), pp16-19; Nesi, Sergio, *Decima Flottiglia nostra. I mezzi d'assalto della marina italiana al sud e al nord dopo l'armistizio* (Milan 1986, 2nd edition 1987), p95.

[25] Borghese would go on to survive the war, being, with his wife, the only Italian Fascists to be saved by the OSS. He may have committed the last act of the Fascist war when he may quite possibly had led a team in 1955 into the Black Sea to blow up the Soviet battleship *Novorossisk* – the war reparations old *Giulio Cesare*. See Jack Greene and Alessandro Massignani, *Black Prince of the Commandos: The Life of Junio Valerio Borghese* due out in 1999.

[26] Mackesy, Piers, in *War in History*, Vol 3, No 1 (1996), pp102-106.

[27] Parish, *Aegean Adventures*, pp203-7.

[28] Nafziger, George F, *Italian Order of Battle World War II* (West Chester 1996), Vol 2, pp50-51.

[29] Ilari, Virgilio, *Il generale col monocolo* (Ancona 1995) p199. In *Warship International* 3 (1991) p297 and 'News of Naval books', in *Warship International* 4 (1992), pp363-4; also Ilari, Virgilio, *Il generale col monocolo. Giovanni De Lorenzo 1907-1973* (Ancona 1994), p57, n39. Also see Huchthausen, Peter A, 'Espionage or Negligence? A Sinking Mystery', *Naval History* (February 1996), pp19-24. Many thanks to Dr Brian R Sullivan for his comments on the matter.

Chapter 24

[1] Among the large literature on this subject see Greene, Jack, and Massignani, Alessandro, *Ironclads at War* (Conshohochen, Pa. 1998).Certainly Trieste could be also used to supply the Allied forces advancing toward Central Europe.

[2] For example Iachino, Le *due Sirti*, p18 and Lewin, Ronald, *Ultra goes to War. The Secret Story* (London 1978), p155. A survey in Ceva, Lucio, *Africa settentrionale 1940-1943* (Rome 1982), pp150-151. Howard, Michael, *The Mediterranean Strategy in the Second World War* (London 1968), p12. The author comments that Hitler's advisors were unable to make this clear to the dictator. This book is rather a reply to the discussions aroused between British and American historians upon the role of the Mediterranean in Allied strategy, i.e. Mediterranean vs. Second Front, rather than an analysis of the Mediterranean in British strategy.

[3] Memorandum of Admiral Percy Noble of 5 May 1939, of thirteen pages. We used the German translation which is in BA-MA, RM7/1347, also quoted by Ciano on 8 June 1939. The document is discussed by Gerhard Schreiber who had traced it in his *Revisionismus und Weltmachtstreben*, pp168-169. Interestingly enough, this was handed over to the Germans by Ciano.

[4] Hitler thought that the destruction of the British Empire would result in advantages to United States and Japan, not Germany. Schreiber, Gerhard, 'Der Mittelmeerraum in Hitlers Strategie 1940', *Militärgeschichtliche Mitteilungen*, 2 (1980), pp69-99, here p73. Hillgruber, *Hitlers Strategie*, *passim*. The fact that this study has never published in English edition probably influenced the view that Hitler could have conceived other plans of war against the Western Powers. A critical review of Hillgruber on the Mediterranean issue is by Ceva, Lucio, 'Il teatro Mediterrameo e il pensiero ipotetico', *Storia contemporanea* (December 1987), pp1513-1528. The offensive proposals towards the south are quoted among others in: Hartmann, Christian, *Halder Generalstabchef Hitlers 1938-1942* (Paderborn 1991), pp218-9; Salewski, *Die deutsche Seekriegsleitung*, Vol I, pp271ff.; KTB/OKW, I/1, 11 (7.8.40); Greiner, Helmuth, *Die Oberste Wehrmachtführung 1939-1943* (Wiesbaden 1951), pp175ff; Warlimont, Walter, *Im Hauptquartier der deutschen Wehrmacht 39-45. Grundlagen, Formen, Gestalten*, pp142 and ff.; Hillgruber, *Hitlers Strat-*

egie, *passim*. Also on 13 February and 14 March 1942 Raeder proposed the offensive against Suez. For this, besides Wagner's minutes in *Lagevorträge*, pp355-356 and 360-361, see the comments of Reuth, *Entscheidung im Mittelmeer*, pp143ff.

[5] See Schröder, *Deutschland und Italien im Spiegel der deutschen Marineakten*, p854 for defensive aspirations. In September the German Navy replied to Halder that landings on northwest coast of Africa by Britain and USA were possible, since it should be remembered the 50 destroyers loan by United States to Britain. Raeder wanted therefore to seize Gibraltar, Atlantic Islands and Suez. See KTB/Skl volume 3: note on 4 November 1939, p4.

[6] Gerhard Schreiber explained this point in several papers, for example: *Der Mittelmeerraum in Hitlers Strategie 1940; Sul teatro Mediterraneo nella seconda guerra mondiale. Inediti punti di vista della Marina germanica del tempo, Rivista marittima* (March 1987), pp77-94 especially p79; and ditto. *Das Deutsche Reich und der Zweite Weltkrieg*, Vol III, *Der Mittelmeerraum und Südosteuropa*, *passim*; Levine, Alan J, 'Was World War II a Near-run thing?', *Journal of Strategic Studies* 1 (March 1985), confirms the results of the research of Schreiber about the significance of the Mediterranean theatre of operation for the British. On 28 July 1940 Admiral Fricke of Skl prepared a memorandum on the Russia campaign in which the navy had little interest, but accepting that this question should be settled.

[7] Schreiber, *Der Mittelmeerraum in Hitlers Strategie 1940*, p92.

[8] Schroeder, Josef, 'Deutschland und Italien im Spiegel der deutschen Marineakten', *Quellen und Forschungen aus italienischen Archiven und Bibliotheken*, (1972), pp833-866, here p841.

[9] Ibid, p849.

[10] *40 Fragen an Karl Dönitz* (Munich 1980 4th ed.) p69, which quotes Cunninghams words from *The Sunday Times* of 25 January 1959.

[11] Schroeder, *Deutschland und Italien*, p853.

[12] Salewski. *Deutsche Seekriegsleitung*, I, p316, quoted by Schröder, *Deutschland und Italien*.

[13] *Das Deutsche Reich und der Zweite Weltkrieg*, volume VI: Horst Boog, Werner Rahn, Reinhard Stumpf & Bernd Wegner. *Der totale Krieg. Die Ausweitung zum Weltkrieg und der Wechsel der Initiative 1941-1943* (Stuttgart 1990), pp942-943.

[14] Schmider, Klaus, 'The Mediterranean in 1940-1941: Crossroads of Lost Opportunities?', *War & Society* (October 1997), pp19-41.

[15] Babington-Smith, *Air Spy: The Story of Photo Intelligence in World War II*, p140. While exaggerated, we see what the lack of good air reconnaissance did to the Italians.

[16] Adopted from Santoni and Mattesini, *La Partecipazione Tedesca*, pp595-616. Note the math error on Table 1 top line for Italian totals.

[17] Sadkovich, *The Italian Navy In World War II*, p333. Nor does this include the badly damaged battleship *Cavour*.

Bibliography

Unpublished Sources

ACS
Carte Graziani, b. 40/B

Australia
AWM 78 item 292/3

AUSSME
Diario Comando Supremo 1445A
Diario Cavallero, bundle 1343
Carteggio Comando Supremo, I4 4, 10, 20 H4 24

AUSSMM
Promemoria di Supermarina, 1940, 1941, 1942, 1943
Scontri navali e operazioni di guerra, 2, 27, 28, 28, 52
Titolario Aquila nave portaerei, 1
Commissione inchiesta speciale, 3, 5, 6

Public Record Office – Kew London
ADM. 199/1048, n. 0112/00212/16 of the 29 January 1941, Report of Admiral Cunningham of Hindhope
ADM 199/797, Reports of the Commander in Chief of the Mediterranean Fleet
    n. 214/00212/11 of 7 April 1941
    n. 0357/00212714, 3rd March 1941
ADM 199/806, Naval Operations in Mediterranean, reports 1941, Final report of the Commander in Chief of the Mediterranean Fleet No. 2466/00214 of 11 December 1941
ADM 116/3534 – 123288, Report Admiral J. F. Sommerville to the Commander in Chief of the Mediterranean Fleet of 4 September 1937

Bundesarchiv-Militärarchiv – Freiburg i.Br.
RH2/1444, 1892, 2936
RH 19 VIII/252, 322
RH 19 X/9, 84
RH 20–10/54,
BA-MA, RH 26–3/16,
RM 12 II/181, 183, 197
RM7/223, 230, 233, 234, 235, 934, 945, 1347
M686 PG45849–45852
RL 9/52
Nachlass Enno von Rintelen, N433/8

NARS – Washington
Microfilm Serie T78, Rolls: 324, 325, 344, 364
             T84, Rolls: 273, 276, 279
             T821 Rolls: 9, 23, 31, 107, 109, 125, 144, 200, 202, 250, 348, 349, 354, 355, 489
             T1022/1892, 2501, 2519, 3015
             T586/4, 24, 405

Published Sources

Aga Rossi, Elena, *L'inganno reciproco. L'armistizio tra l'Italia e gliangloamericani del settembre 1943* (Rome 1993)
Agostino, Incisa della Rocchetta, *L'ultima missione della corazzata Roma* (Milan 1978)
Aichner, Martino, *Il Gruppo Buscaglia* (Milan 1991)
Allaway, Jim, *Hero of the Upholder* (Shrewsbury 1991)
Ando, Elio and Bagnasco, Erminio, *Navi e marinai italiani: nella seconda guerra mondiale* (2nd edition Parma 1981). Solid scholarship, filled with great pictures. Prime candidate for an English edition.

Angelucci, Enzo and Matricardi, Paolo, *World War II Airplanes* (Verona 1976)

Arena, Nino, *I Paracadutisti* (Parma 1996). Recent large format and heavily illustrated volume on the Italian parachute service. Pictures tell a thousand words, and it puts into perspective just how far this arm was independently developed up to and into the Second World War.

——, *La Regia Aeronautica 1939–1943* 4 vols (Rome 1981–86). Heavily illustrated large format history.

Auphan, Paul and Mordal, Jacques, *The French Navy in World War II* (Annapolis 1959)

Bagnasco, Erminio, *I Mezzi D'Assalto della Xth Flottiglia MAS* (Parma 1991)

——, *Le Armi Delle Navi Italiane* (Parma 1978)

——, and Rastelli, Achille, *Sommergibili in guerra. centosettantadue battelli italiani nella seconda guerra mondiale* (Parma 1994). Also solid scholarship and filled with great pictures. These two authors have probably been more influential in producing and publishing colourful and accurate books on the Italian Navy geared for the general public more than any others and have done a remarkable job.

Babington-Smith, Constance, *Air Spy: The Story of Photo Intelligence in World War II* (New York 1957).

Bargoni, Franco, *L'impegno Navale Italiano durante La Guerra Civile Spagnola (1936–1939)* (Rome 1992). Scholarly, official, and well-illustrated study.

Barnett, Correlli, *The Audit of War. The Illusion and Reality of Britain as a Great Nation* (London 1986)

——, *Engage the Enemy More Closely* (New York 1991). Good for including the effects of ULTRA and poetic, but filled with annoying minor errors of detail.

Bassett, Ronald, *HMS Sheffield* (Annapolis 1988)

Baum, Walter and Weichold, Eberhard, *Der Krieg der 'Achsenmächte' im Mittelmeerraum. Die 'Strategie' der Diktatoren* (Göttingen 1973)

Bernardi, Giovanni, *Il disarmo navale fra le due guerre mondiali (1919–1939)* (Rome 1975)

Bernotti, Romeo, *Cinquant'anni nella marina militare* (Milan 1971). An accessible volume from one who was there until the outbreak of war.

Bertini, Marcello, *I sommergibili in Mediterraneo* 2 vols (Rome 1972).

Blair, Clay, *Hitler's U-Boat War* (New York 1996). A first-class history which has sections on the Mediterranean. Contains some minor errors of detail concerning the surface and air operations in the Mediterranean

Boffa, Charles J, *The Illustrious Blitz* (Malta 1995). An 'I was there' account by a prolific Maltese writer

Bonvicini, Guido, *Decima marinai! Decima Comandante!. La fanteria di marina 1943–1945* (Milan 1988)

Borghese, Junio V, *Sea Devils* (Chicago 1954). Good history of the X-MAS until 1943 but a bit disingenuous about his own role in the war. The Naval Institute has republished a partially updated version.

Bragadin, Marc' Antonio, *The Italian Navy in World War II* (Annapolis 1957). Dated history.

Bryant, Ben, *Submarine Commander* (New York 1980)

Breyer, Siegfried, *Battleships and Battle Cruisers 1905–1970* (Garden City 1973). A classic study that needs to be expanded and updated.

Brice, Martin A, *The Tribals* (London 1971)

Brown, J D, *Warship Losses of World War Two* (London 1995)

Brown, D K, *The Design and Construction of British Warships 1939–1945. Vol II: Submarines, Escorts & Coastal Forces* (London 1996)

Bulkley, Robert J, Jr, *At Close Quarters* (Washington 1962). PT-Boats, written for the President who had served on one in the Second World War.

Burdick, Charles B, *Germany's Military Strategy and Spain in World War II*, (Syracuse 1968). Little on British preparations, thorough on Germany's.

Buxton, Ian, *Big Gun Monitors* (Teignmouth 1978). Excellent study of a neglected area – limited to British monitors.

Campbell, John, *Naval Weapons of World War II* (London 1985). Good but not definitive on Italian weapons.

Carsten, F H, *The Reichswehr and Politics 1918 to 1933* (Oxford 1966)

Casali, Antonio and Cattaruzza, Marina, *Sotto i mari del mondo. La Whitehead 1875–1990* (Bari 1990)

Cave Brown, Anthony, *Bodyguard of Lies* (New York 1975)

—— (ed), *The Secret War Report of the OSS* (New York 1976). Some interesting aspects to espionage and North Africa.

Ceva, Lucio, *Africa settentrionale 1940–1943* (Rome 1982)

——, and Curami, Andrea, *Industria bellica anni trenta* (Milan 1992). Lucio Ceva is one of the elder statesmen of Italian historians. Over the past few years he has jointly published several books with Andrea Curami, who has many varied talents in his own right, including working in five different languages, including Japanese.

Clerici, Carlo Afredo, *Le Difese Costiere Italiane Nelle Due Geurre Mondiali* (Parma 1996). Well-illustrated introduction to Italian coast defences in the Second World War.

Chirico, Giuseppe, *Il sacrificio della prima divisione a capo Matapan* (Naples 1995)

Cocchia, A Aldo, *La Difesa Del Trafficao con L'Africa Settentrionale* 3 vols (Rome 1976, 1977, and 1964). Third volume is by Giuseppe Fioravanzo.

Connell, G G, *Mediterranean Maelstrom: HMS Jervis and the 14th Flotilla* (London 1987). Quite thorough and entertaining account that contrasts the brilliant career of this flotilla with HMS *Kelly* of Mountbatten fame.

Coutau-Begarie, Herve and Huan, Claude, *Mers-El-Kebir* (Paris 1994)

Cruickshank, Charles, *Greece 1940–1941* (Newark 1976)

Cunningham, Andrew, *A Sailor's Life* (New York 1955). Aging but still quite good.

Davin, D M, *CRETE* (Nashville 1997). Reprint lacking the coloured maps of the original.

Dear, I C B, and Foot, M R D, *The Oxford Companion to World War II* (Oxford 1995). Corrects many errors and the Italy heading is quite good, though some minor errors of fact such as the *Ark Royal* being sunk by planes creep in.

De Courten, Raffaele, *Le memorie dell'ammiraglio De Courten (1943–1946)* (Rome 1993)

D'Este, Carlo, *Bitter Victory* (New York 1988)

Dumas, Robert, *Le cuirasse Richelieu* (Bourg-en-Bresse 1992)

Dumas, Robert, *Les cuirasses Dunkerque & Strasbourg* (Bourg-en-Bresse 1993) Beautiful, expensive and thin large format book with many photographs. Part of an outstanding series.

Evans, David C, and Peattie, Mark R, *Kaigun* (Annapolis 1997)

Filippo, Lupinacci Pier, *La Difesa del traffico con l'Albania, la Grecia e l'Egeo* (Rome 1992).

Evans, David C, and Peattie, Mark R, *Kaigun* (Annapolis 1997) (Rome 1992)

Fioravanzo, Giuseppe, *La marina dall'8 settembre 1943 alla fine del conflitto* (Rome 1962)

——, *La marina italiana nella seconda guerra mondiale*, vol. I: Dati statistici (Rome 1972)

——, *Le Azioni Navali in Mediterraneo*, 2 vols (Rome 1970)

——, *L'organizzazione della Marina durante il conflitto*, 2 vols (Rome 1973)

Fock, Harald, *Afrika-Zerstörer 'ZG3' Hermes* (Herford 1993)

——, *Fast Fighting Boats* (Annapolis 1978)

Funk, Arthur Layton, *The Politics of Torch* (Lawrence, Kansas 1974)

Gabriele, Mariano, *Operazione C3: Malta* (2nd ed Rome 1990)

Garzke, William and Dulin, T, *Battleships: Axis and Neutral Battleships in World War II* (Annapolis 1985)

Gatchel, Theodore L, *At the Water's Edge* (Annapolis 1996)

Gay, Franco and Gay, Valerio, *The Cruiser Bartolomeo Colleoni* (London 1987)

Gelb, Norman, *Desperate Venture* (New York 1992)

Germany and the Second World War Vol. 3 (Oxford 1995). Eventually all ten volumes will appear – quite good.

Gill, G Hermon, *The Royal Australian Navy 1939–1942* Vol 1 (Canberra 1957)

Giorgerini, Giorgio, *La battaglia dei convogli in mediterraneo* (Milan 1977)

——, *Da Matapan al Golfo Persico. La Marina militare italiana dal fascismo alla Repubblica* (Milan 1989)

——, and Nani, Augusto, *Gli Incrociatori Italiani* (Rome 1971). Large format and well illustrated.

Godson, Susan H, *Viking of Assault* (Lanham 1982)

Graziani, Rodolfo, *Ho difeso la Patria* (Milan 1948)

Greene, Jack, *Mare Nostrum* (Watsonville, privately printed, 1990). Out of print and produced just after the Loma Prieta earthquake

——, and Massignani, Alessandro, *Rommel's North Africa Campaign: December 1940–November 1942* (Conshohocken 1994)

——, *Ironclads at War: 1854–1891* (Conshohocken 1998)

Groener, Erich, *German Warships* (London 1990), Vol 1 and 2

Gundelach, Karl, *Die deutsche Luftwaffe im Mittelmeer* 2 vols (Frankfurt 1981)

Hammel, Eric, *Air War Europa* (Pacifica 1994)

Hart, Liddell B H (ed), *The Rommel Papers* (London 1953)

Hattendorf, John B (ed), *Doing Naval History* (New Haven 1994). A must read for any naval historian.

Headrick, Daniel R, *The Invisible Weapon* (London 1991)

Held, Werner and Obermaier, Ernst, *The Luftwaffe in the North African Campaign* (West Chester 1992). They produce a nice line of heavily illustrated books on the German military effort in the Second World War, many of which are German translations.

Herde, Peter, *Pearl Harbor* (Milan 1986)

Hezlet, Arthur, *Electronics and Sea Power* (Briarcliff Manor 1975)

Hillgruber, Andreas, *Hitlers Strategie, Politik und Kriegsführung* (Koblenz 1984)

Hinsley, F H, and Stripp, Alan (eds), *Codebreakers. The inside story of Bletchley Park* (Oxford 1993)

Hinsley, F H, *British Intelligence in the Second World War*, 4 vols (London 1979). Excellent study, though avoids some sensitive areas.

Hood, Ronald Chalmers III, *Royal Republicans* (Baton Rouge 1985). Discussion of the make-up of the French inter-war officer corps, little on the ships themselves.

Howse, Derek, *Radar at Sea* (Annapolis 1993)

Howson, Gerald, *Aircraft of the Spanish Civil War* (London 1990)

Hubatsch, Walter (ed), *Hitlers Weisungen für die Kriegsführung* (Koblenz 1983)

—— (ed), *Kriegstagebuch des Oberkommandos der Wehrmacht* (Munich 1982)

Iachino, Angelo, *La sorpresa di Matapan* (Milan 1957)

——, *Le due Sirti* (Milan 1953)

——, *Tramonto Di Una Grande Marina* (Milan 1961)

Ion, Hamish A, and Errington, E J (eds), *Great Powers and Little Wars* (Westport 1993)

Ireland, Bernard, *The War in the Mediterranean* (London 1993). A pleasant read with several errors of detail. One of the most glaring is when the *San Marco* regiment becomes six divisions of 70,000 men for the planned invasion of Malta.

Irving, David, *Hitler's War* (New York 1977)

——, *The Trail of the Fox* (New York 1977)

Jellison, Charles A, *Besieged* (Hanover 1984). Required reading for anyone wanting to understand Malta during the war, but is weak on the Axis.

Kehrig, Manfred. *Die Wiedereinrichtung des Deutchen militaerischen attachedienstes nach dem Ersten Weltkrieg (1919–1933)* (Boppard am Rhein 1966)

Knox, MacGregor, *Mussolini Unleashed* (New York 1982). One of the better academic studies so far produced.

Koburger, Charles W, Jr, *The Cyrano Fleet* (Westport 1989)

Kursietis, Andris J, *La Regia Marina 1919–1945, the Order of Battle and Admirals of the Royal Italian Navy* (Ark Publications, 1995). This thin self-published booklet must be used with care, but is helpful in keeping track of the officers.

Lassaque, Jean, *Les contre-torpilleurs Epervier et Milan* (Bourg en Bresse 1995)

——, *Les C.T. de 2400 tonnes du type Jaguar* (Bourg en Bresse 1995)

Lazzero, Ricciotti, *La X MAS. La compagnia di ventura del principe nero* (Milan 1984)

L'Italia in guerra (Rome, AUSSMM, various). This is a series of papers with a book for each year of the war with volume 1 on 1940 appearing in 1991. A scholarly selection with coverage on many and various topics but not comprehensive

Lodi, Angelo, *L'aeronautica italiana nella guerra di liberazione 1943–1945* (Rome 1961)

Lowry, Thomas P, *The Attack on Taranto* (Mechanicsburg 1995)

Lucas, Laddie, *Malta: The Thorn in Rommel's Side* (London 1991)

MacDonald, Callum, *The Lost Battle* (New York 1993)

March, Edgar J, *British Destroyers* (London 1966)

Marder, Arthur J, *From the Dardanelles to Oran* (London 1974)

Mars, Alastair, *British Submarines at War 1939–1945* (Annapolis 1971)

Mars, Alastair, *Unbroken: The Story of a Submarine* (London 1953)

Massignani, Alessandro, and Greene, Jack, *Rommel in africa settentrionale* (Milan 1996). Italian edition of *Rommel's North African Campaign*, slightly expanded and corrected.

Matloff, Maurice, and Snell, Edwin M, *Strategic Planning for Coalition Warfare 1941–1942* (Washington DC 1953)

Mattesini, Francesco, *Il Giallo di Matapan* 2 vols (Rome 1985)

——, *La Battaglia Aeronavalae di Mezzo Agosto* (Rome 1986)

——, *La Battaglia Di Punta Stilo* (Rome 1990). Well-illustrated, including some colour photographs.

Maugeri, Franco, *From the Ashes of Disgrace* (New York 1948). The Italian version was suppressed for many years as it was viewed as the work of a traitor.

Millett, Alan R, and Williamson, Murray (eds). *Military Effectiveness*, Vols II and III (Winchester 1988 and 1989)

Montagu, Ewen, *The Man Who Never Was* (London 1953)

Montanari, Mario, *Le operazioni in Africa settentrionale, vol.III: El Alamein* (Rome 1989). His four-volume series on the fighting in North Africa is indispensable for any modern study

Morehead, Alan, *The Desert War* (London 1965)

Morison, Samuel Eliot, *Operations in North African Waters* (Oxford 1947). One of the earliest histories in his famous series, it badly needs a 2nd edition.

——, *Sicily-Salerno-Anzio* (Boston 1954)

Morris, Eric, *Salerno* (New York 1983)

Musco, Ettore, *Gli avvenimenti del settembre 1943 e la difesa di Roma* (Rome 1962)

Nesbit, Roy C, *The Armed Rovers* (Shrewsbury 1995)

Nesi, Sergio, *Decima Flottiglia nostra . . . I mezzi d'assalto della marina italiana al sud e al nord dopo l'armistizio* (2nd edition Milan 1987)

New Interpretations in Naval History (Annapolis, various). This annual contains selected papers from the Naval History Symposium; many are of good value.

Newton, Don, and Hampshire, A Cecil, *Taranto* (London 1959)

Ollard, Richard, *Fisher and Cunningham* (London 1991). An insightful and pleasant read, though repeating some old errors.

Pack, S W C, *Night Action off Cape Matapan* (London 1972)

——, *The Battle for Crete* (London 1973)

——, *The Battle of Sirte* (London 1975)

Parrish, Michael Woodbine, *Aegean Adventures 1940–1943* (Sussex 1993)

Pedriali, Ferdinando, *Guerra di Spagna e Aviazione Italiana* (Rome 1992)

Petersen, Jens, *Hitler e Mussolini: La Difficile Alleanza* (Bari 1975). A German scholar who has made wide use of Italian source material over the years and is good friends with many Italian military scholars.

Pirelli, Alberto, *Taccuini 1922/1943* (Bologna 1984)

Playfair, I.S.O. and others. *The Mediterranean and the Middle East* (London, various dates). We used the first five volumes in the series.

Poland, E N, *The Torpedomen* (London 1993)

Poolman, Kenneth, *The Kelly* (London 1954)

——, *Night Strike from Malta* (London 1980)

Pope, Dudley, *Flag 4* (London 1954, reprinted 1998)

Pricolo, Francesco, *La Regia aeronautica nella seconda guerra mondiale (novembre 1939–novembre 1941)* (Milan 1971)

Pratt, Lawrence R, *East of Malta, West of Suez* (Cambridge 1975). Good but limited to British sources

Raeder, Erich, *My Life* (Annapolis 1960)

Rahn, Werner, *Reichsmarine und Landesverteidigung 1919–1928* (Munich 1976)

——, Schreiber, Gerhard, and Maierhofer, Hansjoseph (eds), *Kriegstagebuch der Seekriegsleitung, 1939–1945* (Bonn 1989)

Rainero, R H with Biagini, A (eds), *L'Italia in guerra. Il primo anno, 1940* (Rome 1991). One volume has been produced for the 50th anniversary of each year of the war with essays on various aspects of the war ranging from the colonies, the government, the fighting services, to the Home Front

Raspin, Angela, *The Italian War Economy 1940–1943* (New York 1986). Needs to be updated.

Rauber, Vitaliano, *La lotta antisommergibile* (Rome 1978)

Raven, Alan and Roberts, John, *British Battleships of World War Two* (Edinburgh 1976)

——, *British Cruisers of World War Two* (Edinburgh 1980)

Risio, Carlo De, *I Mezzi D'Assalto* (4th ed Rome 1992)

——, *L'aviazione di marina* (Rome 1995)

Rocca, Gianni, *Fucilate gli ammiragli* (Milan 1987)

Rodger, N A M (ed), *Naval Power in the Twentieth Century* (London 1996)

Rohwer, J, *Allied Submarine Attacks of World War Two, European Theatre of Operations, 1939–1945* (Annapolis 1997)

——, and Hummelchen, G, *Chronology of the War at Sea 1939–1945* (Annapolis 1992 and 1996). Excellent, but does contain some minor errors of detail.

Roskill, Stephen, *Churchill & the Admirals* (London 1977)

——, *Naval Policy Between the Wars*, 2 vols (Annapolis 1976). Probably his best work.

Sadkovich, James J (ed), *Reevaluating Major Naval Combatants of World War II* (Westport 1990). Uneven series of essays.

——, *The Italian Navy in World War II* (Westport 1994). Sadkovich over the years has produced a large body of work on the Italian Armed Forces in the Second World War. He has given to the English reader a tremendous amount of information, but it must be sometimes taken with a pinch of salt. He is the closest scholar to an apologist for the Italian military currently writing.

Sainsbury, Keith, *The North African Landings 1942* (London 1976)

Salewski, Michael, *Die deutsche Seekriegsleitung 1935–1945, Vol 2: 1942–1945* (Munich 1975)

Santoni, Alberto, *Da Lissa alle Falkland. Storia e politica navale dell'età contemporanea* (Milan 1987)

——, *Il vero traditore* (Milan 1981). A classic that should be translated into English. Santoni made great use of the British archives.

——, *La seconda battaglia navale della Sirte* (Rome 1982)

——, *Le operazioni in Sicilia e in Calabria* (2nd ed Rome 1989)

——, and Mattesini, Francesco, *La Partecipazione Tedesca alla guerra aeronavale nel mediterraneo* (Rome 1980). A fine candidate for an English translation. It was a groundbreaking study in comparing the war efforts of both Axis powers under, on and over the Mediterranean.

Santoro, Giuseppe, *L'aeronautica italiana nella seconda guerra mondiale*, 2 vols (Rome 1957).

Schofield, B B, *The Attack on Taranto* (Shepperton 1973)

Schramm, Percy E (ed), *Kriegstagebuch des Oberkommandos der Wehrmacht, Vol. III, 1943, Part I* (Munich 1982)

Schreiber, Gerhard, *Die italienischen Militärinternierte im deutschen Machtbereich 1943–1945. Verraten, Verachtet, Vergessen* (Munich 1989)

———, *Revisionismus und Weltmachtstreben. Marineführung und deutsch-italienische Beziehungen 1919 bis 1944* (Stuttgart 1987)

Schroeder, Joseph, *Italiens Kriegsaustritt 1943. Die deutschen Gegenmaßnahmen im italienischen Raum: Fall Alarich und Achse* (Göttingen-Zürich-Frankfurt a.M. 1969)

Selected Papers on British Warship Design in World War II (London 1983)

Seth, Ronald, *Two Fleets Surprised* (London 1962)

Shores, Christopher, and Cull, Brian with Malizia, Nicola, *Malta: The Hurricane Years, 1940–41* (London 1987). Shores, along with others, has been compiling a series of histories on the war in the air during the Second World War. He has this and four other volumes on the war in the Mediterranean. While small errors of detail occur, his work should be applauded and he works in languages other than English.

Sierra, Luis de la, *La Guerra Navale nel Mediterraneo (1940–1943)* (Milan 1987)

Simpson, Michael, *The Somerville Papers* (Aldershot 1995). A great addition though a bit more on the Spanish Civil War period would have been helpful, if that material exists. Simpson in his preamble to Part II repeats some common errors, such as the Italian lack of radar.

Smith, Peter C, *Action Imminent* (London 1970). A very good study recently given a facelift with a 2nd edition

———, *Pedestal* (London 1980)

———, *The Great Ships Pass* (Annapolis 1977)

———, and Walker, Edwin, *The Battles of the Malta Striking Forces* (London 1974)

Smithers, A J, *Taranto 1940* (Annapolis 1995)

Spiteri, Stephen C, *The British Fortifications* (Valletta 1991). Large format book loaded with drawings and pictures of the numerous forts and fortifications on the island. Recently reissued.

Spooner, Tony, *Supreme Gallantry: Malta's Role in the Allied Victory 1939–1945* (London 1996). A pleasant read but largely limited to English source material – and reflects that.

Sullivan, Brian, *Thirst for Glory* (Zeeland 1984). Sullivan has produced next to Sadkovich the greatest body of work in English and is the most balanced established scholar working in the field working primarily in that language. When will his excellent thesis on the war with Ethiopia be published in book form?!

Thetford, Owen, *British Naval Aircraft* (London 1991)

Thomas, R T, *Britain and Vichy: The Dilemma of Anglo-French Relations 1940–42* (New York 1979). A scholarly overview of Vichy.

Thompson, Julian, *The War At Sea* (London 1996). Great photographs, great period quotes, but the text on the Mediterranean must be taken with reservations.

Torsiello, Mario (ed), *Le operazioni delle unità italiane nel settembre-ottobre 1943* (Rome 1975)

Toscano, Mario, *Pack of Steel* (Baltimore 1967)

Tute, Warren, *The Deadly Stroke* (New York 1973)

Unia, Carlo, *Storia degli aerosiluranti italiani* (Rome 1974)

Valle, Giuseppe, *Uomini nei cieli. Storia dell'aeronautica italiana* (2nd ed Rome 1981)

Van Creveld, Martin L, *Supplying War* (Cambridge 1977)

Vian, Sir Philip, *Action This Day* (London 1960)

Warner, Geoffrey, *Iraq and Syria 1941* (Newark 1974)

Warner, Oliver, *Admiral of the Fleet Lord Cunningham of Hyndhope* (Athens, Ohio 1967)

Waters, S D, *The Royal New Zealand Navy* (Wellington 1956)

Weinberg, Gerhard L, *A World at Arms* (Cambridge 1994)

Westphal, Siegfried, *The German Army in the West* (London 1951)

Williamson, Murray, and others (ed), *The Making of Strategy* (Cambridge 1994)

Wingate, John, *The Fighting Tenth* (London 1991)

Young, Robert J, *In Command of France: French Foreign Policy and Military Planning, 1933–1940* (Cambridge, Mass. and London 1978). A good starting-point. The Navy and the role of Italy is mentioned only in passing.

Zamagni, Vera (ed), *Come perdere la guerra e vincere la pace* (Bologna 1997)

Index

Page numbers in *italic* refer to maps